Professional Newswriting

Professional Newswriting

Hiley H. Ward
Temple University

Harcourt Brace Jovanovich, Publishers
San Diego New York Chicago Atlanta Washington, D.C.
London Sydney Toronto

To
Joan Bastel
My favorite journalist

Cover photo: © Ken Karp

ISBN: 0-15-572010-4

Library of Congress Catalog Card Number: 84-81490

Printed in the United States of America

Copyrights and Acknowledgments appear on page 599, which constitutes a continuation of the copyright page.

Preface

To be professional means to compete successfully with and to outdistance other reporters. To be professional means to learn to be first and best. This book identifies that something extra that makes one reporter better and more professional than another. For example, the professional writes not only accurately but interestingly as well. Topics in this text range from learning efficient ways to take the most accurate notes to learning how to borrow techniques from humor and short story writing to enliven writing style.

To be professional also means to work hard. This book encourages activism among students. The would-be reporter, like the hospital patient, needs to get up and walk around in order to grow in strength. A student who is satisfied simply to sit in a classroom may do better in another profession.

To be professional means to publish. Students should make an effort to get out and publish under the direction of instructors. For instance, campus papers can give students excellent opportunities to publish. Also, weekly newspapers are eager to publish reports about students from their areas. For them, students can identify an athlete from a small town, interview him or her, and send an article about that person to the small paper, with a return envelope for the clipping.

Other opportunities to publish are often available for student reporters. Many editors of small newspapers are happy to use students to cover meetings and other events. Some newspapers use students for late-night sports coverage. Most papers will use "stringers" in areas where they do not have staff available. Campus news bureaus are often eager to receive write-ups about campus events to send off in releases. Students should always be looking for ways to publish as they take this and other newswriting courses. They should keep a complete file or book of clips, for clips are essential in landing a job. (Chapter 22 deals with "stringing," or part-time item-by-item reporting, as well as seeking the first job.)

"Newswriting" is used in the title in order to emphasize the importance of reporting—gathering the facts—as well as to underline the importance of writing dynamically and thinking intelligently when reporting the news. Chapter 9 on writing with style is aimed at helping reporters also become good writers. In a newspaper, journalists use various kinds of writing. Chapter 18 gives some attention to writing at the "rim," the copy desk. The copy desk serves as an entrance point for many new journalists. This book also gives attention to the undramatic, smaller personals and obituaries which newspapers cannot overlook.

Professional advice in this book comes from reporters and editors in all 50 states. No one person's view—no regionalism, no strictly big or small paper viewpoint—takes over here. Ideas come from all kinds of papers, including ethnic and minority papers.

Extensive quotes from reporters and editors give a ring of authenticity; they help make the book comprehensive; they serve to balance each other with various points of view and suggestions that work in different parts of the country. Students and instructors should find some information of interest from reporters in their own area. Also the broader inclusive approach appeals to today's new reporters on the move, who should prepare to work in different parts of the country. The book identifies and solves the kind of real life problems which reporters face.

The book offers a firsthand approach to learning how to report. Not only does the author have 30 years of reporting and editing experience, but for this book he has accompanied other reporters on their beats in various parts of the country.

The electronic age is here in the newsroom. The information about working on video display terminals (VDTs) in Chapter 20 helps prepare students for contemporary work in journalism, as does a section on developments in reporting equipment and what to expect.

A good textbook should also be worth keeping for future reference. Therefore, the reference sections provide information and sources to which students can continue to refer after they start their professional careers.

This comprehensive book will provide aspiring reporters with the skills, role models, and inspiration they need to become professional.

Acknowledgments

The author is grateful to the many persons who helped make this book possible. Special thanks go to reporters and editors in all 50 states who provided materials, responded to letters and questionnaires, or made themselves available for interviews. Their names appear throughout the book and in a list alphabetically by state which follows the individual acknowledgments.

The author wishes to thank former Temple graduate assistant-researchers Robert Orenstein, John Serbell, William Wedo; Yvonne Wright, secretary to the author when he was chairman of the Temple journalism department; Temple journalism librarian Bob Roberts; Temple professors Lee Carl and John De Mott (now at Memphis State) for providing file clippings in science and law-ethics, respectively.

He also thanks those, cited at the beginning of some chapters, who wrote a section or some pages of a chapter, as well as John Gillespie, an editor and a financial writer, and A. Joseph Newman, Jr., financial editor, both formerly with the Philadelphia *Bulletin*, for helpful advice and information for the business writing chapter.

In addition he thanks Joan Bastel, managing editor of the Horsham (Pa.) *Montgomery County Record*, who read the entire manuscript and (as the author's wife) offered helpful advice at all stages of the manuscript; and the readers of drafts of some chapters: Dianne Ward, assistant city attorney, St. Paul, Minn., Police, Courts; Art Geiselman, formerly of the Philadelphia *Bulletin*, Government, Courts; Chuck Newman, Philadelphia *Inquirer*, Sports; John De Mott, and Paul Sullivan, Law-Ethics.

And finally he offers thanks to his manuscript editor at Harcourt Brace Jovanovich, Gene Carter Lettau, whose skills smoothed out the manuscript; also other members of the HBJ staff: Bruce Daniels and Kate Duffy, production editors; Ann Smith, designer; and Fran Wager, production manager, for their many contributions. And he thanks free-lance typist Nora Peterson, who probably had the biggest job of all.

The following newspapers, editors, and writers are sources of information and clippings in the book. In most cases, their names also appear in the book. (Although some people have since gone on to work for other media, the newspapers at which they were contacted for the most part are listed here.)

Some of the unsigned article excerpts in the book—from the Detroit *Free Press*, Miami *Herald*, Washington *Post*, *Newsday*, Philadelphia *Inquirer*, and *USA Today*—are by the author.

Contributors to *Professional Newswriting*

These are among the media, editors, and reporters—most of whom are mentioned in the book—who helped with the book. In most cases they responded to questionnaires and provided comment and clips. Some persons were interviewed. In several instances, their names were on clippings approved for inclusion by their editors.

Alabama
Tom Jennings, John I. Sellers, Mobile *Press Register*; Bill Plott, Montgomery *Advertiser and Journal*; Kenneth Shorey, Birmingham *News*; James E. Jones, Jr., Birmingham *Post Herald*; Ellison Clary, Doris Flora, Tuscaloosa *News*.

Alaska
Keith Olson, Fairbanks *Daily News-Miner*; Anchorage *Daily News*.

Arizona
Tom Anderson, Globe *Arizona Silver Belt*; Frank E. Johnson, Tucson *Daily Star*.

Arkansas
Roy Ockert, Jr., Batesville *Guard*; Jack Kilgore, Ft. Smith *Southwest Times Record*; Walter Dean, Little Rock *Democrat*; Donna Moore, Springdale *News*.

California
Will Hearst, Los Angeles *Herald Examiner*; Frederick S. Holley, George Skelton, Los Angeles *Times*; Barbara Herrara, San Diego *Tribune*; Dan Walters, Sacramento *Union*; Carol Olten, San Diego *Union*; Robert Maynard, Oakland *Tribune*; Jack Miller, San Francisco *Examiner*.

Colorado
J. Edward Murray, Boulder *Daily Camera*; Carol Green, Denver *Post*; Dru Wilson, Colorado Springs *Gazette-Telegraph*.

Connecticut
Edward W. Frede, Danbury *News-Times*; Bob LaMagdeleine, Kenneth Hooker, Hartford *Courant*; Jeff Belmont, New Haven, *Register*.

Delaware
Evelyn Nilsson, Wilmington *Morning News*; Phil Milford, Wilmington *News-Journal*; Ronald McArthur, Seaford *Leader*.

Florida
Kent Cockson, Pensacola *News-Journal*; Mary R. Heffron, Orlando *Sentinel Star*; Kerry Duke, Jacksonville *Times-Union*; Janice Law, Fort Lauderdale *News*.

Georgia
Jim Merriner, Atlanta *Constitution*; Joe Wilson, Gainesville *Times*; Jim Satterly, DeKalb County *News-Sun*.

Hawaii
Buck Buchwach, Charles H. Turner, Mike Middlesworth, Honolulu *Advertiser*.

Idaho
Ralph D. Berenger, Shelley *Pioneer*.

Illinois
Clayton Kirkpatrick, Clarence E. Page, Gary Washburn, Chicago, *Tribune*; Thomas Picou, Chicago *Daily Defender*; Mike Bailey, Elgin *Courier-News*; Jim Deal, Rock Island *The Argus*; Mardy Fones, Decatur *Herald and Review*; Arthur J. Snider, Robert C. Marsh, Chicago, *Sun-Times*.

Indiana
Skip Hess, Indianapolis *News*; James Adams, Indianapolis *Star*; Steve Marschand, Kokomo *Tribune*; Bill Oakes, Byron Parvis, Lafayette, *Journal and Courier*; Gayle Zubler, South Bend *Tribune*.

Iowa
Gary Clarke, Ames *Daily Tribune*; John Moe, Perry *Daily Chief*; Don Muhm, Des Moines *Register*; John Robertson, Cedar Rapids *Gazette*.

Kansas
Jeff Williamson, Jon Roe, Wichita *Eagle-Beacon*; Robert K. Entriken, Jr., Salina *Journal*; Patty Moore, Atchison *Daily Globe*; Leslie Champlin, Topeka *Capital-Journal*; Ray Call, Emporia *Gazette*.

Kentucky
Ron Herron, Frankfort *State Journal*; Nancy Landis, Madisonville *Messenger*; Carol Sutton, Louisville *Courier-Journal*.

Louisiana
Lynn Stewart, Shreveport *Times*; Gary Hines, Shreveport *Journal*; Vicki Ferstel, New Iberia *Daily Iberian*; Nancy Wood, Lake Charles *American Press*; David Snyder, Gil T. Webre, New Orleans, *Times Picayune*.

Maine
Marshall L. Stone, Bangor *Daily News.*

Maryland
John H. Murphy III, Baltimore *Afro-American*; Terry Rubenstein, Baltimore *Sun.*

Massachusetts
Joseph Hopkins, Springfield *Morning Union*; David Sterritt, Robert P. Hey, Boston *Christian Science Monitor*; Joe Heaney, Boston *Herald American*; Earle Stern, Lynn *Item.*

Michigan
Louis Cook, Detroit *Free Press*; Debi Craft, Barryton *Courier*; Susan Stark, Lucille DeView, Detroit *News.*

Minnesota
John R. Finnegan, St. Paul *Pioneer Press*; Dewey Berscheid, St. Paul *Dispatch* and *Pioneer Press.*

Mississippi
Kathie Jarmon, Tupelo *Daily Journal*; Charles D. Mitchell, Vicksburg *Evening Post.*

Missouri
Joseph Pulitzer, Jr., Alan Buncher, Martha Shirk, St. Louis, *Post-Dispatch*; Maria K. Thompson, Benton County *Enterprise*; Robert Butler, Kansas City *Star*; Jo Johnston, Maryville *Daily Forum*; Monroe Dodd, Kansas City *Times.*

Montana
Gayle Shirley, Missoula *Missoulian*; Kevin Giles, Helena *Independent Record*; Ed Mohler, Boseman *Daily Chronicle.*

Nebraska
Nancy Hicks, Lincoln *Star*; Steve Jordon, Carl Keith, David J. Oestreicher, Omaha, *World-Herald*; Dewaine Gahan, Fremont *Tribune*; Don Pieper, Lincoln *Journal.*

Nevada
Barbara Burgess, Fallon *Eagle-Standard*; Robert Brown, Las Vegas *Valley Times.*

New Hampshire
William Loeb, Manchester *Union Leader*; Aline L. Jacobs, Laconia *Evening Citizen*; John Stylianos, Nashua *Telegraph*; Tom Kelsch, Dover *Foster's Daily Democrat.*

New Jersey
Laurie Stuart, Camden *Courier-Post*; S. Walter de Lazaro, Elizabeth *Daily Journal*; J. Richard Pellington, Ocean County *Times Observer.*

New Mexico
Susanne M. Burks, William L. Hoffman, Albuquerque *Journal*; Arthur

Latham, Maria Puente, Santa Fe, *New Mexican*; Dr. Robert E. Cates, Mike Newell, Hobbs, *Flare*; Paul L. Noskin, Valencia County *News-Bulletin*.

New York

Wilbur Lewis, Rochester *Democrat and Chronicle*; Edward Cowan, William H. Honan, Irwin M. Horowitz, John Lee, Le Anne Schreiber, New York *Times*; David L. Russell, Niagara Falls *Gazette*; Renee R. Cuddleback, Newburgh *Evening News*; Craig Ammerman, Clive Barnes, New York *Post*; Ed Edelson, New York *Daily News*; Gene Grey, Binghamton *Evening Press*; Robert H. Johnson, *Associated Press*, New York City; Stuart A. Seidel, *Newsweek*, New York City; Rudolf S. Rauch III, *Time*, New York City.

North Carolina

Carole Currie, Asheville *Times*; Sue Robinson, Greensboro *Daily News*; Bob Kolin, Raleigh *News & Observer*; Edward Hill, Jr., Winston-Salem *Chronicle*.

North Dakota

Frank Hornstein, Pierce County *Tribune*.

Ohio

Ken Blum, Orrville *Courier-Crescent*; Marge Higgins, Kent-Ravenna *Record-Courier*; Frank Hrudy, Cleveland *Press*; Jim Schottelkotte, Cincinnati *Enquirer*; Roxanne Mueller, Cleveland *Plain Dealer*.

Oklahoma

Bert O. Tucker, Ardmore *Daily Ardmoreite*; Tom Jackson, Lawton *Constitution*; Larry Names, Broken Arrow *Daily Ledger*; Nancy Gilson, Oklahoma City *Journal*.

Oregon

Charles Humble, Portland *Oregon Journal*; Quinton Smith, Albany *Democrat-Herald*; Rick Bella, Eugene *Register-Guard*; Doug Higgs, Klamath Falls *Herald and News*; Anne Thomas, Cottage Grove *Sentinel*; Mary Ann Campbell, Medford *Mail Tribune*.

Pennsylvania

Henry Darling, Tom Gibbons, Dave Kushma, A. Joseph Newman, Jr., Sam Pressly, Philadelphia *Bulletin*; Tyree Johnson, Robert Strauss, Philadelphia *Daily News*; Larry Eichel, Charles Fancher, Jr., Chuck Newman, Dwight Ott, Samuel E. Singer, Philadelphia *Inquirer*; Gary Kocher, William Wedo, Allentown *Call-Chronicle*; Constance Y. Bramson, Harrisburg *Patriot-Evening News*; Emilie Lounsberry, Doylestown *Intelligencer*; Karen Korman, Ida Leiby, Centre County *Democrat*; Neil C. Hopp, Carlisle *Sentinel*; Bob Lange, Ardmore *Main Line Times*; Harry Stoffer, *Calkins Newspapers*, Harrisburg.

Rhode Island

John P. Sulima, Rick Booth, Westerly *Sun*; Joseph L. Goodrich, Providence *Journal*.

South Carolina
Warren McInnis, Columbia *State*.

South Dakota
Bette Burg, Huron *Daily Plainsman*; Gordon R. Garnos, Watertown *Public Opinion*; Robert Imrie, Clark County *Courier*.

Tennessee
Laffitte Howard, Knoxville *News-Sentinel*; Sara Morrow, Nashville *Banner*; Ray McDonald, Chattanooga *News-Free Press*.

Texas
Bob Buckel, El Campo *Leader-News*; Randy Cummings, Arlington *Citizen-Journal*; Lou Hudson, Blair Justice, Fort Worth *Star-Telegram*; Don Pickels, Houston *Chronicle*.

Utah
Lavor V. Chaffin, Salt Lake City *Deseret News*; Will Fehr, Salt Lake City *Tribune*.

Vermont
Burlington *Free Press*.

Virginia
Dan Moreau, Jerry Lazarus, Richmond, *Times-Dispatch*; Julia Wallace, Norfolk *Ledger-Star*; Margaret Edds, Richmond *Virginian-Pilot*; Hugh Robertson, Richmond *News-Leader*; E. W. Scripps, *Scripps League Newspapers*, Charlottesville.

Washington
Ray Ruppert, Seattle *Times*; Bill Stewart, Vancouver *Columbian*; Steve Lachowicz, Wanetchee *World*; Rob Feuerstein, Aberdeen *Daily World*; Carol Pucci, Bellevue *Daily Journal American*; Harry McFarland, Ferndale *Westside Record-Journal*.

West Virginia
Edward Peeks, Charleston *The Charleston*.

Wisconsin
James E. Siepman, Milwaukee *Sentinel*; Kurt Mueller, Sheboygan *Press*; Jim Dowd, Janesville *Gazette*; Reid K. Beveridge, Madison *State Journal*; Doug Koplien, Appleton *Post-Crescent*; Dennis Hetzel, Racine *Journal Times*.

Wyoming
Carolyn Bower, Riverton *Ranger*.

Washington, D.C.
Katharine Graham, *Washington Post Co.*; Ted Shields, *UPI*.

Foreword

If you ask an American newspaper editor what journalism schools should emphasize, the answer you hear most often is "the basics." Professor Hiley Ward has heard this plea, and in this comprehensive volume he dispenses ample doses of practical, down-to-earth information for the beginning reporter.

Ward's advice—plus an extensive listing of reference sources and rules of grammar and style—could even arouse new vigor among seasoned newsmen willing to take the time to browse through this work. Having been a reporter himself for many years, Ward writes with the perspective of a veteran newswriter. Not content with just his own experiences on the beat, he quotes scores of reporters and editors throughout the country. Their advice and counsel are invaluable.

In defining what "professional" means, the author says that successful reporters outdistance their rivals because they strive for accuracy, work harder, do their homework, dig for details, and out-write and out-think their colleagues. These are no small achievements, and the author would be the first to concede that his book, or any other, will not guarantee that students will walk out of the classroom as polished reporters.

What Ward does do is encourage students to stretch their brains as well as their legs, inside and outside the classroom, and to go the extra mile—both literally and figuratively—to satisfy their curiosity and ensure accuracy. He points out to students how they can use enthusiasm, planning, and diligence to turn ordinary stories into page-one sparklers. And in this book he is able to guide young journalists along the path to what he calls the "joy of reporting."

H. L. Stevenson
Former Editor-in-Chief
United Press International

Contents

Professional Newswriting

Introduction: Why Be a Newswriter?

The money is not good for a beginner (you have to work your way up). The jobs are few, some say (the jobs are there but you have to be good—and also assertive—to get them). People court your favors for what you can do for them; in private they may say unkind things about you as a reporter. The pressure—the long hours and the weird hours are certainly there. Most daily newspapers are now morning papers which means most staff have to work into the evenings.

When *Time Magazine* carried a cover story on the media, "Accusing the Press: What Are Its Sins?" (Dec. 12, 1983), the blurb in the inside index announcing the cover story said: "The controversy over excluding the press from Grenada (in connection with the U.S. invasion or police action there in 1983) revealed a growing public hostility toward journalists. The media are increasingly perceived as being arrogant, biased and apt to abuse their power." The article itself proceeded to chronicle the abuse, indignation, and distrust heaped on the media across the nation.

Who needs abuse, poor pay, and tough hours?

First of all, the aspiring journalist should note that the "dues" the reporter pays may not be all that different from the "dues" neophytes in other professions pay. The salary at the outset compares to the profession of teaching. Other professions find there are very costly dues—doctors have long required hours of study and internships before they can practice; new lawyers have trouble getting the first job and usually settle for low-paying clerking positions; ministers put in long years of graduate study and usually start off in poor-paying obscure country parishes; and politicians begin serving on poor-paying township and county boards.

Chapter twenty-two takes up the prospects of getting a job and how to go about it with strategies and information about resumes.

Beyond the comparisons with other professions and similar

game plans and expectations are unique reasons for being a reporter and editor. The reasons are some of the best in the world.

You may want to be a reporter because:

- ***You want a sense of importance and meaning for your life.*** Of course, if you feel important, you may have to battle with arrogance. But you can battle with arrogance on even the most menial job. In reporting and writing for a newspaper (or radio, TV, or video-text words on screen delivery systems), you can relay the great and small events of the times in your own words. You are a mouthpiece of news. You can apply your skills, techniques, understanding, and sometimes your visions, as you do background pieces for the events of the day.
- ***You are a part of history.*** Historians generally write by referring to primary sources, including newspapers. You have a sense of writing for posterity, as well as for the day. Never believe that what you write is forgotten in hours. It becomes a part of a permanent record, a part of recorded history for the future.
- ***You meet interesting and prominent people.*** Any general assignment reporter over a period of time, mixing with the lowly and the great, meets movie stars, sports heroes, great persons of literature, even presidents and other heads of state.
- ***You are always learning.*** In a way, to be a successful reporter you have to like being a student. You are learning every day. Some people are happy with one-way straight jobs—they learn the skills and do their jobs exactly the same way for 30 years, give and take some change in technology. The reporter, on the other hand, interviewing politicians, professors, researchers, scholars of all sorts, and famous leaders and personalities works in a perpetual classroom—and not just an ordinary classroom. Your teachers will be the best—the people who are making the news and the discoveries.
- ***You will have your emotions stirred deeply.*** Reporting is a sure way to join the human race. You will see suffering; your heart will bleed. While some journalists or people in other professions may become cold and detached, as a journalist you do have the opportunity to deepen your sense of compassion.
- ***You will share in the victories of the human spirit.*** The comebacks of the handicapped, the victories of the little man, and the triumph of justice over corruption.
- ***You will earn an array of personal trophies.*** There will be awards—citations, plaques. While the Tuesday night bowler puts up a new trophy occasionally, you as a newspaper writer will have your own "trophies" and "honors" to cherish.
- ***You will have a key to a writing career.*** Many books were first newspaper articles and series. Certainly the newspaper piece can be the basis for

developing an article for a national magazine. A newspaper article is the first step on the ladder to wider publication.

- ***You will have training respected in other professions.*** Certainly newspaper writing offers great credentials for other writing professions—such as magazine writing and public relations. Actually, newswriting is good training for most other professions; reporters and editors have even run for the presidency.
- ***You will have a chance to travel.*** Among the possibilities: following candidates around the state and nation. Or you may work into a specialty. A travel editor goes many places; a drama critic goes to New York; a film critic travels to Hollywood and the Cannes festival in France; a religion writer visits Rome and the Near East; a science writer goes to archaeological digs and space launchings; an education writer and others travel to national and international conventions.
- ***You will work away from an office much of the time.*** To a degree you will work independently and at your own initiative, enjoying a measure of freedom and responsibility.
- ***You will be recognized.*** You will have bylines.

While newswriting is exacting—some consider it to be a profession only for young people of strong wills and bodies—hardly a profession is more rewarding, more creative, more intellectual, and more exciting. Yet, as in all careers, professionals strive to be even better. The aim of this book is not to deliver you at the door of final accomplishment, but to introduce you to skills, to make you think, and to start you along the path of excellence.

Springfield (Ill.) *State Journal-Register* State House Chief Jeff Brody interviews Representative Mike Curran on the floor of the House of Representatives. Photo by Chris Covatta

PART 1

The Basics

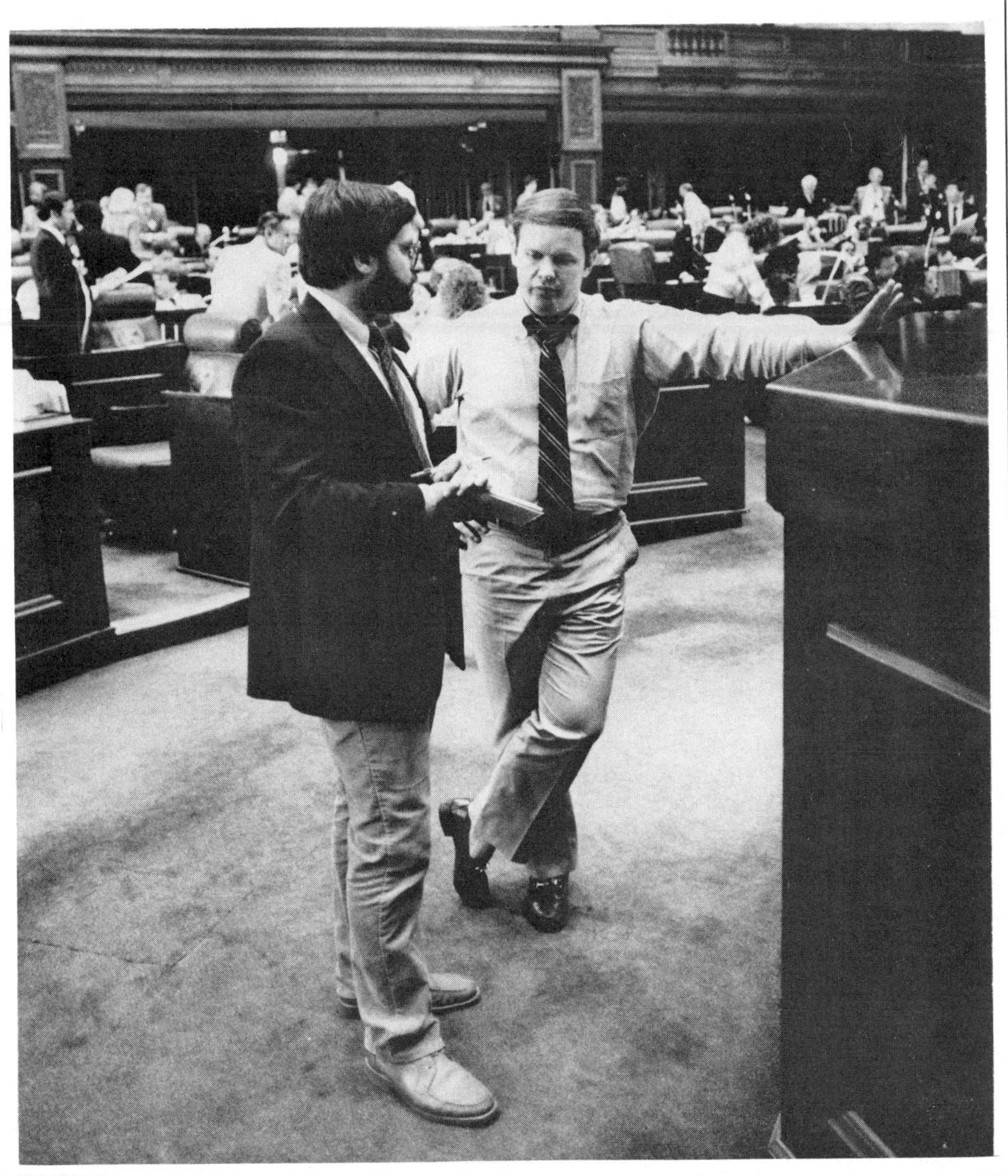

1

Understanding Newspapers and News

What is a *news* paper? What do journalists consider *news*? The answers to these questions will help you understand newspapers and what goes into them.

Journalism historian Edwin Emery says that a genuine newspaper must come out at least weekly; it must be printed "to distinguish it from the handwritten 'newes letters'"; *anyone* willing to pay the price must have access to it; all material must be "of interest to a general public, as contrasted with . . . religious and business publications"; it must have appeal to average citizens; "it must be timely"; and it must be stable.[1]

Historically, the great men had their formulas for newspapers, among them Joseph Pulitzer. He outlined his view of a newspaper in later life in a letter to one of his editors:

> . . . Every issue of the paper presents an opportunity and a duty to say something courageous and true; to rise above the mediocre and conventional; to say something that will command the respect of the intelligent, the educated, the independent part of the community; to rise above fear of partisanship and fear of popular prejudice. I would rather have one article a day of this sort; and these ten or twenty lines might readily represent a whole day's hard work in the way of concentrated, intense thinking and revision, polish of style, weighing of words.[2]

Among modern definitions of newspapers, some prominent U.S. editors offer their answers to the question "What is a newspaper?"

Katharine Graham, publisher and board chairman, Washington *Post*:

> One of the best definitions of a newspaper was Philip Graham's description of the work of journalists. He called it "the first rough draft of history that will never be completed about a world we can never really understand."

E. W. Scripps, chairman and president, Scripps League Newspapers, Charlottesville, Va.:

> . . . I believe that newspapers are objective rather than subjective and that they should be designed to serve their subscribers and not to serve the egos of those who produce them. In my judgment, the final judges of good newspapers are the subscribers who buy and pay for them.

John H. Murphy III, chairman of the board, *Afro-American* Company, Baltimore, Maryland:

> A newspaper is the vehicle used to carry out the mission of the newspaper. Most newspapers have a defined mission to make people aware of those things which will improve their way of life.

Will Hearst, assistant managing editor, Los Angeles *Herald Examiner*:

> A newspaper consists of printed words and pictures which chronicle the events of a particular community—usually on newsprint.

Clayton Kirkpatrick, editor, Chicago *Tribune*:

> A newspaper is a publication offering a daily summary of world-wide events in such a way that it fills the role of informal educator, helpful counselor, edifying commentator, and amusing companion.

Thomas Picou, executive vice president and editor, Chicago *Daily Defender*:

> A newspaper is a vehicle to provide news, goods, and services. Our newspaper also has the platform (as a black daily) to serve the needs of our community and also to bring down the barriers of discrimination.

NEWS ORGANIZATION

As other contemporary businesses are complex in management, so is the modern newspaper. The institution of a newspaper has a hierarchy of staff as does any other major corporation. In some cases, newspapers are actually a part of a conglomerate, a subsidiary or business among a group of businesses under one ownership. Or the newspaper may be a part of a newspaper "chain"—one of a series of newspapers linked by one overall management, as the Knight-Ridder chain which operates 35 daily newspapers, or the Gannett chain, which operates 86 daily newspapers with 4.6 million circulation.

Locally, a newspaper, even if it is a part of a conglomerate or chain, usually functions independently, using what ties it has with a central administration and sister papers to bring in additional stories. Knight-Ridder, for instance, has a special high speed wire that permits sharing of stories among its newspapers. The Knight-Ridder chain also has a group of national and international reporters who serve its network. The newspaper group allows its member papers a wider pool to draw from and more financial security, which makes it difficult for some independent newspapers to compete with papers belonging to a group.

The organization of a metropolitan newspaper might look like the ranking in Figure 1.1. (The departmental executives, such as the news executive, might hold additional titles, such as vice president, and serve on the administrative board of the newspaper and sometimes on the board of the chain organization.)

On a smaller newspaper, in the 25,000-circulation category, for instance, the organization might be:

- Publisher (owner)
- Editor
- Associate Editor (editorial page)
- Managing Editor
- News Editor
  - Section Editors (Sports, Lifestyle)
    - Reporters
    - Photographers
    - Layout Editor—Copy Desk
- Advertising Director
- Circulation Director
- Production Manager

There are variations on the theme, of course. For example, the 42,000-circulation Doylestown (Pa.) *Intelligencer*, belonging to the Calkins Newspapers chain, has its news operation organized as in Figure 1.2.

The associate editor in this model supervises the newsroom, graphics, and page one. The national editor supervises the wire, syndication material, the inside pages, and the computer system. The night editor functions as a city editor and is generally in charge of the reporters, most of whom work at night on this morning newspaper. Two editions of this paper serve Upper Bucks County and Central Bucks County. A separate paper, the Montgomery County *Record*, uses many pages from the *Intelligencer*.

FIGURE 1.1
Organization of a Metropolitan Newspaper

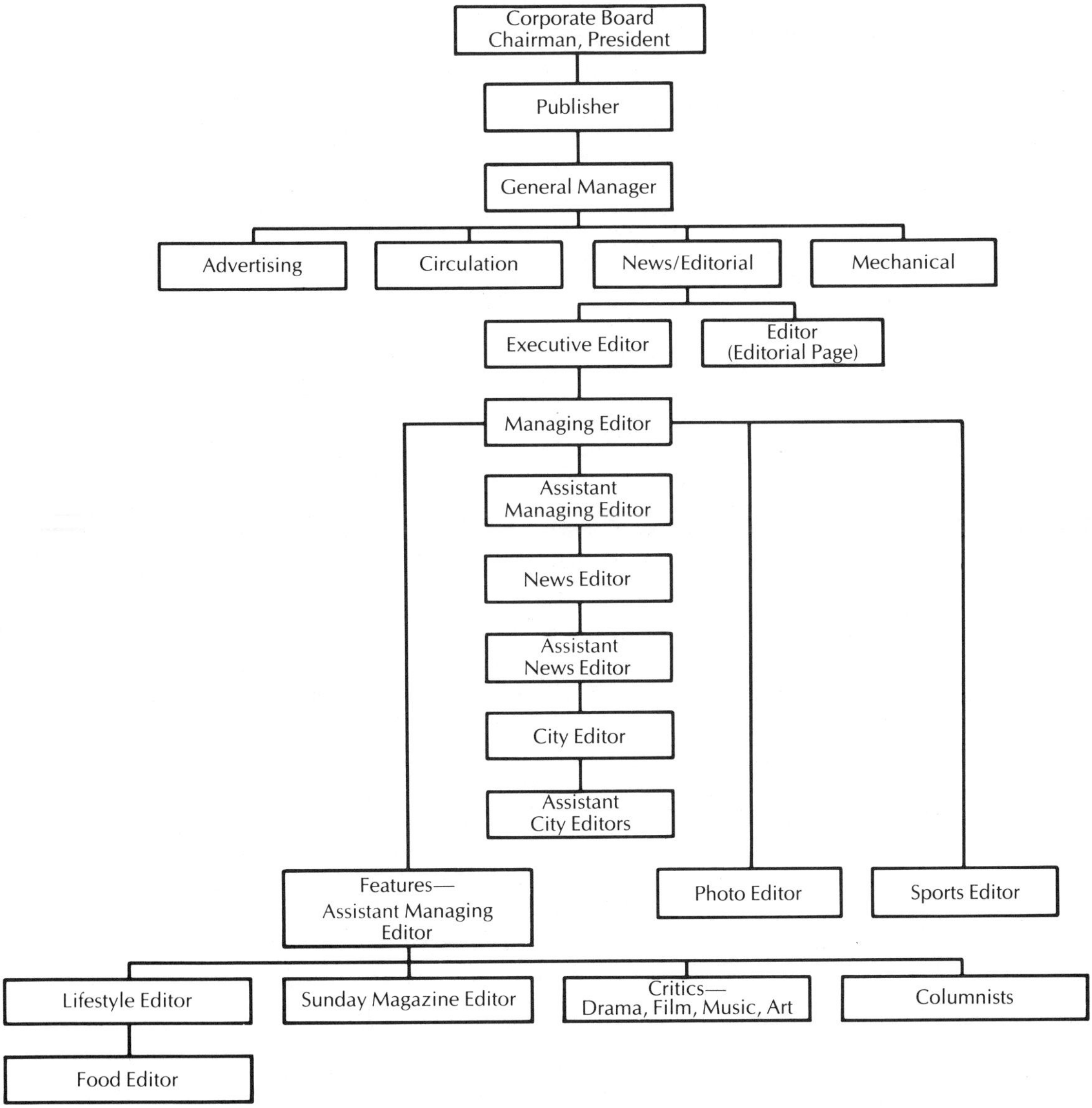

Corporate Board
Chairman, President

Publisher

General Manager

Advertising
Circulation
News/Editorial
Mechanical

Executive Editor
Editor (Editorial Page)

Managing Editor

Assistant Managing Editor

News Editor

Assistant News Editor

City Editor

Assistant City Editors

Features—Assistant Managing Editor
Photo Editor
Sports Editor

Lifestyle Editor
Sunday Magazine Editor
Critics—Drama, Film, Music, Art
Columnists

Food Editor

THE NEWSPAPER AS AN INSTITUTION

Newspapers are profit-making corporations and in some respects are like other institutions of business and industry. One big difference is a clearer separation between departments. The news department

FIGURE 1.2
Organization of the Doylestown (Pa.) *Intelligencer* (42,000 circulation)

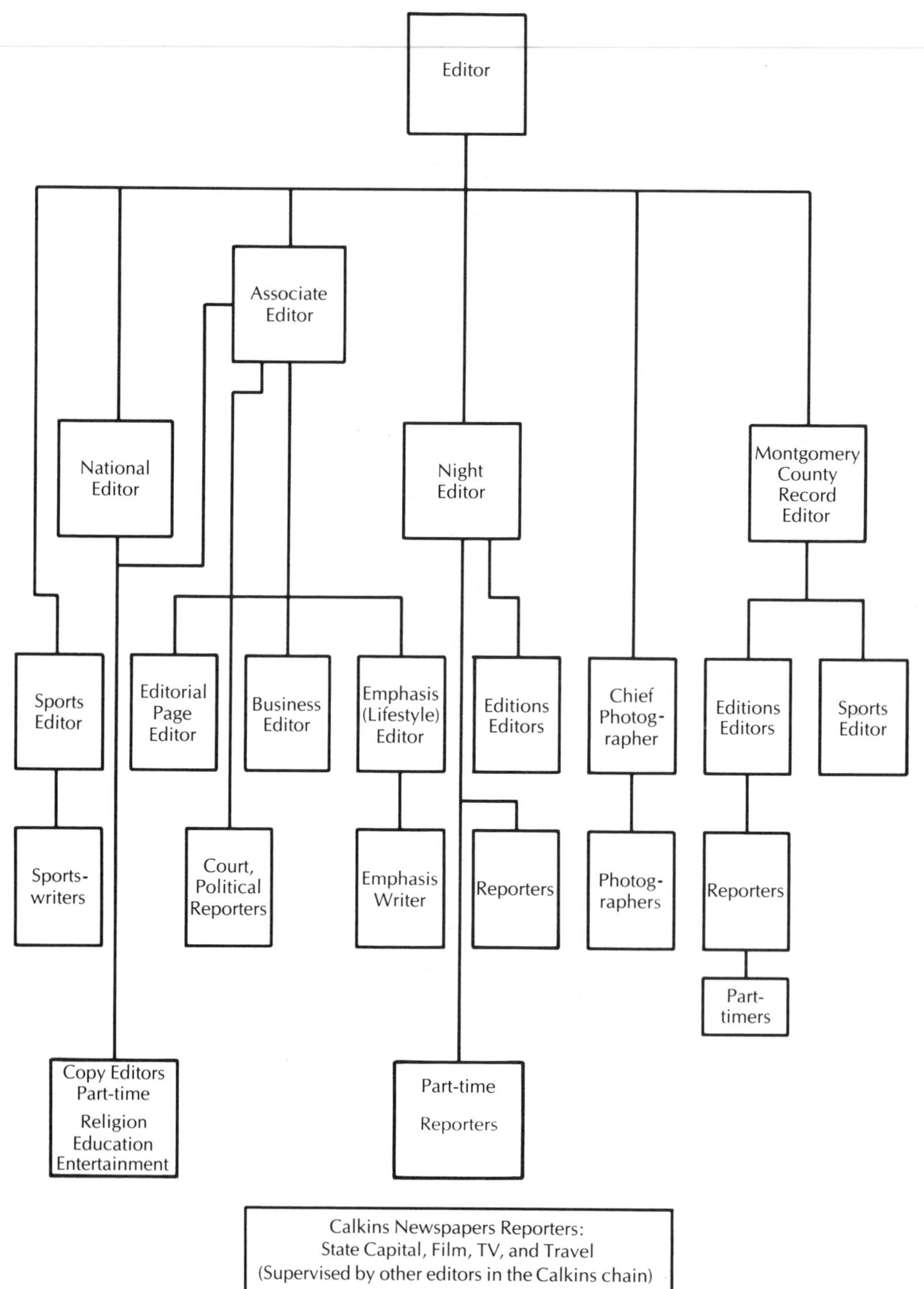

gathers news; some of this news may not be consonant with the views of management. The business and advertising departments are relatively independent of the news-gathering operation—at least ideally so. In other U.S. corporations, all departments tend to reflect the philosophy of a single management. This duality of publishing of news in possible conflict with the official position of the newspaper is a peculiarity of the American newspaper.

A newspaper, as a well-known and often respected institution, can influence what a community thinks and does. The late columnist Walter Lippmann talked of media "putting pictures in our heads." By directing thinking on matters of public concern, the newspaper often influences what the community considers important. The newspaper may influence how members of the community think about a specific matter, such as a new candidate in the race. The way it deals with subjects—the selection of which candidates to write about, the angle or approach in treating subjects, the paper's stated editorial views, and the frequency of stories may affect community response.

Researcher Paul Lazarfeld talked of the power of media to mobilize public response during a political campaign. A study in 1968 in Chapel Hill, N.C., showed a correlation between a newspaper's viewpoint and how the community votes. Said Bernard C. Cohen in his *The Press and Foreign Policy*:

> . . . The press is significantly more than a purveyor of information and opinion. It may not be successful much of the time in telling people what to think, but it is stunningly successful in telling its readers what to think *about*. And it follows from this that the world looks different to different people, depending not only on their personal interests, but also on the map that is drawn for them by the writers, editors, and publishers of the papers they read. . . . The editor may believe he is only printing the things that people want to read, but he is thereby putting a claim on their attention, powerfully determining what they will be thinking about, and talking about, until the next wave laps their shore.[3]

WHAT IS NEWS?

The Subjective Quality of News

Events happen everywhere all the time, but no event is news until someone tells someone else about it. One definition of news, then, is: The communication of reports and events. News does not exist in isolation. News is news when readers receive it—and perceive it. The

Loch Ness monster can come ashore and walk and strut around, but its appearance is not news until someone sees it and reports it. Flying saucers can zip down Main Street, but their antics are not news until people see them and communicate their presence to others.

News, then, depends on you—as *reporter*, as *editor*, and as *reader*—and upon others who must sift through stories and open the way for items to get into the paper.

With this said, can we still arrive at a definition of news? By what rationales do items get into most papers? What are the common denominators and generally consistent factors?

One definition of news goes: "News is whatever the editor says it is." This definition is correct, but news is also what YOU say it is. If you are an *editor*—on campus, for instance—certainly you can help pick out the stories, and tell your reporters how to use them. As a *reporter*, you also have some control over the definition of news. If you think an item is a front page story, your enthusiasm and diligence in investigating and writing might show more. If you think an item is a "nothing of a story," the item will likely end up as nothing big, rightly or wrongly. Your opinions—no matter how subtle—are important in defining the news.

A definition of news that takes into account views of editors, reporters, and a varied audience could be:

> News is what people will read, or what editors, reporters, and management think people can, should, want to, and will read. News can be anything, with priorities usually given to information/utility and human interest values (whatever they are).

News as Novelty

A definition of news must include that which is new. News comes from the Greek *neos*, the Latin *novus* and from later versions of it, the German *neu*, and Middle English *newe*. News is novelty. Summed up in the famous dictum of Charles Dana's city editor, John B. Bogart, on the New York *Sun* in the 19th century: "It's not news if a dog bites a man, but if man bites dog, then it is news!" News is novel; news is something different.

Yet "novelty" isn't that simple. For even very old and very conservative traditions revive and become today's novelty, and therefore news. The youth cults of the 1960s sought to pattern themselves after older primitive groups. Any effort today to imitate an earlier pattern is nothing new, but it is novel. Perhaps the better word is anachronistic—*that which is out of place* is news.

News as Commodity

News is also a commodity to be bought and sold. Many idealistic young people—and older editors, too—rebel at the thought that newspapering is first and foremost a business. But editors do put out a product, and they try to convince people that they need the product as much as they need loaves of bread, boxes of cigars, or suits of clothes. Editors and their newspapers give people what they want. Editors and reporters are a part of the mass culture and naturally extend their own wants and needs—and biases and expectations—to please large masses. This is not a satisfying definition. Nevertheless, newspapers are a commodity, to be bought and sold and consumed like any chattel or food.

A newspaper appeals to people in many ways—people buy it for its ads, news, and comics—like anything else they buy. And editors, whether they admit it or not, know it. The parking lot behind the Wichita *Eagle* and *Beacon*, Knight-Ridder papers in Wichita, Kans., tells the story: Three kinds of parking places designate "news staff," "photographers," and "customers." The sign does not say "readers," but "customers." The newspaper is for customers.

In his *Discovering the News*, an interpretation of journalism history, Michael Schudson observes: "Newspapers are directly dependent on market forces. They appeal directly to popular opinion. Journalism is an uninsulated profession."[4] He also notes that in the U.S. after the first century of newspapers, in the 1820s, more than half the newspapers published in the big cities had "advertiser," "commercial," or "mercantile" in their titles. Some such names survive today: The Honolulu *Advertiser*, Memphis *Commercial-Appeal*, *Sun-Commercial* (Vincennes, Ind.), *Commercial Mail* (Columbia City, Ind.).

News as Conversation

A third aspect of news is that it has conversational value. The "conversational" aspect of news has been a part of the definition from the time of the town criers to today's era of newspapers and broadcasts that get people talking. Charles Dana, of the old New York *Sun*, once said news was "anything that will make people talk." Joseph Pulitzer gave the St. Louis *Post-Dispatch* the task not only to publish important news but also the "original, distinctive, dramatic, romantic, thrilling, unique, curious, quaint, humorous, old, apt to be talked about" news. And William Randolph Hearst said he wanted to elicit a comment—a "Gee Whiz"—with each story.

Editors recognize the conversational value of news, even if they do not always appreciate it. One editor who does recognize this value of news in making editorial judgments is Ken Berg, editor of the highly modernized Mankato (Minn.) *Free Press*. "Readers understand what affects their everyday lives," says Berg, who equates "conversational" with "interesting." "If it is dull, nobody will want to read it," he adds. "If it is interesting, it will be talked about and be useful to the reader."

The feedback of news that is or becomes conversation invariably leads to more use of such news. Berg, who also writes a column, is particularly encouraged when he hears that people are talking about his column; he then knows he is "communicating."

If a news story has considerable "conversational" value, it is likely to have one or several other ingredients important to a news story. It includes information, educational value, entertainment, human interest, or other material relevant to needs of the reader.

Tests of News

Apart from formulating a definition, certain factors make for news.

Timeliness. Nobody wants yesterday's news. News is perishable. News reports on what has happened today or since the last issue. News also means last-minute news.

Conflict. Wars, politicians squaring off at each other, and differences in ideologies make news. Certainly sports news—from the gridiron to the prize-fighting ring—depends on conflict.

Closeness to home. People receiving national honors mean nothing to a community far away, but if they are hometown people, then their honors become news. City politicians far away are generally not news, but those close to home are.

Prominence. Readers may not have a genuine interest in their politicians, but they do recognize names. Readers have heard of the governor, mayor, council member. What these public officials say and do will affect readers. And when in a leisure moment a councilman pokes somebody in the nose at a party or his son or daughter is arrested in a drug raid, readers are interested.

Numbers. If six people die in six separate auto accidents in the state, they will be a part of a story that counts the victims: "Six Die in

Crashes Over Weekend." But if six die in one wreck, the story will be on the front page. One average person killed in an air mishap is not big news, but 100 is.

Curiosity (and "prurient" interest). Most editors like to point to other publications such as the *National Enquirer, Midnight,* or *Tattler*—the supermarket tabloids—when subjects of sex, perversion, the occult, psychic phenomena, and violence for its own sake come up. But even the most gray "old ladies," as some of the more staid respectable dailies across the U.S. are called, report on prurient interests in their own way. Besides carrying fluff, such as astrology columns and gossip columns, conservative papers have their share of articles about beheadings, torture, nude motorcyclists, executions, battered children, family feuds, and public drunkenness of movie stars. One editor defended his paper as less sensational because it carried one less such story than a competitor.

People forget that the distinguished Joseph Pulitzer's New York *World* started out as sensational as any supermarket tabloid. Journalism historian Edwin Emery points out the sensational formula of Pulitzer at the outset of Pulitzer's venture in New York City with the New York *World*. Pulitzer's front page stories included an account of a million-dollar storm in New Jersey, an interview with a condemned murderer, the story of a Wall Street suicide, a Pittsburgh hanging, a riot in Haiti, and the sad story of an abused servant girl. The 22,000-copy press run sold out by noon. Only the *Herald* had matched him in sensational coverage.

While most professional journalists today will agree that serious newspapers should avoid sensationalism, such stories still do make news. The generally conservative Charles Dana's own creed at the New York *Sun* was: "I have always felt that whatever the Divine Providence permitted to occur I was not too proud to report."

Cuteness. Children touch heartstrings. A paper can always use pictures of children doing almost anything. But some newspapers overdo cuteness. How many times have you seen a picture of a nun on a ball diamond with a baseball bat, or at Christmas or Easter, a choir boy with a black eye?

Information. Some information people must know and will read. The weather is important to many—will it rain on the picnic this weekend? People want to know about school closings because of a storm and an election postponed because of a flood.

Self-help. Consumer news helps people sort out good and bad products, introduces new products, and informs readers about how to spend their money wisely. Gardening, real estate planning, medical columns—any "how-to," self-help article or column, with special tips and advice—provide news that readers need and want.

Entertainment. Since people read newspapers voluntarily, they need some pleasure along with serious news. Readers—groggy in the morning, tired on their way home in the evening—will stay hooked to the newspaper if they experience some enjoyment in reading. A dull paper may become a paper of record—one that some people in the know must read to be fully informed—but will never be at the top of the circulation heap if it is not fun or interesting to read.

Ritual. People get in the habit of expecting certain kinds of stories. Each season must be covered on schedule: Santa at Christmas, the ground hog and St. Valentine in February, the Easter bunny, and the June bride. Also, once a breaking news event gets coverage, the good newspaper must re-examine it each day, ritualistically, whether anything happens or not. During upheavals—such as the long ordeal in Vietnam or other national struggles, as in Iran in 1979 and 1980, or more recently in Lebanon and Central America—readers expect a story and a repeating of background facts each day.

Symbolism. Closely related to news as ritual is the linking of news to old symbols that stir up emotions such as hate or love. The swastika of Hitler's Germany is one such symbol. In Philadelphia, one loner, whose true identity remained in doubt and who could not be located later, was able to wave the swastika symbol and dominate headlines for several weeks. After playing up the possibility of a Nazi rally based on the mysterious loner's application for a rally permit, the Philadelphia *Inquirer* continued with the lastest developments in the lead story in the Metropolitan section:

> If James Guttmann does not appear in federal court at 10 a.m. today, the federal permit allowing a Nazi rally at noon Sunday near Independence Hall will be withdrawn, U.S. District Judge Clifford Scott Green said yesterday.
>
> Green said that Guttmann, whose identity and whereabouts remain a mystery, had been subpoenaed and that the U.S. attorney's office would make a "good-faith effort" to find him. . . .

Inquirer columnist Dorothy Storck in the same issue asked the obvious questions about the ritualistic-symbolic frenzy that editors get caught up with:

What is this, anyway?

A 21-year-old punk who spells his name three ways and needs to have his mouth washed out has, for the past week, managed to get headlines, editorials, top spot on TV news and a lot of silly pomposity from a lot of organizations that should know better.

He has done this quite simply. He phoned up everybody and told them he was a Nazi and wanted to hold a rally.

Nobody, apparently, checked the guy out. They don't even have a good address or telephone number on him.

Everybody heard the word "Nazi" and fell into ritual rage.

It was as if a stage director had yelled, "Places, please" and the actors followed a well-rehearsed script. . . .

Educational Significance. When a major story breaks in unfamiliar territory, the reader needs some background to understand the event. If a president may be impeached, the reporter needs background and history about prior impeachment attempts. If the president has a new energy plan, readers want to know why the government did not implement such a plan before. Readers also want to know its potential influence on energy crises and fuel scarcity in the next decade. Backgrounding and news analyses are an important part of modern newspapering.

Interesting trivia. Human beings are fascinated with nostalgia—they collect things from old matchbooks to old baseball cards. Objects of no apparent value at all take on significance. So it is with events. Descriptions of details—the turn of a hand, a slipped word, a wrong glance, a gesture—all get into newspapers. Readers can understand the little details that get their attention. Trivia is one of the blessings of American newspapers. Without it, you would have only great statements, documents, and records of abstractions from the party in power.

Celebrities. Celebrities are not only important on their own merit, but their very presence gives meaning to other events. The Associated Press, covering a reunion of Rhodes scholars, led off first of all with the most prominent celebrity present:

OXFORD, England—Queen Elizabeth II sipped tea Monday with 850 former Rhodes scholars, including 376 Americans who returned to Oxford University to celebrate the 80th anniversary of the famed scholarship program.

The queen and her husband, Prince Philip, met dignitaries from throughout the English-speaking world who had taken advantage of the scholarships set up by English empire-builder and diamond-mining tycoon Cecil Rhodes.

"It's the best use to which diamonds have ever been put," said one returning "Yank at Oxford," former Indiana Congressman John Brademas, now president of New York University.

The garden party on the grounds

of Rhodes House opened a three-day reunion of former Rhodes scholars.

Among them were Gen. Bernard W. Rogers, Supreme Commander NATO Forces in Europe; former CIA Director Adm. Stansfield Turner; Pulitzer Prize-winning poet and novelist Robert Penn Warren; former Speaker of the House Carl Albert and Sen. Larry Pressler of South Dakota. . . .

—Robert Gless, Associated Press, in the Burlington (Vt.) *Free Press*

In the final analysis, with all of its complexities, news is what people say it is—the reader or participant or observer who alerts the editor, the editor who makes the assignment, and you as reporter who must write the story, after selecting the facts, deciding on the opening or lead and the direction of the development of the story. The news is people.

Basic Newswriting Terms

Some words you should know concerning the organizing, writing, and using of news stories:

Add: Additional material to be included in the story; means of numbering pages—second page is FIRST ADD, third page, SECOND ADD.

A-matter: Material prepared in advance—background information, with the lead called in from the scene of the news event.

Angle: Special quality of interest or marketability that makes idea usable.

Bed: A newspaper put to bed is ready to be put on the presses to be printed.

Book: A page of copy is called a book; see also "take."

Box: Border put around a story to set it aside or call attention to it.

Break: Place where story is continued to another column or page.

Breaking: A breaking story is one which has just happened or is continuing to happen.

Brite (Bright): A short item—maybe only a paragraph—that brings a chuckle or is upbeat in some way.

Budget: A list of stories—with priorities indicated—for the day.

Bull dog: First edition of the day.

Bulletin: Short item—usually a paragraph—of great importance, usually arriving too late to be developed into a story.

Bullets: Round dots (often in place of numbers) to highlight one-paragraph topics or items in a list.

City Editor: Editor in charge of local assignments.

Column: Standard line width of printed type in a newspaper with a standard depth; an opinion, analysis, or entertaining piece of writing, usually of predetermined length with byline.

Copy: Article or material prepared for newspaper.

Copy Boy/Copy Girl: Young person, usually high school or college age, who runs the errands and does the menial jobs around the office. Many have gone on to become noted editors.

Copy Desk: Where material is edited, headlines put on, and so on.

Copy Editor: One who edits—for example, a staff person who takes out extra words, rewrites copy, and puts on headlines.

Correspondent: A non-staff person who writes a story—often a regular contributor representing a distant area.

Dupe: An extra copy of a news story.

Edition: Total unchanged press run; when new material is added to a new run within the day and it is so designated, this is another edition. Large papers have as many as a half dozen editions in one day.

Editorial: An unsigned article or essay—often very brief—appearing on an editorial or opinion page, usually expressing the views of the management of the paper.

Enterprise: Effort to find news or picture idea on one's own.

Feature: To make a story look more prominent in the paper, to lead off with it; name for a human interest, non-timely article (in contrast to hard or breaking news).

File: Sending (by wire) or calling in a story.

Fluff: Vague and often unimportant copy; poor writing, nonfactual writing; also, light, non-serious topic.

General Assignment: Availability to cover any topic.

Hard News: Straight, factual news, usually of a compelling nature.

In-depth: Emphasis on the "why" and background of a story.

Jump: Part of a story that is continued on another page or column.

Kill: Eliminate designated words, stories, or parts of stories.

Lead (Lede): The beginning of a news story.

Lift-out: Sentence or paragraph from story repeated with headline for display purposes.

More: Notation at bottom of page indicating more is coming.

Move: A story is sent by wire or edited copy is sent into production.

Must: A label put on a story that indicates to editors it must be used that day.

News Hole: Space available for news stories in an issue after advertising space is allocated.

Newsprint: Paper used for newspapers—cheaper, poorer grade paper.

Peg: Idea or event on which story is based.

Play: The way a news story is handled in the paper, such as where it appears and how much space is given to it.

Rewrite: A person who edits and rewrites stories; a person who takes calls from reporters on breaking stories and writes them in the office.

Second Day: A story on the same topic that appears a day later.

Sections: Parts of a newspaper dedicated to one topic—the sports section is a good example.

Sidebar: An additional short news story that is split off from the main story but which is printed alongside it, often in a box.

Slant: Direction or emphasis to appeal to certain kinds of readers.

Slot: Top inside edge of a horseshoe-shaped copy desk; also, key copy editor who sits there.

Spot News: Breaking news; also, firsthand, on the spot.

Stringer: Correspondent; often a part-time, out-of-state contributor who calls in stories. Sports desks, for example, use local stringers in peak seasons.

Story: News article or feature.

Take: A page of copy.

Top-off: Put a new lead on story.

Trim: Cut back length of a story; also, portion that is trimmed.

Update: Add more recent facts to story.

Notes

[1]Edwin Emery and Michael Emery, *The Press and America*, 4th ed. (Englewood Cliffs, N.J.: Prentice-Hall, 1954, 1978), p. 4.

[2]Don C. Seitz, *Joseph Pulitzer: His Life and Letters* (New York: Simon & Schuster, 1924), p. 286.

[3]Bernard C. Cohen, *The Press and Foreign Policy* (Princeton: Princeton University Press, 1936), p. 13.

[4]Michael Schudson, *Discovering the News* (New York: Basic Books, 1978), p. 9.

Assignments

1. News gets into the newspaper for many reasons. Using this chapter, make a list of such reasons and definitions of news, adding any observations of your own. Then rank three reasons and definitions by number as to which are the most important tests of news.
2. Find a story in a newspaper which has strong news values from several dimensions. Likewise, identify a "non-news" story in the paper, perhaps a story that should not have run. Explain your choices.
3. Create a complete, but concise, definition of news. How does it differ from other definitions of news?

4. Prepare an organization chart on your local town newspaper and on your campus paper. Contrast the two.
5. Create a model organizational diagram for a modern newspaper as you think it should be. Explain.
6. A "gatekeeper" is one who lets information into the paper, the person who decides on moving a story ahead to publication. Take a foreign correspondent's story. What "gates" do you think the story went through before it saw print in the paper?

2

Starting and Organizing the Story

American journalists continue to debate about how much to pack the first paragraph with facts. Some argue that all the essential facts should be there; some will say they can be worked in within the first few sentences. Both groups agree that certainly the most important or most interesting fact should be available right away. But the second group allows more than the other for the facts to be worked in along the way and not all dumped in the first paragraph. With the growing emphasis on style, perhaps this second group is winning out.

GENERAL PRINCIPLES

Both groups subscribe to three axioms:

1. Start the article the best way possible. The editor and reporter make that determination based on judgments as to what is interesting and important.
2. The reader should know what the reporter is talking about right away.
3. All the basic facts should be at the "top." To the formalist this means all at once in a strict inverted pyramid form. To the stylist this means as soon as possible in the first four or five paragraphs. A good reporter-writer will likely use both forms of writing—packing the lead with information (on stories such as disasters)—working the facts in gradually in stories such as a personality profile.

THE FIVE W'S

The basic formula for newswriting—and for packing the opening paragraph—is what is known as the Five W's and the H.

Stories with all of these in the lead will have facts that tell WHO the story is about, WHAT happened, WHERE it happened, WHEN it happened, and WHY, along with HOW it happened.

If one packs all the information into the lead, it may be just right:

> MIAMI (UPI)—The FBI today searched government records to identify a Spanish-speaking man who hijacked a jet to Cuba with a "bomb" that later turned out to be a bar of soap.

Most facts of the basic formula are here: WHO (FBI and a Spanish-speaking man); WHAT (hijacker-identity search); WHERE (Miami dateline, action between Miami and Cuba—man was taken into custody in Havana, according to second paragraph); WHEN (today); WHY (hijacking—motives not known); HOW (bar of soap "bomb").

But packing the basic information and details into the first paragraph can make the first paragraph heavy. The following is based on a lead that appeared in an Eastern newspaper:

> A 76-tire tractor carrying 15 steel plates weighing 60 tons moved through the city Thursday in a dry run of the nuclear equipment delivery route from the (name of company) loading dock at the harbor to the nuclear power plant eight miles away.

Breaking Up the Five W's

There are variations on the Five W's and the H which are effective, such as changing the order, even starting with HOW. But often it is just too much to pack every lead paragraph with all the facts. For one thing, not every fact is interesting or important.

Thus it may be more effective to pick out the W or the H that is more interesting or important and let it stand by itself or with only one other basic ingredient.

For example, only WHO and WHAT are in this lead:

> It's open primary season for the Warminister Democratic organization.
>
> After almost two hours of discussion, the party voted 32–28 not to endorse any more township candidates for the May primary election.
>
> —Bob Orenstein, *Today's Spirit*, Hatboro, Pa.

On occasion, the newswriter can get by with only one of the Five W's or HOW in the lead. For example, the following story has only a WHAT lead:

There were at least a dozen kinds of meatballs. The total menu—ready-to-serve and portion-packed seafood, veal, lamb, beef, pork, potatoes, pizzas, wieners, vegetables, drinks and desserts—was several hundred items long.

—Bill Collins, Philadelphia *Inquirer*

This story has only a WHO lead:

Duane David Bartholomew Bobick. It's a name for the chairman of the board, or maybe a bank president. Certainly not a pugilist, even a former choir boy from Minnesota. So, they modified it slightly and called him "The Great White Hope."

—Jack Hawn, Los Angeles *Times* Service

After giving the most important fact succinctly, the reporter should present the other information as soon as possible.

Do not lose sight of the Five W's and H, but do not be their slave. Be warned of this paradox: If reporters cannot write a Five W and H story, they do not understand what the newspaper business is about; if they write that way all the time, they can be branded as hacks. One young man bluffed his way into a newspaper job and did marvelously well with the formula Five W's and H stories. He simply made himself a chart. If there was a fire, he followed his model for a fire story; the same with an accident. But when management caught him one day looking at his chart to rewrite the stories that came in, they realized he was only an untrained, unskilled fellow and fired him.

INVERTED PYRAMID

The basic newswriting story can be seen as an "inverted pyramid," and in case of doubt as to how to write a news story, you should resort to this approach. The inverted pyramid simply means that the foundation of the story, the most important information, comes first, and the rest of the information follows in descending order. The least important information appears at the end of the story. This form has several advantages, one being that busy readers can glance at the news readily, sample the first few paragraphs and move on. The "inverted pyramid" way of writing—getting the Five W's and

H and the most important supporting information at the top—also means that the most significant facts will get into the newspaper. If the original story comes out to 12 inches, but the advertising department sells 10 more inches, only the first two inches of the story may get into the paper.

Many analogies help to put the basic news story into perspective. For example, think of the immediate happening or hard news story as a model of a hammer. The mallet or head of the hammer is larger. Think of all the main facts packed into this part of the hammer. The wooden handle indicates only supportive information—you could leave any part of it out without seriously distorting the story.

Edward J. Smith, of the University of Oklahoma, has suggested that the model could be that of a screw. In *Journalism Educator,* he writes:

> The screw model rejects the idea, inherent in the inverted pyramid, that news story information is readily rankable with respect to importance. Any newsman who has sat through a five-hour, 10-agenda item city council meeting knows that often arbitrary selections are made of what items should be at the top and what items should be at the bottom of the story. Generally, the idea that news story information is rankable by importance is indefensible in practice. Obviously, in some stories major facts stand out, but in others they do not. But even in cases where a few items of information are clearly of greater importance than others, somewhere along the continuum of items they begin to level out and exhibit approximately equal importance. . . .
>
> The screw model acknowledges this reality . . . the screw model adopts a top portion of the inverted pyramid but then levels off along the shank of the screw. This leveling illustrates the likelihood that information will, in fact, reflect equal importance. The shank of the screw continues until clearly discernible minor details are evident. . . .[1]

DEFINING LEADS

The beginning of a news story is generally referred to as a "lead" (some write it "lede"). It may be one or several paragraphs.

There are two major kinds of leads: a story can be either hard news, with most of the important facts told right away, or the story can be a feature with a "walk-in" or soft lead. Many possibilities exist within these categories. Much depends on the context: what else has happened since the first report, how often such events have happened before, where the possibilities for humor, pathos and/or other emotional approaches are. And how does the reporter handle these possibilities in a particular instance? Some stories might be funny in one community or at one time—for example, the escape of a harmless, fun-loving boa constrictor. But if the community has recently seen stories about fatal snake bites, the story will not appear funny. In that instance the story should be a straight account.

How the reporter should approach the story is up to the editor. If the editor wants a human interest story for the snake escape, then that is the way the reporter will write it; if the editor wants to alert the community about a problem, then the reporter will play it straight.

Of course, the reporter can often mix hard news and feature approaches. For example, an article on snakes can start with a human interest account of a person being bitten by a snake or with a brief story of snake lore. Then the article can move on to hard information and somber warnings from authorities.

When a Lead Is Good

Some things make a lead good, and some make it bad. A lead is good when a reporter keeps in mind what news is. Definitions of news include that which is (1) informational, (2) educational, (3) entertaining, and (4) conversational—that which people will talk about. When writing a lead, you should remember these criteria. Also, you should keep in mind the major criteria for news—ranging from timeliness and conflict to humor.

A good lead includes some newsworthy action or result. No one wants to read about a person walking down the street. But if that person is shot while walking down the street, then you have a news story.

A good lead appeals to a wide readership. Even if you are writing for a specialized section of the paper, keep a wide audience in mind, including the 12-year-old reader, the factory worker, and the headline writer.

A good lead often gives readers some human interest. Sometimes, although a lead may not report significant action, it may give some sidelights that make a good story. The human situation—with human needs, emotions, and hopes—appeals to readers.

A good lead provides information the headline writer needs without having to read the whole story. When a copy editor must reach down to the fifth or sixth paragraph to find enough substance to write a head, something is wrong with the lead. No matter how soft a lead may be—for example, a lead for a personality profile—some summary facts at the top should identify what the article is about.

When a Lead Is Bad

A bad lead contains uninteresting verbs. "Chairman Robert Jones, member of the city council, *spoke* to the women's society at. . . ."; "The meeting *opened* with an invocation. . . ."; "Two hundred persons *attended*. . . ."; "The 15th annual picnic of the Animal Lovers Society was *held*. . . ." Rather, start off with some substance, such as what the person or persons said or agreed on. Or look for some other angle, such as contrast: "Attendance doubled at the annual picnic," and follow with "why" it doubled.

The reporter forces the lead to conform to a clever idea or something cute, such as a pun. Don't get in the rut of trying to be clever all the time. "The number of horses in the county has stabilized" can create a groan instead of an invitation to read the article.

The reporter himself intrudes. Avoid using the first person. "I've got opinions, too," said Frank Angelo, former managing editor of the Detroit *Free Press*. "But I can't give them any place in the paper. Nobody cares about my opinion and nobody cares about *yours*." His point was clear. Even if the young reporter has the greatest idea in the world, so what? Who is he or she anyway?

Of course, you can include ideas, but you should attribute any comments to an authority. Let somebody else voice them. Your job is to report them. Unless you write a column, which builds up its own credibility and identity through frequency and specialization, you should not use unattributed ideas and opinions.

A person's title dominates. Don't spend the first two lines of a lead or any paragraph identifying someone. Use abbreviated titles on first reference. Use phrases such as "The president's top legal aide," "the head of an urban planning agency," "a leading consumer advocate said today"—then in the second or third paragraph, let the reader have the full title. Remember, basic facts should be toward the top, but they don't all have to be in the lead. (Paragraphs have their own leads—keep the beginning of paragraphs interesting.) The long title is best given in full at the end of a paragraph, perhaps again after another reference to the speaker or source.

The reporter assumes that readers have prior knowledge. A Richmond, Va., newspaper recently ran a front page story about a state candidate whom the president was coming to town to help. However, nowhere on the front page or elsewhere did the newspaper say what office the man was running for. Presumably, local readers knew. But there are always visitors in a community, and they may not know. Let readers know whom you are talking about. A good rule to follow is the "airplane rule." Pretend you are flying over a city and reading its newspaper in an airplane. What do you want to know? You do not even know the name of the governor. So be sure to include the politician's first name and title in the identification. Likewise, when an ongoing story continues for several days or weeks, you should remind readers in each issue what has gone before. For example, if your paper has run earlier stories about a murder trial, spend a few words recapping the charges and events to date. Do not presume prior knowledge.

A bad lead contains little or no information or content. If after reading the opening lead, the reader (1) has not learned anything or (2) has no idea about what is going on, then obviously the lead is bad. Even if the lead is clever or appeals to some senses, the lead needs to be more than a hook to get attention. The lead should get attention, but it should also convey information and indicate the theme or direction of the article. An anecdote or story may lead the article, but it should do more than entertain. Let the lead convey information and/or set the theme of the article.

Set Some Taboos

A reporter, like others, grows and matures when he or she acquires discipline. One way to do this is to set rules for yourself. These can include "taboos"—things to avoid.

To start a taboo list, you can identify tiresome, wearisome, easy-to-do leads. Three leads that you could put on a taboo list in the interest of sharpening up your style are leads that use (1) quotes, (2) "you," or (3) questions.

Quotations. How often have you seen news articles that begin with a quote from a speaker, followed by "so-and-so said" or "That is the opinion of Dr. John Jones, professor of physics at True University"? You can find exceptions to every rule, but in leads generally avoid quotes followed by a demonstrative "that" or "those." Such an approach is a very lazy way of writing.

Yet, if you exercise the "this" and "that" and "those," quotes do work sometimes. For example, a quote works well when it is separate from the story—when the story can run with or without the quote. In seasonal copy, a Christmas mood piece might begin with a verse about the wise men coming from the East, printed in italics; then you could follow with the body of the article discussing astronomy and the "star" of Bethlehem. Such an article can stand on its own, with the Scripture quote joined to the article, set aside, or not used at all. A column on the late Father Charles Coughlin, famed radio political priest of the 1930s, began with a quotation from a book about Father Coughlin. The St. Petersburg *Times* played up the quote in large italics. The Washington *Post*, using the same column, did not use the quote at all. The article was usable either way.

A second way in which you might use a quote in a lead is if it is a natural part of a scene-setting technique. As dialogue, it might be part of an anecdote, a part of a short story, or an incident setting a scene from real life.

A third way to use a quote in a lead is when the information in the quote is the most important of all. Start with the quote, but remember the taboo on "this" and "that" and "these words were said by." Simply use the quote, and then walk away from the quote into the copy without the abrupt use of "this," "that," and "these."

For example:

> "The end of the world as we know it is very close."
>
> The lean-boned professor from Harvard sat on a desk in the classroom and continued:
>
> "It will come because of. . . ."

"You." Do not use the second person pronoun "you." Although media writers use "you" in all kinds of stories, it is a lazy way out: "'*You* had better tie your dog up next summer, if *you* don't want to lose him,' dogcatcher Mange E. Hound says," or "*You* will find apartment hunting easier this fall. . . ."

These types of leads—often appearing in consumer stories—pose another problem, besides being lazy leads. They are usually untrue. "You" may not have a dog, "you" may not be hunting for an apartment. They are rhetorical leads, appealing to an anonymous, general person out there, and this loss of precision makes them unacceptable in good newswriting. A good writer gives the name of a real person who has a dog or a problem or who is apartment hunting. This takes more work, but is better reporting.

Again, an exception proves the rule. "You" can have a shock value and immediacy, particularly in a universal situation. All people must die. So a story on the Detroit morgue for the Detroit *Free Press* by James Harper started something like: "You are on a slab. You came in at midnight. The tag around your toe says you are number 338. . . ."

Questions. More acceptable than the other two taboos (the quote lead and "you" lead), a question lead is one of those easy ways out, and it can become addictive. Use one question lead, and without knowing it, question leads will be popping up in many stories. Journalists and professors disagree whether question leads are good or bad, but one point is clear: you should not use them too often. Use them only when a question is the best way to write a particular story.

A question is a good way to begin a discussion piece: "Just how realistic is the new Mideast peace plan offered by Syria or Israel?" "Who will be the presidential candidates in 1988?" "What are the best beaches in the county? Judged by their use, they are. . . ."

Here writers use questions in a weather story, a lifestyle story (both of which ran front page), and a mood piece from overseas:

> Think yesterday was a scorcher? It was just a warmup.
>
> It's going to be even hotter today.
>
> The temperature soared to 94, breaking the old record set in 1936 by two degrees.
>
> And it may hit a sizzling 95 today, said National Weather Service forecaster Tom Grant. . . .
>
> —Michael Hechtman, New York *Post*

> Who's minding the people who are minding the kids?
>
> If the kids are under two or over five, no one, according to the chief of the bureau of licensing, New Jersey Division of Youth and Family Services.
>
> And the situation is making him—and other child care professionals—very uneasy. . . .
>
> —Fredda Sacharow, Burlington County (N.J.) *Times*

> SURIN, Thailand—"Elephant boy, what's your name?"
>
> Seated 12 feet above the ground, on the neck of his elephant, the young man pondered the question a moment from behind a pair of dark sunglasses.
>
> "Me? Or my elephant?" was his reply.
>
> He was Theing. His elephant was Bunmah—"bearer of merit." And this was the Surin elephant roundup. . . .
>
> —Rod Nordland, Philadelphia *Inquirer*

THE BLIND LEAD

Reporters write many stories about unknown people—people kill, get killed, they steal, they are victims, and they win honors. Actions or events make news, not names, unless, of course, a name is known in the community. Then the name itself makes news. Running a stoplight is not news, but if the mayor or governor does it, then it is news.

To start an article with the name of an unknown, such as, "Robert Jones, 25, of 1111 Maple St., son of a police officer, died when . . . ." is dull. Better: "A 25-year-old son of a city police officer died today when . . . ." Then starting the *second* paragraph: "Robert Jones, of 1111 Maple St. . . ." Holding the identity until the second paragraph is called using a blind lead.

A point to keep in mind with blind—and all—leads: Look for the emotive or familiar word to which people can relate. People sit up and take notice of "police," "death," "crash," "food," "dog," "cat," "horse," and "fun." Names of people previously unknown provide no recall value to the reader, and the reader will probably not remember the name after he reads it.

Stick with the familiar and immediately work in the important information, such as identification. The blind lead usually means that the precise information—the identification—will come immediately at the start of the second paragraph, after the reader learns what happened or finds out who the subject of the article is.

Some examples of blind leads:

TIJUANA, Mexico (AP)—A search team found the decomposed body of a 16-year-old boy, apparently dead from heat exposure, in a remote area between Mexicali and Tijuana, officials said Saturday.

The body of Aristeo Roman, which was found Friday, was the fourth discovered since six friends set out on an ill-fated hiking trip a week ago and subsequently ran out of water, authorities said. . . .

—Burlington (Vt.) *Free Press*

WASHINGTON—A well-known metallurgist has developed a new method of producing fuel gas with low sulphur content from high-sulphur coal.

Rheinhardt Schuhmann Jr. was granted patent 4,094,960 last week for the apparatus and method. . . .

—Stacy Jones, New York *Times* Service

UPDATING THE LEAD

Newspapers are day-to-day affairs—often hour-to-hour—as editions are updated. Particularly in cities where newspapers compete with other newspapers and radio and TV, the most recent story must be different from the earlier story. Updating means working in—usually leading off with—the latest information (while also summarizing again the initial event). For example, prisoners make a jailbreak. As clues develop—as the men are seen along the railroad track, as they disappear again, as search dogs sniff out the scene—the reporter will include the latest facts in the lead as they happen.

With the facts as they are at the start of a day, the good reporter asks what is going to be the most important, the most interesting, and what is the latest fact for the edition in which the article will appear.

In a competitive situation, when all parties have the same information, the reporter may want to go behind the superficial information. Thus, a reporter for one newspaper might repeat the basic events, a reporter on a second newspaper might present the latest information, and a reporter for a third newspaper, in a competitive situation, might project what experts expect to happen on the basis of the latest information. But the experienced reporter will be aware of deadlines and competition. A reporter for a weekly in a non-competitive area, for instance, may decide to summarize the main events in the lead and play down the aftermath, since a weekly does not have to come up with as many different stories and leads. Also, reporters may get too far ahead of a story and lose sight of the basic facts which they have not fully reported.

KINDS OF LEADS

The following leads point up some of the many ways to start a news report or feature. Note that each of these leads works for a certain kind of story. Thus, remember again, the specific information will determine the best kind of lead. Like a photographer taking pictures of a news event, the reporter may not be able to determine what is going to make a good story until the event actually happens. Before writing a lead, the reporter must get the facts in hand and understand the context.

1. ***The backdating lead.*** Start with an earlier fact to put the story into context:

> Three years after the government filed suit to strip a Detroit area clergyman and accused Nazi war criminal of U.S. citizenship, the matter still has not gone to trial. . . .
>
> —Susan Morse, Detroit *Free Press*

> LANSING (UPI)—Gov. Milliken kept his promise and vetoed legislation Tuesday that would have funneled $10 million to county sheriffs' departments. . . .

2. ***The stacked parallelism lead.*** List two or more unrelated items (facts, vignettes, and so on), giving each about the same space, and then link them:

> Dave England has been a pilot with United Airlines for 22 years, his wiry frame, lean features and crew cut a reminder of his younger days as a military flier.
>
> Gail Gorski, 26, has been with United for just a few months. Her good looks, statuesque figure and flowing blonde hair are a reminder that she was elected 1972 Queen of the Kentucky Derby.
>
> The two met for the first time recently in the cockpit of United's Flight 754. . . .
>
> —Michael Satchell, *Parade*, June 25, 1978

3. ***The comparison lead.*** Also in this category would be leads indicating a contrast in views or setting up a debate.

To some people, bore worms are a disgrace. Other people pay a premium to own furniture with the tiny round holes the worms make as they burrow into wood.

Gail Rowland, an Anchorage antiques appraiser, has found she must use tact when telling clients their furniture has worms. "Some people treat it the way they would ringworm in their child's hair," she says.

Rowland has been in the antiques appraisal business five years. . . .

—Evey Ruskin, Anchorage *Daily News*

Penny Capstick says the offer for her house was fair; Ruth Swift says the offer she got was not.

Both women are among the first 10 families that have agreed to sell their homes in Times Beach to the Federal Emergency Management Agency, known as FEMA. . . .

—Laszlo K. Domjan, St. Louis *Post-Dispatch*

4. ***The history lead.*** Remind readers of history and link it to the present.

STATE COLLEGE, Pa. (AP)—Clyde had his Bonnie, but the famous man-woman crime duo was the exception half a century ago and is the exception now, according to a university researcher who says men prefer men as partners in crime.

"Men who populate and control the world of crime prefer to work, associate and do business with other men," said Darrell Steffensemeier, associate professor of sociology at Pennsylvania State University. . . .

—Burlington (Vt.) *Free Press*

5. ***The straw man lead.*** State a fact or condition and then contradict it.

Advertising is a madcap industry where businesses and their employees and clients tend to come and go with the speed of an Anacin headache—right?

"Wrong!" says Don Johnston, chairman and chief executive officer of J. Walter Thompson Co. . . .

—Barry Rohan, Detroit *Free Press*

6. ***Literary devices.*** See also chapter nine on style. There are many possibilities here, from alliteration (use of words with the same initial sound) to repetition of a subject with a certain cadence to the comparative techniques of simile and metaphor.

7. ***Use of literature.*** It can be a direct reference or a play on the reference, substituting a word or so.

In the eyes of the bards, it seems that trees can do no wrong.

He who plants a sapling, Henry van Dyke said, "provideth a kindness for many generations." To other writers of verse, trees represent hope, love and a friend to the sun and the sky.

But Patrick Howard is not a poet. He is the assistant director of the Street Maintenance Bureau of the Los Angeles City Public Works Department.

And to Howard, he who plants a tree plants a potential headache. . . .

Although the city's 660,000 street trees (defined as those in roadway medians and parkways in front of homes) should be clipped at least once every six years, Howard said, city workers are struggling to maintain a 16-year maintenance cycle.

Consequently, the city's timber—from the magnolias and carobs of Westchester to the ficuses and pines of the Harbor area to the ashes, elms and fruitless mulberries of the San Fernando Valley—is growing out of control and falling on cars, homes and people in dramatically escalating numbers. . . .

—Paul Feldman, Jan Klunder, Los Angeles *Times*

If all the world's a stage, then everyone's a critic.

Only a few, however, actually get paid for having opinions. . . .

The real difference between paid critics and the general public—apart from literary expertise and background in the field—is that they have a forum: newspapers to print their words, radio or television stations to air their views. . . .

—David Stabler, Anchorage *Daily News*

8. ***The humor lead.*** See also chapter nine on style.

You could call it the ultimate manufacturer's closeout sale.

After all, the last model of trilobite rolled off the cosmic assembly line, say, 300 million years ago, give or take an epoch.

And at fossilist Judy Owyang's shop, it's 50% off on the stony corpses of those extinct critters, bargain prices on petrified lizard dung, and door-buster discounts on a pair of fossilized mammoth molars that look like a matched set of standing rib roasts.

On Thursday, at a back-to-school/autumnal equinox sale at her Westside boutique, Fossils, Etc., people who realized that they just don't make 'em like they used to—and in fact, don't make 'em at all—were snapping up sundry dinosaur bones, shark's teeth and the like at, well, rock-bottom prices. . . .

—Patt Morrison, Los Angeles *Times*

And there's always the perennial pun:

A diplomatic end has been written to the battle of the blueberries, rescuing former Secretary of State Henry Kissinger from a jam.

Kent, Conn., snug in a pastoral valley amid the Berkshire mountains, seemed hardly the place to gain international attention.

But the press corps arrived in force when soon-to-be-resident Kissinger found himself target of the town's blueberry lovers.

It began simply enough in late August when the *News-Times* of nearby Danbury reported Kissinger and his wife, Nancy, were buying a 50-acre retreat for $470,000. Besides a white house, pond, swimming pool and tennis court, the land included five acres of blueberries.

About 4,000 blueberry bushes were going to be ripped out. . . .

—Timothy McQuay, *USA Today*

And jokes:

There is a macabre joke circulating in nuclear arms control groups. It goes like this:

"According to the Swedish journals, there are 13,000 megatons of nuclear bombs in arsenals worldwide and 58,000 warheads. . . . We have a true gap in that we have more weapons than targets."

The storyteller, who asked that his name not be used, privately related the tale yesterday at a press conference to illustrate the "senseless" stockpiling of nuclear weapons by nations around the world.

Each representative of the six nuclear freeze groups, which called the press conference, commended ABC-TV for its scheduled airing on Sunday of the controversial movie, "The Day After." The film, a painfully graphic account of the destruction of Kansas City by Soviet nuclear missiles, was described as "frightening," "alienating" and "hopeless."

The groups were unusual in that each represented a profession: nurses, lawyers, physicians, educators, musicians and some of the most conservative businessmen in the city. Their combined membership totaled more than 1,300 area residents. . . .

—Kitty Caparella, Philadelphia *Daily News*

9. ***The exclamation lead.*** You can alert the reader with a sudden gasp or words of exasperation.

Has David Brenner got good news for Philadelphia!

Four million (count them)—*four million*—of the city's jobless can find work, Brenner proclaimed last night. How? Brenner is glad you asked.

Just put them to work cleaning up the Schuylkill.

One catch. The man with the idea was *comedian* David Brenner, not the newly appointed city commerce director, David W. Brenner. But that was all right with Mayor-elect W. Wilson Goode, who actually laughed at the idea—really laughed.

Brenner presented his idea to the city last night at the Philadelphia Golden Slipper Club's award dinner at the Franklin Plaza Hotel, where both Brenner and Goode were honored guests. . . .

—Edward Moran, Philadelphia *Daily News*

10. ***The moralizing lead.*** Begin with advice drawn from the facts.

It pays to check out new housing developments even before the models are finished. There have been several instances lately in which introductory prices were raised before the models were completed and the subdivision formally opened. . . .

—Jack Woerpel, Detroit *News*

11. ***The rhyme lead.***

You scream, I scream,
We all scream for ice cream!

Whether we demand it or put in a polite request, most of us get our share of ice cream.

The U.S. Department of Agriculture's statistical reporting services shows that the per capita consumption of ice cream for 1981 was 17.8 pounds.

What's in all that ice cream we eat?

According to federal and state standards, milk fat and other milk solids must make up at least 20 percent of the weight of ice cream. . . .

—Mary Parkinson, Gannett News Service, Burlington (Vt.) *Free Press*

12. ***The appeal to senses lead.*** Since readers are all physical creatures—an all too evident fact—you can give it special attention. Included here are feeling, sight, and sound.

Ahhh . . . this is the life. Stretched out on a blanket on the beach, your body sizzling in the blazing sun. Objective: a glorious, glowing tan.

The great American quest for a beautifully bronzed body has begun in earnest at beaches, in back yards, in pools and on sundecks. . . .

—Barbara Yarro, Chicago *Sun-Times*

The mere glimpse of a tall shell of frothy lager will bring tears to the eyes and drool to the mouth of a true beer lover.

And this summer, rising U.S. beer prices and the favorable—or favourable—exchange rate make this a good time to travel across the border. . . .

—Marty Hair, Detroit *Free Press*

Bubumf!

The sound sends chills up the vibrating spines of drivers on area roads. And it's been sending cars hobbled by flat tires and bent rims to area auto repair shops.

It's the sound of a pothole claiming another victim. Many an area wheel has fallen prey to these bothersome craters. . . .

—Bill Power, Hatboro (Pa.) *Today's Spirit*

13. ***The chronicle lead.*** Take your subject moment by moment.

CHICAGO—In the owner's mezzanine box in Comiskey Park, Chicago White Sox President Eddie Einhorn sits with a lap full of congratulatory telegrams. Slowly, he opens each one and digests the best wishes on his team's division championship.

Every minute or two, the phone rings next to him and Einhorn says, "Thank you" in a dozen different ways. Somehow, he never misses a play on the field as he keeps his scorecard as earnestly as though it were a religious talisman.

A fan asks Einhorn to autograph the front page of the Chicago Tribune—the newspaper that owns the rival Chicago Cubs. The headline reads, "Sox Toast of Chicago."

Suddenly, Harold Baines breaks for second base, then, as the Minnesota catcher throws to second, Baines stops dead in his tracks. Before the second baseman can recognize the trick and throw back to home, Tom Paciorek has slid across the plate with a delayed double steal, one of the prettiest plays in baseball.

"Now that's ugly. Very ugly," says a beaming Einhorn. . . .

—Thomas Boswell, Washington *Post*

14. ***The viewpoint or point of view lead.*** The story begins as seen through the eyes of one person. Variations on this technique appear in chapter nine on style.

When Beverly Stabler put on her formal dress to watch Zsa Zsa Gabor perform Tuesday at the City Line Dinner Theater, she expected a special evening.

It's not often that she and her 15 fellow residents of the head-trauma unit at the Woods Schools in Bucks County get the opportunity to catch a nightclub act.

But their evening ended abruptly and hurtfully. Miss Gabor refused to go on with the show unless Miss Stabler and five other head-trauma patients who watched the performance from their wheelchairs were moved from their tables near the stage.

"She made me feel so ashamed," said Miss Stabler, 44, who suffered brain damage when she was hit by an automobile 30 years ago. "We can't help that we're in wheelchairs. It's just by the grace of God we have them to get around." . . .

—Henry Goldman, Philadelphia *Inquirer*

15. ***The impersonal lead.*** While leads with people in them are usually best, sometimes you choose a totally impersonal approach.

This hasn't been a fun year for buying new homes. It hasn't been much fun building them, either. . . .

—Dorothy Weddell, Detroit *Free Press*

There's a mountain of wood chips two stories tall behind Camden's main sewage-treatment plant. There's a new concrete slab bigger than a football field nearby. There are 25 million gallons of waste water flowing into the plant each day.

It's ready now. Tomorrow at 11 a.m., Camden's new $3 million sewage-sludge composing project will be dedicated. . . .

—Philadelphia *Inquirer*

16. ***The suspense-mystery lead.*** Catch your readers' curiosity so they will want to know how the story comes out.

Tyrone Scott boarded an MTA bus in West Baltimore late Wednesday night, took a seat and then picked up a brown shopping bag that he thought had nothing in it but an old sheet—until the bag "moved."

"I put the bag down and looked in it," Mr. Scott said last night. "I said, 'Hey, bus driver, somebody left a dog garn baby in a shopping bag.'"

Sure enough, wrapped in that old sheet was a baby girl—no more than 4 days old. A note, handwritten on a piece of white notebook paper inside the bag, said: "Please take care of her." . . .

—Ann LoLordo, Baltimore *Sun*

17. ***The prolonged moment lead.*** Describe a race to the finish, an agonizing moment after a crash, the slow-motion details of an explosion, to provide your readers with a realism more intense than life itself.

Between cross-hairs, Sgt. Annice Gay sights her green-uniformed targets. She pushes a button. A silent flash betrays her in the darkness.

She retreats but soon will know whether she has accomplished her mission.

One minute later, Sgt. Gay peels an underexposed but adequate Polaroid snapshot from its backing. . . .

"I take pictures of graduating classes. . . ."

—Rick Ratliff, Detroit *Free Press*

18. ***The personification lead.*** Remember the TV series "Knight Rider," and many years ago, "My Mother, the Car"? You can breathe life into inanimate objects, from "pet rocks" and money trees (remember those crazes, too?) to cars . . . and footballs. . . .

Nearly 800 Model A Fords came home to the Motor City Friday.

The vintage vehicles . . . created an old-fashioned traffic jam as they tooled through the Dearborn Rouge complex. . . .

—Patty Montemurri, Detroit *Free Press*

. . . Deep in the green-painted lower levels of Veterans Stadium today, Rusty Sweeney, equipment manager for the Eagles, is blowing up the 24 little leather soldiers that will make it all possible.

It is the day of the wild-card playoff game against the Chicago Bears, and while the Philadelphia fans may have point spreads and perhaps even a Super Bowl on their minds, Sweeney has his eye quite literally on the ball.

His 24 charges will be the game's unsung heroes: battered, punted, tossed around, slammed into the Astroturf during end-zone ecstasies. But it takes a Sweeney to really take them seriously, to watch over them as they must be watched. . . .

—Rick Nichols, Philadelphia *Inquirer*

And people relate to animals described like humans.

The ducks at the Furman University lake stood silently on the bank, their heads turning in unison as their eyes followed Lyell Whyte down the lakeside footpath.

After he passed, they broke into a chorus of quacks, as if saying to each other, "What in the world was that?"

People have made such comments when they spied Whyte walking beside the lake with a 28-foot-long wooden object balanced on his head. They also have hailed him at stoplights to inquire, "What is that thing on top of your car?"

Whyte explains patiently that it's a scull, and. . . .

—Diane Sechrest, Greenville (S.C.) *Piedmont*

19. ***The overstatement lead, and understatement.***

Overstatement:

The protesting of the children around the candy store had the makings of a full-scale revolution. . . .

Understatement:

He has a little bit of power in his forefinger.

It is his finger that would press the button and destroy the world.

20. ***The test or quiz lead.***

DALLAS—True or false: People who eat food live longer than people who do not eat food.

Decide which word doesn't rhyme: "bar, car, far, jar, miscellaneous, star, tar."

By now you probably realize that you don't have to be a genius to answer those questions.

"And that's the whole idea," explains 29-year-old Steve Price. "I've started a club for people who are going crazy with high-IQ jabber."

His organization is called DENSA (which stands for Diversely Educated Not Seriously Affected). It's a spoof of Mensa, the group that requires potential members to pass an intelligence test. . . .

—Maryln Schwartz, Dallas *Morning News*, in Denver *Post*

Have you ever been kicked out of a public library for being too quiet?

Did you buy cable TV for the 24-hour weather channel?

Do you think Walter Mondale is a pretty funny guy?

Do you go to bed at 8 p.m. . . . to sleep?

If you answered yes, you're Joseph Troise's kind of guy: dull.

Troise, a tallish, baldish fellow with a drowsy air about him, is the leader of the Dull Pride movement in America. He's the founder and president of the International Dull Men's Club, and author of a just-published manifesto of moderation, *Dare to be Dull* (Bantam Books, $2.95). . . .

—Colin Covert, Knight-Ridder News Service, in Miami *Herald*

NEW YORK—Umberto Eco is:

A. The title of a Wharton School seminar on Italian commerce.

B. The scientific name for the name "Umberto" reverberating.

C. Italy's leading philosopher and journalist.

D. America's surprise best-selling

novelist whose first book of fiction, *The Name of the Rose*, now holds the No. 2 spot on the New York Times best-seller list.

The last two answers will both be accepted.

"Usually a man in his 50s escapes to Monte Carlo with a chorus girl to find again his youth," jokes the zesty, 51-year-old scholar of semiotics (the theory of signs), waving a cigarette over his smoked salmon and a couple of martinis in the lobby dining room of the Intercontinental Hotel.

"I, on the contrary, wrote a novel." . . .

—Carlin Romano, Philadelphia *Inquirer*

21. ***The zoom "camera" lead.*** As if you're on top of a mountain with a movie camera, you gradually come in for a close-up, taking more detail in view as you go along.

LEBANON, Ky.—From the highway, it looks like the typical big cemetery in a Kentucky county seat.

The grass is manicured, the graves are sodded, the weeds are pulled, the trash is picked up and the tombstones and monuments are straight and well-kept.

This is Ryder Cemetery, on a hill overlooking the east side of Lebanon. Along what first appears to be its rear boundary runs a fence topped with barbed wire.

Beyond the fence and a parallel gravel road lies a jungle of weeds and blackberry briars, the ground strewn with dead trees, debris and piles of dirt.

A closer look reveals that this is a cemetery, too—with graves covered by dirt, and markers askew, broken or missing.

Except for a road that forks into the overgrown section, there is no indication that it is part of the same cemetery as the section so well kept by Ryder Cemetery Co.

The basic difference isn't in the landscape of the two sections, but in the skin color of their occupants. Those buried in the manicured section are white; in the overgrown part, black. . . .

—Al Cross, Louisville *Courier-Journal*

22. ***The letter lead.*** It reads as if you are writing a letter to someone.

Consider the plight of the poor loving wife.

"I've got a problem," she writes. "I love romance, but my husband is about as romantic as a Clydesdale. What can I do?"

Don't fret, romantic wife. Don't despair. Romance is here.

Or, rather, "Romance!" is here, ready to rescue men and women whose lives and relationships have gone a little flat.

Langdon Hill, the man behind "Romance!"—a column on how to put romance into your life—will find a way to get the bubbly back in your champagne.

He doesn't profess to be the most romantic man alive. What he does claim is a large reader audience in 70 to 75 newspapers and good suggestions for those with problems.

And he does have romantic credentials.

Consider his past.

Now only 26, Hill has studied in France, traveled to 35 countries and learned three languages fluently. . . .

—Judy McConnell Steele, Gannett News Service, in Burlington (Vt.) *Free Press*

DEAR JUDGE:

I know you've heard this one a million times, but honest, I didn't realize I was going that *fast*. Gosh, I'm just a country boy, and where I come from, we think a tractor goes too fast.

Detroit iron is pretty exotic, let alone some imported fancy rally-racing French car. Does Your Honor know the speedometer on that little car is in kilometers per hour? That can confuse a fellow.

The allegations that this tiny little 1.4-liter, mid-engined two-seater Renault R5 Turbo 2 could blow a Ferrari 308 or a Porsche 911 off the road are purely preposterous, as any rational man can plainly see. First off, the French car doesn't *look* fast, does it? . . .

—Peter G. Chronis, Denver *Post*

Or it could take the form of a memo:

Female hockey buffs, take note. Perry Turnbull, the blond, brown-eyed left winger for the St. Louis Blues, will just about bare it all for Paco, the "indescribable" men's cologne, when he appears Thursday in a downtown department store display window.

Like the "Paco man" in the award-winning national magazine advertisement and television commercial, Turnbull will be in bed, talking on the telephone with someone special—customers of the Famous-Barr store. . . .

Turnbull, 24, a 6-foot-2 hunk of a hockey player, will be promoting Paco, the cologne made for the "sophisticated man of today." . . .

—St. Louis *Globe-Democrat*

23. ***The crisp dialogue dramatic lead.*** It's almost as if you were reading the script of a play.

Dan Greenburg and Suzanne O'Malley, his wife of "three-and-a-third years," are munching on house salad and talking about marital revenue sharing.

"Actually, I brought more assets into the relationship," he says, chasing a crouton around his plate with a fork.

"True, he did," she says.

So they got triple checking accounts: "His," "Hers" and "Theirs."

"I use all three," he says.

"You *what*?!" she says.

"Only if I need to."

"Wait a minute."

"Well, it's not that often."

"It better *not* be."

"Money," he explains, "is a touchier subject than sex—excuse me, honey, could you please pass the butter?—Everybody these days talks about what they do in bed. But if you ask them how much they have in the bank, that's really inappropriate."

"Sharing financial information," says his wife, "can be a real expression of faith—what happened to *your* butter?"

The chapter on money, they both agree, was the hardest one to write in their new book, "How to Avoid Love and Marriage" (Freundlich, $9.95), a humorous joint venture they're hoping will prove a valuable source of family income. . . .

—Bill Thomas, Baltimore *Sun*

24. ***The symbolic lead.*** You take an object, give it special meaning, and let it represent your main point.

The bullet—the one with the Broncos' name on it, the one Denver had nimbly dodged for two games—finally found its mark in Mile High Stadium Sunday afternoon.

Pulling the trigger were the Philadelphia Eagles, a team that put an end to the Broncos' winning fantasy with a 13-10 victory. Place-kicker Tony Franklin, who had never won a game in his five-year National Football League career with a field goal, concluded that trend Sunday when he punched a 43-yarder through the uprights with 57 seconds remaining in the fourth quarter. . . .

—Gene Wojciechowski, Denver *Post*

25. ***The "headline" lead.*** Headlines sound different than leads. Headlines summarize stories in a few words that may not constitute a complete sentence. However, the crisp summary headline-sounding lead can work on rare occasions, especially for the quick-pace sports story. Note how the first sentence sounds like a headline.

> NEWS ITEM: Yanks retrieve Larry Milbourne.
>
> This is merely the first step in a major overhaul of the New York Yankee infield. It is a stopgap move to contend with the repeated injuries to second baseman Willie Randolph. Down the road, when it comes check-writing time, the Yankees will take their shot at Manny Trillo, who hasn't been exactly ecstatic over his residence in Cleveland. . . .
>
> —Dick Young, Burlington (Vt.) *Free Press*

> Sentry welcomes Kohl's customers. Kohl's welcomes Sentry customers.
>
> In newspaper advertising at least, a war of words has been declared by the two long-time supermarket rivals here.
>
> On Tuesday, Sentry Food Stores, apparently capitalizing on the news that A&P plans to buy Kohl's Food Stores, ran an advertisement in The Milwaukee Journal welcoming all Kohl's customers. "Sentry Foods welcomes you as a customer. Use your Kohl's Foods check cashing card at the Sentry Food Store," read the ad, which indirectly implied that Kohl's was disappearing from the supermarket scene.
>
> Wednesday, Kohl's retaliated with a full-page ad emphasizing that Kohl's is not going to disappear. "Shop Kohl's with confidence," read the ad. "We are here to stay . . . and so is our quality and service." . . .
>
> —Helen Pauly, Milwaukee *Journal*

The list of different kinds of leads could go on. You can make your own list by studying the variety of leads in newspapers. Even if you observe a taboo list of what not to use, you can always find plenty of options for an appropriate lead to get to the point and get the reader into the story.

THE BODY OF THE STORY

How one approaches a story depends on the story. For a feature, you may want to pick the best theme or "news peg" and select additional material that ties in best with that emphasis. Then you can work in background facts along the way, and use the less interesting important facts toward the end.

For a hard news-breaking story, you decide what the key action is and simply say it. For the rest of your article you merely add information in descending order of importance, using the inverted pyramid pattern.

No one formula provides total organization. Of course, your article must hold together and move along logically, from the first statement of fact or theme to the last item of information. The section on transitions later in this book will help you learn how to cement the structure. However, some overall models of structure beyond models that emphasize leads may be helpful to you now.

1. ***The unfolding model.*** Encompassing both inverted pyramid, top-heavy hard news writing, and good feature approaches, the unfolding model assumes the fluidity of a narrative style. Like a letter home to parents, you tell the news anxiously and quickly, and, as time permits, you add details. Just as you would tell your parents what they need to know or what might interest them, so you tell your readers those facts which may affect or be of most interest to them.
2. ***Personality model.*** You introduce the reader to an interesting cast of characters. You impose a sense of order such as a common summary theme in the lead. Or you may give your readers a sense of order by presenting the most important or most interesting descriptions of the people at the top (such as you may want to do in reporting a hearing).
3. ***Dialectic model.*** You tell about an event such as an election, a riot, or a political meeting. Then you seek out reactions. You can intersperse reactions with facts or block them together in segments. You can stress balance and equality in your treatment of viewpoints.
4. ***Conflict.*** As in writing a short story, you set the scene and state the conflict. The "barriers" or problems emerge, a solution or climax occurs, and denouement or winding down concludes the story. In newswriting, you can follow this process or you can reverse it. In reverse form, you can set the stage with a summary paragraph, state the climax or solution quickly, then discuss and develop the barriers and conflicts, and provide some description at the end.
5. ***Counterpoint.*** The order comes in segments. You may insert quotes of pathos at regular intervals, such as every third paragraph, in order to highlight the poignancy of a tragedy, or you may use other refrains referring back to the first paragraph as the story develops.
6. ***The reasoning model.*** An article could proceed in a logical argumentative development. You could state a main, general fact. Then, from the known information and clues, using attribution of sources, you can trace the steps and causes which lead to that event. Or you can use induction. Tell the plight of several people who are represented in statistics, then quote the statistics and lead into addressing the whole problem.
7. ***Catalogue of ideas.*** In newspapers using tight formats, reporters are often content with listing ideas, grouped together, in summary fashion. This is a technique used by *USA Today.*

Wall Street Wednesday took its biggest jump in eight months, spurred by good news on interest rates, the economy, inflation, individual income and consumer spending.

The Dow Jones Industrial Average climbed 30.74 points to close at 1227.86—its biggest one-day gain since November and ninth largest in history. Volume was 109,310,000 shares, most since June 22.

"Institutions wanted to come back

into the market and they needed a reason," said Trude Latimer of Evans & Co. "Now they've got one and they came back very significantly."

Behind the buying binge:

- Federal Reserve Board Chairman Paul A. Volcker told Congress the central bank isn't going to rein in the money supply sharply, which could have driven up interest rates and shut off the economic recovery. Volcker endorsed a gradual tightening, in which rates should level off or drop.
- The Feds estimate the gross national product will rise 6 percent in 1983; inflation will range from 4 to 5¼ percent.
- Interest rates fell again on the bond markets.
- The Commerce Department said consumers had more money—and spent it more eagerly—in June. Personal income rose 0.5 percent; spending on consumption rose even faster, at 1.0 percent.

—Mike McNamee

In all cases, stay on the key point—fact, idea, or human interest—and do not lose sight of the lead. A good test of a coherent story is to read it not only from the first important point to the finish, but also to read it backwards, reading the less significant final paragraphs first. If your readers still know what you are talking about, you have a well-structured story.

Notes

[1]Edward J. Smith, "Screw Model has Advantages Over Inverted Pyramid," *Journalism Educator* (January, 1979): p. 17.

Assignments

1. Make a folder of examples of different kinds of leads. Find examples of the leads identified in this chapter. Identify an additional 10 kinds of leads.
2. Bring to class an example of the worst lead you've seen in the past week, and an example of the best. Explain.
3. Study a feature story in the paper. Explore all the many different ways it could have started. Why did the writer "go" with the lead in the article?
4. Take a set of hard facts—perhaps a report of a crime, fire, or accident. Experiment with six leads by splitting off each of the five "W's" or "H." That is, see how it sounds if the first sentence (and paragraph) gives only one of these six ingredients. Then try several combinations. Compare with other class members' efforts. What is the best lead?
5. Be an artist. This chapter talked about some graphic descriptions of leads, such as the inverted pyramid, screw, hammer lead, for instance. Suggest some other models for leads. Select three leads from the paper and diagram them symbolically.
6. Compare the first paragraph in various kinds of writing: the editorial,

essay, column, feature, hard news story, magazine article, a non-fiction book, a novel, a short story. Summarize your observations.

7. Take three stories in the paper, and with three or more phone calls, proceed to write an update lead for the next class session. Each week, for three weeks, continue to update the same story with a new lead.
8. Test out the theory that a good lead—or top of the story—permits a good headline to be written from it. This is not always true, especially in sports pages. Compare headlines and first paragraphs in both the front news section and the sports pages. What do you think?
9. With a history book before you, write leads on 10 great stories in history (or do this with the great events of the past 100 years); then in class, using one of the famous front-page books, such as published by the New York *Times*, compare your leads on great events with those actually used in history.
10. What "taboos" do you set for yourself—what kinds of leads will you for the most part want to avoid?

3

Getting It Right

Reporters must be accurate. Reporters, free-lance writers, and student interns in the media who get facts wrong will end up looking for other jobs.

Accuracy comes from the Latin *ad* which means "to" and *curare* which means "to care for," "to take care of." Accuracy means "to take care," and, says *Webster's New World Dictionary,* it also means "free from mistakes and precise." Good reporters care. They check over their material and work hard to be as precise as possible.

Joseph Pulitzer's motto for the New York *World* was "Accuracy! Accuracy! Accuracy!" Three years after his retirement, in 1910, he was still talking about accuracy:

> It is not enough to refrain from publishing fake news; it is not enough to avoid the mistakes which arise from the ignorance, the carelessness, the stupidity of one or more of the many men who handle the news before it gets into print; you have got to do much more than that; you have got to make every one connected with the paper—your editors, your reporters, your correspondents, your rewrite men, your proof-readers—believe that accuracy is to a newspaper what virtue is to a woman.[1]

Like virtue, accuracy is a trait that reporters have to work at. They can never take it for granted. Studies show that newspaper stories are error free about half the time. Experts who have researched accuracy find newspapers are 40.1 percent accurate (332 stories in two non-metropolitan dailies checked by William Blankenburg of the University of Wisconsin); 54 percent accurate (591 stories in Minneapolis papers checked by Mitchell Charnley of the University of Minnesota); 59 percent accurate (145 stories from 42 small-town Oklahoma newspapers checked by Charles Brown of Pennsylvania State University). These studies are not conclusive, of course, for (1) they depend on those who returned questionnaires, (2) they generally accept the views of those referred to in the articles as to the accuracy of the articles, and (3) they do not allow for source checking and source correction by reporters.

When some people charge inaccuracy, they may mean lack of clarity, imprecision, or overstatement (or understatement). They then may say that since these articles give an incorrect *impression*, they are "inaccurate."

Be cautious about using such words as "many," "some," "a few." Relying on words such as "many" or "some" can mislead. "Many" may be as few as three or as many as thousands. "Many of the city's elite attended the wedding of the mayor's daughter. . . ." The reporter probably could only identify a few or a dozen local luminaries. The city might have several thousand such people. "Many" becomes not only meaningless but misleading. If the reporter wants to be precise, and thus more accurate, in this instance—although when used intelligently, imprecision and the deletion of unimportant detail can be a matter of style—the reporter says, "The president of the City Council and the head of World Food Chain were among the guests at the wedding of the mayor's daughter Saturday. . . ."

Not only does imprecise reporting lead to misinterpretation, but it allows bias to creep into writing. For instance, in covering a rally of a group the reporter doesn't particularly like or is indifferent toward, he or she might play up the negative: "A group of protesters mingled with the New Year's Day ethnic parade. . . ." If the parade included members of the reporter's own ethnic or religious background, he or she might be positive and precise and say exactly, "Three protesters . . . ." which emphasizes there were three.

Reporters who are imprecise because of ignorance or lack of energy usually cannot cover up their weaknesses for long. Little twists in wording, the use of vague words, quotes that don't ring true, key information gaps, phraseology which such reporters obviously don't understand, or using unexplained technical information will give them away.

WHERE ARE INACCURACIES FOUND?

Inaccuracies can occur anywhere in a newspaper—from the front page to the comic pages. The front page of a Kansas daily, late edition, reported a hotel fire that took eight lives in a rural town. The fire chief's name was reported by the wire service (depending on an untrained stringer) as "Bomb": "Fire Chief Bomb said. . . ." The next day's editions reported correctly that the chief's name was "Baum."

Copy editors can confuse release dates for comics. Comics have tiny datelines to tell when they should appear. A task of the copy desk is to check comics, crossword puzzles, and syndicated stories for the correct release date. The wrong set of answers to a crossword puzzle can be as disastrous to a reader as reading a wrong name, sometimes even more so. Even Scripture in a Billy Graham column has appeared incorrectly quoted or with a key word left out, probably due to typing or transmission error.

Wilbur Lewis, of the Rochester (N.Y.) *Democrat & Chronicle*, wondered just how many errors his paper had. He noticed one day that a local priest performing a wedding was inadvertently listed as father of the bride. Lewis reported this horror tale:

> In a much shorter period than we care to admit, *Democrat & Chronicle* copy readers shifted the site of a political campaign, wedded a bride to her father-in-law, dumped a man into Lake Ontario instead of Irondequoit Bay, elected the wrong man village fire chief, admitted girls to school dropout classes when the plan was merely under consideration, pushed an engaged girl into wifehood, killed a budget when it was increased, and paralyzed a man who had suffered only minor injuries.
>
> Writers confused a witness with the victim in a traffic fatality, created a Sunday school superintendent when there was one already on the job, postponed the Civil War until the 20th century, built a temple two miles from its site, quoted a candidate in support of his opponent, placed an injured girl in the wrong car, cited Alexander Hamilton as the defender of John Peter Zenger, tossed a Korean veteran into a Japanese prison camp, and summoned James P. Mitchell back into office as secretary of labor.

Lewis then asked:

> Can any newspaper equal that record? If you dig beneath the topsoil I think you'll find that most of them can—at least some of the time. . . .

How do you stop inaccuracy?

You can't stop errors any more than you can create a perfect vacuum, or synthesize a crystal without flaw. But you can flag errors down in the hope that some day they will be only a crawl. That calls for a personal attack, a ruthless and unrelenting harassment of offenders and the establishment of inaccuracy as a personal crime.

Fallible humans, however, can take some comfort in knowing that the computers storing and channeling copy can goof things up, and since they are supposed to be more efficient than humans in some respects, they can goof things up more efficiently, too. Consider this explanation in the Camden (N.J.) *Courier-Post* by the paper's executive editor, Jerry Bellune:

Many *Courier-Post* readers were puzzled—and some angered—by a story in Saturday's editions.

The story, bearing a Washington dateline, came from the Associated Press. It concerned a federal judge's decision to impose life sentences on two anti-Castro Cubans convicted of killing a former Chilean ambassador.

The 12th paragraph and five subsequent paragraphs, however, were not transmitted by the AP. They were part of the working outline of a story on George Guilfoyle, bishop of the Camden Diocese.

The six paragraphs, none of which had been edited or were intended for publication at this time, had been stored in one of the *Courier-Post*'s two computers. They were part of a larger story on Bishop Guilfoyle and the diocese. Their appearance in the paper was not only premature but out of context in the total article. . . .

In layman's language, the error took place in the *Courier-Post* computer. Our best guess, at this point, is that a new "program," which is a set of instructions telling the computer what to do, malfunctioned.

Confused by its instructions, the computer mixed the Associated Press story from Washington with part of the working outline of the story on the bishop.

The *Courier-Post* and CSI, the computer program designer, are working to solve the problem.

According to a survey at the Medill School of Journalism at Northwestern University, Evanston, Ill., human errors are caused by these factors:

- Time pressure which may require basing the story on major facts, letting minor facts slide.
- Failure to check reference books, such as street guides, phone books, and city directories.
- "Pooling" of information or "lifting" of stories from other papers and thus compounding one reporter's errors by duplicating the misinformation in all papers.
- Using second-hand sources of information.
- The human element involved in mechanical reproduction of stories as they pass through rewrite and typographical processes.

INACCURACIES IN QUOTES

Incorrect information and impressions often appear in quotations. Recording everything accurately is impossible, of course, so the reporter often has to supply a few words. These "few" words, however, can make a tremendous difference. For instance, the difference between *a* and *the* can be considerable, yet few reporters write down the articles *a* and *the* in note taking (more on note taking later). "He will play center in *a* game of the season" means something different than "He will play center in *the* game of the season." (The homecoming game?)

What the speaker meant exactly in a quote can present problems. Don't guess—if you don't know, ask the speaker for clarification, or leave out the quotation.

A survey of 200 stories in 42 small-city newspapers by the University of Oklahoma journalism school took up the problem of inaccuracy in quotes:

> . . . the survey revealed a rather reckless disregard of the sacredness of quotation marks—that they declare to the reader: "These are the exact words of the speaker." One story, quoting a school leader, said: "'This meeting will be a good start if the governor really intends to give us what we demand,' she said, but added she felt the call was mostly a stall on the governor's part." The respondent, complaining of being misquoted, said: "I used the word 'move'; 'start' was used. I used the word 'ask,' not 'demand.' I did not say the word 'stall' at all."
>
> One respondent criticized an attribution to him in quotation marks which he did not remember saying, another stated that some remarks were not his words although the meaning was correct, and still another said he did not remember making a certain statement but that it was true and "worded better than I could."
>
> The conclusion is almost inescapable: an editor wishing to improve the accuracy of his newspaper must see to it that his reporters perfect their techniques in taking notes and in asking questions that bring out all the needed information.[2]

James Kilgallen tells of learning of the sacredness of quotation marks the hard way and never forgetting. In his report on his life, he says:

> . . . Then one night I was sent out to the South Side to cover a housewives' protest meeting against the high cost of living.
>
> A butcher named Glutz, as I recall, elected to defend the high cost of pork chops. In the midst of a hot debate, a refined housewife whom I will call Mrs. Smith arose and said:
>
> "Mr. Glutz, I beg to differ with you."
>
> The verbal clash that resulted made great copy. Back to the Tribune I went determined to demonstrate that I could do a real job on this story—my big chance. When I came to the point where Mrs. Smith was differing with Glutz, I took literary license and quoted her as shouting:
>
> "Tut, Tut, Mr. Glutz!"
>
> My story made Page One. Next day on my way to the office by streetcar, I read the story again and again and again. . . .

> I thought I was going to get a raise when Jimmy Durkin said the boss wanted to see me. . . .
>
> He came to the point. Did Mrs. Smith say "Tut, Tut, Mr. Glutz," as a key line in the Tribune's headline had stated?
>
> "Not exactly," I stammered. "She said, 'I beg to differ with you, Mr. Glutz.'"
>
> The boss eyed me coldly. There was a pause. Then he said:
>
> "Well, Kilgallen, I should fire you. But maybe you have possibilities. Go back into the local room, and never again while you are on this newspaper 'Tut Tut' again."
>
> In my long newspaper career I never "Tut-Tutted" again. I learned then and there that accuracy in journalism pays off.[3]

Sometimes even the words a reporter uses in attributing a quotation bring a response. The late J. Edgar Hoover, head of the FBI, reacted to this statement in the Akron *Beacon Journal* in 1970:

"The FBI has concluded the campus shooting by the Ohio National Guard which led to the deaths of four Kent State University students was 'not necessary and not in order.'" Hoover objected to the word "concluded." He told John S. Knight, head of the Knight chain at the time, that the word "conclude" made the FBI look like it was a prosecuting and judicial agency. Knight apologized: "We should have used 'reported' rather than 'concluded.' I regret this mistake." Knight, however, lectured Hoover for getting too worked up over "an exercise in semantics" and for a "hostile" tone that went beyond the substance of the criticism.[4]

Besides being on guard when quoting oral statements, reporters should be aware of the hazards of quoting printed information. Reporters should check EVERYTHING quoted from a printed text against the published document and never rely on memory.

An article by Dr. Richard Asher in the *Journal of the American Medical Association*, referred to in *Christian Herald*, has this advice:

> Look up everything you quote. You may be certain there is a book called *Alice in Wonderland*, and that it mentions a "Mad Hatter," that there is another book called *Alice Through the Looking Glass*; that Sherlock Holmes said, "Elementary, my dear Watson"; and that in the Bible story of Adam and Eve, an apple is mentioned. In all five cases you are wrong.
>
> The first book cited was originally *Alice's Adventures in Wonderland*. It refers only to the "Hatter," never to the "Mad Hatter." The other Alice book is *Through the Looking-Glass*. The Holmes passage runs: "'Excellent,' said I; 'Elementary,' said he." Finally, Genesis mentions no apples.[5]

HOAXES

There are always people out there who like to fool people. They range from the college prankster to the professional hoaxer who turns up a false story for the money, maybe collecting a bet.

In the old days, some hoaxers were even on newspaper staffs. Richard Locke wrote a false account of life on the moon seen through an allegedly new giant telescope. In 1835 Locke told readers of monsters of "bluish lead color." Other hoaxes that have made print include: Clifford Irving's book on the late Howard Hughes; the birth of sextuplets in Chile; the Piltdown Man, the faked "missing link" in man's history; the Cardiff Giant, a petrified man allegedly from prehistoric times—two Yale professors said the 10-foot statue found buried on a farm near Cardiff, N.Y. was for real, in 1889; a fake report of kidnapping of the wife of movie magnate E. M. Lowe in 1964; the fake report of a Detroit reporter, reporting his own kidnapping in 1973; the famous Martian landing broadcast of Orson Welles in 1938; the Chicago disc jockey's report that John F. Kennedy was still alive in Dallas.

Some people have a penchant for putting their friends' names in wedding announcements or obituaries. This report from Wenatchee, Wash., appeared in *Editor & Publisher* some years ago:

> . . . Need for new cautions reached an instantaneous shock climax when 22-year-old Mary Lou Long walked into the city room of the Wenatchee *World* Dec. 15 holding a clipping from the *World* of the preceding day telling in three paragraphs of her own demise and told reporter Beulah Davenport: "Look, I'm not dead."
>
> The obituary was a three-paragraph item in a news column on page 11 next to paid funeral notices and telling of Mrs. Long's death "Sunday in a Spokane hospital." It was seemingly authentic with her exact date of birth and residence in East Wenatchee, and with the correct names included of her husband and her parents.
>
> A quick editorial conference resulted in a decision to play the retraction high, wide and handsome. . . .
>
> Fully reported was the terrifying situation that some relatives had taken to their beds in shock, before the truth was made known. Also told was the story of the deluge of calls that came in, the father's panicky race when at his place of work the obituary was first called to his attention, and the painful check that husband and father made through the Wenatchee funeral chapels and authorities, even after they knew Mary Lou was alive and healthy.
>
> Office investigation of the matter revealed that the *World* had been badly taken in by a sobbing "cousin."

Among recent elaborate hoaxes was a fake story about the death of a leading humor magazine editor, only the magazine had never heard of the editor. The story made the rounds in some areas before an enterprising editor checked with the magazine and stopped the story.

Jennifer Beals, star of the film "Flashdance," had her picture on the front page of the New York *Post* in December 1983 with the headline "'Flashdance' beauty and exec Thai the knot." Only the story was phony. *Editor & Publisher* (Dec. 24, 1983) told what happened:[6]

> The alleged marriage of "Flashdance" star Jennifer Beals tied a knot in the stomach of *New York Post* editors who published reports and a page-one photo that the actress wed in Thailand Dec. 16.
>
> Metro editor Steve Dunleavy expressed extreme discontent with United Press International, which ran the story of the supposed marriage over the wire.
>
> "Not only are we paying them, we're paying them to be wrong," Dunleavy said.
>
> "We're very embarrassed," he said. "This is very annoying. It makes us look bad and UPI intimated it was our mistake. We had to pay to replate, besides."
>
> Dunleavy said the error was corrected in the Post at 1 a.m. Saturday morning, when the paper replated the page and offered a retraction, headlining the mistake a Bangkok hoax and the star's wedding a "flash in the pan."
>
> UPI spokesman Dave Wickenden said the story originated in Bangkok, where a reporter for the *Bangkok Post* approached a young bride whom he purported looked exactly like the film star.
>
> The American woman claimed to be Beals and granted an interview with the reporter for the following day. A public relations agency in Bangkok supplied the reporter with a photo of the ceremony, specifying the bride as film star Beals, Wickenden said. The *Bangkok Post* published the wedding portrait and a caption heralding the nuptials as Beals and her new husband Robert Simmons.
>
> Meanwhile, Associated Press dispatched the photograph of the happy couple for a "short time" to approximately 70 papers throughout the country. Beal's father, living in Arizona, read of the event and called his local newspaper to say his daughter was at Yale University in New Haven, Conn., where she was studying for final exams, and not honeymooning in Asia.
>
> "We believe this is an elaborate hoax," Wickenden said. "The exact details are not clear. We're trying to track it down."
>
> AP's assistant general manager for foreign news Nate Polowetzky said the story did not move on AP's wires, although the photo did.
>
> "A man on the desk spotted the story and thought there was something wrong with it," he said. "We checked with her agent in California who said it was all a mistake."
>
> Hal Buell, AP assistant general manager for news photos, said the fallacious photo was curbed by one of the photo editors, but managed to slip through the cracks into a special circuit.
>
> Buell said the photo "smelled, frankly" and was killed when the wire service could not "get it authenticated 100%."

The newswriter cannot check everything, but columnist Tom Fox of the Philadelphia *Inquirer* wished he had checked a certain letter from an "admiral." A letter signed by a rear admiral who identified himself as the senior officer in the U.S. Navy at Philadelphia, on the admiral's stationery, took Fox to task over what the letter writer felt were Fox's views on a controversial housing project. Fox said the letter troubled him (which should have tipped him off to check it out). The letter suggested that columnist Fox was a racist because of opposition to public housing. (Fox says in his answer, "I oppose public housing of all kinds.") The name-calling made Fox angry, when he should have kept his cool and checked on the letter. Fox said: "I thought, perhaps, that Adm. (F. F.) Palmer might have something intelligent and constructive to offer regarding the Whitman Park (housing) issue, but, alas, the admiral is just another broadbrush artist. . . ."

The next day, a correction box called the letter a hoax—an apology was offered on behalf of the paper and Fox and promised further word from Fox on the next day.

Fox wrote in his next column:

This is difficult to say. I have committed a grievous wrong. I have demeaned and degraded a good and decent man.

And as a good and decent man myself—and an honest and forthright newspaperman—I must right the wrong I have committed.

I write a column for this newspaper, a column in which I am given unbridled freedom to express my personal views and opinions on any and all subjects. It is a great and rare privilege for a newspaperman, but like all privileges and freedoms, it carries with it an awesome responsibility.

I must always be right with my facts. There is no margin for error. I understand this. It is a code by which I live. It is my creed as a newspaperman.

Now, having stated all this, I must confess in public print that I have violated this code—this sacred creed by which I labor as a truth-seeker.

Two days ago I wrote something here that was not factual. And because it was not factual, I besmirched and sullied a good man's name, and for that I feel a deep and gnawing shame. . . .

I did not check the letter's authenticity with the admiral. It was my responsibility to do so, but the letter seemed so authentic that I neglected my responsibilities, and that was a grievous error.

Rolfe Neill, my old editor at the Daily News, used to say, "Fox, if your mother tells you that she loves you, check it out."

It was sound advice, but I unconsciously violated the Rolfe Neill Law and I ended up in an incredible jackpot.

It turned out that Adm. Palmer did not write the letter. The letter was a hoax, written on stolen Navy stationery by a thief and forger who used the admiral's good name and office to spew his own sick view and I was taken in like a rube from the cornfields.

I learned all this Tuesday when I met with Adm. Palmer and two aides in the office of the editor of this newspaper.

I apologized to the admiral, of course, and he was gracious enough to understand.

"Mr. Fox," he said softly, "I think we were both set up."

The admiral's grace and dignity did much to ease the situation, for I felt like a great fraud in his presence. But his grace and my contrition will hardly undo the indignity he has suffered. . . .

College pranksters also get into the act. At William Jewell College in Liberty, Mo., pranksters announced that the college would show a series of six fictitious movies on sex education weekly on campus. The announcement was prepared in the form of a release or announcement story for the local paper. The pranksters waited until the last minute before deadline to drop the typed release off at the Liberty *Tribune*. They typed the name of a biology assistant on the release for reference; the accompanying phone number was the general number of the main men's dorm. The roommate of the chief prankster took the call—"Yes," he was the person listed (he was not) and "Yes, it was OK to use the article." It appeared on page one. The biology department was embarrassed, but so was the newspaper for announcing the new series with titles such as "The Sex Life of the Turtle," "The Life Cycle of the Kangaroo." In the next issue the paper printed a front page apology.

The mere motions of checking were not enough in this case, especially when a story as whimsical as this invited suspicion. A more foolproof means would have been to check for other phone numbers of the persons listed, comparing phone numbers with the phone directory, and checking with the head of the biology department and other officials.

In 1984, the Temple University *Temple News* had to recall one edition in which a student reporter had VDT access to another reporter's story and inserted a reference concerning a sexual function in an article about a "tireless" woman worker. Reading final page proofs in this case might have helped. Again, a front page apology and possible legal suits.

VERIFICATION

"Verification" comes from the Latin *verus* ("true") and *ficare* ("to make"), thus literally meaning "making it true." In the newspaper reporting assignment, reporters can best determine truth inductively—as in the scientific field—by getting *all* the information from various sources. At a Kansas university, a student reporter prepared a very effective series on shenanigans—including kidnapings, hazings, and orgies—in on-campus fraternities. Both university and fraternity officials made efforts to discourage, if not suppress, the story before it appeared. The professor in charge of the assignment verified the story in various ways. One way was to parcel out parts of the same assignment to other student reporters who had not seen the article, but when they came back with the same information, it seemed clear that the first reporter had not misunderstood anything. By the time the story appeared, the story was so foolproof and polished in the facts it used that criticism and reaction were not forthcoming. In fact, the sororities invited the journalism department to put on some skits about the fraternities at an annual campus show (the invitation was declined).

Watergate investigators Bob Woodward and Carl Bernstein verified their information with two other sources before putting the information into print. But people forget that two supporting sources were not enough at times to assure veracity, even for Woodward and Bernstein. When dealing with obscure, private (not presented generally to the public) information, two sources *may not be enough*. And the two sources, even if they themselves do not give incorrect information, may—by their means of communication or other limitations—transmit false information.

Once Woodward and Bernstein had four sources and still did not get the correct information:

> . . . Simons told the reporters he would feel more comfortable if they had a fourth source. It was past 7:30; the story could not hold beyond 7:50. Bernstein said there was one other possibility, a lawyer in the Justice Department who might be willing to confirm. He went to a phone near Rosenfeld's office and called him. Woodward, Simons and Sussman were going over the story a final time.
>
> Bernstein asked the lawyer point-blank if Haldeman was the fifth person in control of the secret fund, the name missing from Hugh Sloan's list.
>
> He would not say.
>
> Bernstein told him that they were going with the story. They already had it from three sources, he said; they knew Sloan had told the grand jury. "All we're asking of you is to warn us if there is any reason to hold off on the story."
>
> "I'd like to help you, I really would," said the lawyer. "But I just can't say anything."
>
> Bernstein thought for a moment and told the man they understood why he couldn't say anything. So they would do it another way: Bernstein would count to 10. If there was any reason for the reporters to hold back on the story, the lawyer should hang up before 10. If he was on the line after 10, it would mean the story was okay.
>
> "Hang up, right?" the lawyer asked.
>
> That was right, Bernstein instructed, and he started counting. He got to 10. Okay, Bernstein said, and thanked him effusively.
>
> "You've got it straight now?" the lawyer asked.
>
> Right. Bernstein thanked him again and hung up. . . .[7]

But the story was *not* solid. In a postmortem on what went wrong when they had more than enough sources confirming the information, Woodward and Bernstein say:

> There were . . . miscalculations. Bernstein should not have used the silent confirm-or-hang-up method with the Justice Department lawyer. The instructions were too complicated. (Indeed, they learned, the attorney had gotten the instructions backward and had meant to warn them off the story.) With Deep Throat, Woodward had placed too much faith in a code for confirmation, instead of accepting only a clear statement.[8]

CONTEXTUAL ACCURACY—WIDENING THE PICTURE

Sights and sounds can mislead reporters—and others. Judges know how differently people experience and see the same event. Ten people witnessing an accident—from different points along a street—will see different details and sometimes different essentials. Maybe five persons remember some of the same elements; the other five will remember others. A reporter who talks to five people may talk to the "wrong" five. So reporters should try to get the *total* picture.

As a reporter, you should find as many people as you can to help you interpret an event. Even if you have researched the assignment well, you must still contend with other variables, such as the limitation of prior available information (was it put in the file a year ago?). After you have gathered enough information to write the hard news story, you should expand your understanding. If nothing else, you may discover that your additional questions turn up ideas for follow-up stories.

An event seen in proper context—even if you have to write a series to develop all your leads—will best serve the cause of accuracy. At the scene, do not be shy. Ask eye witnesses such questions as: "How do you see it?"; "What do you think this means?"; "Have you seen this happen before?"; and "Do you think you'll see it happen again?" In an article in *Christian Herald*, "Accuracy Is a Winner's Policy," free-lance writer Evan Hill says: "At its best, accuracy is a painstaking, caring, patient and reasonable faculty of mind. And ultimately it is creative, too. For it not only looks up facts, it discovers them in the first place."[9]

Make a special effort to appreciate the background of an event by studying clippings or making phone calls to knowledgeable people before going on assignment. For example, find out before the county supervisors meeting as much as you can about County Supervisor Jones. How does he usually respond to issues? Is he open on zoning changes? Any change in his patterns might cause you to probe in different directions.

Recognizing social dynamics is often important for your accurate assessment of situations. What racial and ethnic tensions exist? What do speakers actually mean with the words they say? Do their words stem from personal convictions or are they the result of group pressures or frustrations? An action that has one significance in one community or neighborhood may mean something else in another. A neighbor giving candy to a youngster might be a charming custom in one area; it might stir fears in another neighborhood where a child once was abducted by a stranger with candy. Knowing the background of customs, recognizing cultural problems, and understanding the history or background of a setting or an event will help you interpret actions and words. A good liberal arts background in college will give you the wide background you need to assess the situations you meet as a reporter and to present your readers with accurate reports.

HOW TO GET NAMES RIGHT

If readers see misspelled names, they will assume that the reporter is careless. But even worse, they will think that the reporter is also inconsiderate and has a disregard for people. Would you want your own name misspelled in print? As a reporter, you must care about people as well as facts. Getting facts right is both a professional and a human endeavor.

Your best sources for the spelling of names are the persons themselves. But even then you may get misspellings.

A few years ago a student, preparing an article during an election campaign on views of farmers in Sedgwick County in Kansas, trudged through mud and followed tractors. In his article he presented both sides—Republican and Democrat views—fairly. Only one thing was wrong. Four of the names looked odd. The student reporter vowed that the men had given their names directly; two of them even wrote down the names for him.

But all four names were wrong. For example, "Alec" was "Alex." The student reporter had not heard two of the names clearly and was unable to read the handwriting of the two who had written their names down.

To avoid such mistakes, ask people to verify the spelling you have noted down, and if in rare instances (for example, foreign names) you ask them to write out their own names, tell them to *print*.

Above all, do not accept a previously printed spelling of a name. Never trust a newspaper clipping for the spelling of a name. The very best newspapers will have names spelled incorrectly. An article on casino gambling in Atlantic City in the Philadelphia *Inquirer* quoted a board member of the Holiday Inn who had resigned rather than become involved in the gambling operation. His name was "Klymer," the article said. A columnist following up on the story assumed the spelling was correct. He talked by phone with "Klymer" in Memphis, Tenn., and only as an afterthought asked him if "K," "Klymer" was the right spelling. "No," the man said. "It's Clymer with a C!"

Another poor source is names printed in programs—dinner theaters, ballet recitals, high school plays. Sometimes the name spellings are not even remotely correct. Sally Mihelich, dancing in *Finnian's Rainbow* in a suburban Detroit production, saw her name printed something like "Maholick." City directories, telephone directories, and national compilations such as *Who's Who* are generally dependable, but not absolutely so.

If the spelling of a name is unusual—or different than usual—for example, a Chinese name "Woo" instead of "Wu"—write in the margin "folo (follow) copy—Woo." Then the editor knows that you are right. Unless you mark the spelling, some people on copy desks may change it on their own initiative.

If a paragraph is absolutely crucial to a story for accuracy and other reasons and you have some reason to think an editor might cut it, write in the margin "MUST" or "lv this pph in." Also, if you think a sensitive story runs long, don't leave the cutting to a copy editor; instead, mark the less important paragraphs "can be cut." Some reporters also mark "cq" to indicate that they have checked each name. Some newspapers require such a "cq" above each name in a story. *Time* Magazine researchers place a black dot over facts they have checked. *Newsweek* researchers underline the words they have checked.

WHEN YOU REALLY DON'T KNOW

Sometimes you may have to report some facts when you are not absolutely sure these facts are accurate. Fortunately, such situations occur infrequently. One example is that of the attendance at some big gathering. Here you have to use an estimate. In a stadium, you know the seating capacity ahead of time. You can make some reasonable assertion after three estimates—your own, the sponsor's, the police's or an attendance official's. You may want to average these. If you're sure the crowd is between 4,000 and 6,000, report that the attendance was "more than 4,000" or "nearly 6,000" persons. You will of course be right, if not in this case precise.

In general, the best advice you can follow to maintain accuracy is: "Any information you cannot verify you should omit!", or, put more epigraphically, "In case of doubt, leave it out!"

Notes

[1]Alleyne Ireland, *An Adventure With a Genius: Joseph Pulitzer*, (New York: E.P. Dutton, c. 1914), pp. 110–111.

[2]Charles H. Brown, "Majority of Readers Give Papers an A for Accuracy," *Editor & Publisher* (Feb. 13, 1965): pp. 13, 63.

[3]James Kilgallen, *It's a Great Life* (INS, 1956): pp. 6–7.

[4]"Knight Upbraids Hoover on Journalism Lecture," *Editor & Publisher* (Aug. 22, 1970): p. 32.

[5]Richard Asher, *Journal of the American Medical Association*, quoted by Evan Hill in "Accuracy Is a Winner's Policy," *Christian Herald* (New York: Christian Herald Association, Inc., c. 1973) 96:6, p. 24. Condensed in *Reader's Digest*, Oct. 1973.

[6]"Hoax in Bangkok," *Editor & Publisher* (Dec. 24, 1983): p. 7.

[7]Bob Woodward and Carl Bernstein, *All the President's Men*, (New York: Warner Books Edition, arrangement with Simon and Schuster, 1974), p. 180.

[8]Woodward and Bernstein, p. 194.

[9]Evan Hill, "Accuracy Is a Winner's Policy," *Christian Herald* (New York: Christian Herald Association, Inc., c. 1973) 96:6, p. 24. Condensed in *Reader's Digest*, Oct. 1973.

Assignments

1. Play the old "telephone"—relaying information—game. Start off with several difficult names—with spellings—whispered into the ear of one class member at one end of the class; the student passes it on to the next and so on. How will it come out with the last student?
2. Select several dozen of the most difficult names from the phone book; divide the names up among fellow classmates, each taking several names. Each student must get the rest of the names orally from the rest of the students and compile them in a list. How accurate will the list be?
3. Take a published or unpublished article involving local names but which has one or several misspelled names. Each student's task is to make calls locally to verify or correct each name.

4. Ask fellow students to come back from assigned attendance at some large gathering with an estimate of the crowd. Discuss the estimates and means by which each determined the crowd size.
5. Make a list of 10 facts, including a person's name, titles, actions in the community, and so on. Acknowledging that the person involved cannot be reached, list under each of the 10 facts the best sources of verification and rank them according to reliability. At which point, with the information forthcoming from these sources, do you and your classmates feel comfortable with writing the story?

4

Discovering News: Sources

THE CREATIVE REPORTER

Newswriting is generally a young person's profession. Many newspaper reporters are under thirty-five; editors prefer to hire reporters in their twenties. A few older reporters do stay on in special beats or move up to management. Others become night police reporters, night copy desk editors, or columnists dealing with local personalities. But young people prevail in many newspaper jobs.

One reason why young people have the edge on reporting jobs is that they show the high levels of energy and creativity that editors want. So recent college graduates need to impress on editors that they are indeed young and have ambition, drive, energy, and the willingness to pursue a story aggressively; that they are open-minded, unbiased, and not stodgy; that they possess a sense of humor; that they demonstrate a certain maturity in judgment; and that they have excellent journalistic skills.

Although older journalists often leave newspaper work partly because salaries traditionally have not been high for reporters, conditions are changing with continual upgrading through union agreements and an improved public image of newspaper people. Also, specialized organizations have emphasized the professionalism of the newspaper journalist. Such organizations include the Society of Professional Journalists, Sigma Delta Chi, an organization which students may join, and organizations such as the American Society of Newspaper Editors, the American Newspaper Publishers Association, and the National Newspaper Publishers Association, which have established standards and adopted codes.

But all the codes in the world won't help a newspaper if the reporters are not creative. Editors periodically criticize staff members who do not come up with new ideas; this is especially true if competing newspaper or broadcast station staffs are producing good stories. A Detroit newspaper once did a study of where ideas originated and found that approximately 49 out of 50 ideas used in the paper on a given day came from the outside; only one came from the staff.

Editors want "plus" people, those who are accomplished reporters who also have creative ideas. Editors want reporters who have more determination and drive than ordinary reporters, who have higher motivation and more ambition that guarantee serious dedication, and who have more and better ideas.

Reporters who cannot generate ideas themselves will depend on other people's; successful competitors will figure out ways of getting good—and unique—stories. Reporters who have no creative ideas will not even recognize good story ideas. Reporters who have no ideas will be plodders, and their papers will be papers of record—good as reference papers but not strong in breaking important stories or following up on events and explaining the ramifications of complicated incidents.

Young people who are recent college graduates with some reporting experience often do offer creativity and courage—at least many editors think so. Recognizing this, the recent college graduate who is seriously interested in working on a newspaper ought to get on the staff of one without waiting too long. Although good jobs—often with good money—await some graduates in public relations firms, if your goal is newspapering, you should go into it right after graduating; if possible, gain experience before graduation through part-time jobs, internships, or hometown media jobs. In fact, many experts agree that if your goal is public relations, you should first spend a few years in professional newswriting on newspapers—a sure way to prepare you to write usable releases and to communicate with newspapers, skills that are essential for public relations.

HOW TO GENERATE IDEAS

Generating ideas does not come easy to many people. Nevertheless, a concentrated search for ideas will pay off. Discipline yourself. Each day come up with an idea for a news story. At regular intervals, such as once a week, share an accumulated list of other ideas with your editor. You will find that the more ideas you consciously call up, the more ideas will come spontaneously. Also consider these suggestions for searching out ideas:

1. *Read.* Read widely, including all available out-of-town newspapers. Ideas are not copyrighted. Pick up good ideas from other papers; localize and update items.

2. *Patronize the library.* Besides reading, browse in the library. See what's new. Examine covers of magazines and new book lists; follow *Publishers' Weekly* and the New York *Times* book section. Be alert to local interest; identify local authors.

3. *Circulate.* Get around town. Once a month attend some kind of event you have not attended before.

4. *Listen.* Reporters—partly because of the intensity of the demands on their time and thoughts—find it hard to leave their work behind them; some are known for being real bores at parties because they talk too much about themselves. Learning comes from the ability to listen—not from the sound of your own voice.

5. *Identify and meet leaders.* Take some key personnel to lunch and plan to run into others at fraternal organizations, in discussion groups, and at clubs.

6. *Read records.* Government agencies are full of records. Search them out. Look over past records to get information about holdings, employment, travel, financial dealings, and other activities of individuals and organizations which may lead to good stories. Be acquainted with new records added to the files. And, of course, know the keeper of the files and at least one assistant or secretary in each office who can help in the absence of the key person and who indeed may be even more helpful. (Some of the particular kinds of information you can examine in court and government agency files are outlined in Part II.)

7. *Be friendly.* Be friendly to *all* people. New reporters enraptured with the success of having landed a job and having people in the community show respect and sometimes even fear, may regard themselves as more important than others. However, the best reporters make friends of street vendors, clerks, bartenders, derelicts, and inmates.

8. *Subscribe.* Get on many mailing lists. A new scientific discovery, a new gadget, or a new policy may be as close as the "junk" mail and monthly magazines at your doorstep.

9. *Entertain opposites.* Good reporters are skeptical and suspect that often the truth is different than it appears. If you hear a report of a kidnapping, for instance, think about the possibility that the incident wasn't a kidnapping, and ask around; if a person in the community achieves high respect and praise, remember that most good has a bad side, and look around. If a person is called a villain, entertain the possibility that the person is not really such a culprit and look for other people or other forces that made the person that way. Try hypotheses that are different

than the announced or revealed facts. Through your checking, you may find that an alternative idea is true, and you may have an exclusive or at least a good follow-up story.

10. *Develop expertise.* A reporter should be somewhat "expert" in all areas. But the reporter who goes on to study or to concentrate on reading in a certain area will be able to probe deeper—in that subject area at least. A reporter with a knack for law—and knowledge gained from law courses in evening college—will spot irregularities in law cases and see vistas to investigate more readily than one without that knowledge. A reporter with special scientific understanding will move ahead of other reporters in covering scientific stories and will be more apt to come up with ideas for more pertinent, important stories than less specialized competitors.

To get good ideas, invest your time wisely, continue pursuing knowledge, and probe, search, and investigate with an open mind.

SOURCES

Kinds of Personal Sources

What are your sources? The more controversial a story is, the more sources the editor may want the reporter to have. Usually a source is a person conveying information, although the information itself may be regarded as a source.

Human sources range from the top official to the person on the street. Human sources of news are called *contact, tipster,* or *informant.* Some slang designations on special beats, such as the police beat, may include such a term as the *snitch* who may pass along information anonymously.

A *contact* is an established, usually visible person available with information, often on specialized topics. The public relations officer of a company is regarded as a contact. The word "spokesman" usually appears in print.

A *tipster* may have information or point to a source. The tipster may have only partial, unsubstantiated information. A tip often refers to the future, to what will or may happen. For instance, a reporter may get a "tip" that a waterway will be polluted or blocked as a result of new zoning action but receive no details. The reporter will get the story from reactions to the tip and explanations from authorities.

An *informant* gives information not available through regular channels. The informant or informer seeking some gain may provide information in exchange for privileges or, if from the state, may ask for protection from prosecution; he or she may inform on a regular basis.

Developing Personal Sources

If you are a new reporter, you can feel out of place in your new surroundings and feel it will take you eons to catch up on sources. But you can begin to cultivate sources almost instantly.

Here are some ways to develop personal sources:

Start your own phone directory. Hold on to every telephone number that comes your way. Classify the numbers and keep an orderly notebook reserved for them. Put tabs on the outsides of the pages so you can turn to the right category readily. For example, under an education tab, you might put PTA, school board, state, federal, community college, university, and union numbers.

Meet the heads of every agency in the community—and their secretaries. Build these names and contacts into your file system, namely into your phone listings. The dual numbers are important. If the registrar of deeds isn't in or doesn't want to talk to you, the secretary or aide might help you, especially if you know that person's name and can dial extension numbers directly.

Invite one key official to lunch each week. Perhaps your newspaper will even pick up the bill since it is to the paper's advantage for you to make such contacts. A lunch meeting gives you both a chance to get to know one another and gives you a better understanding of the person and your access.

Visit the scene. If your beat is education, then visit all the schools by appointment over a period of weeks. If your beat is the police station, try to visit all the departments—if courts, all the courts. A good way to get around to all the areas your beat covers, for instance, is to let the liaison person—or another reporter—take you through the departments or locations and introduce you to the people you'll need to know. Make a point to pick up at least one name of a cooperative person from each department. If you have a directory at hand, you can put down a special notation next to the names of those who seem the most friendly.

Visit fraternal and church groups. Show an interest in their projects. Join in panel discussions and classes if you have time. One reporter in Minnesota discovered that most of the city's elite were members of churches or synagogues. He found that because he visited adult discussion groups in Sunday school at three of the biggest churches, he developed cordial relations with most members of the city council, with judges, and with the keeper of records, as well as with attorneys, doctors, business leaders, and influential farmers. Parochialism is very important to most leaders. For instance, at a Baptist church, if you sit around the table in a discussion group across from several city council members, you will develop a rapport with them. They will probably accept you as one of them. Over a period of time, you can also attend programs at the Presbyterian church and then the Methodist. You can also visit Catholic and Jewish programs. Be sure to get back to each group occasionally. You can work the same kind of routine for the Rotary, Lions, and Kiwanis clubs, and don't forget the First Friday Catholic lunches for lay persons. You will have sources for the whole political and agency structure of the community and access to wider sources—sources your competitor never dreamed of. Although you may not have time to keep attendance up at all of them, making such contacts is a good way to start off your first year as a reporter in a community.

Send letters and cards. As you pick up information, you find out about birthdays, graduations, awards, and illnesses. Send a few birthday or congratulation cards (don't overdo it), and always send a get-well card when a key news source or celebrity is ill. For example, a reporter who genuinely liked—but did not agree with—the elderly Charles E. Coughlin, controversial radio figure of the 1930s, sent the old gentleman a birthday card each October. Shortly before his death at 87, Coughlin was not seeing reporters, but he did make a point to see that reporter; the interview appeared in the Washington *Post* and other major papers.

Acting out of humane and humanitarian motives pays dividends—sometimes many years later and in unforeseen ways. The reporter who did the Coughlin story was out of the newspaper business for awhile but kept sending the cards. When the reporter was back writing for newspapers again and asked Coughlin for the exclusive interview, Coughlin obliged.

Make friends with everyone. If you've seen the movie (from the play), "The Front Page," about Chicago journalism in the 1920s, you will remember that Jack Lemmon, playing the reporter, got ahead of all the others. He was not afraid to humble himself. He spoke to and was kind to the scrubwoman (Carol Burnett). When the mayor was shot, she was the only witness. And whom do you think she told about it?

The street vendor who has been standing at the same corner every day for most of his life and the retiree living in an old hotel who likes to drop in on meetings here and there can provide you with tremendous leads and news tips. They know ahead of time from conversations with store officials when the leading department store is going to close, for instance.

Socialize with everyone you can. Newspeople like to socialize with each other at nearby bars—some spend six or eight hours together almost every evening. If you want good sources, get away from the newspaper herd, at least once in a while. Socialize with judges, politicians, agency chiefs, and others.

Evaluating Sources

Be alert to the possible influence a source may have on your news judgment. To use a source properly and to avoid having the source use you, you should understand that a reporter's relationship to a source is never simple. Many factors such as the following might tarnish the value of a source–reporter relationship.

Motives. Few people do something for nothing. This also applies to the altruistic. They do their deeds of charity, from helping the needy to providing information for the benefit of society, because they get a good feeling of helping to change society. They are not without motives, and they want something in return, however idealistic. Try to find out what the source "wants."

Possessiveness. Some sources may feel they need a reporter as an ally and may appear to give information generously and without selfish motives. But even experienced reporters should *always* beware of information from sources and check such material. How long and to what extent, for example, should a reporter uncritically accept information from an attorney or press officer of a group such as the late Jim Jones's Temple?

Awe of persons. Few reporters can maintain professional objectivity with the President or other heads of state. We all have a built-in awe of the great. Some of us are afraid of falling from the glow of power if we should offend the powerful one. Some of us develop a hate relationship toward the one in power. The esteem in the first case and the hatred in the second show in the kinds of questions we ask. Also, the charisma which some famous people exert can affect even seasoned reporters.

Bias. What perspective does the source have? Is the source's viewpoint what you would expect from the source's social and economic class? You should find out about the social and economic background and world view of the source and weigh that against the information.

Lack of responsibility. Some irresponsible sources get themselves or others into trouble. For instance, consider the person from a foreign country who wants to go home but who talks too openly to the press. A responsible journalist may humanely protect the welfare of the source by eliminating or playing down the source's critical remarks about his or her native government.

Misunderstanding. Sometimes a reporter cannot understand what a source has said. The source may have had a confusing accent or use words in an unusual context. The reporter should avoid any misunderstanding by getting back to the source, by testing the information on others, and certainly by holding the story until all doubt is removed. The more hazy a source is, the more cautious a reporter should be in working a story.

Time difference. On the other hand, sources and their information can become out of date. What a source says at one time may have a different meaning later. Try to use information from sources as soon after thorough checking as possible.

Games. Dealing with a source may become a game. Who can get the most and who can use the other are parts of the game. The reporter should keep one step ahead, always asking where will this take us, who is in control, who is affected, and who is helping whom? Both sides add some information. Sometimes the roles are switched. The source may now gain the upper hand in getting information from the reporter.

Class status. If the reporter's middle-class self-sufficiency is obvious, to either the very rich or the very poor, the source may be reluctant to share information. Generally the reporter should not dissemble, but sometimes changing style when relating to the cultural groups of the source can be advantageous. Low-cut dresses don't work at a conservative gathering, but may work at a disco. A red coat and bright tie may not impress a stockbroker source, but may be just right at a race track. And sometimes the unsavory appearance of reporters and photographers—beer breath or general sloppiness—has turned away potential sources.

Health. Many personal factors—physical and psychological—can affect a source-reporter relationship. The reporter should be sensitive to the personal crises a source may be having. A source beset with disappointment may be more reckless, and a reporter should be aware of disenchantment or euphoria and use sources with such attitudes cautiously.

In checking a source, look for characteristics such as the following which will give the most benefit to the source–reporter relationship.

Knowledgeability. People who have lived in an area all their lives are good sources for local information. The views of some oldtimers who have experienced many local floods and backups and have seen proposals that have not worked would be valuable in an article on drainage in a neighborhood. Experts with experience or research degrees on the subject would probably also have good information.

Acceptability to others. A loner can give the reporter tips, but a source with some community standing will more likely have material the reporter can use more directly. Look to the source who has demonstrated leadership or been given some status by his or her peers—a gang leader, a spokesman for a city block, or a respected educator.

Credibility. An eyewitness at the scene of an accident certainly will be a better source than one who arrived after the fact.

Fearlessness. The source should be unafraid of the police. One graduate student working the front desk of the Central YMCA in Oakland, Calif., found he had many judgments to make such as who could get a free bed in the Y's dorm. The student worked out a simple test. To the down-and-outer who wanted a free night's lodging, the student would mention that the police had cooperated with putting people up and asked the person to wait while he made a call. If the person disappeared immediately, that was that. If the down-and-outer just stood there and looked doleful, then the student behind the desk made no effort to call the police but simply gave the person a bed.

Accuracy in relating details. The source who is correct in details will certainly be useful in helping the reporter discover the totally correct picture. Be sure to isolate some details from a source, and check for accuracy. Even then you should never take direct information from a source as fact without attribution. A source who is "always right" may slip up once, and unquestionable acceptance of the usually correct source can get a reporter into trouble.

Protecting Sources

When a source gives incorrect information or turns on a reporter, he or she may want to break the agreement of confidentiality with this source. The celebrated Bob Woodward and Carl Bernstein in their zeal were willing to—and did—reveal a confidential source in one case where they thought they received wrong information (from an FBI agent). They went to the source's boss, told him what happened, but later had second thoughts and felt guilty.

> The reporters spotted one of the agent's superiors in the hallway. Their next move represented the most difficult professional—unprofessional, really—decision either had ever made. They were going to blow a confidential source. Neither had ever done it before; both knew instinctively that they were wrong. But they justified it. They suspected they had been set up; their anger was reasonable, their self-preservation was at stake, they told each other.[1]

Reporters can be tempted to re-interpret and rationalize complex procedures for dealing with sources. Reporters and editors may reason that they shouldn't reveal a source—as Woodward and Bernstein did—but if a source has given a reporter incorrect information, then the relationship is over. If a source—whether intentionally or unintentionally—gives incorrect information, then the reporter should drop the source and not resort to betraying trust.

> . . . Woodward observed that they had the option of naming their source because any agreement with a source was broken if he had given bad information. Rosenfeld (Harry, metropolitan editor) was unsure. Bernstein was against it.
>
> Bradlee [Benjamin, executive editor] signaled for quiet. "You're not even sure whether you've got it right or wrong." He was agitated, but displayed no anger. "Suppose you name sources—they'll just deny it and then where are you? Look, fellas, we don't name our sources. We're not going to start doing that."[2]

A relationship between reporter and source should at all times—as long as the source desires it—be confidential. Again, there are exceptions to the rules, but even the exceptions are debatable: for example, the source is accused of murder or is murdered, and the reporter's testimony concerning his or her presence with the source is relevant at a trial; perhaps the testimony would help to convict a murderer or help free a person wrongfully accused. What the reporter should do in such a situation depends on the individual's own orientation and understanding of the facts. But to set conditions weighted in favor of the reporter as to when he or she can break a confidence is only to advertise that the reporter does not respect confidences.

The reporter can protect his or her sources by various means. He or she can make a point, if necessary, of taking phone numbers and names down in codes that would make the material meaningless to those raiding the files. For instance, several digits of a phone number can always be reversed in notes. Only the reporter will know what the real number is.

An alias like Bob Woodward and Carl Bernstein's "Deep Throat" can protect sensitive sources (they used "X" for one bookkeeper). Some reporters mix symbols from Greek, Russian, Chinese, and other languages in their notes. If a few of the letters are scribbled and reversed, the notes will be even less comprehensible to anyone else.

Some reporters take their sensitive files home, to vacation cabins, or to attics of friends—to any place where the law or others are not likely to probe. Notes are not absolute: their authors can destroy or alter them so that they are often totally unintelligible to the outsider (and even to some reporters themselves after the third day). But in the age of closer surveillance when the police have the right to hold surprise raids on reporter files, as with the student Stanford University *Daily News* in 1978 (action upheld by the U.S. Supreme Court), reporters and editors must protect sources in their notes on sensitive investigations.

What to Print About a Source

The former Philadelphia *Bulletin* led off a story which said:

> Informant Charles Allen has told federal investigators that Teamsters Union President James R. Hoffa hired two killers shortly before his 1975 disappearance to murder North Jersey mobster and Teamster boss Anthony Provenzano, informed sources say. . . .

In a story about juvenile authorities interviewing children of the MOVE commune, which was involved in a shoot-out with police, the Philadelphia *Inquirer* noted:

> . . . The children's statements were released to 11 MOVE defendants during pretrial hearings and were obtained by The Inquirer yesterday through a source. . . .

Charles Seib, who writes on media matters for the Washington *Post*, has noted in his column that ". . . perhaps one-third of the news stories read by the American public rely wholly or in part on sources known to the reporter, and perhaps to his editors, but not to the reader. . . ."

Some newspapers have been rethinking the extent of attributing information in stories to anonymous sources. The Louisville *Courier-Journal* and *Times* have set up these guidelines for using anonymous sources:

1. The reason for the source's anonymity should be explained in the story as fully as possible without revealing the source's identity. (If the reason isn't a good one, then the source shouldn't be quoted.)
2. Information from an anonymous source should ordinarily be used only if at least one other source substantiates the information.
3. A supervising editor should be consulted every time an anonymous source is going to be quoted.
4. We should avoid letting anonymous sources attack someone's character or credibility. If, in a rare instance, it is necessary to do so, we should not print the assertion without first giving the victim a chance to respond.[3]

The American Society of Newspaper Editors and the Associated Press Managing Editors have guidelines on using anonymous sources. The ASNE, in its statement of Principles (adopted in 1975) says: "Unless there is clear and pressing need to maintain confidences, sources of information should be identified." A 1975 APME Code of Ethics says: "News sources should be disclosed unless there is a clear reason not to do so." The New York *Times* stylebook now includes a statement on anonymous sources:

> The best news source—best for a newspaper and best for its readers—is the source that is identified by name. But it is also true that a

> newspaper, to give its readers information vital to them, must sometimes obtain it from sources not in a position to identify themselves.
>
> The decision to permit anonymity of a source must first of all be justified by the conviction of reporter and editor not only that there is no other way to convey the information, but also that the information is both factual and important.
>
> When it is established that the anonymity of the source cannot be avoided, the nature of the source must be specified as closely as possible.

In dealing with the press, sometimes government officials will protect themselves by giving conditions for and defining the kinds of attribution allowed when they give information. J. F. terHorst, who served briefly as President Gerald Ford's press secretary, put out a memo outlining the kinds of attribution used at the White House and by some federal agencies:

> *On the Record:* All statements are directly quotable, by name and title, to the person who is making the statement.
>
> *On Background:* All statements are directly quotable, but they cannot be attributed by name or specific title to the person commenting. The type of attribution to be used should be spelled out in advance: a White House official, an administration spokesman, a government lawyer, or whatever.
>
> *On Deep Background:* Anything that is said in the interview is usable but not in direct quotation and not for attribution. The reporter writes it on his own, without saying it comes from any government department or official. . . .
>
> *Off the Record:* Information given "off the record" is for the reporters' knowledge only and is not to be printed or made public in any way. The information also is not to be taken to another source in hopes of getting official confirmation. This form is mainly used to prevent reporters from speculating along inaccurate lines. . . .
>
> *Guidance:* Reporters often will ask for "guidance" on the particular timing or status of an event. In this case, they believe they are receiving the information on a "background" basis, and not "off the record," and the information will be used in stories which say, "White House sources predicted that the appointment would be made this week." It must be made clear when giving a reporter "guidance" whether he can use the information in a story.

> Those who choose to talk to reporters on something other than an "on the record" basis should be aware that they, as well as the reporter, have a responsibility for keeping the conversation confidential. An official who tells someone he has been interviewed by a reporter can't complain if he is later identified with something written by the reporter.
>
> Finally, the Press Office strongly recommends that White House officials speak "on the record." It is by far the safest policy.[4]

Confidential Sources and Legal Hazards

A debate continues in the United States as to whether reporters need special legal protection, or "shields," to keep over-anxious jurists from forcing reporters to reveal their sources or notes.

The 9th Circuit Court of Appeals, in the case of U.S. vs. Caldwell, said that newspersons should have special privilege in gathering the news:

> To convert news gatherers into Department of Justice investigators is to invade the autonomy of the press by imposing a governmental function upon them. To do so where the result is to diminish their future capacity as news gatherers is destructive of their public function. To accomplish this where it has not been shown to be essential to the Grand Jury inquiry simply cannot be justified in the public interest. Further it is not unreasonable to expect journalists everywhere to temper their reporting so as to reduce the probability that they will be required to submit to interrogation. The First Amendment guards against governmental action that induces self-censorship.[5]

The First Amendment to the Constitution says:

> Congress shall make no law respecting an establishment of religion, or prohibiting the free exercise thereof; or abridging the freedom of speech, or of the press; or the right of the people peaceably to assemble, and to petition the government for a redress of grievances.

In the Caldwell case, Earl Caldwell, a *New York Times* reporter covering black militant groups in California, was ordered to produce his notes and tapes concerning the aims and plans of the Black Panthers. Caldwell argued that to do so would result in "driving a wedge of distrust and silence between the news media and the militants." Caldwell refused to appear before a grand jury as a result of a subpoena and received a citation for contempt. The appellate court reversed the decision.

Later, however, the high court limited the privilege of newspersons. It reversed the lower Caldwell decision by upholding convictions of Paul Branzburg, a Louisville *Courier-Journal* reporter who witnessed the illegal synthesizing of hashish from marijuana and later spent several weeks interviewing drug users. The high court, 5 to 4, said that state or federal grand juries could require newspersons to appear and testify before such juries without abridging the First Amendment. This judgment removed the protection newspersons had traditionally had when they concealed criminal behavior of sources and possible evidence.

In the case of Myron Farber, a reporter with the *New York Times*, the U.S. Supreme Court let stand a New Jersey Supreme Court ruling that the *Times* and Farber were in contempt for not turning over files in the investigation of the deaths of 13 patients in a hospital 10 years earlier. Farber spent 40 days in jail before the doctor on trial, Mario Jascalevich, was acquitted. New Jersey had a "shield law" protecting reporters, but the New Jersey Supreme Court had ruled that First Amendment rights, even when protected by shield laws, must give way to a defendant's right to a fair trial. The U.S. Supreme Court did not comment in the Farber case, which was complex: Farber sold rights to a book on the case before it was adjudicated; this sale indicated to the jurists that he might have some monetary interest in the outcome of the trial. Contracting books in advance is a standard and acceptable practice, but in this case confused the issues. Most observers feel that the Supreme Court still has not ruled definitively in this area. Movements are afoot to secure national legislation to reinstate newspersons' privileges.

In the early 1970s, a rash of bills before state legislatures gave special privilege to reporters, much as lawyers, doctors, and clergy are protected from coercion to reveal confidentialities. The bills and laws fell into two classes—absolute privilege to decline to give information or names of sources, and qualified privilege with some conditions under which the newsperson does not have protection. Over two dozen states now have shield laws, with slightly more favoring the absolute privilege shield laws.

California has had a shield law since 1935 as a part of the Code of Civil Procedure. It now also includes radio and TV and applies to newspersons at the time the news happens and not just at the time of the challenge. It protects unpublished as well as published material, too.

The section in the California law that deals with newspersons' privilege says:

> A publisher, editor, reporter, or other person connected with or employed upon a newspaper, or by a press association or wire service, or any person who has been so connected or employed, cannot be adjudged in contempt by a judicial, legislative, administrative body, or any other body having the power to issue subpoenas, for refusing to disclose, in any proceeding as defined in Section 901, the source of any information procured while so connected or employed for publication in a newspaper.
>
> Nor can a radio or television news reporter or other person connected with or employed by a radio or television station, or any person who has been so connected or employed, be so adjudged in contempt for refusing to disclose the source of any information procured while so connected or employed for news or news commentary purposes on radio or television. (Evidence Code, Section 1010, California Code of Civil Procedure)

Although observers have considered it an absolute shield law, this law has not always proven so. In 1971, in Farr vs. Superior Court, an appeals court questioned the law's constitutionality. Los Angeles *Herald-Examiner* reporter William Farr at the outset of the trial of the Charles Manson "family" on multiple murder charges wrote an account of a prospective witness who said the Manson gang also intended to murder show business personalities. The judge wanted to know where Farr had gotten the information. Farr simply said he had received information from two of the six attorneys in the case and from another source. However, under oath, all six attorneys denied having given this information. Experts saw Farr's case as constituting an exception to the privilege law. His refusal to divulge his sources specifically led to a contempt of court citation, and he was jailed.

In Minnesota, which has a qualified shield law, a judge can still force a disclosure of sources when all three of these conditions are met:

1. That there is probable cause to believe that the source has information clearly relevant to a specific violation of the law other than a misdemeanor.
2. That the information cannot be obtained from any alternative means or remedy less destructive of first amendment rights, and
3. That there is a compelling and overriding interest requiring the disclosure of the information where the disclosure is necessary to preserve justice.

Whether qualified privilege shield laws are really desirable is debatable. With such limitations, with good reasons given, a reporter is in danger of being asked to be an arm of the law in turning over material that might be used in the defense or prosecution. Also such shield laws, some believe, define the rights of the reporter too closely, treading on the spirit of the First Amendment.

A set of "pros and cons" for shield laws appear in a booklet, *The Courts and the News Media*, by Albert G. Pickerell and Michel Lipman. Among the arguments opponents of shield laws use, they say:

> A shield law could conceivably be a step leading to further governmental encroachment on the press. The news media should not be in a position of petitioning Congress for their rights since Congress would be placed in the role of defining *who* is protected by the statute—or *who* is a newsman. The next step could be a licensing process, since the news media have asked to be placed in the same category as the licensed, screened professions receiving such privilege—for example, attorneys, doctors and priests.[6]

Press Releases as Sources

Announcement stories that companies or individuals send out often plague the newspaper office. As one editor put it, these announcements or press releases arrive as a giant snowstorm each day. Obviously, a newspaper can use very little information that comes into the office this way—even if it is high quality—because of space limitations. But most releases that come by mail are worthless, especially for the bigger paper which cannot publish information on every activity of a company and its personnel. While most releases are self-serving, telling the general public what the person or company wants the public to know, nevertheless, sometimes releases can provide sources and ideas for news.

Press Releases as Reference Material

However, releases *are* valuable for setting up a directory of potential sources. The professional release has the name and address of the PR officer and the company which can be contacts, as can the names of new heads of divisions and other personnel mentioned in releases. For example, if a scientific researcher is the subject of a release—maybe he or she is just back from a trip—the information on the trip is probably not of general interest, but basic information on the person may be useful as he or she may later be able to supply information for a scientific article. An educator may be useful for an education article or a theater director for a future piece on the arts.

The reporter should not throw too much away without at least an evaluative glance.

Some small weeklies without adequate staff use releases directly. Most newspapers rewrite any releases they decide to use, for several reasons. First, an editor can never be sure of the veracity of all releases; often the lowest person on the totem pole, a trainee in the company, has worded the release. Certainly many releases are incomplete, and the newspaper person must make a call to flesh out or verify information. For instance, a good writer or editor will want the reader to know where an event will take place, a point that a release may overlook. An announcement of a campus event by a university may make sense to campus readers, but the general readers will need to know the address of the lecture hall.

Most standard releases have a release date, or "embargo" line, which tells the paper when to release or print. Editors should respect these restrictions, but they do pose a problem.

Embargo comes from *embargar*, Spanish for "to arrest," "to seize" (and Latin, *in*, "in" or "on," and *barra*, "bar"). In commerce, embargo has meant a restraint of ships. In journalism, embargo means that a hold or restraint is to be put on the use of information until a specified time indicated on the release. For example, a major corporation is calling a press conference which will likely say the company is expanding or going out of business, but the company is not to make the announcement until 9 a.m. on a certain day.

For the newspaper which may be on a different schedule, this is bad timing. A 9 a.m. time favors the wire services and afternoon newspapers. A morning paper's main deadline is likely to be 5 p.m. the day before. The morning paper reporter favors a 3 p.m. press conference when the competing afternoon editions are all put to bed for the day.

As a morning newspaper reporter, what do you do when the biggest industry in town says it will have an extremely important announcement the next day at 9 a.m. at a press conference in the ballroom of a local hotel? At this point, all you have is an announcement of time and place and no content. Some purists would argue that all you can do is sit back and wait. Others would tell you to get on the phone, call anyone you know or can find out about at offices in other branches of the company across the United States. With a general hint about the topic, a skilled reporter may be able to zero in on specifics.

Conventional newsrooms almost always put embargoes on stories until the time of the speech or event. Or, if a major story is breaking, press officers will schedule a press conference early in the day before the big announcement. For example, a national nonprofit agency had prepared grandiose plans for reorganization—board officers had heard that much about the plans in a general meeting two days before the scheduled announcement in Detroit. Reporters from New York, Washington, and the wire services gathered for the 7 a.m. announcement breakfast. But to their amazement, the local morning paper was already on the street with a banner headline on the story. The other reporters were all very bitter toward the local reporter who had secured the story and who even developed it with reaction from other sources. The reporters argued: "You broke the embargo!"

The energetic reporter countered: "What embargo?"

"It's in your box in the press room!"

"You may be right. But I haven't been in the press room or looked in my box. I have not seen any embargo."

Of course, the energetic reporter, suspecting that there would be an embargo on the story, had avoided formal press room arrangements, sought out the document from a delegate who had a copy of the reorganization plan in his packet without any embargo restriction.

Investigative Sources

One of the best examples of the importance of reporters developing sources is the classical Watergate case back in the 1970s. How far would Carl Bernstein and Bob Woodward have gotten in the Watergate investigation without a basic source—"Deep Throat," the insider—who whetted their appetite for information and supplied enough to keep them going? They also had a myriad of other sources:

Telephone books. They were able to make a profile of James McCord, one of the people arrested at the Watergate headquarters, who was at the Watergate complex after the break-in at Democratic headquarters—without talking to him. The reporters followed up on an Associated Press report that McCord worked with the Committee for the Re-Election of the President (CRP). In the telephone book they found the number of the private security consulting firm McCord ran. When they called, no one answered. They then checked the criss-cross telephone directories which listed phone numbers by addresses. Here they found neighbors in the same office building as McCord. When they called these people, some were able to supply information, others were not. Eventually a profile of McCord emerged.[7]

Washington *Post* police reporter. A *Post* police reporter had information of a Howard Hunt connection with the White House from one of his sources and passed it along. Address books of two of the men the police arrested had the same name and number: Howard E. Hunt with White House identification.[8]

Library of Congress. Here Bernstein and Woodward were able to find a cooperative clerk who showed them everything that Hunt had read. Included was material on the Kennedy Chappaquiddick incident, when a young lady with Edward (Ted) Kennedy had drowned and which Kennedy did not report for several hours. Contacts in the White House had said that Hunt conducted an investigation of Democrat Kennedy because the White House feared a Kennedy presidential campaign.[9]

Personal telephone sources. Persons provided information on calls and directed Bernstein to Miami for telephone listings subpoenaed by a district attorney. Bernstein was able to confirm a New York *Times* story about money being laundered through Mexico.[10]

***Post* researcher.** The CRP guarded a list of the 100 people who worked at the national headquarters as if it were a classified document. The *Post* obtained a copy through a researcher for the paper who had a friend at CRP. From this, Bernstein and Woodward were able to make their nightly visits to people by using their addresses and knocking on doors. The most valuable information came from a bookkeeper who told about a slush fund and said that the FBI investigation had not asked the right questions and had, therefore, ignored some things.[11]

FBI and Justice Department sources. "... the reporters checked regularly with a half-dozen persons in the Justice Department and the FBI who were sometimes willing to confirm information that had been obtained elsewhere. The sources rarely went further, often not that far."[12]

Call from an unknown lawyer. The lawyer had nothing to do with the Watergate investigation. But he told Bernstein that Donald Segretti (a political trickster) had a friend, Alex Shipley, who had been approached by an Army friend about doing some "political work" for the Nixon campaign. Bernstein eventually called Shipley in Tennessee and Shipley told Bernstein about Segretti. Bernstein was given names of other Army friends and eventually tracked Segretti down.[13]

Court records. Bernstein called District Attorney Earl Silbert who was handling the Watergate grand jury investigation and asked him if he could have the jury roster. Silbert refused and rejected Bernstein's argument that the list was public record. Woodward asked a friend in the clerk's office about the list and the friend told him the same thing. Woodward identified himself as a reporter. The clerk said that he could look at the list but that he could not copy any names or take notes. Woodward found the Watergate grand jury list, memorized four or five names and addresses at a time, and slipped off to the washroom and wrote the information down. He repeated this procedure until all the names were written. He and Bernstein visited some of the jurors but were unable to get information. They held back after Judge John Sirica warned against contacting grand jurors.[14]

Federal courthouse reporter. Lawrence Meyer on the *Post* came across a confidential copy of a routine legal agreement of prosecutors and attorneys for the Watergate break-in defendants. Although it contained little new information, one thing stood out. A phone in the White House with the billing address of a Kathleen Chenow had been disconnected. Looking through the crisscross directory, Bernstein located a former roommate of Chenow. Through the roommate, Bernstein traced Chenow to Milwaukee where she had moved. It turned out that she had been a secretary to the secret White House group known as the "plumbers" which was investigating leaks to the media.[15]

Address on envelope. When Bernstein was in District Attorney Earl Silbert's office, Bernstein saw a letter on the desk which proved to be from a company where McCord had bought the bugging equipment. Bernstein made a mental note of the address and proceeded to contact the company. He wrote a story on how much money McCord paid the company—$3,500 in thirty-five $100 bills.[16]

Plain sleuthing. Most of Woodward and Bernstein's information came from digging. The reporters continued to expand a list of names which they kept checking. These included people who were working in or had worked in the White House, the Justice Department, and the FBI. By checking out every lead, the reporters found new leads which resulted in new connections.

Using Records

Transactions between people are recorded many ways. And various kinds of records, although they may not always appear to be interesting, can communicate fascinating information—and proof or evidence—about what people do. Studying records can add depth and conviction to a story, but you can also find many ideas for new stories by looking through records for unusual facts and matching these facts against other information. Besides police, court, and specialized resources noted in other chapters, some records and sources you may want to check out follow here. (Be sure to check your state open record laws concerning access.)

Birth records. The county clerk or health department (or a bureau of vital statistics) keeps birth records. If you suspect that people are lying about their ages, checking records can help set things straight. Such research can also help in identifying who parents are—information which you may want to report in some stories.

Death records. The county medical examiner can supply information on the location, time, and cause of death.

Marriage. The clerk in the marriage licensing bureau can tell you who has applied for licenses.

Divorce. The start of a suit is public. The name and action are available from the court clerk. You can find information about subsequent developments—except for grounds—in the prothonotary, or chief clerk's office, indexed by the party's name, alphabetically by month or year. You will usually need some idea of when the action started.

Wills. You can read the books of copies of wills as well as the original documents from a register of wills kept by clerks of specific courts (in Philadelphia, the clerk of the Orphans Court) or by a prothonotary. Wills are filed by year and number.

Real estate. The registry of deeds or the registry unit of the department of records keeps information which allows you to trace the ownership of a piece of land all the way back to the first owner. You need to know the address so that you can consult the special map which gives a plan number. You can look at the plan which pictures the address you are interested in. Such plans may have more than one file number on them because lots or tracts are sometimes realigned over the years. With these numbers in hand, you can obtain the abstracts, which are usually on microfilm. An abstract will contain the date of sale, the seller's and the buyer's names, and the size and location of the lot or parcels. A special section in a deed, called a "recital," traces the owners and means of sale or transaction. These can include public grant (patient), foreclosure (sheriff sale), will, private grant (deed), or condemnation.

State tax stamps affixed to the deed can give you an indication of the sale price of the property.

Property tax records. The assessor's office has legal descriptions of land tracts and records of assessment.

Neighbors on a city block. Crisscross phone directories (your newspaper and public library have these) list streets alphabetically, with street addresses and residents. You can use these to identify people living on each block. Also, city directories list people alphabetically and by street and telephone numbers, and include information about employment and spouses' names.

Building permits. On the surface, such permits may not appear to tell you very much, but they include information on renovations and additions and on contracting firms; they also provide you with a master plan of the property. By studying such permits, Jack Tobin identified a number of persons working with the contractors or subcontractors at Richard Nixon's house at San Clemente, Calif. By talking with these workers, Tobin learned that they were being paid with a government check from the National Park Service.

Bankruptcies. The clerk of the U.S. district court has papers on bankruptcy cases filed in that particular district. Such papers give a total look at the assets and debts of a person. In the bankruptcy procedure, the creditor may have instigated a "205A examination" in which the creditor's lawyer questions the debtor. The title of the investigation comes from the part of the bankruptcy code directing the procedure. If the clerk does not want to make additional material available, you can remind the clerk about the ruling supporting access (Winton Shirt Corp. vs. Elizabeth Trust Co., 104 Fed Reporter, 2nd Series, 777, 3rd Circuit, 1939).

Judgments. County clerks' offices keep records of persons collecting a debt through the judgment of the court. Such records reveal the debtor's credit standing.

Corporations. Businesses file incorporation papers first with the secretary of state in the state capitol. Eventually these papers go in the county clerk's office in the county where the new company is located. These files give the company's purpose, its board of directors, its address, and a record of stock issued. *Moody's Industrial Manual* names U.S. corporations, with staff members, history, officials, and budget.

Voter registration. In the register of voters you can find a person's address, birth date, profession at the time of registration, voting record, and physical appearance.

Auto records. The secretary of state keeps vehicle records, including information from license applications.

Payroll records. If the person is working for the state, the payroll record is public. Check with the civil service department.

Professional records. Regulatory boards in a state keep public records available on the professional groups they control, such as doctors, lawyers, nurses, funeral directors, realtors, hairdressers, and technicians.

Permits and inspections reports. The department of licenses and inspections has public records of citations against any licensed establishment. The health department can make available weekly food inspection reports of area restaurants, schools, and other institutions. The fire department should provide you with reports of inspections at public places.

Traffic accident reports. In the records department of some cities, you can get a copy of an accident report for a modest fee if you provide the driver's name and the place and date of the accident.

Military records. The Pentagon can supply you with names of men and women on active duty. The *Army Register, Navy Register,* and *Register of Commissioned and Warrant Officers of the Navy and Marine Corps* list the names of officers.

Income tax records. You may see the tax forms of nonprofit corporations by filing Form 990 with the Internal Revenue Service, but this can take several months. Members of religious and cult groups, for tax-free status, must fill out a form under Section 501(c)(3) of the Internal Revenue Code.

Telephone records. For billing purposes, the telephone company keeps lists of long distance telephone calls. Sometimes a personal acquaintance in the company can supply these; some government agencies with special powers can also subpoena them. In their *Investigative Reporting* book, David Anderson and Peter Benjaminson add:

> It is also possible to obtain these records by trickery. At least one reporter we know would stoop so low as to call the telephone company business office, and, posing as the person being investigated, claim that he didn't recall making certain long-distance calls that had been charged to him. He would then ask the phone company to check the numbers and dates of the calls and report back. (The same gambit is sometimes used by reporters who wish to check on the money a person has borrowed. They simply call the credit company to "reconfirm" the loan. A similar technique can be used to check on someone's airplane reservations.) Obtaining such information from the phone company, however, works both ways. So, if an experienced investigator is intent on protecting a source's identity, he or she may call from a remote pay phone or from the paper's subscription department rather than from a home or desk phone.[17]

A useful book for more detail on using records is John Ullmann and Steve Honeyman's *The Reporter's Handbook: An Investigator's Guide to Documents and Techniques*, a project of the Investigative Reporters & Editors, Inc. (New York: St. Martin's Press, 1983). The book, for instance, includes names and addresses of places to write in all 50 states for birth, marriage, divorce, and death records.

Many out-of-the-way and little-known sources from groups may be very useful to you. The annual minutes of the United Methodists in one area in Illinois proved to be important information in profiling the Democratic candidate for the presidency in 1972. A tip that candidate George McGovern had been a seminarian (a fact which he did not include in his fact sheets) led a reporter to interview his former instructors. They in turn pointed to recorded minutes that identified the candidate as a clergyman in his early years. Further sources included interviews done with people in the town where he had been the pastor, yellowed newspaper clips, and reminiscences that a reporter tracked down from old-timers across the country. When the research was done, the article with a reaction from McGovern to the information made national news:

THE BRIEF CAREER OF REV. McGOVERN
NEWSDAY

Diamond Lake, Ill.—The Rev. George S. McGovern—politician, senator, presidential aspirant—has done more than kiss the babies, as most bigwig politicians are known to do on the campaign trail.

In his career, the South Dakota senator has baptized them.

Although his press handouts make no mention of McGovern as clergyman, the minutes of the Rock River (Northern Illinois) Conference of the Methodist Church in 1946 and 1947 list him as a pastor of the rural Illinois parish of Diamond Lake, 40 miles northwest of Chicago.

If he should go all the way to the White House, he would be the first preacher to reside there since the 20th President, James A. Garfield, who had a regular circuit of churches in northeast Ohio for the Christian Church—Disciples of Christ—before he became President in 1881.

McGovern was a compassionate, promising—if not organized—young pastor, who was near the top of his class in church courses at the Methodist Garrett Biblical Institute (now called Garrett Theological Seminary) in Evanston, Ill.

Interviews with McGovern's former professors in Chicago and Evanston show that he was highly regarded. His courses ranged from economics to worship. He earned an A− in "Economic Issues and Christian Ethics" from the Rev. Dr. Murray Leiffer, the recent past president of the United Methodist Judicial Council. The Rev. Mr. Leiffer described McGovern in an interview as "particularly sensitive, showing considerable insight." In the course "Worship in the Church," required for all student pastors, the Rev. Dr. Rockwell Smith remembers McGovern "as a very pleasant student—the kind you feel when you are dealing with him, that you are dealing with a man who could make good use of what you give him."

Dr. Smith did not divulge McGovern's grades.

McGovern, son of a Methodist pastor, served during 1946 and 1947 at Diamond Lake at $1,000 a year. Membership under him went up from 133 to 170. Although not ordained to full orders, McGovern was licensed, a procedure that comes on recommendation of Methodist officials. It entitles one to conduct the church's full rites, including marriage and baptism, in a particular parish only. . . .

But what were McGovern's clerical days like in the eyes of his parishioners? Was he a success or failure? Just why did he quit after doing well in seminary and after giving his rural parishioners indications he was going to stay on? Church diaries for the period in the Diamond Lake Methodist Church (now called Mundelein Methodist Church) indicate that the McGoverns had just bought a house shortly before he quit, not the action of a man planning to leave the area.

McGovern seemed to have had little use for the establishment of formal ways of doing things, but at the same time, he kept the essence of faith before him. His style of baptizing—at least 17 persons were baptized by him at Diamond Lake—revealed a disenchantment with formality.

McGovern baptized Mrs. Vivienne Umbdenstock and her five children in her living room (Mr. Umbdenstock already was baptized). There were no members of the congregation with him, the Umbdenstocks recall. In fact, McGovern was so informal he went into the kitchen and got a kitchen bowl for the water, and had it all done in short order with a few sprinkles.

The oldest of the five children, now Mrs. Elaine Teltz of Lake Villa, Ill. recalls: "We all lined up in the living room according to age, which was also according to height. He (McGovern) was a very tall and good-looking man. Since we were older than most who are baptized, he thought it would save some embarrassment to baptize us in the house and not have to stand up in church. . . ."

Mr. and Mrs. Robert Whitney had their daughter Kay baptized Aug. 3, 1947 by "the reverend down the corner" without preparation.

Mrs. Whitney was a Catholic, her husband a Baptist. "We were not accepted in the Catholic faith, so we went to the church on the corner, six blocks away. I explained we were not of the Methodist faith, but Rev. McGovern said it did not matter. So we went over to the church at 2 p.m. one Sunday afternoon, and the reverend sprinkled her head with his fingers.

"My husband offered Rev. McGovern a donation in an envelope ($5), but he would not accept it. He said he was happy to baptize our daughter and that it was a service the church gives. All he wanted, he said, was to 'see you and the baby sitting in our pews.'"

The Whitneys did return to the corner church. But they did not see McGovern again and did not attend church for four years. Ultimately, the family became very active there—Mrs. Whitney taught Sunday school for 18 years, and her husband was Sunday school superintendent for 11 years. Kay sang in the choir for 16 years.

Now Kay Sabatka, 25 and working as an accountant at a Lake Zurich, Ill., paint firm, says: "When growing up, I didn't think much about it. Now it's very thrilling, and a thing of pride."

McGovern apparently was successful in getting the church's Men's Club off the ground, and once appeared in one of their minstrel shows. He was less successful in getting a youth program going. And the current pastor, the Rev. George Groh, believes "McGovern was the world's worst record keeper, but then again they didn't stress this in seminary in those days." . . .

At the Shreveport (La.) *Times*, an article series using a wide range of personal and record sources led to the resignation and indictment of the city commissioner of public safety. One of the writers of the series, Lynn Stewart, recalls: "Our initial confidential source was a high-ranking police department official. Using the background information he gave us, we went to records at city hall to prove our case. Later we studied payroll records, purchase orders, telephone bills, and other internal records."

The series, which printed a ledger of the checks issued to the commissioner, began:

Large sums of taxpayers' money are being spent by some city officials who give no public accounting of those expenditures, a *Times* survey of records has revealed.

The funds are being obtained by officials with only a vague indication of their eventual use. In each case they are requested by a commissioner and approved without question by Finance Commissioner George Burton.

They include 43 payments totaling $17,300 paid in the last 15 months to Commissioner of Public Safety George

W. D'Artois personally.

Each payment was for $400, with the exception of one $500 check, and, since Jan. 1, 1975, these have been issued on an average of twice a month.

The only information on file in the Finance Department to indicate what the funds are being used for are brief letters from D'Artois. In most cases, the letters state that the funds were being requested "for obtaining evidence and information from informants on organized crime cases."

D'Artois was asked by the *Times* for records concerning those expenditures. He produced only a manila folder filled with miscellaneous pieces of paper that included various copies of offense reports, torn scraps of papers and some receipts.

Unlike other divisions of his department, he could produce no tabulated list reflecting date, payment, and case, and said the amount he had received during 1975 was "whatever the finance department says it is."

An unusual turn of events occurred during the *Times'* study when Police Chief T. P. Kelley said he did not know that D'Artois was drawing any funds for such investigations or conducting investigations requiring the use of such funds. . . .

—Charlotte Burrows, Margaret Martin and Lynn Stewart, Shreveport (La.) *Times*

A second article went further back in the records and studied the pattern of the check payments:

Monies paid to Commissioner of Public Safety George W. D'Artois personally by the City of Shreveport increased dramatically the same month that George Burton was first sworn in as Shreveport finance commissioner, a *Times* study has revealed.

Up until December, 1971 city funds to D'Artois, other than his paycheck, averaged about $600 a year. In the portion of 1971, prior to Burton's election, D'Artois had received only $420.

But in December of 1971—the month that Burton was elected and sworn in—D'Artois drew $600, bringing the total for 1971 to $1,020. His payments since then have never dropped below $5,100 a year and in 1975 they soared above $13,000. . . .

When questioned by the *Times* enterprise team about the increasing number of payments to Commissioner D'Artois since his election, Burton replied: "He requested funds to purchase information and I honored his request."

Asked about the markedly lower payments to D'Artois in prior years, Burton answered, "I didn't bother to check. . . . I don't have any idea of what he got before. I don't see the significance of it.

"I don't know his sources of information. I do not have personal knowledge of his sources of information," the finance commissioner said, and, referring to informants, Burton added, "I don't want to be responsible for someone's safety. Who he designated is not my business."

During the period in which the large payments on a regular basis to D'Artois began, there was neither an experienced finance commissioner nor an auditing firm familiar with the city's past financial practices. . . .

Finance department records show that from 1963–1969, checks issued to D'Artois averaged about four payments a year, and most were in the $100 to $200 range. There were no checks—other than paychecks—to D'Artois recorded in 1970. . . .

—Margaret Martin and Lynn Stewart, Shreveport (La.) *Times*

Access to Public Records

The right to inspect government records does not exist by itself by any natural, moral, or common law, but is defined and limited by statutes of the state and federal government.

In many states, groups or committees—often connected with Sigma Delta Chi, Society of Professional Journalists—have published guidebooks on what is available from various branches of government and agencies and how to go about obtaining it. In Pennsylvania there is the Pennsylvania First Amendment Coalition which has put out a booklet, the *Media Survival Kit*.[18] It offers the following advice on what to do when you are denied access to the records of any court, agency, board, commission, or department of the executive branch:

1. Make a written request for access to the documents. If the records were sealed by a judge, make the request to that judge. If access to the documents was denied by the Prothonotary or Clerk of Court, the request should be presented to the Chief or President Judge.
2. The request should identify the documents which you seek to inspect as narrowly and with as much detail as possible.
3. Do not state the reason why you want to inspect the documents.
4. If the written request is denied, ask that the denial be placed in writing, together with a statement of reasons for the denial.
5. There is no statute covering the right to inspect court records. You may petition the court to open the records, following the same procedure as with closed courtrooms.
6. If you lawfully obtain access to a document which was ordered sealed by the court, you may publish it; however, the court may initiate proceedings to determine who provided you with the document.

The *Media Survival Kit* outlines what records fall under the Pennsylvania Open Records Law (you will need to check your own state). In Pennsylvania the following records are available; they have been held subject to the Open Records Law:

1. Examination papers and scores of all applicants for Civil Service jobs.
2. Records of retired state employees.
3. Attendance record cards of professional employees of school district.
4. Building record side of property records maintained by county board for assessment and revision of taxes, containing information as to construction specifications.

5. Individual salary records of community college employees.
6. Accident reports prepared by accident investigation division of police department.
7. Completed reports prepared by Department of Labor and Industry pertaining to safety and health in industrial plants.
8. Review and refund docket of Board of Finance and Revenue.
9. List of names and addresses of kindergarten children in school district.
10. Police payroll records.
11. List of persons taking CPA examination given by Commissioner of Professional and Occupational Affairs.
12. Address to which a school district forwarded the scholastic record of a former pupil.
13. List of delinquent taxpayers.

The following records have been held *exempt* from the Open Records Law:

1. Field investigation notes made by a staff member of city planning department for purpose of a report to a city council member.
2. Departmental budget reports required to be provided to the budget secretary (held to be a statement of facts and events and not an "account," which consists of debit and credit entries).
3. Names, addresses, and amounts received by welfare recipients.
4. Contents of teacher's personnel file maintained by school district.
5. Financial disclosure statements voluntarily submitted in response to executive order requesting such statements from members of the governor's cabinet and members of certain agencies.
6. Financial information regarding the operation of state-related university.
7. Physical fitness reports and promotional evaluation reports of police department.

In Pennsylvania, if you are denied permission to inspect and copy documents of any agency, board, commission, or department of the executive branch, the *Media Survival Kit* also suggests that you appeal the denial of access under the "Right To Know" Act. A sample form of appeal is available from the Coalition.

On the federal scene, the Freedom of Information Act of 1966 provides access to many documents, and almost every week you read of some disclosure from the past revealed for the first time because an enterprising reporter decided to check on certain documents. In general, the Act provides that all records in the hands of agencies of the executive branch of the federal government can be inspected, unless the documents are covered by one of nine exceptions.

Excepted are classified national defense and foreign policy items; internal personnel matters; items prohibited from disclosure by a statute; privileged and confidential trade and commercial information obtained from an individual; information which would be privileged in a civil lawsuit; "unwarranted invasion of personal privacy," such as medical documents; investigation files where one of a half dozen special bad effects would occur; specified bank records; and oil well information.

To obtain records from a federal agency, write a letter to the agency, being specific and describing in detail the document sought. This request must be answered in 10 working days. If there is no answer, or the request is denied, you can write a letter to the head of the agency. Some suggest you include a legal reason for your appeal, although this is not necessary. Having it sent by an attorney might give it more serious consideration, but not necessarily so. Groups such as the Pennsylvania First Amendment Coalition provide sample appeal letters. This appeal must be answered in 20 working days. If denied, then the next recourse is to file a complaint in the federal district court. The Coalition (headed by Sandy Oppenheimer, Bucks County *Courier Times*, Route 13, Levittown, PA 19057) has sample complaint forms.

Using Libraries

Time spent browsing in libraries can turn up prospective story ideas. You may find an overlooked author in your area. You will find consumer reports which you can localize. Glance through magazine articles. They deal with the relevant themes in contemporary life, many of which you can adapt and discuss for readers in your locality. You can also pick up a few ideas from out-of-town newspapers. Libraries not only contain resources for story research, they can also be the source of new ideas, background information, and fact verification.

Libraries also have books about reference books and materials. Among them are *The New York Times Guide to Reference Materials* (New York: Popular Library, c. New York *Times* Co., 1971) and Rivers, William L., *Finding Facts* (Englewood Cliffs, N.J.: Prentice-Hall, 1975). *The Writer's Resource Guide*, edited by William Brohaugh (Cincinnati, Ohio: Writer's Digest Books, 1979), has listings with addresses for various information services, including consumer topics, sports information offices, museums, archives, embassies, community services, and finance and banking.

The list of reference materials goes on endlessly, but some books you might want to know about are:

Biography

Barnhart, Clarence L. *New Century Cyclopedia of Names*. New York: Appleton-Century-Crofts, 1954.

This three-volume work presents facts about people, both living and deceased.

Barone, Michael et al. *The Almanac of American Politics, 1976*. New York: E. P. Dutton, 1975.

The author gives biographies of senators, representatives, and governors, listed by state. He also includes their records in office, description of districts, past elections, and ratings.

Dictionary of American Biography. New York: Scribners, 1928–74. 13 volumes.

This book covers only deceased Americans in lengthy but informative articles.

Ethridge, James, ed. dir. *Contemporary Authors*. Detroit: Gale Research, annual. 1962 to the present.

The editor presents living authors, both well and less well known. The annual is subtitled *A biographical-bibliographical guide to current writers in fiction, general nonfiction, poetry, journalism, drama, motion pictures, television and other fields*. In *Contemporary Authors*, Permanent Series, Vols. I and II (Detroit: Gale Research, 1975, 1978) Ethridge presents the authors contained in regular series that no longer need revision.

Hyamson, Albert M. *A Dictionary of Universal Bibliography: Of All Ages and of All Peoples*. 2nd ed. New York: E. P. Dutton, 1951.

This reference presents thumbnail sketches.

Who's Who in Finance and Industry. 20th ed. 1978–79. Chicago: Marquis, 1978.

This work contains international profiles of important people in the field.

Who's Who in Government. 1st ed. 1972–73. Chicago: Marquis, 1972.

Who's Who in American Law. 1st ed. Chicago: Marquis, 1978.

Who's Who in Religion. 2nd ed. 1977. Chicago: Marquis, 1977.

Who's Who Among Black Americans. 2nd ed. 1977–78. Northbrook, Ill.: Who's Who Among Black Americans, 1978.

Who's Who in America. 42nd ed. 1982–83. 2 vols. Chicago: Marquis, 1982.

Who's Who in the East. 19th ed. 1983–84. Chicago: Marquis, 1983.

Who's Who in the Midwest. 18th ed. 1982–83. Chicago: Marquis, 1982.

Who's Who in the South and Southwest. 18th ed. 1982–83. Chicago: Marquis, 1982.

Who's Who in the West. 18th ed. 1982–83. Chicago: Marquis, 1982.

Who's Who in the World. 6th ed. 1982–83. Chicago: Marquis, 1982.

The International Who's Who. 47th ed. 1983–84. London. Europa Publications, Ltd., 1983.

The International Year Book and Statesmen's Who's Who. West Sussex, England: Thomas Skinner Directories, Ltd., 1983.

Who's Who of American Women. 13th ed. 1983–84. Chicago: Marquis, 1983.

Kunitz, Stanley J., and Haycraft, Howard. *Twentieth Century Authors*. New York: H. W. Wilson, 1942. 2nd printing, 1944.

Kunitz, Stanley J. *Twentieth Century Authors*. First Supplement. New York: H. W. Wilson, 1955.

Louis, Rita V., ed. *Biography Index*. 1945 to present. New York: H. W. Wilson.

This index is issued three times a year with annual cumulations, and appears in bound volumes for three-year periods. The index presents a guide to biographies appearing in periodicals, individual and collected works, diaries, letters.

Stuart, Sandra Lee. *Who Was What When*. Secaucus, N.J.: Lyle Stuart, Inc., 1977.

This book ranges from sports and fashion winners to railroad men of the year to national drama, book, and film award winners.

The New York Times Obituary Index. 1885–1968. New York: New York Times Co., 1970.

This index is good for obits of not so famous people as well. It has more than 353,000 alphabetical listings with the date of the *Times* obit. Famous people have additional coverage.

Facts (General)

Facts at Your Fingertips. Washington: U.S. Department of Health and Human Services, 1981.

This publishes lists of health surveys and National Center for Health Statistics surveys.

Facts on File. New York: Facts on File, Inc., 1941 to date. From 1941 to present.

This publication is compiled weekly.

Flanagan, Timothy et al, ed. *Sourcebook of Criminal Justice Statistics*. Albany, N.Y.: Criminal Justice Research Center, 1982.

Flanagan presents the nature and distribution of known offenses, characteristics of criminals, correlation, and interpretation of criminal statistics.

McWhirter, Norris Dewar, and McWhirter, Alan Ross. *Guinness Book of World Records*. New York: Bantam Books, annual.

This book publishes a vast variety of all kinds of records—from the best beer drinker to the fastest marathon runner.

Kane, Joseph N. *The American Counties*. 4th ed. Metuchen, N.J.: Scarecrow, 1983.

Kane gives the origins of names, dates of establishment, size, population, and historical detail of more than 300 counties in 608 pages.

Kane, Joseph N. *Facts about the Presidents*. 4th ed. New York: H. W. Wilson, 1981.

Here Kane compiles biographical and other data on presidents and vice presidents.

Kane, Joseph N. *Famous First Facts*. 4th ed. New York: H. W. Wilson, 1981.

This records first events, discoveries, and inventions in the United States.

Kane, Joseph N. *Nicknames and Sobriquets of U.S. Cities and States*. Metuchen, N.J.: Scarecrow, 1970.

Population Handbook. Washington, D.C.: The Population Reference Bureau, 1978.

Columbia Journalism Review says: "Boon to all those who find themselves wrestling with demographic facts, (the handbook) defines terms, describes calculations, presents examples and notes commonly made mistakes in reporting. . . ." It includes population statistics, extensive lists of information sources, telephone numbers, and a glossary.

Facts (History)

Carruth, Gordon et al. *The Encyclopedia of American Facts and Dates*. 5th ed. New York: Thomas Y. Crowell Co., 1970.

Chronological with index. The authors present a wealth of information on Americana.

Ketz, Louise B., ed. *Dictionary of American History.* Revised edition. New York: Scribner's, 1976.

This has seven volumes with an index.

Webster's Guide to American History. Springfield, Mass.; Merriam–Webster, 1971.

This is arranged chronologically with maps and tables, and descriptions of historical periods. It also contains biographies and an index.

United Nations

Delegations to the General Assembly. Annual since 1945. New York: United Nations.

This work lists committee members and delegations. Entries for U.S. delegates and staff advisers include telephone numbers.

Everyman's United Nations. 8th ed. New York: United Nations, 1968.

This book is subtitled a complete handbook of the activities and evolution of the United Nations during its first twenty years, 1945–1965. A supplement has been published for the years 1966–1970.

United Nations Judicial Yearbook. 1963–present. New York: United Nations.

This yearbook includes treaties, legislative texts, international laws, and the legal acts of the UN organizations plus bibliography.

United States Documents

Bernier, Bernard Jr., and David, Charlotte M. *Popular Names of U.S. Government Reports*. Washington, D.C.: Library of Congress, 1970.

This publication lists 753 significant reports by the popular name, for example the Warren Report or Kerner Commission Report. Identification in libraries does not follow the popular name of person heading committee, thus the Kerner Report is listed as the Supplemental Studies for the National Advisory Committee on Civil Disorders. From 1800–1970.

Directory of Federal Statistics for Local Areas: A Guide to Sources. 1966. Washington, D.C.: Superintendent of Documents, U.S. Government Printing Office.

This guide covers sociological and economic topics.

Pocket Data Books: USA. 1973. Washington, D.C.: Superintendent of Documents, U.S. Government Printing Office.

These books present statistics on various topics.

Schmeckebarn, Lawrence F. *Government Publications and Their Use*. Washington, D.C.: Brookings Institution, 1969.

This is an excellent source for anyone needing anything to do with the federal government. It lists congressional publications, federal laws, court decisions, presidential papers, foreign affairs documents, and where to find them.

Healy, Robert E., ed. *Federal Regulatory Directory*. Washington, D.C.: Congressional Quarterly, Inc., annual.

The editor has collected background on government agencies, what they do, recent actions; regional directory, and so on.

U.S. Department of Justice, Federal Bureau of Investigation. *Uniform Crime Reports*. Washington, D.C.: U.S. Government Printing Office, annual.

This presents statistics on all crimes, compiled by local law enforcement agencies.

Books–Magazines

Book Review Index. Detroit: Gale Research, annual since 1965.

This gives comprehensive indexing of book reviews from more than 300 periodicals. Lists authors and titles alphabetically. Bi-monthly with annual cumulations.

Book Review Digest. New York: H. W. Wilson, since 1905, monthly with annual accumulations.

This digest gives condensations of reviews from more than 70 journals listed by the book author's name. Includes citations to complete reviews. Subject and title index.

Business Periodicals Index. 1958 to date.

This is published monthly with annual cumulations and contains a subject index to wide range of business periodicals.

Humanities Index, Social Sciences Index. New York: H. W. Wilson. Separate indexes as of 1974; from 1956–1974 called *Social Sciences and Humanities Index*; from 1907–1965 called *International Index to Periodicals*.

This series has a monthly subject index to scholarly literature in broad disciplinary topics.

Media Law Reporter. 1976 to present. Washington, D.C. Bureau of National Affairs, Inc.

This publishes updates every two weeks. It is a loose-leaf report information service that includes user's guide, topical index, table of cases (by jurisdiction), and full text of each decision, as well as important law cases related to the media.

National Directory of Newsletters and Reporting Services. Detroit: Gale Research, 1978.

Each of 759 entries in all categories includes a description of subject matter and scope plus vital statistics. This directory is cross-indexed.

Poole's Index to Periodical Literature. 1802–1906. Gloucester, Mass.: Peter Smith.

Public Affairs Information Services Bulletin. 1915 to date. New York: PAIS Inc.

This bulletin appears monthly with cumulations; there is a subject index to current information sources such as books, government reports, law periodicals, public and private agency reports, and conferences. It has excellent coverage of political science, government, and mass media issues.

Readers' Guide to Periodical Literature. 1900–present. New York: H. W. Wilson.

This is published semi-monthly with annual cumulations; it contains subject and author indexing from more than 160 magazines. The first volume was published in 1905.

Topicator. Annual. 1968 to date. Golden, Colo: Topicator.

This appears monthly with annual cumulations. It contains a subject index to trade publications of communications industry, including *Editor & Publisher, Advertising Age, Broadcasting,* and *Columbia Journalism Review.*

Federal Agencies

Among federal agencies which provide information at little or no cost on "companies" from banks to universities are (according to a list compiled by Washington Researchers, 910 Seventeenth St., N.W., Washington, D.C. 20006):

Airlines, air freight forwarders, commuter carriers and air taxis: Bureau of Operating Rights, Civil Aeronautics Board, 1825 Connecticut Ave., N.W., Washington, D.C. 20428, (202) 673-5088.

Airports: Air Traffic Service Division, Federal Aviation Administration, 800 Independence Ave., S.W., Washington, D.C. 20591, (202) 426-8472.

Bank holding companies and state members of the Federal Reserve System: Freedom of Information, Board of Governors of the Federal Reserve System, 20th Constitution Ave., N.W., Washington, D.C. 20551, (202) 452-3684.

Banks, national: Public Disclosure, Controller of the Currency, 490 L'Enfant Plaza East, S.W., Washington, D.C. 20551, (202) 447-1832.

Barge and vessel operators: Federal Maritime Commission, 1100 L Street, N.W., Washington, D.C. 20573, (202) 523-5876.

Cable television systems operators: Cable T.V. Bureau, Federal Communications Commission, 2025 M Street, N.W., Washington, D.C. 20554, (202) 632-9797.

Colleges, universities, vocational schools, and public schools: National Center for Educational Statistics, 400 Maryland Ave., S.W., Washington, D.C. 20202, (202) 245-8511.

Commodity trading advisors, commodity pool operators, and futures commission merchants: Commodities Futures Trading Commission, 2033 K Street, N.W., Washington, D.C. 20581, (202) 254-8630.

Consumer products: Office of Product Safety Commission, 1750 K Street, N.W., Washington, D.C. 20207, (202) 492-6608.

Electric and gas utilities and gas pipeline companies: Federal Power Commission (DOE), 825 N. Capitol St., N.E., Washington, D.C. 20426, (202) 275-4006.

Exporting companies: American International Traders Register, Office of International Marketing, U.S. Dept. of Commerce, Washington, D.C. 20230, (202) 377-2206.

Federal contractors: The Renegotiation Board, 2000 M St., N.W., Washington, D.C. 20446, (202) 254-8266.

Federal land bank associations, and production credit associations: Farm Credit Administration, 490 L'Enfant Plaza, S.W., Washington, D.C. 20578, (202) 755-2170.

Foreign corporations: World Traders Data Reports, Department of Commerce, Washington, D.C. 20230, (202) 755-2170.

Hospitals and nursing homes: National Center for Health Statistics, 5600 Fishers Lane, Rockville, MD. 20852, (303) 443-1613.

Land developers: Office of Interstate Land Sales Registration, Department of H.U.D., 451 7th St., S.W., No. 9253, Washington, D.C. 20411, (202) 755-7077.

Mining companies: Mining Enforcement and Safety Administration, Department of Interior, C & 18th Streets, N.W., Washington, D.C. 20240, (202) 343-8735.

Nonprofit institutions: Internal Revenue Service, Freedom of Information Reading Room, 1111 Constitution Ave., N.W., Washington, D.C. 20224, (202) 964-3770.

Nuclear plants: Nuclear Regulatory Commission, 1717 H St., N.W., Washington, D.C. 20555, (202) 643-1380.

Pension plans: Office of Employee Benefit Plans, Department of Labor, 200 Constitution Ave., N.W., Washington, D.C. 20216, (202) 523-8782.

Pharmaceutical, cosmetic, and food firms: Commissioner of Compliance, Food and Drug Administration, 5600 Fishers Lane, Rockville, MD. 20852, (301) 443-2410.

Notes

[1]Bob Woodward and Carl Bernstein, *All the President's Men* (New York: Warner Books Edition, arrangement with Simon and Schuster, 1974), p. 214.

[2]Woodward and Bernstein, p. 216.

[3]"Use of Unnamed Sources Limited by Guidelines," *Editor & Publisher* (Feb. 7, 1976): p. 7.

[4]William Metz, *Newswriting: From Lead to "30"* (Englewood Cliffs, N.J.: Prentice-Hall, c. 1979, 1977), pp. 91–93.

[5]Donald M. Gillmor and Jerome A. Barron, *Mass Communication Law: Cases and Comment,* 2nd ed. (St. Paul, Minn.: West Publishing Co., 1974), p. 498.

[6]Albert G. Pickerell, and Michel Lipman, *The Courts and the News Media,* Conference of California Judges, Project Benchmark, 2150 Shattuck Ave., Berkeley, Calif., n.d., pp. 95, 96.

[7]Bob Woodwood and Carl Bernstein, *All the President's Men* (New York: Warner Books Edition, arrangement with Simon and Schuster, 1974), p. 21.

[8]Woodward and Bernstein, p. 23.

[9]Woodward and Bernstein, p. 33.

[10]Woodward and Bernstein, pp. 36–45.

[11]Woodward and Bernstein, p. 60.

[12]Woodward and Bernstein, p. 105.

[13]Woodward and Bernstein, pp. 115–123.

[14]Woodward and Bernstein, pp. 230–250.

[15]Woodward and Bernstein, pp. 240–244.

[16]Woodward and Bernstein, pp. 253, 254.

[17]David Anderson, and Peter Benjaminson, *Investigative Reporting* (Bloomington, Ind.: Indiana University Press, 1976), p. 63.

[18]*Media Survival Kit,* Pennsylvania First Amendment Coalition, prepared by Samuel E. Klein (Philadelphia: Kohn, Savett, Marion & Graf, P.C. n.d.) cf. pp. 5–10.

Assignments

1. Study an in-depth article in a newspaper and list what you think the sources might have been for the reporter. Make a composite list of the sources in class, then ask the reporter who wrote the article to come to class to discuss sources as far as he or she is free to do so.
2. Select a story you or another person has written and list sources suggested in this chapter which might have strengthened or given more depth to the article.
3. How many class members have been sources (not subjects) for articles? Explain.
4. Go to the library and come back with 10 ideas for interesting articles (but not tied in with the day's headlines) based on resources in the library.
5. Write a press release with explicit information for a follow-up, namely, three phone numbers and addresses of persons whom a reporter might want to contact in developing a story from the release.
6. Discuss "embargoes." Most would consider them absolute. Can they ever be circumvented? Is anything absolute? Are there exceptions for emergency and medical considerations? Suggest 10 rules for regarding embargoes.
7. Each student should choose one kind of record as discussed in this chapter, go to where these records are located, and look for one specific point of information.
8. Find a library reference book or resource not mentioned in lists in this chapter and report on it.
9. To some people "investigative reporting" simply means "in-depth" reporting. Find a subject that would have high interest but which would involve research and "digging." Summarize in one page what your article would be about and the direction it might go (you don't need to write the article). Also, on a second page give some sources and resources which you could use to get the facts for the article.
10. Look through books about reporting and reporters (or journalism history texts). Prepare a report on a famous "in-depth" story by a reporter in U.S. history.

Doris Flora questions U.S. Senator Howell Heflin during one of his "town hall" meetings in Northport, Alabama. Photo by Calvin Hannah, Tuscaloosa (Ala.) *News*

PART 2

Gathering the News: Groups and Individuals

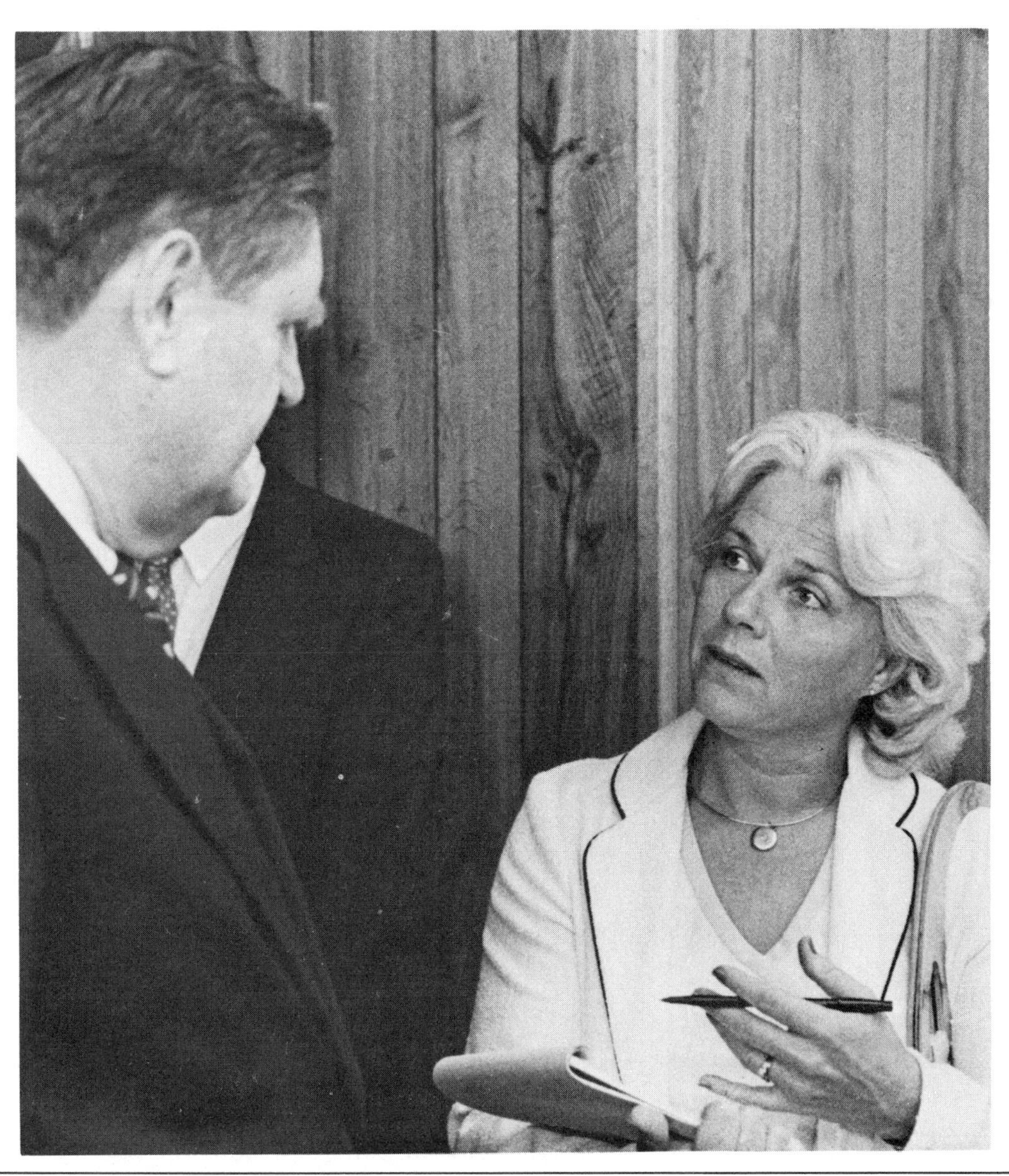

5

Covering Press Conferences

Press conferences make information available at a definite time and place. Important people who do not have time to see each newspaper representative individually present their information and allow reporters to ask them questions for a specified time.

Some press conferences may not be newsworthy. Some people call a press conference just to get the attention of the media: a person wants to start a small business, parents want to launch their daughters as singers with the help of press conferences (Aretha Franklin's father did this with his daughters), or citizens want to announce that they are running for obscure public office or that they are among some 60 persons filing for the mayoral primary. Two questions you may want to think about: Is it really your job to help promote people simply because they have invited the press to a formal press conference? Does a press conference really make some event or accomplishment important?

Great news stories *can* come out of press conferences—a grand jury reports its findings, astronauts tell their experiences, or a coroner gives the scientific findings from a criminal investigation.

But even in these situations personalities may dominate, and more public exposure helps to prepare possible candidates for future races for public office. Press conferences are sometimes public relations events and, of course, sometimes news events. But since they are also official rites, celebrated with handouts or releases, the reporter needs to be aware of the theatrical atmosphere and the dangers of manipulation and the egomania of some public personalities.

WHERE THE REAL STORY IS

One new reporter in Detroit was sent to cover an automotive convention. He was an hour or so early for the press conference, so he looked around and found most of the reporters socializing among themselves. But he used his extra time to look over the convention program and realized that a researcher on women drivers was possibly the most interesting person scheduled to take part in the program. A check with the hotel showed that the researcher had not arrived. So the young reporter called up the researcher in New York and took an interview on the phone. When the press conference proved to be of little interest, the young reporter wrote his story on what the scheduled—but absent—prospective speaker had found about women drivers. Everybody else wrote about the press conference and wondered how the new reporter came up with the sharper story.

Now suppose the same expert on women drivers did appear at the press conference. Still, the aggressive reporter could try to find the expert in his hotel room earlier in the day or the night before. An interview would give more depth. Then the reporter could attend the press conference to pick up further information. Or, with the interview in hand, he might skip the press conference, meet an earlier deadline, and get on to another project.

Collecting background information is often helpful. Relevant clippings ("clips") in the newspaper files, particularly when they are from outside sources such as newsmagazines, national newspapers, or news services, may yield information which the reporter can use to obtain further information at a press conference. Being armed with statistics and other information such as what a candidate said on another occasion can be useful in prying more information from the subject.

Experienced reporters also use other sources to prepare for press conferences. *Who's Who* has biographical and professional information on most personalities. Yearbooks, directories, periodical indexes, and library clipping files (particularly on entertainers) can yield leads for further research. Talking to experts in the same field as the topic of the press conference can help equip you. In an interview, Al Carmines, the New York playwright, suggested that the reporter who was going to interview Kurt Vonnegut, Jr., ask Vonnegut "what he hates." The reporter did; this question put Vonnegut on the defensive and elicited his detailed views on life.

Although questions and answers usually comprise the main part of a press conference, often reporters will also receive a "handout"—a prepared statement on behalf of an official or expert. But press conferences may be more complex. A press conference could include panelists, or it could combine a featured (noted) speaker, a panel to quiz the speaker, and questions from reporters and other members of the audience.

Where *is* the story at a press conference? Student reporters (and others) often report on what the person says in a speech and perhaps on what the panel says. But questions from the audience may hold clues to a better story. A noted New York *Times* newspaperman gave a speech on press topics at a university in Minnesota; the student paper duly reported what he said. But the paper might have developed a livelier and perhaps more significant story from the confrontation he had with challenges from the audience. During that program, a Harvard-trained lawyer noted inconsistencies in the speaker's presentation and suggested the speaker's views bordered on racism. Reporting this lively give-and-take would have provided readers with a better perspective of the speaker than the dutiful and uninspired reporting of the speech itself.

Yet the best story at a press conference *may indeed be* the handout of the speech rather than what the responses were to questioning. One reporter learned this when he was assigned to keep track of one group of corporation officials at semiannual meetings. He did a lot of buttonholing and ferreted out a lot of angles until he finally realized that his competitor merely reported what was said or distributed at a press conference. The aggressive reporter was ignoring the basic handout information, which happened to be good material.

WHEN IT'S OFF THE RECORD

If a subject which reporters could probably find out about comes up at a press conference but is put "off the record," what do responsible reporters do? They now know about the subject for the first time from the press conference. Although they could have discovered it elsewhere, writing about it would break the confidence between the reporters and the person who disclosed the "off the record" subject.

Some ways around the dilemma:

1. *Leave the press conference at the first mention of "off the record."* When a person says he or she is going off the record, consider the press conference over and leave. You can proceed to find out what the guarded information was from other sources if necessary. And if you don't find out, nothing is lost since the information was to be off the record anyway.
2. *Cut off the speaker.* Stand up and say, respectfully, that you do not wish to waste the speaker's time or your time by having information "off the record." Suggest that the speaker say only what is on the record. Then no misunderstanding can arise later as to what was on the record and what was not. One thing to remember is that most people will say what they

were going to say anyway. So, if the speaker eliminates "off the record" remarks at the reporter's request, the speaker will probably tell everything on the record.

3. *Report the exact words of the speaker.* When he elects to go "off the record," report that the speaker went off the record on a certain topic. The reader can guess what the speaker discussed. Such a procedure discourages the speaker from resorting to the "off the record" device.

THE PRESS CONFERENCE SETTING

The facility for a press conference may be inadequate. Too often the place is a tiny sideroom in a hotel, and more people are present than the room can hold.

You should get there early and sit in the front row if the press conference really seems important. You need to be able to see, hear, and be heard if you have questions.

Some press conferences turn into riots. For example, when the late Nelson Rockefeller, as vice-president designate, appeared before a small press conference of the National Newspaper Association convention in a Toronto hotel, a half dozen radical labor socialists from Canada refused to let him speak. They shouted him down in the press conference. One reporter did not really care, for he had gotten his story beforehand. Using the dogging-the-subject technique, he had crowded into the governor's entourage from the ballroom, walked along with the governor, and ridden on the first long escalator in a series of escalators. The reporter had moved out of the picture for a few moments and then returned on the next escalator. The reporter had time for two follow-up questions before the press conference. News conference or no news conference, the reporter already had a news story from the governor.

Too many reporters are satisfied with a sit-down routine. In very large press conferences—such as the Pope may hold with some 800 newsmen—you may elect to stand up so that you can see both the subject and the person who is asking the question (sometimes important in follow-up pieces on factions and agencies). You can step out yourself and command attention more readily if you want to ask a question. But most important of all, you can study traffic patterns and see means of exiting with the celebrity; then you can move ahead quickly in the current that takes you to the famous person for a question or two of your own, while the "sitters" will never get out of their chairs before the celebrity exits. Also, standing up in sluggish, overheated rooms may not be comfortable, but it keeps you awake and literally on your toes.

WHAT TO DO AT A PRESS CONFERENCE

Ordinarily, at press conferences, try to:

1. ***Make good use of your time.*** Other reporters or walk-ins may get off on tangents that do not interest you or your paper. Big press conferences will sometimes set a "ranking order." Members of "the working press"—representatives of dailies with immediate deadlines—have permission to ask questions before representatives of magazines, freelancers, and others. Similar problems exist in a small-town setting. Although the reporter may be the only bona fide reporter who shows up, a contingent of local students may have instructions to ask questions. The working reporter has a right to get his or her questions out of the way first. Most public relations directors and subjects of press conferences, such as candidates, are more interested in the working reporter than in the others anyway.
2. ***Secure documents.*** Ask for the speech ahead of time. Most noted speakers bring extra copies. But copies of the speech, background packets, and/or copies of an author's book may be in short supply. Try to get your hands on this auxiliary information before the briefing starts.
3. ***Don't tip off the competitors.*** Most newspapers exist in one-newspaper towns. However, papers with overlapping circulations from throughout the county, as well as the broadcast media, may have representatives at the same press conference. Some of their media coverage—radio and TV—will get to the public before your news story appears in print. If you ask pointed questions at a press conference and the electronic media or your competition airs or publishes the answers first, you may be upset; you will have scooped yourself!

   Good reporters can avoid revealing too much at a press conference. One quality helps: *humility.* Reporters don't have to show how smart they are by asking the most pertinent questions. Some of the best reporters remain nearly silent in press conferences and ask only what they have to. They let their competitors ask the most important questions. Sometimes they even ask questions about things in which they are not interested in order to throw the competition off the track.
4. ***Questions to ask.*** If the time to ask questions is limited, what do you ask and how? After being recognized by the speaker or moderator, you should do the following:
   a. *Give your name and the name of your newspaper.* This helps to keep the exchange professional and to the point. The speaker should not have to guess or ask to whom he or she is talking.
   b. *Keep out of the question.* The press conference is called to listen not to the reporter but to the speaker.
   c. *Consider using a brief transition or lead-in clause.* Start out with phrases like "A report last month said. . . ." or "What do you say now

about. . . ." to soften the question so the subject can mull it over and organize his or her thoughts. The lead-in also gives a chance to refer to a prominent fact, indicating that you want new information and not a recital of past achievements or old ideas.

   d. *Know what information you want.* Ask for this information in several ways so the answer will be clear and complete.

5. ***Be ready with follow-up questions.*** Ask a series of questions as rapidly as possible, since you will often not get a second chance. Start with one complete question. Then, when the speaker has answered the essence of the question and takes a breath, interrupt this pause with a related one-word question such as "How?" or "Why?" Encourage the speaker to discuss the subject in some depth.

Remember that the press conference is for you, the reporter, and ultimately for your readers. Be humble, but do not let the speaker manipulate you. Make the most of your time and opportunity.

Assignments

1. Contact local politicians, educators, and business PR officials to find out about an upcoming press conference. Have your class cover it together, with each student writing it up afterward. Compare your articles with local press and broadcasting coverage.
2. Collect a half dozen PR handouts from the news bureau of your school. Apply editorial judgment. Which ones would you, as an editor of a local daily, use? How much of each release would you use? Can you combine them? What's missing from the information that you should ask individually or at a press conference?
3. Prepare in advance for a Presidential press conference which is to be televised. What questions would you ask? Watch the conference and then:
   a. Write a one-page assessment of the questioning of the President that evaluates press performance. Were there examples of "grandstanding"? What was the best question?
   b. Write the first two paragraphs of a news story based on the President's answers; do not look at the morning paper until you come to class. Compare leads in class.
4. Conduct a press conference in class with a local official such as a city council member or police chief. Prepare in advance a knowledgeable list of questions, pick the question you want to ask most and then ask it, with follow-up questions.

6

Interviewing

The interview provides an active method of gathering news. In the interview the reporter has control of the news gathering situation, unlike the press conference in which press officers may try to manipulate the reporter. The reporter or editor determines whom to interview and arranges the time and place of the meeting and maintains control of the line of questioning. Of course, interviewees can refuse interviews, terminate interviews, refuse to answer certain questions, or even ask questions of their own. But the interview remains a principal technique of the reporter. In a way, all of the reporter's professional dealings with people—even much of the style of the press conference and backgrounding for events and meetings—are forms of interviewing.

SEEKING A CENTRAL THEME

A main effort of the interviewer is to find one central theme of interest or importance that will hold the interview story together.

Consider two stories in the Philadelphia *Inquirer,* each held together by a unified theme. One story deals with a Zairean missionary couple that escaped the terror of invading rebels; the other story is an interview with Dom De Luise by Jack Severson.

The Zairean story starts out:

> Harold and Elsie Amstutz folded their hands and bowed their heads in the busy lunchroom of a New York hotel and prayed the simple grace that many pray:"Thank you for this food and bless it to the strength of our bodies and us to thy service."
>
> The prayer was unlike the desperate prayers they had been praying in recent days. It was unlike their prayers a week before in Kolwezi in the troubled Shaba Province of southern Zaire where an invasion by Angola-based rebels left more than 700 dead, among them more than 100 foreigners. . . .

The article proceeded to catalog the prayers of the missionaries in hiding when the rebels were camped in their back yard. Each prayer helped to enunciate the anxiety and terror of the moments.

The end of the story:

> On board the Belgian transport, Elsie recalls, "I just lifted my arms to Heaven and had a good old time!" An officer looked at her and smiled.

To the reporter interviewing the couple on their arrival in New York and watching them pray, the variety of prayers in their lives under incredible circumstances suddenly seemed to be one idea to hold the story together from the beginning to end. Once "prayer" was identified as a possible "peg", or pivot point, for the story, questions elicited other "prayers" concerning danger.

Consider the story about comedian De Luise:

> Backstage at the Valley Forge Music Fair, Tuesday night, Dom De Luise is interviewing a reporter.
>
> Yes, you read that right—the cherubic comedian is interviewing a reporter who came to interview him.
>
> "Are you warm—was it warm in there?" he asks, perspiration already beginning to soak through the fresh shirt he put on seconds ago.
>
> De Luise has just done 40 minutes in the round—40 minutes of rollicking humor and cavorting that left a sell-out audience standing and applauding and left De Luise wringing wet and "high as a kite."
>
> Another question. "Did I tell you I get terrified when I go out there?" . . .

The feature article continues to report the questions that De Luise asked, each question telling the reader something about De Luise himself. The article concludes with De Luise asking the reporter:

> "What are you going to write? I'll bet you know exactly what you're going to say about all this."
>
> No comment. End of interview.

Dom De Luise's unusual way of dealing with an interview by reversing roles and asking the reporter questions offers a natural focus on which the reporter can develop the write-up. From beginning to end, the article consists of the revealing questions that De Luise asks.

This thematic approach may leave much out but results in a successful, unified feature that stays with one idea. In the case of the Zairean missionary couple, the reporter left out many facts such as an incident when the couple wrapped themselves in bandages and ketchup to appear as wounded people under Red Cross care. But once the theme was set, in the newspaper story, that additional episode and others did not fit the scheme the interviewer had established.

WHO TO INTERVIEW

Most student editors, like some other editors, are celebrity conscious and will go after every celebrity who comes along, from the presidential candidate to the latest recording artist, sometimes even ignoring other possibly good interviews. Perhaps many student reporters-editors spend too much time interviewing persons the local daily has already interviewed. Students, however, can get a different angle—one which will appeal to students. Perhaps they can get celebrities to talk about restraints in society, give personal views on proposed marijuana legislation, or tell about their own college-age children.

Student editors who have the chance and want to do some real in-depth interviewing and profiling should recognize that their readers are predominantly students. In-depth profiles on students take more effort and skill than interviews with "walk-in" celebrities. Richard Ben Kramer of the Philadelphia *Inquirer* won a Pulitzer prize in 1979 for foreign reporting because he broke away from the pack and chronicled the fears and aspirations of the common citizen in the Near East during peace negotiations.

The situation is analogous to a campus where the better reporter may not be covering the celebrity but the forgotten student instead. One campus newspaper advisor challenged staff members to go out and find one living, breathing student and write about him or her. Staff members were at a loss, for they were conditioned to rewriting administration handouts and reporting on campus visitors.

These staffers were unlike Ernie Pyle, one of the most famous of World War II correspondents. His interest was to chronicle the war the way it really was by writing about the men who lived it. Pyle refused special treatment, lived with the men in the foxholes, and was eventually killed while at the front. He was so obviously different from the other correspondents who traveled together and wrote about the "big story" that *Newsweek* once started an article with the comment that covering the war in a particular war zone were several score correspondents—and Ernie Pyle. Pyle is the one remembered today.

The best interviewing is selective; so, like Pyle, you should identify in advance the kinds of people you want to interview. Pyle's soldiers were living the war, and through them he could chronicle the war. Student reporters doing interviews for a discussion topic should think about how relevant the responses are going to be for the specific topic and choose the best people to interview. Some student reporters invariably interview boyfriends or girlfriends and/or roommates! The lack of variety and the shallowness show. The results are records of people speaking spontaneously, perhaps interestingly, but without knowledge or authority.

If the subject is what a new development in relations between China and the U.S. means to the average local citizen, the reporter shouldn't interview every Oriental on campus (most of whom are American-born) but instead seek out the experts on China: economists, political analysts, and the China-born. Similarly, the reporter cannot justly treat expected effects of new zoning regulations with "quickie" interviews with passersby but must interview proponents and opponents active in the decision-making process. The reporter should talk with people whose land may be rezoned, zoning planners, sociologists, and others who have faced similar rulings in other counties. Interviewing the right people is very basic to successful reporting.

HOW TO GET AN INTERVIEW

Most celebrities, especially politicians and entertainers, have press officers paid to deal with the press. Sometimes their jobs focus on keeping the press away. At other times they try to save time by corralling reporters into press conferences; in some cases they use press conferences to control the celebrity's image, since the reporters all receive the same information.

But you can often reach the busy celebrity for some individual, unscheduled questions. How *do* you get to a gubernatorial candidate in the busy last week of the campaign; to a public figure such as Billy Graham during a Madison Square Garden crusade; to Edward Kennedy, overprotected as the last of the Kennedys; or to Johnny Carson or other big-time entertainers?

To reach the busy political candidate, phone his or her aide for permission to interview during the ride in the candidate's car from one engagement to the next. For someone like Billy Graham, make sure his aides see the value of newspaper articles in your particular geographical area as a way to increase his listening audience; if you are an out-of-town reporter, you may get an exclusive interview using this approach.

In his pre-presidential campaign days, Edward Kennedy appeared as the luncheon speaker at big conventions. Reporters were told they had to buy a lunch ticket and sit in the back of the room; they had no chance of talking with Kennedy who left immediately after his speech. One reporter got around this at a Washington luncheon. He came in without a ticket (tickets were collected at the tables), sat in a vacant seat down front after the lunch had started, told the waiter he was just sitting there, and didn't eat. Kennedy came in beaming and made his way to the head table; in about 40 seconds all the grandmothers and teens in the crowd of 2,000 would be crowding toward the head table for Kennedy's autograph. The reporter immediately stepped up, leaned across the head table, and got in three questions before the autograph-seekers descended.

The answers to three questions on the most current issues are enough to give you a good news peg, especially if you have done your homework and have secured the text of the speech from the press office.

Catching the celebrity on the run requires planned strategies.

One technique is to identify the exit aisle at a meeting or conference ahead of time, stand in it or in the doorway, and get in a few words when the government leader or celebrity leaves.

Another is to study the routes the elite usually take to or from conferences. In hotels, look for the escalator or elevators with security officers positioned nearby. Join the celebrity on the escalator or elevator. Anita Bryant, en route to a large press conference in Atlanta with two security aides, answered a few questions for a reporter who walked along with the three. The late Chief Justice Earl Warren answered questions for a reporter who followed him on an escalator. Some celebrities actually appreciate aggressive but polite reporters and would just as soon talk to one on the run as to a gang in a press room.

But for most interviews, you will have to go through the press representatives. To get information about a politician, call Democratic or Republican headquarters for phone numbers of his or her closest aides.

Who's Who lists home addresses of key politicians and entertainers. A letter sent to this address often gets a personal reply; at least the celebrity will see it. For entertainers, call the business office of the place they are appearing; you'll eventually get the name of their promoter or manager. Often people around town know where the guests normally stay.

Even when celebrities try to dodge the press, there are ways to find them. Find out what entertainers' favorite charities are—they probably visit them when in town. Who handles the police escort? Entertainers stay at certain hotels. A call to hotels asking for the entertainers to be paged may bring the response that they are not in yet or some comment that will serve to confirm that they are in the hotel. Standing in a lobby and observing the people coming and going will give you some clue as to where the celebrities are in the hotel.

Getting to important people has been much of the life of Los Angeles *Times* Syndicate correspondent and columnist Georgie Anne Geyer. Her advice on how to get to the difficult international types is not without relevance in dealing with local and national figures.

> . . . Dealing with guerrilla movements and leaders is something else again. Since I have had inordinate luck in getting to guerrillas, let me go into this.
>
> The first thing is trust. You present yourself to them, you present your case with dignity and honesty and tell them what you can do for them and then give them time to think it over. I have always said, honestly, to them, "Take all the time in the world to check me out—I don't want to be endangered by any of *your* sloppiness." They must trust you absolutely—and you'd better be sure they do.
>
> In my experience, too, the worst thing is to flatter them, to tell them you are a believer in their cause, and so on. People involved at this level of often fanatical conviction sense the slightest suggestion of pandering or untruth. Just tell them you'll be honest.
>
> Then there are other little things I do quite naturally. When they are taking me, for instance, to see someone like Arafat, I make it a point never to watch where I have been. I don't want to know. I do not ask extraneous questions. I do not want to know the real names of terrorists or anything like that. You have to know the limits.
>
> In these cases, I am convinced it helped to be a woman. To guerrillas, American men are the imperialists; not so American women.
>
> I know that young journalists would like some one-two-three answers, but the fact is that you get important interviews through some rather complicated and subtle ways: 1) Know your subject. Deeply. Know the culture. 2) Be pleasantly persistent and use anger only

> calculatedly and carefully. 3) Have realistic arguments for them as to what you can do for them. 4) Be open to the unexpected. I will never forget the night in Cairo when a censor I had befriended told me all the details of Sadat's throwing out of the Russians!
>
> Frankly, I find most leaders far less interesting than normal people, probably because I don't much like fanatics or egocentrics. They have no relative arguments; everything is absolute. There is little whimsy. But there is fun in the getting to them . . .[1]

Those who have seen Geyer in action and worked in competition with her agree that she is assertive. Other reporters know when she is at an event; she is at the front asking questions. Her ability to speak foreign languages, especially Spanish, is a great asset. More than once she has engaged a subject in his or her own native language and left the English-speaking journalists out of a significant conversation.

WHERE TO INTERVIEW

The press room at a convention may not be the best place to interview. If other people are in the room, they will interrupt; if they are newsmen, they will probably steer the interview off course and use the answers to the best questions themselves. If the celebrity's secretary is there, that is fine, but get rid of the visiting local people and various hangers-on if you can—they will interrupt and try to tell you what to ask.

Hotel rooms are excellent. They are far from the banquet hall, few people drop in, and they provide quiet and comfort. Avoid hotel lobbies. Somebody always recognizes the celebrity, a parade of handshaking begins, and soon the reporter is told that time is up. If you meet in a coffee shop, select a quiet one, preferably at least a block away from the convention hotel.

Most social events are sacrosanct. However, an enterprising reporter should not miss an opportunity to attend these when interesting and important people attend. Usually you can gather some information if you are tactful and not too assertive in conversation. Sometimes restraint pays off. For example, you might say, "I don't want to trouble you with any questions tonight, but how about letting me see you for 15 minutes some time before 4 tomorrow afternoon?" Celebrities appreciate people who look out for their schedules, and in so doing the reporter can be looking ahead to a story.

MULTI-SOURCE INTERVIEWS

Although the common concept of an interview as a direct relationship between interviewer and subject persists, the in-depth modern interview generally involves many sources. The completed major interview article reflects both direct contact and "backgrounding"—studying the facts of the subject's life and accomplishments—and should include material from other sources such as opponents, family and friends, business associates, and community leaders.

In some cases, the reporter never actually talks with the subject and must rely on diverse sources to provide information for the profile; using such sources forces the reporter to dig deeper for information. An *Esquire* writer once prepared an extensive profile on Frank Sinatra even though Sinatra had declined to talk to the reporter.

Ida M. Tarbell, noted investigative reporter (or "muckraker," as such reporters were called early in this century), prepared an extensive "character study" on John D. Rockefeller. Tarbell was unable to interview the press-shy Rockefeller, so she trailed him to a Sunday school where the pious Rockefeller was to give a short talk. Tarbell wrote:

> Mr. Rockefeller came into the auditorium of the church as soon as Sunday school was out. He sat a little bent in his pew, pitifully uneasy, his head constantly turning to the farthest right or left, his eyes searching the faces almost invariably turned towards him. It was plain that he, and not the minister, was the pivot on which the audience swung. . . . My two-hour study of Mr. Rockefeller aroused a felling I had not expected, which time intensified. I was sorry for him. . . . Mr. Rockefeller . . . was afraid, I told myself, afraid of his own kind."[2]

If you have time, when doing a major newspaper magazine or Sunday feature profile, prepare as though you would not be talking to the subject. Talk to the subject when you have already accumulated solid background information. In most profile interviews of important people, the reporter gets only one opportunity to talk with the subject. This subject may set a time limit of 15 minutes or less. (An in-depth interview can take one-and-a-half to two hours.) The reporter who has done homework—talked with the subject's friends and colleagues, questioned background experts, and consulted clippings—can ask questions to update and clarify information already gathered and perhaps probe in areas other reporters have overlooked.

USING THE TELEPHONE

Personal interviews are preferable. The reporter can sense the nuances, study the expressions on a face, and assess the subject's size and demeanor; all of these, when detailed in the article, help the reader see the subject. If the article is a profile or a human interest piece, then the reporter should try to do the interview in person. However, the reporter doesn't have to do all stories in person.

In a metropolitan area a reporter may easily take half a day to do one interview in person—50 miles out, 50 miles back. A well-planned, well-done phone interview can cut the time to about half an hour.

One advantage of the phone interview is that you can get right to the topic without distractions, although the distractions—the house pet, the children, or the off-beat decor—often enrich features. The phone interview has an additional advantage in that you can type notes as you go along and they will be easier for you to read.

Another advantage of the phone interview is that you can often get your story ahead of your competitor. Suppose a banquet speaker or the author of a popular new book is due in town, but the newspaper will have already been put to "bed" before these events. If you call the person up in New York or wherever the person is before he or she leaves by plane, you may get just the information you need to meet your deadline.

Of course, you can get caught if you write stories ahead. A Detroit reporter called the president of a New York educational institution on a Sunday morning. The educator was due in Detroit for an 8 p.m. speech. First deadlines were three hours before the time for the speech. The reporter wrote the interview for the early edition and told a director of the forum in Detroit to call if the speaker did not show up. The speaker didn't show, but the director never called the reporter. The speaker's plane did not land in Detroit because of fog, and he never gave the speech. But the Monday morning article had the man in Detroit—giving the speech—the night before. If you use this phone interview technique, you should not say explicitly that the remarks were said in the city, instead say, "John Jones, who was scheduled to speak at the Town Forum Sunday, said. . . ." Or:

> By the year 2000, the forests will be dead and the only wildlife left will be in the sea, a leading environmentalist said Sunday. Dr. Itsa Allover, of the World Future Institute, Chicago, said it is already too late to stop the destructive process.
>
> Dr. Allover was listed as the main speaker at a forum Sunday night at the new Educational Institute annex. . . .

If the speaker, Dr. Allover, arrives on schedule, such an article based on information from a phone interview before he took his flight makes sense; it even makes sense if he never takes the plane. Of course, the article can be updated for later editions if and when he arrives.

PREPARED QUESTIONS

After they have been in the business for some time, reporters find that interviewing has become second nature. They instinctively ask the right kind of questions at the right time and have a further instinct to know when to shift gears. However, even the most seasoned reporter can forget a basic area of questioning, and it is certainly easy to forget a vital statistic such as spelling, name, age, or home address.

Reporters have to discover what works best for them. Although some old-timers pride themselves on never taking notes in an interview, subjects may not even recognize their own quotes since the reporter has in his mind changed (even distorted) the subject's words and ideas.

However, a compromise method combines advance preparation with spontaneity. Use a reporting notebook for the interview; in addition, take along questions typed at the top of a vertically folded sheet of typing paper. Hold this paper behind the reporter's notebook, and slide it unobtrusively up and down to see your questions.

Sometimes, however, you can assure your subject that you have done the necessary research by having prepared questions in full view. You will have accomplished an important task: developing rapport with the subject and making him or her believe you know the topic. CBS interviewer Dan Rather had a clipboard full of questions with him when he interviewed President Jimmy Carter on the eve of the 1980 Democratic Convention for "60 Minutes."

If Lois Lane (Margot Kidder) in the movie "Superman" had had a list of questions, she might have done better with the rooftop interview with Superman (Christopher Reeve). Even pros such as Lois sometimes get enamored with their subject and forget questions or have a day when their minds wander. Lois's experience went like this:

LOIS: Are you married? . . . girl friend? How old are you?
SUPERMAN: Over 21.
LOIS: How tall are you? How much do you weigh?
SUPERMAN: 225.

LOIS:	Rest of body functions normal? What's your background? your past? . . . Do you eat?
SUPERMAN:	When I'm hungry.
LOIS:	True, you can see through anything?
SUPERMAN:	Just about.
LOIS:	Impervious to pain?
SUPERMAN:	So far.
LOIS:	What color is my underwear? I think I embarrassed you.
SUPERMAN:	The planter must be made of lead. It's hard to see through lead. Lois is your name? Pink.
LOIS:	What?
SUPERMAN:	I meant your underwear. Now I think your underwear is pink.
LOIS:	What's your background?
SUPERMAN:	Far away outer galaxy . . . Krypton.
LOIS:	C-r-i . . . ?
SUPERMAN:	K-r-y-p-t-o-n.
LOIS:	Do you like pink?
SUPERMAN:	I like pink. Very much.
LOIS:	Why are you here?
SUPERMAN:	To fight for truth, justice, and the American way.
LOIS:	Just how fast do you fly?
SUPERMAN:	Don't know. Never timed myself. Let's find out. . . .

If Lois Lane had had a list of questions, she might have seemed more professional. Note, however, that even though she was flustered in asking for some basic data, she did remember to mix in some human interest questions. She of course was too involved emotionally to do a good interview with the biggest story subject to hit Metropolis. She could also have used more follow-up questions such as: "Do you eat cereal, steak, oranges?"; "What's your background?"; and "Who were your father, your mother?"

In a prepared list, abbreviations or symbols reminding the reporter to ask about "bg"—background, age, address, and full name—come at the top. Then follow questions on subjects the reporter wants to know about most, plus some open questions. Ultimately come the throwaway questions, such as queries about the subject's hobbies or family.

Since an interview may be cut short, the reporter can put asterisks by three or four of the most important questions. The reporter may number the others.

Here are the kinds of questions you might type up before an interview with a noted book author:

- Name, age, home?
- How many books have you written? Novels, non-fiction, sci-fi?
- Danger in getting the information?
- Most dangerous experience?
- Close calls?
- What would you do differently?
- *Did the President really say "__________"?
- How do you know?
- Any other sources?
- *Any threats, attempts to censor?
- Are you publicity conscious?
- What should the President have done?
- Is world peace endangered by the info on the President?
- *Time* said about your book. . . . Do you agree?
- *There has been a lot of controversy about your book since it came out. What have the reviewers overlooked? What else is controversial?
- Where did the President go wrong? Why?
- What do you think of the Secretary of State? The Secretary of Commerce? Why?
- If you were to do the book over, what would you do?
- *Next project? Why?
- *You've made more money than you did on your last book? How much?
- Hobbies?
- Family?
- Travel?
- Buy any new real estate? Vacations. . . ?

Note that when preparing such a list the reporter knows exactly what he or she wants, but is also flexible. The questions with asterisks should have priority. One line of questions tries to further pin down the author on an existing controversy on the book. Another line of questions fishes for something new that other reporters might not ask. One way to avoid getting mere "yes" and "no" answers is to ask "or" questions. ("Do you think construction on the pumping station should be continued or do you think it should be halted?") The person may choose one or the other, but is also likely to give a reason.

Incidentally, you can call up an author before the book comes out. Some good exclusives come about this way. Try to stay clear of the publisher and talk directly to the author. Irving Wallace gave an interview long distance to a Detroit reporter about *The Word* a few months before the book came out. The article was premature, but it was ahead of the other reports. The author of the controversial religious book, *Was Jesus Married?*, talked freely to a reporter before publication. The reporter had seen pre-publication advertising in *Publisher's Weekly.* Although the publisher had promised an exclusive to the New York *Times*, the author did not care to whom he talked. The book publisher then tried to prevent further "leaks" until the *Times* could do its story on the book. (Moral: In a competitive news situation, don't always wait for the stories. Go after them, but expect difficulties including prior "exclusive" arrangements.)

Some Interview Tips

Keep out of the interview. Time spent talking about home towns and shared friends, for instance, cuts into total interviewing time. After some cordial opening, simply say that the subject's time is valuable (so is yours) and get to the questions.

Avoid off the record. Advise a person, if necessary, that if anything is off the record, the person shouldn't say it. Reporters will disagree on this, and of course no rule is absolute. As the discussion of press conferences noted earlier, as a general rule you're better off not to have to commit yourself to an off-the-record promise. You can tell the interviewee, "Don't tell me if it's off the record—that way there is no danger of misunderstanding about its use; besides, our time is short, let's stay on the record."

Be as positive as you can. When a Temple University student reporter received an assignment to find out how various hospitals in Philadelphia kept and treated their cadavers for medical research, one pathologist called the student's professor and asked how the student was going to use the story. He had a legitimate concern. The professor said the student reporter was handling the story sensitively. The professor added that the article contained directions on how people could donate their own bodies for research. In fact, the professor said, the article was so sensitively written that he himself felt like donating his body to research. The doctor was pleased and appeased. The article ran in the Philadelphia *Daily News*—with a picture of a doctor and a wrapped cadaver—and the author, William Wedo, now with the Allentown (Pa.) *Call-Chronicle*, won a Society of Professional Journalists, Sigma Delta Chi citation in feature writing.

In general, do not let a subject review your copy before publication. On rare occasions you may allow this for very technical subjects when there is enough time, and when you are confident the subject is not going to try to obstruct publication of the article.

On most occasions, if the subject must check something, call the person back and read the questionable portion aloud for checking. Some people in society readily approve an article about themselves. But, as you will learn, some people, such as some professors, scientists, philosophers, and sociologists, may be difficult to please. They will quarrel down to the last detail.

Camouflage note-taking when writing down an answer on which the subject might have second thoughts. If no notes are allowed at all, leave the room for a few minutes and write down notes. In normal interviews where you may take notes, and you anticipate sensitive areas, do not write while significant answers in those sensitive areas are coming quickly; instead, immediately ask innocuous questions (about family and hobbies), and while the subject is answering these questions, write the answer to the more important previous questions.

Stop when the interview is over. When you have asked all questions, prepare to leave. If you linger and bore the subject, he or she will remember and may avoid you in the future. Besides, your time is valuable, too. Some photographers have a way of lingering and wanting to chat. Sometimes you may want to take a separate car to the interview rather than rely on the photographer.

As you leave, get the phone number where you can reach the subject for the next two or three days in case your editor has questions, or events related to the subject develop that require you to get back to him or her.

Countering "Dirty Tricks"

Jane Evinger, of the University of Hawaii at Manoa, has a lot of fun with her classes by inviting a "cantankerous" person to be interviewed. Only the class does not know ahead of time that the person is so mean-spirited. She asks the person being interviewed to use all the dirty tricks possible. Most of the students figure out what is happening before the interview is over.

The interviewee follows this list of tricks as the students try to get information:

1. Denounce the press in general—"never get quotes right" or "you people are only interested in bad news and in getting people."

2. Turn the question around and interview the interviewer—"What do you think?" or "What would you do?" This is fun; some students will bite and answer several questions before the light dawns.
3. Go off the record, either before or after answering the question, to see what students will do.
4. At some point, deliberately misstate a fact everyone should know, such as "Vice President Howard Baker said" or "As the 49th state, Hawaii is . . ."
5. Be hostile to someone—"That's a stupid question." "You didn't do your homework or you would know the answer to that question." "That's none of your business" (a response that is particularly effective if it deals with something that is a matter of public record).
6. Wander wildly off the track. Students often are too polite to try to bring an interviewee back to the question.
7. If there is an opportunity, answer only "Yes" or "No" and see if you get a follow-up question.
8. Instead of answering a question, refer the interviewer to some difficult-to-obtain or time-consuming source—"I refer you to my book X, in which I discuss that question thoroughly."
9. Be inconsistent—say one thing at one point in the interview and another, contradictory, thing at some other point, to see if anyone catches it.
10. Talk jargon to see if anyone is sharp enough to insist on plain English for the "average" reader.
11. Answer a question with a folksy but inappropriate anecdote. If possible, make it a very appealing anecdote so the questioner will be tempted to use it.
12. Ask to see the stories before they are published.
13. Mumble or speak softly so the interviewer will be forced to ask that the answer be repeated.
14. Answer a question, then say "Now, I want you to quote that, it's important. But don't use me as the source—that would get me in a lot of trouble and I'll deny it. Just say the quote came from a knowledgeable source or something like that."
15. Defame someone—call a lawyer an "ambulance chaser" or a doctor a "quack."

In most cases, the best way to handle the mean-spirited character is to ignore most of the tricks and comments and pursue your story. However, sometimes some dialogue helps, and Evinger suggests you might consider:

1. Trying to convince interviewees who denounce the press that the reporter is accurate and trustworthy, or letting the interviewees vent their hostility, in hopes of then proceeding calmly with the interview.
2. Answering inquisitive interviewee's questions in hopes of creating rapport or saying "I'm sure our readers are much more interested in your opinion on that."
3. Explaining the need for attribution to interviewees who try to go off the record and urging that the material be placed on the record for the sake of credibility, or returning to the material later with related questions in hopes of getting the information on the record, or flatly refusing to accept off-the-record information.
4. Correcting misstated facts or asking for clarification.
5. Telling hostile interviewees about the sources checked before the question was asked or explaining why the answer to the question is necessary.
6. Allowing wandering interviewees to ramble in hopes it will lead to something useful or bringing them gently back to the question by saying "That's interesting, but. . . ."
7. Phrasing questions so that they cannot be answered "Yes" or "No" or asking "Could you elaborate?" or "Why do you say that?"
8. Pleading deadline pressures or asking for a summary of interviewee's views when they refer reporters to other sources.
9. Seeking clarification or stating the inconsistency to self-contradicting interviewees.
10. Asking jargon-speaking interviewees for definitions or explanations understandable to lay readers.
11. Expressing interest in the inappropriate anecdote, but asking how it relates to the subject, or whether interviewees have a more appropriate anecdote.
12. Refusing to allow sources to see stories before publication because this violates a newspaper's policy, but, if policy permits, agreeing to check major points by telephone.
13. Asking mumbling or soft-spoken interviewees to speak more clearly, explaining that "This is such interesting information that I want to be sure I get it all."
14. Pressing sources who refuse to be identified for on-the-record attribution and, if that fails, testing just how far the identification can go beyond "knowledgeable source."
15. Pointing out the defamatory material to interviewees who defame someone and asking for documentation.[3]

GROUP INTERVIEWS

Sometimes you may want the opinions of a six-member panel or the views of a scout troup or a school class of 30 students. But interviewing many individuals takes too long, and if you interview the group as a unit, you may not get enough information. Members of the group may all say the same thing. They will correct one another or think of the same answer, and somehow all will be reduced to one level.

But the way to give each one in the group a chance to express his or her views individually and with maximum creativity is to give the panel or class written questions. Let each person fill in the answers. Ask the same question several ways. Usually you will not use all the answers, just some of the best.

You can interview 30 people in three minutes of your time. If you want responses from a typical class, call a school principal or teacher and arrange for him or her to give five questions orally to a class. This works for the fourth grade—say, at Halloween time—and it works for a graduate class in philosophy if you are probing in that area. The students write down the answers individually, then turn them in. The school official can even deliver the questions to the reporter's desk. The only time the reporter spends is in giving the questions over the phone.

If you use this technique, be sure teachers understand that they are not to discuss the questions with the students. A comment from the teacher or classmate reflects in the answers. If the teacher keeps his or her hands off and lets the students come up with their own answers, *in writing,* without any discussion whatever, a gold mine of quotes and ideas can result—and the reporter has invested only three minutes.

INTELLIGENT USE OF QUOTATIONS

Your interview will produce a lot of possible quotations to use. Invariably the beginning reporter wants to use every quote, but not every one is usable or readable. Remember, what separates a reporter from a secretary is that a reporter selects from an array of material. A secretary takes it all down. To get good quotations, you have to go fishing for them—use follow-up questions, press the person being interviewed for more information, and ask the person for one more story. Be wary of advice that tells you to use a lot of quotes. Such advice may be fine for many articles, but not all. If you must use a lot of quotations, use a lot of *good* quotations.

Don't use informational quotes, ones that repeat obvious information such as the distance between cities, a person's age, or an identification of an occupation. A fact is a fact. You don't have to put quotes around it, although some information presented as fact which may or may not be true needs to be attributed. But even then you don't have to put everything in direct quotes.

Look for quotes that appeal to some emotion or that is plain interesting or cleverly put. For instance, there is nothing exciting about someone saying, "I was born 20 years ago and grew up in Chicago." But these quotes have a life to them:

> "I believe that dirty wash which is not laundered in public does not get clean."
>
> —Jacobo Timerman, formerly imprisoned editor from Argentina (*Newsweek*, Dec. 20, 1982).

> "You don't argue a case after you've argued *United States v. Nixon*."
>
> —Leon Jaworski, Watergate prosecutor, shortly before his death (*Newsweek*, Dec. 20, 1982).

> "When I was 10 and 12 and 15, I only went to R-rated movies. I would refuse to go to PG movies. Who wants to see people talk and have a good time? I wanted to see violence and hanky-panky."
>
> —Arnold Schwarzenegger, star of "Conan the Barbarian" (New York *Times*, Chris Chase's column, "At the Movies," May 14, 1982).

> "There is nothing a priest can tell me about God. My experience is more profound than his."
>
> —Fernando Parrado, on the 10th anniversary of the air crash in the Andes, where survivors were kept alive by faith and cannibalism (Associated Press, in Philadelphia *Inquirer*, Oct. 18, 1982).

> "He hurts you in so many ways. He doesn't have to score a point to play a flawless game."
>
> —Philadelphia 76ers coach Billy Cunningham, commenting on Los Angeles Lakers guard Magic Johnson (Ron Thomas, *USA Today*, May 31, 1983).

> "I knew before that you cannot make from a story a movie. As my Aunt Yentl used to say, 'You cannot make from a borsch a chicken soup.'"
>
> —Isaac Bashevis Singer, commenting on Barbra Streisand's movie, "Yentl," in an article by Linda Matchan, Los Angeles Times Syndicate, printed in the Philadelphia *Inquirer*, Jan. 25, 1984.

REPORTER'S NOTEHAND

Reporters' notepads contain strange, sometimes even exotic languages in which they scribble. The languages are usually not real languages, but a system of abbreviations, shortcuts, and symbols that aid rapid recording of what is said. Probably no two reporters take notes in the same way. Says one Minnesota newsman (in response to a questionnaire): "I take notes poorly. Occasionally I have seen the notes of others here in the office. They always seem more legible and more complete than mine. I wonder how I survive!"

He is not alone in his concern, for very few reporters are equipped with any secretarial or recording skills (outside of having perhaps taken a course in typing). How do they get by? What creative solutions have newsmen developed? What does a "practical" note-taking system look like? Reporters were asked: (1) What are some of the symbols or markings you use in your note-taking? (2) How do you take down a key statement verbatim when necessary? (3) How do you keep identifications straight? (4) How do you mark or code your notes for items that need further verification or clarification? and (5) What do you take notes on?

A compiled list of reporters' notehand symbols looks like this:

ausa: assistant U.S. attorney
bg: background
bk: book
cg: Congress
cr: classroom
c/r, ctrm: courtroom
cty: city
da: district attorney
Dx: Denver
e.g.: for example
est: establish
f: father
fed: federal
g: guard
gg: going
hpnd: happened
i.e.: that is
invu: interview
j: judge
l: lawyer
m: mayor, mother
M: Michigan; ***Mn:*** Minnesota, and so on.
mk: market
nfa: not for attribution
o/c: organized crime
or: off record
pple: people
px: police
rdi: ready
rep: representative
sap: soon as possible
sch: school
sitn: situation
std: standard
SX: San Francisco
th: that or there
to: turnover
trsy: treasury
u/: under
u/stndg: understanding
u r: you are
viz: namely
WA: Washington
w/: with
w/o: without
wh: whether
wr: wide receiver
wt: what
xgr: legislature
Xn: Christian (***Xnty:*** Christianity)
y p: young people

Also used are math and other symbols:

#s: numbers
>< or ↑ ↓***:*** greater than or less than
∴***:*** therefore
△***:*** change
U.S., U.N., MSU (Michigan State University): ordinary abbreviations
thru, enuf, tho: phonetic spellings

In addition to these notehand symbols, consider omitting vowels—except in important words—and the articles *a, an,* and *the*. Also try using only the first and last letters of words.

GETTING IT VERBATIM

Sometimes recording exact wording is very important. A legal statement, the reading of a code or law, the announcement by a politician that he or she will not run again, or a sudden confession (that to repeat to the source would bring a retraction or rewording of "off the record" comment) all require you to record word for word.

Also sometimes circumstances make repetition impossible: the subject exits, a competitor gets the text first, or the deadline is a minute away.

When every word counts, how do you get it down? Some professional advice:

Paraphrase, and put quote marks around the 'most important' words or phrases.

—Tyree Johnson, Philadelphia *Daily News*

Listen for key phrases, and do not try for extended verbatim notes.

—Edward Cowan, New York *Times*

Take it down word for word in Gregg shorthand.

—Barbara Herrera, San Diego *Tribune*

Use combinations of shortened words (as long as you'll be able to understand them exactly), abbreviations, and shorthand.

—Samuel L. Singer, Philadelphia *Inquirer*

Write slowly, and use large, distinct characters. Perhaps read back as a check.

—Jeff Williamson, Wichita *Eagle-Beacon*

Mentally memorize each statement, and try to get it down as quickly as possible.

—Roxi Mueller, Cleveland *Plain Dealer*

(In the phone interview) Take the notes on the typewriter. We use IBM Selectrics and they are FAST.

—Charles Humble, assistant city editor, *Oregon Journal*, Portland Ore.

Put down only the first letter of every word, and spell out key words, or about every fifth or sixth word, as time permits; then immediately go back over this key paragraph, and fill out all the words as the press conference, broadcast, or whatever, continues.

Some techniques help to sort out a group of names around a conference table as each one speaks:

- "Unusual, but smart, was the reporter I saw using red, blue, and green lead pencils at a conference," said one reporter. "Three people were speaking. Blue for Smith, Red for Jones, and Green for Williams."
- Identify carefully each speaker each time he or she speaks. Put a code number or initial before what is said. Draw a line across the page after each speaker concludes, thus clearly separating his or her remarks from another's.

Query Symbols

There are always some things that you will need to check later:

- Did the speaker say a "billion" or a "million"?
- A former politician is referred to; how do you spell his name?
- A law is cited; did the speaker have it right?
- A book title.
- The name of an institution (seldom cited correctly by anybody).
- The actual title for an official.

If reporters do not mark these items in question in the notes, they may neglect to check the spelling or wording, and an error may creep into print.

Ways to make sure one verifies doubtful information include:

(?)—Check it out. (Sp?)—Check the spelling.

—Carol Green, Denver *Post*

CQ?—Check later.

—George Skelton, Sacramento bureau chief, Los Angeles *Times*

CK:—Check out a fact with a certain authority.

—Constance Y. Bramson, lifestyle editor, Harrisburg (Pa.) *Patriot-Evening News*

Also some use "ch" after anything that needs to be checked.

Arrows, stars, circles, underlines and question marks.

—Clarence E. Page, Chicago *Tribune*

✓—It's accurate. While a question mark means to check, a check mark means it's accurate.

—Lavor K. Chaffin, *Deseret News*, Salt Lake City, Utah.

Circle a word for spelling, put question marks beside information to be checked.

—Jan Schaffer, federal courthouse reporter, Philadelphia *Inquirer*

My only symbol is to put a question mark in parentheses after words I doubt, or to bracket a passage that needs further amplification.

—Jeff Williamson, Wichita *Eagle-Beacon*

I draw a box around such information.

—Ray Ruppert, Seattle *Times*

The reporter who is working on a magazine piece with a lot of lead time and the traveling reporter who must gather information on a half-dozen stories before he or she returns to the office can have problems, not only with reading notes, but with understanding just what exactly the notes mean after a long interval between reporting and writing.

The "two-pencil" technique works well. Take notes with a ballpoint pen—it moves quickly across a page. But at the first chance—usually on airplanes or in motor vehicles between assignments—use a pencil to complete words and fill in gaps. Thus you know that the ballpoint entries are literal and the pencil markings are fill-out editing and context clarification.

Another way is to put the added spelling and contextual information or the fill-out of a quote in the note in parentheses. Again you will know exactly what the subject said literally, and you will be able to identify words or letters added later.

NOTEPAPER

Reporters will write on anything from reporter notebooks and typing paper folded vertically in half or quarters, to the back of an envelope, cocktail napkins, plane and train tickets, and backs of checks and checkbooks. Martha Shirk, of the St. Louis *Post-Dispatch*, says she sometimes writes ". . . on whatever scraps of paper I can find in my purse—credit card receipts, envelopes, gum wrappers, paycheck stubs. It's often quite embarrassing, but it only happens when I find a story by chance, a murder on the way home from work, for instance!" Skip Hess, of the Indianapolis *News*, says he has made use of grocery sacks, whereas Jim Merriner, political editor of the Atlanta

Constitution, writes on "matchbook covers, shirt cardboards, anything available." Pocket-size cards are used by one San Diego *Union* reporter, while one New York *Times* reporter makes notes in the margins of handouts.

While many abide by the use of the reporter notebook, one investigative reporter from *Newsday* says he never uses one: "Too bulky, a turnoff to witnesses." Some use yellow legal pads, such as the San Diego *Tribune's* Barbara Herrera. Chicago *Tribune's* Clarence E. Page likes a big pad but has switched to the smaller, narrow reporter notebook. His reasoning is a bit unusual: "I used to write out notes on a legal pad because a former girlfriend-journalist did it and I thought it was cute. Then, we broke up and I stopped using legal pads because they reminded me of her and I found it hard to concentrate on my work!"

Robert Strauss of the Philadelphia *Daily News* says: "One guy used to write notes on his arm. . . . One time he took off his shirt and went down his side . . . don't know whether he ever got confused with his tattoo."

TAPE RECORDERS

Using a tape recorder has these advantages:

- Reading illegible notes at a later date is not a problem.
- Tape preserves actual words of the person.
- Tape gives the reporter the flexibility to check back on nuances and tone of voice which may affect meaning.
- Tape has reference value, particularly for interviews with celebrities or politicians if you have an occasion later to come back to the figure for an in-depth piece.
- Reporters have more freedom to react to the subject when not encumbered with note-taking.
- Tape provides the ultimate value of having totally accurate recall.

The disadvantages of using a tape recorder are that:

- The reporter gathers too much material. Instead of having selected notes, the reporter has an hour interview to check over—unless he uses the digital counter. Whenever the subject says something that seems especially important, the reporter notes the number on the tape recorder at that moment. The reporter's auxiliary notes indicate which sections of the tape to check for the key points: 183, 241, 460, and 542. So the reporter can still perform the selection function while taping.

- Some offices do not provide tape recorders, and the amount of personal expense for equipment may be prohibitive.
- Tape recorders may malfunction. Erasures, garbled tapes, and dead batteries are common. Most reporters in key interviews take some back-up notes beyond the mere indexing with the digital counter.
- While inflections and voice tones may be preserved, a reporter may lose the context: the body language, the interaction of the subject with his or her aides, the grimaces and smiles. Also, although the answer may be clear, the question—especially one that someone across the room has asked—may be inaudible, and many answers are useless without the questions.
- Some people get very self-conscious when being taped (although some are more relaxed).
- Habitual mumblers often become more rigid and stentorian on tape. But speaking distinctly has its advantages—not only will the subject be understood, the subject who speaks distinctly is probably doing some thinking. This self-consciousness may be acceptable for stories eliciting ideas but may not be so successful for stories of human interest, in which the asides are often worth noting.

Even with the digital counting system and ability to plug back into the cassette at any point, writing slowdown occurs. Formerly reporters had tapes typed out—a time-consuming activity. Even now with the ability to get information off the tape quickly, you have to go back and forth between audio and print material. It is not possible to glance at a group of ideas on tape, as in print. Also, you can't cut and paste together spoken words on paper or link them as you can with words on a video display terminal.

Buying a Tape Recorder

Most tape recorders today do not need external microphones because condenser microphones are built into the machines. The sound quality of these condenser microphones is often very good. In fact, many radio stations use tape recorders with condenser microphones because they are easier to use (no worrying if the microphone cord is connected) and the sound quality is good. A tape recorder can be placed on a nearby table or desk; the recorder can easily pick up sounds within 10 feet.

Cassette tapes add convenience to using tape recorders. Just insert the cassette, close the cover, press the record button, and the machine begins taping.

Cassette tapes come in different lengths, identified by time: 60, 90, and 120 minutes, for both sides of the tape. It is better to use high-grade C-60 or C-90 tapes, since C-120 tape, which is very thin, tangles and tears easily.

All recorders, except the very small microrecorders, use what is called the standard-size cassette. For the kind of work a reporter does, the minirecorders, slightly larger than a paperback book, and portable cassette recorders, about nine inches long, are adequate.

Phone Taping

You can hook up most tape recorders to a telephone. Simple suction-cup attachments are available to be stuck onto the phone handset and plugged into the recorder, with clear results. Some use official telephone company taping equipment which puts out a "beep" every 15 seconds to let the other party know he or she is being taped. The Federal Communications Commission Act of 1934 says in Section 605 that unauthorized disclosures of radio and wire communications are prohibited, and FCC's Tariff 263 calls for a "beeper" on all interstate calls. Some believe the FCC is not clear on this, and the use of a 15-second beeper is the result of telephone company sales efforts. Subsequent rulings appear to have made the beeper unnecessary.

Lopez v. United States, 373 U.S. 427 (1963), said it is not illegal for one party in a telephone conversation to record and make known the conversation without the consent of the other party, and that such information is even admissible as evidence. In the wiretapping and electronics surveillance section of the Crime Control Act of 1968, 18 U.S.C.A. #2510 et seq., a person in a conversation is allowed to intercept it as long as the interception is not for a criminal purpose.

Apparently, according to federal law, only one party needs to know the information is being taped. However, the issue of taping without permission is still not settled. State legislatures dealing with wiretapping laws vary in interpreting what an "interception" is. Does an "interception" involve one, two, or three parties? Some states have followed the federal government policy of requiring only the consent of one of the parties, some require the consent of both parties, and others—about half of the states—have no regulations concerning consent.

Notes

[1]Georgie Anne Geyer, "Securing the Elusive Interview—Geyer Tells How She does It," *Editor & Publisher* (February 10, 1979), 112: 6, p. 28.

[2]Ida M. Tarbell, *All in the Day's Work* (New York: Macmillan, 1939), p. 235.

[3]Jane Evinger, "Dirty Tricks Teach Interview Pitfalls," *Journalism Educator* (Winter, 1984): p. 28.

Assignments

1. Interview a fellow class member now; at the end of the semester, interview the same student and compare the second article with the first.
2. Although an interview can be complex and may depend a lot on psychology, time, and other factors, some basic questions are useful in most interviews. Make a list of 10 questions you can ask in most interviews. For example, "Was there anything in your life that almost kept you from reaching your goal?"
3. Translate a short article into note-taking symbols—some from this chapter, some you devise yourself.
4. Do brief library research on a famous person in history. In class, compile questions that an interviewer might have asked in an interview with that person.
5. Invite a public official to class. Tape the interview. Write the interview from your notes. Compare accuracy of yours and other student's quotes with the tape version. The student who most faithfully reported the words of the speaker can comment on his or her successful techniques in quoting.
6. Analyze a feature interview article in the newspaper. Identify: (1) the theme of the interview, if there is one, (2) what gives it a sense of location, (3) what tells what the person looks like, and (4) the best quote. Discuss what the reporter could have left out and what the reporter might have asked, but apparently did not.

7

News From Meetings and Speeches

At meetings, important people say important things they might not say elsewhere. Important civic transactions take place; new ideas take shape. The reporter who attends meetings can report on speeches, chronicle political decisions, and follow up on ideas which are becoming actions. The meeting and speech setting provides the reporter with a regular source for current local news and for future news and features.

ANNOUNCING THE MEETING

Before reporters receive assignments to report on meertings, they must often write announcements of them. When reporters present announcement information, they should tighten up the copy. For example, this is too loose:

> The Bow and Arrow Club will hold its most important yearly meeting late this month on Thursday, Jan. 31, at 6 in the evening in the home of Anna Marie Sullivan. . . .

This is better:

> The Bow and Arrow Club will meet at 6 p.m., Thursday, Jan. 31, at 111 S. Main St. Hostess is Anna Marie Sullivan. . . .

In rewriting announcements and similar notices, also emphasize facts which will appeal to your readers. Let the first few words convey action and information. For example, do not start this way:

The 22nd annual meeting of the parents of the Friggens School will be held 5 p.m. Sunday at Waterdown Park.

A bicycle race will be provided for the youngsters who bring bicycles after the supper. . . .

Start with "bicycle" in the lead:

A bicycle race will highlight the annual outing of the parents of Friggens School Sunday at Waterdown Park.

The race for youngsters who bring their own bicycles will come after. . . .

Or, consider how to doctor this one up:

Members of the Serpentine Garden Club of Oakdale will meet Friday at Sarah Gibbons's home, 1606 Leftover St. Various reports will be heard.

Martha Roundtree will tell of plans for a rooftop flower garden on top of the Forgotten Old Folks Home where she lives. . . .

Start off with:

A rooftop flower garden will brighten the Forgotten Old Folks Home, 1000 Stationary St.

Martha Roundtree, a resident of the home, will tell members of the Serpentine Garden Club of Oakdale about the plans during the club's monthly meeting at 5 p.m. Friday at the home of Sara Gibbons, 1606 Leftover St.

The journalist should know the value of words, especially words that touch an emotion and words that stir a wide understanding and empathy. *Night* conveys suspense; *boys* and *girls* are universal topics and "spontaneous" in essence. People can relate to them. So, start with *night* or *boys and girls:*

A *night under the stars* awaits boys and girls. . . .

Not:

The school district is planning a night under the stars.

Again, your lead-in about young people will get readers interested if you start with the young people.

> *Boys and girls* will compete in a one-mile race for the first time at Apple Junior High.

The lively words get swallowed up here:

> Coach John Burns announces plans for a one-mile race for boys and girls at Apple Junior High. . . .

"Sunrise" is a word that conveys imagery and elicits feeling, so start with it.

> *A sunrise service* along the Lazy River will herald the start of Easter Sunday. . . .

The main point of interest—sunrise—is obscured if you do this:

> Services for Easter Sunday in Hankstown will include sunrise rites along the Lazy River. . . .

HOW TO COVER A MEETING

Reporters have these suggestions:

1. ***Get a copy of the agenda.*** A clerk can read it over the phone.
2. ***Make sure to have in hand some background on each item.*** Call an expert on each item. If there is a critical issue coming up in a voting meeting and you know you won't have much time at the end for questions, ask an expert in advance for two quotes: one to use if the vital measure passes, another to use if the measure fails. Or get the home phone number and alert the person you need the quote from to expect a phone call after the action. You can get a brief quote in a matter of seconds if you have arranged the call in advance.
3. ***Secure other documents ahead of time and/or immediately on arrival.*** Sometimes only one extra copy of a report is available; the person who gets up front first will probably get it.
4. ***Identify the spokesman or expert of the group.*** Stake out a chair next to that person. If the meeting is hostile and people are shouting and

walking out, stay near the door so you can catch people on their way out and talk to them. However, the vacant chair next to an expert is always a good place for you to sit for a while. Once seated you can check information with your source.

5. ***Watch identifications.*** Ideally, the reporter knows who the people attending the meeting are. If you don't know them, be sure to check for correct spellings and titles and get phone numbers where you can reach them.
6. ***Don't take down everything.*** Take notes on key issues, and make marginal notes of ideas for future topics.
7. ***Do not participate in the meeting.*** Minimally, nonparticipation can mean not voting or standing up in any head count. Some conventions are so loose they count everybody including guests. Other groups are angry at any interference. But exceptions prove almost every rule. Some groups welcome an honest question from a reporter which brings out some overlooked discussion point.
8. ***Look for the key agenda items.*** Being there when important issues come up is crucial.
9. ***Seek balance.*** If you take down the views of one side, be sure to take down the views of the other side.
10. ***Be prepared to switch gears.*** An entirely new agenda item may emerge. If this catches you by surprise, immediately pull an expert from the meeting for fill-in on the new development. Move around; you may want to crouch in the aisle to talk to people about the new proposal while you are listening with the other ear for further developments.
11. ***Single out key people—but not just officials—from the audience to get explanations of relevant points.*** Seek additional comment from those who will feel the effects of the action, such as property owners who will experience the impact of a new school tax.
12. ***Have in mind how to start the article.*** Although your idea for a lead may change, you should come up with a tentative lead and spend time seeking supporting information for the lead you think you may use. If something happens to change your idea for a lead, you can start the process over again. It is discouraging to get back to the office to find that you have a good one-paragraph lead and that all your other information deals with other topics.

Remember, a meeting that "met" is neither important nor interesting and is not news. But what the members of the group at the meeting *do* may be newsworthy. If members vote on something crucial, they may make news and a headline such as "Board Votes New Bonus" or "Council OKs New Swim Pool."

The Hostile Meeting

Although reporters prefer to work in a favorable climate, meetings, often steeped in conflict, are frequently not the happiest places. Sometimes participants at meetings do not want reporters to hear the dissension between factions, and so they try to exclude reporters.

Reporters should take responsible actions on their own behalf and on behalf of their papers and the community. Some professionals advise reporters not to leave a meeting without a protest. While this may be good advice in some instances, there are some other considerations. Reporters with low profiles who keep after stories may be better off. For one thing, reporters, unless they have specific instructions from their editors, risk censure from editors for acting overly aggressive or for storming out of a meeting. Recently, a southeastern Pennsylvania official refused to talk to one reporter but said he would talk to the other reporters in the room. The reporter whom the official discriminated against protested and walked out. (The others should have, too.) But his managing editor chewed him out for protesting.

On the other hand, a soft answer and a humble response can protect the reporter. A quiet, gentle person is hard to fault. Although storming out and speaking out loudly at meetings in order to serve some possible legal action has its place at times, generally a reporter who does so risks being regarded as arrogant or plain hotheaded.

Reporters may also be less interested in proving that they should be allowed to stay in the meeting because the reporter's main concern is getting the story. The editor does not send reporters out to prove a point but to get stories. Being humble will not make enemies. With a low profile, reporters can stand outside and elicit comment from those who exit. Also, people who feel sorry for expelled reporters are more likely to help.

Some reporters, particularly on bigger newspapers, have trusted sources they can send incognito to meetings. Such reporters don't appear in meetings where they anticipate problems. The moderator is then more relaxed and may say more, never knowing that the source or informant is securely planted in the meeting and is possibly recording the meeting.

When the meeting of a nonpublic group is closed to reporters, they can still find ways to get the story directly, sometimes by "eavesdropping" or by actually becoming a member of the group. Articles on the John Birch Society were prepared by a Detroit *Free Press* writer who joined the group incognito. Articles on the Ku Klux Klan have appeared from time to time written by reporters who had become members in order to write exposes. In 1979, a Chicago *Tribune* reporter became a secretary to a group of doctors and was able to blow the whistle on a multimillion-dollar illegal drug dispensing business. Reporters have gone so far as to join religious groups. Sometimes they have even become meeting "crashers." Consider this report in the Philadelphia *Inquirer* from the Investigative Reporters and Editors, Inc., convention in Denver in 1978:

DENVER—An investigative reporting technique, sometimes used as a last resort to get information, is posing. The reporter pretends, by not telling the whole truth, to be somebody else in order to get a story.

The religious groups have had their news "imposters." A reporter "joined" one of the choirs at the Second Vatican Council to get an inside look at the deliberations. Another reporter posed as a waiter during the formerly closed secret meetings of the U.S. Catholic bishops in a Washington hotel.

Other reporters have infiltrated the controversial Children of God, occult movements, and the young Jesus People communes.

Although participatory journalism is frowned on in many circles, some of its proponents were among those who gathered in Denver for the annual meeting of Investigative Reporters and Editors, Inc.

Posing to get stories came up here at panels and at a luncheon featuring Pamela Zekman of the Chicago *Sun-Times*.

Zekman told about the Mirage, a bar bought in Chicago by the *Sun-Times* and staffed with reporters as bartenders and waitresses. The *Sun-Times*' efforts resulted in nailing several corrupt city inspectors and others involved in kickbacks.

In religion reporting, Edward Plowman, news editor of the generally conservative *Christianity Today* magazine, is widely known. In an interview here, Plowman confessed to using posing techniques on occasion.

Plowman is infiltrating the tourist industry to expose abuses and failed promises by some of the religious tour organizers. He sometimes poses as an average tourist on some of the questionable flights. He also tags along with chaplains in six states and looks at prison conditions, without authorities knowing that he is a reporter.

Plowman, who on Sept. 1 becomes senior editor of the 155,000-circulation *Christianity Today*, commented on posing: "We do not lie. Mostly it's a case of not telling everything, and in some circles, that would be called deceit. . . ."

And deceit is not always bad. For example, in the time of war, the hiding of airplanes is acceptable, Plowman said.

The *Sun-Times*' Mirage Bar approach, apart from the question of using bars, Plowman said, was great. "The extent of corruption in Chicago and the complexities of the bar codes made it difficult to document this corruption through normal channels. They (the reporters) had to become first-hand witnesses."

A more reserved outlook in posing was offered in an interview with Gary Thatcher, of the *Christian Science Monitor*'s Atlanta bureau.

Reporters as customers mingling with others is all right, but "if, in the undercover work, your presence would affect the outcome," Thatcher believed, the *Monitor* would "opt for not doing it."

About infiltrating an organized group, such as a questionable youth movement, Thatcher said, "A reporter brings critical skills and one would not get a totally accurate picture" of the group.

The same would be true of a hand-picked member of the group as an informer. "We prefer to interview someone and not rely on one who has a stake in the outcome," Thatcher said.

Norman Udevitz of the Denver *Post* said that as a rule of thumb, "Do not represent yourself as one who can compel information, such as a priest, a doctor, and so on. All the rest is fair game. . . ."

Reporters have these observations about outright hostile meetings where they are clearly not wanted:

I try to be courteous but persistent. Tell them you have a job to do and that you plan to persist. Always try to keep your composure. In South Carolina, we have a freedom of information law so we can't be asked to leave a public meeting except for specific reasons like personnel discussions.

—Warren McInnis, staff writer, *The State*, Columbia, S.C.

In the first place, we don't leave if it's a public meeting because New Mexico has an open meeting law. Stick it out, refuse to leave, be persistent. Tell people who refuse to give information the public has a right to know and if they still refuse, emphasize you are going to quote them as refusing. But keep trying to get the information.

—Susanne M. Burks, city hall reporter, Albuquerque (N.M.) *Journal*

Remain calm and professional. Be ready to cite laws relative to open meetings, open records. Reason with individuals, do not threaten. Take down quotes and say you'll print exactly what went on, ask for reasons.

—Neil C. Hopp, managing editor, Carlisle (Pa.) *Sentinel*

Remain as detached emotionally as possible. Know your rights and express objections for the record when necessary. Don't get into a physical confrontation or cuss-fight.

—Roy Ockert, Jr., managing editor, Batesville (Ark.) *Guard*

Report the hostility.

—Ron Herron, city editor, Frankfort (Ky.) *State Journal*

The Detroit *Free Press* once reported a hostile county supervisor's meeting by giving all the unkind remarks board members said about each other. In Philadelphia, city council meetings can be a battleground. Few meetings get as exciting as this one, but if they do, the reporter writes about something besides agenda, plans, and voting:

State Rep. Milton Street and a band of his supporters turned the City Council's regular weekly meeting yesterday into a violent clash with Philadelphia police.

Plainclothesmen and uniformed officers, some wielding blackjacks, dragged Street, his brother John, and at least a dozen other followers out of the council chambers on the fourth floor of City Hall.

Before order could be restored, City Councilman Francis Rafferty, a vehement critic of Street, punched Councilman Lucien E. Blackwell in the face after Blackwell had denounced police for having used blackjacks to quell the disturbance.

Such protests and disruptions by Milton Street and his supporters have been commonplace recently during council meetings. The violence was new.

Altogether, police arrested 13 persons, including Milton Street, who precipitated the 10-minute melee by hurdling a three-foot-high railing onto the council floor, his brother John, a lawyer, Thomas Blackwell, 20, and Lucien Blackwell, Jr., 21, both sons of the councilman from West Philadelphia.

Police said that two officers required medical treatment. Freddie Velez of the civil affairs unit, who was hit on the head with a cane, was treated at Hahnemann Hospital, and Frank Brown, 52, suffered chest pains and was admitted to Hahnemann, where he was reported in stable condition, police said.

The issue behind Milton Street's protest is the city's plan for spending $64 million in federal Community Development funds. Street and his followers contend that the city has not allocated enough money for slum areas in North Philadelphia.

The administration of Mayor Frank L. Rizzo has provided some funding for North Philadelphia, but the thrust of the city's housing effort has been in neighborhoods of marginal housing, where city officials feel the infusion of funds can more successfully check deterioration than would be the case in poorer areas.

The council session began boisterously, but not unlike many other City Council meetings that Street and his followers have attended.

Shortly after 10 a.m., as council members filed in from the Democratic caucus room across the hall, Henry DeBernardo, a Street supporter who was one of those arrested, began leading the protesters in a deafening chant: "We're all fired up! We ain't takin' it no more!"

In an effort to call the meeting to order, City Council President George X. Schwartz exchanged his microphone for a bullhorn, but he was still drowned by the incessant roar of the crowd of about 200 people.

Schwartz then gestured to several council aides, and they began walking toward DeBernardo, who was standing in the spectators' gallery on the north side of the chamber. Suddenly, on the east side of the room, Milton Street leaped over the railing that separates the gallery from the council floor, where council members were seated at wooden desks. The force of Street's jump nearly carried him into the arms of Councilman Alvin Pearlman, who rose with a start from his desk. . . .

—William K. Marimow, Bob Frump and Dick Cooper, Philadelphia *Inquirer*

In preparing to cover a hostile meeting—one in which there may be some effort to exclude the reporter—you must know the laws. Secure a copy of state open meeting and open records laws, if they exist.

In some states, you can get printed miniature copies of the laws, so small you can hold them in the palm of your hand or fit them into a billfold or purse. Often the local chapter of the Society of Professional Journalists, Sigma Delta Chi prints these for its members. In Arkansas, a reporter challenged at a meeting can pull out a miniature card, 1½ × 2½ inches, and read aloud from the Arkansas Freedom of Information Act of 1977:

> . . . Except as otherwise specifically provided by law, all meetings, formal or informal, special or regular, of the governing bodies of all municipalities, counties, townships, and school districts, and all boards, bureaus, commissions, or organizations of the State of Arkansas, except Grand Juries, supported wholly or in part by public funds, or expending public funds, shall be public meetings . . . (Act 652, Section 3).

In Pennsylvania, the state Open Meeting Law (1974) says:

> The meetings or hearings of every agency at which formal action is scheduled or taken are public meetings and shall be open to the public at all times. No formal action shall be valid unless such formal action is taken during a public meeting. (Act 175, Section 2).

In South Carolina, the Freedom of Information Act of 1976 provides for open meetings of the state legislature, the legislative committees, and the state agencies, and in most instances permits taping of these meetings.

The "Boring" Meeting

Attending a seemingly useless meeting doesn't have to be a total waste of time for a reporter. Besides picking up ideas, experienced reporters develop some aspect of the meeting into a feature or even a human interest story. Some reporters can also turn a boring meeting into a humorous feature. A Minnesota editor of a weekly serving the Rainy Lake area on the Canadian-Minnesota border covered a meeting by reporting on the people who wandered in and out in between doing their shopping and other duties. He concentrated on what they had done all day rather than what was happening in the meeting.

John Neville, a naval officer and attorney who sometimes writes for several Ohio papers when he is on leave, covered a boring meeting by writing a humorous column on the smokers, describing their foibles and rituals in lighting up.

James Adams of the Indianapolis *Star* wrote about tablecloths. He recalls:

> I covered a luncheon meeting of labor groups backing a boycott of J. P. Stevens products. People discovered that all the hotel table linen was Stevens-made and removed all tablecloths and napkins and piled them in front of the rostrum. This made my lead.

Quinton Smith of the Albany (Ore.) *Democrat-Herald* wrote about the ordinary farmer in a crowd. "'Candidates Fairs' around election time can be boring or hard to zero in on because there are dozens of candidates to speak," says Smith. But at one such fair, Smith found an interesting angle:

> I asked a farmer in the crowd if I could sit by him and record his reactions as the politicians and would-be pols marched on stage. Then I wrote the story through his eyes: why he came, what he could be doing if he didn't attend, and what he thought of the fair in general.

> This method can be used sometimes—possibly when a meeting focuses on one issue and a participant (council member, for example) makes a key vote. Then you record the participant's comments and talk to him afterwards about what influenced his or her decision. Sometimes it works great and other times not so great.

Ron Herron of the Frankfort (Ky.) *State Journal* went back into some history to make a boring meeting interesting. "Subdivision plat approval is routine business," he says. "But previous developments made this one more interesting":

> Several years ago, plans were unveiled for a luxury hotel at the intersection of U.S. 60 and 127 in West Frankfort.
>
> Inn Kentucky was to have offered culinary traditions of the Bluegrass. Mint julep brandy "nightcaps" for guests and possibly even a thoroughbred horse in residence.
>
> That never materialized.
>
> Instead, there now emerges "Hudson Park," a considerably less ambitious plan that would put four fast-food restaurants, perhaps an office building and undetermined other enterprises on the 12-acre site.
>
> The City-County Planning Commission gave partial approval Thursday night to a preliminary plat subdividing the land into commercial lots for sale.
>
> Realtor Jack McDonald, agent for Inn Kentucky, Inc., in efforts to sell the property, said one lot has already been sold to Captain D's seafood restaurants and numerous other fast-food chains are also interested in the location.
>
> Explaining the failure of the hotel plans, McDonald said, "The energy crisis stopped the lenders from getting into that business."
>
> The plat presented to the planning commission Thursday night divides the side into three sections; further subdivision is planned later as the lots are sold. . . .

A meeting called to discuss a new building addition can be boring; it can be lively, however, if there is a cat in the story! Consider this classic account by Emery Hutchison back in the mid-1950s on the front page of the Chicago *Daily News*:

> The board meeting of the First Methodist Church of Glen Ellyn was torn asunder Tuesday night.
>
> All had been harmony among the 50 members attending during discussions of plans for the Church's $350,000 addition.
>
> * * *
>
> THEN Ridgely A. McCrary, a board member who is a buyer for Marshall Field & Co., dropped a bombshell with this question:
>
> Should Tabby, the church cat, be retired?
>
> McCrary so moved and was seconded and the fight was on.
>
> * * *
>
> SOMEONE asked why retirement?
>
> He was reminded that Tabby had a bad habit of wandering out to the pulpit during addresses by guests—recently Dr. Charles Ray Goff of the Chicago Temple, for example.
>
> One board member suggested that this merely enlivened the speeches.
>
> But he was harshly reminded that the merriment of the congregation should not be weighed against a guest's embarrassment.

* * *

DURING ALL of this the brown and white cat, whose innumerable kittens are in homes scattered all over the Glen Ellyn area, could be seen through an open door, pacing the church corridor.

A proposal was made that the cat be caged during guest appearances.

It failed when no one volunteered to be chairman of the committee for caging the cat.

Clay Steele, secretary-treasurer of Hart, Schaffner & Marx, then started a heated discussion with a request for a definition of "retirement."

It finally was decided that this did not mean execution, but rather the finding of a suitable home.

* * *

THE REV. James D. McKelvey, the pastor, ventured the opinion that they might not have a right to retire Tabby.

"Last summer I received an anonymous gift of $10 for an operation on Tabby to reduce the population of kittens around the church," he recalled. This operation was performed.

"Did anyone," he asked, "know that donor, who might claim ownership?"

Yes, several board members admitted, they knew the donor, but each was true to his trust. They refused to identify him.

* * *

CLARENCE McGee, assistant treasurer of Quaker Oats, wondered aloud: "Isn't a cat a church necessity for keeping mice out of the organ?"

Mrs. Vera Erickson scoffed at this. 'Hadn't anyone ever heard of mousetraps?" she asked.

Someone said that this was all a waste of time, since the durable cat had survived several previous church boards.

* * *

BUT AT LAST it was put to a vote.

A chorus of "Ayes" from those in favor of retirement was matched by an equal chorus of "Ayes from those opposed.

* * *

THE REV. Mr. McKelvey then asked for a show of hands. The count of those voting was 18 to 19.

The verdict was retirement.

So the word was going around in Glen Ellyn Wednesday: Does anybody want to take over the custody of the old church cat?

GETTING IDEAS AT MEETINGS

Demonstrating how ideas that emerge at a meeting can bloom into features, Ron Herron first wrote only three paragraphs on a meeting:

The City Commission agreed unanimously today to join a self-insurance plan with other cities and counties throughout Kentucky that are trying to cut costs of Workmen's Compensation coverage.

City Manager Paul Royster recommended the city try the new approach, which already has Franklin County government among its participants. It is sponsored by the Kentucky Association of Counties and the Kentucky Municipal League.

Anticipated are initial savings of 10 percent off the $99,000 premium charged by a private insurance company and the eventual prospect of dividends after the statewide fund has grown to a comfortable level.

Then Herron decided information on the kinds of claims that come in—and other background information—would make a feature, and wrote:

A city policeman runs up over $1,000 in medical bills after a car he stops for alleged drunk driving is backed into his cruiser. Another officer is kicked in the stomach by a man he is arresting. A dog attacks a worker at the Animal Shelter, possibly necessitating surgery on his hand. A garbage man picks up a can loaded with concrete and strains his back. Another garbage man, terminated after being off two weeks without notice, notifies the city through an attorney that he expects compensation for a back injury sustained on the job. A fireman using a plaster hook gets struck in the eye by falling plaster. A Street Department employee gets particles in his eye while cutting grass.

These are a few of the cases for which city employees have filed Workman's Compensation claims in recent months. They are not unusually numerous or severe. City Personnel Director John Cheshire says he was "amazed" at the low rate of job injuries among city workers when he left private industry to join local government a year ago.

Just the same, the city's premium for Workmen's Compensation insurance had doubled since 1975 and was going to cost $99,000 this year until the City Commission decided last week to drop its private insurer and join a self-insurance plan sponsored by the Kentucky Municipal League and the Kentucky Association of Counties.

City Manager Paul Royster traces the burgeoning growth in insurance costs back to 1972, when the state legislature liberalized Workmen's Compensation rules and, in his opinion, made it almost impossible for employers or insurers to calculate their risks.

"I certainly am not personally opposed to laborers being adequately protected," Royster stresses. "However, we now have a bill that interprets almost any kind of disease that happens to be contracted by an employee during his employment as being a job-related disease. For example, if you have a fireman now who suffers a heart attack, lung disease, cancer or even a hangnail, we don't have a prayer of being able to defend against a claim."

He adds that there has been little evidence of exploitation among city employees, but that has not held down the rates for Frankfort.

"The insurance industry isn't looking at what's happening in Frankfort," Royster explains. "They're looking at the industry performance as a whole."

Even though the job safety record may not be that bad among city workers, every young employee added to the force represents a potential liability of $300,000 if he should be disabled on the job and yet retain a normal life expectancy.

The result, according to Royster, is that many companies do not even want to write Workmen's Compensation policies. The city was summarily dropped by the company and put in an "assigned risk" pool by another, adding 8 percent to the premium.

Meanwhile, other city and county governments in Kentucky were having the same problem, so they got together to form a self-insurance fund that will cut the initial costs and may even repay dividends in future years if premiums substantially exceed claims payments. . . .

Susanne Burks of the Albuquerque *Journal* picked up on "a mayoral failing" which was being commented on at a meeting. She had previously felt the subject merited attention. The meeting was a reminder.

So with her idea, which surfaced at the meeting, she later came up with:

Mayor David Rusk has not appointed members to two city boards created by the City Council almost a year ago, city spokesmen acknowledged this week.

But Rusk has made 161 appointments to boards and commissions, including several new ones, since taking office Dec. 1, 1977, mayoral aide Ronda Stoddard said.

She said there are 59 city boards and commissions composed of unpaid citizens and serving various functions.

City councilors have criticized Rusk in the past few months for delay in filling vancancies on existing and new boards.

The most recent public incident occurred Jan. 15, when Councilor Sondra West criticized the mayor for failure to appoint an Economic Development Advisory Committee created by an ordinance she sponsored.

The ordinance was adopted by the City Council on Feb. 21. Mrs. Stoddard, who handles appointments to boards and commissions, said last week, "We are working on it now."

The other board still not appointed is a Law Enforcement Consolidation Task Force established in a resolution passed March 6 and including members from other governmental bodies. . . .

Bette Burg of the Huron (S.D.) *Daily Plainsman* came up with an idea when she covered a meeting between Canadian and U.S. senators in Winnipeg which dealt with establishing an international wheat agreement. At the meeting, she found that most agree that many American farmers do not understand the Canadian grain marketing system. Before leaving the meeting, she talked with Canadian senators and some Canadian wheat growers to find out about their system. This then became a separate story in addition to the main story on the senatorial meeting.

COVERING SPEECHES

Many techniques for covering meetings and press conferences apply to covering speeches, too. Reporters should get to the event on time and try to get a copy of the speech ahead of time, as they would try to get the documents ahead of time at a press conference or meeting. Speeches are generally easy to cover, but reporters may still need a fill-in by the speaker or another to help interpret it, react to it, or to help explain some of the difficult terms that come up.

Will Fehr, city editor of the Salt Lake (Utah) *Tribune*, offers five rules for covering a speech:

1. *Do some homework on the topic.* Many times the speaker is talking to a group with "inside" knowledge and some of his or her references may have no meaning at all unless the reporter explains them to newspaper readers.
2. *When in doubt about any statement, get back to the speaker.* Find out precisely what he or she means. Quoting a speaker accurately does no good at all if the intent of the quote is not crystal clear.

3. *Always stay for any question and answer period after a speech.* Many times, the question and answer period is more interesting than the speech itself.
4. *Never trust a printed program.* Often the speaker's name is misspelled and the title is wrong.
5. *If a speech is dull, don't think you have to write a long, dull story.* Too many new reporters feel they have to faithfully record everything a speaker says and to report the items in the same order. An experienced reporter knows he or she has to be very selective.

In the speech and article that follow, notice how Fehr picks one idea out of the speech and follows through with a discussion of that one idea. Only in the final paragraphs does he touch on anything else the speaker said.

Robert B. Hansen, attorney general of Utah, was speaking before the 10th Circuit Seminar of the Association of Trial Lawyers of America in Salt Lake:

> . . . I would like to urge our distinguished guests to use their very considerable influence to aid the cause of justice and the advancement of our profession in two particular areas. First, by supporting Antitrust Enforcement Act of 1979 now pending before Congress which would overturn the rule established in the United States Supreme Court decision in the case of *Illinois Brick*. This legislation is necessary in order that those parties injured by violations of our federal antitrust laws will be able to even have access to court to present their claims. Present law closes the courtroom door before the merits of their case can be presented—usually involving long recognized and traditional violations of antitrust laws.
>
> Secondly, by urging enforcement of the bar's canon of ethics banning trial of cases in the media. Recently there have been two flagrant violations of this canon in my opinion. One was on national TV in CBS' "60 Minutes" broadcast dealing with the Lee Marvin palimony case where counsel on both sides were blatantly arguing the merits of their respective causes before trial. The second occurred locally when the former Salt Lake County attorney just before he relinquished his office last month argued the merits of a rape case which is now pending on appeal before the Utah Supreme Court. If there is merit in this canon, and I believe there is, it should be enforced. If this canon is not going to be enforced it ought to be repealed so everyone will know what the rules are and the danger of discriminatory enforcement removed.
>
> Before concluding, I would like to take this opportunity to urge the Utah attorneys here to support passage of H.B. 218. This bill will remove any bar politics from the licensing and disciplinary phases of the legal profession. It will also permit a very limited participation of

laymen in this process and that is salutory in my opinion in that it should go a long way toward removing the "them vs. us" attitude so much of the public now has. I was very happily surprised to read in the Utah *Holiday* article referred to previously that James Lee, our most recently retired bar president, does not oppose the removal from the bar commission of its disciplinary activities. In fact he even approves of the transfer of this function to the Department of Business Regulations which would be a far more drastic change from past practices than H.B. 218 which places that responsibility upon the staff of the Utah Supreme Court so there is no constitutional question regarding any breach of the separation of powers provision of the Utah Constitution. I have several copies of the summary of that bill for anyone who would like more details concerning it.

Finally, I am as concerned, as you undoubtedly are, with the public image of lawyers, which image is principally set by trial attorneys and attorneys serving in public office. I hope with renewed efforts we can improve that image for the good of society and the benefit of mankind.

Here is Fehr's article:

Utah's attorney general wants the legal profession to enforce its canon of ethics banning "trial" of cases in the media.

Robert B. Hansen, speaking before the 10th Circuit Seminar of the Association of Trial Lawyers of America, at Hotel Utah, pointed out two "flagrant violations of this canon."

One was the "60 Minutes" television report on the Lee Marvin palimony case. The actor is being sued by Michelle Triola Marvin for $1 million. She lived with him for six years and claims he promised to support her for life.

On the national television show, "Counsel on both sides were blatantly arguing the merits of their respective cases before trial," Mr. Hansen said.

The other was former Salt Lake County Attorney Paul Van Dam's discussion of the merits of a rape case now pending appeal before the Utah Supreme Court, Mr. Hansen said.

Before he left office, Mr. Van Dam commented on 3rd District Court Judge Bryant Croft's reversal of a jury's conviction of a rape case.

"If there is merit in this canon, and I believe there is, it should be enforced. If this canon is not going to be enforced, it ought to be repealed so everyone will know what the rules are and the danger of discriminatory enforcement removed," Mr. Hansen said.

The attorney general also argued for support of the Antitrust Enforcement Act of 1979, legislation currently before U.S. Congress which would allow access to court by individuals injured by violations of the federal antitrust laws.

He also spoke in favor of Utah H.B. 218 which would bar politics from licensing and disciplinary phases of the legal profession.

Some speeches can be covered very briefly by listing ideas:

DENVER—Schools are failing to teach the skills high school students need most to succeed in the high-tech society of the '80s—speaking and clear thinking, education officials from across the USA were told here Wednesday.

Industry needs employees who are "trained to be trainable, who can learn something else when their job is replaced by a machine," said IBM's William Howard at the convention of the Education Commission of the States.

High schools, Howard said, need to teach:

• Logical thinking—the ability to gather data and draw logical conclusions.

• Basic economics, including an understanding of the forces that drive industry.

• Personal finances—some graduates, he said, "can't even balance a check book."

Beverly Anderson, formerly of the National Assessment of Educational Progress, agrees.

"We are not making improvements or even holding our own in higher level reasoning and problem-solving skills."

Examples:

Fewer than 30 percent of high school seniors can figure a 15 percent tip on a dinner bill.

Only 56 percent can determine a car's gas mileage, with or without a calculator.

—Pat Ordovenski, *USA Today*

Edward W. Frede, managing editor of the Danbury, Conn., *News-Times*, adds his five rules for covering speeches:

1. *Try to avoid canned speeches altogether.* They're dry and boring and usually say nothing.
2. *Read the text* as the speaker gives his talk. Note when the speaker departs from the text.
3. *Look for the bombshell* which some speakers drop in departing from the text.
4. *Attend just for the speech.* Stay away from the freebies. Too many make you drowsy.
5. *Play up the byplay and reaction to a speech*, or lead with it, and bring in the text where it fits. Sometimes the byplay and reaction are more interesting than the speech itself.

Since they must often meet early deadlines and beat competitors, reporters may write up speeches from prepared texts. Nevertheless, if the speaker is important, reporters should go to hear the speech anyway and look for any new angles; if there is a later edition of that day's paper, they phone in any significant additions or deletions from the prepared version. If there is no later edition, a second-day story may take care of the new information and other developments.

Edward Frede's Danbury *News-Times* ran two articles on a speech by the same writer, Tom Ahern, on two different days. The speech was the January 3, 1979 inaugural address of the late Connecticut Governor Ella T. Grasso. Since she was not to give the speech until 2 p.m.—"two hours past our press time" said Frede—the reporter had to write the story from the advanced copy of the text with reference to the "prepared text."

HARTFORD—Gov. Ella T. Grasso officially began her second term today by offering a rosy view of the state's future and then warning that lean years ahead could wilt the picture considerably.

Grasso's inaugural address, scheduled for 2 p.m., highlighted the ceremonial opening of the 1979 Legislature. The state's 187 senators and representatives were sworn in during the morning and Supreme Court Chief Justice John P. Cotter administered the oath of office to Grasso in early afternoon.

As the legislators bustled about, painters and carpenters strolled down the majestic halls of the state Capitol building, making final arrangements for offices and committee meeting rooms. The workers, clad in white coveralls, seemed oblivious to the gathering sense of expectancy building up for the inaugural ritual.

Neither the workmen, nor the nameplates that gave mute testimony to occupants of many offices from years past, dampened the excitement, though.

Lt. Gov. William A. O'Neill, who did get his name exchanged for predecessor Robert K. Killian's outside his new third-floor office, hosted an early morning coffee for reporters and photographers.

State Sen. Richard Bozzuto, R-Watertown, hustled about, conferring with his troops from his new minority leader's office, even though his name still hung outside another room down the hall.

The legislators, after taking their oaths of service to the state's 3.1 million citizens, went to the nearby Wadsworth Athenaeum for a midday banquet before returing to the Hall of the House for Grasso's first speech of her second four years in office.

The governor's prepared remarks seemed a not-too-distant echo of many campaign promises from the fall.

Twice, she was to promise no new or increased taxes, a familiar theme of the November election when she was returned to office by the near-landslide margin of 190,000 votes.

She combined this with a note that federal aid cutbacks to local communities force them to "re-evaluate programs or reduce services despite the state's effort to lessen the gap."

The state faces similar cutbacks, her speech said, but she chose not to add that this forces similar re-evaluation and reduction at the state level.

Instead, she added, state efforts "will also be restricted by the insistence of our people that we live within our means" and the text followed with "inflation has again become the cruelest tax, destroying the value of the dollar and adding new costs to every purchase."

"This plight is worsened by the ominous portent of further increases in energy costs," her speech added.

These forecasts of a tight budget and high expenses contrasted with her renewed "pledge to economic growth, humane service and effective organization of government."

—Tom Ahern

The next day, January 4, on the front page with a four-color picture of the governor and others, the reporter wrote about the speech for the second time, with more detail of the ceremony and some reactions:

HARTFORD—Pageantry eclipsed serious business yesterday as Gov. Ella T. Grasso took her oath of office to the tune of a 19-gun salute and the 1979 Connecticut Legislature opened up shop for another session.

Democrats and Republicans called Grasso's short inaugural speech typical because it touched many problems. Some legislators seemed disappointed it offered few solutions, especially considering the powerful position she holds by virtue of her 190,000-vote victory last fall.

State Rep. Joseph Walkovich, D-Danbury, said Grasso's address struck him as a "pretty general look toward the future." Sen. Wayne Baker, D-Danbury, termed the speech "in character" and added he didn't expect "any ingenious innovations."

Rep. Clarice Oslecki, R-Danbury, said the speech was "glorious in its unspecificity."

Grasso asked for progress in economic development and help for the handicapped and elderly, education, crime prevention, environment and public transportation. She warned legislators they could count on limited funds to cope with these problems.

In contrast to New York Gov. Hugh Carey's inaugural speech, interrupted 13 times by applause, the crowd packing the Hall of the House at the State Capitol Building stopped Grasso just once.

That time, Republicans began the applause after the governor tossed words of praise their way by noting the importance of a vigilant minority party. In our society, the majority rules but the minority retains rights too, she said, quoting Thomas Jefferson who warned the alternative is "tyranny."

The audience gave her a 40-second standing ovation at the end of her speech. Dressed in a trim navy-blue dress, she smiled and waved from the podium while her supporters whooped it up.

Among those there were U.S. Reps. William R. Ratchford, a Danbury Democrat elected to his first term this fall; Anthony Moffett, D-6th District, Christopher Dodd, D-2nd District, both re-elected; U.S. Sen. Abraham Ribicoff and former Gov. John Dempsey.

The governor's foot guard in high fur helmets, and a detachment of officers on horseback, escorted her to the Capitol steps where a National Guard contingent fired cannons 19 times. . . .

After Mrs. Grasso answered, "So help me God" to the oath of office delivered by Chief Justice John Cotter, the governor told the collected members of the 1979–80 General Assembly that the tough times aren't over.

Grasso did not mention the plight of urban poor, a point obviously worrying delegates from the state's larger cities.

Sen. Sanford Cloud, D-Hartford, the only black in the Senate, and a supporter of former Lt. Gov. Robert K. Killian in the September gubernatorial primary against Grasso, said later, "We haven't seen the budget yet but the tone of the governor's message showed that the programs dealing with the poor are not a high priority."

Grasso will submit her budget message in February. The initial proposal her administration worked on contained a 4.3 percent spending increase.

Although the governor "renewed" her "pledge to economic growth, humane service and effective organization of government," she reserved personal support for just a few areas, none of which cost the state money. The governor spoke of the absence of a direct primary system for selection of major statewide candidates, and the "deplorable cost of campaigning for public office." She said, "Together we can alter these inequities."

She repeated her fall campaigning promise of "no new or increased taxes," saying "the voices of November are not lost in the winds of January." She told legislators, "Your efforts to enact further limitations . . . will provide additional tools."

—Tom Ahern

Assignments

1. Prepare "A-matter"—or advance material—on a meeting that is about to happen. Look at previous clippings and talk with leaders of the organization about key issues coming up. The article should be complete enough so that all it needs is a lead called in from a reporter at the meeting.

2. Call the editor of a small weekly newspaper and make arrangements to cover a meeting for that paper.
3. Take a meeting story out of the daily newspaper. Find five ideas in the story that you could develop into a longer feature.
4. Accompany a daily newspaper reporter to a meeting. Write up the meeting, and compare your article with the professional reporter's story the next day.
5. Report a meeting strictly on the basis of phone calls to the participants.
6. Secure a speech given at a meeting or a document to be presented at the meeting. Write an article based on the speech or document. (You may duplicate one speech or document for each member of the class to work on.)
7. Do a follow-up on a meeting story in the newspaper. In this second story, update or develop one key idea that came up at the meeting.
8. Go to a meeting and, in addition to any coverage you might do, identify a human interest idea (humor, interesting personality, an individual's achievement) that is perhaps unrelated to the meeting, and write a story about it.

8

People Facts and Personals

People make news. Sometimes they make big news. Everyday actions of a President and other politicians who take part in significant events may appear on the front page. Or a group of persons dies in a plane crash. Or a young girl, Samantha Smith, of Manchester, Maine, visits the Soviet Union at the invitation of Soviet leader Yuri Andropov. Events that are out of the ordinary involving people reach the front page. But the basic events of people's lives also appear in newspapers, such as births and weddings. And most certainly most people may be sure of getting into print at least once—when they die.

Shorter items about people include birth announcements, social activities of locally and nationally prominent people, professional promotions, engagements and weddings, and obituary or death notices. Some columnists deliberately mention as many recognizable names as possible. Also, straight news columns present short, often humorous, items about noted people. (See also Chapter Eleven concerning daily up-front people news columns.) Special people columns offer such material as weekly profiles of children available for foster homes.

Editors used to print as many names as possible. Now that larger circulation makes even newsprint expensive, editors cannot mention as many people, especially since names alone do not significantly raise circulation (even assuming that a certain percentage of those mentioned would become subscribers). Newspapers are getting away from the indiscriminate use of "personals."

TRENDS IN PERSONAL INFORMATION

Kent Cockson, managing editor of the Pensacola (Fla.) *News-Journal*, which does not publish personals, defines personals as "news about who is visiting whom in town, where the neighbors went on vacation, and how many prize-winning petunias Mrs. McGilicutty entered at the county fair."

Clearly, society personals are on the way out. "Ten years ago, we had a woman calling and writing personals," says an editor of the Charleston (W. Va.) *Gazette*. "There were about three columns worth on daily and on Sunday two columns. Now we have none."

The *Independent Record*, in Helena, Mont., no longer has a full-time person covering personals. "We avoid this fluff," says Kevin Giles, lifestyle editor. "We concentrate on strong 'people' stories and hard news."

Says Marie B. Pulvermacher, associate editor of the *Capital Times* in Madison, Wis.:

> Personals have been practically eliminated from our paper. We do run meeting notices if the meetings are open to the public, if there is a speaker worthy of special notice, or if the event is a charity affair. Gone are the birth announcements (except in the record columns), the church circle meetings.

Her paper has also cut down on wedding announcements, confining them to the Saturday editions. Her paper now charges for obits and "the copy is handled by the advertising department."

She continues:

> The stress now has shifted to "lifestyle" articles, consumer items, and so on, with an emphasis on day-to-day problems, such as how to cope with inflation. Some years ago we incorporated our "Society Department" into our feature section, called the PM section, which also includes the arts, comics, and television pages.

Yet some editors make a good case for running personals. People are still news, and the down-to-earth situations have a certain warmth and friendliness to them. Bill Adams, news editor of the Hilo (Hawaii) *Tribune-Herald*, sounds a warning about cutting them back too much. He observes that he notices after 10 years as a reporter-editor that ". . . most coverage of personals is getting tighter . . . less friendly and familiar, and more objective. In the main, this is healthy, but it can get too cold, too pithy in certain circumstances."

Among smaller community papers which have space for personals, some evolution is taking place. Says Barbara Burgess, editor of the Fallon (Nev.) *Eagle-Standard:*

> Names make news in a small daily such as the *Eagle-Standard*.
>
> Several years ago, actually it's more like 40 to 50 years ago, obituaries and wedding announcements were considered page-one

material. Even if the individual had resided in Fallon for only five years and was killed in an auto crash in Oklahoma, the news found its way to the front page.

Wedding announcements included everything from what the bride wore to what type of necklace the groom's grandmother wore. If it was a prominent family, the entire account of the ceremony was front page.

Now, an obituary is carried on page one only if it is the notice of a leading citizen's death. . . .

We still have personal columns submitted to us by older women from the various districts in this large county. The women report on who is visiting the area and who is sick. Not too long ago, these reports also included news that so and so had just purchased a new Ford sedan. That really is not considered news now.

On page one, we carry a column called "Bits and Pieces." It contains the birthday greetings, anniversary notes, and other tidbits of information about people in the community. Up until two years ago, we had a column written by the publisher about little pieces of gossip he had heard on the street. . . .

Although instructors in college and university journalism courses say little about "personals," recent journalism graduates on their first job may find themselves assigned to take care of personals. One student on his first job on a weekly in Minnesota wrote a letter describing his own experiences:

. . . The biggest problem I had when I started this job was to get used to what constituted news in a small town. . . .

Journalism students today are taking many jobs on small dailies and weeklies. If the reporting courses only taught what to expect in a small town newspaper situation, they would be prepared. For example, the first week I was here, an obituary came in (untyped) that I thought was about two pages too long. Of course, I edited it for length and sent it on. After the paper came out, two irate ladies came to the office and complained because we hadn't printed every last word.

Also, small town newspapers often run many stories that pass for "news." They really are only thinly disguised advertisements. Reporters on small papers don't turn up their noses at any information that comes in, no matter how mundane or bad they may think it is. If a story involves local people, the paper PRINTS IT.

In spite of the small town focus, I am enjoying the job because I am getting some good experience, and I am my own boss. I can write whatever I want.

A journalism student should be familiar with small town newspaper practices.

The young man's point is a good one. Although professors and students may have more fun producing more in-depth and dramatic articles, they should not forget that, for many professionals, newspaper reporting includes work on small town papers: putting together personals, wedding announcements, obits, and free publicity for local merchants.

The training you receive on how to write the in-depth article should not keep you from being able to write personals. If anything is worth doing at all, it is worth doing well. And how much experience and training do you need to edit and print personals? Basically the same principles apply to all newswriting. As a trained journalist you should be able to write various kinds of articles and to do all writing assignments well. Just because one newspaper is very unimaginative in its outlook does not negate your need to know a full range of skills. You can use good news and feature skills at all levels.

GLEANING IDEAS FROM PERSONALS

Sometimes ideas for other articles come to mind as you read personals. A notice about a garden show can suggest a feature on the newest hybrid in town or the prettiest plant in the show and how to grow it. Personals mentioning children always suggest possibilities, such as ways to meet their needs. In fact, one small weekly of 2,000 circulation in Bellefonte, in the mountains of central Pennsylvania, made an appealing feature from material on local children and Father's Day. The Centre County *Democrat* filled most of the front page on June 14, 1979 with "What is a Father?" Under 23 pictures of smiling children, a story appeared describing what they thought of their dads.

The *Democrat* also prints personals from stringers such as Ida Leiby in Boalsburg, Pa., and Karen Korman in Centre Hall, Pa. As you look over reports of personals such as theirs, you may get ideas for future features reporters could write based on the personals.

BOALSBURG
The Boalsburg Garden Club met Friday evening, June 1, at the home of Dorothy Burick, Boalsburg. Before the meeting, with twenty members and a guest, a tour of Hillside Gardens, Bailey Lane, was taken with Tig Burnett, owner, as guide.

Mrs. Laura Stoner, president of the club, presided for the business meeting. The annual flower show will be held at the Boalsburg Fire Hall August 16.

A workshop will be held at the home of Mrs. Lynn Doran, of Kaywood, Boalsburg, Friday evening, July 6, at 8 o'clock. The co-hostess for this meeting will be Mrs. John B. Thomas. Refreshments were served during the social hour by Mrs. Burick, and co-hostess, Mrs. Orvel Schmidt.

Mr. and Mrs. Lawrence Callahan

have returned to their home in Baltimore, Md., after visiting Mr. Callahan's sister, Mrs. Ruth Green, and his brother and sister-in-law, Mr. and Mrs. Harold Callahan of Boalsburg; his sister, Mrs. Clayton Martz of Tusseyville, and a sister-in-law, Mrs. Verna Callahan, of Centre Hall RD.

Five confirmands were received into the Zion Luthern Church of Boalsburg Sunday morning, June 3.

The Rev. Lloyd Seiler is pastor of the church. The confirmands were: Kenneth C. Hall, Daniel A. Kyper, Mark W. Morgan, Ian S. Keith, and Dorothy J. Vesper.

After the church service, the confirmands were honored at a reception given by their parents: Mr. and Mrs. Jon Hall, Mr. and Mrs. Alec Keith, Mr. and Mrs. Arthur Kyper, Mr. and Mrs. William Morgan, and Mr. and Mrs. Carl Vesper.

Mrs. Hazel Rossman, of Port Matilda, and Mr. and Mrs. Clair Fisher, of Warriors Mark, visited Mrs. Edna Bloom and Richard.

—Ida Leiby

CENTRE HALL
Recently Miss Bertha Sharer attended an Alpha Delta Kappa sorority social in Altoona. The social tea was held for five new teachers at the home of Mrs. Eugene Tipton.

Mrs. Margaret Grove, of Mechanicsburg, spent the last two weeks with her son and daughter-in-law, Mr. and Mrs. Samuel Grove, of Centre Hall. During her visit Mrs. Margaret Grove spent an afternoon with Mr. and Mrs. Arthur Thoman. Mrs. Margaret Grove also visited with Mrs. Grace Lingle, of Tusseyville.

Senior Citizens from Bellefonte, State College and Centre Hall traveled to Elizabethtown College for the 19th annual convention YMCA Senior Power (federation of retired persons club). Some of the people representing Centre Hall were: Mrs. Alma Grove, Mary Bierly, Polly Homan, Polly Hout, Adaleine Mark, Anna Runkle, and Mrs. Eleanor Wert.

Girl Scout Troop 1202 and 1203, under the leaders of Mrs. Wilma Shuey and Margie Korman, and Brownie troops 1200 and 1201, under the leaders of Mrs. Judy Spotts and Peg Cole, went to Camp Oakwood, near Lewistown, for the weekend for a campout.

The Scouts and Brownies participated in a hike, a nature scavenger hunt, an alphabet scavenger hunt, fingerprints, leaf prints, and so on. The girls had a campfire and a camp sing. This was a culmination of the activities for the school year.

—Karen Korman

Some of the questions that reporters could ask if they are looking for feature stories hidden in the Boalsburg personals are: What's new in Hillside Gardens? Are there any changes in the new annual flower show? What do the Callahans' relatives do in Baltimore?; Are they important people? How about pictures of a confirmation? Is five a large or small number? Why? What is confirmation?

From the Centre Hall personals: What do the new teachers at Centre Hall have in common? How about a feature on YMCA Senior Power? How about tagging along on a girl scout campout? Could we chronicle a nature scavenger hunt and help the reader to have fun and learn along with the scouts?

GUIDELINES FOR PERSONALS

Follow the general rules for writing all personals—society tidbits, birth, wedding, and death announcements—by making sure they are:

1. ***Complete.*** Include a person's full name (first name or first two initials), address (street, avenue, or court).
2. ***Accurate.*** The rules mentioned in Chapter Three apply here. Because pranksters (see the discussion on hoaxes) often call the personals columns, you need to check items which invite fakery. Verify items of romance or new engagements (particularly around Valentine's Day) and death news which comes from other than established sources.
3. ***In good taste.*** Some people have strange hobbies and food habits you may not want to talk about; information about recent illnesses is also often taboo.
4. ***Up-to-date.*** If Jane Jones went to Vail at Christmas, don't publish the information at Easter.
5. ***Geographically within your reading area.*** Personals from another county without reference to the immediate circulation area are meaningless to local readers.
6. ***Fair.*** If Mrs. Smiley's story appears in print, then so should Mrs. Jolly's.
7. ***Free of innuendos, bias, and judgments.*** People all know each other in a small town, so you have to keep your own feelings and opinions out of your writing.
8. ***Appealing to many readers.*** Does anyone care about the information besides the subject? One can get up at 5:30 a.m., but that is not significant. If someone gets up at 5:30 a.m. in order to do the farm chores for a sick neighbor, however, others in a rural community may want to read about it.
9. ***Non-commercial.*** People try to slip in stories which further their commercial interests or which promote products. Generally you should refer such people to the classified ads desk. Try to keep the news free of advertising. A Clifton, N.J., editor was indicted in the summer of 1979 for extortion. He was accused, among other things, of threatening to write bad stories on local merchants who did not advertise with his paper. Another kind of extortion is for a reporter to promise to refer favorably to an organization or product (in personals or elsewhere) if a firm places advertising.
10. ***Terse.*** Says Kevin Giles of the Helena (Mont.) *Independent Record*:

> My suggestion for the beginner dealing with obits and personals is that he or she adhere to the rules of good journalism: tight, terse, tele-

graphic. Don't get persuaded to join the scrapbook syndrome. Ask: "Is this news, or is it simply self-serving for a club, a person, or an organization, for inclusion in their scrapbooks?"

WEDDINGS

Even a paper as large as the New York *Times* includes engagements and weddings. Like a smaller newspaper, the New York *Times* goes into some detail:

Catherine Calvert Silver and Robert Keith McNamara were married yesterday in the Church at Point O'Woods, Fire Island, L.I., by the Rev. James Lowell Shannon, an Episcopal priest.

The bride is a daughter of Mr. and Mrs. R. Bruce Silver of Point O'Woods and Akron, Ohio. Mr. Silver is executive vice president of the Akron Chemical Company, which was founded by his late father, J. R. Silver Jr.

Mr. McNamara is a son of Mr. and Mrs. Keith McNamara, also of Point O'Woods and Columbus, Ohio, where his father is a lawyer.

The bride graduated from the Old Trail School in Bath, Ohio, and Skidmore College. She attended the Villanova Law School.

Her husband, an alumnus of Wesleyan University, received a master's from the Fletcher School of Law and Diplomacy of Tufts University. He plans to attend the Stanford University Business School in September. Until recently, Mr. McNamara was in the international division of the Chemical Bank in Brussels.

* * *

The engagement of Marcy Ellen Wilkov, daughter of Mr. and Mrs. Harry Wilkov of Stamford, Conn., to Christopher M. Waterman, son of Dr. and Mrs. Arthur J. Waterman of Huntington, L.I., has been announced by the prospective bride's parents.

Miss Wilkov, a graduate of Mount Holyoke College, is a third-year student at New York University School of Law, where she is senior note and comment editor of The Law Review. Her mother is a high-school teacher in Stamford. Her father is senior partner of Wilkov & Smyth, Stamford public accountants.

Mr. Waterman, an associate with the New York law firm of Mudge Rose Guthrie & Alexander, is an alumnus of Yale University and Catholic University School of Law. His father, professor emeritus of political science at the C. W. Post Center of Long Island University, is a retired Foreign Service Officer who worked in the Rome and Beirut embassies.

Printing costs, which limit the size of a newspaper, and the growing size of circulations in consolidations, which means more general interest news, account for a cutback in the use of wedding news. Perhaps the growing divorce rate and some attention to alternate lifestyles are also factors.

The women's liberation movement also may play a role. One Montana lifestyle editor has made changes "to eliminate sexism. For example, the cutline no longer reads, Mr. and Mrs. John Doe, but rather, John and Jane Doe. Lengthy descriptions of the bride's mother's dress and other such hysterical holdovers from American-Victorian journalism have been eliminated."

Most newspapers let the couple themselves provide the information by filling out a form. Again, the danger of a hoax always exists, but when people have to come to the newspaper office to fill out a form, they are less likely to be playing a joke. Nevertheless, you may want to check the wedding information. The performing magistrate or clergy person is a good person to call. You only need to verify if the wedding is scheduled.

Typical of an engagement form is this one from the Central Maine *Morning Sentinel*, Waterville, Maine:

ENGAGEMENT ANNOUNCEMENT

CENTRAL MAINE MORNING SENTINEL
25 SILVER STREET WATERVILLE, MAINE 04901

WOMEN'S NEWS EDITOR

(Engagement announcements and pictures should be published at least 30 days BEFORE the wedding ceremony. Please include middle initials and home residence addresses. These facts will be held confidential until the proper time for publication.)

Full name of bride-to-be__________ of__________
Daughter of__________ of__________
Full name of
bridegroom-to-be__________ of__________
Son of__________ of__________
Date of wedding__________ Place__________
Bride-to-be's education__________
indicate whether graduated

____

Employment__________ Address__________
Bridegroom-to-be's education__________
indicate whether graduated

____

Military Service: Branch__________ Rank__________
Stationed at:__________
Employment__________ Address__________
Telephone No. (daytime)__________
Photo accompanies: yes no (circle)
Photo taken by__________
Signature of parent or guardian if under age__________

Wedding forms sometimes ask for more than basic information. The Oklahoma *Journal* in Oklahoma City requests a good picture, which indicates its interest in format and layout. The *Sentinel* in Waterville, Maine, also uses the wedding form to look for ideas and unusual facts.

A newspaper reporter should always be looking for the unusual. And sometimes people have unusual weddings. Some examples: the ceremony is based on a medieval one; the ceremony takes place aboard a raft going down the river, or on the wings of an airplane; the bride and groom wear wedding garb 2,000 years old; or the wedding party treks from church to reception in antique cars, as happened in Royal Oak, Mich.

OBITS

The obituary announcement, like weddings and other personals, requires you to be dedicated to accuracy and sensitivity to people. You have to be able to get along with all kinds of people on the phone, from busy, business-like morticians to hard-of-hearing survivors. The newspaper puts much of the burden on the funeral home, and in many newspapers funeral homes handling the arrangements pay for the obits. Some papers carry both paid ads and separate news listings. In such cases the reporter limits coverage to news and leaves details of the funeral to the paid ad.

Here is an example of an obituary form from the Hawaii *Tribune-Herald*. An obit follows written on the basis of the information provided in such a form:

HAWAII TRIBUNE-HERALD
INFORMATION BLANK FOR OBITUARY
(Deadline: 8 a.m. Monday through Friday; 4:30 p.m. Saturday for Sunday Tribune-Herald)
(PLEASE TYPE. CROSS OUT PHRASES WHICH ARE NOT APPLICABLE.)

Mr. Mrs. Miss (other)____________________________
(Name of deceased in full)

______, of_______________________________
(Age) *(Address of deceased)*

died____________________________________
(Day and date of death)

at/in___________________________________
(Place of death—Hospital, home, accident scene or other locations)

He was/She was____________________________
(Identification—occupation/position, etc.)

____

Funeral arrangements are pending, with______________________in charge.
(Name of Mortuary)

Friends may call at______________________________________
(Place)

from________________to__________________ __________________
(Time) *(Time)* *(Day and date)*

A wake service will be held at/
The Rosary will be said at________ ______________________
(Time) *(Day/date)*

at____
(Place)

Friends may call______________from______________to______________
(Day/date) *(Time)* *(Time)*

at____
(Place)

Funeral services/A Mass/Private family services/Memorial services/
Combined wake and memorial services/Services over the cremated remains/
____________________was born in______________________________
(Last Name of deceased) *(Place of birth)*

He is survived by his wife______________________________________
She is survived by her husband__________________________________
________sons____
(Number) *(Full name/address if not living with parents)*

____

____

________daughters____
(Number) *(Full name/address if not living with parents)*

____

____

He/She also is survived by____
(Parents/brothers/sisters/with address)

____

____

____

and________grandchildren and______________________great-grandchildren.
(Number) *(Number)*

(Name of mortuary)

Other information:______________________________________

____

____

(USE SEPARATE SHEET IF NECESSARY)
(THE ACCURACY OF ABOVE INFORMATION AND THE MEETING OF DEADLINE ARE THE RESPONSIBILITIES OF THE FUNERAL HOME)

Funeral Home______________________________Phone______________
Information submitted by____________________Phone______________

ETSUJI SUYAMA

Etsuji Suyama, 91, of Hilo, died Thursday at his residence.

He was a retired salesman for I. Kitagawa and Co.

Friends may call Sunday from 5:30 to 7 p.m. at Dodo Mortuary chapel. Services will begin at 7 p.m. Cremation will follow the services.

Survivors include a son, Earl Mineo Suyama of Hilo; five daughters, Mrs. Yaso (Emiko) Abe of Wahiawa, Oahu, Mrs. Kenji (Momoye) Kaneku-ni, Seiko Suyama, Yooko Suyama, and Esther Keiko Suyama, all of Hilo.

He also is survived by a brother, Yoshisuke Suyama of Honolulu; two sisters, Mrs. Michiyo Tsuruda and Mrs. Kazuyo Kawazoe, both of Japan; and by three grandchildren.

Mr. Suyama was a member of Hawaii Shima Yamaguchi Kenjinkia and the Kapiolani Kumiai Association.

Many factors can make the death of an ordinary, unheard-of person front page news. For example, if a sidewalk swallows a person:

CAIRO (AP)—A pretty young bride dropped from her husband's side when a sidewalk in Alexandria gave way, and disappeared without a trace.

After a fruitless five-day search, the governor of Alexandria ordered frogmen Saturday to probe underground cisterns in the city dating to the days of Julius Caesar and Cleopatra.

Residents of Alexandria recall that about 30 years ago the ground cracked and swallowed a young mother who was walking with her husband and son. She was rescued, alive, after three days.

The city is built over a series of 700 underground basins built by the Romans, some of which have two or three stages.

The latest accident happened Monday evening as journalist Anwar Said of Al Gomhouria and his 20-year-old bride Mervet were walking home from an evening movie. He was taken to a hospital suffering from severe shock.

Civil defense crews probed the hole the first night, but found only a bracelet.

Water company officials said water from a cracked pipe had created a vast underground reservoir, covered only by the thin sidewalk pavement. When this slender covering gave way and the woman fell, the reports said, she was apparently swept away by the underground water.

Or if monkeys are the culprits:

JAKARTA, Indonesia (Reuters)—Hundreds of monkeys bit and scratched a 9-year-old boy to death in a southern Borneo animal preserve after he and three other boys had refused to give up their lunch box, the news agency Antara said yesterday.

Of course, when prominent people die, the story gets full treatment. A practiced writer captures the essence of the celebrity's life, appreciates the person's style, creates nostalgia for an era in which the person served and lived, and assesses the person's place in history.

Consider a front-page report in the Philadelphia *Inquirer*, compiled from the wire services, on the death of a familiar broadcaster:

WASHINGTON—To those he covered and those he competed against, Frank Reynolds was, above all, a reporter who cared. He defined his job in simple terms: "To help people understand what's going on."

Reynolds, the chief anchorman of ABC-TV's "World News Tonight," died early yesterday after three months of battling viral hepatitis—brought on, a colleague said, by "a bad blood transfusion." He also had multiple myeloma, a form of bone cancer.

Reynolds, 59, was a familiar figure in broadcasting for more than 30 years, anchoring the live coverage of such events as the assassination attempts on President Reagan and Pope John Paul II, space shuttle launches and landings and national political conventions.

He co-anchored the late-night specials during the Iranian hostage crisis that led to creation of the ABC-TV "Nightline" program, and he played a major role in development of the multiple-anchor format used by "World News Tonight."

Reagan called him a "warm, considerate friend." A spokeswoman for Nancy Reagan, who spoke to Reynolds by telephone several times during his illness, said Mrs. Reagan, and perhaps the President, would attend the funeral Saturday at St. Matthew's Cathedral.

Reynolds will be buried in Arlington National Cemetery at his "last request" conveyed by his wife to Mrs. Reagan in a telephone conversation, the spokeswoman said.

Reynolds, who was awarded a Purple Heart for service in World War II, qualified for burial at Arlington as a veteran.

In an interview last night with ABC News, Reagan reminisced about Reynolds:

"I think that Frank had a perception of me that was kind of based on an image that was prevalent in the East about that wild westerner out there. I think we both learned to like each other. I think he was quick to decide that the image didn't fit.

"He was a friend, but more than that, he was a professional also. He never let friendship interfere with what he felt had to be said, nor would I have expected him to. He was a very decent man, not only in the way he lived but in the way he did his job."

Reynolds and his wife, Henrietta, had been friends with the Reagans since he did a story in 1976 on how Reagan handled his failure to win the Republican presidential nomination.

Reynolds died at 12:40 a.m. yesterday in Washington's Sibley Memorial Hospital. A few hours later, ABC had some of his colleagues and competitors on its morning news-talk show.

"Frank Reynolds reported the news as though it were happening to him," said Ted Koppel of "Nightline."

"Frank felt other people's pain very deeply, and he showed the pain of others very deeply, and what we now know about him in retrospect is just to what extent he succeeded in hiding his own pain. He showed everybody's pain but his own."

Reynolds had undergone surgery March 17 for a leg broken when he slipped on ice. The hepatitis was diagnosed April 29, and Reynolds had not appeared on the news program since then.

Koppel said that Reynolds apparently "got a bad blood transfusion and contracted viral hepatitis" and that "although we later found out that he had cancer, it was the hepatitis that killed him."

When Reynolds left, "World News Tonight" dropped from second to third in the audience ratings.

Dan Rather, anchor of the "CBS Evening News," said, "The Reynolds competition was always class all the way . . . If you were (competing) against Frank Reynolds, you knew that you were going to be beaten some of the time, but you would never be beaten unfairly."

To Tom Brokaw of NBC, Reynolds was "a kind of 24-hour-a-day newsman" who never lost "his sense of awe, his sense of delight at being where he was."

Reynolds' emotions were on nationwide display as he anchored the running story of John W. Hinckley Jr.'s assassination attempt of Reagan in March 1981. After reporting that press secretary James Brady had died, Reynolds learned the report was erroneous. Angrily, on camera, he lectured his reporters: "Let's get this straight."

The anchorman was widely criticized for the remark. Roone Arledge, president of ABC News, said Reynolds, "perhaps the most caring reporter that I've ever known . . . could never understand, nor could I for that matter, why he was criticized sometimes for feeling so personally the story that he had to report."

Reynolds co-anchored the "ABC Evening News" with Howard K. Smith from May 1968 until December 1970, when he lost the post to Harry Reasoner, who moved to the network from CBS.

Reynolds, who once told a friend his career was "Lazarus-like," made his return to the anchor slot eight years later, joining Peter Jennings and Max Robinson on "World News Tonight."

He joined the network news division from ABC's Chicago station WBKB—now WLS-TV. For 12 years before that, he was a newsman with WBBM-TV, the CBS station in Chicago.

A native of East Chicago, Ind., Reynolds also had lived in nearby Hammond, where he met his wife. He lived with his wife in suburban Bethesda, Md.

In addition to his wife, Reynolds is survived by five sons. One son, Dean, is the White House correspondent for Cable News Network.

On the day after the death of a famous person, a followup on one detail—such as the cause of death—can be the story:

WASHINGTON—Viral hepatitis, probably contracted through a blood transfusion, was the immediate cause of anchorman Frank Reynolds' death Wednesday in Sibley Memorial Hospital, Washington, D.C., says ABC spokeswoman Kitty Bayh.

Hepatitis is rarely fatal, but Reynolds' case was complicated by a previously unrevealed case of bone cancer called multiple myeloma.

About a tenth of those who receive transfusions, as Reynolds did after surgery for a broken leg March 17, may become infected with hepatitis, though most never know it and the body fights the disease naturally, says Roger Dodd, head of transmissible diseases and immunology for the American Red Cross.

Reynolds' case had a complication: "Multiple myeloma is a cancer that affects part of the immune system. Any person with advanced cancer is subject to any number of infections and diseases," says Dodd.

Though Reynolds' family knew of his cancer for several years, his coworkers at ABC had no idea how ill he was when he was admitted to Sibley early this month. "We were stunned," Bayh says.

Reynolds hurt his leg during a January vacation in Key Biscayne, Fla. He reinjured the leg in February, when he slipped on ice in Washington.

"He was finally diagnosed as having hepatitis on April 29," Bayh says, "but he had been ill off and on for weeks before that. He kept thinking he was battling a flu."

Symptoms of hepatitis include fever, weakness, loss of appetite and sometimes muscle pain or jaundice.

About 55,000 cases of hepatitis—an inflammation that impairs the liver's ability to function—are reported each year. About 1 percent are fatal.

—Anita Manning, *USA Today*

In feature obits, include in the lead the key thing for which readers should remember the person:

Marsh Dozar, noted for his philanthropy and community service and as founder of Marsh Dozar Auctioneers, the nation's largest auctioneering firm dealing exclusively in real estate, died Tuesday at his home in Beverly Hills after a long illness, his family announced.

Dozar, who was 62, was honored by the California Assembly, the Los Angeles City Council and the county Board of Supervisors for his humanitarian activities. He was president for two years of Gateway Hospital and Mental Health Center in Los Angeles and sat on the board of directors of that facility. He also served as president of the Pinerock Ranch Foundation for Emotionally Disturbed Children and was on the board of directors of The Guardians, the support group for the Los Angeles Jewish Home for the Aged.

Dozar was active as a Shriner and Mason and was honored in 1975 as Man of the Year by the Westwood Shrine Club. He contributed to the City of Hope and various Jewish charitable appeals.

A native of Winnipeg, Canada, Dozar came to the United States in 1943 and became a citizen. He worked in the restaurant supply business and owned a hotel and motel before founding Marsh Dozar Auctioneers in 1960. The Beverly Hills firm is the largest in the United States dealing only in real estate, according to Dozar's partner and son-in-law, Stan Kottle.

Funeral services were scheduled for today at 3 p.m. at Mount Sinai Memorial Park.

—Los Angeles *Times*

Vic Wertz, former Cleveland Indians' first baseman best known for swatting a long fly ball to deep center field in New York's Polo Grounds in the first game of the 1954 World Series that Willie Mays of the Giants made a time-honored over-the-shoulder basket catch on, died yesterday during open heart surgery at Harper Hospital in Detroit.

Wertz, 58, died at 7:34 a.m. as surgeons attempted to perform a coronary bypass and replace a valve in his heart. He suffered a heart attack on June 23 and was admitted to the hospital, where he suffered a second heart attack Wednesday.

In a film replayed every year around World Series time, Wertz came to bat in the eighth inning of the first game, with the score 2-2. He lofted a pitch by reliever Don Liddle, but Hall of Famer Mays made a spectacular catch about 460 feet away. The Giants went on to win the game, 5-2, in 10 innings and swept the Series.

In the 1955 season with the Indians, Wertz was stricken with polio Aug. 26 and hospitalized until Sept. 13. His illness was diagnosed after high fever and neck stiffness.

"There is no sign of paralysis, but the condition is polio," Dr. Don Kelly, former Indians' team physician, said at that time.

At the time of his illness, Wertz said, "I've got two strikes on me, but I'm still a long way from being out. I know I have polio, but I'm going to lick it. They tell me this thing may end my baseball career, but they'll never make me believe it."

Wertz backed up his words by earning American League Comeback Player of the Year honors in 1956 when he hit 32 homers, batted in 106 runs and batted .264 with the 1956 Indians. The homerun total was a career high. . . .

—Cleveland *Plain Dealer*

The essence of a person's outlook on life, or charisma, can be part of an obituary, especially that of a celebrity.

BEVERLY HILLS, Calif—The organ at Good Shepherd Roman Catholic Church played "Ink-a-dink-a-do" and "Give My Regards to Broadway" as Mass was celebrated for comedian Jimmy Durante, who died Tuesday at 86.

More than 500 friends, colleagues and admirers heard the comedian eulogized by Bob Hope and Danny Thomas at the rites Thursday night. The Lennon Sisters sang for the Communion rite.

But all eyes returned again and again to the battered old hat atop the coffin.

"He did have a million of 'em—not jokes . . . friends," Hope said.

"At least Al Jolson and Bing Crosby won't be lonely, now. They waited a long time for a piano player who could play their kind of music. Now they've got one."

Thomas, who was godfather to Mr. Durante's daughter, Cecilia Alicia, paid tribute to the entertainer's "childlike simplicity that was in complete contrast to his ability to perform. He was a real pro."

"Jimmy," he said, "was a holy innocent who did no one any harm. He had no envy in him. He never thought there was anything different than the way he spoke. He thought everyone sounded the way he did.

"What a wonderful world this would be if we all spoke, and lived and loved, like Jimmy Durante."

The rare turnout of Hollywood greats gave additional testimony to Mr. Durante's standing among them.

Marlon Brando, whose public appearances have been exceedingly rare, walked quietly and sadly into the church.

Others at the service included comedians Red Buttons, Don Rickles, Marty Allen and Jack Carter; actors Desi Arnaz, Robert Mitchum, Peter Lawford, Cesar Romero, Margaret O'Brien, Doris Day, Fess Parker, Ernest Borgnine and Angie Dickinson; director Frank Capra, composer Meredith Willson, singer Phil Regan and Los Angeles Mayor Tom Bradley.

Arriving in a wheelchair was Eddie Jackson, solemn-faced and grieving, the surviving member of the comedy team of Clayton, Jackson and Durante.

At private burial services yesterday at Holy Cross Cemetery in Culver City, Calif., Mr. Durante was given his final round of applause.

As the service ended, Borgnine called out: "Let's hear one last one for the Schnoz," and the crowd of 50 people gathered around his graveside broke into spontaneous applause in the morning sunshine.

—Philadelphia *Inquirer* Wire Services

Kent W. Cockson, executive editor of the Pensacola (Fla.) *News-Journal,* has worked out an elaborate guide for writing obituaries:

- ADDRESSES—Double-check all addresses for accuracy. Every obituary should have an address. If there is no number in a street address, consider locating the home better by mentioning what intersection it is near.

  Use the abbreviations Ave., Blvd. and St. only with a numbered address:

1600 N. Pace Blvd.

Spell them out and capitalize when part of a formal street name without a number:

near the intersection of Blount and Normal streets.

All similar words are always spelled out. There are no abbreviations for alley, circle, court, drive, lane, place, port, road, route, terrace, and so on.

Spell out and capitalize First through Ninth when used as street names. Use figures with two letters for 10th and above:

1 E. First Ave.

2205 N. 59th St.

- BIOGRAPHY—No biographical details should be considered insignificant. If there is much personal history offered, perhaps that is a tip-off that the deceased was prominent in the community and warrants an obituary story rather than a simple death notice.

  We should make an effort to search out at least one "humanizing" thing that further identifies the deceased in his obituary—his occupation, an unusual hobby, significant club membership role, or simply his occupation and where he or she worked. Beyond that, no extra information need be solicited.

- CITIES—If the city is NOT in Florida, indicate what state it is in for the first reference. States are always abbreviated when preceded by the name of a city, except those eight listed on Page 209 of the AP Stylebook. (One of those states NEVER abbreviated is Texas.) If the city is in Florida, do NOT use Fla. after the name of the city. . . .

- DIED—Always use died. Never say passed away, succumbed, left us, went to the great rest home in the sky or other such bombastic euphemisms.

- FAKED OBITUARIES—Beware of faked obits. If a caller informs us that a relative or close friend has died, ask them what funeral home is handling the arrangements and CALL THE FUNERAL HOME. All obituaries should be verified through a funeral home.

- FLOWERS—We will NOT use the phrase "in lieu of flowers." Nor will we make any reference to flowers, EXCEPT when the mortuary indicates in the obituary that the family has requested that flowers not be sent. Because of conflicts with flower advertisers, we should ensure that the "no flowers" request is made by the family. When such a request is made, we are bound by the wishes of the family, taking precedence over the wishes of floral advertisers. The family is paying for the obituary, putting them on equal par with the flower advertisers.

  If the family indicates it will accept memorial contributions, we will say WITHOUT mentioning flowers:

  The family prefers that memorials be sent to. . . .

  Contributions may be sent to. . . .

- FUNERALS ELSEWHERE—If a body is to be transported to another city or geographic location after local funeral services, you should attach a paragraph at the end of the obituary saying, for example, "Commander Funeral Home is in charge of local arrangements."
- GRANDCHILDREN—We will use the names of grandchildren IF they are the only surviving relatives or if there is some special newsworthiness. The same applies to special friends, cousins, and so on. Normally, we will publish the names of brothers, sisters and all children who are survivors.
- HUSBAND, WIFE—Use husband, not widower, in referring to the surviving spouse of a woman who dies. Similarly, use wife, not widow, in referring to the surviving spouse of a man who dies.
- IN, AT—Use of the word *at* is preferred to *in* when referring to hospitals, cemeteries, and so on in an obituary.

  Ruth Nelson, 69, . . . died Thursday at a hospital.

  Burial will follow at Pleasant Hill Cemetery.

  Webster says that basically *at* is the preferred preposition of general (usually static) location, and that *in* is preferred when more specific or detailed location is required, as in: A body is buried at a cemetery in a coffin that is put into a six-foot-deep hole.
- LATE OBITUARIES—Every effort will be made to get in a "late" obituary, even if it is an hour after your deadline but still in time to be published. After all, that's the name of the game in this newspaper business. But do not do so at the expense of accuracy and quality.
- LIBRARY CLIPPINGS—Be wary of library clippings in obtaining background information. Such information should be checked through the funeral home. The deceased is not in the newsroom to defend himself against his files. And the clipping may contain a 20-year-old error that was never corrected or tells only part of the story. Consult with the desk editor in charge whenever there is a question.
- LOCAL—Avoid the redundant use of the word. For persons who reside in Pensacola and die at a Pensacola hospital, it is enough to say:

  Jack R. Jacobsen of 225 E. Jackson St. died Saturday at a hospital. He was 59.

  You need not point out where the hospital is unless the obituary concerns a resident of one city or county or state dying at a hospital, nursing home or convalescent center in another city, county or state.
- LONGTIME—It is one word when used as an adjective.

  He was a longtime resident of Walton County.
- NAMES—All names must be spelled right, from that of the deceased through the survivors, funeral officiates and pallbearers.
- ONE-TIME—This word is hyphenated when it is used as an adjective.

  He was the one-time Florida director of public services.

- PALLBEARERS—Never say "Pallbearers include . . ." because only complete lists of pallbearers are given. The sentence should begin, "Pallbearers will be . . ."
- ROSARY—It is *recited* or *said*, never "read" or "performed." The word is always lower case.
- STEPFATHER—It is one word, not hyphenated. Same for stepbrother, stepson, stepmother, stepdaughter, and so on.
- SURVIVORS INCLUDE—If there are more than two, use this form. If there are less than two, write Mr. Jones is survived by. . . . In conjunction with this, never write *one son*; use *a son*, etc.
- TIMES—Write it this way:

  Funeral services will be 2 p.m. Thursday . . . and forget the use of the word "at."
- UNPUBLISHED MATERIAL—When there is material the family does not wish published—age or cause of death for instance—we will handle the matter with sensitivity and diplomacy. The editor in charge will make the appropriate judgment. We tactfully will try to get ages of all the deceased that appear in our obituary columns. Ages are essential parts of obituaries, but obit writers will not be argumentative or obnoxious about getting such information.

  Occasionally we may publish material the family wishes we didn't. We should do so having made an editorial judgment, and not by accident.

To help you comply with these rules, an example of a typical obituary follows, incorporating many of the guidelines already listed:

HOPE FUNERAL HOME

Jones

CRESTVIEW—John K. Jones of 550 W. 17th St. died Sunday of cancer at an Escambia County hospital. He was 63.

Mr. Jones was the processing-plant maintenance supervisor at St. Regis Paper Co. He was a native of Florala, Ala., but had resided in Crestview for the past 35 years. Mr. Jones was a member of the Baptist church and Masonic Lodge No. 122 F&AM. He was a veteran of World War II.

Survivors include his wife, Mary Elaine Jones of Crestview; a daughter, Beverly Sills of Pensacola; two brothers, Jack Jones and Casey Jones, both of Birmingham, Ala.; a sister, Mrs. Paul L. Berry of Munson; a stepsister, Rita Skorka of Birmingham; 18 grandchildren; and 23 great-grandchildren.

Funeral services will be 2 p.m. Tuesday at Good Hope Baptist Church with the Rev. H. R. Block and the Rev. I. R. Stanton officiating.

Burial will be at Magnolia Cemetery with Masonic rites at graveside. Hope Funeral Home will direct.

Active pallbearers will be Henry Jacobs, Martin Stallworth, Henry Martin, Buddy Hackutt, H. O. Train and Alfred Neuman.

Honorary pallbearers will be Thomas Hall, Dr. James Goodpaster, Harold R. Smith, Jesse M. Pearl,

Anson I. Jansen and members of Mount Sinai Sunday School.

Friends may call Monday after 2 p.m. at Hope Funeral Home. The body will be taken to the church an hour before services.

The family prefers contributions be made to the American Cancer Society.

Assignments

1. Underline the local names in an issue of the daily newspaper in your area. Construct a policy statement or set of guidelines which the paper appears to follow concerning local persons. Who gets into the paper—in columns, featured obits, marriage announcements, and so on?
2. What is the style for titles and similar information in the personals? Compare with AP stylebook.
3. Write obits of one another in the class, using local newspaper obit format or one used in examples in this chapter.
4. Discuss the following questions:
   a. Should the paper give the cause of death?
   b. Should the paper mention suicide and the method of suicide?
   c. When would you put a wedding story on the front page?
   d. Assume your paper's policy is to feature on weekends the partying and comings and goings of the rich and well-known. Is there any comparable coverage that the paper can do for the poor?
   e. How about lottery coverage? How much should you play up the winners and/or the losers?
5. Take a page of your newspaper. Put an X on any people coverage you find offensive, a question mark on any personal where more facts are needed, and a plus sign on people information you like and which you feel is complete.

Ed Edelson, New York (N.Y.) Daily *News* science editor, takes notes as Dr. Rochelle Hirschorn explains an experiment taking place in a graduate clinic. Photo by Kappock, New York (N.Y.) Daily *News*

PART 3

Lively Writing

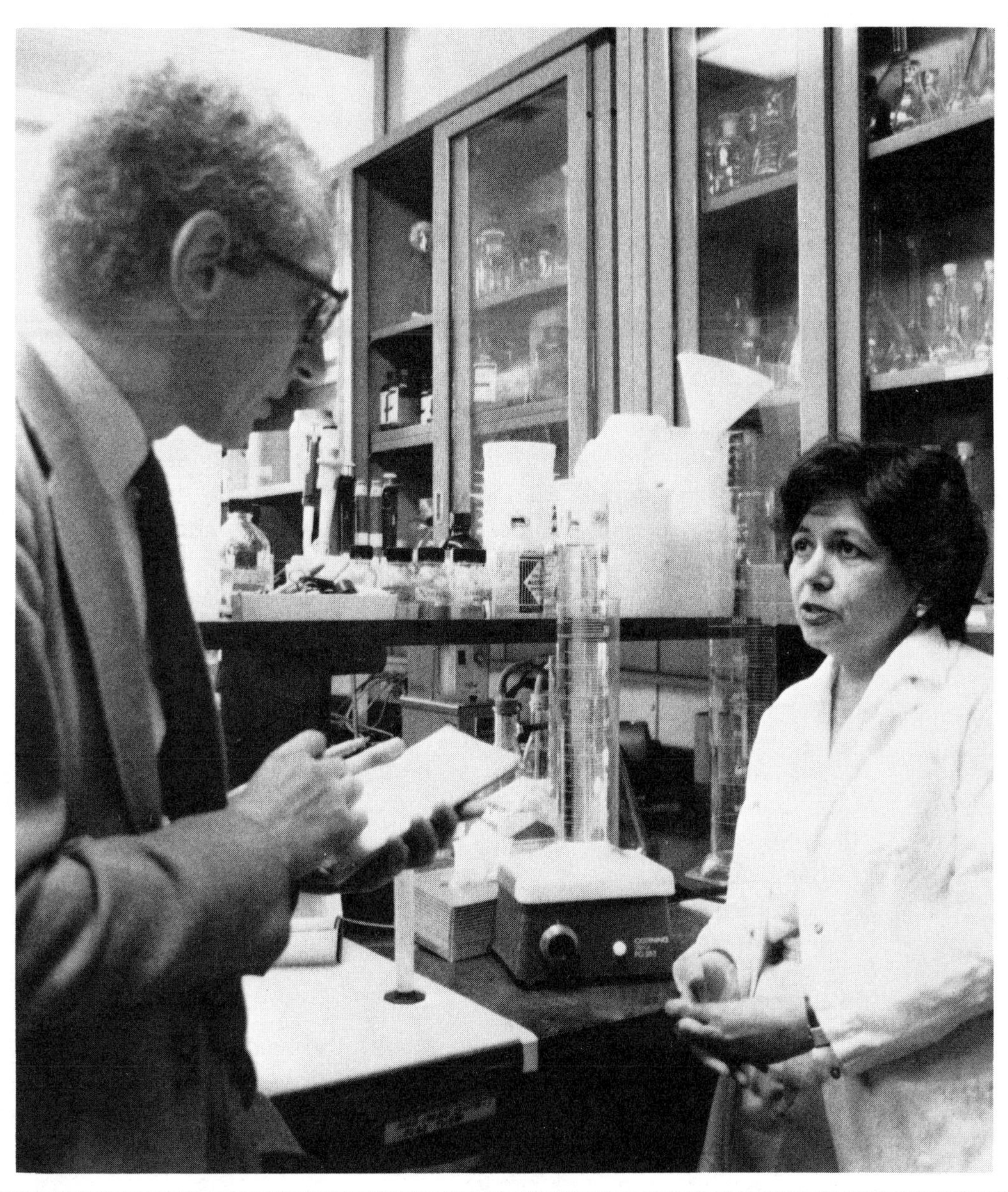

9

Writing With Style

> WANTED: A reporter of four or five years experience, hard-working and dedicated. We are looking for someone who is a good writer as well as a good reporter.

Editors want staffers to be able to report *and* write. One metropolitan daily advertised for an investigative reporter and received some 700 applications. Even then it was hard to select the right person because the successful applicant also had to be a good writer. Good reporters who are good writers are hard to find.

Many things go into good newswriting, and certainly among them are proficient language skills and reporting techniques. But editors also look for something else: the enigmatic sense of style which is to writing as charisma is to personality. People flock to those who have charisma, but nobody knows exactly how to get it. People admire a writer with good style, but nobody knows exactly how a writer gets it. However, there are some clues.

"Style" in the media usually means two things. There is "a style" and "style." *A* style is a particular way of putting words and marks of punctuation together, a writing habit, the use of certain terms and colloquialisms, and a commitment to follow certain rules and conventions. This idea of style is like an accent. A writer uses a certain style, such as a news style, a creative style, or an essay style.

But the kind of style we will be discussing here—writing *with* style—is more than just a writing pattern, although certain writing and reporting skills interact with the general sense of style that people identify as good writing.

One ingredient which affects both the techniques of *a* style and also the general tone and organization involved in writing *with* style is how the writer looks at life. This personal view is the beginning of all style. What color are the writer's inner eyeglasses to the world? Do they have the hue of gloom or the tint of an ideology or the clarity of purpose? If the writer views the world with creativity and curiosity and with some kind of organizing principle—a philosophy or even a method of searching—the writer stands on the ground of style. If the writer is boring inwardly—that is, in the inmost thoughts and outlook (even though the person may be an extrovert and the life of the party on the surface)—this person will lack style. Unless some character trait or guiding light or commitment to ideas, including a commitment to the human race—some kind of altruistic principle beyond ego and self-preservation—energizes the writer, the hope for style in this person's writing is distant indeed.

Some who write about style say an "outlook" is imperative. Says Paul Tillich in his *Theology of Culture*:

> Every style points to a self-interpretation of man, thus answering the question of the ultimate meaning of life. Whatever the subject matter which an artist chooses, however strong or weak his artistic form, he cannot help but betray by his style his own ultimate concern, as well as that of his group, and his period.[1]

Says Jerome Thale in *Style and Anti-Style: History and Anti-History:*

> Within a given context or a given writer there is indeed a correspondence between the rhetorical, syntactical, grammatical patterns and the writer's way of looking at the world. And when there is a high degree of regularity in the use of these patterns we may guess that the pattern comes from, and therefore reveals something of, the writer's habitual way of seeing reality, and that the pattern is one of the ways in which a similar way of looking at the world is created for the reader.[2]

Style is not innate or born anew by declaring that one is to be a reporter or writer. Style comes out in process; it is forged and perfected in the kiln of practice. Richard Eastman, who quotes both Tillich and Thale in his *Style: Writing as the Discovery of Outlook*, believes the central question of style is outlook, but also that outlook is related to practice: "From a man's writing you can determine his outlook, his own way of taking hold of things."[3] And: "in the process of writing one both creates his outlook and discovers it."[4]

A SENSE OF ORDER

A person who writes with style is one who thinks powerfully. Although writing with style may look easy, such writing involves not only the larger rational processes, such as understanding one's grounds of commitment, but also a host of small choices. And education—increasing the store of information and options in subject matter—helps with the shaping, or "discovery," of style. Says Eastman:

> You can't easily use language without making choices (sometimes unconscious ones) of words, details, sequence, stress, and so forth—and those choices express your values, the experience to which you are most responsive, your judgment of what really counts. If you learn all that you have to choose from, your style can answer more sharply to your own nature. Again, by expanding your knowledge of possible choices you become aware of more in your experience itself. Your style and your experience build into each other: that is why the development of style belongs near the center of a first-rate education.[5]

A news story or feature written with style doesn't just happen. The reporter may write it in the white heat of 30 or 40 minutes before deadline, but the writer's consciousness and willfulness determine how the piece will come out. Like the execution of a poetic line which requires the poet to bend the language to his intellectual will, perfected prose style requires a concentrated deliberation by the skilled reporter.

For style, a sense of order must exist on various levels. In addition to the writer's personal view of life, writing with style also involves "organization." Among organizing processes necessary for you to know in order to write with style are:

1. ***Organization of ideas.*** You need to ask what your goals for writing are: what do you want to accomplish?

   Do you want the reader to feel the terror of trying to escape from a hotel fire that threatened or actually claimed lives? Or do you want the reader to feel the suffering and pain of violence or prejudice?

2. ***Organization for the audience.*** You have to know for whom you are writing.

   Reporters who write with style do not think of the reader as one entity. Those who write with style see the children, the men and women, the elderly, the wealthy, and the dispossessed among the readers as they write. "Writing is a social act," says Eastman. "It is carried on with readers and because of readers. The presence of your reader . . . can become your greatest stimulus. In learning exactly how to relate to him, you learn more about what you really make of your subject."[6]

3. ***Organization of sentences.*** The right choices for the first word of the paragraph and the first word of each sentence are essential. The first

word should serve one of two purposes: it should link the new sentence with the previous sentence, or it should have sufficient power or interest to convey the reader into the new sentence and/or paragraph. The right choice of the last word of a sentence is also important in order to maintain the reader's interest.

Organizing sentences also means constructing them in a simple way: using a subject, verb, and object in sequence and seeking to make most independent clauses into separate sentences.

Howard Heyn and Warren Brier in *Writing for Newspapers and News Services* observe that:

> The best *simplified* sentences convey their meaning without fuss or fuzziness. While order and length are paramount, other qualities enhance this delivery process:
>
> 1. Active verb forms are the fastest vehicles. Direct sentences are the easiest to read, and active verbs travel the direct route between writer and reader. Passive verb forms lengthen the sentence, making the reader work harder, and may even confuse him.
> 2. Wherever possible, active verbs should also be colorful verbs. These command attention, sustain interest.
> 3. Tense and number must conform, for reasons of clarity as well as grammar.
> 4. Subjects and objects must be immediately identifiable. In other words, watch those pronouns![7]

Some good ways to control the use of pronouns in sentence organization are: (1) repeat the noun frequently, so your reader will not lose track of what you are talking about; (2) use the same pronoun for the same subject throughout the article; and (3) keep the pronoun in the same position in sentences as the noun was when first used. For example:

> The *News-Herald* named *John Jones* the man of the year. The newspaper named him because. . . .
>
> or
>
> John Jones is the man of the year. . . .
> He became the first . . . according to. . . .

4. ***Organization of words.*** Writers with style are highly selective—they won't use just any word. English provides a right word for each place in each sentence. In newswriting the right word is usually the simplest and most easily understood, and the best word stirs some feeling or conveys some mood. A good test of writing with style is to look at several sentences and ask yourself if each word is essential. If all the words are important—and interesting—the result is writing with style.

One criterion is to keep writing clear and simple. Rudolf Flesch has worked out a "yardstick formula" for blowing the whistle on cumbersome words and sentences. He comes down particularly hard on words with prefixes and suffixes: short additions such as "ad" or "ex" at the beginning of words, and suffixes such as "ish" and "ed" at the end of words. In his system of determining readability, the reader counts the number of words in a given number of sentences, the number of affixes, and the number of personal references such as pronouns and names. The reader then consults a chart. Short sentences with few affixes and many personal references put the writer's style in an approved category. Flesch discusses his views and formulas in *The Art of Plain Talk, The Art of Readable Writing*, and *The Art of Clear Thinking*.

5. ***Organizational process after the writing.*** Certainly the reporter must be able to write an article in haste and be prepared for an editor to call it up on the screen as is. But the process of writing with style may include a chance for the writer to edit copy. If you have half an hour to write the story, do it in 25 minutes; then plan five minutes to read, transpose, and trim.

   As Norman Mailer put it in an interview concerning his writing in his *The Executioner's Song*:

   > All I had to watch out for was taking out things that were excessive. It was really like scraping the last pieces of meat off a bone. I wrote a poem years ago: "I like poems/to be like bones/and shine silver/in the sun." I kept thinking of that when I was working. I wanted the paragraphs to have that look of the sun having bleached out something.[8]

TRANSITIONS

Writing with style often demands some reordering of sentences and words, particularly when you do longer pieces.

As you budget time; plan to spend some time organizing the story before you start.

Proper organization of ideas, paragraphs, sentences, and words creates a smooth, coordinated style which you can test through the effectiveness of your transitions. A transition gets you from one idea to the next, from one paragraph to the next, and from one example to the next. If elements do not flow together in a logical or natural way, something is wrong with your master plan and with your style.

Preparing a quick outline is an organizational procedure that can help you with transitions. Before writing, jot down some plan or order to follow. In newswriting, such an outline can be very informal. Simply write down the topics you want to cover, then decide in what order to use them. Number each point in order and follow the numbers. Transitions become easy this way, when ideas follow one another in an interesting, natural, and logical sequence. Such outlining or sketching also has another practical value. In a newsroom where the phone rings and there are constant interruptions, such an outline can serve to get you back into your story quickly and help you meet deadlines.

In your copy, some techniques to make paragraph transitions effective include:

1. ***Transitional words***
   a. Conjunctions and connecting words such as "but," "however," and "nevertheless."
   b. Words of addition such as "also" and "in a second incident."
   c. Words of movement and time such as "when," "since," and "while."
   d. Words of attribution such as "according to" and "John Jones said."
2. ***Highlighting the theme.*** If the article is about roses, refer back to the roses often; if it is about the primary election, mention the election often. Also, a mood, once established and continued, will hold the article together: Say that the night was dark as Halloween and repeat the reference to the darkness.
3. ***Repetition.*** Lead off one paragraph after another with the name of the subject in a feature or news story.

   John Smith likes new cars.
   Smith drives three cars—all new.
   Smith uses his compact when he drives in town.
   On the road, Smith cruises in his Rolls-Royce.
   There is a reason for the third car. Smith believes. . . .
4. ***Logic.*** A question precedes an answer. Or a national problem precedes its ramifications for the local scene. Your reader can predict expected results once you have set up a logical sequence of statements or questions.
5. ***Punctuation.*** Use numerals or bullets (round dots) to accent items in a list or series of self-contained paragraphs; this will help you to hold a group of sentences or paragraphs together. The reader's eye sees these readily and automatically links them.
6. ***Balance or contrast.*** If you give a woman's view, you can use the man's view for contrast or vice versa. Or if you give a quote from a debate on one side, your quote from the other side may follow naturally.
7. ***The "camera" technique.*** Describing a scene graphically throughout a story can help to hold a story together and keep the transitions tight. If you are interviewing the President, for example, you may begin the article with a partial description of the President's oval office. You may then want to describe changes in the daylight entering the room as your interview progresses, or you may want to "pan" paraphernalia around the desk, pictures on the walls, furniture in various areas of the room, or others present.

LITERARY DEVICES

The discipline of writing poetry and short stories can help you face the problems of continuity and transition. Learning to write with a consciousness of the value of each word in a narrative storytelling way can help bring a natural flow and solve transition problems. In addition, poetry and literary prose can help you in ways other than transition and coherence. Such writing also makes you aware of the basic "outlook" and "organizing" requirements of writing with style.

Poetic Devices

Among poetic devices used by those writing with style are:

Alliteration. When words that are in close proximation start or end with the same letter. If you use this, be sure it comes naturally. You should never force writing into such a pattern. From the *Washington Post*, note the "h":

Hastings-on-Hudson, N.Y.—The Japanese lieutenant who required 30 years to achieve surrender and stop fighting World War II in the Philippines took a look at the lox and bagel on his plate and indicated to his honorable hostess here in suburban New York that he was not all that hungry. . . .[9]

More obvious alliterations are the "f" and "s" sounds in this story, also from the *Post*:

Fresh young faces, flushed with cold and excitement. Flaring miniskirts, flashing, slender legs, splayed in the air in symmetrical formation. Shouts and yells, screeched to the crowd in forceful unisons, answered by thunderous roars. It's the cheerleaders, doing their stuff for the big game, the culmination of the season, the ultimate prize.[10]

Onomatopoeia. When a word or group of words sound like what they describe. For example, Tennyson writes, "Murmur of innumerable bees. . . ." Richard Eastman gives another example of onomatopoeia: "She skipped through the dry fallen leaves, delighting in their CRACKLE AND RUSTLE, SCUFFING her heels so as to stir the leaves into CRISP WHISPERS and BRITTLE HISSES."[11]

Metaphor. When a writer compares two unlike elements, the description is called a metaphor: "The mountain-high building," "the dungeon-weary room," or "the tiger-faced man."

Simile. When a writer uses "like" to make the comparison. "There it was, like a gold-knotted ribbon at the bottom of the fish bowl," said a mood piece in the Detroit *Free Press* on the life and death—the death especially—of a goldfish.

Meter. When poems have a certain number of beats to a line. Sonnets and other classical forms of poetry have meter. Sonnets have five two-part beats to a line, with the arrangement called iambic pentameter. The sonnet sounds like a "one, two, one, two . . ." with the emphasis on the "two." In the column on goldfish, see if you can identify some hint of meter:

> I never paid too much attention to my little friend with the transparent tummy and gargoyle eyes, until one day he or she—I never did know which it was—took a turn for the worse.
>
> It had had its moments of peril before. Like when Fluffy, the calico cat in our house, sat humped up for hours with its soft nose right on the water, watching. . . .
>
> Or when the little fish flopped around in the sink while the bowl was being shined up. Or when little hands probed in the fish bowl.
>
> And my nameless goldfish survived famine, and over-feeding by a two-year-old and by neighbors' two-year-olds, and the generations of bigger kids who fed the fish as generously as they would feed a lot of hogs.
>
> But now, I looked up from the ocean of junk on my desk, and I saw trouble in the goldfish bowl.
>
> * * *
>
> Solitary, with no cat or kid around, my finned friend looked about finished.
>
> Once a birthday gift by a daughter, somehow the little fish had survived for 18 months.
>
> I sprinkled in a little food—who knew how long since it had been fed.
>
> But there it was, like a gold knotted ribbon at the bottom of the fish bowl, its silvery-gold frame barely responding to a heart beat.
>
> A change of liquid—a firm hand to hold it . . . nothing helped.
>
> "Shishy!" shouted my two-year-old pointing at the goldfish bowl.
>
> "He's sick today . . . no, no, get your hands out of there . . . all right, just a little food. . . ."
>
> * * *
>
> Later the two-year-old came back and inquired about "Shishy."
>
> I shook my head. "He's gone . . . dead . . . I mean, sleeping. . . ."
>
> Then, I wondered, why should I avoid giving the child a little lesson in life's reality of death? So when she came back, I said, "he's dead," then ushered her out and started her playing with something and was spared the full thunder of a child's grief.
>
> * * *
>
> I didn't have the heart to flush the dead little fish down the drain. For surely if I did, some kid would ask what I had done with it and it's hard to tell a lie. So I put it to rest in the garbage can, and nobody asked. . . .
>
> —Detroit *Free Press*

There are various rhythms here, including iambic patterns: "no cat, no kid around," "on the water, watching . . . ," "I shook my head, 'He's gone. . . .'"

Repetition. When certain elements are repeated for effect. Writing with style uses repetition in various ways. As we have seen, in effecting transitions the repetition of the subject, almost with a cadence, assures unity and readability. In the above column, the first person subject is repeated (usually you write in objective nonpersonal terms, but note again that this is a column). There is a repetition of ideas and of unusual words, such as "Shishy," the child's name for the fish. Repetition or parallelism—particularly the balance of statements that are similar—is an old form of Near Eastern poetry. For example, in the familiar 23rd Psalm—"The Lord is my shepherd; I shall not want"—there is a parallelism of ideas. Both segments mean the same. There is parallelism in this line also: "He maketh me to lie down in green pastures; he leadeth me beside the still waters."

LEARNING FROM THE SHORT STORY

Most short stories deal with real and "real" imagined people; in other words the characters are believable. And as in newswriting, the details must be authentic and true.

Short story writers concern themselves with a lot more facts than reporters do. They describe the air, the scent of flowers, the wind, the sounds of insects, the shape of a sidewalk or a gate, or the lean of a tree. Because of this, the powers of observation of short story writers need to be great.

Significant Detail

Both newswriters and short story writers have an obsession with significant details. Both kinds of writers must be able to select only the best details—the important, the significant, and the intriguing. How many articles are ruined by insignificant detail? A joke in one Michigan newsroom told about one young assistant city editor who had a passion for facts, but for the wrong ones. Reporters mocked his outlook by saying that he would tell them, "Make sure you get the shoe size of the witness." The same assistant city editor, however, was also apt to edit out crucial WHO, WHAT, WHERE, WHEN, WHY, or HOW facts in stories!

But the right details make a difference. If the robber has a red beard or purple track shoes or a bright tie and coat, you will want to report those details. Such facts are significant in creating a visual image of the subject for your reader; such facts are also significant in increasing the public's ability to recognize and apprehend the culprit. So both a good short story writer and a reporter will pay attention to such details.

From your standpoint as a reporter using the short story as a way to learn how to use details, what are the significant ones in the beginning of this story from *Teens*? Which details help you to relate to the setting, the plot, and the development of the main character?

THE BIG WINDOW

The old ladder was creaking and Jim was afraid it'd give way. With all the strength of his slim arms he grabbed the top rung. His body was heavy, but he swung his feet over onto the narrow ledge and pushed himself from the ladder. It was no place to stop. He hugged the side of the barn, scraping his skin, and slowly, gradually worked his way to the big barn window. His legs were shaking, and he could feel splinters in the bottom of his feet. He was scared—too scared to look down.

Finally he took one big step, nearly losing his balance in doing it, but made it to the big window at the top of the haymow. He was panting, but he felt better when he took a deep breath. A cool breeze hit him, and for a minute the sweat stopped rolling down his back.

He hung on with all his might to the window. The huge pasture was stretched out before him and he could see the tiny cattle in it. The old willow tree was there, and the rocks, and the little stream that crept out of them.

This was the first time he had been so high, and the side of the old cattle barn was so warped it seemed that everything was shaking with him. When Jim had mustered enough courage, he took a quick glance around. Sneezer, a little white bundle down in the straw, was still barking.

Jim's eyes caught hold of something and he soon forgot his scaredness. Right by his feet was what he came up for. Two young squabs—they couldn't have been very old with the yellow pinfeathers all over them. They looked so young—so eager—such a ball of life. He reached into the nest and picked one up. His heart pounded hard. He wished he could take both of them in one trip, but it was hard enough getting up and down as it was. . . .

In this newspaper account from the Wichita *Eagle*, can you spot the significant details?

Ruth Gowing's candy dish is gone from its perch on a filing cabinet outside the police department offices on the fifth floor of City Hall.

The dish will be missed not because of the candy it always held. Its absence hurts because it will be a reminder of the absence of Ruth, undoubtedly the single most loved member of the Wichita Police Department.

Keeping the dish full of candy for officers and visitors was just "one of the little things" that police recalled Monday about Ruth, 47, who died Saturday from a heart ailment.

"She always thought of others and never of herself," said Lt. Harlan McClaskey, who echoed the words of many other officers.

Ruth, a secretary for the police

department for 11 years, was "quite a girl." "A hell of a lady." "A wonderful woman."

The praise came unsolicited. Throughout the department, spread among three floors of City Hall, employees were talking about Ruth.

They remembered what Lt. Charles Oswald called "the little things that probably wouldn't seem important to a lot of people."

Things like sending cards on birthdays, weddings, the births of officers' children, illnesses and deaths.

"She always had a present for an officer when he transferred sections," another policeman recalled.

"Everyone who has an office around here has some memento on his desk from Ruth," said Capt. E. J. Kuntz.

"You writing a story about Ruth?" asked a detective. "You ain't got enough room in the whole paper to list all she's done for people. She took care of everybody."

"Taking care of everybody" cost more than a secretary makes. So Ruth took another job, part-time work with a local answering service, just to make enough extra to keep on helping the officers she called "her boys."

Lt. Barbara Ray, one of Ruthie's closest friends, remembers what she called a typical story about Ruth.

About three years ago, police employees got together to turn the tables on Ruth—to give her a present for all the gifts and thoughtfulness she had showered on others.

There was a collection of money to help pay back a little of the money Ruth had spent over the years. But they should have known better. Lt. Ray said, "Ruthie" found out about a couple of officers who needed the money and she gave it to them.

And the city got its share of gifts from Ruth over the years—in the form of donated work. Officers said they frequently saw Ruth at her typewriter on weekends and into the wee hours of the morning—trying to get some work done for someone else.

The police department and officers weren't her only charity. Ruth also was a volunteer worker at the Veterans Administration Hospital and the Salvation Army.

"It seems sometimes like the good Lord takes the good ones and leaves us the bad ones," said Detective Tony Godinez.

Ruth's funeral services Wednesday afternoon at Byrd-Snodgrass Colonial Chapel "is one funeral no one will have to be ordered to attend," a veteran officer said. "We'll all be there."

In typical selflessness, Ruth refused to concern herself with her health in recent years. Lt. Ray said she had tried to get Ruth to go to a doctor more than a year ago, when Ruth complained of weakness and pain. Ruth finally went in March and was hospitalized immediately.

Her doctor told her she had already suffered two heart attacks.

Despite the severe illness, which left Ruth drawn and weak, she continued to visit the department, to see "her family."

But Saturday, in what was a sad irony to those who knew her, Ruth Gowing, whose heart had gone out to so many, became the victim of a bad heart.

—Craig Stock

Dialogue

Like the short story, you select the words to be said and make them count.

In both short stories and news articles, you need to show who is talking. Don't quote one person and then start the next paragraph with words of another. Indicate first if there is a change of speakers.

Make transitions between dialogue and between quotes. One rule is to not quote a person until he or she is mentioned or referred to in some way in the previous paragraph. For example:

> The father and three *daughters* stood together before the charred frame of what had been their home. "It's terrible, it's terrible," John Smythe, 43, said.
>
> One of the *daughters*, Maryanne, looked up, with wet eyes, and said: "I can't believe it."

It's best to avoid dialect; it's hard to read and usually offends the group whose way of talking is being highlighted.

About using "said": Remember, you want to highlight the words being reported; you do not want to slow down the reading by using a lot of heavy, often meaningless and dull substitute words for "said", such as "maintain," "declare," "stated," or the totally useless "added."

There are occasions for variety, however. Some excellent advice is offered by Louise Boggess in her book, *Fiction Techniques That Sell*. She suggests a cycle of terms—starting with and returning to the basic "said." In fiction, the writer is interested in rising action and progression that is moving toward either more complication or a solution. Thus she suggests that in "emotional dialogue," begin with the neutral "he said."

> *As the conflict becomes more heated, insert an adverb* or an adjectival phrase to show emotionally *how* the character said the words, as "he said hotly." A *said substitute*, "he shouted," implies even stronger emotion. *At the crisis peak of the scene, drop the said* entirely for the strongest emotion. In this manner, the *said* moves the characters through a revolution of emotion:
>
> | | |
> |---|---|
> | he said | he said |
> | he said *how* | he said hotly |
> | he said substitute | he shouted |
> | no he said | "I dare you." |
> | he said | he said |
>
> The *said* revolution may begin at any point and take any direction or use any combination. You may need only a part of the revolution.
>
> he said substitute
he said how
no he said
he said
>
> This reveals a character who moves from hot to cold and back.

> he said
> he said how
> he said
> he said substitute
>
> . . . So in writing emotional dialogue, identify the speaker, let him speak in the next paragraph, tell how he speaks, then point to the next speaker. Continue the process until you create a scene cycle.[12]

Likewise, in newswriting keep a "cycle" in mind. Do not depart from the use of "said" just to use another emotionless word. Use the variety or change of pace to introduce an element of emotion, feeling, intention, or character insight.

Setting a Scene

Which of these paragraphs starts a news story, and which starts a short story?

1. Farther down the mountain, in the dense woods of birch and spruce and fir, there are fox, deer, bobcat and bear. But in the winter, only one animal climbs this high to brave the bitter cold and howling winds that make Mount Washington as alien and dangerous as another world. That animal is man.

   The challenge of the arctic world. . . .
2. Whether you think professional wrestling is a sport or not is up to you. . . .

The first example is from the front page of the New York *Times* (March 2, 1982); the second, a story from *Boys' Life* (August, 1981).

"Setting a scene" and allowing the reader to see a context or setting is important. Give some details about the place, just enough to make it seem concrete and real. People don't just read—they see. Help the reader to see the story. It's no accident that the news article is commonly referred to as a story. (A rule to remember: Put one "concrete" or descriptive reference in each story.)

David Boldt, editor of the Philadelphia *Inquirer's* "Inquirer Magazine," likes to tell students to give a "sense of place" in their interview articles and stories. For example, he suggests that in reporting a talk by a guest editor in a seminar room, the reporter should give the reader some mention of the table—its hardness, color, or its shape.

From the study of the short story, you can learn to set a scene, or series of scenes, in an article and give it a narrative sense. The narrative—and especially a rounded-out narrative entity that stands by itself—is an anecdote. The use of the anecdote—the backbone of news-feature writing and longer hard-news pieces—owes much to short story scene-setting techniques.

The anecdote is one of the most important tricks in a writer's bag. If reporters can tell little stories or anecdotes well, they can use this device, rooted in facts, to begin articles—especially features—and then continue to use it throughout these articles. Of course, they will develop anecdotes that convey important and relevant information. Anecdotes such as the ones in the article on Ruth Gowing are the most difficult to find. Once a reporter has these, however, filling in with the "mortar" of additional detail and facts is often easy.

In newswriting and in magazine and feature writing, the anecdote, a one-incident scene written in a few lines or a few paragraphs, introduces the article or moves it along. The anecdote or short narration is not static but moves ahead within itself, as well as serving to move the total body of the article along. A successful scene—or anecdote—"must push a story forward," as William Byron Mowery puts it in *Professional Short-Story Writing*. For Mowery, early in the scene setting there is a "picture-peg," some words describing and locating the scene. "Rising action" follows and then comes a peak or climax, then a "slope-away" from the climax, and finally transitional copy before the next scene.[13] However, not all newspaper anecdotes are so complete.

There are different kinds of anecdotes. For instance:

Complete story. An incident is told or retold at some length. The elements include a hero, a barrier overcome by the hero, a climax, and a denouement or final outcome. In a news story telling about the ceremony of awarding medals to firemen, the story might start by recounting a heroic rescue: a building is on fire, a child cries within the building, and a fireman ignores his own safety and rushes in; the smoke and fire become increasingly dense, but the fireman emerges safely with the child. The account would close with comments or responses from bystanders. The anecdote has its own action and moves along; once it is completed, the article moves into a discussion of the larger theme, the heroics of firemen in general or some other topic for which the anecdote has served as an example.

One scene unresolved—a setting. The firemen arrive with hook and ladder and prepare to go to work—there is no development, no climax to the scene. This information can be a few lines, enough to place the firemen at a fire with equipment.

Short anecdotes, such as the single setting, can be stacked so that they appear one after the other.

> The fire engine from Company D screeched to a stop at the corner of Willow and Grove. The hoses soon snaked toward the smoldering cottage.
>
> Across town, equipment from Company D arrived at Maple Glen and Smith streets. A roaring holocaust with a fallout of sparks threatened the whole block.
>
> On the south side, another alarm brought. . . .

Part of a scene. Just a few descriptive words can function as an anecdote and leave a scene or fragment of a scene in mind.

> The bandit's face had been knotted in fury, the witnesses agreed.
>
> When the police arrived the look of fury was gone. The bandit lay dead at the foot of the counter. . . .

Mere identification.

> Patty Hearst, allegedly kidnapped, the woman with a gun. . . .
>
> She stood before Judge. . . .

There is no development here. Yet from these few words the reader is able to recall considerable imagery because the subject had received national attention for months, even years.

Implied anecdote. The more sensational papers certainly make use of this.

> Movie celebrity Mix Masters was seen leaving his uptown apartment with Mary Lovely. The two had arrived at the apartment late yesterday. . . .

No information is known whether the two had married, as was rumored, or whether they just spent the night in the same building. The writer sticks to the observable facts and leaves the reader to fill in with his or her imagination. National tabloids thrive on such gossip, as do movie and nightclub columns in respectable papers.

Serious reporters always try to avoid the implied anecdote, but cannot always do so. For example, if the President is taken from the White House on a stretcher and noted cardiologists are later seen in attendance, the mere mention of this information, when no other information is available, permits readers to entertain implied anecdotes of the President having possibly suffered a heart attack.

Manufactured anecdote. You should also generally avoid the manufactured or fabricated anecdote, although sometimes you may have to use it, especially when you are dealing with private clinical information and with information about juveniles. You can protect vulnerable people by blurring their identities. You can sum up their characteristics and attach new names to them. For example, a psychiatrist will say, "I can't give you the real information, but I'll give you a composite case. Call her Mary. Her case is typical. We have 17 like her." In such a case, it is a good policy to say in the article that the subject is being referred to under another name and that he or she is a composite.

In the day-by-day run of stories, it is sometimes bad practice to put average names on average situations with no real person in mind:

> Mary Scott stood and looked in the store window at Jake's dress shop.
>
> Mary Jones joined her a few minutes later, and then Alice Smith came along. They all looked at the royally dressed mannequin. . . .

The problem with manufactured anecdotes in innocuous situations is that they sound phony—the reader can spot what is real and what isn't. The glibness, the choice of names, and the lack of specific identity give away the phony anecdote. You should remember that you are in a real-person business, and you should strive to identify real people at all times. Avoid using the directly manufactured anecdote if possible.

You can use a tentative manufactured anecdote positively as a preliminary mold for the real anecdote. If you want the best possible anecdote for your key story, you can think it out ahead of time and then call sources until you find a real person who fits the mold you need. Then you can use names and precise information.

Viewpoint

One way to help impose a central focus on the article—and on any component anecdotes that might be used—is to have a well-developed sense of viewpoint. The use of viewpoint here does not refer to "what" one thinks but rather "how" one looks at the world. Authors of short stories achieve the viewpoint they wish by telling the story through a certain character's eyes or by having an impersonal narrator. When the narrator is a child, the reader sees what the child sees in a room described in the language that the child uses. If a parent comes into the room, the writer does not describe the parent as a person with a certain appearance walking down the hall and opening the door. Rather, the author describes the event from the child's perspective: the child hears the approaching parent's footsteps and sees the parent appearing in the doorway. The description would be in the simple words of the child.

In newswriting, such singleness of viewpoint generally applies to the article as a whole—you will not interchange pronouns such as "I," "he," "she," "it," "we," "you," or "they." Most news stories are in the third person singular ("he" or "she"). The factual range is limited to that which outsiders can observe.

Normally neither your reader nor you are conscious of viewpoint unless the article is a feature. But in writing an in-depth feature article you must decide on a viewpoint. You can write profile features from any viewpoint: the author ("I"), the reader ("you"), the group ("they"), or a single other subject ("he," or "she" or "it"). However, once you decide on a particular viewpoint, you should maintain it throughout the article.

Consider the interruptions a mixed viewpoint brings:

Jane Lark came home to rest today.

We stood there at her graveside as the tiny body in a heavy gilded casket was received into the ground.

The crowd had other things on its mind.

I knew I was not alone.

Shirley Marie Smith in the back row thought, "By the grace of God, there go I."

More consistent would be:

Jane Lark came home to rest today.

Her tiny body in a casket was lowered into the ground.

Around her descending coffin, the crowd stood silently, and looked into the grave. Jane in her short lifetime had come to know what was on their minds.

She had known Shirley Marie Smith well. And in the background, Shirley Marie Smith was heard to say. . . .

Among possible viewpoints and variations are:

First person singular—"I". News stories are not written in the first person singular, but sometimes in journalistic writing you may use this form. Features allow you to use any approach that works. Certainly "I" works well for reminiscing. When movie star John Wayne died, Detroit *Free Press* drama critic Lawrence DeVine wrote:

> John Wayne and I came down out of the Colorado Rockies into the short grass country of Southern Wyoming and rode across the Platte River on the specially painted blue-and-gold train rolling west toward the Great Salt Lake. . . .
>
> It was a fine bunch of Americans on that good train, highballing across a genuine John Wayne landscape of rocky hills that took on a pinkish cast in the early sunlight. There were train men and journalists. . . .

Second person singular—"you". Remember that although the temptation to use "you" may be great when you write news leads, it should remain one of your taboos. "You" works in some writing, but in most newswriting it is too limp, too uninteresting, too rhetorical, and too lazy a way to write.

> You were there.
>
> You arrived too late. The body was already being carried out. . . .

Third person singular—contrived. Although the subject may not be real, "he," or "she," or "it" does sum up the characteristics of a group. This viewpoint is rarely used in newswriting.

> The criminal who steals ducks out of a pond is a strange duck.
>
> Take Elmer Down. He is typical of the duck pluckers who. . . .

Third person singular—real. This is probably the most common and the most used. It allows some subjectivity:

> Miriam Reston was feeling some anxiety. She wrinkled her nose and coughed. The idea was strange, and she said. . . .

Third person singular—real, plus author. Related to the one above, this is the ultimate viewpoint in the author's mind even though the pronoun is third person. This is perhaps the most honest viewpoint, for the reporter cannot know what is in the mind of another.

> Michael Reston wrinkled his nose and coughed.
>
> His apparent difficulty in breathing increased. . . .

Dan Moreau writes an excellent example of this combination of author and third person in this article from the Richmond (Va.) *Times-Dispatch*. He gives the basis for subjective speculation and presents the information conditionally by using the word "may":

> The young father driving with his family on a rural Henrico County road may never have seen the dark green sports car until it was shattered across the front of his truck early Saturday.
>
> The vehicles met too fast for Danny Gantz to hit the brakes. No skid marks were found behind his truck.
>
> But in the split-second before the crash, David Bell had been trying desperately to bring the Corvette out of a slide. His car left grooves and tire marks on the pavement of Creighton Road as it careened westward.
>
> Both men died. . . .

Third person singular—judgmental commentator. The author possesses all wisdom. He is a "pankrator," a Greek word for "all-powerful judge." The facts are in. History is making its judgment.

> The former president of the transit authority sat in jail.
>
> He contemplated his record of the past few years.
>
> It was a sorry record he. . . .

You had best leave the use of this judgmental viewpoint for editorials. Generally you should avoid commenting from a superior moral viewpoint unless your article appears under an editorial head. In the news story, you should allow your reader to make deductions from the facts without your commentary, or you should be able to attribute such judgments to authorities.

Third person singular—impersonal. "It" can be a subject. But whenever possible you should try to use either a person or a named object as the subject of your sentences.

> It happened on the 21st of March.
>
> It wouldn't have been that way if. . . .

First person plural—"we". For instance, a group of editors or reporters might use "we," particularly in launching a series.

> We sat in on the governor's special commission on housing.
> We are a group of 16 reporters from around the state.
> We found. . . .

First person plural—majestic. "We" is used for "I." Best known examples are kings and queens and popes who issue documents starting with "we"—one person speaks in the name of a collective body of people. Reporters, who for some reason had to or felt they had to mention themselves in a story, have on occasion used "we" as a more humble approach than "I." Columnists sometimes do this, and "we" is used in editorials to represent an anonymous collective position.

First person plural—contrived. This would lend itself more to exhortation and speech-making: "We, the people, must take new initiatives. . . ."

Second person plural—"you". This is more rare than the use of singular "you."

> You—Battalion 101—are still with us.
> Your wars have come and gone, but you still have things to fight for.
> Your annual reunion—and a new set of goals—show that. . . .

This, of course might appear in newspaper promotional copy: "You, the readers, will be treated in the Sunday editions to. . . ."

Third person plural—contrived. "They" are not real people. The composite case history discussed earlier fits here as well.

> Mark Smith will make an appearance in juvenile court tomorrow.
> Jim Hanson will be there, too.
> Mark Smith has a mental problem.
> So does Jim Hanson. These are not their real names. They are among the residents at Forever Farm. . . .

The characters are not real as such, but facets of their descriptions are drawn from various real inmates.

Third person plural—real. The plural subjects actually exist as substantial entities.

> They were off to a good start.
> The first three horses—Mable, Singapore, and Rubber Cement—held onto the lead.

Third person plural—poetic. The identity of the subject(s) is not known nor is it necessary.

> The old men sit on the park bench across from the liberty statue in Washington Park.
> They do not talk to each other.
> They do not know each other's names. . . .

Omniscient. Although a single viewpoint is generally preferred in short story technique (and in news-feature writing), fiction writers—novelists in particular—allow themselves the technique of having the author enter the minds of *all* the characters. In character development a novelist may devote a series of early chapters to developing characters, one chapter for each character at the outset, and then have the characters interact in later chapters. The omniscient viewpoint—entering the minds of all equally—is more difficult to do convincingly in shorter formats.

WRITING WITH STYLE AND HUMOR

For some, writing with style culminates in successful humor writing. Choice of words, timing, sense of purpose or outlook, and a use of organizing principles are elements of humorous writing which make it the most difficult of all to write. Humor can be a dangerous or risky form, for it can fail; misunderstood, humor is a quick route to libel. On the other hand, the power of humor is incontestable. Says Robert Yoakum, a syndicated humor columnist: "Humor can blow fools and hypocrites off the landscape faster than any other ammunition. Humor can sometimes make a point in a few lines that would otherwise take a tome."[14]

Among some classifications of humor are:

1. ***Satire.*** The satirist points out human weakness to readers as being humorous. In satire, "The author is the initial aggressor against a political

personage or social institution," says Charles E. Schutz in his *Political Humor: From Aristophanes to Sam Ervin*. "By his comic genius he has translated his anger or resentment into a satirical attack in which his target is made the butt of humor for an audience."[15] Like other forms of humor, most satire appears in feature columns. Some reporters on small papers may have the option of writing such columns, but a nose for satire can also be useful when news reporters are ferreting out quotes or covering public and political events. They may be able to show readers contradictions in society through satire.

2. ***Wit.*** A person with wit is clever and has a good sense of timing. Wit presents ideas in a new way in association with something that is familiar, but usually with an element of surprise. A witty writer is able to use the incongruity between a new idea or event and some counterpart in the past and put these elements into an unconventional context. The resulting humorous contrast elicits a laugh. The lead of a front-page story on Governor Lester Maddox of Georgia told of his apparent confusion during budget hearings at the state legislature and described Maddox as bouncing around as though he had a swamp turtle fastened to the seat of his pants.
3. ***Parody.*** A sports story could begin by describing a coach with a "once upon a time" approach and use the imagery of "Alice in Wonderland," "Snow White," or some other fairy tale. While quoting other people, the article might make the comparison between the coach and the storybook figure (this is a license you will more likely find in sports than in other news writing). On occasion a reporter might use the same organizing technique to describe a day in the life of a politician or mayor. Indeed, comparing the John F. Kennedy clan in government with "Camelot" was a form of parody.

   A Kansas reporter parodied a beauty pageant for the first round of selection for Miss Kansas by describing "princesses" (contestants) lined up at the "castle" (auditorium). Although such opportunities for parody are rare and are hard to do effectively, parody done well can increase reader understanding and enjoyment.

Among those who make humor their business is comedian Ben Berman, who has been an instructor of humor at Wayne State University, Detroit. He has categorized four techniques of humor.

The Freudian Fumble is the honest mistake which results in humor. In the "old" days of TV, Art Linkletter got a number of honest, funny mistakes out of his questions to children.

The Unexpected is the "switch," the surprise, the non sequitur. The humorist or comedian leads you to expect one thing and then pulls a switch on you. Groucho Marx talked about shooting an elephant—in pink pajamas. A switch. Of course, elephants do not wear such things.

The Needle, like a needle pricking a tube or balloon, bursts the bubble of normal expectations. Phyllis Diller and her jokes about people who are extremely fat or skinny are totally deflating; fortunately, the audience sees her fat woman, who takes three chairs to sit down on, as somebody other than themselves. Celebrity roasts (Don Rickles style) and annual press club put-downs of the great and near-great use the needle technique.

Word turns—the use of words in unusual or unexpected ways—produce laughter. Awkward dialogue, such as that of a drunk, brings laughs. And the world is full of the perennial play on words, the pun. In the gas crunch of 1979, you could expect to find headlines such as "Things You 'Auto' Know About Your Car," and "Learn to Use a Car 'Break.'" in John MacDonald's novel, *Ballroom of the Skies*, the hero, conditioned to live on another planet, and his intended are about to be married. Since the couple is empowered with enhanced intellectual abilities, an observer says, "It is, to pun badly, a mating of the minds."[16]

Experienced newswriters are not comedy writers, but they often know where their readers' "tickle bones" are and how to give them a nudge. Those who know something about humor are likely to know something about writing with style from having practiced tight editing, having developed a sense of timing, and having learned to appreciate the sound and effect of words.

But journalists have to exercise some caution when working with humor. Buck Buchwach, executive editor of the Honolulu *Advertiser,* says to editors: "Don't let reporters write 'humorous' news stories about un-humorous events and don't permit copydeskers to put 'funny' heads on non-funny stories."

Bob Krauss, a columnist for the *Advertiser* and writer of features, did find a funny event: youngsters in an elementary school taking part in a muscle and body building contest. Humorous and appealing photographs accompanied the story.

Arnold Schwarzenegger he is not. But neither is Ronald Cuizon, age 9, a 97-pound weakling. He is a 55-pound muscleman who will never get sand kicked in his face.

Yesterday, Ronald flexed his biceps (not to mention his triceps and forceps) before an admiring crowd at the Pearl Ridge Elementary School cafetorium.

His body, all 55 pounds of him, glistened with baby oil.

He strode out of the wings and stepped up on the platform in the center of the spotlight. Girls whistled. Miss Pearl Ridge, age 12, waited in the audience to kiss the winner of the Summer Fun Male body beautiful contest.

What greater reward can there be for a muscleman?

Ronald lowered his arms, as big around as pool cues, and let his shoulders sag, tensing his chest muscles. This pose is called the "crab." The Hulk stands that way in TV ads.

Then, moving with the ease that comes of long practice before the living room mirror, Ronald lifted his arms and clenched his biceps in the famous Charles Atlas pose.

What he lacked in biceps he made up for in rib cage. You've never seen a finer set of ribs in your life.

Next came the side chest pose, reminiscent of Rodin's "The Thinker." However, when Ronald turned to the side, there was even less of him to see than there was from the front.

The last standard pose is called a lattisimus dorsi spread. The lattisimus dorsi is the heavy back muscle under each shoulder. To spread the lattisimus dorsi you put your hands near your waist and tense up.

When Arnold Schwarzenegger does this, the heavy slabs of his lattisimus dorsi stand out like wings on a hang glider. When Ronald Cuizon did it, he looked like he had to go to the bathroom.

One problem for many of the musclemen in the contest is practicing at home where there are likely to be sisters who do not always understand there is more to a double front biceps than meets the eyes. Baby oil, for instance.

"I practice in my room and in front of the living room mirror," said Kevin Spencer, age 10. "First, you gotta dump on lotta oil, baby oil, any kine oil. Put plenny on. It makes you look good and shiney, man."

Angel Pablo, 13, has a sister, 14. "She gets mad at me 'cause I pose in front of her too much," he confessed.

This was not the response yesterday in the cafetorium. Miss Pearl Ridge, May Grace Esperitu, said the show was "Terrific. I like to watch."

Twelve-year-old Kenny Gottlieb, a competition swimmer, had the teenyboppers whistling like stevedores.

Every time Kenny flipped 'em a lattisimus dorsi spread, the girls let out howls. Edee Doseo, a junior leader, went mad over his right side chest pose.

"Hold me back, hold me back," she cried.

By the time all 18 contestants had displayed their muscles, or lack of them, most of the girls had definite ideas about who was going to win. And he did.

Kenny Gottlieb was crowned Mr. Pearl Ridge of 1979. He got a trophy (which the dealer let Summer Fun have at a discount), a kiss and the applause of the admiring multitude.

Mac Coleman, 13, came in second. Jason Lee, 11, won third. Angel Pablo got fourth and 9-year-old Scott Coleman won fifth prize.

Kenny Gottlieb was picked "most muscular," Mac Coleman "best abdominals" (those are stomach muscles), and Jason Lee won "best legs."

I saved my cheers for Ronald who got a trophy as the most inspirational body builder. Indeed, he is that to us strong, silent types who stood before the mirror when we were 9 and flexed what passed for biceps.

Animals can be excellent topics of humor. Joe Heaney and Bill Dooley of the Boston *Herald American* made a front page "whodunit" out of the death of a parakeet:

LOWELL—It was Lowell's first case of "birdicide" and burly 6-foot-4, 220-pound Richard P. Wojcik yesterday stood accused of killing the one-ounce victim.

A crime of passion in some ways, police said, because Pepper, the parakeet, was strangled after a quarrel.

And there was also vengeance, District Court Judge Elliott Cowdery was told, because Wojcik, 26, of Willie Street, knew the blue and green bird was "the most prized possession" of his friend, Joanne Pickels of 31 Mt. Vernon St.

Not only did Wojcik slay the tiny feathered creature, the charges read, he tried to flush the still-warm body down the toilet. But it floated, and police recovered the body as evidence against the unemployed weightlifter.

Alan Davidson of the Lowell Humane Society called it cruelty and the first case of "birdicide" in Lowell's rough and tumble history.

Policeman Gerald McCabe brought the other charges: making threats, breaking and entering in the daytime and open and gross lewdness.

Davidson and McCabe recreated the crime this way for Judge Cowdery:

In broad daylight Tuesday, Wojcik went to Ms. Pickels' second floor apartment in a yellow house in the Acre section of North Lowell.

He had tried to get a key to the residence from another friend of Pickels, Michael Kluck. When that failed, he broke in.

After the killing, Wojcik telephoned Pickels' friend, Linda Ryan, who also lives on Mt. Vernon Street, and allegedly confessed without compassion.

Then Ryan and a friend, David Ilg, called police and Davidson.

Davidson testified that when Wojcik learned he had been implicated by Ryan and Ilg, he strolled to the sidewalk outside their apartment, dropped his pants and threatened them.

"He told Kluck he was going to kill the bird," said Davidson. "Then he told Ryan and Ilg he did it."

But before Judge Cowdery, Wojcik denied even being in the neighborhood and pleaded innocent.

Judge Cowdery continued the case until Jan. 10, ordered a psychiatric exam for Wojcik and released him on his own recognizance.

A weeping Pickels last night bemoaned the fate of the pet she bought 18 months ago at the local Woolworth's. "It was the only thing I had," she sniffled. "I don't have the money to afford another one."

Pickels is a telephone operator for the A and L Taxi Company in Lowell. She said she had kept Pepper in a yellow wire cage on a stand between her kitchen and her living room.

At police headquarters, a seasoned desk officer said dryly: "Murderers who kill people are loose on the streets and people get all excited about someone killing a bird."

Personification, discussed in Chapter Two on leads, is an excellent approach to humor, especially when the subject is a "hog's hog." This article by Tom French of the Indiana *Daily Student*, Indiana University, won first place in feature writing in a recent William Randolph Hearst annual newswriting competition:

Up on his farm in Elwood, under the skies and in the mud of central Indiana, Harold McDermit keeps a pig.

He keeps about 85 other pigs as well, all of them a breed known as Durocs, and anyone willing to drive up Indiana 37 to the farm would find them waiting out back, squealing and rooting and doing the kinds of things pigs like to do.

But one hog commands particular attention. Upon first introduction, people are inclined to notice the size of this Duroc, because he weighs more than half a ton and resembles a hairy golf cart set on "auto."

Just as some men are men's men, this animal is a hog's hog. This is the slab of lunchmeat that all tiny swine must aspire to be, if in fact they aspire toward anything other than their next feeding.

The sight of this pig is at once a disturbing and stirring tribute to the perseverance of the American farmer. It is amazing anyone could raise such a beast in their backyard; it is even more amazing anyone would want to.

McDermit seems fairly used to the idea, though. He and his wife Evelyn have lived with this pig since it was born four and a half years ago, when it was just a little squealing bundle of three pounds. They like to call him "Junior."

They do not give a great deal of thought to why they raise a pig this size. Harold McDermit just shrugs his shoulders and says it's "just to see if we can do it."

Junior is not the only giant hog on the McDermit farm. The pig's father, a 7-year-old boar known as "Funk," is there to keep him company. Funk is mammoth, but not as mammoth as his son. He only resembles a small cow whose belly skims too close to the ground.

Although many people would find Funk and Junior grotesque, the McDermits say they feel affection for the animals. "I'm afraid so," says Evelyn McDermit.

They like Junior, but the McDermits say Funk is their favorite. "After you have kept it for this many years, after you have fed it and worked with it," says Evelyn McDermit, "there is bound to be some affection. He's been around here so long, he seems like one of the family."

The McDermits talk like runners exchanging batons. Harold will start to answer a question and will get no further than "Well, I reckon . . ." and his wife will complete the thought for him.

Harold McDermit does not seem to mind; he rarely speaks for longer than 10 seconds, and his conversation is a combination of phrases and half-completed sentences.

And when he stands next to Junor or Funk, the size of the pigs is exaggerated into even more incredible proportions. McDermit is thin and about 5 feet 3 inches tall. Both hogs come up to his chest, rather than to his stomach as they would with most men.

Family relations between Funk and Junior are a bit strained. They keep their company at a distance, in separate lots out of sight from one another. McDermit says they might kill each other if stuck in the same pen.

About the only time Junior and Funk get to see each other is every year at the Indiana State Fair, when McDermit enters them in a contest which decides the largest boar in the state.

Together, the two pigs are one walking ton of the McDermit farm, and the McDermit farm doesn't fare too badly at the fair. In the last eight years, his hogs have dominated the contest mercilessly, establishing the kind of dynasty most National Football League coaches never dream of. The McDermits won their first title with another pig in 1972. Then Funk won in 1975 and 1976, and Junior won in 1978.

By the time this year's contest came around three weeks ago, the McDermit pigs knew what they had to do—get in there and be fat. The competition offered by the two has been so devastating in recent years that the field has dwindled; this August, only one other mammoth pig dared show his snout on the fairgrounds.

But as Funk and Junior and their sole competitor moved into the arena at the Swine Building, preparing to be weighed, McDermit's face was not awash with confidence. Back at his farm, there is no scale big enough to weigh the hogs and he can only estimate their size.

Quiet and nervous, he looked on as the judges weighed the first pig in at 882 pounds. Funk was next, and he weighed in at 985 pounds.

Even then, though, after he knew a fifth title was his, McDermit did not relax. Junior's turn at the scale was up, and he had a chance at history. Last year, he won at 1,077 pounds. But as far as McDermit knows, the largest pig ever at the contest weighed about 1,140 pounds.

And as far as he knows, this is the only contest of its kind around. So in his mind, the winner of the competition at the state fair is, unofficially at least, the largest pig in the country, if not in the world. To own the largest pig ever to be entered in this contest, then, is to own perhaps the largest pig in history.

Here in the heartland of America, the accomplishment cannot be denied. After all, Americans have always, as a matter of tradition, taken pride in having the biggest. They like having big cars, big houses, big breasts. Why not the biggest pig?

Junior walked out into the arena, taking short, halting steps, like a woman in a tight skirt. Five men pushed him onto the portable cattle scale stationed in the arena and came to know the pig's hindquarters in intimate detail. When the five men stood back and the hog stood still, the scale registered at 1,150 pounds. . . .

When Junior won the title three weeks ago, he was surrounded by a mass of people who wanted to see this great hunk of an animal for themselves. The McDermits say Junior tends to be temperamental and a little nervous around so many strangers, but he stood immobile among the crowd, looking dumbly at the flashing lights.

His patience wore thin, however, when Sandy Hill of "Good Morning, America" and her camera crew tried to interview McDermit.

Hill was dressed in a farmgirl outfit of jeans and red-and-white checked shirt and was chewing gum loudly. She said, "My, that is a big pig, isn't it?" when Junior decided that he'd had enough.

The mammoth Duroc began lumbering forward through the crowd, gaining speed as he moved away from the lights and the questions and the sound of chewing gum. Men and boys with sticks and boards chased after him, while the announcer kept telling them, "That pig is going to do whatever he wants.' . . .

Problems can lend themselves to humor and be a basis for an in-depth topical feature. Henry R. Darling of the former Philadelphia *Bulletin* wrote about pacemakers and heart disease:

Every six weeks or so a friendly young lady calls me on the telephone and has an intimate conversation with my armpits.

I don't know what the three of them are saying because they talk in an electronic beeper language that sounds like your car when you forget to fasten the seatbelt.

But I do know that in the course of their conversation the friendly young lady, a registered nurse named Mary Castle, can tell whether the Pacemaker tucked under my skin just below my right shoulder is doing its proper job—keeping me alive.

When Mary Castle calls, I unwrap two electric wires from a pocket-radio-sized device called a CardioBeeper. At the end of the electric wires are two little black plastic pads. These I place under my arms. Then I hold the beeper to the phone and press a button.

In the Pacemaker Evaluation Center at Paoli Memorial Hospital in Chester County, Mary Castle translates the beeper noise into an electrocardiogram of my heart. After a minute, she tells me to release the button.

"You're doing fine," she says. "How do you feel?"

How do I feel? I feel great, which is an improvement over the way I felt a month ago. But the truth is, I didn't feel all that bad when I went into the hospital.

Mine was no dramatic arrival at the emergency room with ambulance sirens screaming. I walked into the hospital on my own feet, and my only concern was that the big toe of one of them was sticking through a hole in the sock which someone was sure to notice if they put me into a bed.

I had had no heart attack, no sudden collapse, no severe chest pains.

True, over recent weeks, I had noticed that the slight rise in the path leading to our house had grown steeper and I was having trouble keeping up with the self-propelled power mower.

So I made an appointment with my doctor, expecting him to give me some pills for low blood pressure. Instead he took my pulse and sent me to the hospital for an EKG (electrocardiogram).

The next thing I knew I was in bed (if someone noticed the hole, they didn't say anything) in a big room with lots of blinking lights, dials, valves and switches, some strange looking plumbing, tubes and bottles hanging around and a scary variety of bubbling and bleeping sounds. . . .

Sin and sex and the whole terrain of human foibles and weaknesses are natural targets for humor. Robert Schwabach of the Philadelphia *Inquirer* wrote about massage parlors:

WILMINGTON—"What do you want to talk about?" she said, unhooking her brassiere.

"I don't suppose you're into Schopenhauer," I said as she reached for her panties.

A small worried frown began to appear on her forehead, the first of many to come.

We were having a nude conversation, Diana and I.

It would have been a nude massage, but there are no more massage parlors in Delaware—the Legislature wiped them out. This was a good thing and worked immediately, because now there are only nude conversation parlors and you cannot get a massage at any price.

For conversation, however, it's 50 bucks.

For 75 bucks you can talk the whole thing over together in the bathtub, a heart-shaped affair sunk into a raised platform covered in what the carpet boys call a sensible shag. For 95 you can gargle with champagne in the long pregnant pauses.

I paid the 50 bucks.

"Don't you want to take your clothes off?" Diana said.

I considered this for a moment. The room was comfortably laid out, but a bit overheated. The only pieces of furniture were a sofa and a bed. Piped music came from a couple of loudspeakers set in the ceiling.

I remembered the admonition of an old friend and mentor never to touch the native women unless you boiled them first. I was also a little anxious because at least one of the owners of these joints had a couple of arrests for assault and was known to pack a rod, as they say.

"I'll leave them on for a moment," I said ambiguously.

"Well I hope you don't mind if I take mine off," she said, completing her number.

Why should I mind? I crossed my legs and lit up a Lucky.

It was back in July that the state established a commission to regulate massage parlors and adult bookstores. Regulation means the right to make regular inspections and establish rules on just what can and cannot be done.

In the wink of an eye, massage parlors became conversation parlors.

Arlen Mekler, the attorney for several parlor owners, said: "I just don't think people realize the market for companionship."

Charles M. Oberly 3d, the state prosecutor, says, "If they really are conversation parlors, they're not evading the law. But I think this is an attempt to evade both the letter and the spirit of the law, and we're going to be on the lookout to try and prove it.

"The bottom line in this is that you can't ever stop prostitution on an individual level but you can try and stop it from being blatantly pushed before the public, and the suspicion remains that that is what these places are for."

The owners of these parlors have vigorously denied allegations of prostitution in the past. Services beyond what is supposed to be provided are normally arranged for under a system of what are called "tips." I did not offer any tips at the Club Elite and none were solicited.

The interview

"What kind of men come here?" I asked fatuously.

There followed a long pause. I went into a meditative state and became supremely conscious of the bridge of my nose. Diana shifted her body on the couch and aimed her hips at me. Her left hand began absently to stroke her left breast.

I asked where she was from, and it turned out she was from Baltimore. She had only been in Wilmington a couple of months, she said, and this was the first place she'd worked.

"What do you do for a living?" she said conversation-wise.

"I'm a newspaper reporter," I said in the practiced, casual manner that newspaper reporters always use when asked that question by nude women. The small worried frown became a longer worried frown.

"I think I better go to talk to the manager," she said.

"In a few minutes," I said. "You can talk with the manager any time."

"Am I going to read about this in tomorrow's paper?"

"No, it's a morning newspaper and it's already too late for the early editions."

"I think I have to talk to the manager," she said, getting up.

"Sit down," I said. She sat down. There appeared on her face that troubled look of a woman who is no longer certain that she is completely in control of the situation.

Bath vs. couch

I felt for her, so to speak.

"Give me a rundown on the preferences for the bath versus the couch," I said.

"This is the first time I've ever been in a conversation room," she said. "I've always been in the bath before.

"It must be murder on your complexion," I said. The worried look changed to a very worried look.

Time was running out on me. It was clear that I had only a matter of moments before Diana either went numb or ran hysterically into the corridor screaming something unintelligible but something that was likely to be interpreted as a need for a show of force.

And I still had not answered what was to me the most important question about a place like this—what kind of men use it and why. There seemed to be plenty of other ways to meet women, and if the Bureau of the Census had not been fooling me with the statistics lately, there were more of them around than us.

I approached the matter discreetly.

"What kind of men use this place?"

"All kinds," she said, edging toward the door. "The same kind you see anywhere."

"Why do they come here?"

"They have problems," she said.

What kind of problems, I wondered. You can buy leather suits all over town these days.

"You know, they have problems with their wives," she said, expanding the available horizons. Perhaps I should interview the wives. Out of the question. Door-to-door in Wilmington. Quiet town. I would be picked up by the cops in no time. Some of them might remember me. Had I paid all my parking tickets? It was getting near midnight.

"I really better go now," Diana said. She had a hand on the knob. I struggled to get up from the couch.

"But we've only been talking a half-hour," I said. "Do you give refunds?"

"No."

"Rain dates?"

"No."

I walked out quickly, before the manager could draw anything more than a conclusion. Two small boys turning the corner jeered at me as I stepped out the door.

"I'm from Licensing and Inspections," I said.

They laughed at me.

Kids, what do they know?

MASTERS OF STYLE

At most newspapers, one—maybe two—journalists are known for writing with style. Their ranks are thin; many covet to write like them, but few achieve it.

Jon Roe of the Wichita *Eagle* can write a story about a celebrity photographer with his pictures in a museum and turn it from a "gee-whiz" exhibition story into a deeply personal testament on behalf of the visitor:

The quiet, fragile man sat exhausted on a bench in the middle of a room that screamed with power and energy.

Seventy-five of his photographs were secured to the walls of Wichita State University's Ulrich Gallery—bold, dramatic photos, heavy with contrast and texture and emotion—seeming to vibrate with the life W. Eugene Smith put into them.

His big body slumped under the despoilation of old war wounds. Smith was tired from a grueling day of interviews and the prospect of a reception and lecture later Wednesday night on the show which will be at the Ulrich through May 22.

But, as he rested amid 40 years of his photographs, he talked slowly and quietly about them . . . and about one in particular—the most important photograph he ever made.

ENTITLED "The Walk to Paradise Garden," it's known to nearly everyone. A small boy and girl walk away from the camera down a dark path that opens onto a blaze of sunlight.

It's important to Smith because it was the first photograph he made after World War II, at a time when he was so crippled from his wounds he didn't know whether he would be able to photograph anything again.

The photo marked his rebirth as a photographer and as a human being.

Today, ranked as one of the world's greatest photographers, Smith balks at discussing his work in terms of art.

"Certainly photography can be art," he said. "But I've never had a picture improved by calling it art. And I've never had one hurt by not calling it art.

"Life is of first importance to me in my photography. If, in capturing life, I create art, well, that's fine."

BORN IN WICHITA in 1918, Smith made photographs for The Eagle and The Beacon in high school, then went on to work for just about every major magazine. His work gained its greatest exposure in hundreds of photos for Life Magazine.

During World War II, he covered 13 Pacific invasions, including Iwo Jima, Wake Island, Saipan, Guam and Okinawa.

It was during the 13th invasion that he suffered wounds on his head, chest, back, legs and hands.

"Mortar fragments took out all the bone on the right side of my face, the roof of my mouth, most of my nose and nearly cut my tongue off," he said. "There were 32 operations performed on my mouth alone."

Which brought him to the subject of "The Walk to Paradise Garden," the photograph that broke two years of frustrating helplessness.

"It was shot at home in New York," he said. "The children are my son Patrick and my daughter Juanita.

"I persuaded them to go for a walk and limped along behind them, not knowing if I would be able to take the photo, not knowing if I'd ever be capable of photographing again."

SMITH HAS WRITTEN about that moment in a collection of his work. Wednesday, he listened as the words were read to him.

"Two painful, helpless years followed my multiple wounds," he wrote, "during which time I had to stifle my restless spirit into a state of impassive, noncreative suspension while the doctors by their many operations slowly tried to repair me . . .

"But now, this day, I would endeavor to refute two years of negation. On this day, for the first time since my injuries, I would try again to make the camera work for me, I would try to force my body to control the mechanics of the camera; and, as well, I would try to command my creative spirit out of its exile.

"I was determined that this first photograph must sing of more than being a technical accomplishment. Determined that it would speak of a gentle moment of spirited purity in contrast to the depraved savagery I had raged against with my war photographs—my last photographs.

"I was almost desperate in this determination. . . . That day I challenged myself to do it, against my nerves, against my reason.

"I felt, without labeling it as such, that it was to be a day of spiritual decision."

SMITH NODDED as he listened.

"My hand was badly smashed up," he said, "and I had trouble operating the camera. Even loading the film was a painful challenge. And there was an infection that made my sinuses run constantly.

"I felt great pain as I crouched behind my children and pressed the camera against my cheek."

And then—in that one perfect instant—W. Eugene Smith pressed the shutter release button . . . and came back to life.

"I felt as soon as I made it that it would be a good, workable picture," he said, running a hand through his thin gray hair. "But I didn't know it would be my most published photograph."

Published in Life, it was reprinted around the world, torn from magazines and pinned to walls.

EIGHT YEARS LATER, when Smith arrived at Albert Schweitzer's jungle clinic to do a photo essay, that photo was on the wall in Schweitzer's office.

It was used by Edward Steichen to conclude the monumental Family of Man exhibition he assembled for the Museum of Modern Art.

"And I heard that a stripper on the vaudeville circuit had the picture pasted to the top of her suitcase," Smith said. "Probably reminded her of her innocent youth or something."

Bold, emotional, human, "The Walk to Paradise Garden" has meant something important to millions of people in the 31 years since it was shot.

But it holds no greater meaning for anyone than it does for Smith.

It told him the war was over—the savage conflagration he had covered with his camera—and his personal war to be whole again, to work again . . . to be alive.

To write in style, Jon Roe says:

1. The flat, unadorned statement is the most powerful you can use.
2. If you find the story movement, transitions will take care of themselves.
3. If a passage leaps out at you as brilliant and can stand without the paragraphs on either side of it, it's probably no good for the story, and should be thrown out.
4. Begin your story at the last possible minute . . . as close as you can to the climax.
5. Action verbs (always action verbs).
6. Adverbs almost always get in the way and slow down the story.

7. Some of the most interesting material you run across is extraneous to THIS story you're writing. Don't stick it in unless it fits with THIS story . . . although the temptation will be great.
8. The length of your sentences will do as much as your words to set the mood and atmosphere of the piece. So pay attention to your sentence structure all the time. (Oversimplified example: short, choppy sentences—action; long, flowing sentences—tranquility).
9. Similes and metaphors are invaluable when they fit. But when they serve to show off your writing rather than to describe your subject, throw them out.
10. The best stories occur when you're able to get out of the way entirely, and let the subject tell the story.
11. The fewer characters in your story, the more effective it'll be.
12. To my mind, the key to every story is organization. I spend more time organizing a story than writing it . . . because, once you've hit on the proper organization, the story writes itself.

Note the sense of organization and style in this serious story which won first place in a recent Hearst competition in general news writing for Mark Arax, a writer for *Insight* at California State University, Fresno. An hour-by-hour chronology is a part of the organization which carries the article along:

Her pink fur-lined coffin measured only 24 inches long and she was buried in a new red velvet and lace outfit that Grandpa bought as a final gift.

Dawn Marie Beckman died when she was only 85 days old. Why? Nobody knows. They call it the Sudden Infant Death Syndrome (SIDS) and 10,000 babies between the ages of four weeks and six months die from it each year. It is the single largest cause of death among infants.

There are virtually no symptoms. A healthy child is put down to sleep and never awakens.

* * *

Wednesday, Nov. 30, 1977, started out as a typical day for John and Doris Beckman of Fresno. John, 30, went to work at the Kentucky Fried Chicken outlet where he is manager, and Doris, 28, stayed at home with her two children—Mark, 5, and baby Dawn.

The Beckmans will never forget the chronology of that tragic day:

1:10 p.m.—Dawn Marie was put down in her crib where she usually slept until 10 p.m. Sometimes, when she awoke, Dawn would cry until she was fed. After feeding, she would usually go back to sleep within a few minutes.

3 p.m.—Mrs. Beckman heard Dawn "fuss slightly" but this wasn't unusual, so Mrs. Beckman didn't feel it was necessary to look in on her.

7 p.m.—Mrs. Beckman had a strange feeling. She went to check on Dawn.

"It just seemed too quiet in there," she said. "Under normal circumstances, I wouldn't have checked up on her that early. She usually slept until 10 o'clock.

"I turned on the hall light instead of her bedroom light. I got right up to the crib. There was no movement. I touched her back and it felt cold, and besides, she was laying in the corner which looked kind of strange.

"So I went back and turned on the overhead light. I picked her up and laid her on the bed. She looked terrible, she was already stiff and cold and she had blood on her chin.

"I was like a zombie, in shock. I knew she was dead but until the paramedics came and told me they couldn't do anything, I still had hope."

John Beckman describes that day:

"I was at work when my mother called and said 'Come home,' and I say why. She just said 'Come home, you're needed.'

"When I saw the police in front of my house, the first thing I think that came to my mind was my wife. I walked in the door and they said that Dawn's dead. I just more or less went into shock."

* * *

The parents of SIDS babies invariably suffer from extreme guilt. Almost every parent blames himself until the facts of crib death are known.

Doris Beckman's guilt has subsided for the most part. But she still regrets not having gone in and checked on Dawn when she heard her fuss at 3 o'clock that afternoon.

"If I had gone in and checked up on her, maybe this wouldn't have happened. At least I could have held her in my arms one more time."

But medical evidence clearly shows that no one can prevent crib death from occurring. Here are some basic facts about SIDS from a pamphlet issued by the U.S. Department of Health, Education and Welfare:

—"SIDS cannot be prevented or predicted, not even by a physician."

—"Research to date indicates that SIDS is not caused by suffocation, aspiration or regurgitation."

—"A minor illness such as a cold may be present but many of the victims are entirely healthy prior to death."

—"There appears to be no suffering and death often occurs very rapidly, usually during sleep."

—"There may be blood or vomit around the mouth area but this is a result of death, not a cause."

—"SIDS is not hereditary and there is no proof of environmental causation."

According to the Beckmans, the public is largely misinformed about the Sudden Infant Death Syndrome.

"There are so many misconceptions and these misconceptions add to the guilt that the parents feel," said Beckman. . . .

An old lady was taken to the races in style—with style—in Billy Reed's article in the Lousiville (Ky.) *Courier-Journal:*

LEXINGTON, Ky.—She was going to the races for the first time in years, so she put on a sparkling silver necklace and a lovely blue dress. And, of course, white gloves. In her day, a lady always wore white gloves when she went to the races.

Mrs. Lucille Markey, the grand dame of racing, is in her 80s now. Her hair is white, her days spent in a wheelchair because of crippling arthritis. She and her husband, Admiral Gene Markey, are unable to go to the race track to watch their horses carry the famed devil's red and blue silks of their Calumet Farm, still the most famous name in racing.

This has been especially sad this year. For the first time in a decade, Calumet has a horse, Alydar, capable of winning the classic race that the farm dominated in the 1940s and 50s—the Kentucky Derby. Until yesterday, the Markeys had never seen Alydar run in person. They were forced to watch his races either on live television or video tape cassette.

But thanks to the thoughtfulness of Keeneland president James E. "Ted" Bassett, arrangements were made for the Markeys to be brought to Keeneland yesterday to see Alydar run in the Blue Grass Stakes, his last major prep race before the Derby on May 6 at Churchill Downs.

So at 3 p.m. on an absolutely

gorgeous afternoon, a green Keeneland station wagon pulled up at the Markeys' mansion. After Mrs. Markey put on her white gloves, she and the Admiral were helped into the car by their driver, Lovell Brown, a Keeneland employee. He wore a black chauffeur's cap because, he said, "This is a special day."

At 3:30 p.m., the station wagon slowly pulled into the secluded lawn adjoining the track's clubhouse. . . .

"They're just thrilled to death," said chauffeur Brown. "They said they had been to Keeneland many times, but never like this."

At 4:20 p.m., the horses came on the track and the crowd of 22,512 gave a roar at the sight of Alydar, the 1 to 10 favorite. Ordinarily, the horses turn right and parade past the grandstand. This time, though, they turned left so they could go past the clubhouse and parade past the green station wagon.

As the horses began to file past, about 10 feet away, Admiral and Mrs. Markey were helped out of the station wagon. Alydar was the seventh and last horse to come by. By the time he got there, the Markeys were on their feet, bracing themselves on the rail. This was the horse they had never seen run.

At the sight of the Markeys, jockey Jorge Velasquez broke into a huge grin. He had on the red and blue silks, the colors worn by Eddie Acaro when he was riding Whirlaway and Citation and all the great Calumet horses. Velasquez stopped Alydar directly in front of the Markeys and addressed himself to the lady in the white gloves.

"Hello, my lady," he said. "How have you been doing? Here's your baby. Don't he look pretty?"

And then he reached down and patted Alydar on the neck and said, "C'mon, say hello."

Admiral Markey asked if Velasquez could bring Alydar closer and the jockey smilingly obliged. "Is that better?" he asked. Then, after a few moments, Velasquez turned Alydar and took off. The Keeneland employees helped the Markeys back into their station wagon.

The next time he came by, Velasquez smiled and waved at the station wagon. Then, finally, it was post time.

At the start of the race, the Markeys sat in the station wagon, listening to Tom Hammond's call on station WLAP. Early on, Alydar was far back. On the back stretch, however, Velasquez asked him to run and he began to pass horses.

As the field turned for home, at the precise moment that Alydar was taking the lead, the Markeys once more were helped out of the green station wagon. And as they stood there, leaning on the arms of the Keeneland employees, their horse, their marvelous horse flashed past in the lead, pulling away, a poem of power and motion in that devil's red and blue. His head was cocked to the right, almost as if he were straining to have a look at his owners.

And the lady in the white gloves smiled at the sight. . . .

Says Carol Sutton, senior editor of the *Courier-Journal,* of Reed's article:

> The piece starts with a good story, simply told. It has a strong, smooth, narrative flow . . . marked by a soft spotlight on the subjects. The writer is there, but he never intrudes. He leads the story development along; he notes it in rich and precise detail, but never gets in the way.
>
> For anyone who has ever seen a great thoroughbred run, for instance, Billy's description of Alydar as "a poem of power and motion in that devil's red and blue" creates a strong image for the reader. So do Mrs. Markey's silver necklace, the lovely blue dress, and, of course, the white gloves.

> The writer also uses quotes with great skill. The quotes are obviously carefully selected, then woven into the story at just the right places, not just dropped in as blobs to change the pace of the writing. . . .

Lucille DeView says she tries to create "word pictures." In the following story in the Detroit *News*, she creates glimpses of the city's "lonely old men" as anyone might glimpse them. She then tries to get inside that loneliness. The style is meant to evoke interest and compassion through words and imagery:

> You see them on the park benches or at the shopping malls or in the dime store coffee shops—the old men with time to kill.
>
> On clear autumn days, they sit hunched in the sun as if trying to soak it up; trying to save its warmth for their brittle bones which will soon be chilled by winter frosts.
>
> They sit. They walk. And they try to look purposeful but they are not.
>
> Their sunken, cloudy eyes look vaguely at everything and see almost nothing—and they talk little, if at all.
>
> Some have been alone so long in life that they have gone inside their shells, and like slow-moving turtles they inch along the sidewalks, withdrawn and aloof.
>
> Others, still frantic with the rush and hurry of earlier years when there were places a man had to be and times when he had to be there, dart and dip like frenzied birds, lighting first here and then there. Old birds. Tough old birds.
>
> They'll be out on even the worst of days, defying rain or sleet or snow just to have something to do. Something. Anything. Just not to sit in a room day after day. Just not to die alone in a chair.
>
> Atlantis Vidloff brings his lunch in a brown paper bag. Many men do. Atlantis likes to sit at the river in front of Cobo Hall and watch the boats while he eats.
>
> His lunch is simple. A bologna sandwich, a tomato, a thin sliver of pickle. He walks downtown from his room in the inner city. His face is thin and nut-brown from long summer days of being outside.
>
> Atlantis speaks hesitantly with an accent. He came from Bulgaria in 1914, but says stoutly, "I'm here now. I'm American." That's important to him. He retired in 1960. "I was an ice cream man. I had all kinds of jobs. You name it," he says and laughs, crinkling his already crinkled face.
>
> He has friends along the riverfront. They meet and pass the time of day. They are "the regulars." They have a special kind of pride. They are not unemployed, not drifters, not that. They worked once. It's just that they do not work now because they are too old.
>
> They have dignity, too, and a sense of privacy. They are loners, not joiners. They disdain groups or clubs.
>
> One man, talking intently to a friend in his native Polish did not want to answer questions. Yes, he came down to the park often but whose business was that? And who would care how he spent his days? And who would dare take his picture? He was angry and he and his friend walked brusquely off to another bench and he spat, showing his disgust.
>
> George McLeod, however, was in a mellow mood. He apologized for napping. He is recovering from surgery and has had sleepless nights and it was pleasant, he said, to lie dozing in the sun.
>
> George and his wife, Marian, often go downtown together from their home in northwest Detroit to spend the day. They go to restaurants for lunch. They like to go to the ethnic festivals at the waterfront. . . .

Writing from San Francisco for the *Christian Science Monitor*, Stewart Dill McBride put the longshoremen in soft focus:

Nothing
Is too good
For the workers. Fortunately
We have plenty of it.
—Folk poem

Outside the waterfront cafe, dawn rusts through a battleship sky. The clock over the door reads 6:55. We have kept Big Red waiting.

He sits, hunched over a steaming white porcelain mug—the brief breakfast calm before the Cyclone fence at the San Francisco Stevedore and Ballast Company on Pier 80 swings open for business.

Red is flanked by truckers spooning greasy hash browns from pink-rimmed plates. Across the table a longshoreman, sleeves rolled above the elbows, drowns a fried egg in ketchup.

"What kept ya?" Red asks us.

"Traffic on the bridge," I answer. Wishing I had a more compelling excuse, I take a seat among the square shoulders and brushcuts.

He grins. "Gave up my five-mile morning run for this, so let's get started."

Big Red, known off the San Francisco waterfront as Bob Carson, has worked as a longshoreman and ship's clerk for the last 16 years, and, while he is not particularly "big," his hair is red, a wavy cadmium. Carson is soft-spoken, with the hands of a piano player and a manner more common to a high school classics instructor than a life-long stevedore, but that's what makes Carson's story worth telling.

The longshoreman's son, born in Hunter's Point, an industrial ghetto south of San Francisco, holds a master's degree in creative writing, is a published poet, and is the editor of a book just released by Harper & Row entitled "The Waterfront Writers." The volume, which has headlined the NBC Nightly News and TV talk shows like "Good Morning America," is a collection of short stories, poems, screenplays, photographs, and sketches by a group of local dockworkers, which Carson helped organize.

The writers and artists are past or present members of Local 10 or Local 34 of the International Longshoremen's and Warehousemen's Union. The book grew out of a series of readings the dockworkers held in an old folkdance hall in the city's Sunset district.

"It's part of a strong working class literature that has been ignored in America," says Carson, staring out into the crowded cafe. "We've been conditioned to believe there is a barrier between work and art. Work is always something you do for money. It's about time America learned that there are faces behind those jobs.

"How long do we have to put up with those encyclopedia ads with the guy in the hard-hat and the caption: 'You don't want your child to grow up like this, do you?'"

In the introduction to the book, Carson writes that the waterfront writers group exists "in vigorous contradiction to the notion of 'artists' inhabiting an ivory tower highrise, isolated and insulated from any sordid grubbing for a livelihood or the mundane facts of life." They also defy the "hard-hat" image and Archie Bunker life-style that the image-mongers decree as role models for the American worker.

If "The Waterfront Writers" does anything, it shatters stereotypes. The selections represent nine writers, and there seems to be something for every reader. The writing is sensitive, though often surly and sententious. At times it is angry, passionate, bawdy, occasionally heavy-handed. The common thread is humanity on the docks. The poems are strongest when read aloud by the longshoremen themselves. . . .

Louis Cook, a general assignment reporter at the Detroit *Free Press* and now a successful editorial page writer and human interest columnist, sums up his advice for writing with style:

> The only sound piece of advice about writing that I ever came up with was in answer to Neal Shine (another good writer, later managing editor) when he asked me 25 years ago when a piece of copy should end. I said, "When you have nothing left to say." Half of our bad stories result from writers coming to that point and then continuing on for 15 paragraphs.

Notes

[1]Paul Tillich, *Theology of Culture* (New York: Oxford University Press, 1959), p. 70, originally appearing in *The Christian Scholar*, XL, 4, Dec. 1957.

[2]Jerome Thale, "Style and Anti-Style: History and Anti-History," *College English* 29 (Jan. 1968): pp. 286–302.

[3]Richard M. Eastman, *Style: Writing as the Discovery of Outlook* (New York: Oxford University Press, 1970), p. 3.

[4]Eastman, p. 27.

[5]Eastman, p. 4.

[6]Eastman, p. 4.

[7]Warren J. Brier and Howard C. Heyn, *Writing for Newspapers and News Services* (New York: Funk and Wagnalls, 1969), p. 23.

[8]Jan Herman, "Up Off the Canvas, With a Troubled Look Ahead," Philadelphia *Inquirer*, 25 Oct. 1979, D–1.

[9]Henry Mitchell, "Samurai's Surrender," *Writing in Style: From the Style Section of the Washington Post*, ed. Laura Longley Babb (Boston: Houghton Mifflin, 1975), p. 117.

[10]Alan M. Kriegsman, "Roots in Dance, Rites of Fall," *Writing in Style*, p. 247.

[11]Eastman, p. 189.

[12]Louise Boggess, *Fiction Techniques That Sell* (Englewood Cliffs, N.J.: 1964), pp. 114, 115.

[13]William Byron Mowery, *Professional Short Story Writing* (New York: Thomas Crowell Co., c. 1953), p. 216.

[14]Robert Yoakum, "The Humor Shortage," *Grassroots Editor* (Fall 1979) 20: 3, p. 9.

[15]Charles E. Schutz, *Political Humor: From Aristophanes to Sam Ervin* (London: Associated University Press, c. 1977), p. 76.

[16]John D. MacDonald, *Ballroom of the Skies* (New York: Fawcett, c. 1952), p. 172.

Assignments

1. Discuss or report on what media news writer you like best. Why? Does it have anything to do with the writer's style? What are the ingredients in that person's style?
2. Take a dull article in the paper about an interesting subject and suggest ways a reporter could rewrite it with a sense of style.

3. Exchange articles with a fellow student. Each of you should suggest ways to improve the transitions in the fellow student's paper.
4. Take a page of *Time* or *Newsweek* and underline transitional words and devices. In articles that have a lot of conversation and quotes, underline words or elements in one quote that anticipate the next speaker and quotation.
5. A short story is concerned with such elements as the following: significant detail instead of insignificant detail; a singular viewpoint (centering on one person's story, seen through his or her eyes); a conflict or central problem to be overcome; a solution; crisp dialogue; scene description; and developing characters. Look for—and note—some of these elements in stories in today's newspapers.
6. Take down a conversation you overhear on a bus, in a diner, in the hallways, or in a classroom. Type up two pages of this dialogue. What part of it would you use if you were writing a story or news article? Why?
7. Take a paragraph or word referring to a place or setting from one of the news articles you have written recently. Write a page and a half of description on that place or setting.
8. Write two anecdotes—humorous short items from your experience. Bring them to class with an envelope addressed to an editor and ready to mail. (Sunday sections of newspapers often use these; the Philadelphia *Inquirer* pays $25. *Reader's Digest* also uses them and reportedly pays $300.)
9. Writing with style in contrast to writing without often means you are presenting your information as a "story." Experts have compared good writing to writing a letter home to your mother and father. As an exercise only, take a straight news article or dull feature and rewrite it (sticking to the facts) as if you were writing a letter home to your mother and father.
10. Write a news or feature piece personifying an animal or object; that is, tell the story from the viewpoint or eyes of that person or object.

Firemen fight blaze in older neighborhood. Better Living Photograph/HBJ Collection

PART 4

"Bread and Butter" Beats

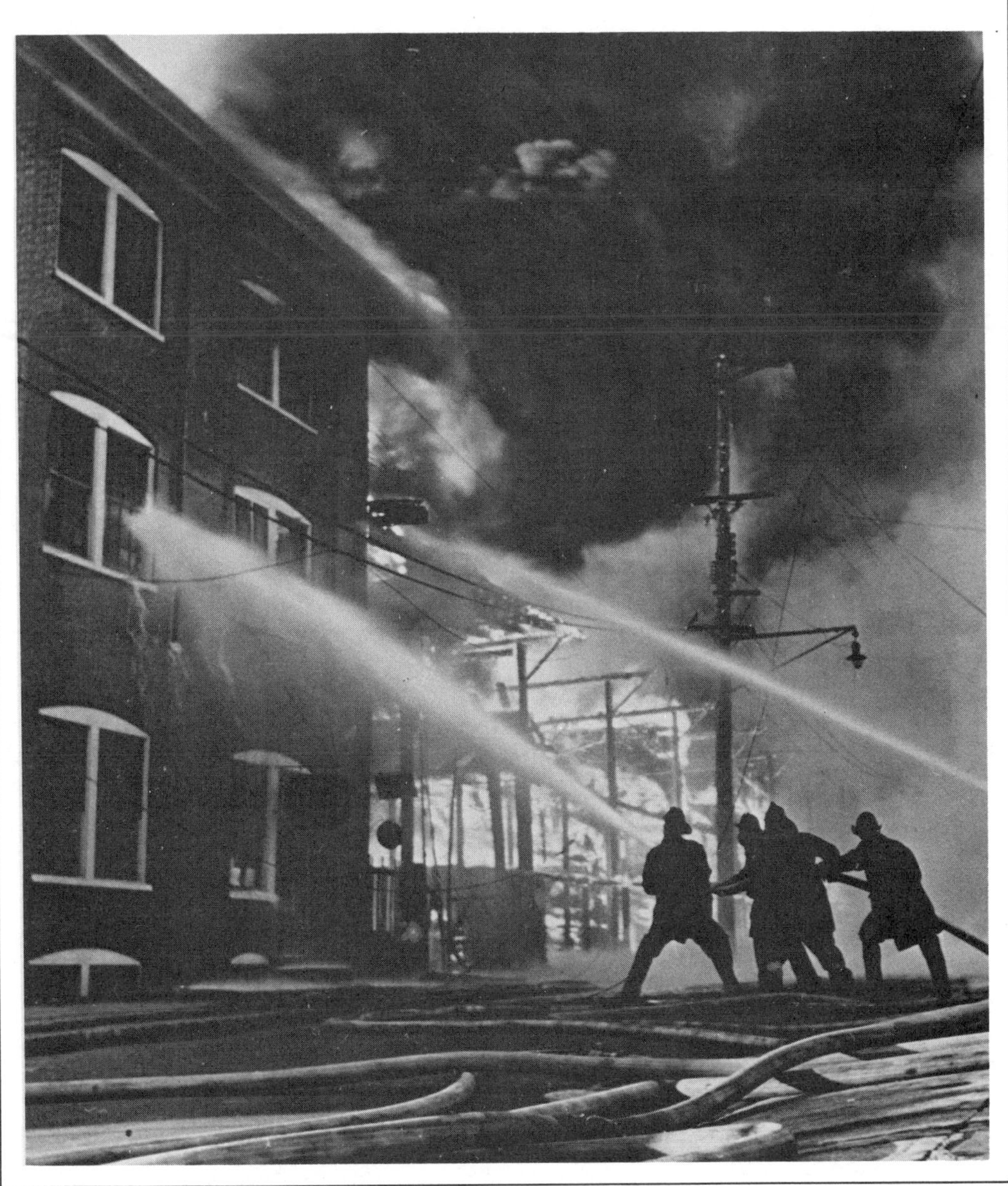

10

Police and Fire

The police beat can be one of the most interesting and also one of the dullest. The police beat is interesting because (1) it deals with people and problems and (2) it centers on things that excite people: violence, death, accidents, and the unknown. On the other hand, the beat can be dull. The setting for police reporters is usually a dingy press room, shared with others, often in an outdated city hall or police station. Reporters often get stories routinely, from listening to a garbled police scanner radio or from reading the "blotter" (log book) or "case jackets" (printout sheets put in a box each day). The people with whom the police reporters sometimes work may not be cooperative, and many of them are suspicious of the media. The beat may be dull even when reporters cover fires or accidents and encounter death and suffering. They have seen it all before. The police beat can be like reruns of many bad movies.

Whether exciting or dull, the police beat is complex. With all the routine, seldom do reporters get anything handed to them. Usually reporters get bits of information. "They [the police] just piecemeal you," says Tom Gibbons, a young Philadelphia *Inquirer* police reporter who works out of the drab police press room in the Philadelphia police "roundhouse." Gibbons, himself a former policeman, has sources that others have not dreamed of, and yet he has to work with what he calls bits of information with little direct cooperation.

The relations between police and press were tense in Philadelphia under Mayor Frank Rizzo, a former police commissioner, who was defeated in a bid for a third term largely due to the opposition from the newspapers. The *Bulletin* (since folded), the *Daily News*, and the *Inquirer* were critical of the mayor and police department. The Philadelphia *Inquirer* won the Pulitzer prize in 1978 for documenting police brutality. The *Daily News* also had little reason to be in the good graces of the police. It went to great lengths to photograph police stomping on and kicking members of a dissident commune.

Nevertheless, covering police business provides the reporter with the challenge of doing some special legwork. For the so-called glamorous side of police reporting—if there is such a side—consider this report of a murder solved by a reporter. Paul Mickle, 29, of the Burlington County *Times* in Willingboro, N.J., questioned the police report that a boy was missing and "possibly abducted." Mickle was able to obtain information that permitted him to say in a copyrighted front-page story that the boy was murdered and secretly buried. The three-year-old victim's mother and her boyfriend were charged with the murder. The executive editor of the paper, Daniel A. Eisenhuth, said, as quoted in *Editor & Publisher*: "Mickle stuck with the story long after it had disappeared from the headlines. The story was the result of ingredients every reporter relies upon—good sources and considerable legwork." *Editor & Publisher* gives this background on the story:

> On January 8, 1979, three-year-old Arthur Luciani disappeared from his Pemberton Township home. His mother, Linda, 23, told police she had sent the boy to the backyard to pick up trash. Within minutes, according to her story, he was gone. Mickle was assigned to cover the disappearance.
>
> —In the days that followed, police questioned the missing boy's mother, the boyfriend who lived with her, neighbors and their children. Tracking bloodhounds were used. One of the dogs apparently picked up the boy's scent and followed it from his home to an abandoned house nearby, giving weight to the story that he had been kidnapped. However, the boy remained missing, there were no arrests, and the disappearance officially was listed as a "possible abduction."
>
> —Several weeks after the boy disappeared without a trace, friends of his mother, who lived near the Burlington County Times office, approached reporter Mickle, saying they had misgivings about the abduction story. The couple said the older sister of the missing boy, five-year-old Tanya Luciani, had stayed with them overnight to help her forget her brother's disappearance. Mickle suggested the couple invite Tanya to their home once more, where he would question her.
>
> —On February 13, more than a month after Arthur Luciani disappeared, reporter Mickle and five-year-old Tanya met in a home in Willingboro. It was the first time anyone, including police, had interviewed the girl privately. Police had questioned her since she was at home the day her brother disappeared, but only when her mother and her mother's boyfriend were present.
>
> Following are excerpts from Mickle's copyrighted story:

"Daddy drowned him," five-year-old Tanya Luciani answered without hesitation when asked what had happened to her missing brother, three-year-old Arthur Luciani.

Holding a red stuffed dog upside down, Tanya showed how Brian Still—the fourth man she has called "daddy"—held Arthur by the ankles and literally dunked his head into a bathtub full of hot water and bubblebath. . . .

After consulting with Burlington County Times city editor Louis A. Chimenti, Mickle took the information he had obtained from the girl to the county prosecutor. On the basis of that information, Mrs. Luciani and Still were picked up for questioning. A few hours later, they were arrested and charged with murder. Police found the boy's body wrapped in a trash bag and buried in a nearby churchyard. . . .

After the clamor died down, Mickle looked back on the experience and said several questions crossed his mind at the time he knew he had murder evidence on his hands.

The first was whether the story told by a five-year-old girl carried enough credence to permit printing it. Mickle asked the girl to repeat the story several times. When she did not waver from her original version of the murder scene, Mickle decided she was telling the truth.

The second question was whether to print the story before notifying authorities. After consulting with editors, the decision was quickly made to take the information directly to the county prosecutor.

The third decision was how much to print, and when to print it. Editors decided that the first day's story would be a straight news account of the arrests and murder charges. It wasn't until two days after Mickle heard the evidence from Tanya—when the newspaper was sure the girl was safely out of reach of her mother and boyfriend—that the full story of the newspaper's involvement in solving the case was printed. . . .[1]

GUIDELINES FOR NEW POLICE REPORTERS

Among basic guidelines for the new reporter on the police beat, police reporters suggest that you:

1. Be patient with police. Remember that they are human, and think about how you would act if you were in their shoes. They have everything to lose at the hands of the public, the victims, and their own superiors if information is misused or misconstrued.
2. Develop good contacts. Find out where officers hang out, and frequent the location. "Learn who has the inside track with the police chief, and who doesn't," says Gordon R. Garnos, news editor of the Watertown (S.D.) *Public Opinion*.

3. Don't be timid or afraid to ask questions.
4. Get to know members of the police force on a first-name basis.
5. Listen for details in reports and conversations.
6. Get to know someone in central records well.
7. Occasionally give an officer credit for an arrest, if your paper permits this.
8. Don't overlook anyone. Get to know everyone from chief to janitor.
9. Don't be afraid to do small favors for an officer. As Gary Clarke of the Ames (Iowa) *Daily Tribune* suggests: "Bring in a picture of the police dispatcher's basketball-playing son."
10. Be courteous to everyone. Kurt Mueller, police reporter for the Sheboygan (Wis.) *Press*, extols the virtues of humility: "Many of the guys you need feel you're some overpaid college punk who gets his name on the stories and all the glory. And they more than likely have different images of cop-reporter relations than you." And he adds: "Nobody likes a smart ass, so don't be one."

Steve Marschand, reporter for the Kokomo (Ind.) *Tribune*, gives further advice on how reporters should conduct themselves:

> Students should be told that when they cover the police beat for a newspaper they are not writing for such publications as *True Detective* or *National Enquirer*. They also are not writing Mickey Spillane novels. They are writing about real people and real situations, and they are writing for the general public. This includes impressionable children, and people who object to sensationalizing graphic murder in the mass media.

On the psychological makeup of the police reporter, Marschand suggests that if reporters have weak stomachs or are not strong emotionally, they should not cover the police beat. Marschand says that if reporters stay long enough, they will:

> . . . see things that are extremely unpleasant. I myself have only been on the beat for about two years, but I have seen people literally torn apart in accidents, have seen people who have been savagely murdered, and, in one case, have photographed for the police the body of a young girl who was killed and left lying in the sun for two weeks. I consider myself to be a strong person emotionally, but I have to admit I had nightmares after seeing both her and a young man who stepped in front of a train on the same day. If reporters don't think they can witness the results of violent crime, they should give up any thought of covering a police beat.

Rick Booth, a reporter for the Westerly (R.I.) *Sun*, offers a self-reliant set of rules:

1. Keep your mouth shut and eyes and ears open at first—a police station is a microcosm, and until you know how it works (and each one is different), you could say the wrong thing.
2. Remember, the desk officer is an underling and might not be able to tell you what you want to know. Work through the shift commander, and develop a rapport with him. Also develop contact with the chief, but never sell out. Police officials must know where your loyalties lie if a conflict arises between your job and the police.
3. Rules of evidence sometimes call for discretion on the part of the reporter in giving details. Small towns, too, might call for discretion concerning lurid crimes. Remember, you have to deal with these people tomorrow and the next day.
4. Keep notes on everything, keep them with a system, and don't throw notes out. They might save your neck, even in the most trivial incident.
5. Remember: If you've got to print something less than flattering about the police, do it. Your responsibility is with the public, and even if the paper has to rotate you off the police beat, you're better off. If the paper fires you, you don't want to work for it anyway. It should protect you.

A typical day from Tom Jennings, police reporter, Mobile (Ala.) *Press Register*:

- 6 a.m.—Arrives at work. Makes routine phone calls to police, hospitals and other law enforcement agencies. Learns of an auto accident in which two are killed; follows up and makes additional phone calls about the wreck; writes and stores the story on his VDT.
- 7 a.m.–10 a.m.—Makes rounds at the Mobile Police Department headquarters, gathers information on crime within the past 24 hours and developments in ongoing cases.
- 10 a.m.–noon—Hurries back to the office. Writes an update on the original accident story. Takes a call from a stringer (or correspondent) in another county; adds a reported fatality to the original accident story. Listens to police calls over the 10-channel police monitor in the newsroom; prepares items (from the monitor) on burglaries, robberies, a rape, and a murder arrest. Takes dictation of a story called in by another reporter.
- Lunch
- After lunch—Tracks down ambulance and police calls recorded during lunch. Rewrites stories while listening to the police monitor.

He says, "On any given day, the police reporter takes phone-in obituaries, reports on fires, and other information which does not fit into a particular beat category."

HOW VETERAN POLICE REPORTERS DO IT

A police reporter will use many sources but is careful to attribute, that is, to say where the information comes from.

Note how the reporters in the following stories attribute the information by giving the sources of their information. From the Elgin (Ill.) *Courier-News*:

Two people were shot to death in Elgin this morning, one in a spectacular flurry of gunfire near the downtown area; the other in a home in Parkwood subdivision in the city's northeast section.

A man, the husband of one of the victims, later surrendered to Hampshire police, telling them he had just shot two people. He was in custody at Elgin police headquarters this afternoon.

Gwendolyn McGee, 21, of 1155 Hecker Ct., Elgin, was shot to death and a companion injured about 10 a.m. when a man believed to be the dead woman's husband, opened fire on them at a service station at State Street and Highland Avenue.

The injured woman was identified as Patricia Holley, 18, believed to be of the same Hecker Court address. Shortly after noon, police were called to investigate a report of a shooting at the Hecker Court address. There, they found the body of Mrs. Irvin Holley, 62, who had been shot once in the head. The shooting is believed to have occurred prior to the service station incident, police said.

Police believe McGee went to the Hecker Court address in search of his wife at about 9:30 a.m. Mrs. Holley had just returned home from work, police believe, and apparently was shot to death at that time.

Police theorize that McGee then left and found his wife at the service station where the second murder occurred.

Mrs. Irvin Holley was believed to be the mother of Patricia Holley.

Police originally believed that Patricia Holley had been shot in the head. She was taken to Sherman Hospital where it was determined she had not been shot, but suffered a deep head wound from flying glass.

The man believed responsible for the slaying, Michael McGee, of 1390 Mulberry, Elgin, turned himself in to Hampshire police at about 10:45 a.m., 40 minutes after the murder. . . .

—Mike Bailey

Bailey explains his sources for the first six paragraphs:

1. I developed the lead from overall information.

2. Information was assimilated from the detectives and Hampshire police.

3. The account came from first patrolman on the scene, as well as from my personal observations (I arrived within minutes of the call).

4. The police radio—I monitored the dispatch to that address. I arrived there and spoke with the sergeant at the scene. A detective supplied me with the information in the last line of the graph.

5. The detective who interrogated McGee told me that he supplied that information in his statement. The last line came from the patrolman who interviewed the dead woman's husband.

6. Again this came from McGee's statement.

I might point out that this is a same day story and emphasizes the importance of good connections. The first shooting happened at 10 a.m.; the second was discovered at 11:15 a.m. We have a 10:30 a.m. (first) deadline but were able to get the entire story in the afternoon edition.

From the Shreveport (La.) *Journal*:

A man who stopped on the Red River bridge of Interstate 20 to help a woman with a flat tire was critically injured this morning when an oncoming car slammed into the parked vehicle. The victim was getting a jack from the trunk of the woman's car when he was struck and pinned between the two cars.

The driver of the oncoming car also was injured in the 8:35 a.m. accident.

Police said the collision occurred on the eastbound lane of the bridge. A car driven by Ginger Scott, 19, of 6000 W. 70th St., had a flat tire and was stopped on the inside lane of the bridge.

Next, James C. Bamburg, 30, of Coushatta, drove by and stopped to assist Ms. Scott. He parked his pickup truck in front of Ms. Scott's car. A car driven by Pam Nunley, 29, of 2225 Beckett St. in Bossier, then rear-ended the auto, crushing the lower portion of Bamburg's body between the two vehicles.

Police said there were no skid marks on the pavement and police estimated the Nunley vehicle was traveling about 50 mph when it hit Bamburg. Witnesses told police Bamburg had his back to traffic and never saw the approaching vehicle.

Ms. Scott, who was not seriously injured, said, "He (Bamburg) was looking in the trunk and the next thing I knew I was flying everywhere." The force of the collision knocked the Scott car onto the median barrier.

Bamburg suffered leg and other injuries and was taken to LSU Hospital. He was in critical condition undergoing surgery late this morning. Ms. Nunley is in undetermined condition at Willis-Knighton Hospital.

—Gary Hines

Sources Hines used:

1. This is a summation of information I gained from talking with police at the wreck scene, ambulance and hospital personnel, one of the drivers involved in the accident, and personal observation.

2, 3, and 4. I talked to three patrolmen who were working the accident to learn details of how the mishap occurred. Names of victims came from ambulance drivers and two local hospitals.

5. I obtained this information from an officer in the identification division who specializes in auto accidents.

6. The driver of the auto with a flat was not seriously injured, so I got in the police car where she was sitting and asked her about the wreck.

From the Lawton (Okla.) *Constitution*:

Police today were investigating the death of a Durant man found stabbed to death today behind the African Breeze Lounge, 116 SW 1st.

The body of Billy Ross Rhea, 39, was found about 9 a.m. lying face up a few feet behind the African Breeze by a passerby, Jerry Canada.

Det. Mark McFarland said Rhea was stabbed in the chest and back several times. He said the worst wound was about three inches wide and two inches deep.

Several pools of blood in the frozen alley north of the Breeze indicated the victim was stabbed at the side of the building and crawled or was dragged around the corner to the back, McFarland said.

McFarland said cuts on the hands and neck indicated there had been a struggle. He speculated that Rhea might have been overcome by more than one assailant.

He said Rhea was killed about 5 a.m. or 6 a.m., according to medical examiner Gary Jackson.

Another violent incident took place near the Breeze about 11:30 p.m. Monday when a man standing at the corner of 1st and B was shot in the leg.

Jimmy Elix, 1607 Georgia, Apt. B, said he saw two men standing behind the African Breeze. He said he heard shots, which he believed came from the direction of where the two men were standing, and felt a bullet hit his right leg after he started running for cover.

A spokesman at Southwestern Hospital said Elix was treated for gunshot wounds in the emergency room and released.

McFarland said he doubted the two incidents were related.

He said the victim's wallet was missing and his pockets had been gone through when the body was searched by detectives, and said the killer or killers may have robbed Rhea. He said Rhea had been carrying "about $200" and that $40 was found in Rhea's jacket pocket.

A 28-year-old man arrested about 7 a.m. near the Breeze for driving under the influence of alcohol was ordered held in city jail for questioning in connection with the stabbing death. Police said it was believed the man might have information concerning the slaying.

The stabbing capped what has so far been a violent week for the African Breeze. Two men carrying a shotgun and pistols were disarmed after a struggle inside the tavern early Sunday by police and arrested for carrying firearms into a business where liquor is served.

Canada said he noticed Rhea while driving down B Avenue. He said he went over to help, thinking the man had fallen and injured himself on the ice and called police when he realized what had happened.

—Tom Jackson

Jackson's sources included:

1. I heard on the radio that police had a "working homicide" at the African Breeze, and when I arrived there a body lay a few feet behind the tavern. A detective told me where Rhea was from.
2. I talked to Canada at the scene—neglecting as you can see to obtain Canada's address—and heard Rhea's name from a man from a funeral home. I got the correct name and spelling from talking to Det. Mark McFarland.
3. I could see the stab wounds myself, but I didn't measure them. McFarland, obviously.
4. It was hard to miss the blood but the theory came from talking to McFarland.

5 and 6. Talking to McFarland again. I saw Jackson arrive and tell the cops that Rhea died not from a shotgun blast but from knife wounds, but I didn't know Jackson's estimate for the time of death until I talked to McFarland.

In Tuscaloosa, Ala., in the second floor newsroom of the Tuscaloosa *News* in October, 1983 Doris Flora had a bigger assignment than she might have expected on a Saturday afternoon.

It had been a quiet October afternoon, with reporters working their tubes (VDTs) and keeping their ears attuned to the Penn State-Alabama football game. Flora, a veteran court reporter who doubles as a police reporter on Saturday evenings, got a call that a youth missing for 10 days in one of the densest swamp areas in the state had been found, and that the body would be brought out in about an hour and a half.

She had the following earlier story and basic information (from the Tuscaloosa *News*, October 6, 1983) in front of her:

Tuscaloosa police, Hale County authorities, Moundville volunteers and Tuscaloosa County Civil Defense workers have discontinued their search of a large wooded area in Hale County for a Tuscaloosa man who has not been seen since Sept. 28, police said.

John Jamison, 28, was being sought in a wooded area behind Pleasant Hill Baptist Church on Hale Road 50, about six miles from Moundville, Tuscaloosa Assistant Police Chief Jerry Fuller said.

Jamison's parents, Charles "Brat" and Martha Jamison of Tuscaloosa, said they do not know where their son is, but they would like to let him and his friends know "there is some concern," Jamison said today.

"Maybe this will bring him out of the woodwork, if he is around somewhere," said Jamison.

The Moundville Rescue Squad, a volunteer organization, started looking for Jamison Sunday evening after his brother, Tommy Jamison, had found his motorcycle and helmet behind the church Saturday.

Mrs. Jamison said her sons frequently hunt on land in that area.

Jamison said they were not concerned at first because their son has "gone off for a day or two before."

The Tuscaloosa Police Department became involved Monday at the request of friends of the Jamison family, Fuller said.

Tuscaloosa Police Chief Winston Morris, Fuller and officers with the helicopter air patrol participated in the search through Wednesday afternoon.

The Tuscaloosa County Sheriff's Department bloodhound team aided Hale County Sheriff Chester Colvin in the search also, covering several hundred acres.

Tuscaloosa Police Capt. Billy Wilkins, who heads the West Alabama Narcotics Squad, said about five men from his squad helped in the search because they frequently work with Hale County authorities and are deputized in that county.

Fuller said police do not suspect foul play at this time. He said the city police frequently assist other law enforcement agencies in searches when they need help or when Tuscaloosa residents are involved.

Jamison said his son is not currently employed and takes classes at night at Shelton State Community College.

With this background story before her, Flora set out for the site near Moundville, 10 miles south of Tuscaloosa. When she arrived at the scene, she was too late.

Two Hale County sheriff cars were still there and two volunteers, but the body, parents, and forensic people were gone. "Ratzo," she said.

She proceeded, nevertheless, to get the facts. Note a soft line of concern in her questioning which made the sheriff and others trust her more.

Here's a part of her line of questioning on the spot following the biggest search party effort in over 35 years in the area:

FLORA: Tell me what you can. . . . How long has the search been going on?
SHERIFF: Since around 1 o'clock.
FLORA: Was it a search party . . . county bloodhound unit? . . . I thought you-all called it off.
SHERIFF: It's been going on since Monday.
FLORA: Helicopter that night? And today? How long you-all been out?
SHERIFF: All day. . . .
FLORA: How many miles?
SHERIFF: Two-and-a-half miles. . . .
FLORA: Was he in water? . . . Look like foul play? . . . But he was found in the water by himself? . . . Gun?
SHERIFF: No gun. . . .
FLORA: Was his helmet found here?
SHERIFF: There was other evidence. . . . Also his parents own property . . . near here.

FLORA: What's back there? Real swamp? . . . Was his father with you-all when you found the body?
SHERIFF: We did not let him come. . . .
FLORA: How many at the scene? . . . Are they your people or volunteers? . . . People good at helping?
SHERIFF: I was just commenting—people all helped. . . .
FLORA: It's hard in a small county . . . you couldn't put them all out.
SHERIFF: I had four all week.
FLORA: A bad way for it to end? . . . You lose hope? . . . How many men came? . . . Back there, is it thick?
SHERIFF: Five miles wide, eight miles long.
FLORA: Was the county coroner here? [She followed with queries as to where she might contact the coroner in the next few hours.] Sheriff, you want to make any comment? Appreciation? Have you had one of these recently?
SHERIFF: Biggest since I've been here; over 35 years [since something like this].
FLORA: Wednesday . . . [is] when you had the most people?
SHERIFF: We've had them since Monday.
FLORA: How many you put in Monday?
SHERIFF: 100.
FLORA: You-all walked or did you go in on horseback?
SHERIFF: A rattlesnake about three-feet big was killed. . . . I was afraid of snake bite—the reason I did as much on horseback. . . . As hot it's been, snakes still out.
FLORA: Sheriff, it looks like the body has been dead several days. . . . Was the body deteriorated?
SHERIFF: In a bag. . . . A friend of the father's brought it out in his 4-wheel drive. . . .
FLORA: So, it's been a long six days? Was it his brother who found the motorcycle behind church? . . . Are you pleased with people in this area? . . . Did you hate it to end like this?
SHERIFF: I expected this. . . . [Talk continued about the density of the swamp area . . . what the victim was wearing—he was fully clothed but barefoot] . . . We figure he lost his boots in the mud. . . .
FLORA: In shallow water? . . . So bad on his mother and daddy, but I know they are most appreciative of all of you. . . .

On the way back, Flora changed her view from "Ratzo" (too late) to "luckier than we thought." She commented: "Saturday night shifts go swiftly. You don't have to worry about what you're going to do."

Back at the office, the editor, Ellison Clary, commended her and suggested getting more on the city police role. She worked her story on the VDT and was interrupted a half dozen times to take and write obits coming over the phone. Fortunately the coroner's preliminary report came in about 9 p.m. in time for her deadline. After additional checking, she wrote for the Sunday paper:

The body of a 28-year-old Tuscaloosa man, missing since Sept. 28, was found shortly after noon today, culminating an intensive six-day search in a heavily wooded and swampy area which borders on Tuscaloosa and Hale counties.

Hale County Sheriff Chester Colvin said the body of John Jamison was found in shallow water about 1 p.m. Saturday by a group of volunteers who had been scouring the area since Monday.

Colvin said foul play in the death has been ruled out following a preliminary autopsy report Saturday night.

"Actual cause of death is not known at this time," he said. "We do rule out any foul play whatsoever at this time."

The effort to locate the Tuscaloosa man was described as the largest search conducted in the area in some 36 years by one of the volunteers, Colvin said.

"I know it was the biggest search we have had since I have been here," Colvin said. He has been Hale County sheriff more than 11 years.

Jamison is the son of Charles "Brat" and Martha Jamison of 73 The Downs, Tuscaloosa.

Colvin said it appeared the Tuscaloosa man had been dead several days when he was found Saturday afternoon.

The body was brought to the Tuscaloosa County Forensic Medicine Facility where an autopsy was performed Saturday night by Tuscaloosa pathologist Dr. Henry Santina. Dr. Santina released a preliminary autopsy report to Colvin Saturday evening.

Colvin said the body was found in shallow water approximately 2 to 2.5 miles from the Pleasant Hill Baptist Church where the Tuscaloosa man's motorcycle and helmet were found Oct. 1.

The church is on Hale County Road 50, about six miles from Moundville. It is near property owned by the Jamison family.

Colvin, who coordinated the search, said efforts to find Jamison had been concentrated in an area "five miles wide and eight miles long, which extended into a portion of Tuscaloosa County." Most of the search area is in Hale County, he said.

Throughout the week, he said, searchers had been through the marshy area where the body was found "several times." The area was so "thick with lily pads and brush, volunteers were 10 feet apart and could barely see each other," he said.

So rough was the terrain, the sheriff said, "The volunteer who found the body had trouble getting back to it the second time."

A green jacket Jamison was wearing also added to the difficulty in locating the body, Colvin said.

When he was found, Colvin said, Jamison was wearing a green "vest-type hunting jacket, flannel shirt and blue jeans." He did not have on shoes.

"We thought he had a gun," the sheriff said, however, no weapon has been found. Boots which Jamison was thought to be wearing were missing also, he said.

The law enforcement official said he "hated to see it end like this. However, I was expecting it to be like this after it took this long."

The Moundville Rescue Squad, a volunteer organization, began the search for the Tuscaloosa man Sunday evening. Jamison's brother Tommy found his motorcycle and helmet behind the church Saturday, Oct. 1.

Assistant Tuscaloosa Police Chief Talmadge Murray said the city police helicopter "was sent down Sunday night and did a spotlight search" of the area.

Colvin said his office "organized the search Monday morning and searched every day."

During the week, the Hale County Sheriff said he and his four deputies were assisted by Tuscaloosa City Police, Tuscaloosa County Sheriff's Department bloodhound team, West Alabama Narcotics Squad, Tuscaloosa County Civil Defense, Dallas Sheriff's Department, Board of Corrections, Alabama Bureau of Investigation, Moundville Police, Greensboro Police and others.

Colvin praised the law enforcement officials and volunteers who turned out to assist.

"We had 75 people or more searching today," he said. Eleven volunteers on horseback helped with the effort on Friday, he said.

"We had the most people searching Monday. We must have had over 100 people out then."

That was the day searchers "found evidence and knew he had been in this area," Colvin said. This included a milk carton and money, he said.

Raiford Johnson, one of the volunteers who spent the week searching for the missing man, said Jamison had spent time through the years at his home and had hunted in the area.

"That is what has us confused," Colvin said. "He was supposed to have known the area."

Murray said Tuscaloosa Police assisted in the search every day except Friday.

"We called the search off Friday to get things together to go back today (Saturday)," Murray said.

Funeral arrangements for Jamison will be announced by Hayes Chapel Funeral Home.

STUDENT REPORTERS AND POLICE

Police reporting is frustrating for most journalists and especially for the student reporter. The student, usually still a novice in skills, public relations, and with few contacts, can hardly expect to excel where even the pros themselves have trouble. Besides, police officials have less reason to talk to a student reporter, for the student reporter is unknown, and cautious police bureaucrats want to minimize the danger of being misquoted.

One way to become acquainted with a police beat is to drop in at a station. If you live in a small town, sit in on the 9 a.m. press briefing or look at the police log book or slips of paper that have the basic information on crime and accidents as submitted by police on duty the day or night before. Although this kind of information is very sketchy, you will find out the basic facts about what happened, when, where, and to whom, and the name of the reporting officer so you can follow up for more detailed coverage.

Another way to begin is to listen to the "flash" announcements on the police scanner radio. With basic information, plus a few calls, you can put together a few accounts for practice and compare your efforts with reports in the daily paper.

As a student reporter, you can undertake police topics. These may include identifying and studying the most dangerous traffic corner near campus (case histories of recent wrecks, annual police statistics) or researching the development and trends in a specific crime against people or property, such as drug abuse, muggings, rapes, bike thefts, or shoplifting from bookstores or cafeterias.

Students at Mankato (Minn.) State University wrote about assaults in and around the campus (they rode with patrol cars). At Wichita State, Kate McLemore investigated a local police raid on an allegedly obscene movie shown on campus and anticipated (and went along with) a police raid on bookstores. (Her story, mentioned earlier, became a headline in the morning Knight-Ridder Wichita *Eagle*.) Following a fatal dorm stabbing on campus, another Wichita State student wrote an in-depth piece on campus murders across the nation, and a letter to the FBI brought personal help from FBI Director Clarence Kelly. At Temple University, Martha Master, a graduate student and school teacher in New Jersey, took local police statistics (after getting acquainted with police through a small classroom report assignment) and integrated the information with anecdotes of real events. She wrote a lead story in a New Jersey daily on crime in schools. The list goes on; police stories do not have to be a forbidden domain of students, but can be a challenge for the uninitiated just as they are for the veteran reporter.

Students in one class at Temple University summarized their experiences in establishing a working relationship with a police department. After making a list of cooperative persons at the Tredyffrin Police Department, Susan Oliver suggested:

- Call in advance and make an appointment to see a particular police official. You are less likely to interfere with schedules.
- Many departments are tired of students coming in and asking for information. Good manners and appreciation of their willingness to help you may open an otherwise closed door.
- Be well-dressed and well-groomed. Be deserving of the time they are giving to you.
- Expect to have difficulty obtaining details about cases which have not gone to trial yet. Ask if you can receive the same information that professional newspaper reporters receive.
- Acquaint yourself with all report forms. Ask to see copies of the reports, and make sure you understand them. Statistics listed in the Uniform Crime Report are especially helpful.
- Thank people who have given time from their schedules to teach you. Your courtesy may enable you to be well-received the next time you ask for information.

Student Jack Lule wrote:

> My first step was to contact the police reporter who covered Upper Darby police department activities for the local paper. From this reporter I received information on the best day to call, the best time to call, the worst time to call, the best person to talk to, and how much time I could expect from this person. I used the information on the day and time.
>
> The reporter suggested that I contact a specific office such as "Traffic Records" and talk to office workers there. Acting on a suggestion from my professor, I contacted an officer high up in the department and requested his help. This step has many advantages: you cut "red tape" immediately, you obtain "orders" for help instead of your own simple request, and you initiate a relationship with a ranking officer instead of a less powerful office worker.
>
> A captain helped me personally on the first project, as we both examined a file of completed cases that would be useful for me in completing my assignment. Other benefits were the courtesy of the police department—and coffee and doughnuts.
>
> This relationship with the captain helped me immensely on the more complex, second assignment. I was working on a traffic problem, but decided to talk to the captain about it. He had an office worker use a computer to get the data I needed, data I would have had to calculate by hand. While this was being done, he also referred me to other agencies that work on traffic problems, such as the Franklin Institute and the Department of Transportation. His cooperation was invaluable.

Susan Weiner, writing her report in the form of a memo, told of getting information in Allentown, Pa.:

> Before you approach the police station, read up on your story in the morgue (newspaper library) files. Talk to other city employees who know what's going on, and get a feel for your subject.
>
> Arm yourself with this preliminary information and get those questions ready. Then you'll be in a good position to call the station.
>
> When you have the name of a sergeant, for instance, find out when the specific sergeant goes on duty. If he's on night shift, as mine was, go in early and wait for him to show up. It's good to catch him at this time when he's free to talk to you rather than calling him at home in the afternoon and chance waking him up.
>
> You never know when you'll run into a hostile person. My subject was suing a journalist who portrayed him as an unsavory character. In these situations, when you start off on the wrong foot, just try to gradually establish trust by leading up to the more difficult questions after shooting the breeze for a while.

Never give up, even though you may unknowingly try to interview someone who's unwilling to talk to you at first. If all else fails, try the officer on the next shift.

USING THE PHONE

Since he is new on his beat and knows fewer people, Dwight Ott of the Philadelphia *Inquirer* uses the phone perhaps more, he says, than a reporter with longer-established sources. Ott calls around until he gets the information. He feels that using the phone offers an advantage because he can call many more people than he can contact by rushing out to the scene (traveling through a big city may take an hour).

Dwight Ott and all police reporters rely on various directories, among them *Cole's Metropolitan Householder's Directory*, published for specific locales. It contains names, addresses, and phone numbers of homes, businesses, and organizations in each metropolitan area. It lists information according to location using a street-by-street and block-by-block system.

When you have only partial information, such as only a name and block of residence, *Cole's* is a fast way of finding the identity, address, and phone number. And it helps to turn to neighbors of story subjects. If a person is murdered, for instance, what do the neighbors know about that person? You can reach a whole block of neighbors quickly from your office.

Ott has before him on his desk a yellow, battered paper with a list of key numbers he and other *Inquirer* reporters need often. The categories here are the kinds of categories you will also need in your own personal telephone list, if you become a police reporter:

- **Narcotics.**
- **Police radio:** Broadcasts the who, what, when, and where of the dispatch.
- **Battalion chief:** Flash information and fire calls.
- **Fire radio:** Gives same basic info as above pertaining to fire dispatch.
- **Night command:** Night duty captain's number. He receives all detailed info on major crimes.
- **Homicide:** Besides homicides, this department handles all crimes committed by or against police, except police shootings.
- **Accident investigation unit:** Takes care of traffic or industrial mishaps which result in serious injury or death.
- **Call room:** Where all prisoners are detained.
- **Arraignment court:** Defendant is read the charges; bail is set.

- **Detectives:** They are assigned to each of the seven districts.
- **House of detention.**
- **Head inspector, narcotics and homicide:** Supervises drug and murder investigations.
- **Medical examiner's office:** Responsible for corpses and attempts to determine time of death, cause and name and address of deceased.
- **Fire marshal's office:** Provides more detailed info on fires.
- **Major crimes office:** Located in detective bureau; investigates major crimes, namely large holdups (but not homicide).
- **Bail room:** Where bail is arranged.
- **Gang control:** Plainclothes unit in the Juvenile Aid Bureau.
- **Morals office:** Investigates all sex crimes.
- **Airport police:** Airport personnel.
- **Lobby desk:** All people coming into the building, including all arrests, are logged here.
- **Civil affairs:** Plainclothesmen investigating demonstrations, strikes.

When Ott makes a call, he sounds authoritative even though he speaks quietly: "This is Dwight Ott, police administration press room on Race St. . . ." He says it in such a way that the listener hears particularly "police administration," and Ott admits that he intends to say it just this way. People catch the "police administration" before the other words and respond more readily, even though he has also identified himself as a member of the press room. Since he is merely gathering information, this is adequate. In more substantial conversations, where reporters are seeking comments and conjectures, they, just as Ott, should also identify the newspaper they represent.

POLICE PROCEDURE

The criminal justice process begins when a crime is brought to the attention of authorities. Usually the crime is observed by somebody and reported.

The first stage of the process is an *investigation* by the law officers. They may respond to a call at the scene of the alleged crime and begin to collect and record data. Plainclothes detectives may also initiate an investigation which can stretch over any amount of time. The investigation may or may not result in an arrest. If a complaint of a person who comes to court initiates the arrest, the judge issues a warrant for arrest.

At the time of arrest, the police must inform the suspect that he or she has the right to remain silent and has the right to seek an attorney then or at any time. After this is done, officers take the suspect into custody and then book him or her. The suspect is photographed, fingerprinted, and a formal record is made of the arrest for a specific crime.

At any of these points—at the place of arrest, on the way to the station, or at the booking desk—authorities must advise the suspect of his or her constitutional rights. The officer prepares a report on the arrest, and if the suspect signs a waiver, questioning can begin. An assistant prosecutor may participate in the questioning for more serious crimes, such as murder.

The person arrested may seek to have *bail* posted in order to be released pending disposition of the case. Rates for bail for misdemeanors or lesser offenses usually follow a scale set by the courts. The court may set higher bail for more serious crimes. Anyone can pay the bail amount, including a bail bondsman licensed by the state to issue loans to pay bail.

A person who is arrested must come before a magistrate within a certain period, usually 48 hours. At this point, a formal complaint or *affidavit* is filed. The person filing the complaint or a policeman signs the complaint under oath.

If a prosecutor agrees with the complaint, a court date is set. In this initial appearance or arraignment, the court advises the accused of his or her rights and of the charge, seeks a *plea*, and if the plea is not guilty, sets bail; if the plea is guilty, the judge can impose sentence for minor offenses.

For a misdemeanor, the judge may hold a *summary trial*. In the case of a felony, the judge will set a time for a *preliminary hearing*. Here the judge can dismiss the charges or bind the person over for trial.

If the person is to stand trial, the prosecuting attorney issues an *information* based on the complaint, or a grand jury issues an *indictment*. If the grand jury collects the evidence, the indictment is called a *presentment*; a *bill*, if the prosecuting attorney gathers it; and a *true bill*, if the grand jury (of 13 to 24 persons) endorses the prosecuting attorney's efforts.

In an *arraignment*, the court hears the plea of the accused. Then the suspect is given a choice between a court or jury trial. The court appoints a public defender, if necessary. The court can order a *pre-trial hearing* at this time to discuss the validity of evidence or confessions and procedures. J. Norman Swaton and Loren Morgan note in *Administration of Justice* that ". . . dismissal of charges is often the result of these hearings since they are frequently held because the judge already suspects there may be a flaw in the people's case."[2]

KINDS OF CRIME

Law enforcement agencies have various ways of classifying crimes. The FBI, for instance, divides reported crimes into two groups: (1) the "serious," or "important," crimes and (2) the remainder. The first group includes murder, rape, robbery, aggravated assault, burglary, and auto theft. As a group these represent the most common local crime problems. In the second category are arson, forgery, embezzlement, sex offenses, violation of liquor laws, disorderly conduct, violation of curfew, and runaway juveniles.

Cesare Lombroso, called by many the father of criminology, talked in categories of the crimes of the born criminal, the insane criminal, the criminal by passion, the habitual criminal, and the occasional criminal. Dutch criminologist W. A. Bonger put crimes in categories of motives: economic crimes, sexual crimes, political crimes, and miscellaneous crimes. Says Gresham M. Sykes, in *Crime and Society*: "In recent years, however, there has been a growing recognition that a crime is a complex social event involving a pattern of interaction between the criminal and his victim in a socially defined situation. If we look only at the criminal, we leave out more than half of the picture."[3]

"Felonies" (from Latin, *felonia*, meaning treason or treachery) are more serious crimes, such as murder; "misdemeanors" (from Latin *mis*, wrong, and Old French *demeanor*, conduct) are crimes of lesser importance.

Today crimes are usually classified this way:

I. Crimes against persons

Abduction: Taking of a female child or woman without consent.

Abortion: Terminating the life of the fetus under certain conditions.

Aggravated assault: Assault with specific intent to kill, rape, or commit serious crimes against a person.

Assassination: Murder—usually of a prominent figure—without immediate provocation for political, social, private reasons, or for hire.

Assault with dangerous or deadly weapon: Attemping or indicating desire to do bodily harm without cause by any instrument which could harm or cause death.

Assault with intent to commit manslaughter: Attempting to harm a person in such a way that if successful the crime of manslaughter would result.

Assault with intent to commit murder: Specifically intending to kill someone while acting by malice aforethought.

Assault with intent to commit rape: Having an intent to commit the crime of rape, with the presence of facts which bring the offense under the definition of assault.

Battery: Assault when any force is used, no matter how slight, applied to another person (such as slapping another person).

Breach of oral contract: Breaking of a promise, such as to marry, resulting in emotional, mental, and other distress.

Common or simple assault: Attempt or indication of intent to hurt another person.

False imprisonment: Unlawful restraint of a person's freedom.

Homicide: Killing of another—it can be ruled justifiable, excusable, or felonious.

Homicide, felonious: (1) Murder, first degree: premeditated with evil intent; (2) murder, second degree: killing with intent and malice but not premeditated.

Homicide, vehicular: Causing death by motor vehicle.

Maim (mayhem): Intentional maiming or mutilation of a person.

Manslaughter, involuntary: Unintentional killing.

Manslaughter, voluntary: Intentional killing without malice.

Rape, statutory: Sex relations with a minor female even if she consents.

Terroristic threats: Intimidation and threats of violence to cause intense fear—often to a group of people—for political reasons.

II. Crimes against property

Cheating by false pretenses: Taking property by false pretenses (confidence games, for example).

Criminal trespass: Encroaching on forbidden property with violence against a person's right or property.

Embezzlement: Taking of property or funds unlawfully by fraud or deceit—usually from a company or government agency—for one's own purposes.

Extortion: Taking money or property of another by force or fear with the person's consent.

Forgery: Changing a piece of writing for deception and/or for gain.

Fraud: A trick or breach of confidence to gain something or an advantage.

Grand larceny: The stealing of a large sum of money (amount varies in individual states), usually a felony.

Hijacking: Robbery in transit, usually from trucks or airplanes.

Larceny by trick: Obtaining property by trick or fraud with intent to put to own use; also includes taking advantage of mistake in surrender of possession.

Malicious mischief: Destroying of property or injuring or killing animals with malicious intent.

Petit larceny: Stealing of a smaller sum, usually a misdemeanor.

Receiving stolen goods: Property received and known to be stolen.

Robbery: Property taken away in the presence of the victim by force or fear.

Uttering forged instruments: Offering a forged document as good.

III. Crimes against habitation

Arson: Willfully and maliciously burning another's property.

Burglary: Forced entry into a building with intent to commit a felony.

IV. Crimes against public morality and decency

Adultery: Voluntary sexual intercourse between two persons, one of whom is married to another.

Bestiality: Relations of a person with an animal.

Bigamy: Being married to two persons.

Fornication: Sexual relations not constituting adultery but not between husband and wife; generally, sex between unmarried persons.

Incest: Sexual relations between closely-related relatives.

Indecent exposure: State of appearance or exposure morally offensive to others.

Lewdness: The state of going beyond norms of decency; unprincipled lust.

Miscegenation: Marriage or the living together of people of different races as forbidden by law.

Obscenity: That which offends the language and idea norms of society, often by sexual or violent expressions.
Polygamy: Being married to two or more persons.
Prostitution: Selling of sexual favors.
Seduction: Persuading an unmarried person to engage in sex relations by deception.
Sodomy: Homosexual relations or relations with animals.

V. Crimes against the public peace

Affray: Fighting in a public place causing fear or terror in others.
Disturbing the peace: Acts of annoyance that disturb people.
Forcible entry: Entering property of another violently.
Gambling: Betting on outcomes that are not predictable.
Gaming: Playing a game where players contribute to a pool of funds going to the winner.
Riot: An assembly or gathering which is lawful at the outset but which later carries out unlawful purpose with violent or disruptive means.
Rout: An assembly or gathering that from the beginning carries out the unlawful purpose of those assembled.

VI. Crimes against authorities

Bribery: Offering money or other incentives to entice a person from normal performance of duties.
Compounding a felony: Helping a criminal escape justice or agreeing not to prosecute one in dodging justice.
Contempt: Disregard and/or disrespect for court or court order.
Counterfeiting: Making money without authority and for deception.
Embracery: Attempt to influence a jury with money or other favors.
Misconduct in office: (1) Malfeasance: doing illegal acts in office; (2) nonfeasance: willfully neglecting duties set by law.
Misprision: Having knowledge of treasonous acts and failing to disclose them.
Obstruction of justice: Interrupting efforts of those entrusted to carry out justice.
Perjury: Giving false testimony under oath.
Racketeering: Organized conspiracy to commit a crime of extortion or coercion.
Seditious conspiracy: Conspiracy to overthrow the government by force.

Subornation of perjury: Getting another person to testify falsely under oath.

Treason: Giving "aid and comfort" to the enemy; betraying the government; trying to overthrow the government.

VII. Crimes against public safety, health, and comfort

This is a miscellaneous category which includes such violations as those of traffic laws, food regulations, and health codes.

Reckless endangerment: Action that may potentially hurt someone, such as scaling a skyscraper.

VIII. Conspiracy in crimes

Accessories after the fact: Person who comforts or aids another while knowing the accused has committed a felony.

Accessories before the fact: Person who is absent when the crime is committed, but who has advised, helped, or ordered the accused to do the deed.

Principals in the first degree: Person who actually causes the crime or who causes it through another.

Principals in the second degree: Person who "aids and abets" (incites) another who is acting in the first degree.

IX. Civil and constitutional rights violations

These include a myriad of subjects such as discriminatory practices, invasion of privacy, and criminal libel.

THE POLICE RADIO

The police radio chatters on, muddled and sporadic, at the police headquarters press room in Philadelphia. Dwight Ott of the *Inquirer* and others are going about their calls and conversations; a man who has just collected $3 from each for coffee services is chattering and peddling a little information. Suddenly police reporters stop what they are doing and look up. Their trained ears have caught a bit of information from the radio. There is mention of a policeman who has been cut. No other information follows. Any injury to a policeman is always worth checking. In this case it turned out the officer was merely hurt by a car door.

Says Dan Moreau, of the Richmond (Va.) *Times-Dispatch*:

> You can listen to the police radio like the changing breezes on a bay. Subtle shifts in the level of noise and chatter can mean real trouble.
>
> Listen for catch phrases such as a request for the coroner or

> medical examiner or the infamous "no lights, no sirens" which invariably means a stakeout or a wildeyed rifleman holding hostages. "We go fire" often slips into the mainstream's chatter unnoticed. It's your signal to go to the blaze.

Small newspapers, although they usually have some working relationship with police, such as being able to check the police blotter or attend a briefing (both of which may hold back information), also make use of police scanners to pick up on actual police calls.

Ken Blum, editor-manager of the *Courier-Crescent* in Orrville, Ohio, notes the value of the police radio. He wrote in one of the bulletins of the National Newspaper Association, *The Byliner*:

> A police band scanner has been the most ingenious and most valuable addition to our office in a long time. It's like having a faithful informer sitting on the desk.
>
> The device is fascinating to watch. Eight mini-lamps are constantly lighting as the radio makes a swift scan. Each light represents a separate crystal. For instance, number one is our fire band, two is sheriff, three is highway patrol, four is police, and so on.
>
> The scan will stop on any frequency in use. After the message, the scan continues. If desired, you can stick to one crystal by operating the unit manually.
>
> Reception on all eight crystals is perfect (actually 16 crystals can be installed but only eight can be used at one time). It can be hooked up in our staff car within seconds by just plugging in the aerial and power source.
>
> Thus far, the scanner has put us on the scene of dozens of fires and accidents within minutes. About 50 percent of the time, we beat the fire department and emergency squad to the scene. Other tips have included a manhunt, train derailment, and truckers' highway blockade.
>
> A word of warning, however. Most if not all law enforcement agencies use code and signal numbers in their radio traffic. We had no trouble getting the list of numbers on a confidential basis. You'll be lost without them unless you spend months trying to decipher the system yourself.
>
> Total cost of a good scanner and crystals is in the neighborhood of $200.

POLICE LANGUAGE

The police beat, as other beats, has a language of its own. Here are some terms, courtesy of Phil Milford of the Wilmington *News Journal*:

Bail: Money or property forfeited to court if person does not appear. Sometimes it is a percentage; this is up to judge to decide.

Secured bail: Court receives the money or property.

Unsecured bail: Individual does not have to post money or property because judge feels confident individual will return; commonly referred to as "released on own recognizance."

Surety: Legal term for bail.

Bond: Paper left with court saying individual will pay if he or she does not show up in court; commonly used as "posting bond."

Bail bond: Same as bond but is used by a bail bondsman (someone who will guarantee the money to the court).

Capias: Latin word used to describe warrant issued by a judge, also called a "bench warrant"; a writ commanding a police officer to take an individual into court, used primarily in Delaware lower courts because of regional differences.

Arrest warrant: Issued by police officer.

Rule 9 warrant: Issued by superior court after a grand jury has indicted an individual (again a regional term; may differ in other areas).

Handgun: A pistol. (Milford says his editor prefers using pistol because handgun is a hackneyed phrase.)

Revolver: Type of pistol with a revolving chamber (generally for six or eight bullets); revolvers do not eject shells after firing (a nonautomatic).

Semiautomatic: The shell casing is ejected after firing and a new one is put in place; trigger must be pulled each time.

Automatic: Fires continuously as long as trigger is held down. It is a federal offense to possess an automatic pistol.

Automatic rifle: Also illegal according to federal law.

Shotgun: Shoots a number of little pellets at one time; used in duck hunting.

Sawed-off shotgun: The barrel of a shotgun has been sawed off closer to the stock; this widens the pattern of little pellets and sprays a larger area, enabling the gun to cut a person almost in half if fired at close range (regular shotgun with long barrel keeps pellets closer together). There is a federal law against owning a sawed-off shotgun—called possession of destructive weapon—because the short barrel can be concealed easily.

Calibre: Millimeter measurement of a barrel's inside diameter; common calibres are .22, .25, .32, .35, .38 (used by many police departments), .44, and .45.

Magnum: This type of shell has extra charge of powder than standard shell.

DWI: Driving while influenced (under alcohol); also DUI, driving under the influence.

DOA: Dead on arrival, generally at a hospital.

SWAT: Special Weapons and Tactics—a highly trained combat team that uses automatic weapons, demolition equipment, and tear gas.

Ten Codes: Used in radio communications; differ from region to region but common ones are 10–4 (OK, message received), 10–36 (what time is it?), and 10–13 (what are the weather conditions?).

The Elgin (Ill.) *Courier News'* Mike Bailey identifies some of the police slang in his column, "Reporter's Notebook":

> Following are samples of police slang that both thrills and mystifies regular listeners of police scanners (radio).
>
> ***Snitch:*** Same as "stool pigeon"; one who stays out of jail by informing police of illegal activities by others.
>
> ***Paper:*** As in "We got paper on him"; a warrant for arrest of a specified individual.
>
> ***Bad paper:*** A person "hanging bad paper" is writing bad checks.
>
> ***Scam:*** A confidence game that generally depends on a "mark's" (victim's) sense of greed for success—which opens the way to more slang. The "pigeon drop" and "bank examiner" are two examples.
>
> ***Flip someone:*** If detectives "flip someone," they have made an agreement with a suspect in a crime for him to testify against another in exchange for immunity.
>
> ***Turn:*** As in "turn a deal," an agreement to purchase drugs.
>
> ***Score:*** An acquisition of drugs or a successful crime.
>
> ***Mope:*** Someone police may deal with regularly, a character who is well known to them—or sometimes any person.
>
> ***Eyeball:*** If a detective "finds an eyeball," he has located an eyewitness to whatever is being investigated.
>
> ***Dirty:*** Someone is "dirty" if they are in possession of drugs or stolen property when they are arrested. It can also mean a criminal record.
>
> ***Theft over:*** A "felony theft," theft of property worth more than $150.
>
> ***Make:*** Identification of a suspect by a witness to a crime through use of photos, one-on-one confrontation, or being picked from a group on a police station stage. (Expression comes from the latter procedure.)
>
> ***Ice, chill, snuff, break-off, terminate, erase, blow away, dust off, cancel:*** All terms for death or murder.
>
> ***Hard time:*** Penitentiary time, as opposed to jail time.
>
> ***Stick job:*** Armed robbery.
>
> ***Smash and grab:*** When someone breaks a store window, grabs the merchandise on display, and runs.
>
> ***Dick:*** Detective.

Diaper dick: Juvenile division detective.

Keeper: Someone 17 years old or older who can be kept in jail.

Cooler, slammer, cross bar hotel: Jail.

Walk: Someone who beats a charge will "walk" or be set free.

Going down: A crime in progress is said to be "going down."

Drop the dime: When an informant calls police to give them information on a crime.

Took a hat: Left town. Also called "Boogie-ing."

Put the button on him: When a detective shows someone his badge.

The man: The police, also known as "the heat" and numerous other names, some unprintable.

Police reporters inevitably must deal with drug terms, from those needed to write drug bust articles to overall background pieces. Here are some of the terms they may encounter. The summary is by John Covaleski, as it appeared in a special section on drugs in the Doylestown (Pa.) *Daily Intelligencer*:

The following is a list of abused drugs and their street names:

Marijuana: weed, pot, grass, reefer, rope. The term marijuana refers to any part of the hemp plant (Cannabis Sativa) which grows in mild climates in most parts of the world. When dried and crushed, it can be smoked or eaten.

Its effects include a euphoric feeling, talkativeness, increased appetite known as "the munchies," drowsiness, in some cases panic, a redness of the eyes and a distortion of time and space comprehension.

The drug's active ingredient is tetrahydrocannabinol, which when synthesized is sold in pill or powder form as product known as THC.

Lysergic Acid Diethylamide: acid, or when adhered to paper—blotter acid. LSD was once the number one hallucinogen in the country and is now making a comeback, according to drug officials.

LSD is usually manufactured in pill form, known as "hits," and creates emotions from euphoria to panic. Users hallucinate, experience impaired judgment. . . .

Formaldehyde, an ingredient used in embalming corpses, is used in the preparation of LSD.

Amphetamines: bennies, pep pills, whites and truck drivers, the first commercial amphetamine was benzedrine.

Amphetamines are stimulants which directly affect the central nervous system. Most frequently found in tablet or capsule form, the drug is also sometimes used in liquid or powder state.

Effects induced by the drug include talkativeness, euphoria, excitability, irritability, hyperactive reflexes, dilated pupils and a marked decrease in appetite. Some amphetamines are medically-prescribed for weight loss.

The drug is known for its ability to increase alertness and activity.

It often makes it to the street through abuse of doctor prescriptions or by production in homemade laboratories.

Methaqualone (Quaaludes): ludes, "heroin for lovers," soaps, quacks, and quads, quaaludes were first synthesized in India in 1955 as an antimalarial medication.

Manufactured as pills or capsules,

quaaludes produce a euphoric effect balanced with calmness. Other mental effects caused by the drug include hallucinations, alteration of one's body image, numbness and anxiety.

The drug is usually swallowed, but can also be ground to powder, dissolved and injected into the bloodstream. Getting high on the drug is called "luding-out."

Cocaine: coke, leaf, snow and happy dust, the drug is expensive. . . .

It is obtained from the leaves of erythroxylon cocae, a bush that grows wild in Peru and Bolivia and cultivated in other countries. It is crushed to powder form and inhaled through the nostrils (snorted).

The drug produces restlessness, excitability, talkativeness, depressed reflexes, a distortion of space and time, irritation of the nasal cavity and dilated pupils.

It is highly addictive.

Heroin: skag, horse, smack, snow and H, heroin is derived from morphine which is a chemical extraction from the opium poppy of Asia.

Regarded as one of the most dangerous and addictive of narcotics, it is injected into the bloodstream or snorted.

The drug was originally introduced as a pain reliever and cough suppressant.

Heroin's effects include hallucinations, anxiety, depression, coordination impairment, constricted and dilated pupils, reddened eyes, cramps, diarrhea, nausea, and severe physical and psychological dependence. . . .

Phencyclidine (PCP): angel dust, embalming fluid, elephant or horse tranquilizer and rocket fuel, PCP has hallucinogenic effects and was associated with at least 80 deaths and 4,000 emergency room treatments nationally in 1977.

It comes in tablet or powder and is manufactured in home laboratories. It is swallowed, snorted, or sprinkled on marijuana and smoked.

It distorts time and space, and creates panic, confusion and laughter in its users. It is considered to be psychologically addicting. Users have been known to experience feelings of strength, power, and invulnerability.

Hydrochloric acid is an ingredient used in its manufacture.

Countless other pills and capsules are abused.

Among those are the barbiturates known as yellows, reds, blues, Christmas trees and barbs. These items fall under the category of "downers" and produce a depressant effect.

In the hallucinogenic list are peyote, which is derived from a cactus plant, and psilocybin, which can be extracted from certain mushrooms.

Other notable drugs include standbys such as glue, which when sniffed produces a depressant effect, and some cough syrups that, in large doses, also act as a depressant.

COVERING FIRES

Police reporters cover their share of fires. Police reporters suggest the following fire reporting guidelines:

1. Learn how to distinguish between a routine trash bin fire and a killer fire by becoming familiar with your police-fire scanner.
2. Establish a line of communication between yourself and two or more persons in the fire department who will always be available to immediately confirm if a fire is serious.
3. On the scene, stay out of the way of the working firemen, but don't be put off by all the action.

4. Check first for loss of life and limb. People are more important than property. "Even if a notable work of art were destroyed in a fire which killed a hobo, I would lead with the death," says Rick Bella of the Eugene (Ore.) *Register-Guard*.
5. Next, find out the problems and the strategy. "Covering a large fire," says Bella, "is somewhat like covering a war. Conditions can change from moment to moment and the firemen, like field commanders, must adjust their strategy. Similarly, the reporter, like a war correspondent, must be able to analyze the effect of the changes. If possible, the reporter should try to anticipate changes in strategy."
6. Stay with the fire. Bella recalls starting home when he thought a fire was just about out, but the winds shifted, and the size of the fire quadrupled.
7. Locate the highest-ranking fire official to learn the extent of the fire and the number of casualties. Try to learn the cause and point of origin and the name of the person who reported and/or discovered it.
8. Find out the names of those in the building, both tenants and/or visitors. This information can come from tenants and from firemen and police at the scene. Red Cross officials, usually summoned to all multialarm fires, may provide another source of such information. The Red Cross also has information on the placement of displaced persons. Finding homeless fire victims can be one of the biggest problems, says Bob LaMagdeleine of the Hartford (Conn.) *Courant*: "Often the victims have dispersed to surrounding homes, have left the area and found shelter with relatives, or are en route to hospitals."
9. Stress additional human angles. Bella suggests these kinds of questions: Were the neighbors evacuated? Were the pets killed? Was the house vacant because the family had moved out the day before?
10. Besides checking information, always talk to firemen for a graphic description of what happened (especially if you weren't there).

Of course, you do not have to follow these steps in order. The circumstances—the developments and progress of the fire, talking with whoever is available at the moment—will determine the best procedure. But as in all reporting, you will want to touch all bases, from contacting officials to seeking human interest, and to be on the lookout for the unexpected.

Note the emphasis on people in this report by Art Latham of the *New Mexican*, Santa Fe, N.M.:

A 2-year-old boy died in a blaze that swept through a second-floor apartment at Rustic Ridge Apartments on Calle Lorca this morning.

A maintenance man who saw black smoke billowing from the apartment ran to the scene, but was unable to save Robert Tito Reynolds, who was apparently trapped in his bedroom by smoke.

Firefighters sifting through the rubble of charred mattresses and burned baby toys on the scene said the apartments do not have fire doors in the stairwells. They also have only one entrance and exit door per apartment and no fire escapes.

"When I came out of my building, I saw this real heavy black smoke going up past the third floor to the roof. The glass broke on the window when I was running across," maintenance man Wally Patcher said.

"The mother was on her hands and knees down by the door carrying her little baby. I asked her who was in there and she said 'Tito,'" he said.

"I got as far as the bedroom door, and that's as far as I could go. It was just too hot, and everything was burning," Patcher said.

Neither the mother, Kathy Reynolds, nor her infant were hospitalized. . . .

The fire was first spotted about 9:30 a.m. by police officer Bill Lopez, on routine patrol in the area.

Lopez and several neighbors saw a woman with two children in the apartment next to the one on fire and formed a human net to catch the children.

"We made like a group and she threw them down to us. They were about two and three years old. By that time, the fire department had gotten there and she got out by the ladder," Lopez said.

Lopez said Tito Reynolds' badly charred body was found in the corner of his bedroom.

"If he tried to get out, he wasn't successful," he said.

The apartment was a total loss, according to Deputy Fire Chief Mil Fleig. . . .

Preferring people over other angles—such as the increase in number of fires and suspected arson—the Elizabeth (N.J.) *Daily Journal* carried this report:

NEWARK—Five persons, including four children, died Sunday night when they were unable to reach a fire escape during a suspicious blaze in a city-owned tenement that was recently condemned. A sixth person was believed missing.

It was the second tragic blaze here in as many days. Three persons died Saturday morning in a two-alarm fire that broke out in two 2½-story private homes in Newark's Ironbound section.

The blazes bring to five the number of serious fires in the northern New Jersey area over the past month, with at least 38 fatalities.

Newark Fire Director John Caufield said the city had received reports of anonymous threats that the tenement, recently condemned, would be burned down.

Caufield said 17 other people who escaped down fire ladders could have been trapped if the blaze had broken out later at night.

The fire official said he "could not comment" whether an accelerant was spread around the first floor to help fuel the flames.

But, he said, "There was no question in my mind that this fire is definitely suspicious" and added tests would be run on debris to determine what was used to set the blaze.

He said several tenants reported seeing "three young men" running from the building shortly before the fire started. . . .

Student reporters also cover fires. Steve Patton of Temple University, working part-time at the Coatesville (Pa.) *Record*, wrote this report, cited in the William Randoph Hearst annual awards competition in the "breaking-news" category:

Ten people were left homeless by a fire which ripped through their ranch house in South Coatesville late yesterday afternoon.

The fire, of undetermined origin, destroyed the home of Marvin Hubbard, 52, at 9 Upper Gap Road.

In the house when the fire broke out were Hubbard's wife, Elizabeth, 53, two children, Mary Louise, 30, and Kim Lee, 18, and three grandchildren, Veronica, 9, Michael, 4, and Ronald Young, Jr., 22 months. All escaped safely.

According to Modena Fire Chief Leon Pluck, the fire spread through the house quickly, leaving no time to remove any of its contents. The Hubbards, who have lived at the house since 1971, lost everything they owned in the blaze.

"No Idea"

"I have no idea at all about what we're going to do," Mrs. Hubbard said, visibly shaken. "The little we had was in there. We worked hard for what we have and now this happens."

Marvin Hubbard, who is self-employed as a junkyard operator, was returning home from work when he saw his home in flames.

"I was driving my tow truck home from work when I saw smoke coming from the house. When I got there, the place was burning. My son (Kim Lee) told me there was nothing left."

According to Mary Louise, Veronica discovered the fire in her bedroom on the first floor of the two-level house.

She then alerted Kim Lee, who ran to Mrs. Hubbard and told her. Mrs. Hubbard then evacuated everyone from the house.

Modena Fire Co. sounded the first alarm at 3:27 p.m. following a call from a neighbor, Mrs. Louise Allen. Firemen were on the scene minutes later.

The firemen's job was complicated by gusting winds and a shortage of water. According to Pluck, the water supply from the equipment at the scene, which included the Brandywine and West End companies, along with Modena, ran out after about 20 minutes.

Tank trucks were called in from Parkesburg, Cochranville, Pomeroy, and Po-Mar-Lin. However, there was a 10-minute span with no water while the tank trucks were en route to the scene.

Use Creek

Modena Lt. Randy Lowry said firemen dammed up a section of a creek on Woodland Ave. and pumped water from it to the house until the tank trucks arrived.

Another problem was the location of the house. It lies at the top of a hill, making it difficult to move hoses into position. The location on the hill also left the house open to gusting winds.

"When a house is on a hill like that, it's wide open to the wind," Pluck said. "The wind was really strong, and it just pushed the flames."

The fire was declared under control at 4:55 p.m. One fireman suffered a small finger laceration.

The blaze spread quickly throughout the dwelling, burning off most of the roof as well as gutting most of the interior. The Hubbards returned to their home to find only smoldering, charcoal-black wood and crumbling cinder blocks. . . .

Notes

[1]"Murder Case Solved by N.J. Reporter," *Editor & Publisher* (Mar. 31, 1979): p. 17.

[2]J. Norman Swaton and Loren Morgan, *Administration of Justice* (New York: D. Van Nostrand, 1975), p. 100.

[3]Gresham M. Sykes, *Crime and Society* (New York: Random House, 1965, c. 1956), p. 45.

Assignments

1. Write a report on a crime or fire based on an oral report—perhaps on a brief TV report. Include information you obtain from additional phone calls and other sources.
2. Attend a briefing by police officials and/or review the logging for the day in the "blotter" book or case jackets on arrests. Select the most interesting and/or important item and write it up.
3. Develop a feature on a police-related topic, such as the most prevalent crime on or near campus, or the most dangerous corner near the school.
4. Prepare a skit (such as a simulated robbery or arrest in the classroom). It will be better if the rest of the class is caught by surprise. Each student should report on the incident. Do all agree on the facts?
5. Create a live "disaster" scene to report on. Divide your class into two groups: (1) reporters and (2) principal characters—witnesses, victims, and officials. For example, the situation could be the aftermath of a 727 crashing in a farmer's field; principal characters would be a farmer, police chief and officers, fire chief and firepersons, and motorists.

   The instructor may take the role as spokesman for the hospital and city agencies. The instructor may also describe the basic scene: the body of the plane is over here, the wing over there.

   The reporters should take notes standing up, as if they were on the scene.

   You will need a second "disaster" for the same class session in order to have roles as both principals and reporters (all need to play a reporter at some point so each will have something to write up). The second disaster can be something like a bleacher has just caved in on the football field or in the gym.
6. Arrange to spend an evening in the police press room and perhaps, if the class is small, go with the police reporter to a fire or crime scene on several different nights.

11

Courts

Few areas demand as much energy as covering the courts. On the police beat, a story breaks—an accident happens or there is a dramatic violation of law. But after the initial story and immediate followup, the reporter usually goes on to other assignments.

On the court beat, reporters not only follow the court actions of violent, titillating crimes, but develop stories on other aspects as well. Personalities and defendants' and victims' backgrounds, environments, and friends often make news. When a case comes to trial, its disposition can take weeks or months, and a reporter may cover its complexities for the duration.

Reporters assigned to courts often cover several courts and at the same time must stay with time-consuming significant trials. Besides, reporters on courts must constantly work the halls—talk to people, predict strategy for trials, and routinely check court files. While slipping out of a trial to check on records, reporters may miss surprise developments in the courtroom.

Emilie Lounsberry, a young reporter who recently finished her senior year in college, worked part-time for the *Daily Intelligencer,* in Doylestown, Pa. She won Pennsylvania state awards for investigative reporting and other awards. But newly assigned to the local court beat, she knows she is up against stiff competition, veteran Philadelphia reporters plus representatives of other media in the populous Bucks County area.

On a typical day, she arrives at the modern courthouse in Doylestown about 9:30 a.m. She already has spent an hour at the newspaper office before coming to the courthouse.

Her first stop is the reception area of the District Attorney's office, a glassed-in room, in the corridor. Here she picks up two lists. One is of arraignments, with attorneys, charges, and file numbers. The other interests her more—the trials scheduled for that day in the four chambers of the Court of Common Pleas.

There are several items that catch her eye. She would most like to cover the much publicized case of the Bensalem Township school principal being tried for armed robbery, but another reporter from the paper has been assigned to that trial. Also there is an attempted homicide in Warwick Township, and there is a rape trial from the same area of prime circulation. She finds other trials which interest her, especially a drug trial, but the defendant is not from the prime area of circulation. Nevertheless, she says, "Drugs we can do. We just did a series on drugs," and a drug trial would ride the crest of that effort.

She flips the pages. "Let's look at the rest of the week . . . tomorrow doesn't look so good. Oh, boy. . . . Here's drugs on Wednesday. . . . We can wait until then. . . . Here's another nut from Quakertown. . . ."

Lounsberry has voiced her philosophy as to what a paper wants: "Nuts, sex, violence, and public wrongdoing!" She mentioned an upcoming case of a socialite to be tried for allegedly killing her lover: "Now, that case has it all!" Lounsberry eventually will have a chance to cover that one.

On this particular day, a Monday, her choice narrows to a rape case: a local youth accused of raping a 10-year-old girl and assaulting a police officer.

It will be several hours before the trial is to get under way. Lounsberry banters with a dozen persons, including reporters from the big city papers, and picks up a little information here and there.

She talks with:

- A New Britain patrolman who had stopped her recently for driving too fast. They joke a bit.
- A Warrington police officer about a death the night before: "Who was killed? . . . shot? . . . stabbed. . . . Really? . . . I need a good thing." But that is not for today.
- Rural police officers: "They have good arrest and conviction records and are good sources" when cases reach trial. "They even chase after people in snowmobiles."
- A member of the DA's office about his family's vacation trip to Disney World.
- A member of the DA's office, who tells her that the rape suspect will plead guilty.
- An attorney who says the defendant threatened to kill one of the attorneys.

She checks around on this lead, then decides to make the rounds of the prothonotary, the civil records office. Standing at the counter with a pencil in her mouth, she flips through a folder, finds one item that interests her, then tries to talk a clerk into putting the item in a special topical file—a trick she learned from a Philadelphia reporter. The aim is to get the item out of the common current file, which everybody sees. The clerk refuses. Lounsberry slips it among some other items. "I know, I'll put it in next to some (items) that no one is interested in. . . ." (It will be there when she comes back later, and hopefully other reporters will have overlooked it.)

Down at the DA's office she checks a theft case in her area. "What is he charged on? Any good?"

She asks about upcoming drug cases.

She gets back to her anticipated main item for the day. She asks a member of the DA's staff: "Any word?" Answer: "I think we'll get a conviction." Lounsberry: "Anything new? . . . He tried to kill you?" Answer: "No, he's scared to death."

When the case finally comes up, she happens to be back upstairs working on the prothonotary item. A friend in the courtroom comes to tell her to hurry back for the rape case.

The judge is defining the law to the defendant: ". . . forcible compulsion . . . carnal statutory rape . . . indecent assault . . . terroristic threats . . . criminal mischief . . . disorderly conduct . . . simple assault. . . ."

The defendant does not satisfy the judge that he knows what the judge is talking about. The judge declares a recess so the defendant's attorney can go over the charges again.

Lounsberry takes the opportunity to interview the assistant DA. Her questions: "How old is the defendant? His present address? Date of alleged incident? And it occurred in a field? Behind bushes? How old was the girl? At about what time? What did he basically do?"

The assistant DA brushes aside Lounsberry's questions about alleged new threats, but tells Lounsberry the defendant will likely plea ". . . terroristic assault and aggravated assault. . . . I guess that should do it."

At the trial, testimony by the assistant DA describes the handcuffed defendant swinging a chair at an officer and shoving and hitting a policeman in the eye. He also gives the details of the rape in the field and states that the victim described the assailant positively from 13 photos. A guilty plea on the rape charge ends the trial. Sentencing will come later. Lounsberry's article in the *Daily Intelligencer*:

A former Warminster man who has reportedly threatened to kill his attorney, a Bucks County judge and an assistant district attorney, pleaded guilty Monday to raping a 10-year-old Warminster girl and to assaulting a police officer at the time of his arrest.

William Schick, 24, who now resides in Philadelphia, faces up to 40 years in jail as a result of the plea before Bucks County Judge Isaac S. Garb, who deferred sentencing.

According to defense attorney James A. Downey, Schick made death threats against the three during conversations with him last week. Joseph Frontino, the assistant district attorney named in the threats, said no charges will be filed.

Schick encountered the girl, whose name is being withheld by The Daily Intelligencer, in a field behind the Lacy Park Elementary School last Oct. 7, forced her behind a clump of bushes and raped her.

He was arrested on the charge after the victim identified him from a photographic lineup.

Schick was also charged with making threats to District Justice James M. Kelly at the time of his arraignment on the charge last Oct. 31. At that time, Schick became enraged at the charges against him, told Kelly, "I'm going to kill you," and flung a chair into a wall at Kelly's office in Warminster, according to charges.

Kelly testified at the preliminary hearing on the charges in November that when police were summoned, Schick began punching Officer Paul Petrun of the Warminster police department. Petrun suffered an eye injury.

On Monday, Schick pleaded guilty to assaulting Petrun, but charges that he threatened Kelly were dropped by the district attorney's office in exchange for his plea.

An additional charge of corrupting the morals of a minor was also dropped in the plea bargaining session. That charge concerned Schick's alleged offer of $10 to an 8-year-old Warminster girl last Oct. 6 in exchange for sexual favors.

Schick, who remains in Bucks County Prison pending sentencing, gave no reasons for his actions. Downey said he believes last week's threats were made "because Schick's afraid he's going to be sent to state prison."

Lounsberry is now a reporter with the Philadelphia *Inquirer.*

KINDS OF COURTS

Court systems vary from state to state. In the following pages, first consider the system on the West Coast, in California, and then in the East, in Pennsylvania.

California

California has two kinds of courts: (1) trial courts which decide cases on the basis of facts determined in court and on the basis of the judge's understanding of the law, and (2) appellate courts which decide if the justice system has used the right law and if the system has made any errors in the application of the law. If the system has made errors, the appellate courts determine if the errors have affected the outcome of the original trial.[1]

The courts are:

Municipal and Justice Courts. The state's counties are divided into judicial districts. These districts elect municipal and justice court judges. If the population in a district is over 40,000, the district has municipal courts with judges; if the district has less than 40,000, it has justice courts with justices of the peace.

Justice courts rule on claims up to $1,000; municipal courts take care of claims up to $5,000. Both justice and municipal courts can convene as small claims courts, dealing with claims of $500 or less. Such small claims courts are informal. Both plaintiff and defendant must appear in court. The plaintiff cannot appeal, and the court keeps no formal records. If the defendant wishes to appeal, the case is tried anew, or *de novo*, before a judge of the superior court.

Superior Court. California has 58 superior courts, each representing a county or city. These courts (one of them, Los Angeles County, has over 150 judges) handle:

1. Cases involving money over $5,000.
2. Divorces, probate issues (sometimes the department of the superior court which handles probate cases is called the probate court), titles to property, and real property foreclosures.
3. Felonies, including capital crimes.
4. Writs. These include special court orders for a citizen to do something, such as pay child support; they can also be orders to determine an issue such as whether a person is being held legally.
5. Appeals from municipal and justice courts.

Juvenile Court. Superior courts have jurisdiction over juvenile cases. The presiding judge of superior court names a judge or a referee (one who has five years of law practice or more, or five years of probation officer work) to hear juvenile cases.

Courts of Appeal. Divided into five districts, California's intermediate appellate court has five district courts of appeal—in San Francisco, Los Angeles, Sacramento, San Diego, and Fresno. These district courts of appeal review cases on appeal from the superior court, except for the death penalty appeals. These courts take cases pending before the state Supreme Court when the state Supreme Court transfers the cases to a court of appeal.

Supreme Court. A court of last resort, the state Supreme Court's decisions are final. The court also has the authority to remove a judge or suspend or disbar an attorney in the state. The court can take cases pending before a court of appeal prior to any action by the court. Usually this is done with the purpose of clarifying the law when previous rulings appear to be in conflict.

Pennsylvania

A "unified court system" was put into effect in Pennsylvania in 1968, replacing a system in which each court operated independently. All courts are now under the supervision of the Court Administrator's Office, headed by an appointee of the state Supreme Court.[2]

In Pennsylvania, the courts are:

Minor Courts. These are "courts of the first instance" and not "courts of record." Cases may begin here and go up in appeal, but if they do, no record from the first court is included. The minor courts include:

1. District justices of the peace. Each of the "magisterial districts" not served by a "community court" has such a justice.
2. "Community courts" with a judge for 75,000 persons. When voted on, these courts replace and consolidate the jurisdiction of district justices of the peace.
3. Municipal and traffic courts, as in Philadelphia, which deal with minor offenses. Philadelphia Traffic Court handles driving offenses. Pittsburgh has Police Magistrates, appointed by the mayor and approved by the city council, who rule on minor offenses.

Courts of Common Pleas. Generally following county lines, 67 counties in Pennsylvania have 59 judicial districts, and each district has one Court of Common Pleas. Areas of jurisdiction include criminal, civil, juvenile, and domestic.

Commonwealth Court. The Commonwealth Court is a result of the 1968 state constitutional revisions and is responsible for cases involving the state of Pennsylvania and its agencies. (Formerly, the common pleas court in a specified county sat as the commonwealth or state court.)

Superior Court. The Superior Court hears appeals from Courts of Common Pleas (if the cases have not been sent to the Supreme or Commonwealth Courts). Appeals in criminal cases (except felonious homicide) come here.

Supreme Court. In the Supreme Court, the ultimate state court, most cases come by the appellate route, but some may come directly from courts of common pleas. Such cases may be felonious homicide, law practice disbarment, or constitutional questions.

TYPES OF LAW

"Law" comes from the Anglo-Saxon, a plural of "lag," something "laid down," akin to the English "lay" and "lie." The Latin "lex, legis" (not related to "lag" or "law") meant to collect and bring together, the basis of the words "legislature" and "legal."

"Law" has had different meanings in history, each determined at times by the cultural and national experience. In primitive society, law was the result of an established routine rather than the result of deliberate action. Customs in primitive societies often acquire the luster of being sacred.

In later societies, as philosophers such as Aristotle observed the "commonness" of experience and the archetypal behavior necessary for survival, the concept of natural law from which one should not depart in order to be truly human formed a guiding basis for members of a group. Embodiments of "natural law" range from the Ten Commandments ("thou shalt not kill," "thou shalt not steal," and so on) to systematization of natural law and the writing of social contracts or constitutions based on natural themes (for example, the Declaration of Independence's "life, liberty, and the pursuit of happiness").

Science and mathematics have their own laws: the laws of gravity, molecular behavior, temperature, aerodynamics, and other rules which, when applied, produce expected results. There are also the laws or principles of multiplication, algebra, and calculus.

Laws that govern our behavior are determined by consensus and enforced by designated authorities. Groups such as ball teams set *regulations*, a legislative body passes *statutes*, local councils pass *ordinances*, and church officials create *canons*. But "canons" can also be seen as natural and essential laws of society, "the canons of society."

The earliest known collection of laws is the Hammurabi Code, named after a king of Babylon in the 20th Century B.C. Ancient laws had the principle of *lex talionis*, "law of revenge," an eye for an eye and a tooth for a tooth. Modern law has a *substantive* side, which defines what is right and wrong behavior, and an *adjective* side, which defines the rules and places the responsibility for implementing them.[3]

In Greece, an early codifier of laws was Solon in the Fifth Century B.C. His name is still used today, as some headline writers will say "solons" for legislators or other policy makers. Solon made laws more supportive of the individual and inaugurated a system of appeal from local magistrates to a group of individuals organized into a court. Despite the democratic values in dispensing judgment from large bodies, the appeals procedure allowed inconsistencies and political tampering. Nevertheless, early Greek law did contribute the idea that law must be for the common good and be representative of the people.

Romans divided their laws into "custom" or unwritten law (*ius non scriptum*) and written law (*ius scriptum*). As with the Greeks, assemblies dispensed justice, but only a magistrate could place a matter before the assembly for a ruling.

When the English system developed, it depended on prior cases and decisions which formed the basis for future decisions. A judge based decisions not on precise formulas, but on precedent cases. Common law justice tended to "let the decision" of previous cases "stand" (*stare decisis*). At first much American law was based on English common law, but today most law here derives from statutory law formulated by legislatures. However, common law does help to interpret the meaning of a particular law in practice. The English also developed a separate court or chancery which imposed immediate remedies. Today, "cases in equity" differ from "cases in law," for judges in a lower court can make "equitable" judgment on their own with injunctions without reference to a tradition of law.

Law usually fits into two categories: public (the state has an interest and is a part of the process) and civil (private or personal) law.

Glossary of Court and Legal Terms

Some legal terms you should know:

Affidavit: A document sworn to be the truth by a police officer, a witness, or a person involved in a legal or criminal action.

Amicus curiae: Friend of the court. This is an official intervention by a third party on the side of one party in a proceeding.

Arraignment: A formal court hearing where the court presents the defendant in a criminal case with a copy of the charges against him or her and gives the defendant the chance to enter a plea to the charges.

Award: The amount a jury decides the winner of a civil suit should receive. An award is not a settlement.

Burden of proof: The prosecutor in a criminal trial has the burden of proving a defendant guilty beyond a reasonable doubt. The defendant does not have to prove his or her innocence. The court presumes the defendant innocent until a prosecutor can prove guilt to the jury.

Change of venue motion: Attorney on either side of a case wants the case to be tried in another district or another county, usually because of pretrial publicity or because the defendant can't get a fair trial in the original location.

Complaint: An allegation, stated in writing, of the basis of the charge.

Class action suit: Filed by a group of people who share a common concern.

Continued: The case has been postponed. "Postponed" is the better word to use.

Defendant: The person charged in criminal court with committing a crime, or the person charged in civil court by the plaintiff.

Domicile: One's "permanent" home.

Demur: A plea that admits the facts are true but insists they are factually irrelevant.

De novo: (As in a defendant being granted a trial *de novo*.) In an appeal situation, the higher court does not hear arguments by the lawyers but convenes a new trial and hears all the evidence again, arriving at a new verdict and possibly passing a new sentence if guilty; in Kansas, usually a municipal court appeal to a district court.

Deposition: A written statement made under oath by a party to the lawsuit and usually sealed in the court file until the case actually comes to trial. (Says Steven C. Lachowicz of the Wenatchee, Wash., *World*: "Depositions can be a great source of background information which occasionally lead to investigative follow-ups.")

Discovery: A proceeding under which a defense attorney may learn facts the prosecutor knows.

Dismissal with or without prejudice: A suit dismissed with prejudice cannot be filed again; a suit dismissed without prejudice can.

Docket: A sheet or page of a logbook on which a judge makes entries concerning the actions taken at each step of a court case. Also a calendar of court hearings.

Eminent domain: The right to claim private property for necessary use by the state. (Used to claim path for new highways and public utilities.)

Entered no plea: In a felony case, the court will decide on the plea. (Courts, however, usually insist on a not guilty plea if a question of guilt exists.)

Escrow: Money or deed held by a third party until completion of promised performance; surety to guarantee the agreement.

Estoppel: A person's action; an acceptance which negates any later attempt to change his or her mind.

Garnishment: Action in which a person's salary, property, or other income is attached to pay a debt.

In camera hearing: Private hearing in judge's chamber ("camera" means "room"); used when confidential business records are necessary for evidence in a case. Also used when the judge reviews questionable evidence which attorneys want the judge to suppress at a pretrial suppression hearing.

Initial appearance (many times confused with arraignment): Where the court formally charges the defendant and sets bond.

Innocent: The proper term is "not guilty." (However, most reporters should use "innocent" only because it prevents the inadvertent typesetting mistake of dropping the "not." "Thus, it really is a newspaper term applied to the courts, and an excellent safety valve," says Robert K. Entriken Jr. of the Salina, Kan., *Journal*.)

Inter alia: Among other things.

Inter alios: Among other persons.

Interrogatories: Questions served on a person before a trial which must be answered under oath in writing. Also, questions asked of witnesses in court.

Intervention: A third person is allowed to become a third party in a suit.

Juvenile delinquent: This means different things in different states; the reporter should be aware of terms in this sensitive area. In some states it refers to any antisocial youth; in others such as Kansas, however, it means a minor charged with a felony crime.

Leading question: Tells a witness how to answer or suggests wording for the answer to a question.

Memorandum of authorities: More commonly known as a "brief," a memorandum explains the issue as one side sees it and offers argument, including citations, from previous case law.

No bill: A statement by a grand jury that it found no evidence for an indictment.

Nolle prosequi,* or *nol pros: The state declines to prosecute on charges, usually in exchange for guilty or no contest pleas on other charges; the court may also use it when the case is unprovable.

Nolle prosse: Dismissed.

Nolo contendere,* or *"no contest": A criminal plea in which the defendant does not admit guilt (he or she merely "does not contest," or dispute, the allegation), but the judge is empowered to make a finding of guilt or pass sentence. It almost guarantees a conviction, but the plea cannot be used as proof of guilt in subsequent proceedings, such as civil action.

Non vult: Person who enters a "no defense" plea to murder charge.

Parole: Essentially the same as probation but applying to persons released from prison early.

Plaintiff: Initiates a personal action or lawsuit against another to obtain remedy for a personal injury or loss.

Plea bargain: An agreement before trial in which a defendant agrees to plead guilty in return for dismissal of other charges, probation, or lesser sentence.

Preponderance of evidence: The most credible evidence (not simply the most).

Presentence investigation: The judge orders an investigation of the defendant's past if the defendant has been found guilty. The sentence depends on this investigation.

Probation: Court-imposed restrictions in return for suspending a prison sentence.

Pro tem: Refers to a substitute judge presiding over a court.

Recognizance agreement: Between the court and a person accused of a crime who, when released from custody, promises to appear at any future courtroom proceedings in his or her case. Under such an agreement no bail or bond is required, only the word of the accused consenting to be available when necessary.

Riparian rights (water law): The principle that whoever has access to free-flowing water has the right to use that water and return it "undiminished" to the stream from which it was diverted. (Riparian comes from the Latin word meaning "river.")

Sentencing: The order of a judge confining a person convicted of a crime to a jail or institution, based on the punishment a jury has prescribed.

Sine qua non: Literally, "without which nothing" (Latin); something that is absolutely necessary.

Stands mute: An option a defendant sometimes exercises in a criminal action. Instead of entering a plea of guilty or not guilty, the defendant may choose to stand mute—not enter a plea. Judges often will not accept this plea.

Stipulation: An agreement of both attorneys admitting certain facts and waiving evidence to prove the facts.

Subpoena duces tecum,* or more commonly *duces tecum: Literally, a subpoena to carry something along. It may be a subpoena for a person to bring documents, usually office files or autopsy notes, to court.

Suspended sentence: Most commonly used when a judge imposes a jail term, orders the defendant to serve only part or none of it, and suspends the rest.

Tender of proof: Testimony that may or may not be relative to the case for which the attorney must prove relevancy to the judge before presenting the testimony to the jury. The attorney presents the testimony to the judge after the jury has been removed from the courtroom. Each side has the opportunity to argue if the jury should hear the testimony. The judge then rules.

Tort: An injury or wrong to a person or property caused without force for which a civil action can be taken.

Voir dire: Examining witnesses or jurors to determine their qualifications.

Withheld judgment: A sentence, which is completed to the court's satisfaction, will result in the dismissal of charges (procedurally different from a delayed imposition).

Writ: An order from a court calling for a definite action; it gives a person or group the right to perform the required act.

Writ of certiorari: An order for review and certification of the decision-making process (most commonly designed to see if a planning commission or board of adjustment or board of elected officials acted properly in a ruling on a land use application). It compels the judge of a lower court to certify return of records of proceedings in a review of an action.

Writ of habeas corpus: A court order requiring a person be brought to court at a definite time for a ruling on the legality of his or her detention—it literally means "You should have the body." The term is most often used in connection with criminal defendants in federal court to challenge a conviction on the grounds that his or her constitutional rights were violated (for example, the defendant was beaten, illegally searched, or seized), and the defendant seeks release from custody on grounds of invalid conviction.

Writ of mandamus: Issued by a judge when a government body has failed to do something required by law. (*Mandamus* means "We command" in Latin.)

Writ of replevin: The issuance of such a writ enables the owner of property held by another to claim possession of that property.

A word of caution: Don't get in the lazy habit of repeating technical terms. Rather, if you must use a technical word, also include a definition set off by commas or parentheses. It is often advisable to ask attorneys and others using technical words to tell you what they mean. Anybody can repeat a big word. As a good reporter and writer, make sure you and your readers know what the term means.

PRETRIAL PROCEDURE

A trial is similar to a drama. The boundaries of a courtroom compare to that of a stage, and the conflicts, with all of their ramifications, unfold before the audience. But the drama is not limited to the "stage." Before the trial, personality conflicts, plot strategies, and the complexities of human psychology unfold as the participants try to clarify issues and determine facts on the one hand, and protect the interests of various parties on the other.

Private persons or firms bring civil suits against other individuals or firms. Criminal cases involve action by the "people"—the state—against individuals or companies.

A civil action begins with the filing of a *petition*, also called a *complaint* or *statement of claim*.[4] Civil actions come under two headings: (1) real and mixed actions and (2) personal actions. A real action involves an attempt to recover the loss of land or the denial of access to land. A personal action seeks to recover personal property or damages for a legal right which allegedly has been violated.

Personal actions deal with breach of contract or an injury with or without force to another person or to that person's property. Among actions taken for breach of contract are:

1. ***Assumpsit.*** This is action taken as a result of a broken promise or agreement, oral or written. (*Assumpsit* is Latin for "he or she has undertaken.")
2. ***Foreign attachment.*** If a party is holding property of one against whom a suit has been filed, a plaintiff can make an attachment against that property even though it has been moved to a third party.
3. ***Replevin.*** Action is taken to recover goods taken from the plaintiff without proper procedure. The action tests the plaintiff's right to have the goods. (From *replegiare*, "to recover the pledge".)
4. ***Action of deceit.*** This attempts to recover damages where fraud was used.
5. ***Trover.*** This action calls for the defendant to return goods which he or she found but refused to return; it is also an action to recover damages for the defendant's illegal use of the plaintiff's goods or the withholding of goods lawfully belonging to the plaintiff. (From the French *trover*, "to find.")

In the filing of a civil action, the action states:

1. Title, name of court, county, names of parties in the action, the plaintiff, and defendant.
2. A short clear statement of facts explaining the action, with each allegation numbered.
3. A call for "relief" to which the plaintiff feels he or she is entitled. A money sum must be precise.

For an action to begin, traditionally some form of notice is given to the defendant, such as a process (court order compelling defendant's attendance in court), writ, or summons. Some courts today assume the action is under way with the filing of the complaint. Reporters should know the policy in their own states, for an intended action may be political or serve some personal cause.

The usual course of a civil suit leading up to a court action is summarized in a booklet from a California judges' group:

—Plaintiff files an action with the court.
—Clerk of the court issues a summons.
—Defendant has at least 20 days to file his answer or demurrer with the clerk of the court. If the defendant fails to respond in the time allowed by law, the plaintiff may file for a default judgment.

—Defendant may answer—that is, admit or deny each of the plaintiff's allegations and set forth any reasons why the plaintiff is not entitled to the relief he seeks.
—Defendant may demur or say that even if everything in the complaint is true, it still doesn't prove his liability. So a demurrer is concerned with the question of whether the facts pleaded to constitute a cause of action; a demurrer may also call attention to some particular defect in the complaint.
—Defendant may cross-complain, making claims of his own against the plaintiff. The parties then become known as "plaintiff and cross-defendant" and "defendant and cross-complainant."
—Plaintiff may demur to the cross-complaint.
—Plaintiff or defendant may move for a summary judgment.
—Plaintiff or defendant may take discovery procedures against the other side; usually each will do so. That is, each takes the depositions or sworn testimony of witnesses on the other side or demands sworn answers to certain written questions or interrogatories. The other side must answer these questions if they are proper.
—Either side may make additional pretrial motions.
—When the case is "at issue," one side may make a motion to set for trial. But before the actual trial begins, there will usually be a pretrial conference with a judge to see which questions can be disposed of by stipulation or prior agreement and whether there is any chance for an agreement or settlement before trial.
—Most of these motions and pretrial hearings are appealable; one side, for example, may feel that a demurrer was improperly permitted or sustained. So it goes to a higher court, usually a court of appeal, for review. This may set off a new chain of hearings and appeals, and sometimes several years may elapse before a case comes to trial.
—Either side may ordinarily demand and get a jury trial. However, the trial may not be a final determination either.[5]

In pretrial criminal procedure the person, following arrest, makes an appearance before a judge to be identified, advised of his or her rights and the charges, and to have bail set. The judge also sees that the person has counsel; if the accused cannot afford a lawyer, the judge appoints a public defender. At the arraignment, the judge asks how the defendant pleads: guilty or not guilty. The court may then hold a preliminary hearing to decide if a crime has indeed been committed and if there are reasons to believe the defendant committed or contributed to the crime. The state presents its evidence.

In federal court, no preliminary hearing is held if the grand jury indicts first. In other words, once a defendant is arrested, either a judge or a grand jury can find probable cause. If the grand jury finds probable cause first, a preliminary hearing is essentially unnecessary.

If the judge orders the defendant to stand trial, the defendant is again arraigned in a process called *rearraignment*. The purposes are the same as the prior arraignment: to identify the defendant, to let the defendant know his or her rights, to make provisions for counsel, to present a copy of the information or indictment, and to take a plea from the defendant on the charges.

In some jurisdictions, the defense attorney may file a number of motions before the trial begins. These motions may seek to set aside the information or indictment for procedural and other reasons, to suppress evidence gathered illegally and deny its use in court, or to seek an insanity hearing.

FEDERAL COURTS

While every state has its own court system to handle state crimes such as murder or assault or civil disputes such as auto accidents, the federal government also operates a court system. Federal courts, however, handle only special cases. For example, federal prosecutors, called U.S. attorneys, may prosecute such federal crimes as embezzlement or bank robberies (because banks are federally insured), racketeering (which involves crimes of interstate commerce), and wire or mail fraud (which involves the use of the telephone or the U.S. Postal Service). Civil suits in federal court will involve violations of federal laws such as maritime claims, discrimination charges, or antitrust claims. In addition, all bankruptcy actions are filed in federal court and are handled by special bankruptcy judges. Finally, all civil suits against a defendant who lives in a different state from the plaintiff will be filed in federal court under the court's "diversity jurisdiction."

Federal court has three levels:

1. ***District courts*** have jurisdiction over many counties and in some parts of the country over the whole state. They are comprised of magistrates, who arraign and set bail for criminal defendants and conduct preliminary hearings or minor trials, and district judges, who preside over major trials. When a case challenges the constitutionality of a law, the judges may sit as a panel of three to hear the case.
2. ***Circuit courts*** hear appeals of federal cases from several states. The judges make a final ruling in the cases in written opinions.
3. ***The U.S. Supreme Court*** hears all federal appeals and some state appeals. Its nine judges are responsible for interpreting the law and establishing precedents that lower court judges will use in deciding cases.

Other federal courts handle tax matters and claims against the government.

TRIAL PROCEDURE

In addition to the judge and attorneys, the principals in a court include the bailiff, who keeps order, and the court clerk, who convenes the session and gives the oath to each witness. The clerk keeps the records of the proceedings. The court reporter transcribes all of the proceedings for the record.

If a jury takes part in the trial, the court calls a panel of veniremen, or potential jurors—usually the number is double those who will serve on the jury. Attorneys and judges question the veniremen. If an attorney thinks a particular person should not serve on the jury, the person is challenged. Challenges can be one of two types: a *challenge for cause* is based on a reason, perhaps resulting from an unsatisfactory answer, whereas a *peremptory* challenge can be made without a reason given. Laws limit the number of such peremptory challenges to five, six, or seven. If the court does not select the jury from the original panel, then it selects additional persons (*talesmen*) for the panel—in some lower courts it chooses from the audience, although this practice is rare.

Steps at a jury trial in a civil case include:

1. ***Opening speeches.*** These are informative rather than argumentative speeches. The attorney for the plaintiff begins by giving the reason for the suit, identifying the parties, stating the damages sought, and summarizing the evidence to be introduced. In some courts, the defendant's attorney may then proceed to make his statement; in other courts, the defendant's attorney may not give a statement until the plaintiff has offered all of his or her evidence.
2. ***Direct examination.*** The attorney who is the first to call a witness to the stand can ask the first questions in this face-to-face or direct examination.
3. ***Cross-examination.*** The opposing attorney follows through with questions to find weaknesses in a witness's testimony. The judge may ask questions at any time; the jurors may do so also, although they seldom do.
4. ***Redirect examination.*** Following the cross-examination, the attorney who introduced a witness may reexamine the witness about any new information that may have come up in the cross-examination.
5. ***Conclusion of plaintiff's evidence.*** The defendant's attorney may ask a "move for a nonsuit" or "demur to the evidence." These are references

to points of law—to demur, or enter a demurrer—which question whether the evidence supports the facts for the purpose for which they are offered.

6. ***Statement by defendant's attorney.*** This may come earlier after the statement of the plaintiff's attorney.
7. ***Direct examination of witnesses by defendant's attorney.***
8. ***Cross-examination by plaintiff's attorney.***
9. ***Plaintiff's rebuttal.*** After the defendant's witnesses have testified, the plaintiff's witnesses often need to speak again, and the plaintiff's attorney may call them to respond to any new material.
10. ***Directed verdicts.*** If the trial so far makes it clear that one party in the trial has failed to make a case, or if a verdict is obvious, the judge can direct a jury to make the obvious decision but leave other matters such as amount of damages to the jury. The motion comes from one of the attorneys, usually after the evidence is in, but can come at any point in the trial.
11. ***Final arguments.*** The attorney for the plaintiff gives the first summary, then the defendant's attorney summarizes his case. The plaintiff's attorney receives one more final response.
12. ***Charge to the jury.*** The judge reviews the evidence on both sides of the trial, reminds the jury that it is to make its decision based on the facts only, and instructs the jury on the law and the necessary elements of the crime the jury must look for in order to convict.

Reporters may find themselves on the stand, cooperating to the point of clarifying facts without surrendering their notes. Testifying is a new experience for most reporters, and they have their moments of trepidation.

If you have the rare experience of testifying in court, you might want to consult the *Handbook of Courtroom Demeanor and Testimony* (Prentice-Hall, 1971) by C. A. Pantaleoni. It contains advice from the International Association of Chiefs of Police, Inc. (excerpted from Training Key #8) on how to respond to tactics of attorneys in cross-examination.

PROBLEMS IN COVERING THE COURTS

Court reporting is a complex job: reporters must be alert every second and plan every moment of their time.

The problems include:

1. ***Keeping track of cases and the progress of trials.*** "There are so many cases and so many delays," says Maria Puente of the Santa Fe *New Mexican*. "Keep a list, keep in touch with DAs on the case, keep a 'tickle' file, talk to judges, check the court clerk's office to look through the files."

   Says J. Richard Pellington of the Ocean County (N.J.) *Times Observer*: "Don't panic, take items one at a time, and use a personal priority system."

   Jim Dowd of the Janesville (Wis.) *Gazette*: "The major problem (after learning the lingo) I have had is keeping track of and obtaining all of the open court records. I have set up specific times when I will be in to check the records."

2. ***Learning the courtroom procedure and jargon.*** "My method of solving this problem," says Jack Kilgore of the *Southwest Times Record* in Ft. Smith, Ark., "was simply by asking questions when I didn't understand something. Of course, a course in covering courts goes a long way."

3. ***Getting court information by phone.*** Says Robert K. Entriken, Jr., of the Salina (Kan.) *Journal*:

   Probably the biggest problem is reporting the other 31 district courts, which must of necessity be done by telephone. Dealing with 31 county attorneys, sheriffs, and judges brings up many variants. While some are open, others are maddeningly secretive—often because they are afraid the reporter is going to blow the case. . . . It also doesn't hurt to do the prosecutor a favor. In a case involving a multi-county burglary ring, I'd let one prosecutor know what happened to the defendant in another county, usually before he'd get the word from official sources.

4. ***Keeping objective.*** Says Ed Mohler of the Boseman (Mont.) *Daily Chronicle*:

   In a small town, rumors are frequently more interesting than fact, and it may be difficult to avoid prejudicial reporting. Efforts must be taken to independently verify allegations that may circulate on the street before issues reach court. Reporters must also be watchdogs of their own accuracy: On small papers, where the quality of copy editing is uneven or lacking, it is especially important for reporters to double-check their copy for possible factual errors and make sure they have written what they want to before copy crosses an editor's desk.

5. ***Beating competition.*** Says Jim Deal of *The Argus*, in Rock Island, Ill.:

   In the west-central Illinois news market, there are three major daily newspapers, three active television news departments and four active radio news departments—not to mention numerous weekly newspapers. Beating the competition here is tough. It is necessary each day to contact every news source on the beat and check every loose piece of paper for possible leads on stories. A reporter must keep track of ongoing controversies and be alert for any tip a news source might let slip in conversation.

Tips for Covering Courts

Veteran reporters, drawing from their own experiences when they were novices, suggest:

Know the background of the case. Before you begin covering anything in the courts, be able to summarize in your own mind chronologically all the events leading up to the trial.

Get to know the court clerk at each court. Judges may be too busy to talk about a case, but clerks of courts will likely be talkative.

Keep a file on arrests. Some, such as Carolyn Bower of the Riverton (Wyo.) *Ranger*, feel that the only way to be a court reporter is to be a police reporter "so you can follow the case from the arrest to the sentencing or dismissal."

Be patient. The wheels of justice do indeed grind slowly. Don't get ahead of yourself. You're not sure anything will happen. "A writer can't even say the jury will have to decide," says Nancy Landis of *The Messenger* in Madisonville, Ky. "The jury may not reach a verdict at all."

Be impartial. Each side has its story to tell. Until the court renders a decision, each story is equally valid.

Verify everything. Courts constitute a very sensitive area. A small error, even a mistyped letter or word, can be libelous more easily in court stories than in others. Says Robert K. Entriken, Jr., of the Salina (Kan.) *Journal*:

> I have found that reporters substituting for me make most of their errors simply by assuming that what was, still is. The classic example is the felony defendant who pleads guilty to a lesser offense. The sub doesn't pick up the reduction and reports him admitting grand theft when in fact he pleaded to petty theft—and that could be libel.

Ask questions. Says Entriken:

> As Linus, in "Peanuts," once noted, even stupid questions have answers. Even if you think you know the answer, ask anyway. It goes back to verifying everything. If something seems funny, ask about it. The

answer may at least make a good quote and . . . may clear up what could have been a libelous error.

Establish ground rules regarding the mechanics of court coverage with the presiding judge. Says Ed Mohler of the Bozeman (Mont.) *Daily Chronicle*: "It is a little awkward to be cited for contempt simply because, for example, you didn't know the judge doesn't like cameras in the courtroom!"

Differentiate between official records and other argument or rumor. Report each for what it is.

Be wary of attorneys. "Some are hired guns," says Bozeman's Mohler. "Some are real hip-shooters who are not above using the press to promote their clients' cases. They may be waiting in ambush. . . ."

Use legal terminology sparingly and correctly. If you use legal terms, be sure to explain them. Make sure your definitions are correct.

Summarize lengthy testimony. Be selective: concentrate on the points that are most relevant to the case.

Get to know the judge. He is not God Almighty.

Be polite in all contacts. Treat everyone, from the court attendants right up to the judge, deferentially.

Keep track of each judge's docket. Know when cases are coming up for trial or for plea bargain or sentencing.

Familiarize yourself with all kinds of legal proceedings. Go to trials—little ones, big ones, hearings, pretrial hearings, sentencings, arraignments, and plea agreements: ". . . anything at all to become familiar with the way EVERYTHING WORKS," says Marie Puente of the Santa Fe *New Mexican*.

Know the system. Know what the steps are after a person is arrested. Also know the law and where to go for further information.

Look for stories in minor cases. "Murders take care of themselves," says Bill Stewart of *The Columbian* in Vancouver, Wash. "But in minor cases you may find some good human interest stories, or such cases may lead you to something more important."

Respect the defendant's right to a fair trial. Hold information that might threaten the just hearing of a defendant.

Get to know people at various levels in the courts. Judges may be too busy to talk about a case, but clerks of courts will likely be talkative. Says Steven Lachowicz of the Wenatchee (Wash.) *World*:

> The deputy clerks in the office can tip you off on what's about to happen or what has just happened. That's the only way you're going to find out what you thought would be a routine ruling on a pretrial motion turned into a contempt sentence when the out-of-town attorney called the judge a dirty name. The lower-level workers will be a much better source of initial information than the judges or the prosecutors or the defense attorneys.

HOW THEY DID IT

Make a list of ideas you get from the following examples of reporting on courts coast to coast. Each of these reporters offers some pointers on how to write court stories.

1. The Headline

"Deliberations Expected to Begin in Damage Suit," by Carolyn Bower of the Riverton (Wyo.) *Ranger.*

The Reporter's Comments

> The only way to write this particular article was to attend the hearing. But background, such as how much the man was asking for in damages, came from the suit filed at the district court. The clerk of court was the source for obtaining a copy of such a document.
>
> Other background was obtained by going over the police report and records the night the incident occurred. However, the events of the night in question became the main topic at the hearing; therefore going over the records wasn't necessary. I must admit though it sure helps in reporting to know what happened that particular night before going into the courtroom. I talked to the policemen involved. The lawsuit gave me the plaintiff's side of the story.
>
> The hardest part of covering trials such as [this one] is being able to get all the questions asked by attorneys and answers by the witness

down on paper before the next question is asked. That is why it is important to know most of the facts before the trial, so you know what needs to be in the story, and what minor facts can be left out. . . .

The Story

A four-woman, two-man Fremont County Distrct Court jury is expected to begin deliberations today following final arguments by attorneys in a damage suit filed by a Riverton man claiming he was battered by a policeman.

Gene W. Arnell claims he was struck by Riverton Police Sgt. James B. Ringer in a malicious manner following his arrest on a number of traffic offenses in September 1976.

The 19-year-old is asking for over $50,000 in compensatory and punitive damages in the lawsuit and names Sgt. Ringer and the city of Riverton as defendants.

After the jury was selected the plaintiff Arnell was the first to tesify yesterday morning. He described the events of Sept. 13, 1976, that led to his arrest.

Arnell was pursued by a police officer after he was clocked speeding on N. Federal beginning at approximately 12:30 a.m. and a chase ensued.

Arnell admitted during the chase he reached speeds of up to 100 miles per hour and ran two roadblocks in an attempt to elude the police.

The plaintiff stated that after he was apprehended at his home on the 500 block of N. First E. that Sgt. Ringer struck him in the eye with handcuffs during the routine frisk.

"He hit me hard enough to knock me off my feet," Arnell testified, adding that he did keep his balance.

After Arnell was transported to the police department he said he "felt out of it" and that his eye was burning and dripping with blood.

Arnell, who didn't ask for medical attention during his overnight stay at the city jail, said he went to the emergency room at the Riverton hospital the following night at 9 p.m. after his mother saw his condition.

The plaintiff said Dr. Ferris, who attended to him that night, told him to see an eye specialist because the doctor didn't have the equipment.

Acting as attorney for the city and Sgt. Ringer, Lakewood, Colo. lawyer Martin W. Burke asked Arnell how much he had to drink the night of the incident.

Arnell, who was 17 years old at the time, said he had two 12-ounce cups of beer within a half hour.

Burke repeatedly questioned the witness of his whereabouts the day of the arrest, but Arnell said he couldn't remember. . . .

Arnell was questioned many times concerning the fact that he didn't go see a doctor until 11 hours after he was released from jail and why it took him five days to see the specialist the emergency room doctor recommended, but Arnell said he didn't want the doctor to mess with it (eye) because he knew it would hurt him.

On re-direct, Arnell's attorney Rich Hollon asked the plaintiff why he didn't ask the police for medical attention at the jail and Arnell responded, "I didn't know I could ask for it."

Dave Libby, a man who said he watched the arrest procedure the night of the incident, was called to testify after the luncheon recess.

Libby, who lived one block from the scene of the arrest, said he got out of bed and dressed because he thought he heard a car roll over, and he went out to help.

Libby testified that Ringer looked tired and shook-up at the scene, when he was asked to describe the officer's behavior. Libby also said he saw Arnell being escorted by two other officers, and that it appeared he needed the help of the policemen to stand up.

"He (Arnell) was crying, his head

was tilted down, and he looked very weary," Libby said of Arnell's appearance. He also said he noticed Arnell's right eye was puffy and that blood was trickling down his face and that there was blood on his jacket.

"Because of what I'd seen I just stood there," Libby continued. "I couldn't believe what I had seen." Libby, who began to expound on the emotional feelings he felt that night, was stopped by an objection by the defendant's counsel.

Billy Weber, Arnell's mother, said when she returned from a trip to Laramie, she accompanied her son to the hospital. She testified her son was not able to see the recommended specialist (Dr. James H. Fontaine) for five days because she couldn't get an appointment any sooner. . . .

Dr. Fontaine, a Lander ophthalmologist, said after he conducted a number of tests and X-ray examinations on Arnell that he found a small hemorrhage on his retina.

During cross-examination, Dr. Fontaine stated the hemorrhage has no permanent effect on the eye and will go away with time.

Sgt. Earl Hinkle and Officer John Fisher both took the stand as adverse witnesses for the plaintiff. Hollon questioned the two repeatedly concerning police arrest procedure and their fellow officer's (Ringer) behavior the night of the arrest. . . .

Fisher was questioned many times by Hollon concerning the use of a gun when stopping a suspect on a traffic violation. "Through my study of law enforcement," Fisher said, "I was taught when someone was fleeing from an officer that he may have something to hide."

Fisher said officers draw their guns for their own protection, and that he felt an officer could initiate an assault on a suspect if he felt he needed to defend himself.

Both police officers were asked to relate scenes of the night, and both told the court of the two roadblocks that Arnell ran and the pursuit that lasted for over an hour.

Hollon told the Ranger following yesterday's session he was planning on calling Sgt. Ringer to testify today. The trial is scheduled to end today.

2. The Headline

"Drunk Driving Conviction Cover-Up Admitted," by Jim Dowd of the Janesville (Wis.) *Gazette*.

The Reporter's Comments

Court clerks were first overheard withholding a traffic conviction. My own investigation showed the case involved a drunken driving charge and also the son of a doctor.

I made personal contact with the judge, who denied knowledge but promised to look into it. The clerk finally released information the next week but refused to say who had ordered it withheld. I wrote the original story saying it was withheld but was unable to report who was responsible.

Ultimately, the judge admitted he did so, based on an inherent power. He stated medical condition of the youth required it withheld. The district attorney ruled otherwise.

The Story

An attempt to cover up publicity of a drunken driving conviction in Judge Gerald Jaeckle's court was admitted today, but the person who ordered the public record to be kept secret remains anonymous.

The case involves Andrew Kronquist, 17, of 349 Greendale, who was arrested for operating an auto the wrong way on a one-way street and operating an auto while intoxicated last October.

Kronquist had been scheduled to go to trial on the two charges last Thursday; however, due to plea bargaining between his attorney and the city attorney's office, the driving the wrong way on a one-way street charge was dropped in lieu of a guilty plea to drunken driving.

Last Tuesday, Jaeckle accepted the plea and fined Kronquist $205 and ordered his license revoked for 90 days.

When a Gazette court reporter attempted to collect results of last week's court action, the Kronquist file was withdrawn from the rest of the records.

Subsequent investigation indicated that the reason clerks in Rock County Court Branch 3 withheld the file was due to a note attached saying that it should not be released.

Jaeckle said Friday that if a file had been kept from the public it was not done on purpose, and he could "guarantee that it was inadvertently done."

A clerk who handles traffic cases in Branch 3 released the disposition of the case this morning at a direct request from a reporter. When asked why the file had not been included with the others last week, she replied, "I was told not to."

When asked who had told her not to release it, she replied, "I can't say. I don't want to get anyone in trouble."

Jaeckle maintained Friday that his court has "religiously" abided by all of the court ethics involving public records and the press. "The Kronquist name doesn't mean a thing to me," he remarked.

When questioned about the matter Friday afternoon, Jaeckle assured the Gazette reporter that he would look into the incident. "I'll find out," he said.

3. The Headline

"Investigators Muffed Case, Jurors Say," by Mary R. Heffron of the *Sentinel Star* in Orlando, Fla.

The Reporter's Comments

Coverage of a trial generally ends with the verdict. But when a major drug trial here ended with a hung jury, my editors and I felt a little more was called for. Initially, I began with a tip that jury tampering might have been involved.

But, after talking with five of the six jurors (in Florida, only capital cases get 12 jurors) in the trial of a prominent local businessman for cocaine conspiracy and possession, I came to the conclusion that rather than some criminal act, the problem was a bungled case by local law enforcement agencies that have had more than their share of internal problems of late. In "headlinese," the investigators muffed the case.

I began by getting the names of the jurors, which are public record but were not in the trial file because the judge's court clerk had not yet transcribed the notes of the trial. To get them I had to go to a couple of offices and ask a couple of questions.

The clerk gave me six names but no addresses. Here I had two choices. I could go to the voter registration office and get addresses for the jurors. But since I am basically lazy, I took the easy way and got the addresses (after a couple of wrong calls and a lot of leading questions) right at my desk in the newsroom—from the phone book. (Voter registration files were always available as a backup.)

Then all I had to do was to get the jurors to talk. (I had to get a couple at work because I couldn't find a home number, but other jurors were able to clue me in to where they worked.) Luckily, one juror was fairly intelligent and extremely talkative. This juror's response was like having my own tape of the deliberations. Another juror was moderately talkative, and two more confirmed what the first two had told me. The fifth—the holdout—was the only actively hostile one.

After a couple of calls for comment from investigators, I had the story—not the blockbuster expose I had envisioned—but still a good story that needed to be done. After all, if our law enforcement officers are accomplishing the same thing by their ineptitude that others might by a criminal act of jury tampering, that's news.

The Story

The personal notoriety of some Orange County law enforcement officers has not been kept discreetly in law enforcement closets for quite some time.

And statements from jurors in a recent drug trial indicate the foibles of these investigators helped create a hung jury.

Specifically, there are indications that the widely publicized troubles of several Orange County deputy sheriffs, together with what the jury may have seen as bumbling, contradictory testimony from investigators for the Orange-Osceola state attorney's office, the Metropolitan Bureau of Investigation and the Florida Department of Law Enforcement, may have led to a mistrial in the Robert Taccia drug case.

Interviews with five of the six jurors in the trial indicated the jury vote was a firm 4-2 for conviction of Taccia and codefendant Robert Michaud on charges of conspiracy to possess and possession of cocaine.

And apparently even the four jurors who voted to convict were bothered because they felt, as one juror put it, the shots were being called on the state's case not by prosecutors or law enforcement officers, but by police informant Michael A. Tischer, who admitted he had made drug deals on the side.

"We had the feeling Tischer was kind of leading the law enforcement people . . . running it from 33rd Street," said juror Jack B. Snell. "It was almost as though the Florida Department of Law Enforcement and Orange County Sheriff's Department were working for Tischer."

The juror who others said was so adamant for acquittal denied being the holdout and would not discuss her vote or reasons with the *Sentinel Star.* But other jurors said that in deliberations she was "negative about the law enforcement people" and believed neither Tischer nor the extensive tape recordings of alleged drug deals made with the two defendants.

"She felt he (Taccia) was set up, that the law enforcement people were out to get Taccia," another juror said. And despite testimony from several officers that the tapes had not been altered, the holdout juror suggested in deliberations the tapes could have been altered as were the Nixon tapes.

The fact that the crucial "driveway tape" of a conversation between Taccia and Tischer in front of Taccia's home in the King's Row section of Maitland was monitored from what was then former Orange County Chief Deputy Leigh O. McEachern's home—even though McEachern had been fired from the department and was under indictment—also bothered jurors.

They knew McEachern's name and were vaguely aware even without a defense reminder that former sheriff's Lt. James Harris—part of the team that listened from the McEachern garage while Tischer spoke with Taccia—was later fired from the Sheriff's Department.

Harris was accused by Sheriff Melvin G. Colman of lying about the existence of evidence in a gambling case against eight Orange County men who were indicted by the same grand jury that indicted Taccia. Harris had denied any wrongdoing.

Defense attorneys brought all that out in the trial—in what the prosecutor, Assistant State Attorney Richard H. Combs, called a "smokescreen.". . .

Harris' testimony that he kept a cocaine sample overnight at his home before turning it in "bothered a lot of people," a juror said. "The law enforcement people really botched the possession thing.". . .

4. The Headline

"Dismissal Sought in Theft Charges," by Doug Higgs of the Klamath Falls (Ore.) *Herald and News*.

The Reporter's Comments

Most of the articles written by me are from information obtained from court records. Some articles are written from actual courtroom proceedings I have attended. The latter usually involve cases of significant public interest. . . .

At no time in the article do I use the usual court terminology because, if I did, most readers would not know what I was writing about.

However, it is important for writers to understand the court terminology so they may translate it accurately into an understandable and readable article while at the same time being accurate.

I attended the particular court proceeding mentioned here. As a rule, I am very reluctant to use any second-hand report of testimony in court. Using such reports can be risky. There is no better witness for what was said in court than the reporter's own firsthand experience.

A court proceeding is important to everyone involved and an

inaccuracy in an article can be extremely damaging and could lead to a libel suit. But, if reporters are dedicated to accuracy, this will not happen.

The Story

Dismissal of two criminal counts against Donald G. Lingren, Klamath Falls, and connected to the theft of four Steinway pianos is being sought in Klamath County Circuit Court.

Klamath Falls attorney Tim Bailey, who is representing Lingren, contends the counts should be dismissed because of an excessive delay in filing the charges against Lingren and two other Klamath Falls men.

Judge Ted Abram said Tuesday he will rule later on Bailey's motions.

Lingren and the two other men, James Claude Bowden and Donald Leroy Compton, all affiliated with Bowden Music Co., 527 Main St., are accused of stealing the pianos from Foreman Piano Service and of receiving the four Steinway pianos from Robert Wells Jacobson with the knowledge they had been stolen on Jan. 12, 1977.

The counts against them are first-degree theft and theft by receiving.

Bailey contends there is no valid reason for the two-year delay in filing the charges against Lingren. He said the unreasonable delay has considerably damaged the defense's case.

According to Bailey, certain evidence, which would have been available two years ago, is not available now. He also stated that witnesses, who would have had a fresh recollection of incidents connected to the charges two years ago, have more difficulty now remembering these incidents.

Klamath County Deputy District Attorney Rodger Isaacson said the Federal Bureau of Investigation handled the case for an extensive period of time.

"The state did not become involved until notified by the FBI that it had decided it was not going to prosecute" Lingren, Bowden and Compton.

Isaacson blamed the FBI for the delay in filing of the charges.

Jacobson was prosecuted by the FBI and was sentenced to three years in prison on Sept. 6, 1977, after being convicted in U. S. District Court of interstate transportation of stolen property.

The FBI said Jacobson took the four pianos from California to Klamath Falls, where he sold them to Bowden Music Co. They were taken during a burglary of the Foreman Piano Service warehouse in San Mateo, Calif., Jan. 5, 1977, the FBI stated.

A nine-foot piano and three seven-foot pianos were stolen, the FBI said. Their estimated total value was between $25,000 and $27,000.

Lingren was scheduled to be tried before a jury Tuesday, but the trial has been rescheduled May 1. Bowden is scheduled to be tried March 20 and Compton on April 21.

5. The Headline

"Suit Challenges Racial Separation of Funeral Homes," by Vicki Ferstel of the *Daily Iberian*, in New Iberia, La.

The Reporter's Comments

On a story about a man filing a class action federal discrimination suit against a funeral home, I decided to get basic. The man came to my house and after a three-hour interview—full of sobbing and pill popping—I got the meat of the story.

Then I checked every allegation with as many people—including lawyers—as I could. Finally, I called the defendants and their attorney. The story won first place in a statewide contest.

The Story

The practice of separate funeral homes for whites and blacks is under fire in a lawsuit brought by a New Iberia man against the owners of Jacquemoud Funeral Home.

Charles C. A. Verdun of Lydia is asking $25,000 for emotional distress, pain and suffering and $25,000 in punitive damages "because of the illegal and racist actions of the defendants."

Those named in the suit are Security Industrial Insurance Co. of Donaldsonville and its president, E. J. Ourso. Ourso's company owns Jacquemoud Funeral Home.

According to Verdun, his mother, Margaret, was issued a funeral insurance policy on March 1, 1972, worth $600. It was to provide the full funeral services such as casket, embalming and wake.

When his mother died Jan. 21, 1974, Walter Dodge, an employee of the funeral home, allegedly told the family they could not hold the wake in the funeral home. Dodge allegedly suggested the family hold the wake at home or in a church.

"I said, 'All right, give me my $600 and I'll go somewhere else for the service,'" Verdun recounts. However, Dodge allegedly told Verdun he would only get back $153.18 of the $600, as that was the amount paid in premiums.

Verdun made arrangements with Fletcher's Funeral Home and when he and two Fletcher employees went back to Jacquemoud Funeral Home to pick up his mother's body, Dodge allegedly refused to release it.

"Mr. Walter Dodge stepped in front of the body and said, 'that body cannot leave here until we get $75,'" Verdun contends. The $75 was for embalming services Verdun claims were never authorized.

Verdun accuses Dodge of then stepping out of the embalming room and "within a few seconds 9 or 10 white men surrounded us."

A Fletcher employee eventually came by with the money and Dodge released the body. Verdun says he then walked up to Dodge and shook his hand. "I thought, 'Mister, I'm going to get you someday.'"

When contacted by the Daily Iberian, Dodge firmly denied ever having sent 10 men into the embalming room.

He did explain why the funeral home would not hold the wake for Mrs. Verdun. "As you know all the white funeral homes don't lay out colored. . . . It hasn't been done in the past.

"We are not the official funeral directors for the colored."

Dodge insists the insurance agent must have told the Verdun family who the official funeral home for blacks was since there are two sets of pamphlets given to policy holders: one for whites and one for blacks. Those pamphlets indicate the official funeral homes of the company.

He noted that Security Industrial Insurance Corp. has contracted with funeral homes in Abbeville and in Franklin to hold wakes for New Iberia blacks.

"It's a ticklish situation," he admits. When asked if not holding wakes for blacks is a policy of the company, Dodge said it is.

As for only refunding $153.18 to Verdun, Dodge says, "You'd either get a premium refund or a percentage of the policy."

Whether he embalmed Mrs. Verdun's body without the family's consent, Dodge again says he does not remember. He adds it was a possibility since at the time there was a state law requiring embalming within 24 hours of the death.

John H. Fritz, vice-president of Security Industrial Insurance Co., declined to comment on the case as it is in litigation. The company is being represented by Talbot, Sotile, Carmouche, and Marchand of Donaldsonville.

Verdun and his lawyer, R. James Kellogg, have filed a class action suit in the Western District of U.S. District Court "on behalf of all black citizens" in the state alleging that "refusing to provide the same funeral services to black persons insured by them as is provided to white persons insured by them is a violation of the rights of blacks to contract the same as whites."

The suit has been assigned to the federal court in Lafayette.

Verdun says he has suffered two nervous breakdowns since the incident. "I was like an animal," he remembers. "I was raging mad."

He said he threatened to kill two Security Industrial Insurance Co. agents when they came to his house after the incident.

"This thing is so pathetic," Verdun said. "We are Americans. I served 8½ years of my life to the military. I don't know what complete freedom is, (but) I found out . . . when I left the U.S.A."

6. *The Headline*

"Judge Takes Obscene Shirt With Probation Ruling," by Steven C. Lachowicz, of the Wenatchee (Wash.) *World*.

The Reporter's Comments

Here's a story that won't win any Pulitzers and won't make page one too often, but it is a common kind of court tale that will get a lot of readership.

The story had its roots six months earlier when the T-shirts first appeared being worn by two men in a Wenatchee restaurant. On them was printed an obscene directive to the Wenatchee P.D. Wenatchee police confiscated the shirts and checked to see if any charges could be filed. Prosecutors said no. I did not personally cover the story at that time since it fell within the City of Wenatchee jurisdiction, another reporter's responsibility. But I was aware of it.

Because I do not have time to sit through all court proceedings, I have to rely a lot on papers filed in the clerk's office to keep track of what happened in court the day before. When I got to the clerk's office the morning of March 6, there was no paperwork on this case since the sentencing had not yet been signed by the judge. But because I have established good rapport with the court clerks, one of them asked if I'd heard about the T-shirts. When I said no, she told me what had happened.

I immediately went to the Superior Court judge and asked for his version. He supplied further detail and background. Next I checked with a friendly deputy prosecutor just to see if there were any other details I might have missed.

Once back at the office I went through my fellow reporter's files and found clippings of the first stories about confiscation of the T-shirts. Those stories did not name the two wearers. I then had to call a friendly dispatcher at the police department who confirmed the defendant in this Superior Court case was indeed one of the same men who had a T-shirt confiscated six months ago.

Then I wrote the story. Total time elapsed from the time I first heard about the case until it was in my editor's hands—about an hour and a half.

The Story

It may not be illegal to wear a T-shirt with a printed obscenity aimed directly at the Wenatchee Police Department, but Greg Radach has had to surrender his anyway.

Radach, 24, of 497 N. Kentucky, East Wenatchee, recently pleaded guilty to charges of unlawful possession of marijuana before Judge Charles W. Cone in Chelan County Superior Court.

Cone learned of Radach's T-shirt through the presentence investigation.

On Monday the judge deferred Radach's sentence three years on condition of probation, a $350 fine, 60 days in jail, taking periodic polygraph tests and turning his off-color T-shirt over to Wenatchee police.

The judge also said Radach would have to go to IRS officials and tell them about his income for the past few years to see if back taxes might be owed.

Radach agreed to the conditions rather than going to prison.

Last October two T-shirts with the same sexually obscene insult to the Wenatchee police were confiscated from Radach and a friend. But city and county prosecutors decided at that time they had no legal grounds to charge the wearers of the T-shirts and the garments were returned to their owners.

7. The Headline

"Three-Year Sentence Brings End to Unsuccessful Career," by Jim Deal, of *The Argus*, in Rock Island, Ill.

The Reporter's Comments

My interest in this case began with Nu-Nu's arrest for stealing baby powder and diapers. He was obviously not typical of most defendants.

Police stories from the city beat and Nu-Nu's frequent court appearances kept me up to date on his progress.

When a judge finally revoked his probation, I felt there was a story in Nu-Nu's career.

My principal sources included the police blotter, the daily court schedule, and the individual criminal files on Nu-Nu kept in the circuit clerk's office.

The Story

By now, Edward White "Nu-Nu" Johnson must feel like there's a dark cloud following him around. He is one of Rock Island's most notorious unsuccessful petty criminals.

Twice county judges have taken pity on Johnson and have modified a 1977 probation rather than commit Johnson to prison. But the third time up to bat, Johnson struck out.

He was sentenced yesterday to three years with the Department of Corrections after Judge Jay Hanson found justification to revoke his original probation for a burglary.

Nu-Nu's problems began on Aug. 22, 1976, when he committed a burglary at the home of Luzell Robinson, 830 12th St., Rock Island. Johnson grabbed a box of Pampers baby diapers and a bottle of baby powder from the home.

He was identified by witnesses and arrested by Rock Island police. On Jan. 5, 1977, he was sentenced to three years on probation, six months in the county jail and was ordered to go to the Community Mental Health Center.

Less than a month later, on Feb. 1, 1977, Johnson violated his probation by stealing a bottle of wine from the Walgreen's store on Rock Island's Great River Plaza. His getaway was spoiled when he slipped and fell, cutting himself on the broken wine bottle.

A petition to revoke his probation was filed by the state's attorney's office, but June 7, 1977, Judge Conway Sparton ordered Johnson to attend Skills, Inc. and to take his medication.

In a little less than three months, Johnson was back in court again on another petition to revoke his probation, this time for unlawful possession of marijuana, aggravated battery, criminal damage to property and resisting arrest.

It seems when police went to arrest Johnson on the marijuana charge, he fought with them, hitting two police officers and damaging the badge and uniform of an officer.

Again, Johnson was given a reprieve. His probation was extended by Judge John Donald O'Shea and he was ordered to report regularly to his probation officer, to attend classes at the Alpha Center and to be home by midnight.

On Nov. 29, 1978, the state's attorney's office filed its third petition to revoke Johnson's probation because he allegedly tried to burglarize a car owned by Arlen E. Huettman and parked at 2821 5th St., Rock Island.

While waiting in the Rock Island County Jail for the courts to take action on his latest probation revocation proceeding, Johnson was stabbed in the chest with a broken spoon after he asked his cellmate, confessed murderer Raul Maldonado, how to spell a word.

Johnson was able to hold his own in the ensuing fight with Maldonado, who was pinned to the floor by Johnson by the time jailers arrived to break up the fight. Johnson's injuries turned out to be minor.

Johnson never did actually break into the car. He was caught trying to open the lock by using a coat hanger. He told police he wasn't trying to commit burglary. He was just trying to help a friend who couldn't get into the car.

Judge Jay Hanson this time put an end to Nu-Nu's probation.

8. The Series of Follow-Up Stories

These five short articles by Robert K. Entriken, Jr., of the Salina (Kan.) *Journal* follow one case from the initial appearance of the defendant to the final sentencing.

The Reporter's Comments

This was a rather minor case and, therefore, typical of day-to-day court reporting. The examples in this case reflect the five basic steps of a criminal case: initial appearance, preliminary hearing, arraignment, plea, and sentencing. (The first story was done by a substitute while I was on vacation.)

Story A: My sub (following my usual practice) visits the county attorney's office daily, simply asking what's new and is told of new cases being filed. In this case, he is shown the petition being prepared against Comfort and the police affidavit accompanying it. Usually in minor cases, I sit on the story until the defendant appears in court, getting from the court record that he has appeared, been charged, and set for preliminary hearing. I do not run PH dates in the story because they always are continued at least once (Kansas law providing for one demand continuance which is taken 99% of the time.)

Story B: The preliminary hearing: I merely ask later that day what happened (source, a trusted court clerk) and am told Comfort waived his hearing and was bound over for trial. The court has a reliable calendar of arraignment dates (exceptions are rare), so I use that date based on the court calendar.

Story C: The arraignment: I make it a point to attend arraignments looking for those who plead guilty. In this case Comfort pleaded not guilty (reported as pleading "innocent"). After doing the brief story, I file this case in my "for trial next court term" file.

Story D: The plea: Late in February, when the judges are making up their calendar of March trials, I check a list of all pending cases. The judge tells me Comfort is expected to plead on March 1 (I never report an expected plea—it announces guilty before defendant has admitted guilt). On March 1, I am present to hear the plea and at that time learn of the dismissal of the felony charge. Had I not been present, I would have specifically asked if he pleaded guilty to both counts charged against him.

Story E: Knowing Comfort was to be sentenced March 26, I later ask the judge (not being able to be present at the time) what sentence he gave. Or, if the judge is not available, I will check his notes on the docket sheet. I mention the now-dismissed felony charge in this story only to let the reader (and my editor) know why I am writing a story about a petty theft case which normally would not rate a story.

A. The Headline and the Story

CHARGED WITH THEFT OF WALLET, FORGERY

Timothy Kirk Comfort, 358 N. Columbia, has been charged in District Court with counts of theft and forgery.

Comfort faces a misdemeanor charge of theft and a felony count of forgery in connection with an alleged Nov. 29 theft of a wallet belonging to Harold Olson, 1515 Bachtold. Comfort is also alleged to have forged Olson's signature on the back of a $31 check on Dec. 23.

Comfort is free after posting $2,500 bond awaiting further court action.

B. The Headline and the Story

MUST STAND TRIAL

Timothy Kirk Comfort, 20, 358 N. Columbia, waived a District Court preliminary hearing Jan. 19 and was bound over for trial on charges of forgery and petty theft.

He is accused of stealing a wallet owned by Harold V. Olson, 58, 1515 Bachtold, and with forging Olson's endorsement to a $31 check taken from the wallet.

Comfort is free on $2,500 bond and is to be arraigned Jan. 29.

C. The Headline and the Story

PLEAD INNOCENT

Pleas of innocent were entered by two men during District Court arraignment Jan. 29.

Appearing were Timothy Kirk Comfort, 20, 358 N. Columbia, and West Kendal McArthur, 22, 15 N. Eastborough Road.

Comfort is accused of forgery of the endorsement of Harold V. Olson, 58, 1515 Bachtold, on a $31 check cashed Nov. 29 at the Conoco service station, 1017 S. Santa Fe, and petty theft of Olson's wallet from which the check was taken. He is free on $2,500 bond.

McArthur is appealing a Municipal Court conviction for driving while intoxicated, on which he was fined $150. He remains free on $500 bond, having surrendered his driver's license in lieu of posting the bond.

D. The Headline and the Story

PLEADS GUILTY TO PETTY THEFT CHARGE

A forgery charge against Timothy Kirk Comfort, 20, 358 N. Columbia, was dismissed March 1 in District Court after he pleaded guilty to a misdemeanor charge of petty theft.

Comfort admitted stealing a wallet Nov. 29 belonging to Harold V. Olson, 58, 1515 Bachtold. He took the wallet while at Olson's home helping Olson's daughter to move.

The forgery charge alleged Comfort signed Olson's endorsement to a $31 check found in the wallet and cashed it at the Conoco service station, 1017 S. Santa Fe.

Judge Morris Hoobler deferred sentencing to March 26. Comfort remains free on $2,500 bond.

E. The Headline and the Story

GETS PROBATION

A six-month jail sentence was meted out to Timothy Kirk Comfort, 20, 358 N. Columbia, March 26, in District Court.

Comfort had pleaded guilty March 1 to petty theft of a wallet owned by Harold V. Olson, 58, 1515 Bachtold. A second charge alleging forgery of a check in the wallet was dismissed at that time.

After pronouncing sentence, Judge Morris Hoobler granted a one-year probation.

9. *The Roundup Summary*

Some newspapers attempt to summarize the actions in a court each day.

The Reporter's Comments

This "District Court" column in the Laconia (N.H.) *Evening Citizen* is by Aline L. Jacobs, who emphasizes ". . . the checking and double checking of names that look wrong."

The Story

David G. Wheeler, 22, of Cherry Valley Rd., Gilford, pleaded innocent to DWI, second offense. The case will be heard on April 24. Surety bail was set at $500.

Matthew F. Batchelder, 20, of Peabody, Mass., was found guilty of DWI. He was fined $165, and his right to operate was revoked for 90 days.

Bruce J. Bean, 22, of Contoocook, who pleaded innocent to DWI, was found guilty. He was fined $165, and his license to operate was revoked for 60 days.

Aurel Chamberlain, 53, of Rte. 140, Belmont, who pleaded innocent to failure to yield the right of way, was found guilty. He was assessed $27.50.

Neal N. Cobleigh, 21, of Plymouth, who pleaded innocent to disorderly conduct, was found innocent.

Robert A. Rothwell, 18, of Ox Box Lane, Gilford, changed his plea to nolo to DWI, second offense. He was fined $550, and his license to operate was revoked for three years.

James Griffin, 22, of 9 Pleasant St., Tilton, was found guilty of two counts of allowing an uninspected motor vehicle to be operated, improper use of repair plates, operation after suspension and two counts of failure to answer summonses. He was fined a total of $292.50. He pleaded innocent to one count of failure to answer a summons. The case was continued to April 11. Bail was set at $100.

Frank Mekkelsen, 21, of 28 Duffy St., Franklin, forfeited $200 bail when he failed to appear on a charge of DWI.

Judge Bernard I. Snierson presided.

Notes

[1]Albert G. Pickerell and Michael Lipman, *The Courts and the News Media* (Berkeley, Calif.: Project Benchmark, Conference of California Judges, c. 1974), pp. 1ff.

[2]Helen N. Redfern, ed. *Key to the Keystone State: Pennsylvania* (Philadelphia: League of Women Voters of Pennsylvania, 1978), cf. pp. 37ff.

[3]J. Norman Swaton and Loren Morgan, *Administration of Justice* (New York: Van Nostrand, 1975), p. 28.

[4]Curtis D. MacDougall, *Covering the Courts* (New York: Prentice-Hall, 1946), cf. pp. 143ff.

[5]Pickerell and Lipman, pp. 18, 19.

Assignments

1. Interview the judge in one court, listen to one of the cases, and identify other court officials in the courtroom. Then write a report on the court and its procedure.

2. Write a "how-to" article with about 10 steps on how to use a court. An interesting subject might be on how to bring a complaint against an individual and follow it through, such as against a neighbor who has barking dogs or dogs which threaten children.
3. Using court records, contrast decisions of judges who deal in the same area. For example, contrast how different judges deal with traffic offenses. Is one more lenient than the other, or do these judges show lenience or harshness depending on the kind of case?
4. Prepare an article on a court case—preferably a nonjury case—that is tried and decided in one morning or afternoon session.
5. Do a feature on an innovative technique or rehabilitation program connected with the criminal justice system. Check with lawyers and judges for ideas. There are many possibilities, from juvenile protection programs to halfway houses for parolees.
6. Role play a court drama in class. Perhaps you can use some of the transcript of a trial or a transcript from a book of a famous trial. Then report the drama as news.
7. Courts usually generate some humor. Go to the local courts for a few hours and write a "brite"—a few paragraphs on one of the humorous cases—or, since judges also have a sense of humor, report on one of the lighter conclusions, remarks, or conditions stemming from the judge.

12

Government

Government reporting includes covering townships, cities, counties, the state and national and international scenes—sometimes with considerable overlap. The levels of government may even share the same office building, and some cities have a city-county building. Each citizen's life is also touched by taxes—city, state, and national—that interlock with each other.

New as well as experienced reporters are likely to be very engrossed in matters of politics and government on a local, county, and state level. They will report on national leaders who are representatives of their state and districts.

THE GOVERNMENT BEAT

Just as for other areas of journalism, developing sources and skills in interviewing and covering press conferences and meetings are essential for all government and political reporting.

Organizing Coverage

In government coverage, newspapers often divide the reporting in two ways. First, if only a few governmental bodies are involved, such as a city and two outlying towns, one reporter may cover the municipal government of each of the three communities, while another may cover the school boards for all three. Still another may be in charge of all features for the three-community area.

When the paper serves many municipalities—cities, towns, townships, and several school boards and the county—the editor may divide beats geographically, with each reporter responsible for all coverage (except sports) of one or two communities. Or one reporter may cover county news while another takes care of agricultural news.

Each method has advantages. In the first instance, if the reporter has a topic such as municipal government or school board, the reporter has a chance to see trends in stories, and to have information for comparison readily at hand. But the disadvantages include lack of variety in story content for the reporter and a possible lack of objectivity.

In newspapers which assign stories on a geographical basis, readers develop a sense of identification with "their" reporters. Reporters actually become experts on their communities, and editors encourage reporters to live in the communities they serve. Yet geographical coverage may mean that reporters are spread too thin over areas where their expertise is even thinner. Also, such reporters have little opportunity to see "trend" stories or to put the news of their communities in perspective with what is happening in neighboring communities.

Regardless of what coverage approach a paper chooses, whoever covers the governmental law-making and regulating board (city council, board of commissioners, or board of supervisors) will work mainly in the area of government reporting.

Local Government Divisions

The U.S. Census Bureau classifies five main categories of local government: (1) counties, (2) towns and townships, (3) incorporated places, (4) school districts, and (5) special districts.

But variations exist. Pennsylvania has boroughs instead of towns. Some 50 of them are big enough (with over 10,000 people) to be cities. Boroughs have a weak executive government. Delaware uses the term "hundred" for township (usually new residential areas outside a town or city).

Traditionally, a town has a population of 2,500 or less. Communities need 2,500 to incorporate as a city, as in Illinois; 200 for a village in counties with less than 150,00 population and 2,500 in other counties; municipalities over 25,000 automatically have home rule government; and communities under 25,000 population have the option of choosing some rule by referendum, according to a U.S. Census book, *Government Organization*, No. 1. (There are some big villages, such as Oak Park, Ill., with 62,500, and some small cities such as Northampton, Mass., the smallest city in the state with 25,000 population.)

Different Attitudes

In his book, *Investigative Reporting and Editing,* the late Paul Williams offers a general attitude for government reporting:

> You need to assume that the institutions of government are under constant and pernicious attack by both external forces seeking special advantage and internal operators who figure that graft is one of the perquisites of office.

Williams was writing about investigative reporting, but if you believe, as many journalists do, that *all* good reporting is investigative reporting, then what he says is worth keeping in mind in the day-by-day routine.

> The assailants (against the institutions of government) are not only corporations but unions, professional associations, and organizations whose stated purpose may sound entirely altruistic.
>
> You need also to assume that within these institutions, most of the people are still essentially honest, unaware of what's going on, or merely jealous of the grafters and graftees. This majority comprises your best resource, your best hope for doing reporting that will effectively describe our systemic problems.

Williams, who won a Pulitzer prize with his investigation of the finances of Boys Town in Nebraska and later taught journalism at Ohio State before his premature death, quotes Louis Rose of the St. Louis *Post-Dispatch*:

> When I see someone in a position to take graft, I try to think of all the worst things they could be doing. What are the inherent possibilities here, what is every single advantage that somebody could get out of this? You've got to train your mind not to accept anything at face value. Put down every single thing you can think of, no matter how incredible it may seem, and then gradually go down the list and cut them off: This can be done in this case, this can't be done, this is a possibility, but can I prove it?

And Williams adds: "Rose's is a sound approach to examining the working government. . . ."[1]

Beginning reporters, of course, should be warned about being overly zealous and trying to put every politician in jail. On the other hand, beginning reporters can also be professional reporters and ask skeptical questions.

Mason Taylor, Pulitzer prize winner and retired editor of the Utica (N.Y.) *Press* and *Observer-Dispatch*, offers an overview for covering government. He tells of "A New Ball Game" in government reporting in an article included in John L. Dougherty's *Learning in the Newsroom: A Manual for Supervisors*:

> Being a local government reporter for a newspaper is a new ball game today.
>
> At the national level, we have seen the proliferation of TV and radio stations and their increasing know-how in handling news and skimming off the cream of top news stories. Now this has filtered down to the local level as electronic newsmen in cities large and small do a better job in covering the stories that make our headlines.
>
> And perhaps because they are easiest to get, they have begun to zero in on city council meetings, county legislative boards and "news conferences" set up by local officials. And they get the utmost in cooperation. For what mayor or county legislator can resist falling in love with his image in full color on the tube?
>
> So, if you want to be a local government reporter on a newspaper, you've got to be able to give the readers something they can't get on radio or TV.
>
> At the national and state level, the better reporters are doing this with interpretive stories and investigative work. If you have the know-how and the zeal, your electronic competition can't come close to matching you in these fields, assuming that your editor will give you the time that is needed. For one thing, your competition is spread too thin. As of now, they're after the high spots of the news. Secondly, most of them lack the know-how.
>
> So that's the first step—making sure you know a lot more about your government than they. A good starting point is studying your city or county charter and all of the laws relating to the powers and duties of the government you are covering.
>
> Once on a new job in a strange city, I did a 13-part series, "Know Your City Government." Just doing it forced me to become familiar with every city department and what it did.
>
> Secondly, establish good, solid news sources. But don't play favorites. Establish a reputation for being fair and objective. Your sources then will develop from two directions: those in government who want good government, and the political opponents, or disgruntled office-holders or employees who will tip you on what's going on behind the scenes or "leak" information to you. Don't ever betray a confidence. On the other hand, make it clear to any source that you will not "cover" for him if he is under fire or in the wrong, just because he has given you valuable information. More often than not, he will respect you for laying it out like that.
>
> If you know your government and have good contacts, doing

interpretive pieces—what it all means—should be no problem. In the main, these are stories that develop the fifth dimension of the story—"why?" . . .

The first rule of good investigative reporting was laid down some years ago by Clark Mollenhoff—the Des Moines *Register* and *Tribune's* top investigative reporter: "Follow the dollar." Keep your eye on the cookie jar—where the money goes and how. If you suspect there's waste, extravagance, or dishonesty, that's the first step in ferreting it out.

That sewer job, let out on a cost-plus basis. Go over the vouchers in the comptroller's office to see what was paid to whom for what. Who are the stockholders in the company? Was the work done according to specifications? Ask another contractor to look it over. (We once turned up an instance where a sewer contractor laid a street sewer three feet shallower than the specifications called for, and didn't even join the pipes together.)

Is the concrete sub-base of that new pavement the thickness called for in the specifications? Go out to a newly-laid strip late some afternoon when work has stopped and measure it. Or bore a couple of holes in newly-laid asphalt and see if it is as thick as the taxpayers are paying for.

Who's on the city payroll? Are they really working? Once in a while publish a payroll—public works, for example—listing each worker's name, address, hours worked and dates. You may get some revealing telephone calls. Once we spotted a political boss's barber on the payroll as a street inspector. (Presumably he did his inspections with a flashlight.) A couple of other guys were driving buses when they were supposed to be driving city trucks.

Check the minutes of all the boards and commissions regularly. If you weren't there or didn't know of the meeting, you may have missed something your readers should know about. I once knew of a city board of estimate which was in the habit of meeting at 4 p.m. the afternoon before Christmas to approve assorted claims against the city. A nice Merry Christmas for the recipients until a reporter came across the minutes of one of those happy holiday meetings.

Take a hard look at those zoning changes and tax refund ordinances that sometimes slip through legislative sessions without a word of comment. Make a hard pitch to get an advance copy of all legislation to give you time to ask questions.

On a dull day, visit the purchasing agent's office and go over vouchers. Seventy-five cents *each* for a gross of ballpoint pens? Wow! (Twenty or thirty years ago, the mayor of a major city was turned out of office mainly because a sharp reporter found out his administration was paying triple the going rate for office wastebaskets.)

How do the real estate assessments of your public officials and legislators compare with those of their neighbors? The same before and after they took office? And do you have communities with such low assessments that veterans, because of exemptions, pay no taxes at all? . . .

With the rise in food prices, there has been greater consumer awareness of farm subsidies. How about finding out the amounts of subsidies paid the big commercial farmers in your area? When we tried this a year ago, we ran into a road block at the federal agency handling them in our territory. But it only took a letter to Washington to have the local agency head told the payments are public records. . . .

And never, never accept an official's statement that "there's nobody in here but us mice." I knew a good reporter who, on a day he felt like "coasting," accepted the word of a county official that the state audit he had just received contained nothing that wasn't "routine." The opposition had a clean beat with one of the biggest stories of the year.

Get in the habit of using a tape recorder. Your stories of the City Council meeting or on the mayor's press conference will be a lot more interesting if you can quote what the guy actually said, instead of paraphrasing it into something that makes him sound as erudite as Adlai Stevenson.

This kind of reporting is often hard work, but rewarding. It probably won't get you any high paid jobs as a political flack—not unless you are of a mind to be bought off that way. The most you get may be the accolade one reporter got from the mayor when he was promoted to editor: "It's a big loss to the city. He kept us all honest."[2]

Reporting on Townships

A township is a municipality other than a village, town, or city. Counties are made up of incorporated and unincorporated cities and other communities. In some states, such as Pennsylvania, the rest of the land is divided into townships, sometimes involving large areas. In some states, a township is thought of as an administrative unit—often in new development areas without full service and not yet incorporated into a contiguous city or town. A township is usually governed by a board of supervisors.

Since in most townships the job of supervisor is only a part-time job, sometimes a township manager runs the administrative business of the government. This manager is an employee of the supervisors and takes orders from them.

The township manager (comparable positions would be city manager or the borough manager) is a natural source of information for reporters. Because the supervisors have other jobs, they are often difficult to contact. The township manager, however, is a full-time employee. Building good rapport with that person early is essential because the manager will be able to explain confusing bond issues or give reporters background on a former controversy about a housing development that is popping up in the news again.

Don't overlook the manager's secretary. Secretaries can be the key to getting a story or losing it to the competition.

Supervisors generally have a lawyer—or a solicitor as they are sometimes called. This person attends the board meetings which may be held once, twice, or even four times a month, depending on the size of the community and the enthusiasm of the board members.

The board of supervisors passes the laws that regulate the township. The board passes ordinances (laws) and resolutions (formal statements) which give approval, commend, or show its awareness of a situation. The members determine the budget for the township, apply for grants, hire employees (including road crews and police), determine zoning changes, take charge of snow removal, approve new construction, and maintain parks.

In addition to the board of supervisors, a township will usually have a planning commission, a park and recreation commission, a public safety commission, a zoning hearing board, and a municipal authority (or water and sewer board).

A planning commission reviews plans for new housing developments and commercial construction. It tries to ensure the preservation of the community and the environment while monitoring the growth of the community. It has no power of its own but merely makes recommendations to the board of supervisors.

The planning commission is probably the second most important commission or board in the township, next to the supervisors' board itself. From the meetings of the planners, the reporter may get a view of the future. When 500 new single-family homes are proposed for an area which is now a lovely woodlands, readers are going to want to hear about it immediately.

The planning commission is appointed and usually elects its own chairman. The township manager serves in an advisory post to this commission and also as a liaison between the planners and the supervisors.

A park and recreation commission can be an important body, but generally news from this source is fairly routine. The supervisors appoint this commission or board. Its members elect their own chairman. Quite often reporters can pick up news from this board over the phone unless they know that an important issue is coming up at a meeting and decide to attend. Again, the township manager knows what this commission is planning; the chairman should also be a good contact.

Some townships have a public safety commission. Working with the police, it may suggest changes in speed limits, add children-at-play warning signs, see that street lights are strategically placed, and prescribe that police crack down on the use of motor bikes on school grounds. Usually this commission does not yield much news, but when the commission does have something newsworthy, the items often surface at a meeting of the board of supervisors.

The zoning hearing board and the municipal authority board are slightly different. Although residents appointed by the supervisors make up both boards, each has some power.

The zoning hearing board holds public hearings which are comparable to a hearing in court. The board takes testimony, and lawyers cross-examine and plead cases. This board holds a session when someone requests a waiver of a zoning regulation. For example, the applicant may want to extend his or her fence closer to the road than the law allows. He or she may wish to pave half of the front yard in order to provide more parking space for the car, the kids' bikes, snowmobiles, or boats.

Both the applicant who requested the exception to the law and the township board of supervisors which made the law can appeal the decision of the zoning hearing board in court.

Zoning board members are a good source of additional information. Kerry Duke, city hall reporter of the Jacksonville (Fla.) *Times-Union*, believes zoning boards do not always provide good information. He says:

> Sources dealing with zoning are invariably the worst of city hall fare. Most tell of some insipid request before a zoning board or city council to allow a commercially intensive use of the property but never do they explain *who* is making the request or *what* power he or she wields, the financial gain that can be expected if the request is granted, *how* the change might affect an area, or *why* a request is granted or denied.

Thus, it is the responsibility of good reporters to ask questions which will provide the public with answers to the *who, what, how,* and *why* which members of the zoning board do not provide on their own initiative.

The municipal authority is in charge of water and sewer services for the community. It usually is autonomous, although township supervisors appoint the members. The municipal authority board generally hires a manager who is the administrator of the water and sewer companies. It also may employ workers to operate the sewage treatment plant, to maintain pipes and wells or reservoirs, and to read meters. The board sets the rates for the customers and bills them. The municipal authority manager is the best source of information concerning the activities of this board. From this person, information concerning rate hikes, new treatment methods for sewage, and construction work on sewage systems is available.

Every good source connected with government also can be a good source for nongovernmental activities within the municipality. The vice chairman of the board of supervisors, for instance, may be an active member of the community chamber of commerce. A police officer may be president of the Lions or Rotary clubs. The township secretary may be a volunteer at a home for mentally retarded youngsters. The road foreman may mention that a man who lives down the block from him has a very large and unusual collection of arrowheads.

Because these people are residents, and often the elected or appointed employees, of the community, they know the community and its people well. Take advantage of their knowledge when you are searching for feature topics.

Although covering local government is a serious responsibility, humor also has a place in small township and other local government reporting. Human interest stories can develop through the selection of topics. Debi Craft, a student at Ferris State College in Big Rapids, Mich., has a government beat so small that one of the township meeting houses still has an outhouse. The Sheridan Township meeting hall on Michigan Route 66 was built in 1867, its cement steps are cracked, all varnish has long been worn off the floor, an old piano and lectern gather dust, and on the walls are a portrait of a nineteenth century matron and a yellowed 1904 certificate of membership in the Ancient Order of Gleaners, a farm group. The township board covers many bookkeeping items, but Debi Craft's one-woman newspaper, the Barryton (Mich.) *Courier*, caught the right news peg with "Outhouse Will Have to Do" on a topic of universal nostalgia:

SHERIDAN TOWNSHIP—For the time being at least, the outhouse behind the Sheridan Township Hall on M 66 will have to suffice.

During last week's meeting of the Mecosta County Board of Commissioners, county officials denied an $8,500 revenue sharing request from Sheridan Township for improvements to the aging township hall. The money was to be used for construction of a basement into which indoor plumbing would have been installed.

But, county commissioners explained, there's only so much revenue sharing money to go around. Thus, the Sheridan request was denied.

At the present time, those using the hall must either "take care of business" before attending meetings at the hall or make use of the solitary, white frame privy behind the building. Because of the lack of indoor facilities, the hall is not used for dances, potlucks and other community events. Instead, use of the structure is confined to township board meetings and elections.

Township Clerk Judith Smith said

Monday the county denial would be discussed at Thursday's township board meeting and, she added, no decision on what future course of action to take has been determined.

Recommendation for denial of the request was made to the full county board by commissioners Michael Govan and James Peck of the Revenue Sharing Committee.

Defending the action, Peck said Monday, "We felt granting the money to Sheridan Township would set a precedent for other townships. I know, if we approved the expenditure, we'd probably get a request right away from Grant Township which is having similar problems. There are a lot of old township halls throughout the county."

Peck added, "I wish there was enough money to go around so we could give everybody some, but there's just not."

Initially, Sheridan officials anticipated digging a basement, then moving the hall onto the new foundation. Township meetings would be conducted in the basement, saving on heating bills. And, indoor plumbing would be added.

Commissioner Bob Stroud of Remus argued against the commission's final decision saying, "I think they arbitrarily made their recommendation without completely investigating the situation. Sure, every township has revenue sharing funds coming their way, but Sheridan Township has a low tax base so there's not that much money available."

He added, "That's what revenue sharing money is for, to distribute among the people of the county to help them make improvements they can't afford on their own."

For the time being at least, those who use the township hall must continue to step back, a few years, as they continue to use the old two-seater.

City Hall

There are three basic forms of local government, as Russell Maddox and Robert Fuquay of the University of Oregon note in their *State and Local Government*:[3]

Mayor-Council. The mayoral candidate goes through a primary, often first getting the endorsement of a caucus or convention. Usually the general public elects council members in a nonpartisan election. Often the council person comes from a ward or district. The ward permits representation from each neighborhood.

Commission government. The major decision-making power is in the hands of a group which controls both legislative and executive areas. An elected commission elects the mayor who serves as "a first among equals," but who may also have power over the police and fire departments. However, since the council or commission itself chooses the mayor, this person enjoys perhaps more power than an elected mayor would because the appointed mayor reflects the inclinations of the commission or decision-making body. This form offers a simple government, but one which makes pinpointing the decision-making process and determining who is responsible for decisions difficult.

Council-Manager. In this form, similar to the mayor-council arrangement, a manager, independent of the general political process, is hired to be the permanent officer of the city. However, power resides in the council which can dismiss the administrative officer, in this case the city manager. In addition, the public may elect or the council may appoint a mayor. Although the mayor's duties may be more ceremonial, nevertheless this official usually has considerable influence.

There are also "hybrid" forms, as Maddox and Fuquay point out.[4] For instance, in some localities the city manager cannot remove some department heads the mayor has appointed. In other areas, department heads are elected.

Many offices and agencies come under city direction. These may include:

> Police, fire, building and safety engineering departments, building bureau, charter revision commission, city clerk, airport, income tax division, physicians' office, planning commission, treasurer's office, civil rights commission, civil service commission, services for youth and elderly, community health and social services center, community relations commission, complaints and information office, controller's office, corporation counsel, and credit union.
>
> Others include data processing, hospital, dog licenses and pound, drug abuse clinics, election commission, food handlers' permits, food inspection, health department, hospitals, jail, library, lighting commission, bureau of markets, cultural commission, manpower programs, commission on alcoholism, transportation, and muncipal court.
>
> Cities may also direct parking authority, parks and recreation, payrolls, pension bureau, permits, planning commission, public works department, purchases and supplies, city treasurer, voter registration, printing division, retirement system, rumor control center, street railways department, charter coach service, water department, weights and measures bureau, public welfare department, youth board, zoning appeal board, and zoo.

At city hall, reporters work closely with the city clerk and city treasurer. The city clerk handles much of the city's day-by-day business such as licensing—dogs, taxis, hunting and fishing, and marriages—and may also be the commissioner of deeds. In addition, the city clerk prepares city council agendas and keeps records of city council meetings. The city treasurer collects property taxes and keeps track of reimbursement for official trips and various contracts, such as repair orders.

In reporting city hall, the reporter watches the agenda and looks for developments and trends. Bonnie M. Anderson of the Miami *Herald* looked ahead:

> The Miami Springs City Charter, called "antiquated" by city officials although it is only five years old, may undergo a revision study which could lead to a November referendum.
>
> In January, the City Council will consider a resolution creating a City Charter Review Board. The current charter was approved in November 1974 when Miami Springs voters changed the city's form of government from a strong mayor form to a city manager form.
>
> "Our charter has many items that are antiquated and need to be reviewed," said Mayor John Cavalier Jr.
>
> ONE SECTION that Cavalier said should be changed regards election procedures. The terms of all five councilmen expire at the same time. . . .

Covering city hall—with its routine, legal jargon, budgets, and matter-of-fact business—can sometimes be tedious. It is no place for the dull reporter. Not only do good city hall reporters have to be sharp and accurate, but they must have some imagination—a canny ability to spot life amid the paperwork and bureaucracy.

One such creative city hall and political reporter is Janice Law. At the Fort Lauderdale (Fla.) *News* she can see a story when nothing happens:

> SUNRISE—There were no land annexations at City Council meeting last week—and in Sunrise that is news.
>
> Each week the council usually approves the annexation of 10 to 40 parcels, involving hundreds of acres. Last week, nothing.
>
> Mayor John Lomelo Jr. said this was because of a provision of the Home Rule Bill which went into effect Oct. 1, which requires 14 days between readings on annexations. Previously it was seven days, according to Sunrise's charter, Lomelo said.
>
> In other action the council approved sale of $615,000 in water and sewer revenue bonds, and authorized Lomelo to invest $245,000 of city funds. Councilman Walter R. Shaw objected that approval was asked after the funds had already been invested, instead of before.

Her paper expects a quota of stories—even during a low time of year. At such times, Law may do a "roundup" or summary story. She says, "If you can tie the roundup into a central theme, all the better." One such roundup summarized, item by item, the troubles that Sunrise, Fla., was having over land acquisition.

In another enterprising piece, Law profiled a group in government, the "old-timers." Some were members of key boards—some retired after long public service. Each paragraph told of an active public-minded person.

Explains Law:

I enjoy reading and writing people profiles. Such profiles are possibilities on almost any government beat. In that article I profiled a number of city activists who were elderly but certainly not sedentary. I crafted a piece by finding an outside yardstick: the "young" radicals, with whom to compare and contrast the piece's central theme. It's the type of piece you have to be on a beat a few weeks to be able to put together, but always consider people participants for profile possibilities. It's a nice change from bond issues, sewers, and ordinances.

Law's sense of humor in addition to her general alertness to think about the facts resulted in this story:

TAMARAC—Charter Board member W. O. Bangart may be the only elected official in U.S. political history to seek to have himself recalled.

Bangart yesterday filed a recall election affidavit for himself and four other board members.

Bangart, 36, charged the board and thus himself, with "playing politics, running up excessive legal fees, and creating a willful atmosphere of conflict." The other four members of the board have issued denials and stated they aren't quite sure what Bangart's specific charges are.

Asked why he did not resign instead of seeking petitions to recall himself, Bangart said then there wouldn't be anyone to recall the other members, or disagree with their allegedly "obstructionist" policies.

He has not attended the last five Charter Board meetings, for which absence the board has censured him.

Bangart now has 30 days to obtain at least 2,000 voters' signatures on a recall petition, which would mean the recall would be put on a February referendum.

Charter Board members are puzzled at Bangart's action, since they say their terms end in February 1974 anyway. Bangart contends their terms end in February 1975. Morris C. Tucker, board attorney, says the terms end in 1974.

The board, an elective body, watches for charter violations and suggests charter amendments.

Charter Board member Mrs. Vicki Beech responded to Bangart's recall effort by saying he was a "sore loser" because a $1 million bond issue, which he supported, was turned down Oct. 30 by voters. Bangart asked for the recall the next day, although the Charter Board had refrained from taking a stand on the bond issue.

"Bangart has a lot of time to grow up. Chronological age is not a sign of maturity," said Mrs. Beech. Bangart is the youngest elected official in Tamarac.

"I hope he leaves his pacifier at home if he ever comes to Charter Board meetings," responded Al Greene, another member.

Charter Board president Daniel Powers said he is "dismayed" at Bangart's charges. "We have tried to cement relationships in the city," said Powers.

Law explains:

Here I took a routine story and did a humorous piece, with some excellent help from the headline writer (the headline said, "Recall me Irresponsible, Tamarac Official Charges").

I got a tip from sources I had cultivated, that Bangart had filed a

> recall petition which I could have done as a two-graph routine piece since recalls are frequent fare in some of the small cities. But I thought about it and realized that if Bangart wanted ALL the board members recalled including him, it would make an eye-catching story. So I try to think not only what the story says, but what its effect or meaning could be.
>
> If I write about an action, I always write about a reaction, too. So I phoned other charter board members, and used their rather pithy quotes in the last third of the piece.

Covering Counties

Jewell Case Phillips points out in *State and Local Government in America* that "the one almost universal unit of local government in America is the county."[5] Phillips notes that nearly all of the land of the U.S. lies within the borders of 3,049 counties. Some county-like forms include the 64 parishes in Louisiana. And Rhode Island's counties are not units of government but judicial districts. There are a half dozen city-counties which the Census Bureau regards as cities and not counties: Boston, Philadelphia, Denver, New Orleans, Baton Rouge, and San Francisco. Among areas that have no county government are Baltimore, the District of Columbia, and Yellowstone National Park. One state, Delaware, has three counties, while Texas has 254.

Counties in the Northeast perform few government duties, while in the south, counties perform many government functions. In Florida, counties are in charge of health, road construction, schools, tax collections, and administration of justice.

County government is often scattered. Says Phillips:

> With a few exceptions, functions of government in American counties are dispersed among so many separately elected officials and boards that it is difficult to identify any one official or board as the executive or administrative head. In 95 percent of the counties the one agency with most administrative authority is a board of three to 50 or more members.[6]

Drawing up a list of checkpoints in counties as well as in any government is a good idea because you can easily overlook some important agencies and sources of information. Consider these sources:

Social services department. People being helped make stories. This agency can give you leads on fire victims and other personal tragedies, and it is certainly a useful place to check for Thanksgiving and other seasonal stories.

Finance or controller's office. Records of all purchases, contracts, and other financial transactions can help you check for conflicts of interest.

Health department. This department handles all health inspections, from food to pollution. The department often has records of birth, deaths, and disease incidence.

Personnel-Civil Service. Look here for records of city employees with information on lengths of service, pay, qualifications, ages, and addresses.

Purchasing department. Here you can find information on bids for public contracts—costs and low and high bidders.

Emergency medical service or department. This service takes care of emergency calls and sometimes handles dispatch calls for the sheriff.

Assessor's office. The assessor can provide you with information on taxes. Check with this office after tax deadlines to see who among city officials has paid—and who hasn't.

Auto license bureau. This office can give you information about drivers' and auto license numbers.

Weights and measures. You can find records of complaints related to measuring and weighing equipment here. Look for complaints concerning scales and meters in stores and also complaints on packaging information and taxi meters.

Attorney for the county. You can check and verify any interpretation or question concerning county legal matters with the county attorney; for example, you may want to know how much authority certain individuals in county government have, or you may be looking for a long lost document.

County commission or board. The clerk of this deliberative body will have information about agendas, minutes, meetings, and decisions, as well as records such as judgments on debtors and incorporation papers from the state.

Treasurer's office. The tax rolls will indicate whom the county is billing for property taxes, thus showing who owns certain properties.

The various offices and boards can provide sources for you to develop information you have picked up at county board meetings. Bob Kolin of the Raleigh (N.C.) *News and Observer* was attending a meeting of the nine-member Board of Health of Wake County in Raleigh when the board's public affairs committee made its recommendations for a new slate of officers.

At the time there wasn't much discussion over the nominees, Kolin—two years out of college—recalls, but later he picked up on a conversation he overheard between two commissioners. "After all the problems he's had with the health department, . . ." one of them said in reference to one of the nominees. Kolin couldn't hear the name of the particular nominee, but looking over the list of four new nominees, he noted that one was a prominent restaurant owner. Kolin went to the board of health, asked to check the file on restaurants, and found that the new nominee's restaurants had a number of citations for violations, among them failing to post a Grade C rating for the restaurant (the lowest rating) as the law required. In another restaurant, there were no bathroom facilities, which brought another citation. The restaurant owner had pleaded guilty to the first charge of failing to display the rating. Kolin's checking of the board of health records gave a new dimension to what would have been a routine appointment story:

A Wake County man who pleaded guilty to health violations at his Garner restaurant last summer has been recommended for a seat on the Wake Board of Health by a committee of Wake County commissioners.

Bobby O. Wilder was recommended for the position Tuesday on a 2-1 vote by the commissioners' public affairs committee.

After receiving complaints Thursday from health board members and Dr. Robert M. Hall, the county health director, the committee agreed to meet with Hall at 9 a.m. today to reconsider the nomination.

The full board is scheduled to consider the appointment Monday.

The health board oversees the health department, which inspects and grades restaurants.

Commissioners Elizabeth B. Cofield and J. Stewart Adcock voted to recommend Wilder; Robert B. Heater opposed him.

At the health board's request, the county attorney's office filed charges last May in Wake District Court against Wilder for seven counts of failing to display a grade card after his Hickory House Restaurant on U.S. 70 received two poor inspections by the health department.

The seven charges were combined for the court action, and Wilder pleaded guilty to one count of health violations, according to court records. Wilder was ordered to pay court costs and comply with the ordinance.

Wilder, a twice-defeated candidate for Raleigh City Council, said he did not think serving on the health board would create a conflict of interest.

"I'm not that small, and I have no selfish motives," Wilder said. "I have no bag of axes to grind."

He said he pleaded guilty to the charge to keep employees who had been subpoenaed "from being dragged into it."

"There is no evidence that I failed to post (the grade card)," Wilder said.

Health department records, though, show that the restaurant had a Grade B rating that was not posted at the time of the inspectors' visit in March. The restaurant received a Grade C rating, the lowest possible, after a sanitation inspection March 29.

N.C. General Statutes require restaurant managers to post grade cards "in a conspicuous place designated by the sanitarian where it may readily be observed by the public."

Inspections at the restaurant April 2, April 6 and May 2 also revealed that the grade card was not posted, according to department files. Health inspectors held a conference with Wilder after the May 2 check and advised him he was in violation for failing to display the card.

Dr. Jane H. Wooten, then-interim director, asked the health board at a May 14 meeting to initiate the court action against Wilder.

Wilder's name was originally submitted to the commissioners by T. Jerry Williams, executive vice president of the N.C. Restaurant Association.

Williams said Wilder had "done a very good job" during his six years as a member of the sanitation awards committee of the N.C. Public Health Association. . . .

Kolin did not rest there. "On a lark," he said, "I decided to check the records of campaign contributions at the board of elections." Kolin found a tie between the restaurant owner and one of the commissioners supporting the restaurant owner's nomination. The next day after the first story, Kolin wrote:

A Wake County man whose nomination to the Wake Board of Health has been challenged because of health violations at his Garner restaurant was a major contributor to the 1978 election campaign of his chief commission supporter.

Bobby O. Wilder, owner and operator of Hickory House Restaurant on U.S. 70, contributed $350 to J. Stewart Adcock's campaign for commissioner, according to reports filed by Adcock with the Wake Board of Elections.

Adcock said in an interview Friday that the contribution was not the reason he continued to support Wilder's nomination, even after the News and Observer revealed that Wilder had pleaded guilty in August to health violations at his restaurant.

"I want someone representing the restaurant industry on the board because that's one of the biggest functions of the health department," Adcock said.

"Bobby Wilder was the only (restaurateur) whose name was submitted, and I have no problems with his qualifications," Adcock added. "I think the world of him personally."

Wilder, a twice unsuccessful candidate for Raleigh City Council, said the contributions consisted of a reception held for Adcock and other candidates at the restaurant and catering food to Adcock's campaign headquarters on the primary and run-off election nights.

"I didn't give him a dime in cash," Wilder said in a telephone interview.

Adcock agreed: "I don't know of any money that changed hands."

Wilder was one of six people recommended Tuesday by the commissioners' public affairs committee to fill the six seats that become vacant Jan. 1 on the nine-member health board. . . .

When the appointment became final, Kolin did not let readers forget the facts, including new information that came to light when tax and other records were checked:

Wake County commissioners Monday named Bobby O. Wilder, convicted last summer of health violations at his Garner restaurant, to the Wake Board of Health.

The appointment came over strong objections of Dr. Robert Hall, county health director.

"The Board of Health should be composed of people sympathetic with the law and the rules pertaining to public health," Hall told commissioners.

Wilder pleaded guilty in Wake District Court last August to one count of failing to display a grade card after his Hickory House Restaurant on U.S. 70 received two poor inspections by the health department.

Because of the conviction, Wilder's appointment could have a "demoralizing effect to the board members," Hall warned commissioners.

Commissioners Robert B. Heater and Betty Ann Knudsen, who opposed the appointment in the 5-2 vote, said Wilder had other problems with the county that made him unsuitable to serve.

They were referring to Wilder's conviction last year for violations of the county soil erosion and sedimentation ordinance on an 87-acre tract of land he owned on N.C. 55 near Apex.

Also, Wilder was listed last year among the county's top-100 delinquent taxpayers. The county recovered $2,587 in delinquent county property taxes after the U.S. District Court ordered the sale of some of Wilder's land to pay federal, state and county taxes.

The department also has attributed 47 cases of gastrointestinal illnesses on Dec. 14-15, 1977, to contaminated chicken and country-style steak at his restaurant.

Chairman M. Edmund Aycock, J. Stewart Adcock, Elizabeth B. Cofield, J. T. Knott and Vassar P. Shearon voted for Wilder's appointment. . . .

Another Kolin story covered the awaited announcement of five candidates for the job of Wake County manager. But the county commissioners revealed only four names. Kolin needed the other name. Kolin has a quiet, unassuming manner, which, along with his reputation for accuracy and fairness, gives him easy access to most offices.

On his rounds at the county commissioners' office, Kolin asked one of the commissioners for the name of the fifth nominee for county manager. Kolin was told that the fifth man had agreed to be a candidate only if his name was not made public, perhaps in an effort to protect his present job.

"Can you tell me a little bit about this fifth man?" Kolin asked. The commissioner told him that the fifth nominee was a city manager but would not say where.

Kolin asked for the phone numbers of the other four. The commissioner pulled out a list. Kolin noticed that the list had five phone numbers. As the commissioner read off the four numbers, Kolin, eyeing the list upside down, also jotted down the fifth number.

Kolin checked the phone book for the area code and found out the number was in Iowa. He called Iowa information and discovered the number was an Ames, Iowa, exchange.

Rather than calling the number directly, Kolin called an Ames radio station and asked for the name of the Ames city manager and his phone number. It was the same phone number Kolin had from the list. Kolin could now be sure whom he was talking to when he called.

He dialed the number and said, "Sir, I understand you're one of the five who are being considered for Wake County manager."

The man told Kolin that if his name were printed, he would bow out of consideration. Kolin and his paper decided to use it. "People have a legitimate right to know who is being considered," Kolin said.

Kolin's story told it all:

Five finalists for the job of Wake County manager were selected by a committee of Wake County Commissioners Thursday.

The three-member committee interviewed one of the finalists. Carl G. Johnson, 58, a local government consultant in Marina Del Rey, Calif. Johnson was county manager of Guilford County from 1963-67.

Courthouse sources who asked not to be identified cited Johnson's North Carolina connections as a positive factor in his consideration. Several commissioners have said they preferred hiring someone with county government experience in North Carolina.

Commissioner Robert B. Heater, chairman of the search committee, said there was no front-runner for the job.

The new manager will succeed Garland H. Jones, who was fired by commissioners in December. Commissioners have indicated that they wanted Jones to serve in a new position as internal auditor, but they have not offered him that job.

In addition to Johnson, the committee released the names of three of the other four finalists:

Lynn R. Muchmore, 36, of Knightdale, project director in the Center of Policy Research for the National Governors' Association in Washington.

Muchmore served as director of the N.C. Office of State Planning in 1974-77 in the administration of Gov. James E. Holshouser Jr. After leaving state government, Muchmore was a partner in the Wendell Knightdale Airport with Wake Commissioner J. T. Knott for about one year.

John C. Gridley, 57, of Clifton Park, N.Y., a member of the Chemung County Board of Supervisors in Elmira, N.Y., from 1953-73. From 1973-77, he served as deputy commissioner for local government for the State of New York. Since then, he has served as adviser to the New York Legislature and the New York State Association of Counties.

John L. Rowe Jr., 34, assistant city manager of Suffolk, Va. He served on the staff of the Norfolk, Va., city manager from 1971-75.

The fifth candidate, whose name the committee withheld at his request, was Terry Sprenkel, 47, city manager of Ames, Iowa, according to sources.

When contacted Tuesday night, Sprenkel said, "If I was one of the finalists, I'm not now."

When told of that comment, Heater said Sprenkel had told the committee he would withdraw his candidacy if his name were made public. "If his interest is no stronger than that, then it really doesn't concern me (if he withdraws)," Heater said. "We have a multitude of other good candidates."

The committee received 142 applicants for the job. If the committee cannot agree on a candidate after interviewing the finalists, Heater said it may consider some of the other candidates who were not included among the finalists. . . .

Kolin makes a point to see the county manager, Carl Johnson, each day. Johnson says of Kolin: "I don't believe in public relations for government agencies—that is for chewing gum people. The best PR concerning government is to have what it does reported accurately," and he credits Kolin with being that kind of reporter.

In the afternoon before returning to the paper to write his stories, Kolin may do an interview with a local official. One is the local librarian, who seeks to get more funds for renovations and hopefully a new building. Kolin's last stop may be a return to one of the county offices, or as on one day, a stop at the elections board, just in case another name may have come in under the wire for an upcoming election.

Good contacts help when county deliberations are closed to reporters. City editor Charles D. Mitchell of the Vicksburg (Miss.) *Evening Post* comments on one county personnel session which shut out his reporter:

> The hiring of an attorney by county supervisors in Mississippi is big news, often controversial, because of the opportunity for lucrative income. Under state law, such personnel matters can be handled in executive session, and I think the story below reflects a bit of the indignation the reporter felt at being excluded—whether this is fair or not is subject to debate.
>
> Sources were the supervisors' president, the new attorney's law firm, the sheriff, and file background on past attorneys and county salaries.

Note also the hitch-on technique of "other action" after the main item:

After some reportedly heated debate and a split vote, the Warren County Board of Supervisors Tuesday chose Gerald Braddock, a partner in the law firm of Ellis, Braddock and Bost, as the board's new attorney.

Neither the Warren County Chancery Clerk nor members of the press were present when the decision was made, but it was later learned that the board's vote split 3-2 in favor of Braddock.

Board President Jimmy Andrews refused to say how each board member voted but would only say that "the motion carried." Andrews, who informed the press after the vote was taken and the discussion ended, said board members had been trying since Monday to reach a decision and that yesterday's vote followed "much heated discussion."

Braddock was out of the state this morning and could not be reached for comment, but a firm spokesman said they would do the best job possible to represent their clients.

The new board attorney is a native of Ripley and received both his undergraduate and juris doctor degrees from the University of Mississippi. He has practiced law in Vicksburg for about 16 years and has been with Ellis, Braddock and Bost for about two years.

John Prewitt had served as the board attorney until recently when he was appointed as a Circuit Judge. Prewitt's son, Mark Prewitt, then had taken over much of the responsibilities of the position until the recent election.

In other action Tuesday, Warren County Sheriff Paul Barrett requested an additional $300 monthly salary increase for his deputies and a $200 monthly increase for all other sheriff's department employees.

That increase, if approved, would constitute more than one third of the present budget allocation for salaries in the sheriff's department and the jail.

The increases, which would amount to approximately $95,000 annually, would not affect the sheriff or chief deputy whose salaries are set by the state Legislature. . . .

State House Reporting

Besides the governor, executive officers in a state include the lieutenant governor, secretary of state, state treasurer, attorney general, superintendent of public education, and auditor.

The lieutenant governor presides over the senate, as well as filling in for the governor when he is away. On rare occasions, the lieutenant governor may try to impose his or her own philosophy in the governor's absence (Gov. Jerry Brown, of California, sued his lieutenant governor, Mike Curb, for making a state appellate court appointment when Brown was in Washington). The lieutenant governor is usually elected with the governor, but in Tennessee the speaker of the senate is the lieutenant governor ex-officio. In Alaska, the secretary of state serves as lieutenant governor.

The secretary of state supervises elections and is in charge of keeping public documents such as the laws passed by the legislature and proclamations by the governor. In some states, the secretary of state's office issues incorporation certificates and drivers' licenses. This is an elective office in 39 states, appointive in 11.

The state treasurer serves as keeper of the state's funds, pays the bills, and may be responsible for collecting state taxes. The attorney general prosecutes or defends cases involving the state. He or she gives legal advice on state matters to state agencies (with power to investigate them) and in some states supervises local prosecuting attorneys. The *Opinions of the Attorney General* appear regularly in most states; the publications do not have the force of law but are seldom challenged in court.

The state school superintendent interprets state laws and decides how education funds are to be distributed. The superintendent also is in charge of teacher certification, school accreditation, and curriculum.

Law-making bodies in states are generally called state legislatures, although officially they may have other names. Nineteen states call their legislative bodies the general assembly; Montana, North Dakota, and Oregon call theirs the legislative assembly; Massachusetts and New Hampshire, the general court. The one-house unicameral legislature in Nebraska goes by the name of senate.

Except for Nebraska, the legislatures are divided into two chambers. The upper house is the senate; the lower or larger group of representatives has different names: house of representatives, house of delegates, or general assembly.

Members submit bills to the legislature, but bills may originate in many ways.[7] State administrators and agencies initiate action on many bills. Committees of the legislature prepare bills. Committees have specific functions:

- Standing committees study and/or prepare bills throughout the legislative session. Some committees may organize to investigate a specific topic.
- Interim or ad interim committees have special assignments between legislative sessions and may investigate an issue in detail before drafting a bill.
- Conference committees work out the differences between similar bills which each house has passed.
- Select or special study committees have a particular purpose and work within time limits.
- Joint committees have members from both houses.
- Committees of the whole include the total membership of a house sitting as a committee, usually to permit a wider range of discussion than might be possible in a smaller committee.

Apart from the committee process, bills may have their inception in a legislative council—a large permanent joint committee with a permanent staff. The legislative council looks into areas of possible legislation and provides background and reports useful in drafting legislation.

Bills may also originate in investigative commissions which the governor or the legislature sets up. The governor with his "legislative program" is also a source for bills.

The following summary for Pennsylvania demonstrates the process of regulations for considering bills.

A number of provisions regarding legislation are included in the Constitution of Pennsylvania:

- No law may be passed except by bill, and no bill may be amended to change its original purpose. (Occasionally, however, the entire language of a bill has been stripped and replaced with provisions relating to a different purpose.)
- No bill may have more than one subject except a general appropriation bill.
- All bills must be referred to committee before being considered by either house.
- Each bill must be considered on three different days.
- All amendments to bills must be printed before they are voted upon or before the final vote to pass the entire bill is taken.
- All bills must pass by a roll call vote, and the names and votes must be recorded in the Journal. Each bill must pass by an elected majority (26 senators and 102 representatives).
- Presiding officers must sign all bills and resolutions in the presence of their respective houses.
- If the Governor vetoes a bill, a two-thirds majority of members elected to each house is required to override the veto.
- The general appropriation bill includes monies appropriated for the executive, legislative, and judicial branches and for the public debt and public schools. All other appropriation bills—generally termed "non-preferred"—must be separate bills, one to a subject.
- All revenue bills originate in the House of Representatives.
- Appropriation bills may originate in either house. Passage normally requires a constitutional majority; non-preferred bills, however, such as those appropriating money for state-related institutions, require a two-thirds vote of the members elected to each house.
- Members may not raise the salary or extend the term of office of any public officer, including themselves, while they are in office.

PASSAGE OF A BILL—A bill passes through various stages before it becomes law:

- introduction and referral to committee,
- committee examination,
- review by caucus,
- three considerations and passage by one house,
- referral to the other house and similar procedures,
- adjustment in conference committee if necessary,
- signing by the leaders of both houses,
- action by the Governor.[8]

A major task for state house reporters is localizing. Harry Stoffer, a Harrisburg (Pa.) bureau reporter for Calkins Newspapers, says, "A reporter has to go for the 'angle' that best suits his readership." Explaining the following story, he says:

> The primary substance of this story for most state newspapers would have been details about the new candidates in the field, but for the Bucks (County) papers (which Stoffer serves), whose readership is probably primarily concerned with the fate of their "favorite son," I chose to concentrate on candidate Lewis's reactions to the enlarging field, with a few interpretative points scattered here and there. . . .

HARRISBURG—The field of candidates seeking the Democratic nomination for U.S. Senate increased last week when two Montgomery County residents formally entered the race.

The newcomers to the field are Peter J. Liacouras of Gladwyne, dean of the law school at Temple University, and Edward Mezvinsky of Narberth, former Iowa congressman and United Nations official.

The two join a field that consists of state Sen. H. Craig Lewis (D-6) of Feasterville, former Pennsylvania Education Secretary John C. Pittenger of Lancaster County and state Rep. Joseph Rhodes Jr. (D-24) of Pittsburgh.

Asked about the new candidates, Lewis used the opportunity to take a jab at them by saying, "I don't see either as a substantial or significant candidate."

Anticipating that another two or three candidates may yet enter the field, Lewis said he does not believe the increasing demand for the contributor's dollar is going to affect seriously his fund-raising efforts in the short run.

Enhances candidacy

If, however, some of the candidates do not drop out by late January or early February, there could be more of a problem. Most of the candidates are talking in terms of needing a half million dollars for the primary campaign. Liacouras said a full $1 million.

As far as political strategy is concerned, Lewis said, the large field enhances his candidacy for the present because it is drawing more attention to the U.S. Senate race. Up until now, most followers of the political activities have been concentrating on the presidential campaigns.

In the future, the Lower Bucks legislator said, he will view the large field from different perspectives.

If former Pittsburgh Mayor Peter F. Flaherty enters the race, Lewis hypothesized, he would prefer to take him on one-on-one, or at least in a limited field. The point is that lesser-known candidates are likely to divide the votes cast by those who don't go for a "name" candidate like Flaherty.

Without Flaherty in the race, a large field could work to Lewis's advantage, he claimed.

Sees potential impact

Lewis, who formally announced his candidacy in August, tried to minimize the impact Liacouras and Mezvinsky—both southeastern Pennsylvanians—will have on his regional base of support.

He said Mezvinsky is an Iowan "but for the fact he decided to buy a house in Montgomery County."

However, he noted, "To the extent that either one stays in the race, and if they make themselves known, they are going to impact on my vote."

He said he expects their strategies are to get some big contributions and get a lot of exposure from the electronic media, but Lewis claimed, "People in Pennsylvania are suspicious of these kinds of things."

Neither Liacouras nor Mezvinsky offers much in the way of experience and a record of public service, Lewis charged.

He said he views Pittenger as a better opponent at this point because he has experience and money and is making the kind of effort—getting around and meeting people—that is needed to run a campaign in Pennsylvania.

Mezvinsky, 42, married a Philadelphian and moved to the state after losing a re-election bid for his Congressional seat in 1976.

Liacouras, 48, was a professor at Temple when Lewis was a student there, but they were never in the same class.

In an interview here Thursday, Liacouras said he thinks his law school work is appropriate training for the U.S. Senate and views himself as a potential "citizen legislator."

On the Republican side, state Sen. Edward I. Howard's campaign for a U.S. Senate nomination got a nudge forward with an announcement by former NATO commander Alexander M. Haig Jr., another Montgomery County resident, that he plans to enter the presidential primary in New Hampshire.

Howard, (R-10) of Doylestown, had said that Haig was one of the possible "name" candidates who could cripple his chances.

He said Thursday, "I think that the more other potential candidates' plans crystalize, the better it is for all of us."

The other announced Republicans are U.S. Rep. Marc L. Marks (R-24) of Mercer County and Warren R. Williams Jr., a borough councilman in Montrose, Susquehanna County.

On the legislative beat, Reid K. Beveridge, senior legislative reporter for the *Wisconsin State Journal* in Madison, Wis., outlines a typical day at the state legislature:

> I arrive at Capitol at 9 a.m. to attend the Joint Finance Committee meeting reporting out the budget bill to Senate. . . . Go to Assembly at 10 a.m. to cover morning session. . . . A few bills passed. . . . Noon, go to lunch with two colleagues and a friend from D.C. At 1:30 p.m., attend meeting of State Building Commission, which is composed of governor and legislators who must approve all state construction and bonding. . . . At 4 p.m., begin writing stories, three of them, from Finance Committee, Assembly and Building Commission. Finish work at 6:30 p.m. and go home.

For Walter Dean, capitol bureau chief for the *Arkansas Democrat* in Little Rock, Ark.:

> There is no typical day. In covering a monster as gigantic and constantly writhing as state government, a reporter must rely chiefly on intuition, news tips, and gleanings from otherwise routine meetings. A day consists of BS-ing with blabber-mouth bureaucrats; floating between legislative and commission meetings; trying to sort wheat from chaff in verbose attorney general's legal opinions and state Supreme Court decisions and reducing self-serving news releases to their true news substance.

Dan Walters, political writer for the Sacramento (Calif.) *Union,* says:

> When it is a particularly hectic week in the Legislature, my day would go something like this: 9 a.m., check into the Capitol bureau, open the mail rapidly and hit the Capitol, pick up files listing committee hearings, attend one or two of them, back at office by noon, eat lunch at desk while writing morning product. Back at committee hearings at 1:30, try to get back into office by 4 p.m. to write those, while listening on squawk box for a couple of late votes from committee. During recesses or during campaigns, schedule would be entirely different.

Marie Puente of the Santa Fe (N.M.) *New Mexican,* describes reporting during an interim between sessions:

> Keep track of what an agency is up to, whether in new programs, administrative disputes, cabinet decisions, gubernatorial directives, problems in particular agencies, firings, and so on. One particular day, we got onto a story about an apparent dispute between one cabinet secretary and another, who happened to be secretary of the most powerful department and the governor's nephew to boot. I would begin by talking with each secretary and finding out the nature of the dispute and what each side has to complain about . . . then talk to other cabinet secretaries or agency heads to find out if anyone else in state government is upset with this particular secretary and the nature of either one's complaints. I write a hard news story on the fact that the powerful secretary thinks his adversary is on thin ice with the governor and then an analysis piece on the fact that the powerful secretary is no longer an equal among equals but practically a surrogate governor. And other agency heads resent it. Stories take some running around to interview people, plus phone work to interview sources who would rather not be identified.

Working the people angle thoroughly, Margaret Edds of the *Virginian-Pilot* in Norfolk, Va., spends her day at the state Capitol in Richmond, Va., with such dedication that she hardly wastes a second.

From a long mezzanine office of the somewhat ancient Raleigh Hotel directly across from the Capitol in Richmond, she organizes her schedule and pursuits for the day. By 10 a.m. she is stepping very fast up the long hill to the Capitol and leaves any who try to keep up with her out of breath.

She knows what her story is going to be for the next day—an announcement of some 95 highway sections, roads, and bridges that an increased state highway tax would help to improve. She must, of course, stop in at noon for the perfunctory brief session of the House of Delegates. But her main effort will be to pursue members of the finance committees of both the Senate and the House and others to gauge the support for the proposed 4% additional sales tax on the wholesale price of gasoline. The governor is proposing a bill but has not submitted it. Edds wants to know the whys, what is likely to be done, who will take what roles, and the long-term outcome of any new tax. She must have a Sunday feature on the subject wrapped up by the next day.

She has a list of all the committees and their members and stops in the lobby of the Capitol office building to put the room numbers after the names of the finance committee members. In the next hour she crowds in a half dozen interviews.

With the Republicans supporting Governor John Dalton, she tries to pin some legislators down, hoping for some new angles for leads and zeros in on new developments and strategy for her Sunday piece.

To Republican Representative Herb Bateman, Edds asks:

> Do legislators have anything specific in mind (about a new bill)? . . .
>
> Do you think a new bill would supply the money needed? . . .
>
> Do you think your colleagues are as concerned about the need for improved highways as you? . . .
>
> Would it have been better if more were done before the opening session, in educating the people . . . and getting the facts out? . . .
>
> Do you think the governor is moving specifically enough on the highway tax bill? . . . What is he doing behind the scenes? . . . Do you talk to the governor regularly? . . .
>
> Any problem why the bill hasn't come down sooner? . . .
>
> Do you see that the fact the bill hasn't been drafted as any kind of problem? . . .
>
> Will it be ready next week? . . .
>
> Should the truck driver differential be increased? . . .

The representative says he hears different reports. She continues: "So, who's telling the truth? . . ."

Then Edds, looking toward another feature for next week, works in some questions about a coastal ecology bill. She wants to know the representative's role in drafting that bill and gets him to talk by comparing his bill to another bill by a colleague that failed the previous year.

"Why do you see this as an acceptable way to go? . . . Will the administration support your bill? . . . Definitely? . . ."

From the Democrats she wanted to know:

Will the Democrats get together and have a proposal of their own? . . .
Are there enough (votes) to pass it? . . .
What is your assessment of their (Republicans') selling job? . . .
Have they made their case? . . .
In terms of the bill not being drafted yet, is there a problem or is it reasonable? . . .
What will be acceptable to you? . . .
Have you been invited over (to see the governor)? . . .

She picks up a statement which the senator has prepared for a newspaper in another town and promises not to use any part of it in her paper without checking with him first.

She stands in the hall and muses: "Let's see . . . what have we missed? . . ." Edds finds a couple of other room numbers on a floor two flights down. She prefers to bound down the stairs rather than lose time using the elevator.

In the state Capitol, she grabs a cup of coffee which she carries with her into the chambers of the House of Delegates as she tries to find some of the solons she's missed for comment. She sits in the front row and glances around as Speaker A. L. Philpott gavels the session to order. Visiting school and senior citizen groups are introduced in the House and a few noncontroversial bills sail through to final passage. In a half hour the session is over. After a quick lunch in the Capitol snack bar, she is off down a grassy slope—it is the shortest distance—to the hotel office. She has talked to a dozen people in a brief time. "So much of political reporting is people perception," she says. "Politics is what people are thinking. Perception can become the reality. You try to see as many people as possible."

Among special topics, Edds and three other *Virginian-Pilot* writers produced a series of articles on conflict of interest among legislators. They studied the laws, discovered Virginia had more loopholes than most states, profiled the backgrounds and interests of legislators, matched their professional interests with the causes they championed, and made it clear the price Virginians might be paying for not having a monitoring ethics committee. The five-part series which ran in the *Virginian-Pilot* was reprinted and widely distributed under the title, "Private Profit, Public Trust."

First of a series

Protected by conflict of interest laws that are riddled with loopholes and virtually unpoliced, Virginia General Assembly members routinely engage in self-serving practices that at least 31 other states have declared illegal.

That is the conclusion reached by The Virginian-Pilot after a two-month investigation of the state's ethics laws and the conduct of its legislators.

In Virginia, legislators can and do accept free trips or speaking fees from special interest groups without either side's disclosing the payments. That is illegal in New York, California, Massachusetts, Wisconsin, South Carolina, Oklahoma, and at least 11 other states.

Virginia legislators can and do represent private clients before state agencies whose budgets they oversee and whose members they appoint or confirm. Many of their appearances would be banned in Ohio, New Jersey, Florida, Connecticut, Alaska, and Hawaii.

Virginia legislators can and do conceal their financial holdings through the use of disclosure forms that often disclose very little. A legislator who supplied only what was required by the Virginia form would be breaking the law in North Carolina, Maryland, Illinois, Pennsylvania, Texas, Alabama, Washington, and at least 15 other states.

Virginia legislators can and do write laws that benefit them or their clients. That practice, while not illegal, is subject to scrutiny by ethics committees in numerous other states. There is no such scrutiny in Virginia.

While the repeated refrain of the legislative power structure is the old homily, "If it ain't broke, don't fix it," The Pilot's study of hundreds of legislative documents and court files suggests that Virginia's ethics laws are—if not broken—at least in need of major repair.

"It's the way the system works," said Raymond E. Vickery of Vienna, a Democratic member of the House of Delegates for six years and an outspoken advocate of stricter controls. "The very interesting thing in Virginia is not that the conflicts are any less blatant than in other states, but that they have become regularized and systematized in such a way that they're legal across the board. It's all so very subtle."

Twenty-one states have formed independent ethics commissions with authority to investigate complaints of legislator misconduct, according to the National Municipal League, and virtually every state legislature has at least designated a legislative committee to handle such complaints. Virginia has done neither.

Asked who would handle a formal complaint about unethical conduct, John Warren Cooke, the retiring Speaker and, after 30 years, the Assembly's rules expert, replied: "I just don't know. It hasn't come up."

And even if an ethics panel existed, it would have no cause to investigate some controversial practices that are not prohibited by Virginia law.

One of the law's most serious shortcomings, critics say, is its failure to control appearances by lawyer-legislators before state regulatory agencies. At least 15 states ban, limit, or monitor that practice. The Old Dominion does not, though it has a far higher percentage of lawyers in its Legislature than any other state. In 1979, lawyers made up 52 percent of the Virginia Assembly. Texas ranked second with 41 percent.

These were among the specific problems and practices uncovered by The Pilot investigation:

• Well over half of the 73 lawyers in the 1979 Legislature have appeared before state agencies on behalf of private clients. A few of them have gained reputations as specialists in arguing cases before particular agencies.

Many businessmen told The Pilot that they believe they will fare better with regulatory agencies if their lawyers have legislative ties. That line of thinking was evident at the State Corporation Commission, where between May 1, 1978, and Oct. 30, 1979, a legislator or a recently retired legislator served as legal counsel in 54 percent of the contested banking cases.

• A survey of 1978 and 1979 files at two regulatory commissions—the SCC and the Alcoholic Beverage Control Commission—supports the theory that lawyer-legislators get better results at state agencies.

The Assembly appoints the three SCC commissioners, confirms the appointments of the three ABC commissioners, and controls the budgets of both agencies. Virginia, incidentally, has the only legislature in the nation that appoints the commissioners who regulate banks, utilities, and other corporations.

• Frequent appearances by lawyer-legislators before the ABC Commission have created a morale problem in that agency, according to many ABC employees. They say the commission and some of its staff are, for political reasons, partial toward legislators' clients.

Two Tidewater legislators, Del. Thomas W. Moss Jr. and Sen. Peter K. Babalas, were cited by ABC employees as lawyers whose clients get preferential treatment from the commission at hearings on liquor license applications or alleged ABC violations. Moss, who handled twice as many ABC cases in 1978-79 as any other attorney in Tidewater, is chairman of the House committee that screens ABC-related legislation. He also is the newly elected House majority leader.

Moss and Babalas deny that their legislative position gives them an advantage in arguing clients' cases before the ABC Commission. . . .

The Philadelphia *Inquirer* also carried an in-depth report of government operations in an eight-part series of articles on the Pennsylvania state legislature in Harrisburg. Reprinted eventually as a 36-page supplement, the 1979 series—as the *Inquirer* put it—sought to lay bare ". . . an entrenched network of systematic corruption—a system set up by legislators to enable themselves and their political allies and organizations to grow fat at the expense of taxpayers." Three reporters spent eight months ferreting through "mountains of records," looking through materials in 67 county court houses, examining payroll and spending account records, and interviewing hundreds of politicians and lobbyists.

Campaign Reporting

From time to time, political reporters' schedules change radically—especially every two years—when they go out on the campaign trail to cover the candidates.

Hugh Robertson of the Richmond *News Leader* suggests that when you are on the road you:

• Always carry a tape recorder. You don't have to record everything. But a notebook can get awfully full. Use the tape recorder to record the important things.

• Keep a file on each candidate and the issues. If the candidate changes on an issue such as the sales tax, you will know. You can look back at the file to see what he said on the topic in another part of the state.

• Have a friend in the office who can get background and who can tell you what the other guy (competitor or the other candidate) is doing that day someplace else.

At United Press International in Washington, Ted Shields, national desk editor, suggests:

- Don't get caught up in doing too many little pieces on each speech, but do over-all articles.
- Get to know the candidate on a personal basis so you can recognize when the candidate is angry, tired or depressed—so you will be able "to throw something at him in order to get an unexpected response."
- The personal side of the candidate may be a far better source and more helpful than the press officer.

When the candidate's schedule makes it difficult to catch the immediate editions, or your story must be a second day story, Earle Stern of the Lynn (Mass.) *Item* suggests that doing a "crowd" piece can work:

BOSTON—There's a certain something about any event involving the Kennedy clan—call it charisma or whatever—and it certainly was in evidence Tuesday night at the Park Plaza.

Sen. Edward M. Kennedy kicked off the fundraising part of his presidential election campaign in grand style, helped by lots of North Shore residents.

For the admission price of $1,000, a couple or an individual guest enjoyed some exquisitely prepared foods, an almost infinite variety of beverages and some rather interesting company.

No one really knows just how much the state's senior senator raked into his campaign coffers last night, but the Park Plaza ballroom was packed with perhaps 1,500 persons, so estimates in excess of $500,000 are not unreasonable.

Rudy Fiore of Saugus and his wife, Rita, were more than happy to be at a party.

Fiore's bus company is back in full operation after a lengthy strike and Fiore, a former Everett policeman, was more than ready for some celebrating.

"I like him, so I'm helping him," he said of Kennedy, noting that he also has involved himself in other political campaigns, including that of Atty. Gen. Francis X. Bellotti, whose wife was among the guests at the Kennedy fundraiser.

Nondas Lagonakis of Salem, owner of Bill and Bob's Roast Beef sandwich shop in Salem, accompanied by his wife, Ada, understandably ignored the huge slabs of roast beef and nibbled instead on some shrimp while talking politics with Angelique Lee of Washington, D.C., a Kennedy campaign aide.

Mr. and Mrs. Richard G. Len of Lynn entered the ballroom at about the same time that former Gov. Michael S. Dukakis put in an appearance.

Other political personalities on hand included State Auditor Thaddeus Buczko, D-Salem, and Sen. Joseph Timilty, D-Boston, along with Lt. Gov. Thomas P. O'Neill III who is a New England campaign coordinator for Kennedy.

Boston Atty. Jerrill Krowen of Beverly Cove, no stranger in political circles, said the party was every bit as good as his own annual New Year's Day bash.

Krowen was mingling with, among others, John Anderson of Everett, president of Radio Component Corp. of Lynn; and Barbara Marberblatt of Marblehead, treasurer of the firm.

Arriving just before Sen. Kennedy's entrance was John Angelopulos of Swampscott, operator of Nandee's restaurant in Lynn.

There were familiar faces everywhere for the North Shore crowd.

At one end of the bounteous buffet table were Diane Hezekiah Mitchell of Lynn, who recently ran an impressive but unsuccessful campaign for a school committee seat, and her cousin, Joyce Hezekiah, also of Lynn.

At the other end of the table were Edward and Marie Casacchio of Lynnfield.

Ed, who operates auto dealerships in Rochester, N.H. and Wakefield, said it was somewhat unusual for him to get involved in political affairs.

"I happened to be talking to a friend of mine who is in the same business and that's why I'm here tonight," he said. . . .

Says Stern:

The Kennedy campaign story was a fun piece and suited a local newspaper's parochial slant. The *Item* is an evening paper, so the Kennedy fundraiser was 24 hours old by the time we hit the streets with it.

Doing that story involved little more than mixing with the crowd and striking up conversations that provided explanations for individual involvement.

Janice Law of the Fort Lauderdale *News* also watched the crowd when Alabama Governor George Wallace was on the campaign trail.

LAKE WORTH—Alabama Gov. George Wallace attracted an overflow crowd of about 3,500 persons here last night and had to speak twice to accommodate fans who stood in four-deep lines stretching more than a block to see him.

Officials said hundreds turned away discouraged when they saw the already-huge crowds and hundreds more might have attended had it not been for rumors that Wallace had canceled his first 1976 campaign trip into Southeast Florida because of torn ligaments in his knee, suffered when an aide dropped him Monday in Pensacola. He did cancel scheduled daytime appearances yesterday.

"Your Lyin' Eyes" and other country and western favorites by a Grand Ole Opry band resounded as persons with parcels or handbags lined up to be searched by security agents. Security seemed extremely tight.

Wallace greeted the crowds with his characteristic military-style salute and told them, "Frankly, I didn't expect to have this kind of reception tonight."

His delivery was dramatic Baptist preacher style, punctuated with familiar slashing and pointing gestures.

"I might not be the best man or woman to be president of the United States, but I am the best candidate in either party running," said the Democratic hopeful.

In his two speeches, Wallace repeated criticism of big government, welfare cheats and the news media.

Some of Wallace's comments:

"The reason New York City is broke is because they took the advice of the New York Times. The people of Alabama haven't taken their advice, and we're fine.

"Nobody minds giving out of the goodness of their hearts, but at least 25 percent (of welfare recipients) are cheaters. . . ."

To repeated applause, he said the average citizen is "king and queen in America now, and they are going to take back the Democratic Party" which he said liberals usurped in 1972.

"The social issue of this election is whether the American middle class, this great class which fought our wars and paid taxes and stood up for America, is going to survive," Wallace said.

Hubert L. Pitts, 57, a plumber from Pahokee, was among the first of those crowding the Palm Beach Junior College auditorium before 6 for the 7:30 p.m. rally.

"It's Jesus Christ first, Wallace second, and my wife third," the tall Pitts said with a huge smile. "I just love every bone in Wallace's body.

"Why? Because he is America, that's why. He is for everything America stands for," Pitts said.

Long-haired Craig Mangie, 20, a student at Westminster College in Pennsylvania, was also one of the first in line.

"I like Wallace because he is for the middle class, and the middle class in America is getting ripped off," said Mangie.

"I like Wallace because he gives wonderful speeches," said Beatrice Shafer, 75, a Wallace campaign worker who sported an American flag in the hatband of her Wallace for President hat.

She and many others in the audience also wore American flag lapel pins.

A competitor, the *Sun-Sentinel* in Pompano Beach, concentrated on what the governor said:

LAKE WORTH—Alabama Gov. George C. Wallace opened fire on big government, the news media, the Democratic party and welfare cheaters as he spoke before an overflow crowd of 2,600 at Palm Beach Junior College last night.

Explaining *her* approach, Janice Law says:

• Review in your mind how you anticipate colleagues might write the assignment, and decide how yours might be similar to, or different from, theirs.

• Do some prior library research. A quick review of the library clips before departing on the assignment told me the "color" background that Wallace had been injured two days before his local speech—and injured in a very unusual way—dropped, in his wheelchair, by one of his own aides. Also, the accident happened in another Florida city, weaving a bit of local color in my second graph.

• Arrive early at your assignment. I've gotten some of my best stories by arriving an hour or more early, as I did here, and just "hanging around"—not with other reporters—and keeping my eyes and ears open. Here I used my early arrival time to interview many of the persons standing in line, and got the colorful and revealing "human interest" quotes which comprise the second half of the piece. Also I took care to select persons from widely differing age groups and physical appearance, and described them with their quotes, which I felt illustrated Wallace's wide appeal. Early arrival also allowed me to note the tight security, which added another "color" dimension to my story.

• Use color (significant detail), especially in campaign stories, because usually political speeches are Dullsville. In my third graph, I mentioned the country and western music, and even the title of one song, "Your Lyin' Eyes." Retrospectively, it occurred to me that my selection of a song title could be construed as editorial comment, but it was not intended as such. With the auditory reference, the visual reference to the long lines, Wallace's salute-greeting, and a description of his hand gestures while speaking, I attempted to give the reader a more complete mental image than a string of Wallacespeak quotes. The piece could have been a big bore, stuck back with the truss ads, but instead it went 1A.

• If it is possible, try to speak with the candidate before or after his or her speech, to see if you can obtain some different quotes than the speech. Here this wasn't possible. But if you can do it, it often gives a little different story than your competitors'.

On the campaign trail in the Louisiana governor's race in 1979, Clancy DuBos of the *Times-Picayune* in New Orleans concentrated on the people. He filed a story from a different town each day. In Sunset, he used local symbolism to capture the mood of politics there:

SUNSET, La.—All the virtues, vices and vagaries generally associated with the Acadian people can be found in and around this zesty little Cajun town.

There is gambling and good food, horse racing and whorehouses—all mixed with staunch Catholicism and parochial, rural-agrarian values.

A good bourre game is as close as the nearest bar, according to one lifelong resident.

As for food, even the local "greasy spoon" serves deliciously spiced plate lunches.

Evangeline Downs in nearby Lafayette offers thoroughbred racing, and Sunday afternoon quarterhorse races at local "bush" tracks—unlicensed tracks with no pari-mutuel betting but lots of wagering among spectators—were once as regular as morning mass.

Houses of prostitution still flourish in St. Landry Parish, but not within earshot of the Jesuit seminary in Grand Coteau. A recent crackdown padlocked three alleged brothels.

No pastime has more universal appeal among Cajuns than politics, however, and in the Sunset area, political fervor is exceeded only by the local passion for cockfighting.

Perhaps there was some relationship between popularity of the two as spectator sports.

The idea of two roosters pecking and clawing one another to death in the center of a noisy, crowded ring, has certain theatrical similarities to a good old-fashioned, mud-slinging political fight.

If nothing else, there are definite winners and losers at the conclusion of each.

Cockfighting enthusiasts from all corners of the globe descend on Sunset several times a year for days of continuous death battles among the finest, fiercest fighting birds known to man.

In nearby Cankton, two lounges

feature regular weekend cockfights.

"Some people get so into it that they follow the genealogies of those gamecocks the way you would trace the bloodlines of a champion show or racehorse," said one observer.

"I know one guy who imported a rooster from Siam because he wanted to get some Asian blood into his gamecocks. He thought it would improve their fighting."

No infusion of foreign blood is needed to heat up local politics. It's already as spicy as the food.

A six-man sheriff's race has captured most of the attention in St. Landry Parish, leaving many voters with a relatively ho-hum attitude toward the governor's race.

Campaign posters for candidates whose aspirations range from police juror to governor cover the walls of every cafe and bar in Sunset. But only in Sunset could one find signs for opposing candidates for sheriff hanging in the same bar—next to one another.

In the governor's race, however, there is no such conflict of loyalties. Paul Hardy seems to have cornered the endorsement of every watering hole in the area.

"Hardy's strong 'round here," said a patron in one of Sunset's older bars. He said it with such authority that no further explanation was needed, and none was offered.

Hardy, Dave Treen and Edgar Mouton seem to be leading the field in St. Landry, according to state Sen. Armand Brinkhaus of Sunset. "But," Brinkhaus said, "every candidate has support around here. I think it's still anybody's race. . . ."

DuBos's editor, David Snyder, says that the reporter's series "gives the reader a feel for the politics of the state, but the emphasis is on people. What they say sometimes knocks holes in old cliches about who has the political power in a given geographical area."

Snyder, assistant city editor, says the article and series have strength because DuBos

> . . . did his homework before making the swing through the state. He had a good background in Louisiana politics. He supplemented and updated this knowledge by talking in depth with several people well-grounded in the practical politics of the state. He planned his itinerary in advance.

In covering a group of candidates, consider highlighting the one with the unique ideas—even an also-ran, a former loser such as George McGovern. The New York *Daily News'* Frank Van Riper wrote in October 1983, as the election year 1984 was looming:

Former Sen. George McGovern, appearing with his six fellow presidential hopefuls, yesterday declared that the United States could achieve "worldwide leadership" as a peacemaker by freezing production of all nuclear weapons.

The position, which no other major Democratic candidate has embraced, was the most far-reaching of any put forward last night during an hour-long debate in Cambridge, Mass., on the nuclear arms race.

All seven of the announced Democratic candidates participated in the session, held at Harvard University's

Institute of Politics at the John F. Kennedy School of Government.

Although Ohio Sen. John Glenn had proposed a moratorium on the deployment of ground-launched cruise missiles in Western Europe, only McGovern, the 1972 anti-Vietnam war Democratic presidential nominee, endorsed so sweeping a step as a one-sided nuclear freeze.

With the exception of former Florida Gov. Reubin Askew, the other candidates all support a "mutual and verifiable" freeze on nuclear weapons.

However, McGovern, a former bomber pilot in World War II, declared that both the United States and the Soviet Union have sufficient nuclear fire power to "annihilate" each other several times over and that "everything we have spent since that day has been wasted."

Former Vice President Walter Mondale reiterated his proposal that the United States begin annual summit meetings between the American President and the head of the Soviet Union as a way to ease tension between the superpowers and in the world in general.

Sen. Alan Cranston of California, who has made the nuclear freeze a centerpiece in his campaign, again declared he was the candidate with the deepest commitment to ending the arms race. Others participating last night were Sen. Gary Hart of Colorado and Sen. Ernest Hollings of South Carolina.

A sense of place, as discussed in Chapter 9, also adds life to the political story and helps you to "see" the story. Larry Eichel, of the Philadelphia *Inquirer*'s Washington bureau, wrote in June 1984 just before the Democratic convention that nominated Walter Mondale for President:

NEW YORK—For all practical purposes, the battle for the Democratic presidential nomination ended yesterday in a posh townhouse on the East Side of Manhattan.

There, in a second-floor study, nominee-apparent Walter F. Mondale and Gary Hart met, for the first time since the end of the primary season, over a breakfast of scrambled eggs and bacon.

And they emerged from a 1½-hour session, most of it private, to tell 100 waiting reporters of their mutual respect, their continuing friendship and their shared concern for party unity and Democratic victory in November.

Mondale, standing on the steps of the house with Hart at his side, called the meeting "most useful," though "a little overdue." Hart talked about how there was "no difference" between them on "fundamental beliefs and fundamental values."

Throughout their post-summit news conference, they appeared relaxed and at ease with one another. They tried to make the tensions and bitterness of their long battle for the nomination seem part of a distant, nearly forgotten past.

"The practical fact is that this Democratic Party has gone through one of the most boisterous nominating processes in our history," Mondale said. "Now we're seeking that common ground and finding it. If the Republicans and President Reagan were betting on a divided Democratic Party, they can forget it."

The rivals said they had not talked about the possibility of Hart's becoming Mondale's running mate, but had focused instead on next month's Democratic National Convention in San Francisco, the fall campaign and the dangers they said were inherent in a second term for Reagan. . . .

Auxiliary Materials

In the small town of Warsaw, on the Osage River in the heart of the Missouri Ozarks, newcomer Maria K. Thompson expects to keep campaign promises of candidates alive in her articles. As a reporter for the weekly Benton County *Enterprise* in Warsaw, she is having the local library order the *Congressional Record*. "I want to see not only what passed, but also what did not." It will help her chronicle activities of the local representative. "All names (in the *Record*) are in bold print and stand up and grab you," and she can follow what the local representative is doing.

She also plans to get copies of bills from the government printing office. She believes small newspapers should find ways to distribute copies (or print summaries) of bills pending in Congress that affect the area. "Then I would invite farmer reaction to the bills and print the reactions," she says.

She believes the local newspaper can set up a "network" of people contacts related to the Congressman from the district. This includes meeting the secretaries in the regional offices of the Congressman in her area. "Once a network is set up," she says, "the people will call you if something is hot."

Al Morris, publisher of the Philadelphia *Tribune* and a vice president of the National Newspaper Publishers Association, suggests continual efforts to keep the real platform of the candidate before the reader. "When the election is over," he said at a meeting of the NNPA in Norfolk, Va., "find some basis to evaluate the platform. Get a copy of the platform and what it says and follow up to see what the elected official has accomplished. Do the platform and the current actions mesh after the election?"

Covering Polls

As election campaigns heat up, editors vie to give an educated and near correct prediction as to whom the winner will be.

Although today's techniques are sophisticated and, if done correctly, can be quite accurate, in the past some polls failed miserably.

In 1936, the *Literary Digest* mailed out 10 million ballots, and with 2 million returned, predicted that Gov. Alfred Landon of Kansas would have 57 percent of the popular vote for the presidency. Franklin Roosevelt was the winner. The magazine made the habit of using available lists, as Philip Meyer points out in his *Precision Journalism*, but the lists were those of car registrations and telephone directories with a bias in favor of the more affluent when, in 1936, many were still poor and suffering from the aftermath of the Great Depression.

The Gallup Poll, which is one of the more reliable today, goofed badly in 1948 when it predicted that Thomas Dewey would beat Harry Truman for the presidency. George Gallup published his poll on Nov. 1 but had stopped polling on Oct. 14, nearly a month before election day. Allowance was not made for last-minute voter shifts.

Polling efforts are standard fare, even among small newspapers. The *Wichita Sun*, an attractive tabloid and once the largest weekly in middle America before it folded in 1977, correctly predicted the outcome of the 1976 election, including an upset by a young Democrat challenger over the Republican incumbent in a Congressional race.

The article relied on random phone calls students made to every tenth voter from the bottom of the voter registration pages. Students also wrote sidebar interpretive articles. The news editor of the *Sun*, Howard Inglish, wrote the main article:

President Gerald Ford and former Georgia Gov. Jimmy Carter are running neck and neck in Sedgwick County, while Dan Glickman appears to be closing the gap against incumbent Garner Shriver in the congressional race, a poll by *The Wichita Sun* shows.

The Sun poll, consisting of 407 telephone interviews of persons selected in a random sample from the Sedgwick County voter registration list, also shows Sheriff Johnnie Darr with a substantial lead over his Republican challenger, Lynn Cole, 54.1% to 23.1%.

In the presidential race, the poll shows Ford barely ahead, 38.8% to 38.3% among all voters polled in the county. Carter, however, leads Ford among Wichita voters, 38.8% to 37.6%. Slightly over 81% of those polled live in Wichita.

Most other polls in the fourth congressional district have shown Carter and Shriver ahead, although no poll to date has focused in on Sedgwick County with as large a sample as this one. *The Sun* poll shows Glickman trailing Shriver among Wichita voters by only nine points, 37.3% to 46.4%, with the remainder undecided.

Shriver's margin was slightly larger in the countywide totals, 12 points, but that included preferences expressed by some county residents who live in the fifth district. Other polls have shown Shriver with an even larger lead.

One reason the congressional race could go down to the wire is that Shriver and Glickman are waging a close battle for the vote of those registered as Independent.

Results of the interviews in *The Sun* poll were broken down by party, age, sex and whether the voter lived inside the city limits, with the assistance of Rich Conlon, research assistant with the Wichita State University Center for Business and Economic Research. The interviews were conducted on Oct. 12-14 by WSU journalism students.

The breakdown shows that among independents, Shriver's lead over Glickman is less than three points, 41.7% to 38.8%.

Another indication that Rep. Shriver could be in for the toughest fight of his 16-year career is that longtime incumbents are considered to be in trouble once their support drops below the 50% level.

Analysis of the data by age groups shows Shriver leading in all four categories (18-25, 26-35, 36-55, and 56 and up), but the 31-year-old Glickman does much better in the 35 and under age groups.

Shriver, perhaps surprisingly, leads Glickman by a wider margin among females than males.

The Sun poll has a probability of error of not more than two percentage points for each candidate, with a maximum error of five points.

Breakdowns within age groups are not as statistically significant, but do show trends.

The poll shows Carter doing better among his own party than Glickman, but with Glickman doing a better job than Carter in garnering the Independent vote.

Ford, on the other hand, has much less success in grabbing Democratic votes than Congressman Shriver does. The poll shows Shriver getting 31.3% of the registered Democrats participating in the poll, while Ford gets only 12.7%.

Still, Ford does better in raiding votes from the opposite party than Carter, as the Democratic nominee got only 7.8% of the votes of Republicans participating in the survey.

Former Senator Eugene McCarthy grabbed 2.7% of the overall vote, showing—as other state polls have—that in a close race in Kansas, McCarthy could be the spoiler candidate.

The undecided vote in the presidential race was 18.4%, similar to figures in most recent state polls. Other candidates drew 1.7% in the presidential race.

(Interestingly, in all three races polled, women and Independents were the categories with the highest percentage of undecided.)

The undecided category in the Shriver-Glickman race was 16.7%. (There is a third candidate, Robert Cowdrey of the American Party who will be on the ballot in the congressional race, but he was not included in the poll.). . .

Students and others often confuse "spot-checking" with "random sampling." There is nothing wrong with "spot-checking"—stopping people on the street or elsewhere and seeking their viewpoints—but reporters should call it spot-checking and draw no special conclusion other than that the views expressed represent only those who express them.

Random sampling is a carefully controlled technique to try to find out what a larger group—the total inclusive group, or the "population" (or "universe")—thinks about a specific issue, with a certain amount of error allowed.

"Random sampling," says Mildred Parten in her *Surveys, Polls, and Samples: Practical Procedures,* "is the term applied when the method of selection assures each individual or element in the universe an equal chance of being chosen. The selection is regarded as being made by 'chance.'"[9]

A detailed examination of sampling is best left to other textbooks, but a reporter should ask some basic questions before taking a poll seriously. Based on a set of guidelines of the National Council on Public Polls, they are:

1. Who sponsored or paid for the poll?
2. When was the poll taken? Is it new or old? What is the possibility of change since it was taken?

3. Who were the interviewers?
4. Who was interviewed?
5. How were the persons selected for interviews?
6. How were the questions worded? Any loaded words?
7. How big was the sample? (The margin of error depends on the size of the sample.)
8. How were the interviews conducted? Mail, phone, or visits?
9. How are the results tabulated?
10. What are the biases of reporters, editors, and others in interpreting the poll?

Cartoons illustrate examples of poor method in a booklet, *Reporting on Polls: Some Helpful Hints,* published by the Canadian Daily Newspaper Publishers Association. One cartoon shows a young interviewer with neat coat and tie talking to a jackhammer operator in hard hat who does not understand a word the interviewer says, but whose head jerks back and forth with the rhythm of the hammer. The caption has the interviewer speaking:

> Excuse me, sir. I'm from Gidiup Surveys. We would like to have your opinion as to whether our politicians are communicating the feelings of real people like yourself in everyday operational aspects of legislative government. Judging from your nod, I feel we can register a "yes." Thank you for your time and consideration.[10]

Even when interviewees understand questions, a problem may arise in the way those questions are worded. To illustrate how reporters can slant the same content to produce exactly opposite answers, Will Adams, a social science researcher at William Jewell College in Liberty, Mo., tells the story of a monk who liked his cigarettes. The monk sought permission from his superior: "May I smoke while I pray?" The answer was "No." In a few weeks, the monk came back with the question rephrased: "May I pray while I smoke?" The answer was "Yes. One can and should pray all the time." By a simple rewording of the question, the monk got the answer he wanted.[11]

Political Glossary

Some terms you should know which reporters have suggested include:

Blast out: If a bill has been tabled indefinitely in a committee, legislators on the floor may move to have the full house vote to "blast it out" of committee so a full house can vote on it or so the legislators can send it to another less hostile committee.

Caucus: Members of a political party or group meet privately to work out legislative strategy or to discuss bills and amendments.

Committee substitute: A committee adopts its own version of a bill instead of the original version the legislator has drafted.

Concur: Legislators in one house approve a bill which originated in the other house. After a conference committee works out the differences between the house and senate versions of a simiiar bill, the legislators accept the compromise.

Conference committee: If the other house does not concur, a conference committee made up of members of both houses meets to hash out the differences and compromise. Usually the general appropriations bill goes into conference committee just before the deadline for adjournment.

Do-pass, do-not-pass: These are names for the vote by a committee on a bill. They represent recommendations to the next committee or house.

Engross or ***engrossment:*** Members of either house give preliminary approval to a bill. Some legislatures require two votes on a bill before it is passed.

Fat envelope: This is slang for a payoff.

Final passage: When a bill has made it through committee, it goes to the house where it originated for a final vote which is subject to debate and amendments on the floor. If it passes, it goes to the other house through its committees and then to its floor. If it passes there without amendments, it goes to the governor. (If there are amendments, it goes back to the originating house for concurrence votes on the amendments. If they concur, then the bill goes to the governor.)

Juice bill: This is a bill involving special interests in which money is a major factor.

Levy limit: The limit as to how much a tax can be raised.

Local bill: This kind of bill does not affect the majority and usually is a special-interest bill of one legislator.

Nonconcurrence: Legislators reject a bill originating in the other house.

Peel off: A legislator, once in favor of a bill, changes his position.

Promulgate: A state executive takes action without first going to the legislature; usually, such actions are statements supporting a holiday or special week or recognition of an individual for an accomplishment.

Reject: The legislators kill a bill or amendment for the rest of the legislative term.

Revenue stabilization: This action keeps legislators from spending more than taxes can provide.

Shared taxes: These are monies collected in state income taxes that are returned to local governments.

Sine die: This means the adjourning "without a day" (Latin) set for meeting again; thus, a final adjournment of the legislature.

Sleazoid: Reporters use this term to describe a politician believed to be corrupt; also, a "greaseball."

Table: This parliamentary maneuver delays a bill for a time or permanently. A motion to table is not debatable.

Up or out: This describes a move by a politician to try for higher office, who in case of failure will leave politics.

Notes

[1]Paul Williams, *Investigative Reporting and Editing* (Englewood Cliffs, N.J.; Prentice-Hall, 1978), pp. 228, 229.

[2]Mason Taylor, "A New Ball Game," in John L. Dougherty, *Learning in the Newsroom: A Manual for Supervisors,* (Reston, Va.: American Newspaper Publishers Association Foundation, c. 1973, 1975), pp. 171–174.

[3]Russell W. Maddox and Robert F. Fuquay, *State and Local Government* (New York: D. Van Nostrand, 1962), p. 467ff.

[4]Maddox and Fuquay, cf. p. 485.

[5]Jewell Case Phillips, *State and Local Government in America* (New York: American Book Co., 1954), cf. p. 347ff.

[6]Phillips, p. 350.

[7]Marie Crape, editor-in-chief, and Helen Redfern, editor, *Key to the Keystone State: Pennsylvania* (Philadelphia: League of Women Voters of Pennsylvania, c. 1972, 1978), p. 28.

[8]Crape and Redfern, pp. 31, 32.

[9]Mildred Parten, *Surveys, Polls, and Samples: Practical Procedures* (New York: Harper, 1950), p. 219.

[10]*Reporting on Polls: Some Helpful Hints,* a booklet by the Editorial Division of the Canadian Daily Newspaper Publishers Association (Toronto, Ontario, n.d.), pp. 3, 6.

[11]Cf., "So You Want the Public Opinion," in *Achieve,* an alumni bulletin of William Jewell College (Liberty, Mo:, May 1979), p. 7.

Assignments

1. Identify ten agencies in local and county governments and develop a descriptive paragraph on the director or administrator of each unit, with telephone number. Also include the name of the secretary and other assistants as possible contacts. Compile all into a directory of contacts.
2. If an election is coming up, see about the possibility of helping with surveys before an election or in a newsroom on election eve. You could also profile a day in the life of a candidate.
3. Take a topic of special interest during an election season and query all the candidates on that one issue for an article.
4. Prepare a profile on a member of the county or local government. Identify the person's main line of business. Then study the voting record of each official.

5. Prepare a feature on a public official without talking to him or her, relying on friends, enemies, items of record, and so on. As a final step, talk to the public official and get answers to any questions raised in your research.
6. Take a leading event in the news and assume the opposite is true, but only as a working hypothesis. For example, in 1983 the Soviets shot down a commercial passenger jetliner over Soviet controlled waters. The Soviets said, among several explanations, that the Korean flight 007 was a spy plane. The U.S. reaction was one of rage. But things are not always as they seem, so for the sake of research consider that the plane—with the curious 007 number of James Bond—*was* a spy plane. Develop strategies of checking out the theory. For example, if the hypothesis is that the Korean plane had been engaged in spy flights, one course of checking would be to talk to other crew, pilots, and passengers on previous flights of 007. Were there flights over Soviet territory before? (Eventually it was shown there had been recent spy maneuvers of other craft in the area.) Pick your own current event. Entertain the opposite. What strategy and questions would you use in checking it out?
7. Prepare an article on how to use or relate to a specific city agency.
8. Go to a township or other meeting of community officials, pick one item from the agenda, and develop a topical article, using some of the officials for comment.

13

Education

Education, an important segment of government reporting, often merits its own specialized reporting.

The United States has some 16,000 school districts. In 25 states, school districts operate public schools. In 20 states, school districts share responsibility with other government bodies. In Alaska, Hawaii, Maryland, North Carolina, and Virginia, local municipal governments administer public schools.[1]

While in Indiana a single elected trustee administers each school district, in most districts authority is in the hands of a plural-member board commonly known as the board of education, board of school trustees, board of school directors, or school board. Voters elect board members in about four of every five independent school districts; in the remainder, a government official or body of officials appoints them. While board size varies from three to 21 members depending on the state, boards commonly consist of three, five, or seven members elected or appointed for three to seven years.

School boards serve within limits set by state constitutions and legislatures, but within those limits they have broad powers. School boards prepare and adopt an annual budget, set the district's tax rate, issue bonds, and choose sites and approve construction for new school buildings. A major school board power is the hiring of a superintendent to whom the board delegates much of the responsibility for developing policy. School superintendents usually are responsible for planning school curriculum, hiring teachers and staff, purchasing supplies, and planning bus routes and schedules. The superintendent is also chief planner and policy adviser to the board.

School board officers usually consist of (1) a chairperson or president who presides at board meetings and serves as the board's general spokesperson, (2) a clerk who keeps minutes of the meetings and has custody of district records, and (3) a treasurer who receives revenues and makes payments as the board directs. In some districts, voters elect these officers; in others, members of the board select them.

School districts vary greatly in size, both in numbers of students and in the geographic area covered. Larger districts often have full-time public information officers to aid the reporter. In smaller districts, one of the administrators handles public information on a part-time basis. However, virtually all school districts hold regularly scheduled public meetings; reporters cover these in much the same way as other municipal government meetings.

REPORTING ON EDUCATION LAWS

High on the list of priorities in preparing for the job of education writing, according to professional education writers, is gaining an understanding of law that relates to public schools—such as their financing and teacher collective bargaining.

Dru Wilson, education writer for the Colorado Springs (Colo.) *Gazette-Telegraph*, says:

> Approximately 90 percent of the business of education is related to an ever-changing morass of laws. Even day-to-day business is related in some way to complying with a law. Without the necessary background, a reporter can become very lost. I find sometimes my research has provided me with some knowledge that even the local school officials don't have. All of it makes for very interesting stories, and understanding helps a reporter recognize the story potential.

Wilson sometimes wrote directly about the laws themselves:

Public Law 94-142—The Education for All Handicapped Children Act of 1975—has provided a specific "bill of rights" for parents and students that will go into effect as of September.

Many parents, though, are not fully aware of those specified rights.

The new federal law insures that all handicapped children age 3 to 21 can have a free and appropriate public education which emphasizes special education and related services designed to meet their unique needs, to assure that the rights of handicapped children and their parents are protected and to assist states to provide such educational programs.

"Handicapped" is defined as mentally retarded, hard of hearing, deaf, orthopedically impaired, other health impaired, speech impaired, visually handicapped, seriously emotionally disturbed, or children with specific learning disabilities who thus require special education.

The act gives first priority to children who aren't receiving an education and secondly to children "inadequately served, with the most severe handicaps."

The key words in the language of the act are "appropriate" and "least restrictive environment."

Guidelines are set for educational agencies or school districts to determine whether the education provided is in the least restrictive environment—the regular classroom, a special class, or a program in a special institution or agency. Many parents are still concerned though, over what may be termed an emphasis on "mainstreaming."

Mainstreaming is a process that places a handicapped child into a regular classroom situation.

Parents have voiced concern that perhaps a severely handicapped child could not function in a normal classroom even with a teacher who has had proper training.

The Council for Exceptional Children said that the provision calling for the least restrictive environment "does not mandate that all handicapped children will be educated in the regular classroom and does not abolish any particular educational environment—for instance, educational programming in a residential setting."

Education in classes with nonhandicapped children will, however, be "to the maximum extent appropriate."

The new law says at least one parent of the child is to be at each meeting involving education planning for the child and that parents must have the chance to participate, including scheduling the meeting at a mutually agreed upon time and place.

It further states that if neither parent can attend, the local education agency shall use other methods to insure parent participation including individual conferences or telephone calls. . . .

ON THE SCENE

If you are going to be a good education writer, you should get involved with the schools and even into classrooms. "As an assignment," says Joe Wilson, education writer for the Gainesville (Ga.) *Times*, "I spent a week in a primary school and wrote a series which opened up my eyes." He goes as far as to suggest that reporters should spend at least a week as a substitute teacher in the classroom.

On occasion, he also spends a day chronicling the life of somebody in the schools. A full-page picture feature told of his day with an elementary school principal:

Mother Nature would have to get up pretty early in the morning to fool V. C. Allison.

The principal of Lyman Hall Elementary School arrives at school promptly at 6 a.m. on cold, wintry days to make sure the school is warm when teachers and students begin arriving. After adjusting thermostats in the building, he goes back to his home in Lakeshore Heights and finishes his breakfast.

On normal mornings, the principal begins his school day at 7. All of the doors have to be unlocked before the others begin arriving. He almost never wears a tie to school. "I have found that students relate better to me if I don't wear a tie."

Morning is a busy time for Allison; he helps the teachers make sure the students get to their rooms and settle down for a quiet day's work, at least quiet enough to hear the morning announcements over the loudspeaker.

The school serves as his family; he has been a bachelor all his 59 years.

A friendly sort of fellow with rosy cheeks, Allison is the type of person who can talk with knowledge on any subject from the weather to psychology. He doesn't believe in *bad* children, only that children have problems from time to time. "Most of our children are well-behaved and we give them every opportunity to prove themselves," he says, glowing a little.

Allison works long hours as principal, and school officials describe him as a workaholic. "A clean desk is the sign of a sick mind," says a small plaque hanging in his tiny office. The last two school superintendents in Hall County both told him to quit coming back to school at night and on the weekends.

"My position as principal is basically public relations," he says invoking a grin. "All of our children are public relations agents for the school. The school is quiet, but we allow them the freedom to be themselves."

* * *

The 8 o'clock bell rings. A school day begins. Allison starts with a bus conduct report on a student turned in by the driver. Bus conduct reports are written on students who cause problems during their trips from home to school. Two reports and the student is suspended from riding the bus.

Allison calls the boy from his classroom and asks him what happened on the bus this morning. "Randy hit me, so I hit him back," the chubby little boy says in the empty library. Allison informs him that a conduct report will be mailed to his home and warns him that if he gets another report he will be suspended from riding the bus, but not from school.

All throughout their conversation, the principal relates well to his student, never raising his voice in anger, but still getting across his point. Later, after the boy has gone back into his classroom, Allison says he wasn't tough on the little boy because he had never received a report on him before.

His counseling session finished, Allison checks on every classroom in the building. The thermostats show 65 degrees in two of the classrooms. "It always takes a long time for these classes to heat up," he says, noticing students and teachers wearing their coats and sweaters.

Everything in order, Allison drifts back into his office to make a few phone calls and sign a few checks. This particular morning, the principal has to attend a meeting of the curriculum committee for Hall County schools at nearby McEver Elementary School. Meetings are an essential part of principal's duties. They allow him to have some impact on policy decisions affecting the whole county. . . .

A lunch of chicken and dumplings is already being served to the students. "It is the only decent meal many of them get," Allison said. The Lyman Hall attendance area represents some of the poorest households in the county. "We did a survey of the educational level of our parents and we only had three parents who had earned college degrees. They were all ministers."

A compassionate man, Allison says he doesn't blame some of the students for not coming to school on cold mornings. "If I were a child, I wouldn't want to get out of bed in a house with no heat and no breakfast to eat."

When students are absent for long periods of time, Allison visits the homes of the children to see what kind of problems they are having. . . .

The poverty of the students creates special problems for the school. Lyman Hall has one of the lowest attendance averages of any school in Hall County. The average daily attendance is usually between 90 and 95 percent and runs close to 80 percent in cold weather. . . .

Despite the obstacles of poverty and hunger which beset the students, Lyman Hall is something of a showcase school for the county. Its students won more 4-H awards than any other school in last year's county and district competition.

An avid horticulturist, Allison has landscaped the school grounds with beautiful shrubs and flowers to make the prettiest school yard in the county. Tropical plants, hanging baskets and a water fountain decorate the interior of the school.

He makes sure everything in the school is spotless. The new school, completed in 1973 after the old school burned down, has never been painted since it opened. Several other schools have had to be repainted in less than five years.

After finishing lunch, Allison visits all of the classrooms again and works with three of his outstanding students on a program to be presented to the county school board at its monthly meeting.

Students begin leaving the school when the bell rings at 2:30 p.m. Lois Hunt, his secretary, informs Allison that one bus will be 15 minutes late. He makes a slight frown.

Ms. Hunt, who has been his secretary for 13 years, says there has never been a cross word passed between them in those years. "He always has the children at heart," she says. "He does very little paddling and you see how quiet it is and how the children love him." He has paddled three students since the beginning of the school year.

* * *

The day may be over for the children, but the teachers have a faculty meeting with their boss. Allison runs the meeting with his casual, easygoing manner, making a few announcements about upcoming programs and meetings and talking about attendance. A teacher in each grade level demonstrates an art technique and he finishes by demonstrating a new art technique.

* * *

Another school day is over. . . .

Debi Craft, editor of the weekly *Courier* in Barryton, Mich., found that some antagonism had built up between the schools and the paper before she took the job, and "it didn't work to beg for education news from week to week in the paper." She solved her problem by getting out into the schools. She got the community education director (public relations officer) to take her around to the schools, ". . . and they saw I was serious and would put news in the paper." She continued going from town to town in the district in Mecosta County. "I found millions of things." Among them, a spelling bee, a second grade class having a birthday party for twins in the class entertained by the twins' sister, a professional clown, and a blind girl coping with public education by using a new device that could scan and read letters for her. Craft also cemented relations with the school by agreeing to take pictures for and helping edit the school board's newsletter.

A study by Charles T. Duncan, University of Oregon, shows that most education writers surveyed (49 out of 52) visit schools at least occasionally, and over half (30) visit regularly.[2]

In addition to using various sources, Anne Thomas, news editor of the weekly Cottage Grove (Ore.) *Sentinel,* advises reporters to evaluate sources: "Be skeptical about what people tell you. In time you will learn who is telling the truth and who has axes to grind or secrets to hide." And she emphasizes: "Keep in touch with teachers about what's happening in the classroom."

Sources that may not be quotable can still lead to others. Says Donna Moore Whitaker, education writer for the Springdale (Ark.) *News*: "I also listen to comments from cafeteria workers, my babysitter, the newsboy—these comments often lead to good stories when I press the administration and board to talk."

Phone calls and letters set Whitaker to writing a report on school expulsions. She checked the school policy handbook, attendance office records, and other information from principals and administrators:

During the past several months, several Springdale School District policies have been the subject of debate in the community, drawing sometimes heated comment for and against the policies.

Questions have been raised about the number of students expelled from Springdale junior and senior high schools and the reasons for their expulsions. The policy which, in effect, expels junior high pupils for a full year, rather than a semester, had drawn some comment. And the policy which prohibits graduating seniors from completing necessary credits by correspondence has also drawn comment.

In an effort to put these policies into some kind of perspective, the NEWS conducted a survey of eight Arkansas school district attendance offices, principals, administrators.

Three of them—Fayetteville, Rogers and Bentonville—were selected for the survey because they are also located in Northwest Arkansas and might be expected to have similar problems.

Two of them, Pine Bluff and West Memphis, were chosen because they are comparable in size to the Springdale School District and also might be expected to have comparable problems. Springdale has an average daily attendance (ADA) of 6,812 students.

Then the NEWS selected three school districts located in large urban areas—Little Rock, Pulaski County and Fort Smith.

The survey revealed that only one of the eight school districts—Little Rock—expelled more students during the fall semester of the current school year.

During that semester, Springdale expelled 97 pupils, 81 for violating the district's attendance policy which requires a student to be dropped from school after missing any one class more than 12 times.

Five of the school districts surveyed had some kind of attendance policy which could lead to the expulsion of a student.

Bentonville, the smallest school district in the survey (ADA 2,607), expelled 15 students in the fall semester, all of them for attendance violations. Bentonville's policy is similar to Springdale's, but students there are permitted 13 absences instead of 12.

Pine Bluff (ADA 7,235) expelled 81 students during the fall semester, 73 of them for violating the district's attendance policy. Under that policy, a student is dropped from a class after missing it 12 times and is expelled from school after being dropped from three classes.

In Fort Smith (ADA 11,455) nine students were expelled last semester and school officials estimated five of those were expelled for violating the attendance policy.

Fort Smith's policy calls for a student to be dropped from a class after missing it 15 times. A student who is dropped from his second class for absences is expelled for the balance of the semester.

Pulaski County, the largest school district in Arkansas with an average daily attendance of 26,514, expelled 67 students in all last semester but school district officials were unable to say how many of these were for attendance policy violations.

Officials in Pulaski County said there is no district-wide attendance policy and that each school sets attendance standards. . . .

Says Nancy Hicks, education writer for the Lincoln (Neb.) *Star*:

> The new education reporter should develop sources at all levels, including students and parents. . . . Get into the classroom level to see what actually is going on. . . . Learn what the jargon means, then remember to use everyday language in the stories. . . . Know your community (and state) well so that you can understand what the schools are about.

She believes that some understanding of the national political and social climate has a bearing on schools.

> It is important to remember that schools are a reflection of the community within which they operate. The local politics, attitudes, and problems are reflected in the schools and play an important part in the administrative decisions on finance and curriculum. The one-room western Nebraska school bears little relationship to schools in the heart of a Chicago ghetto. Yet education reporters should not be so naive as to think that some national or big town issues will not be found in their local schools.

HIGHER EDUCATION

Larger dailies will often have a person to cover higher education. These college beats are much different than public school beats. Charles B. Fancher, Jr., a staff writer covering higher education for the Philadelphia *Inquirer*, says:

> I focus more on national trends. Through them I develop a sense of what to look for on local campuses. The key to covering national higher education trends is how they affect local colleges.
>
> I'm on almost everybody's mailing list. I read the *Chronicle of Higher Education* closely. I also look very carefully at material coming from the various educational associations and periodically call them up. I rely very heavily on researchers in these various groups.
>
> There are roughly 70 colleges in our circulation area, so it's impossible to keep up with what's going on at each of them on a daily basis. I turn most of my attention to four or five representative schools. But I'm very much a telephone jockey, and I try to stay in contact with administrators as much as possible. I have stringers on some of the campuses, and rely on them to keep me informed. Campus newspapers are of use in terms of things that are going to happen.

Sam Pressley, who covered higher education for the Philadelphia *Bulletin*, said:

I tried to keep abreast of what's taking place nationally. I spent a lot of time reading stuff just to see what's going on. Locally, I just buttonholed people on campus. I found the best people to talk to are students.

SCHOOL BUDGETS

An enterprising education writer, Gary Kocher of the Allentown (Pa.) *Call-Chronicle*, has come up with an advisory for a proposed flyer on how to cover education budgets. While geared to one specific state—Pennsylvania—his information and suggestions are helpful for new education writers:

> Some key questions that you usually want to answer in a budget story are:
>
> How much are the taxes going to be next year?
>
> How does the tax rate compare with the previous year (or several years)?
>
> If taxes are up, why? If down, why?
>
> Will programs and services remain at the same level as last year? If not, what's being cut and why? If programs are expanding, how much is the added cost?
>
> Some key things you want to avoid in a budget story are:
>
> Long strings of numbers, unless confined to one of the lowest paragraphs strictly for the sake of getting the data "on the record."
>
> Explanations that are in bureaucratese.
>
> Accounting data to which the reader cannot relate and has no reason to anyway.
>
> For example, the lead on a typical budget story might be, "The Lower Paddleback School Board last night adopted a $300 million 1978–79 budget with a property tax of 100 mills, up from 98 mills this year." It tells a story, but lacks flair.
>
> Maybe this would be better: "While taxpayers in the Lower Paddleback School District dig deeper into their pockets next year, Johnny will have to fight for more elbow room in class. The school board last night adopted a $300 million 1978–79 budget which held real estate millage increases to two mills by raising average class size from 22 to 28 students." Or, "Tax bills in the Lower Paddleback School District will be going out Friday, and they'll be two mills higher than this year's."
>
> It might help you to arrange an appointment with the superintendent or business manager to go over the budget with you privately in advance of the budget meeting, so you can resolve any uncertainties you have. This is best done early on the day on which the meeting will

be held: That way he is assured you can't release anything early, and you're assured you're not suppressing information that could leak to other reporters.

When should you make your appointment? That brings us to the subject of. . . .

Budget Time Sequence

Under state law (Pennsylvania), the school district must *tentatively adopt* its budget by or on May 31. *Final adoption* must be by or on June 30. Between those two dates, changes may be made. The reason for the seeming duplication is to allow time for public inspection and comment. In your May story, be sure to note that the budget has not been finally adopted.

Some boards that meet just once a month will introduce the budget at the regular May meeting. Those with two meetings per month may introduce it at the first meeting, then vote for tentative adoption at the second meeting. Other boards hold special meetings just to study the budget. In other words, there is no set rule when the budget will first pop up.

Your best bet is to check with the superintendent or business manager before May 1. Check whether any special meetings are planned.

Where The Money Comes From

There are three principal sources of revenue—federal, state, and local.

FEDERAL—this usually makes up a small part of the budget, perhaps 10 percent. One large item you might hear about is "Title I," which is short for Title I of the Elementary and Secondary Education Act. This law authorizes money for disadvantaged kids, of whom even the richest districts have some. . . . All federal money comes under programs for specific purposes and cannot be summarily dumped into the general pot.

LOCAL—School districts can enact only those taxes allowed by state law. All except the property tax have an upper limit. Since most districts are at the upper limit of the other taxes, it is the property tax that keeps rising. The various taxes are:

Property tax: This is also called "real estate tax." It is figured on the value of the property you own. Properties are valued (assessed) at different rates in different counties. Right now, property in Lehigh County is assessed at 50 percent of its value on the open market. Thus, a house purchased for $20,000 would be assessed at $10,000. The tax rate is expressed in MILLS. A mill is one-thousandth of a dollar. Thus, each mill of tax on the $10,000 house would be $10; 10 mills would result in a $100 tax, 40 mills in a $400 tax, and so on. It often helps in your story to give an example to help the reader figure what his tax will be. For example, "Under the new 44-mill levy, a Lower Paddleback

> resident owning a home assessed at $10,000 will pay $440 next year, up from $400 this year."
>
> *Per capita tax:* A "head" tax levied on every resident (18 years and older). Authority for them comes from two different state laws, so sometimes two are listed in the budget resolution. Just add them together.
>
> *Occupational privilege tax:* A tax paid by every person employed in the district.
>
> *Real estate transfer tax:* A maximum 1 percent tax levied on the value of any real estate transaction. The law allows municipalities in the district to claim half of this tax. Most do.
>
> *Earned income tax:* Also called the "wage tax." It's a maximum 1 percent tax withheld from workers' paychecks. Like the real estate transfer tax, it is usually shared equally with the municipalities.
>
> *Occupational millage:* It is like the occupational privilege tax, but instead of being a flat rate it is graduated according to job categories.
>
> *Other local revenues:* Various non-tax revenues include interest, fees, and miscellaneous receipts.
>
> STATE—The state gives money to the district under a variety of formulae (transportation, sparsity, density, special education, etc.), but the main one is the *basic instructional subsidy.* . . .

LABOR RELATIONS

School district labor relations are important. A local of either the American Federation of Teachers or a state education association represents most teachers. Contracts usually expire just before the new school year begins, but district and union negotiators begin their meetings months in advance.

"Usually nothing much is established in the first few sessions," says Dave Kushman, education writer for the former Philadelphia *Bulletin*.

> Hard bargaining doesn't start until the city and school district pass a budget, then bargaining usually heats up in the summer months to a crescendo in August.
>
> Representatives for both sides are only too happy to tell you how unfair the other side is, so there's no problem getting information. If they reach an impasse, a state mediator will be called in and might impose a news blackout on the negotiators. Then you have to rely on sources.

Once you know that a decision has been made, you must set out to find what happened. You can't wait until a decision is handed to you formally at a press conference.

The lack of an announcement did not stop the Milwaukee *Journal* from reporting what happened on an agreement on a new contract:

> Negotiators for the Milwaukee Teachers Education Association and the School Board reached agreement about 4 a.m. Thursday on a new three-year contract.
>
> Details of the contract were not disclosed, but it was learned from a variety of sources that the pay increase for the more than 5,000 teachers would be roughly between 5% and 7% for each of the three years.
>
> Raises of more than 5% for the teachers and other employees in the MTEA would be considerably higher than the raises given some other employees in the school system.
>
> Settlements in recent months with other employee groups include raises of 3% and 4%. Normally, raises for most employees in the Milwaukee Public Schools have been roughly comparable. But school officials said teachers' raises had to be compared with other teachers in the state, not with other school system employees.
>
> The old contract between the board and the union expired June 30, 1982, but terms of it were extended beyond that date while negotiations continued.
>
> The new agreement would cover the period from July 1, 1982 to June 30, 1985. The raises would be retroactive, meaning that teachers could expect to get relatively large checks later this year, assuming they ratify the agreement.
>
> It is also believed that the new contract will allow administrators more flexibility in running the schools because some parts of the old contract were removed after the Wisconsin Employment Relations Commission ruled that the board was not required to negotiate those items.
>
> Patrick O'Mahar, a spokesman for the union, said the MTEA's executive board would consider the proposed contract at 4:30 p.m. Aug. 31, and that teachers representing all the schools in the city would consider it Sept. 7. Teachers will get copies of the contract after Sept. 7 and have until Sept. 15 to vote on it.

If it comes down to a strike, there are always some routine angles. What are the kids doing? Are any groups setting up strike classes? What are the effects of the strike on working women with school-age children? What do picketing teachers have to say?

School Glossary

Educators are known for their big words. Here is some jargon you will need to know and translate into everyday language:

Advanced placement program: Highly qualified high school seniors take these exams in the spring for placement as sophomores in four-year colleges without taking the freshman year.

Alternate school: Students alternate between their home room and specialization rooms.

AMT: This is the degree of Master of Arts in Teaching.

Apperception test: This tests a child's personality, using a series of pictures to encourage the child to use imagination.

Articulation of instruction: This teaching program arranges continuous learning experiences from grade to grade.

Associative discussion: Teachers encourage youngsters to link their group experiences in school with comparable experiences in the outside world.

Aural: This means "that which is heard"; educators use an aural approach in teaching languages.

Battery of tests: This is a group of tests administered together.

Bibliotherapy: Doctors and psychotherapists use selected readings to improve a reading condition. Also, this method helps minorities to improve self concepts.

Bilateral school: Such a high school provides two programs side by side, such as academic and vocational.

Blocked time: This system organizes periods in the school day for more efficient use of teachers' time.

CA: This represents chronological age.

CAMP: This means computer-assisted menu planning.

Catechetical method: This pedagogical method emphasizes rote learning; catechetical school refers to a church school.

CE: This stands for comparative education.

Certification: This gives proof that candidates have met certain standards; qualifications for teaching vary by states and usually include four years of college, often both a bachelor's and master's degree, and sometimes a loyalty oath and proof of good health.

Change agent: The person plays a key role in a change or development process.

Common learnings: All students take part in the same learning experiences.

Cognition: The process of knowing is based on such elements as perception, recognition, thinking, and memorization.

Conditioning: This involves modifying a response to a stimulus in an effort to change behavior.

Consortium: This refers to a library or school that combines resources.

Cooperative School and College Ability Tests (SCAT): These tests determine skills and abilities learned from school experiences.

Dual system: This is a euphemism for segregated schools.

Dyslexia: This is a learning disability in which the student perceives letters in reverse order, in mirror image, or transposed.

EA: This stands for educational age.

Enrichment: This expanded educational program includes opportunities for a wider learning for gifted students.

Exogenous: Something caused from the outside, such as mental retardation as a result of brain injury.

Exceptional children: Children who need special adaptations of school programs because of mental or physical disabilities.

Field studies: Students investigate by doing experiments in their environment instead of in the laboratory or classroom.

Full-time equivalent: This refers to the number of part-time students or part-time faculty expressed in terms of the equivalent number of full-time students or full-time faculty.

Functional literacy: This means the ability to read and write well enough to function normally in society.

Fused: These are overlapping subjects which educators can teach using an interdisciplinary approach.

GED: This stands for General Equivalency Diploma.

GRE: The Graduate Record Exam is the test for those going on to graduate school.

Heterogeneous grouping: Educators put students together in classes without considering their individual abilities and differences.

Homogeneous grouping: Teachers group students with similar abilities together.

Interage groups: Teachers put children of different ages in one classroom.

Magnet school: Such a school offers courses not normally given in high schools and attracts students from many schools.

Middle school: This school teaches students who are between the lower grades and high school; usually they are 10 to 14, in grades five through 8.

Modular scheduling: This system groups small units of time, or modules, around a theme with a unit of teaching containing several modules; a science course might have lectures, several small labs, and library time.

Montessori method: Maria Montessori, an Italian psychiatrist-educator, founded this sytem which trains preschoolers by emphasizing daily activities, heightening the natural curiosity of the child, and acknowledging the great ability of the child to "absorb" culture unconsciously before the age of three and consciously after that age.

Open school: This kind of school holds classes in one big room or hall instead of classroom divisions; such a school is usually student-oriented and less rigid.

Peer group: This is a group comprised of students who are the same age and who know each other.

Pupil: This is now synonymous with student; traditionally pupil has referred to a child attending kindergarten or elementary school.

Standard Metropolitan Areas (SMA): Such an area has at least 50,000 persons in a central city or group of cities where at least 65 percent of the workers are not farmers.

Tenure: This means the permanent appointment of an educator to a teaching staff.

TWI: This refers to Training Within Industry.

Upper secondary school: This is a school with students in the top two grades of a high school and the two junior college years.

Notes

[1]George Blair, *Government at the Grass Roots* (Pacific Palisades, Ca.: Palisades Publishers, 1977), pp. 134–7.

[2]Charles T. Duncan, "The 'Education Beat' on 52 Newspapers," *Journalism Quarterly* (Summer 1966) 43:2, p. 338.

Assignments

1. Secure a copy of a board of education budget; invite a board of education member to class to interpret the budget line by line. Prepare a story.
2. Talk with other students to identify a topic of concern. Do some background research. For example, look into regulations of the state, see if they are being complied with, and find out what other schools have done with a similar problem. Then record what your school officials plan to do or not do and why.
3. Call the parent leaders of several local PTAs. Identify a common concern, research it, and prepare an article.

14

Business—Real Estate—Farm—Food

Business merits a special department in many newspapers. Two editors, five or six reporters, and a clerk make up the typical staff covering business on a large newspaper, according to a survey for the Associated Press Managing Editors Association. In these papers, the business writing department often has its own office and wire machines. Even middle-size papers have business newsstaffs, usually an editor, two or three reporters, and a clerk.[1]

The trend is to step up business coverage. By the end of the 1970s, major papers such as the New York *Times*, Washington *Post*, Louisville *Courier-Journal*, Chicago *Tribune*, and Chicago *Sun-Times* had expanded staff and facilities.[2] In Philadelphia, one of the papers doubled coverage of business news and financial tables (as the result of a new early a.m. edition).[3] In jointly owned papers, such as the morning *Democrat and Chronicle* and the evening *Times-Union* in Rochester, N.Y., business coverage has increased. Each of these two papers has added space and redefined business coverage to include more variety and in-depth reporting.[4]

Efforts to train business writers have increased as well. The New York Financial Writers Association puts on an annual seminar for nearly 100 potential business writers from colleges and universities. The Foundation for Economic Freedom, an educational wing of the conservative National Association of Manufacturers, has workshops on business writing at journalism schools and for business writers and editors in major cities.[5]

Specialized weekly business publications have sprung up. Two have begun in Chicago, following a format of a Houston business paper. Chicago *Sun-Times* financial writer Jerome Idaszak calls them "a hybrid between a newspaper and magazine."[6] The Philadelphia area has three. Mainline business magazines are also doing well. In the 1970s, *Forbes's* circulation nearly tripled, from 228,000 to

668,000; *Business Week* went from 302,000 to 768,000, and *Fortune*, from 296,000 to 628,000.

Papers have also upgraded their staff. Myron Kandel, financial editor of the New York *Post* and former president of the Society of American Business and Economic Writers, recalls how people used to fall into the business beat. One seasoned general reporter had studied the stock market reports very carefully for years; when his paper needed a financial writer, it turned to him. But this reporter had followed the stock market not because of a great interest in the nation's economy, but because he had been left a few shares of stock. Today, Kandel says, financial writers need more interest in the field than mere personal reasons for studying the progress of some stocks.

With inflation concerns dominating opinion poll research in recent years, business and financial news has moved from the "section behind the sports pages" to a much more prominent slot closer to the front page, both in location and in importance. On any day a number of front-page stories may concern the economy, inflation, recession, the dollar, and international economic concerns.

"Financial writing is a field that is growing rapidly," Kandel told journalism students attending a New York Financial Writers' seminar a few years ago. "Financial journalism has come of age. People in the financial section are treated more importantly than before. . . ." He continued, "Financial journalism is not an isolated area, but an area that touches every part of our personal lives."

Financial writers at the seminar emphasized different educational routes for prospective financial page writers. Some professionals suggested studying economics, others accounting, some finance, and still others said a combination. The most important requirements, as for any journalist, are to have good writing and reporting skills. Good reporters can learn anything, they said.

The professionals offered these hints for people interested in working as business and financial writers:

1. ***Read financial publications.*** These will familiarize you with the language, terms, and the special publications in the field. These publications, of which there are many (*Journal of Commerce*, the *Wall Street Journal*, *American Banker*, and the *Oil Daily*, to name a few), may also provide employment opportunities.
2. ***Read books about the stock and trade exchanges.*** Also, read booklets which the different exchanges publish about themselves.
3. ***Talk to people in the industry.*** Go to an annual stockholders' meeting. You may have to search to find a company that allows outsiders into its

meeting, but some do. Then write a story about the meeting for a class assignment or for yourself and compare it to a newspaper account of the same meeting.

4. ***Know reports and records.*** For example, corporations must file what are known as 8–K and 10–K forms with the Securities and Exchange Commission. These forms contain information that the firm does not have to disclose in its annual report. SEC libraries have copies of these reports.
5. ***Get to know people sources other than those in the companies.*** These can be security analysts, market analysts, stockbrokers, and academics. As with any source, you should be aware of experts' biases.
6. ***Keep a "reverse file" of people who have left the industry.*** A former financial or business expert will still be valuable as a source of information, especially for background information and perspective.
7. ***When you start out as a financial writer, talk to other reporters.*** Although they will probably not give out their best sources, their experience can be of assistance.

OVERCOMING AN ADVERSARY ROLE

Reporting business brings a different kind of challenge. When dealing with private agencies, you will find more insulation for the agency and less access for the reporter than in many other areas of newswriting. For example, you don't have access to the accounting and tax forms as you would with public or nonprofit organizations. Often there is little access short of buying stock and attending stockholder meetings. Top executives do not have to hold press conferences; they can slip out of the skyscraper any time of day to a waiting limousine that shuttles them to some distant suburb isolated from the public.

A nonproductive "adversary" relation is sometimes hard to avoid, so you may need very good skills in public relations and patience to get an important story.

"The principal difference in business reporting is accessibility," says an east Florida newspaper business page editor who did not want to be named. "A mayor who refuses to talk to the press is a maverick rarity; businessmen who refuse are legion. How you approach people is critical. Strive to be considered tough, but fair, scrupulous about confidentiality and equal treatment."

Rob Feuerstein, business writer for the Aberdeen (Wash.) *Daily World*, says:

> I really only have one specific tip for business writers. Remember that the people you are dealing with are under no obligation to talk to you.

> Public servants, government officials, and even politicians, in a sense, are required by their payroll to supply information and even at times opinion.
>
> Private businessmen are not. My biggest mistake has been to handle business people as sternly and pointedly as public officials. The result has often been that they clam up. Under the circumstances, I probably would, too.

Starting out in an adversary position can be uncomfortable and unproductive. Writing in the New York *Times*, David J. Mahoney, chairman, president, and chief executive officer of Norton Simon, Inc., makes an important point:

> A reporter recently interviewed a business manager about corporate bribery, kickbacks, international boycotts, illegal political contributions, personal use of stockholders' property, class-action lawsuits, charges by consumers' organizations, and sex discrimination.
>
> When the manager suggested that readers might also be interested in sharply increased earnings as a percentage of sales, the reporter snapped: "This is no puff piece; ours is an adversary relationship."
>
> I think that the reporter was mistaken. The relationship between the press and the government is, as it should be, adversary—a two-century tradition that has been strongly reaffirmed in this decade. But the relationship between the press and other less powerful institutions—business, the labor movement, education, religion, others—ought to be inquisitive and coolly interpretive and neither adversary nor promotional. . . .
>
> Success in journalism ought not to depend on the skill with which the student demolishes success in business, but on sophistication brought to bear on trends shown in companies and industries that affect consumer decisions and foreign affairs.
>
> Success in business ought not to depend on the ability to avoid, evade or bamboozle the press, but on a willingness to provide quick answers to straight questions that will help investors and customers make informed decisions that will ultimately benefit the stockholders and the public.[7]

THE LANGUAGE OF BUSINESS

As with other beats, language is important—business reporters must understand what they are writing about. Most readers are ". . . fed a daily diet of authoritative ignorance, most of which conveys a cheap shot hostility to business and businessmen," says Louis Banks, former managing editor of *Fortune*.[8]

Joseph Poindexter, a free-lance business writer, recalls the story of a wire service reporter

> . . . who showed up at an annual meeting of American Telephone and Telegraph and during a vigorous quizzing of the chief financial officer displayed his ignorance of the difference between stocks and bonds. Less flagrant misuses of the press conference abound. For example, when William M. Batten, new president of the New York Stock Exchange, gave his inaugural press conference, it became badly bogged down when a reporter from the New York *Times* attempted to pin down Batten's salary and determine whether a chauffeured car was one of the fringe benefits.[9]

Many business pages are overloaded with wire stories. Wire stories may be more hastily prepared than others, sometimes by inexperienced stringers or nonspecialist, one-man bureau chiefs in some obscure parts of the country. Such stories may also be second-hand because many wire bureaus are understaffed; members often rewrite and transmit stories that other media in the area have already worked.

One member of the audience at the Wharton Seminar for Business Writers at the University of Pennsylvania some years ago said:

> It seems to me that if you chronicled a lot of business complaints about the press, that a very high percentage of them might well come down to reporting by the wire services. While much of the media has moved away from the limitations of the strictures that are placed on us by deadline reporting, the wire services haven't to a great extent. They may have somewhat, and they do more interpretive pieces, but AP and UPI are still locked into various fast, speedy reporting and much of it disaster and profit stories, and these are very often things that are cited by business.[10]

Stories, written in haste by nonexperts, will, in whatever medium, likely repeat jargon. The business reporter on a regular beat needs to have a feel for the language and not let vague and technical language slip through just because a story from a news wire or PR wire does it that way.

One participant at the Wharton Seminar for Business Writers discussed the basic question of "audiences":

> There is the question of whom do we write our sections for? The L.A. *Times* says . . . coverage aimed very much at the consumer in general. . . . When you get business persons outside of their own fields,

> they're on a par with other people in a great many fields. So, I think that we really should try to appeal to the broadest reader. . . . The type of story we tried to develop in recent years is what I call an ABC story. . . . We take . . . an approach to explaining current events in which you both cover the event and explain it in the very beginning. It teaches the reader . . . and the editor what's going on. You go back and force yourself to get the explanations. . . .[11]

Among the terms you should know and be able to translate in your stories:

Accountant: One who is trained to keep financial records. A C.P.A. (certified public accountant) has passed a test and is certified or designated as qualified.

Accounts payable: Money a company owes to firms from which it has bought goods or services.

Accounts receivable: Money customers owe to a company.

After-tax income: Money a wage-earner has to spend after taxes.

Accrual basis accounting: Method of recording the expenses at the time a transaction is completed, not at the time of payment. The company records the price at the time customers walk out with items, not the price when customers pay their bills.

Amortize: The spreading of a cost of an item over a period of time. If something costs $50 over five years, it will show in the records as costing $10 a year.

Anti-trust laws: Laws which curb monopolies and encourage competition.

Articles of incorporation: A charter which the state gives allowing an organization to set up and function.

Asset: That which is of value, such as property, cash, or stock certificates.

Asset, current: That which can be converted to cash within a year.

Asset, fixed: That which cannot be converted into cash without interrupting business procedures.

Assets, intangible: Things of value that cannot be reported directly, such as copyrights, patents, trademarks, franchises, and licenses.

Audit: A review and verification of records.

Bad debts: Money owed which debtors will not pay.

Balance sheet: A statement, usually at the end of a business day or year, giving the financial position of the company.

Bear market: The prices of stocks are going down.

Big board: New York Stock Exchange.

Blue chip stock: Stock of corporations with proven records of making profits, with dividend payments in good and bad times.

Bond: A promise in writing to pay a designated sum at a future time.

Bonds, registered: Paid only to the person named in the bond.

Book value: Entire assets without liabilities; net worth.

Broker: An agent who sells stocks and bonds for a commission.

Bull market: The prices of stocks are going up.

Cash flow: Actual cash generated in a set time, apart from accounting and billing.

Collateral: Assets such as cash, stock, or bonds which a person uses to guarantee repayment of a loan.

Commodity: Anything that is bought and sold; an item of trade. Commodities: goods.

Common stock: Stock which carries with it a portion of ownership in a company—ownership of what is left over after costs.

Compound interest: Interest paid on both principal and previous interest.

Corporate bond: Bond which a corporation issues.

Deferred income: A liability created when a company is paid in advance, as in magazine subscriptions, when the company must deliver the product after receiving payment.

Deficit financing: Operating at a loss on borrowed money.

Dividends: Money paid to investors and stockholders out of income in return for the investment.

Escrow: Money deposited with a third party to be used on certain conditions, such as paying taxes or paying a down payment on real estate.

Fiscal year: An annual reckoning of accounts at some time other than the start of the calendar year.

Gross national product: Market value of goods and services a nation produces within a year.

Insolvent: Condition of someone who cannot pay his or her debts.

Levying: Instituting a tax.

Liquid: Having plenty of cash or assets which can be converted to cash.

Mutual fund: An investment corporation which invests for individuals and pays dividends on the earnings.

Net profit: That which is left over after all business operation costs have been deducted from income.

Preferred stock: Stock which is given priority in paying dividends; stock that shows ownership in a corporation.

Regressive tax: Tax that puts a greater burden on the poor than on the rich; a sales tax is a regressive tax.

Revenue: Money taken in by or due to a company; income of a government.

Secured loan: A loan guaranteed by a signature other than that of the signer or by property or collateral.

Securities: Stocks and bonds.

Stock certificate: A document or certificate showing ownership of stock in a corporation or of a share of the company's capital.

Tariff: Tax on imported goods.

Title: Proof of ownership.

Trust: The management of a person's money or property by a bank.

Yield: Return on investment, namely on corporate securities.

Stock quotation: Listing of trading and value of a stock for a given day. For example:

52 weeks								
High	**Low**	**Stocks**	**Div.**	**Sales in 100s**	**High**	**Low**	**Close**	**Net Change**
80	67¼	IBM	3.44	305,800	67⅞	67⅜	67½	−¼

Here IBM reached a high of $80 during the year, with the lowest at $67¼; on this particular day, 305,800 shares were sold—prices ranged from $67⅞ down to $67⅜. The last sale for the day was $67½. This was $¼ lower than the day before.

Here are additional credit and loan terms prepared by Philip Heckman for *Everybody's Money*, a quarterly of the Credit Union National Association.[12]

Acceleration clause: Lets the lender require entire payment of the loan as soon as you are in default.

Adjusted balance: Method of determining a credit card balance by subtracting your payments for the billing period before calculating the finance charge.

Adverse action notice: Formal notice of a lender's decision to refuse credit at the requested terms or terminate or reduce the amount of an existing open-end loan agreement. Discloses the reason(s) for a refusal, or informs you of your right to such an explanation, and identifies the credit bureau or other reporting agency involved, if any.

Amount financed: The amount you receive from the lender after prepaid fees, if any.

Annual percentage rate (APR): The cost of credit over a full year, expressed as a percentage of the amount financed. All else being equal, the lower the APR the better the bargain.

Average daily balance (ADB): Method of finding your credit card balance by adding the account balances for each day in the billing period, dividing by the number of days, and using that figure to calculate the finance charge.

Balloon clause: Allows a final loan payment substantially larger than regular payments. Look for it in the payment schedule.

Basis point: One-hundredth of one percent. (Compare points.)

Chattel: Movable personal property.

Cosigner: One who agrees to assume responsibility for a loan if the borrower becomes unable or unwilling to repay. Comaker is sometimes used as a synonym despite a subtle legal distinction.

Credit bureau: A reporting agency that assembles information about borrowers to help lenders evaluate credit worthiness.

Credit card fee: Service charge for the possession of a credit card for one year or month; finance charges are extra.

Credit disability and credit life insurance: Insurance that makes loan payments during a time of disability or pays the remaining balance if the borrower dies.

Credit rating: Evaluation of your ability to handle debt according to a statistical analysis of your finances or a list of guidelines.

Daily interest rates: (See periodic interest rate.)

Default: Failure to carry out the terms of a legal contract. For borrowers, this usually means missing one or more loan payments, but may include the failure to meet any loan agreement terms.

Delinquency: Failure to make a loan payment on time.

Delinquent fee: (See late charge.)

Demand feature: Allows the lender to call for the repayment of the entire outstanding loan under specified conditions, such as loss of income or depreciation of security, or simply the creditor's wish to call the loan. (Compare acceleration clause.)

Equity: Full value of property minus the borrower's debt; a measure of the degree of ownership. Owner's equity increases as loan principal, not interest, is repaid.

Finance charge: The cost of credit in dollars and cents including interest and all other defined charges. Certain fees not included in the finance charge must appear separately in the Truth-in-Lending disclosure.

Grace period: Time, if any, during which you may repay open-end credit without a finance charge. The date the finance charge goes into effect must be clearly stated.

High balance charge: Fee assessed if a borrower's open-end balance, including the finance charge, exceeds the approved credit limit.

Holder-in-due-course: The lender in a third-party loan agreement. In certain transactions, the consumer can withhold payment to the lender if the seller's product proves defective or service poor and the seller refuses to make good. Any loan subject to this rule must carry a notice to that effect.

Insurance premiums: Payments for credit insurance coverage, which may be excluded from the finance charge if the coverage is optional and that fact is disclosed. You must sign to accept the policy. Premiums for property insurance also may be excluded if the fact it is available elsewhere is disclosed. In both cases, the lender must reveal the terms of the coverage. When this insurance is a mandatory part of the credit plan, however, it must be included in the finance charge.

Itemization of amount financed: A listing the lender must give or offer to give that shows where the money you borrow goes, for example, to you in a check, or to various creditors.

Late charge: A common penalty for overdue instalments, expressed as a flat fee or a percentage of the scheduled payment, interest, or principal due.

Liability: Responsibility for unauthorized debt. Credit card holders can be held liable for only the first $50 of purchases with their lost or stolen card. This liability may be disclosed at any time before you report unauthorized use.

Lien: A creditor's claim on a debtor's collateral.

Methods of calculating finance charge: Ways to figure interest on an unpaid balance, which vary according to how the lender defines the outstanding balance. The lender must explain its method. (See adjusted balance, average daily balance, and previous balance.)

Payment schedule: Description of the number, amounts, and due-dates of required instalments.

Periodic interest rate: APR divided by the days, weeks, or months in a year. For example, an APR of 18 percent would have a monthly interest rate of 1.5 percent or a daily rate of 0.0493 percent.

Periodic statement: A record of open-end credit transactions. Borrowers must receive a statement each billing cycle, which must be at least quarterly. The statement must contain: closing date of the billing cycle, previous and new balances, amount and date of each credit advance (purchase or cash advance), each loan payment, finance charge, APR, and periodic rate. Most include the minimum payment required.

Pledge of shares: The use of some or all of a credit union member's savings as security for a loan. Pledged shares are unavailable to the member until the loan is repaid.

Points: A one-time fee mortgage lenders charge to bring the earnings of a loan in line with market rates. Each point equals one percent of the loan principal. Although the seller may have to pay points, the finance charge includes only the borrower's fees. (Compare basis points.)

Prepayment penalty or refund: An extra charge or a rebate of prepaid or accelerated interest, if any, when you pay off your loan early.

Previous balance: Way of figuring finance charge based on your credit card balance before payments made during the billing period are subtracted.

Required deposit: Savings held as a loan condition. The APR does not include money committed in this way.

Right of rescission: Your right to cancel a credit contract during a waiting period of three business days if your home is used as security. (Mortgages to finance the acquisition or construction of a home are excluded.) Can be waived in a "bona fide emergency" if you need the money sooner.

Secured loan: One that pledges certain property to the lender in case of default.

Security: Property the borrower offers to back up the promise to repay. Also known as collateral.

Security interest: Gives the lender the right to claim collateral or items purchased with credit but not yet paid for and sell them to try to recover a defaulted loan balance.

Third-party transaction: Purchase involving buyer, seller, and lender.

Total of payments: The sum of all instalments.

Total sale price: Refers to credit purchases; it is the sum of the down payment, amount financed, and all finance charges.

Unsecured loan: One backed only by the borrower's reputation; no security is involved. Also called a signature loan.

Variable rate loan: One whose APR varies according to certain economic conditions. The lender must tell you what would increase the interest rate; what limits, if any, apply to the increases; and how the amount or number of your payments would be affected.

Things to Watch Out For

Identifying problems that can hinder business writers may help to make life a little easier for the novice. Some of the pitfalls, according to business writers:

Deceptive language

> When earnings are poor, companies always emphasize their "record sales" in news releases. Don't be fooled. Figure the profit margins and report them in language people can understand—cents earned on each $1 of sales. This shows how efficiently the firm is operating.
>
> —Carol Pucci, business editor, Bellevue (Wash.) *Daily Journal American*

The hyper promoter

> Sometime during the first week, the new business reporter is going to run into a promoter, someone whose skill is talking money out of investors, business out of corporations and publicity out of business reporters. Nothing has the potential to deposit egg on your face more than this. Ask yourself: If this guy has 5,000 copies of my story reprinted and starts passing them out, am I going to come off as an

objective reporter or an accomplice? The answer is caution and backstopping. Find the expert in the subject matter and check him out.

—A business editor, Florida daily

Imbalance

Businessmen and most industrial management persons are basically conservative. Listen a lot, and try not to leap into controversies without giving business time to comment. Sometimes you can alienate your business contacts by not giving them a chance to respond immediately to accusations in another segment of the community or by a competitor.

—John I. Sellers, business editor, Mobile (Ala.) *Press Register*

Depending on handouts

Sometimes handouts—public or private—are deliberately misleading, but more often than not, they are poorly written. Call the firm or source, make sure the handout says what it means and means what it says. If figures are spurious or contradictory, get clarification.

—Edward Peeks, business-labor editor, Charleston (W. Va.) *The Charleston*

John Stylianos, managing editor of the Nashua (N.H.) *Telegraph*, adds: "Rewrite handouts. Use names of person being promoted in lead, not the president or any executive in the company. Be alert on figures and percentages."

Business writers also offer suggestions on what a reporter should watch for in reading a financial report or budget:

Be alert to percentages in loss and gain columns. Look at the bottom line.

—John Stylianos, managing editor, Nashua (N.H.) *Telegraph*

After the proverbial bottom line, read the footnotes. Unusual situations are typically handled as footnotes. Also look for trends, over five years or more. If the company breaks out its segments of business, is the emphasis changing? Is the company selling more but making less money?

—A business editor, west Florida daily

On a financial report, above all, read the footnotes. That's where the real stories are to be found in many instances.

—Joseph L. Goodrich, financial editor, Providence (R.I.) *Journal*

[Check the] . . . changes in earnings, revenues and volume for corresponding periods. Readers want to know to what extent a firm is

> growing or falling back. Read carefully the usual statements by the president and chairman. Weigh the alibis, if any, and take note of future plans and predictions.
>
> —Edward Peeks, business-labor editor, Charleston (W. Va.) *The Charleston*

> [Determine] . . . total expenditures, net profits, payroll (because that touches your local economy indicators) and funds for capital expenditure.
>
> —John I. Sellers, business editor, Mobile (Ala.) *Press Register*

> [Look for] . . . uncomparable figures, the arithmetic, unusual acquisitions or divestitures that would skew the figures for one or two years, losses. Just use common sense; anything that seems odd probably is and should be looked into.
>
> —Jeff Belmont, business editor, New Haven (Conn.) *Register*

> [Look for] . . . write-offs and extraordinary income, shareholders equity, long-term and short-term debt load, growth of volume and ratio of profits to growth.
>
> —Robert Brown, editor, Las Vegas (Nev.) *Valley Times*

> [Check] . . . liquidity—see where capital money is going. Check debt/equity ratio. Compare year-to-year earnings per share and retained. Also check leases to see if debt is being avoided through leases.
>
> —Doug Koplien, business-labor editor, Appleton (Wis.) *Post-Crescent*

> [Find] . . . inventory write-offs and growth in administrative expense.
>
> —Laffitte Howard, business editor, Knoxville (Tenn.) *News-Sentinel*

> [Examine] . . . variances from previous reporting methods; change of focus from previous reports; refusal to supply information on recent periods (that is, nine-month reporting instead of third quarter); major difference in year-to-year levels of various accounts; company refusal to explain.
>
> —Kenneth Hooker, business editor, Hartford (Conn.) *Courant*

In summary, Steve Jordon, reporter for the Omaha (Neb.) *World-Herald*, says:

> Check the basics. Companies may hide net losses by emphasizing gross sales instead. If there are questions about financial statements, call the company; check for hidden bombshells: changes in operations, mergers, sales.

WHERE TO FIND STORIES

The sources in business writing, as with other reporting, range from documents and reports to personal contacts.

Business writers, asked for "several key sources of information for business writers, with special attention to lesser known sources," suggest paying attention to:

- University business colleges and research bureaus.
- Secretary of state's office: corporate information filings.
- Auditor of public accounts: information on government bonds issued to private firms.
- Proxy statements for annual meetings.
- Analysts' reports from brokers.
- Bankers and members of the investment community.
- Any regulatory agency covering a specific business.
- Former executives of competing companies.
- Commercial real estate brokers.
- County assessors.
- State stock registration offices.
- 10–K, 10–Q, and 13–D reports of the Securities and Exchange Commission.
- Statistical reports, such as the *U.S. Industrial Outlook*, published annually by the U.S. Department of Commerce.
- Credit reporting agencies.
- Publicity departments of business and industry.
- Newspaper business columnists, such as Sylvia Porter.
- State offices: industrial development and employment, for example.
- Federal offices, besides the SEC: Comptroller of the Currency, Commodity Futures Trading Commission, Federal Deposit Insurance Corporation (FDIC), Environmental Protection Agency (EPA), Occupational Safety and Health Administration (OSHA), and so on.
- Reference services: Standard and Poors, Dun and Bradstreet, as well as research departments of stock exchanges and stock brokerages.

In general, A. Joseph Newman, Jr., financial editor of the former Philadelphia *Bulletin*, says:

> I would regularly look at the *Wall Street Journal*, New York *Times* business section, *Forbes*, *Business Week*, *Fortune*, and maybe *Barron's*—not necessarily read, but check all the heads and read stories of interest.
>
> Not just stories about companies and industries you follow, but about those you ought to be interested in—which could be practically everything. Also the trade press of the industries you follow: like the *American Banker, Women's Wear Daily,* that kind of thing. Every trade has at least one trade publication.

Also the annual reports and proxy statements of companies you're interested in. Read *Acres of Diamonds*. Go to annual meetings, of course, for stories and background.

Get on lists of brokerage houses for reports on companies. Analysts' meetings also very useful, for same reasons.

Read, read, read as much as you can about business, economics, to familiarize yourself with jargon and trends. You might even get to enjoy the stuff. Not to mention story ideas and tips. Quality of writing and reporting in *Wall Street Journal* is the best in the biz.

Attend business conventions as much as possible. You learn from speeches, informal talk in corridors. . . .

Even encyclopedic kinds of information—such as guidelines from an information source—can make a story, especially when topped by an account of a real event. Kathie Jarmon, consumer writer for the Tupelo (Miss.) *Northeast Mississippi Daily Journal*, used guidelines from the attorney general's office:

Nobody likes to admit he's a sucker. That's why it took a lot of courage for a Tupelo resident to call and talk about losing $6,000 in a business opportunity scheme. This is her side of the story.

The ad she read sounded exactly like what she had in mind, a way to make money in her spare time while she cared for her young child. The ad said the investor had a "potential" to make $8,000 part time and $40,000 full time.

Calling the toll-free number in the ad, she made an appointment to speak to a company representative who came to Tupelo. The representative said the company would provide her with toys and display racks and help her find stores in which to place the toys. The representative said she would be the only distributor within a 40-mile radius and told her to ignore the part of the contract which stated the company did not guarantee exclusive territory.

The next day after the interview, the representative came to her home and delivered another high-pressured sales pitch, she said. Falling for it, our victim wrote a $2,000 check. Another $2,000 check was to follow the next day.

That was about a year ago. Within that time, she has made no profit and has numerous complaints against the company for misleading her. . . .

In correspondence between the company and the attorney general's office, the company admits no misrepresentation and claims the complaints stem from personal conflicts.

In 1978, the state of Wisconsin filed a complain in Marathon County Circuit Court against R. J. Wiley Marketing Systems, Inc., the same company involved with the Tupelo residents. The complaint charged the company with violations of Wisconsin law in the promotion and sale of business opportunities relating to toy and pet supply display stand distributorships. The company is alleged to have misled and deceived prospective purchasers. The state is seeking injunctive relief and restitution.

Since Mississippi has no such law and cannot go out of state to file charges, there is very little the state can do to restore the Tupelo residents' money, except negotiate for partial payments, a spokesman for the attorney general's office said. The individuals don't have the money to sue personally. . . .

If you are interested in working on your own to supplement your income by investing in a business opportunity, the attorney general's office suggests following these rules.

Because some firms are in and out of losing ventures, ask about the firm's background. How long has the company been in business with this product? Where is the company's headquarters? What are their references? Insist on a copy and check with them. Who are the owners of the business and what is their background and experience? Will the salesman give you his name and address? How long has he been with the company? . . .

Because many unhappy investors are given excuses blaming others for the delays in shipment, ask about time factors. How long will it take for your investment to be fully operational? Are there any anticipated slow delivery problems? Are there manufacturers or middlemen who deliver the product? If so, who are they and where are they located?

Because profits are tied to high traffic, high sales locations, ask about location or retail accounts. Does the company guarantee locations/retail accounts? Does the company promise high traffic locations? Are any examples given? Do they hire a professional locator? Who? What is their background? Is there any charge (hidden cost or extra)? Do you have a right to refuse a location? If nonproductive, how can new locations be selected? How many miles will you have to drive to service accounts or locations? At the price of gasoline and car upkeep, can you still assume a profit?

Because the product may neither be needed, useful, saleable or priced competitively, ask about the product. Can you see an actual model of the product? What about a warranty? Who handles repairs or defects in merchandise? Will salesmen give you price lists to compare with other suppliers' costs? From whom do you order restocking merchandise? Are their prices competitive? Are there minimum reorders or amounts of sales that are required? Is there to be media promotion by the company to boost sales or do you do it on your own?

Because people are given unrealistic "facts" about profit potential, ask about income projections. What are the income projections based on? They should spell out the percentage of real live investors who have actually earned projected income. Also ask about geographic basis for income claims.

Most importantly, demand names and addresses of investors who have actually earned the profits promised. Is this an "exclusive" dealership? If not, how many others in your area will be sold?

Has the firm complied with the Federal Trade Rule (effective July 21, 1979) covering business opportunities, that is, given you a full disclosure document and documentation of all income projections? . . .

LABOR

Labor negotiations can stretch out over a long period. There are the human stories of hardship, of powerful persons with their followings, and of groups trying to get others to yield. And reporters have to wait for developments at meetings, usually outside closed doors.

On covering the long, difficult negotiations, experienced reporters comment on some of their problems.

> Any labor organization meeting is difficult. I simply take as many notes as possible, or if a strike is involved, talk to as many pickets as possible, plus employers, of course.
>
> —James L. Adams, Indianapolis *Star*

> Longshore negotiations [were the most difficult. The problems were solved] by going to a union source who gave me the information after the meeting. The source had been carefully "nurtured" for years and was reliable.
>
> —Charles M. Turner, labor writer, Honolulu *Advertiser*

Turner's report of another difficult labor meeting, relying on his sources, came out like this:

Contract talks between the striking Iron Workers union and structural and reinforcing steel companies resumed yesterday in an effort to end a walkout which has idled more than 10,000 construction workers throughout the state.

There was no report from the meeting, which began at 2:30 p.m., and a source close to the talks was not optimistic that they would succeed.

The iron workers began their strike Aug. 17 with about 860 members on the picket lines. Members of other construction unions, although not on strike, respected the picket lines, shutting down most major job sites.

The Iron Workers union said Tuesday it had agreed to let other union workers cross picket lines and work, but according to a General Contractors Association spokesman, a return-to-work movement did not materialize except at scattered job sites.

One of the companies involved in the strike, Pioneer Properties, asked the National Labor Relations Board (NLRB) yesterday to act quickly on an injunction to halt the walkout.

Pioneer Properties earlier filed suit for more than $5,000 per day because of the strike, plus $500,000 in punitive damages, on the ground that an illegal secondary boycott is being conducted.

Charles K. Fletcher, board chairman of Pioneer Properties, accused the Building Trades Council of throwing up "a smokescreen" by saying that it had urged members of unions other than the iron workers to go back to work if their conscience was clear.

Fletcher said such statements by union leaders are aimed at avoiding "the massive liability in the hundreds of thousands of dollars now facing the Building Trades' unions in numerous lawsuits, and further to avoid public criticism for the devastating effect of these union actions on the economy of the state."

Fletcher said that about 20 men showed up for work yesterday at his company's Pioneer Plaza project.

"However, when they approached the neutral entrances, they were approached and induced by a union official to refuse to work," he said.

"For over 20 years," he added, "this kind of secondary boycott has been declared illegal."

He said Congress has "confirmed that the American people will not tolerate or permit this type of illegal interference with the livelihoods of neutral employees and of those companies they work for."

He said a telegram has been sent to Natalie Allen, regional NLRB director in San Francisco, urging immediate action to halt the boycott.

The company asked the NLRB last week to obtain "appropriate injunctive relief to halt this illegal activity," Fletcher said.

A spokesman for the Iron Workers union and the Building Trades Council said he was trying to check out Fletcher's report that an unnamed union official had "induced" the 20 workers to "refuse to work" after they showed up at the site of the 21-story office building in downtown Honolulu yesterday.

Here are some labor terms you may find useful in your stories:

Agency shop: Workers must pay union dues but have the option of not joining the union.

Arbitration: A disagreement between two parties is settled by a third party; binding arbitration: parties must follow the decision of the third party.

Check off: The employer deducts union dues from the paycheck and sends them to the union.

Collective bargaining: A group of workers bargain with management through a labor union.

Collective bargaining agreement: A contract between a union and management.

Conciliation: Consultations with outside persons or groups to try to settle a dispute; the decision is advisory rather than binding.

Closed shop: Employees must join a union before they can be hired; the Taft-Hartley Act of 1947 made this illegal.

Craft union: A union organized on the basis of one skill or trade.

Escalator clause: A statement in a contract which says wages will keep pace with the cost of living.

Employment Act of 1946: Gives the government the task of encouraging full employment, economic growth, and stability of prices.

Featherbedding: Curtailing of work output in order to use all employees, thus preventing termination of unnecessary employees.

Industrial unions: Unions organized by industries, such as the United Auto Workers.

Landrum-Griffin Act: Called the Labor-Management Reporting and Disclosure Act of 1959, it attempts to protect the rank and file union member from corrupt leadership by requiring unions and management to report basic information to the Secretary of Labor.

Lockout: Management keeps a union out of a plant until a dispute, often with other unions, is settled. For instance, if one of a dozen unions is on strike at a newspaper, management may "lockout" the other unions in order to avoid paying wages.

Mediation: A third party brings together union and management and offers suggestions for settling the dispute.

Open shop: Ensures the right of an employee to join or not to join a union.

Right-to-work laws: State laws which prohibit the union shop.

Scab: A strikebreaker; one who crosses picket lines to go to work.

Sweetheart contracts: An agreement between a union leader and management favoring that union's interests but not necessarily the interests of workers as a whole.

Wagner Act: The National Labor Relations Act of 1935 emphasizes the right of workers to organize without intimidation by management; the Act outlines unfair management practices.

Wildcat strike: A strike that does not have the authorization of union leaders.

Yellow-dog contract: A contract which requires workers to agree not to join a union. Made illegal by the Norris-LaGuardia Act of 1932.

REAL ESTATE

One of the biggest weekly sections in a newspaper—usually appearing Friday or Saturday and often also on Sunday—is the real estate section. Many big dailies have a voluminous amount of real estate advertising, and editors feel it is necessary to cover and top off a large grouping of these ads with real estate copy. Unfortunately, many real estate pages look like a repository for filler and handout material. When a really big real estate story breaks, it finds its way to the front of the paper.

But some real estate pages put a high premium on enterprising reporting and effective features. Gary Washburn, real estate editor of the Chicago *Tribune*, gets people into his stories by taking a readable, down-to-earth approach:

Lew and Jan Toms own two homes today, but they certainly didn't plan it that way. They're stretched out financially, faced with possible foreclosure, and they're wondering what will happen next.

The Toms are victims of a guaranteed sales program that backfired and real estate sources say there are other families in the Chicago area who could be in danger of financial ruin because of similar programs.

The Toms listed their Streamwood home for sale with a northwest suburban real estate brokerage firm that promised to buy it for $53,000 if it didn't sell in 112 days. Confident that they would get their equity out of the house because of the purchase guarantee, the Toms bought another home in Hanover Park.

But when the time came for the real estate firm to take the Streamwood residence off their hands, it backed out of the guarantee on what Mrs. Toms, 23, says was a weak excuse.

Now there are monthly mortgage payments to make totaling $828. In addition, the Toms must pay interest amounting to $403 every three months on a $16,000 short-term loan they got for the second house's down payment.

Behind by two months now in the first home's mortgage payments, they have been threatened with foreclosure.

"If that home goes down, the one we are in right now could go down, too," Mrs. Toms lamented. "We are on the verge of losing everything we've worked for."

The Toms have a lawyer and may sue the broker, but they say relief may not come fast enough.

Sales guarantees have been offered enthusiastically in recent years by some Chicago-area brokers to attract listings from people selling their homes. They've been sought just as enthusiastically by people who want the security of knowing their present homes are sold as they buy new ones. Sellers looking for the highest guaranteed sales price have heightened the competition among brokers.

Guaranteed sales programs present no real problems when the home buying market is strong as it has been in the last few years because brokers actually have to purchase very few homes.

But in recent months high prices, high interest rates, and seasonal factors have slowed sales dramatically and some brokers who have offered the guarantee have been faced with "eating" more homes than they have money or credit for. . . .

For Laffitte Howard of the Knoxville (Tenn.) *News-Sentinel*, "people are more interesting than square footage." He notes that people who used to live in a house or at a particular site can make a story. "Land has been around a long time," he says. "What was it used for before it was built on? What were buildings used for before the present use? . . ."

Gary Washburn also suggests exploring the design of buildings for "interesting architecture angles."

Jack Miller of the San Francisco *Examiner* met readers' needs and chronicled consumer complaints about building contractors by checking the files of the Contractors' State License Board:

The state has been swamped with so many consumer complaints about building contractors that it has been forced to overhaul its regulatory machinery which has bogged down under the overwhelming work load.

The staggering complaint volume that has the Contractors' State License Board reeling "is far and away more than the total" the Department of Consumer Affairs receives for any of the 14 other independent boards under its wing. The Contractors' Board, which has jurisdiction over approximately 150,000 licensed contractors, gets about 36,000 complaints a year.

Richard B. Spohn, Consumer Affairs director, says the complaint backlog is running between 18,000 and 20,000 cases with some going back about six months. "This is totally unacceptable. Three years ago, complaints were disposed of in about six weeks," he says.

The board also is under the fire of the building industry which is seething about the delay in granting new licenses. Spohn estimates about 35,000 have been issued in the last three years. He attributes much of this torrent of activity to aggressive recruiting efforts by schools selling training courses to meet state examinations. Most have been in the Los Angeles area, he says.

"The passage rate was about 90 percent until last September when examinations were made more meaningful," says Spohn. When the exams were made "more job-related" so an applicant had to show he "knows how to swing a hammer and build a house," the passage rate dropped to 55 percent, he added, indicating the board is under pressure to tighten up further on examinations.

The board's problems, which are being attacked by new legislation that goes into effect the first of 1980, stem from antiquated regulations, inadequate management and staff and several years of record home building plus a booming growth in home repairs and expansions.

Aggravating the mess: Some 20,000 to 30,000 "outlaw operators," which Spohn describes as "small fly-by-nighters" in many cases. They virtually snub their noses at regulatory officials who are almost helpless in fighting this "serious problem." . . .

Gil T. Webre of the *Times-Picayune* in New Orleans, who writes on real estate and other subjects, says:

> To make the real estate page or section interesting, it is wise to write stories on trends—why are condos becoming popular? What is happening in shopping mall design? Why are building lots in short supply? How much will it cost to ready a lot for construction?

In one "why," or behind-the-scenes, story in the 24-page Saturday real estate tabloid in the *Times-Picayune*, Webre compared selling prices over a decade and proceeded to discuss reasons for the increase in real estate prices.

Trends, based on reports of the industry, make important real estate stories. Note the concise, point by point organization of this story by Charley Blaine in *USA Today*, which customarily splits off another group of facts into a side article or sidebar.

Where is USA real estate heading?

The Real Estate Research Corp., the Chicago-based appraisal and consulting company, thinks there are 32 long-term trends that people interested in real estate should watch.

Listed in the company's report, *Emerging Real Estate Trends in the 1980s*, the trends include developments in:

• Housing—Homes will be smaller and lenders will include fewer savings and loans.

• Commercial—Changing preferences of retailers and consumers will force builders to change the way they design and locate retail outlets.

• Political concerns—Cities want more from developers; and Congress is considering reducing the tax advantages the real estate industry enjoys under the 1981 Economic Recovery Tax Act.

Company Vice President Lewis Bolan says the trends are speculative but argues that they still are likely to affect local markets and future home-buying and real estate investing plans.

An increasingly popular trend involves the demands local governments are making on developers before they will allow projects to proceed.

In San Francisco, for example, a ballot measure, if passed, would require developers to pay a fee of $9.80 a foot for the strain their projects place on transit services and housing availability.

The issue was so closely fought that the outcome depends on more than 7,000 absentee ballots that weren't expected to be counted until late Wednesday night. Trends are gleaned from more than 80 interviews RERC, the USA's largest real estate consulting company, conducted with clients and real estate professionals this summer.

This sidebar was boxed at the end of the article:

The trends

Here are five emerging real estate trends you should watch, according to Real Estate Research Corp.

• The number of savings and loan associations will shrink from 4,000 to 1,000 by 1990, but a new generation of S&Ls engaging in specialized lending and customer segments could emerge.

• Aggressive S&Ls that lend too much money too fast and to the wrong clients could fail, further shrinking the market.

• Energy prices will rise gradually

throughout the 1980s.

• House sizes will decline as builders struggle to make their products affordable.

• Expect growth in university-dominated small and mid-sized cities.

Real estate writers suggest:

1. Beware of puff. It comes at you all the time, sometimes by forceful public relations representatives of brokers or developers. Keep in mind real estate agents are in business only to sell property.
2. Study the area. Neighborhoods must have meaning to the writer if the reader is to get anything out of the story at all.
3. Try to meet as many people in the business as possible. Take note of who gives reliable information.
4. Realize that many deals come in several stages. Know people at all levels—members of local boards of realtors, savings and loan presidents, bankers who make mortgage loans, developers, and as many real estate persons as possible.
5. The reader comes first. Avoid propaganda. Try to give the reader information that will help him or her make intelligent decisions.

CONSUMER ACTION LINES

Many newspapers have consumer writers. Usually covering consumer topics is a one-person assignment. The consumer reporter is attached either to the business department or the lifestyle section. Gayle Zubler, consumer writer for the South Bend (Ind.) *Tribune*, advises others:

> Become very familiar with local, state and federal consumer laws and establish good contacts at enforcement agencies on all levels. A consumer writer who successfully combines the clout of the media and the government can be very effective. These days, government agencies are most willing to cooperate with reporters regarding consumer matters. Some—NHTSA, CPSC, FDA—have established rather sophisticated information services. Consumer writers ought to take full advantage of the fact that government agencies are anxious to make a positive public showing.
>
> A consumer writer shouldn't hesitate to hand a tough problem over to the county prosecutor or the state attorney general. Doing so tells the business you're not going to get bored and go away. Sometimes a form letter from the state attorney general is just the nudge a reluctant businessman needs to get him to settle up.

Zubler conducts an Action Line column, the popular kind of column in which the reader can call and write about a problem and get help from the paper—often using the paper's clout. The items may involve considerable telephone work, and large papers have an entire staff doing the Action Line column (which may be called by other names, such as "Contact," "Quest," "Hot Line," "Help," or "Trouble Shooter"). In 1979 there was even a national convention of Action Line editors. Action Lines began in 1961 in the Houston *Chronicle* where the column was called "Watchem," and the concept spread in the U.S. and Canada. For years such columns were on front pages; now most Action Line columns are found inside the papers.

A typical Action Line request and reply comes from Zubler's column in South Bend, Ind. (a column will print three or four of these requests-answers a day):

We lived in Michigan all our lives until we moved to Northern California last July. Now we have a problem that perhaps you can help us with. My husband purchased Beltone hearing aids for both ears from Acoustic-Audio Services of South Bend. They were delivered in June before we moved to California. Before we left, he was having problems with them. When we got to California, he got a letter asking him to send them back, which he did at his own cost. He was sent another pair. These aids fall out unless they're taped in. When they're turned on to where he can hear, they squeal and squawk and they go off and on at every movement of his head. The first letter he wrote about the problem wasn't answered. The last letter was Feb. 12. They said if we would come back there, perhaps they could exchange the aid for another type. And they said the aids would be serviced by any Beltone dealer. We were led to believe it would be free of charge. We went to the Beltone dealer in Redding, Calif., and found that is not so. Also, after examining my husband's ears and the aids, he said there was no possible way they could ever fit. He could do nothing but advise him to get new ones. He said we would get practically nothing for the old ones. The aids he has cost $795. We feel Acoustic-Audio Services aren't dealing fairly with us.

—Mrs. J. I., McArthur, Calif.

Your husband's hearing aids will be completely remade at no cost to you. Mr. I. Stanley Thomas, president of Acoustic-Audio, wouldn't talk to us about your problem. So we discussed it with Anthony Luber, Thomas' attorney. Luber said Thomas would pay for the remolding necessary to make the aids fit and that Charles Howard, the Beltone dealer in Redding, should contact Thomas. Because the simplicity of this arrangement apparently hadn't been made clear to you, we thought we would cut a little red tape by calling Howard ourselves. Howard said he wasn't aware Thomas had agreed to pay for anything. He told us the aids aren't even close to fitting and it's obvious they never were. If he were in Thomas' position, he said, he would assume full cost and responsibility for having the aids completely remade. Remolding them alone won't do the job, he said, because hearing tests your husband had in California indicate the aids aren't designed to meet his hearing needs. With this info, we phoned Beltone headquarters in Chicago and told the whole story to Barbara Leafman, a consumer specialist. Ms. Leafman conferred with Howard and called back to tell us Beltone would assume the expense of remaking the aids if Thomas wouldn't. Ms. Leafman's final word on the subject came after she discussed the problem with Thomas. He has agreed to pay the bill, she said.

A good reference for consumer writing is *Consumer Sourcebook: A Directory and Guide*, edited by Paul Wasserman and Gita Siegman. The fourth edition, a two volume work of almost 1,500 pages, was published in 1983 by the Gale Research Co. of Detroit. These volumes list government agencies—local, state, and national—consumer information centers; clearing houses; toll-free private and government numbers; consumer-oriented associations, centers, and programs; and media services. A bibliography is included.

FARM WRITING

Farming is one of the most basic—and certainly one of the oldest—businesses. "It's a great beat," says Byron Parvis, farm editor of the Lafayette (Ind.) *Journal and Courier*, "because it affects the lives of all people."

Many newspapers, particularly those in agricultural areas, give pages regularly to farm news. Some have editors in charge of farm news—among them are the Birmingham *News*, Phoenix *Republic*, Sacramento *Bee*, Miami *Herald*, Indianapolis *Star*, Topeka *Capital-Journal*, Omaha *World-Herald*, Tulsa *World*, Houston *Chronicle*, and Chattanooga *News-Free Press*.

Farming, as a business, is both big and small. Many will argue that it is big business. The word "agribusiness" ("agri" is from the Latin words "ager," a field, and "agere," to drive, do—thus "ager" is also a place where cattle are driven) combines the two. The Richmond (Va.) *Times-Dispatch* even has a Monday column in section A of the paper called "Agribusiness," a compilation "from wire dispatches and other sources" by staffer Jerry Lazarus.

Farm writers must be familiar with both "big business and farming. Small vs. big—it is the major issue of the next decade in farm reporting," Parvis believes.

Patty Moore, area editor of the Atchison (Kan.) *Daily Globe*, highlights the big vs. small problem in one of her columns:

In gathering material for the 1979 Globe Agribusiness Edition, I found three recurring opinions voiced by most farmers interviewed.

It was also interesting to note these themes cropped up in interviews and information collected by Atchison County Extension Agent Ray Ladd in contributing stories on Kansas Bankers Association award winners in Atchison County.

The statements which were made again and again—sometimes voluntarily, sometimes in response to questions—in separate interviews were:

"I would not encourage anyone to go into farming today UNLESS he had considerable established backing or unlimited financial resources.

"My operational costs have doubled (more than doubled, or tripled) in the past five (two or three) years.

"Income just isn't keeping up with outgo, farmerwise."

One man said he had not even encouraged his only son to go into farming when the young man was graduated from high school several years ago, due to increased costs of getting started. The son did go into farming, but it's been much more costly and difficult for him to get established than it was for the generation before him.

Mentioned less often, but still a frequent complaint, was annually increasing "paperwork" piled on the farmer by government, particularly federal government. . . .

John Moe, managing editor of the Perry (Iowa) *Daily Chief*, says, "Farmers know their business and I feel a farm writer must know exactly what he is talking about. He can't bluff; farmers can tell if the writer is just assuming something or if he actually has knowledge of the field." Moe suggests five things the beginning farm writer should know:

1. The actual operation of a farm.
2. Priorities of a farmer.
3. Problems the farmer faces each season.
4. Market trends and their importance to the farmer.
5. How the farmer feels about government programs and government officials.

The Farm Tradition

While the so-called new militancy of farmers—with their tractor cavalcades and other marches on Washington—may seem a little out of character, contemporary reporters should know something about the militancy of farmers in American history, from Daniel Shays's Rebellion in Massachusetts in 1786–87 to the populist movements and their variations of the late nineteenth century. In fact, militant farm organizers have run many newspapers. In 1885 the founder of the National Newspaper Association was a Red Wing, Minn., farm organizer and editor of the *Grange Advance* and subsequent papers. The Grange, a grassroots movement, meant "farm" or "homestead." B. B. Herbert in his *Grange Advance* sounded almost Marxist (he was quite conservative in later years). He pledged the *Advance* as the "sworn enemy of monopolies and humbugs," as an early issue of the paper declared. Another militant farm editor was R. H. Thomas of the Mechanicsburg (Pa.) *Farmer's Friend*. Thomas was a guiding light and officer of the Grange and one of the presidents of the NNA (Herbert was the first).

Farmers have been issue-oriented and may be members of either political party. The farm reporter must know what the farm issues are. These issues include not only the "small vs. the big," as the Lafayette *Journal and Courier's* Parvis points out, but other conflicting forces as well: ". . . the farmer busting his butt trying to make a profit and the consumer raising hell about prices of food. It's a study in frustration."

Finding Features

Observes Patty Moore of the Atchison (Kan.) *Daily Globe*: "As long as there are weather, the government, county fairs, grasshoppers, the import-export business and one farmer on the face of the earth—there will be feature material. It only takes initiative."

The reference to grasshoppers is not far-fetched. Journalism student Joyce Smith of Wichita State University was given a class assignment early one spring to contact state agriculture officials to predict whether a grasshopper invasion—or a fall-off—was in store for the coming summer. The previous summer had seen grasshoppers as if they were cast in a biblical plague. She did her piece, found that experts predicted a sizeable grasshopper infestation, and reported on it for about 20 papers. One student wrote about the crows that darkened the sky of Wichita (and splattered windshields with droppings). Another, Jim Galloway, published a piece on trends in the bird population in the area for the Omaha *World-Herald*.

There's no end to bug stories. Marge Higgins of the Kent-Ravenna (Ohio) *Record-Courier* wrote about Japanese beetles:

The Japanese beetles are "here in force" as most everyone in Portage County knows by now.

Bruce Brockett, county extension agent, said his office has had complaints from everyone from gardeners to corn growers. Apparently the right combination of weather and soil conditions has led to the superabundance of the plant-destroying pests this year.

Brockett said the beetles will eat just about everything. "Generally, they aren't in commercial orchards because of the regular program of spraying there. But a single apple tree, they'll strip," he said.

In Canfield last week, he noticed a row of newly planted apple trees. Two-thirds of the top tender leaves had been eaten, leaving only a shrub-like stalk on the bottom.

Spraying with sevin, a mild, relatively safe pesticide, can be used to control the beetles. The only trouble is, if your neighbor doesn't also use it, the beetles will fly into your yard from his, Brockett said.

"Economically, the greatest fear is that the beetles will go west. We're trying to keep them from the plains states," Brockett said.

He expects the heavy infestation to last until frost. "We notice them more now because they are feeding more heavily while they are breeding and laying eggs. They'll seem less prevalent later, but they'll be around until frost," he said.

Eggs are laid in the soil and the grubs feed on grass roots.

The U.S. Department of Agriculture has a Japanese Beetle Laboratory on the campus of the Ohio Agricultural Research and Development Center at

Wooster. Entomologists there, T. L. Ladd and M. G. Klein, said the insect has been reported doing widespread damage throughout the state. They note that the Japanese beetle eats the foliage and ripe fruit of about 300 plants.

Ladd said the damage is the highest he has seen in Ohio in a decade. The scientists feel the snow helped keep the grubs from freezing and the moisture this spring and summer has helped propagate the high populations being reported.

Klein warns farmers to keep an eye on their cornfields as they come into silk. "Japanese beetles can do great damage to corn by eating the silk before the kernels are set on the cob," he said.

He and Ladd also advise the use of sevin, malathion or methoxychlor. But they said the pesticides should be used only on plants for which they are indicated and directions on the containers should be followed to the letter.

Ladd questions the effectiveness of beetle traps. Care must be used since improperly placed traps could lure beetles from other areas to foliage you are trying to protect, he said. . . .

Don Muhm, farm editor of the Des Moines (Iowa) *Register*, talks with people to find ideas. "I visit with my editors to find out what they are interested in, but then I head out into the country and visit with farm folks, go to the co-op meeting or a farm sale, and find out what's on their minds there." He believes in keeping a keen ear tuned to everything. He even warns you to: "Watch your competitors closely to see what they are up to in the way of covering the farm beat. You will always learn something from them, just as you will by listening to (and not arguing with) your own editors." He also draws on press conferences, government reports, even TV programs.

Farm Terms

If you have always lived in the city, you may not know some of these terms:

Aftergrowth: The second crop grown in a field in a year.

Agribusiness: The total process of raising and distributing farm products.

Alfalfa: A plant of the pea family, with cloverlike flowers, used as hay or feed.

Bale: A tight bundle of hay, straw, or cotton.

Banding: Putting bands on legs of birds and animals or otherwise marking them in order to identify them later.

Barrow: Castrated male hog.

Bovine: A member of Bovidae family, such as a cow or bull.

Bull: Uncastrated bovine, elk, or moose.

Burro: Donkey.

Caul: Fat around the stomach of cattle or hogs.

Chaff: Outer layer of grain.

Cheese: Made from curds or solid parts of milk combined by the work of a coagulant culture or yeast.

Disk: Blade part of plow that cuts the soil.

Doe: Adult female deer, goat, or rabbit.

Drought: Dry condition caused by lack of rainfall.

Ewe: Female adult sheep.

Foal: Unweaned young horse.

Frost: Temperature drops below 32° F.

Guinea: Chicken-like bird—a popular kind has purple-grey feathers dotted with white—that has some flying ability and moves faster on the ground than chickens.

Heifer: A cow which has not borne a calf.

Legumes: Plants with pods, such as peas or beans.

Maggot: Larva of a fly.

Mole: Long-nosed animal that burrows and lives beneath the topsoil.

Pelt: Skin covering, such as fur.

Pig: Young swine weighing less than 120 pounds; some markets set 130 pounds as the limit.

Pollen: Male fertilization element of plants, often dust-like.

Prune: To take off parts of plants to improve growth pattern.

Rye: A bread grain, used also for cattle feed and for whiskey.

Sage: Gray-green herb that is dried and used to flavor sausage and other meat.

Salami: Pork sausage with 10 to 30 percent beef.

Silo: Tall cylinder-shaped structure used for storing green crops, which are preserved in an eating stage by some fermentation.

Sorghum: Grain plant used to make some pancake syrups.

Stallion: Male horse used for breeding.

Steer: Castrated bull; also, an ox.

Sump: Area or hole in which water is diverted to be pumped out.

Topped: Sorted animals ready for market; tree trimmed off at top.

Whey: Part of milk separating from the curds (or thicker parts) in the making of cheese.

FOOD REPORTING

Reporting on food and meal preparation is changing. The food pages are usually attractive, with clever color illustrations. A growing professionalism is developing that often makes the food pages as exciting and newsworthy as others in the paper.

Among the changes:

> As the price of pulp goes up, management tends to cut back on space allotted to food and family sections. No more can you simply plug in the handouts from food PR people and call it a food section. The writers must be able to keep up with the changing food scene and not be suckered in by food fads. Nutrition and cost are most important.
>
> —Renee R. Cuddleback, assistant news editor, *Evening News*, Newburgh, N.Y.

> There is more emphasis on cost, fast preparation methods, fewer sugar-laden desserts—wider choices (health foods).
>
> —Carole Currie, women's editor, Asheville (N.C.) *Times*

The old formula of getting people's names in the paper applies, and Currie has a "Trade Secrets" column that runs recipes and other information from readers.

Mardy Fones, lifestyle reporter of the Decatur (Ill.) *Herald and Review*, takes the audience participation a bit further:

> We recently started a test cook program where local cooks test some of the canned food copy we get in. Each week, people from the community volunteer for the job. We give them the choice of an area—meats, breads—then send them three or four recipes to try. They evaluate the recipes, I do a little personality piece and they get a picture in the paper.

She also runs readers' recipes on Sunday.

Among tips she has for the new food writer:

- Use only recipe copy which includes ingredients that are available in your area—don't use papaya recipes for Alaska.
- Where possible, make sure the recipes work.
- Respond to reader requests for specific recipes.
- Be cognizant of special groups in preparing recipes—diabetics, vegetarians, or special religious groups.
- Try to key recipes to special holidays, seasons, or other gimmicks.

Sue Robinson, food editor of the Greensboro (N.C.) *Daily News*, takes a solid news approach to food writing. Five things she says the modern food writer should know are:

1. Food is not always feature material. Food reporting should be handled as a beat and food writers who fail to take this approach miss valuable stories. A good food writer takes responsibility for consumer reporting

(inflation, prices, product evaluation, and availability) and many stories that fall in the hard news area: state-funded nutrition education programs, food-related social service programs, nutrition issues (nitrites, contaminated foods . . .), and crop situation in the area if no agriculture beat is assigned. The food writer who lets news reporters handle the "heavy" stuff is missing the boat in terms of readership, experience, and knowledge.

2. Learn how to separate the wheat from the chaff. The food writer may come in first in the junk mail sweepstakes (it helps to develop a good working relationship with the mail clerk—you see a lot of each other).

   Just because a release from the mushroom association says peanut butter stuffed mushrooms are nutritious and delicious doesn't make it so.

   Just because the raisin spokesman says the crop's a record and prices should drop doesn't mean it will be so in your area.

   Just because a release says mayonnaise inhibits bacterial growth doesn't make it so.

   NEVER DEPEND ON A NEWS RELEASE FROM A FOOD COMPANY FOR ACCURATE INFORMATION. WHEN IN DOUBT, DON'T PRINT IT or depend on it for background information.

3. Know that everyone who eats is an expert on food. You'll receive story suggestions from everyone in the building, your mother, your husband or wife, your readers . . . don't hesitate to use those suggestions when they merit a story.

4. Don't be afraid to say "I don't know," but know where to find the answer. You'll receive phone calls about all aspects of nutrition and food preparation ("why has my brandied fruit grown mold?" "Why doesn't my egg have a yolk in it?" or "How do you cook wild boar?"). You'll never have all the answers, but you'll have the sources who do. Take the reader's number, seek out the answer, and return the call. You learn a great deal, and you develop a personal relationship with your readers (they'll love you for it).

5. Nutrition is not an exact science. Nutritionists and dietitians do agree on many points, but if you're dealing with a controversial subject NEVER depend on one source. Many areas in nutrition are very muddy, and it's your job to give the reader the whole picture. Never depend on a medical doctor for nutrition information unless he's teaching foods at a university or medical school. Doctors receive only minimal instruction in nutrition and depend on home economics professionals for diet planning and nutrition counseling.

Robinson has a lively style, and her food features, with four-color illustrations and display type, snap right out.

Here are examples of the range of her stories:

- The lure of herb growing. The headline: "Home-Grown Herbs Flavor Dishes."

Corsican mint. Rue. Creeping thyme. Cuban oregano. Lemon balm. Salad burnet. Fennel.

The names roll off the tongue in a whisper suggesting . . . black magic . . . bubbling cauldrons . . . creepy bundles tied in the rafters.

But there's no mystery in a rue vinegar, no magic in a salad burnet seasoned salad, no quivers in a basil jelly for herb gardener Dorothy Spencer. She weaves kitchen magic from a love of growing things and fine food. . . .

- Searching out strawberries. The headline: "It's Strawberries Time: Where to Pick 'Em."

Dust off the old straw hat. Shine up your sun specs. Shake out the overalls. Get your picking fingers ready.

The strawberries are here and the pickings are bountiful.

Pick-your-own farms are luring supermarket snobs, back to nature lovers and strawberry addicts to the patches again. 'Tis the season for freezing, jamming and . . . ah . . . shortcake.

Early warm weather brought the crop into full flower earlier than predicted and area growers hope favorable conditions will continue. . . .

Average cost per quart is 50 cents, a far cry from the up to 99 cents per pint price in the grocery produce department. Your sweat doesn't count. . . .

- New creative ideas on fixing chicken. The headline: "Chicken for A Month of Sundays."

Chicken is one of your very best buys this year. Lower in saturated fat than beef or pork, chicken is high in protein and lower in calories than many other protein sources.

What's important these days with red meat prices going up, up, up is that chicken remains a good buy.

The versatile bird adapts to a number of flavor combinations as these recipes show. Poultry is suitable for special dieters as well.

A chicken in every pot every Sunday used to be the rule.

If your budget can't swing a rib roast every week, try these super chicken dishes for your Sunday meal.

(Recipes follow this introduction on chicken, one for each Sunday of the month, with the layout like a calendar.)

- Low-cost nutritious meals. The headline: "Suppers on a Shoestring."

A little knowledge goes a long way in planning nutritious suppers on a shoestring.

Nutrition is the byword (and buyword) and the four food groups the foundation for shopping, serving and saving. An adult requires 2 or more servings from the milk group, 2 servings of meat or protein, 4 servings of fruit and vegetables and 4 servings of grain daily.

If supper is the main meal, chances are you'll allow 1 meat serving, 1 milk, 2 fruit and vegetable portions and 1 grain serving. You can often cut costs—and improve your family's health in the bargain—by trimming when you dish it up. At many tables, "serving size" far exceeds the recommended portion.

A fruit/vegetable serving is ½ cup; meat, 2 ounces cooked; grain, one slice bread; milk, one 8-ounce glass. Take a look at plate waste and waistlines to see if your tablemates are literally eating up your food budget.

Substitutions can save money. For instance, one ounce of cooked meat roughly equals 1 egg, 1 slice American or Swiss cheese, 2 tablespoons cottage cheese or ½ cup beans or peas in protein value. Animal proteins (meats) are the best protein resource and the most expensive. By substituting and balancing proteins you can serve better meals for less. . . .

Think before you throw away. Not-so-fresh vegetables can be used for soup stock. Bits and pieces add up. Use small amounts of cooked fish, chicken, meat or cheese in tossed salads, casseroles or omelets. Stale cake and cookies can be crumbled and served with ice cream or in puddings.

Shop the sales and cook in quantity to save food and energy. Think unit price and cost per serving and your battered budget will feel better.

- A "participatory" feature on school lunchrooms, where Robinson went to the schools and sampled—and compared—the lunches. The headline: "Lunchroom Fare Is More Than Fair."

Eating in the school lunchroom isn't like it used to be. It's better.

Since I often don't eat lunch, sampling the food at three area schools was a pleasure. Lending credence to the fact that a full belly makes the mind quicker, my afternoon went smoother after eating rather than abstaining.

On the whole, parents should be satisfied with what their children eat every day. It may not be gourmet fare, but it's the closest thing you can get to mama's cooking at 45 to 55 cents. Most homemakers would, I imagine, love to put as balanced and attractive a meal on the table for under a dollar a plate.

Cafeteria food wasn't as bad as I remember through public school and college dining, or maybe it's improved.

The atmosphere is the same, formica and slightly antiseptic. But the noise level at Brown Summit, Eastern Guilford and Page was more agreeable to good digestion than in my school days. No food fights. No bedlam. Not too many pointed glares from teachers. No spilled milk.

At the elementary level, the little boys, if at all possible, staked out a table removed from the fairer sex. For high schoolers, the match game and gossip appeared more tempting than anything the cafeteria workers could dish up.

One thing that hasn't changed much are the rituals. Each elementary child has his own way of digging in. Some are pickers, eating only a little bit of everything. Some are leavers, eating all of one thing and leaving the rest untouched. Some are grabbers, eating anything—especially sweets—that the more discriminating tablemate leaves. Some are gulpers, barely breathing between bites. Some are players, artistically rearranging everything on the tray.

Now to specifics.

At Brown Summit, it was spaghetti with cheese, peaches, tossed salad, roll, peanut butter cake and milk. The spaghetti was hot—if you ate as soon as you sat down—and was better than Chef Boyardee. The tossed salad, basically chopped lettuce, was fresh and crisp. Seasoned with salt, pepper and French dressing, it met rabbit food lovers' approval.

The canned peaches were well chilled and counted as a favorite with the diners. The rolls were homemade, as all school breads are, and yummy. I could have eaten half a dozen. The peanut butter cake, again homemade, was delicious.

Apparently, the cake is an all or nothing thing. Some love it. Some leave it. A few prefer the icing minus the cake. Eating dessert first is one of the real pleasures of eating at school rather than under mom's watchful eye. After all, explained first grader Michael Bailey, it all goes to the same place in the end.

Blue-eyed Larry Bullis had two complaints. He'd rather bring his lunch because "I have a Steve Austin lunchbox at home but mom won't let me bring it." And, the food, he claims, "it isn't hot." But countered his classmate Terri Smith diplomatically, "it's warm though."

All in all, not bad eating. The children seemed to like the spaghetti which is a close cousin of the avowed favorite, pizza.

At Eastern, there was a choice: barbecue with bun, cole slaw, French fries, rolls, milk, and applesauce or macaroni and cheese, green beans, French fries, roll, milk and apricots.

Barbecue was spicy, piping hot and served on a fresh bun. The green beans also received a "A" rating for excellent seasoning. The slaw, though a bit warm, was well prepared and tangy.

I passed on the French fries for figure's sake but the consensus among my dining partners—Robin Thompson, Kathy Wilson, Lisa Clapp, Lou Ann Koonce, Martha Andrew, Sharon Alcon, Sheila Merph and Debbie Lamm—was that a meal's not a meal without fries. Preferably, oozing with catsup.

At Page, with a choice of ala carte, a chef's salad or the plate meal of fish sandwich, au gratin potatoes, slaw or mixed vegetables, applesauce, peanut butter cookie and milk, I went the ala carte route.

I ended up with a slightly mealy cheeseburger at room temperature and one of the finest pieces of cake I've ever tasted. Cafeteria manager Mrs. Marian Merrill could do a commercial for her super moist applesauce cake with butter cream icing if it came out of a box but it's made from scratch. . . .

Notes

[1]"A Survey: Resources Allocated to Business Coverage," *APME Business and Economics '77*, a report to the Associated Press Managing Editors Association by its business and economics committee, n.d., p. 1.

[2]Jerome Idaszak, "The Business News Boom: Today's Money Is on the Money Beat," *Quill* (June 1978): p. 29.

[3]"Business News Hole Enlarged in A.M. Edition," *Editor & Publisher* (June 23, 1979): p. 26.

[4]"Rochester (N.Y.) Dailies Change Business Sections," *Editor & Publisher* (June 23, 1979): p. 24.

[5]I. William Hill, "Foundation Earmarks Funds to Business News Projects," *Editor & Publisher* (Oct. 1, 1977): p. 11.

[6]Idaszak, p. 29.

[7]David J. Mahoney, "On Ending an Adversary Relationship," New York *Times*, July 7, 1977, c. 1977, 1979, p. 19, col. 1.

[8]Louis Banks, "The Failings of Business and Journalism," *Time* (Feb. 9, 1976) vol. vol. 107, p. 78.

[9]Joseph Poindexter, "The Great Industry-Media Debate," *Saturday Review* (July 10, 1976), c. 1976, Saturday Review Magazine Co.: p. 18.

[10]"Draft for Revision," transcribed from a cassette tape recorded at the Wharton Seminar for Business Writers, Nov. 17, 1976, p. 16.

[11]"Draft for Revision," pp. 18, 19.

[12]Philip Heckman, "Come to Terms with Credit," *Everybody's Money* (c. 1983, n.d.), published by Credit Union National Association: pp. 16–18.

Assignments

1. Invite a stockbroker or corporation official to class for an interview. Ask the person to use the big words and jargon of their work but be willing to back up and explain the word, even over and over again, when pressed by students.

2. Some business article ideas: businesses, even small ones, in town who do export business; what's happened to household help—maids are making a comeback when both husband and wife are employed; new businesses in the area; trends in closings; the unemployment picture.
3. Some real estate article ideas: how to sell a house without a real estate agent; trace the history of a house through register of deeds; the new real estate advisors or brokers who help and advise a client for a small fee but do not sell or take percentages; check out discrimination in selling and zoning; forecast interest rates.
4. Some farm article ideas: a day on a typical area farm; junior and teen achievers; the plight of current crops; forecasting success or failure for the year; new equipment and new ways of doing things; the farm wife and family; the government's changing role; the amount of local crops going overseas.
5. Concerning food, check out methods for dating each food item and how to tell the quality and freshness of a product. Also compare price fixing—usually ghetto areas pay more for food (the people are not mobile) and affluent areas pay less. Look into reports on shoplifters and security measures. Compare restaurants from country clubs to the fast food outlet by city and county food and health inspection reports.
6. Profile the Better Business Bureau or another consumer protection agency.

15

Sports

When veteran sportswriter Chuck Newman of the Philadelphia *Inquirer* talks about sports reporting, he likes to think of Barry Ashbee.

Barry Ashbee was a Philadelphia Flyer hockey player and assistant coach who didn't particularly like or understand reporters or their functions. But he could spend most of a night arguing with reporters trying to convince them that he was right.

Newman was often one of the reporters debating with Ashbee. "We sat five hours once in the Marriott (Hotel), until three in the morning debating the subject," says Newman.

Newman remembers asking: "Barry, what is a reporter?" And Barry insisted: "A reporter . . . you guys, you put in the paper what people like to read." Then he added: "You should be one of us. You should be for the home team."

Newman answered: "No, Barry, we are not 'one of us.' We cover, report . . . we are not 'one of us.' That is what a publicity man does."

Such statements used to upset Barry Ashbee, a player who toiled in minor league cities before expansion gave him a chance. The moral of Newman's stories about Ashbee:

> As much as he would yell at me, and that was often because of my style, I never feared him . . . others feared him. . . . I felt he was one of the most honest of players and coaches. You knew where he stood and he always let you know. I respected him even if I could never agree.

Newman had reason to reflect about Ashbee.

Ashbee died of leukemia . . . at 37.

Ashbee was a journey defenseman whose life was hockey. He had played through the season with a crushed disc in his back. It was nearly impossible for Ashbee to lift his arm. When hit by a puck in the Stanley Cup playoffs, Ashbee lost 80 percent of the sight in one eye.

"He was an athlete's athlete," recalls Newman. "If anything negative was said about him or his teammates, he would yell. Yet he respected objectivity."

Newman, reminiscing about Ashbee, cited the frankness of the relationship between Ashbee and himself as the best possible relationship, that of honest adversaries. Barry disliked PR types. And so does Newman. "I hate 'housemen,'" says Newman. "Anyone who writes what a club likes and does it all the time is a prostitute. You would be amazed at how many reporters are like that, because it is easier or because of fear."

And athletes are good at sizing people up, says Newman. "Believe it or not, an athlete reads you more than you read the athlete."

Sports reporting is hard work and is especially difficult during peak seasons. You can spend all day dogging certain coaches and sports staff personnel and then stay into the late evening covering a game and doing a deadline story on the game. As a sports reporter, you can work nearly around the clock on some nights, especially on Friday nights. Reporters on the early Saturday morning shift at the Mankato (Minn.) *Free Press* more than once found a sports reporter who, after working all night, was asleep on the couch with a coat over his head.

Sports reporting requires the same discipline that other reporting does: the reporting has to be factual; names of players and teams have to be right; and, as with all reporting, the writing has to be interesting.

FIRSTHAND DRAMA

Although sports reporting, because of deadline pressures and the feature-entertainment aspect of the art, tends to be breezy, it is a true form of reporting and offers an excellent way to begin a career in journalism. Few beats on a newspaper require so much of a firsthand approach to the subject. A quote from the handbook, *Learning in the Newsroom: A Manual for Supervisors*, edited and compiled by John L. Dougherty, managing editor of the Rochester (N.Y.) *Times-Union*, points this out:

> We're all news reporters, but cityside reporters work mainly with familiar people under conditions that rarely require them to be eyewitnesses. More than all the rest, sportswriters are required to be *eyewitnesses*, reporting on what they see and weaving it in with what they've heard.[1]

Readers like to relive the experience. They want to be there—at ringside or in the stands. And when the bell rings for another round or the pitch is off, reporters want to bring it to life for their readers. Most likely readers have heard the scores on radio or TV and know the basic facts already. But even so, newspaper reporters' tasks are also visual. Sportswriters attempt to prolong or intensify the experience of the event. Spectator sports are entertainment, and the fans want to prolong—and understand—the entertainment experience, in a word, to continue "seeing" the game in print and pictures.

Sports are also people, and fans want to know about the athletes as people. "Sports are not just games," says Robert H. Johnson, assistant general manager of the Associated Press in New York, ". . . sports are aspects of life that reflect other aspects of life. People are no longer interested in athletes as stamped out rubber heroes running up and down the field. People want to know what people's lives are really like."

To Le Anne Schreiber, sports editor of the New York *Times*, ". . . a part of sports is personality. There are human dramatic situations of a novel or soap opera. In every game, there are real things at stake, not only for the team but for each player as an individual." Personal highs and failures—records, losing streaks, injuries, illnesses, and families—are all a part of the human story of sports, a key ingredient of sports, Schreiber believes.

The role of the sportswriter is also that of a dramatist, says Schreiber, who came to her job after studies in chemistry at the Rice University School of Engineering, Houston, and English at Stanford University. She has nearly completed a Ph.D. in literature at Harvard. Her dissertation area: "Modern American Novel: Ideology of Murder." She has also written for *Time* magazine. "Sports are basic drama," Schreiber says; just as people go to theaters, ". . . people fill a stadium. People are hooked on the drama of sports." She believes the drama, conflicts of personalities, and the "plot" are important. "One temptation is to belabor that sports is serious," she says. "Some want to show it is serious and therefore emphasize the scientific, political or economic side of sports. There is a dimension of that, but there is a profound side, too, that of drama." The dramatic approach, she says, is one way to avoid "leaden prose."

To prepare for sports writing, she suggests reading Shakespeare and the Greek tragedists, in order to "understand simple structure" of the drama dealing with "gain and loss." For learning to write about personalities in sports, she recommends "immersing yourself in the best of fiction—the classics, Elizabethan drama, Greek tragedy and comedy." Also, "the Nineteenth Century novelists help one to perceive character," she says. Her favorites are George Eliot, Jane Austen, and Henry James.

Says the AP's Robert Johnson:

> Students should be voracious. They should want to know something about everything. The best are generalists but with a background not only in writing and English but in all areas. They should read widely—novels, sociology, history, and government. Sportswriters now need to know about labor law. In contract matters, in Congressional hearings, in discussion about a free agent, one has to know what the hell people are talking about.

All in all, sportswriters can have the best of a number of worlds. They can be generalists, specialists, entertainers, harbingers of the daily events, oracles and soothsayers, and, above all, dramatists. Sports reporting brings certain satisfactions to sportswriters because (1) it offers a narrow topic which requires wide general experience and a broad education, and it enables reporters to become experts in one subject (even in one sport); (2) sports reporters have latitude in the topics they select, from hard news to features to columns and trivia; (3) a whole section in the paper each day guarantees considerable space in proportion to other topics in the news; (4) sports reporting permits humor and encourages creativity in style (but reporters do have to beware of the pitfalls of slang and too much creativity in style); and (5) sportswriters have their own followers, a source of satisfaction for all writers.

GREAT SPORTSWRITERS

In reading—in preparation for being a good sportswriter—you might look at the classics in sports writing. You can find these in anthologies containing sports stories such as those by Grantland Rice, Red Smith, Arthur Daley, Frank Graham, Gerald Holland, Bill Vaughan, John Lardner, Tom Siler, John Kieran, and Charles Dryden.

Ralph D. Berenger, publisher of the Shelley (Idaho) *Pioneer*, points out that Grantland Rice's "four-horsemen" story in the New York *Herald Tribune* is what ". . . most sportswriters feel was the greatest sports story ever written." Berenger recalls that when it appeared it had only a one-column head and was easily overlooked on an inside page of the sports section.

In Rice's writing, you will find imagery, style, and a freshness of language (although many of Rice's phrases became cliches when reused and overworked by others).

In an anthology which contains "The Four Horsemen," Herbert Warren Wind gives this background on Rice's classic:

Fashions change, and today it is much harder than it used to be to devise nicknames and labels for sports heroes that stir the public's imagination and stick forever. If Grantland Rice were living today, though, there is a fair chance that many of the modern stars would be bedecked with strangely satisfying sobriquets, frequently alliterative, for Rice had an exceptional gift for this. It was he who first called Red Grange "The Galloping Ghost," for instance, and Jack Dempsey "The Manassa Mauler." His most inspired descriptive appellation, however, was "The Four Horsemen," the name he gave to the great Notre Dame backfield of Harry Stuhldreher, Jim Crowley, Don Miller, and Elmer Layden. Sports fans were enchanted by it, whether or not they were aware of its derivation—a rather inappropriate one at that—which Rice spelled out at the start of his account of the 1924 Notre Dame–Army game. That account, reprinted here, is an excellent example of Rice's point of view and his style. An unabashed romantic where sports were concerned, he usually managed to provide his stories with a soaring "lead" and a flock of high-flying, bright-plumed metaphors even when he was battling the pressure of a deadline. It might be added that he was as kind and chivalrous in his relations with his friends and colleagues as with heroes.

By present-day standards, the Four Horsemen were pretty much of a pony backfield. Stuhldreher, the sharp little quarterback, weighed 152 pounds; Crowley and Miller, the halfbacks, each weighed only 156 pounds; Layden, the smashing fullback, weighed no more than 162. They were rugged and fast, though, and above all, they worked together beautifully as a unit. During their three seasons, 1922–'23–'24, Notre Dame won twenty-nine games while tying one and losing only two, both of them to Nebraska by a single touchdown. In 1924 the team went undefeated and the Four Horsemen bowed out on an appropriately high note by leading Notre Dame to a 27–10 victory over Stanford in the 1925 Rose Bowl Game.

In Grantland Rice's "Four Horsemen" there is suspense and drama from the outset:

Outlined against a blue-gray October sky, the Four Horsemen rode again. In dramatic lore they are known as Famine, Pestilence, Destruction and Death. These are only aliases. Their real names are Stuhldreher, Miller, Crowley and Layden. They formed the crest of the South Bend cyclone before which another fighting Army football team was swept over the precipice at the Polo Grounds yesterday afternoon as 55,000 spectators peered down on the bewildering panorama spread on the green plain below.

A cyclone can't be snared. It may be surrounded, but somewhere it breaks through to keep on going. When the cyclone starts from South Bend, where the candle lights still gleam through the Indiana sycamores, those in the way must take to storm cellars at top speed. Yesterday the cyclone struck again as Notre Dame beat the Army, 13 to 7, with a set of backfield stars that ripped and crashed through a strong Army defense with more speed and power than the warring cadets could meet.

Notre Dame won its ninth game in twelve Army starts through the driving power of one of the greatest backfields that ever churned up the turf of any gridiron in any football age. Brilliant backfields may come and go, but in Stuhldreher, Miller, Crowley and Layden, covered by a fast and charging line, Notre Dame can take its place in front of the field.

Coach McEwan sent one of his finest teams into action, an aggressive organization that fought to the last play around the first rim of darkness, but when Rockne rushed his Four Horsemen to the track they rode down everything in sight. It was in vain that 1,400 gray-clad cadets pleaded for the Army line to hold. The Army line was giving all it had, but when a tank tears in with the speed of a motorcycle, what chance had flesh and blood to hold? The Army had its share of stars in action, such stars as Garbisch, Farwick, Wilson, Wood, Ellinger and many others, but they were up against four whirlwind backs who picked up at top speed from the first step as they swept through scant openings to slip on by the secondary defense. The Army had great backs in Wilson and Wood, but the Army had no such quartet, who seemed to carry the mixed blood of the tiger and the antelope.

Rockne's light and tottering line was just about as tottering as the Rock of Gibraltar. It was something more than a match for the Army's great set of forwards, who had earned their fame before. Yet it was not until the second period that the first big thrill of the afternoon set the great crowd into a cheering whirl and brought about the wild flutter of flags that are thrown to the wind in exciting moments. At the game's start Rockne sent in almost entirely a second-string cast. The Army got the jump and began to play most of the football. It was the Army attack that made three first downs before Notre Dame had caught its stride. The South Bend cyclone opened like a zephyr.

And then, in the wake of a sudden cheer, out rushed Stuhldreher, Miller, Crowley and Layden, the four star backs who helped to beat Army a year ago. Things were to be a trifle different now. After a short opening flurry in the second period, Wood, of the Army, kicked out of bounds on Notre Dame's 20 yard line. There was no sign of a tornado starting. But it happened to be at just this spot that Stuhldreher decided to put on his attack and begin the long and dusty hike.

On the first play the fleet Crowley peeled off fifteen yards and the cloud from the west was now beginning to show signs of lightning and thunder. The fleet, powerful Layden got six yards more and then Don Miller added ten. A forward pass from Stuhldreher to Crowley added twelve yards, and a moment later Don Miller ran twenty yards around Army's right wing. He was on his way to glory when Wilson, hurtling across the right of way, nailed him on the 10 yard line and threw him out of bounds. Crowley, Miller and Layden—Miller, Layden and Crowley—one or another, ripping and crashing through, as the Army defense threw everything it had in the way to stop this wild charge that had now come seventy yards. Crowley and Layden added five yards more and then, on a split play, Layden went ten yards across the line as if he had just been fired from the black mouth of a howitzer.

In that second period Notre Dame made eight first downs to the Army's none, which shows the unwavering power of the Western attack that hammered relentlessly and remorselessly without easing up for a second's breath. The Western line was going its full share, led by the crippled Walsh with a broken hand.

But there always was Miller or Crowley or Layden, directed through the right spot by the cool and crafty judgment of Stuhldreher, who picked his plays with the finest possible generalship. The South Bend cyclone had now roared eighty-five yards to a touchdown through one of the strongest defensive teams in the game.

The cyclone had struck with too much speed and power to be stopped. It was the preponderance of Western speed that swept the Army back.

The next period was much like the second. The trouble began when the alert Layden intercepted an Army pass on the 48 yard line. Stuhldreher was ready for another march.

Once again the cheering cadets began to call for a rallying stand. They are never overwhelmed by any shadow of defeat as long as there is a minute of fighting left. But silence fell over the cadet sector for just a second as Crowley ran around the Army's right wing for 15 yards, where Wilson hauled him down on the 33 yard line. Walsh, the Western captain, was hurt in the play but soon resumed. Miller got 7 and Layden got 8 and then, with the ball on the Army's 20 yard line, the cadet defense rallied and threw Miller in his tracks. But the halt was only for the moment. On the next play Crowley swung out and around the Army's left wing, cut in and then crashed over the line for Notre Dame's second touchdown. . . .

The Army brought a fine football team into action, but it was beaten by a faster and smoother team. Rockne's supposedly light, green line was about as heavy as Army's, and every whit as aggressive. What is even more important, it was faster on its feet, faster in getting around.

It was Western speed and perfect interference that once more brought about Army doom. The Army line couldn't get through fast enough to break up the attacking plays; and once started, the bewildering speed and power of the Western backs slashed along for 8, 10 and 15 yards on play after play. And always in front of these offensive drives could be found the whirling form of Stuhldreher, taking the first man out of the play as cleanly as though he had used a hand grenade at close range. This Notre Dame interference was a marvelous thing to look upon.

It formed quickly and came along in unbroken order, always at terrific speed, carried by backs who were as hard to drag down as African buffaloes. On receiving the kick-off, Notre Dame's interference formed something after the manner of the ancient flying wedge, and they drove back up the field with the runner covered from 25 to 30 yards at almost every chance. And when a back such as Harry Wilson finds few chances to get started, you can figure upon the defensive strength that is barricading the road. Wilson is one of the hardest backs in the game to suppress, but he found few chances yesterday to show his broken-field ability. You can't run through a broken field until you get there.

One strong feature of the Army play was its headlong battle against heavy odds. Even when Notre Dame had scored two touchdowns and was well on its way to a third, the Army fought on with fine spirit until the touchdown chance came at last. And when the chance came, Coach McEwan had the play ready for the final march across the line. The Army has a better team than it had last year. So has Notre Dame. We doubt that any team in the country could have beaten Rockne's array yesterday afternoon, East or West. It was a great football team brilliantly directed, a team of speed, power and team play. The Army has no cause for gloom over its showing. It played first-class football against more speed than it could match.

Those who have tackled a cyclone can understand.[2]

What makes the difference between a mediocre sportswriter and a great sportswriter?

Today's editors and writers know. They suggest the great sports writers are:

1. ***Dedicated.***

Between mediocre and great there is fair, average, good, and excellent. The thing that makes a better than average reporter of any kind is desire and commitment. Technical skills are necessary but nothing beats "fire."

—Dr. Robert E. Cates, editor and publisher, Hobbs (N.M.) *Flare*

One thing: love of your job and sports. If you don't passionately love your area, its athletes, and the sports you're covering, then the long, hard hours of work will be just that, work. Nothing more, nothing less.

—Dewaine Gahan, Fremont (Neb.) *Tribune*

2. ***Creative.***

The great sports reporter has . . . creativity and drive, the willingness to search out the behind-the-scenes stories. Sports is scores and personalities, and the sportswriters who go beyond these will see a whole new expanse of ideas open for them.

—Robert Imrie, sports editor, Clark County *Courier*, Clark, S.D.

3. ***Able to write leads.***

A good deal of it has to do with leads. Your lead is an indication of your perspective and your style; it is your advertisement. An attractive lead tells the reader that it is worth his or her time to read what you have done. You have to be able to make something interesting even though it perhaps was not. You have to make your three-thousandth game seem as new and exciting as your first.

—Bob Buckel, sports editor, El Campo (Tex.) *Leader-News*

4. ***Restless.***

A great sportswriter doesn't sit in the press box during the game. He or she roams the sidelines with ears wide open. The real tempo of a game is on the field, not in a box.

—Harry McFarland, *Westside Record-Journal*, Ferndale, Wash.

5. ***Incisive.***

A great sportswriter tells you more than you'd have known if you saw the game-event yourself. A great sportswriter knows how to turn a phrase without inventing a new cliche, occasionally makes people laugh, and watches "the game" rather than just the home team.

—Keith Olson, *Daily News-Miner*, Fairbanks, Alaska

6. ***Humble.***

Not straining too much (in columns) to be the greatest. . . . Also, enthusiasm that does not wither into boredom.

—Tom E. Anderson, *Arizona Silver Belt*, Globe, Ariz.

7. ***Knowledgeable.***

   The best writers know that particular sport inside and out. That enables the writer to better understand what happens during a game and also lets the writer ask more penetrating and technical questions of a coach or player afterwards.

   —Bob Lange, sports editor, *Main Line Times*, Ardmore, Pa.

8. ***Persevering.***

   . . . creativity, individuality, talent . . . the list is endless.

   —Jim Satterly, sports editor, DeKalb (Ga.) *News-Sun*

9. ***Hard-hitting.***

   The best is a . . . hard-hitting feature style—don't pull any punches—and it has a flavor to it . . . leaves you feeling you know the subject. . . . We need a mean (person) to take (the subject) by the throat and shake it.

   —Craig Ammerman, managing editor, New York *Post*

10. ***Unbiased.***

    A person with judgment and an unprejudiced eye. The realization that it was just a game. . . .

    —Frank Hornstein, Pierce County (N.D.) *Tribune*

11. ***Positive.***

    Among things of great importance . . . writing not only of what you saw and didn't like, but also writing of the good things.

    Of first importance is . . . the ability to write, not just report. . . . Another thing might be the ability to comprehensively understand what is happening in the event (such as being able to figure out when a play is done on purpose, when the coach made a key decision, or picking out a team player who is valuable despite not contributing directly to the scoring).

    —Paul L. Noskin, sports editor, Valencia County *News-Bulletin*, Belen, N.M.

12. ***Humorous.***

    Almost anyone can be taught to write good copy, but the wit which goes into a superior story or column is the secret to success.

    —Larry Names, sports editor, Broken Arrow (Okla.) *Daily Ledger*

In summary, Ronald MacArthur, sports editor of *The Leader* in Seaford, Del., suggests: "A mediocre writer doesn't really put heart and soul into stories while a great one uses his or her background, interest and knowledge to get the best story."

A lot of sportswriters have come through the doors of the Montgomery (Ala.) *Advertiser and Journal*, founded in 1828. One who has had a hand in training new sportswriters for the paper in recent years is Bill Plott, the executive sports editor. He tries to keep sports writing up to high reporting standards. Plott came to the sports beat himself after 13 years as a reporter, Sunday editor, and editorial page editor; he also published a book on sports.

Says Plott:

> I had long felt that if sportswriters and editors had to follow the same rules of style and conduct as reporters and editors on news side, the result would be a much better product. I have been able to accomplish some of my objectives but have found others impossible to deal with effectively. The very nature of sports makes it virtually impossible to eliminate the buddy-buddy relationship between writers and jocks-coaches that has been nurtured over the years.

Among his recommendations for the sportswriter-to-be:

- Don't be a cheerleader. I have had to deal with veteran sportswriters who think their job is to boost the local team. On my staff, their job is to report the local team's events, not to lead the cheers. This applies not only to your writing but also to your behavior at sports events. I see nothing wrong with a sportswriter applauding a good play, but it can very quickly get out of hand, particularly in an exciting game. Some press boxes—unfortunately not enough of them—have established rules prohibiting cheering of any kind.
- Avoid play-by-play writing. Most sports fans would rather read about the reactions of coaches and players than a dull recitation of how each point or run was scored in a game. Young sportswriters need to master as quickly as possible the ability to sum up scoring. This will not only make for more succinct stories but also will help prevent the stories from being cut and the editor from being frustrated. Just remember that no sports section ever has enough space. In the South, 20 years ago, pro football was nothing more than the Washington Redskins on syndicated television. Today, it requires almost a full page of the Monday paper.
- Shun first names. I am appalled at how many writers . . . are allowed to refer to sports personalities by their first names. It shows a distinct lack of professionalism and an open display of the buddy-buddy relationship. All too often, it is done in a manner that says, "Hey look, everybody, Coach So-and-so is a pal of mine."
- Strive for objectivity. This is more difficult in sports writing than it is in news reporting. Nevertheless, the better story is still the one that is basically objective. If you feel the need to editorialize, do it in a column that is clearly labeled as such. Stories should inform readers about sports events, not your opinions of those events.

- Read something other than sports. All too often sportswriters are locked into rather simplistic writing styles because they are aware of nothing in the world except sports. A passing knowledge of what is going on in the world at large gives a sportswriter a wealth of materials for that really sparkling lead. Also, with so much sports activity taking place in the courtroom today, it would be very much to the sportswriter's advantage to have some basic knowledge about courts and how they function.
- Take your job seriously, but don't take sports seriously. There are enough fanatics in the world without adding sportswriters to the group. Fans, especially football fans, lose all powers of reasoning when discussing their team. Certainly their team is important; it plays an important role in the social and economic life of the community. Yet, the team plays games that have little effect on the standard of living and the quality of life outside of the entertainment function.
- Be courteous. That advice is not nearly as silly as it may seem on the surface. One of the biggest pains in the neck to the sportswriter is the score-seeker. Some newspapers have created a buffer between the writer and the score-seeker. They have a telephone operator or a recording device to provide scores. Most newspapers do not enjoy that luxury, however. No matter how irritating it is to take those calls, just remember that people don't have to read newspapers. Television and radio provide them with a wealth of sports news today. It may be irritating to deal with them, especially if you are on deadline, but the day they stop calling is the day you may find your job has become obsolete.

VARIETY OF STORIES

Sports stories range from straight accounts of games in a nutshell to larger features and sidebars and columns. Here are examples of kinds of sports stories, with comment by the writers of the stories:

1. ***"Straight News" Story.*** "Jayvees Fall to Wharton Here," by Bob Buckel, sports editor of the El Campo (Tex.) *Leader-News.*

A seven-run third inning and the blazing fastball of Jeff Frazier keyed Wharton to a 12-4 victory over the El Campo junior varsity in a baseball game at Wharton Tuesday.

Frazier, a freshman mound sensation for Wharton, settled down after allowing El Campo three runs in the first inning, to dominate the game the rest of the way while the Tiger bats did their work.

Wharton got a single run in each of the first two innings off starter Barry Smith, before exploding for seven runs in the third inning and sending coach Joe Mackey to the bullpen for reliever Jerome Dorotik.

Smith gave up seven hits and nine runs in two and two-thirds innings, walking six and striking out one. Dorotik came on in the third to strike out one batter and retire the side. He gave up three runs, all in the fifth inning, and allowed three hits while striking out five and walking one.

El Campo's first inning rally

started when Smith reached base on an error. After one out, Kenneth Poncik singled to bring Smith home, then Troy Washington singled and Kevin Green brought in two runs with another single.

Wharton narrowed the El Campo lead to 3-2 with single runs in the first and second innings, before taking control of the game in the third frame. Two singles, a walk, two more singles and another walk brought five runs in before the first out. An error and another walk made it 9-3 before Dorotik came on to get El Campo off the field.

A triple, a single and a hit batter aided Wharton in pushing three more runs across in the fifth, but Frazier allowed only one more Ricebird run to keep a firm hold on the win.

Smith singled in the fifth inning, then scored on a base rap by Travis Hadash. Kenneth Poncik followed with a double, but he and Hadash were left stranded.

Says Buckel:

This story was written on the basis of the scorebook and a few words from the coach. The scorebook told me about the seven-run third inning, and the coach told me about the kid's fastball. Other than that, it was all routine.

A good variation in sentence lengths is important to keep the reader from being lulled to sleep. You have to think about this and do it consciously; it doesn't just happen.

This was a minor game. Anyone who gets into sports writing will write hundreds like this. What you want to do is communicate the information accurately and in a pleasant, readable style.

The information gets less important as the story goes on. This is helpful when making up the pages, as the story may have to be cut. When you do your own composing, as I do, you learn to do yourself favors like that.

A sprinkling of "sports terms" is nice, but many writers go overboard with fancy adjectives and synonyms for common things. Anything that clouds communication is bad, no matter how clever it sounds.

2. ***"Putting It in Perspective" Story.*** "Local Soccer Games Heat-up," by Mike Newell of the Hobbs (N.M.) *Flare.*

The wild race in Division I of the 4-5-6 year old soccer league became even more mixed up Saturday.

Broadmoor Insurance and E. H. Well Service battled to a scoreless tie which threw the top spot into a three team tie.

Broadmoor Insurance was sparked by the defense of Chris Bilbo and Chad Wiley on defense.

Crechet Brooker and Ritchy Richards were outstanding on offense for Broadmoor.

E. H. Well Service was led by the play of Drane Chavez and Shane Morgan on the defensive end, while Matthew Botone and Karen Myers played well on offense.

Other results in Saturday's soccer action were as follows:

4-5-6 Division I

Craig Electric 2, Jim's Ignition 0 . . .

Heritage Realty 2, Hobbs Mack Service 0 . . .

4-5-6 Division II

Hill's Engine 4, Kerr McGee 0 . . .

Says Robert E. Cates, editor and publisher of the *Flare*:

> Relating a game to other developments in the league is standard procedure in a lead. Note also how the writer packs in local names for a small community in which the names are known. "Nothing appeals to the public more than familiar names—especially their own or their children's."

3. ***"Pinpointing Strategy" Story.*** "Colts Catch Rebs Off Guard," by Randy Cummings, sports editor of the Arlington (Tex.) *Citizen-Journal*.

Randy Porter's sharp eye gave the Arlington Colts their third district baseball victory in five tries Tuesday.

The Colt coach, whose team was nursing a narrow 3-2 lead at the time, saw a miscue by the Richland Rebels in the top half of the seventh inning and with it, his Colts preserved the lead and took the triumph.

Unfortunately for the Rebs, the play occurred on the final out of the game, which in turn, caused a controversy and vocal questioning on the part of Richland coaches.

With one out, Richland placed the tying run at third after pitcher Greg Neifert lashed a triple. The next batter grounded out to third baseman Phil Yates, but on the throw to first, Neifert attempted to come home for the score.

In a collision at the plate with AHS catcher David Patterson, Neifert was called safe after Patterson had dropped the ball. To Porter, who was watching from the Colt dugout, it appeared that Neifert had never touched the plate and so he appealed the play.

"I told David he had missed the plate and so he went over and tagged him (Neifert) and the umpire said he was out," said Porter. "When they met, apparently Patterson had knocked him off the plate when he slid."

The double play then ended the contest and boosted the Colts to a 3-2 record, which gives Porter and his Colts a sliver of a chance for a first-half playoff spot.

It's not the easiest of situations, but Porter attempts to explain:

"If Haltom beats Cleburne that will really change the outlook," he said. "It will leave a lot of ifs to be settled. If we win the next two and Sam Houston beats Cleburne (today's game) and Haltom wins their last two, there's the possibility of a four-way tie.

"But what we really need is for Haltom to beat Cleburne. I've still got my fingers crossed."

Arlington jumped to a quick 2-0 lead in the bottom portion of the opening inning. A triple by shortstop Curt Culbertson landed David Fuller, who had reached on a fielder's choice and Culbertson later scored on a ground out by Carlos Battle.

In the fourth, the Colts tacked on one more following a pair of sacrifice plays. Patterson clobbered a double and was moved to third by a Don Burghardt sacrifice and finally allowed to score when Danny Galvan knocked a long fly to the outfield.

"We didn't get that many hits (4), but we took advantage of the ones we did get," Porter said. "We did what we had to do to score."

Eric Alm was the pitcher of record for the Colts, upping his season's mound mark to 4-1 with the win. Over the seven innings he worked, Alm gave up seven hits and two walks while striking out nine.

Arlington will square off with the Buffaloes this afternoon in a 4 p.m. game at the AHS diamond.

Knowing the subject and the normal line of reasoning of a coach or player—knowledge acquired by "living" the sport—is helpful.

Says Cummings:

> Get new and different angles to stories, and then get the people involved to talk about it. In game stories, for example, many people

who saw or listened to the game will read your story—therefore, make it exciting, interesting, and informative.

Ask coaches to help by calling in information. Depending on the situation, sometimes you can trade information with other writers covering the story. Be attentive, listen, and take notes—little items can be made into longer stories.

4. ***"Conversational" Story.*** "One Cheeseburger and a Championship, Please!" (with the topline, "For Deming's Borderites"), by Harry McFarland, news editor of the *Westside Record-Journal* in Ferndale, Wash.

BLAINE—"If he doesn't pin this guy in forty-one seconds, he owes me a cheeseburger and milk shake," Blaine wrestling coach Randy Deming told his assistant Ron Kowalke, while Nick Kiniski wrestled in the 190 lb. final.

"Then let's not help him," Kowalke responded with a smile.

"Why do you think I'm sitting back and just watching?" Deming quipped, as he leaned further back on the chair.

Kiniski didn't need much help as he won the championship match 12-1 over Nooksack Valley's Tim Skinner to help the Borderites take the Whatcom County Wrestling Championship in a very convincing fashion.

Blaine scored 190 points, leaving Mount Baker far behind with 136 and Meridian with 136. Lynden took fourth and Nooksack Valley fifth.

All 13 Borderites in the tournament qualified for Saturday's regionals at Mount Baker by finishing at least fourth in the league meet.

Six Borderites won championship matches.

Blaine's top-seeded Scott Hacker (122) and Tim Cundiff (129) got the festivities going for Blaine.

Hacker stomped Lynden's Keith Kayser, 16-0, while Cundiff decisioned Meridian's Bruce Bosman, 22-0.

The Sharp brothers, Darryl and Dave, showed their prowess at 158 and 141 pounds respectively. Darryl gave up two escapes to Lynden's Joe Libolt to win 14-2, while Dave stayed on top of Mount Baker's Troy Baisden for a 8-2 victory.

Blaine's Jeff Slevin would have won the "Happiest Champion" award as he jumped around the mat for nearly a minute, following his convincing victory over Meridian's Scott Ableman 11-5 at 168 lbs.

The grueling pace of the day was never more evident than the 135 lb. match between Blaine's Russ Mocquin and Lynden's Dan Roy. They were stumbling most of the third period; Roy took the match by one point, 6-5.

Blaine's John Murphy and Mount Baker's Bryan Gudde wrestled to a 5-5 tie with one minute left; then Gudde scored a cradle hold take down to win 8-5.

Lynden's Dan Bosman scored one of the two pins during the finals, when he beat Mount Baker's James Cooper midway through the second period.

In the final match, heavyweight Kelly Welch of Meridian pinned Nooksack Valley's Rob Meyers with four seconds left in the first period.

Mount Baker's Robert Baisden scored an impressive 10-0 decision over Meridian's Terry Littleton. The Mounties' third champion Robert Dillard decisioned Blaine's Kevin Weatherill, 12-2.

Meridian's second champion was Kevin McIntosh at 108.

Mount Baker and Meridian each qualified 11 wrestlers for the district tournament.

Deming will have this week to enjoy his cheeseburger and milk shake before his team goes against both Whatcom and Cascade League champions.

Knowing Deming, he's probably trying to get Kiniski to bet a steak dinner.

Retelling actual conversation can be a vehicle for the story and give a sense of immediacy. In preparation for such stories dealing with so many names, McFarland says: "I study the league teams before a season. That gives me less work, trying to get all those names, numbers, and so on."

McFarland uses conversation picked up during the match. He believes in "giving the story color, not cliches."

5. ***"Dramatic" Story.*** "Upset Bid Fails in Last Second" (with the topline, "Russets Even Record at 2-2"), by Ralph D. Berenger, publisher of the Shelley (Idaho) *Pioneer*.

With the score tied and one second showing on the clock Friday night, Kelley Thompson of the American Falls Beavers strolled to the free throw line.

He had seen his team grab lead after lead in the contest against the Shelly Russets—each time the lead evaporated in the tense air at the Shelley gymnasium. Just 35 seconds previously, Shelley had a three point lead, but his team had bounced back.

It had been a tough contest. Neither team amassed enough points on the scoreboard to grab a commanding lead, enough points to ice the game.

Thompson dribbled twice, paused and took a gulp of air.

Moments before the gym was a beehive of activity and noise. Now it was silent as Thompson glanced up at the clock and noted the 62-62 deadlock.

Though he had seven points in the contest this was the biggest basket. Earlier he had one chance at a free throw and made it. Now the pressure was on.

Thompson pumped and flicked his wrist and in a second the ball swished convincingly through the hoop. His second shot was also good and American Falls, the No. 1 ranked team in A-2 basketball had made Shelley's impossible upset dream impossible.

But Shelley nearly pulled off an upset in a game that was close from the starting buzzer.

Led by senior Paul Niemeier's 23 points and sophomore Hugh Foster's 16 points, the Russets battled the Beavers right down to the line.

American Falls had only one man in double figures—Neal Flyg with 10—but two had nine points, two eight and three six, a balanced attack.

The Russets had several scoring opportunities in the late-going but were unable to convert 1-1 free throw situations.

The statistics show how tight a game it was.

Both teams had 25 field goals, but the story was from the free throw line. American Falls converted 14 of 17 attempts, while the Russets hit 12 of 20 attempts.

The Beavers had a two-point lead at the end of the first quarter, but Shelley tied the game at half, 27-27, and again at the third frame, 47-47.

Though Friday night's loss evened Shelley's record at 2-2 on the season, the Russet hoopsters Wednesday night put the most points this season on the scoreboard in a nonconference game with the Preston Indians. Shelley won the lopsided contest, 86-67.

Jumping off to a good start in the first period, the Russets never trailed in the contest.

Three Russets were in double figures, led by Scott Sargent who netted 24 points on the night. Ken Louk, who was the big man on the boards all evening, picked up 16 points and Paul Niemeier scored 15 points.

"Drama of a few seconds builds up reader interest," says Berenger. Time is telescoped, and the crucial seconds are relived.

6. ***"Personality" Story.*** Jim Satterly, sports editor of the DeKalb (Ga.) *News-Sun*. "Down, But Not Out" (subtitled "After Recovering From a Severe Knee Injury, David Titshaw Leads Briarcliff to a State Gymnastics Title").

David Titshaw will never forget February 20, 1978. That was the day the doctor told him he'd likely be a cripple for the rest of his life.

He was 16 years old, a junior at Briarcliff High School, and just two weeks earlier he'd ripped apart all five ligaments in his left knee during a gymnastics meet. But until he and his parents made the trip that day to Columbus, Georgia, to see a special orthopedic surgeon, he didn't realize just how serious his injury was.

Suddenly, the fearful projection rained down upon him like a storm, a sentence far worse than anything he could have imagined.

"At first I didn't cry," he recalled, the memory of that day vividly preserved. "But I was fighting back the tears, and when I looked over and saw my dad crying . . . I just couldn't help it."

BUT nobody was crying last Saturday night at Sequoyah. Briarcliff walked off with its third straight state boys gymnastics title, as expected, and Titshaw, the captain, was a convincing winner in the horizontal bar and a close second in the vault—something no one could have ever imagined not long ago.

"I can't believe tonight, because I keep remembering what the doctor told me about maybe getting 50 to 60 percent of the use of my knee back," bubbled David, a likable, articulate young man with a blond helmet of hair that seemingly bounces askew only during a routine, otherwise remaining at parade rest. "I didn't think I'd ever be able to walk again—it really surprised me."

NO wonder. After the operation, his leg was in a bent-knee cast for two months. The leg had atrophied badly from disuse, and, after undergoing a rehabilitation program for a month and a half to be able to use the leg again, he began grueling daily workouts on a weight machine and a stationary bicycle. Finally, he started practicing again in July with some less strenuous work, and by August he was able to land again.

He still can't straighten the leg fully and, he says, it still hurts on cold mornings. "It's swelled up on me a few times—bad enough to keep me from working out," he notes. "but I've never missed a meet."

"He really has been a miracle, he really has," adds his mother, Florine. "I really feel like this was a testimony to God's grace."

TITSHAW modestly states that he deserves none of the credit. "I owe everything to Coach (Mike) Raines and Coach (Robert) Nowell, my parents, the doctor, and God—they did it all. . . ."

IRONICALLY, serious injury seems to dog Briarcliff. Two years ago Joel Rosenfeld came back from a bad knee injury, and last year Mike Gary, the state all-around champ, returned after having suffered a broken neck the summer previous. Appropriately, those were two that provided much of the inspiration and encouragement. "And I have a really great group of friends on this team, too," David adds. "They helped a lot."

After regaining the use of his leg, Titshaw suffered more misfortune, breaking his arm in December during practice. "He was really disappointed," Bill, his father, recalled. "They told him he'd be out three more months and that he might as well forget the season. Well, he was out for a month."

THE future is bright. This weekend he'll go with three of his Briarcliff teammates—Phillip McWilliams, Ray Stainback and Keith Taylor—to the National Boy Invitational in Philadelphia with the Atlanta School of Gymnastics team. He's also recently been accepted to Georgia Tech, where next year he hopes to add two more events (one that he discontinued because of his injury) to his repertoire. . . .

People—and conflict—make good short stories and features; in sports, drama and the will to attain offer a strong basis for people stories. Says Satterly:

> Anyone can report sports, but writing about it with intelligence and insight is another matter. . . . I think there is a difference between sports reporting and sports writing. . . .
>
> A sportswriter is more similar to a movie or theater reviewer than a beat reporter. Certainly he must be able to write a news story, but he must also be able to evaluate, interpret, and featurize. And a good one will have both background and ability—there is no substitute for either.

ACHIEVING STYLE

As noted in Chapter 9, writing in style depends in no small measure on the ability to highlight significant details and to concentrate on those details. Sports writing also achieves an element of style when the right detail or details capture the essence of a person, game, or event.

Ron Green, assistant sports editor of the Greenville (S.C.) *Piedmont*, covering a football game between Clemson and Duke in Durham, N.C., in October 1983, concentrated on the facial features of a winning coach:

> The face of Danny Ford showed an odd mixture of emotions as he leaned against a wall outside the Clemson locker room moments after his Tigers had held off Duke 38-31 at Wallace Wade Stadium Saturday.
>
> There was a smile of contentment, the product of his team's 15th consecutive Atlantic Coast Conference triumph. There was a creased brow, evidence of the nerve-wracking nature of the victory which wasn't assured until the final minute.
>
> And there was a look of frustration in his eyes as he sought to find the elusive answer to his team's successful, yet highly inconsistent, nature.
>
> Rather than a sense of triumph, Ford seemed to have a sense of relief. Until James Robinson swatted down Ben Bennett's fourth-down pass at the Clemson nine in the final 60 seconds, it had appeared the Tigers might become Duke's first victim in six games.
>
> But just in the knick of time, Clemson did what it does best—play well enough to win. . . .

Highlighting a theme or the essence of a person or situation achieves style. *The National Leader* ("The Weekly Newspaper Linking the Black Community Nationwide") describes the "smoothness" of Los Angeles Lakers' Jamaal Wilkes:

LOS ANGELES—His motion on the court is constant, his style of shooting unique. Whether it be a gliding one-handed layup, a 20-foot corner jumper with his arms cocked back over his head, or the simple practice of filling a lane on the fast break called "Show-time," Jamaal Wilkes of the Los Angeles Lakers earns his living by being one of the smoothest, steadiest stars in the NBA.

Since his freshman year at UCLA, Wilkes has been called "Silk" because of his smooth, graceful style on the court. He has a knack for making each and every move seem effortless, a quality as luxurious in the sport of basketball as the cloth he's named after is in the garment district.

"I've always tried to do things as easily as possible," Wilkes said, "in terms of making the most consistent plays, conserving energy, not having to do anything more than necessary. I think that sometimes makes what I do look easier than it is."

Many contend that what Wilkes does best is score by running the wing on the Lakers' fast break.

"He's deadly. He's deceptive," said Boston Celtics center Robert Parish. "He doesn't look quick, but he's very fast. His big asset is he runs the floor very well."

The 6-foot-6, 190-pound forward can also hold his own under the basket, so his frail appearance is deceiving.

"Even with his size he sneaks in there to dish out a little punishment," claims Parish. "He draws a lot of fouls and uses his body well—the little bit he has."

Lakers Coach Pat Riley agreed with Parish but he pointed out a deeper part of Wilkes' game. "Jamaal's one of the smartest players in the game. He's the kind of player who has an arsenal of everything, and it starts with his brain," Riley told USA TODAY's Ron Thomas. . . .

Perhaps the highest compliment paid to Wilkes came from John Wooden, his former coach at UCLA. When asked to describe the ideal player, Wooden said, "I would have a player be a good student, polite, courteous, a good team player, a good defensive player and rebounder, a good inside player, outside shooter . . . why not just take Jamaal Wilkes and let it go at that?"

Yes, let it go at that.

Singling out an object and endowing it with special awe and mystery—by not even naming it at the outset—gave the Boston *Globe*'s Tony Chamberlain's article style and suspense. His story—one of several that day in September 1983 on the Australians' winning America's Cup in sailing—simply talked reverently of the "thing" that took away the cup from the U.S. for the first time in the 132-year history of the race. (This is not an approach that can be used often, but there was high familiarity on the part of readers with the event, and note Chamberlain's crisp, colorful, even emotional approach that sends the reader into the article at a fast clip.)

NEWPORT, R.I.—And so at last, there it hung in all its silent, dangerous glory.

Weapon-like. Sci-fi sleek. In some ways, rather beautiful. In other ways, more like one of those modern sculptures in front of civic buildings that folks complain about.

Outside the chain link fence on the Newport docks, lines of people with cameras gathered in the morning sunshine yesterday to go in and see it.

A guard tended the gate, and every 10 minutes or so he would hustle out the people inside, and let in another bunch.

It was just the kind of line you would find waiting to get into a trailer to see Al Capone's car or a space capsule back from the moon.

The thing is what they wanted to see. Through pictures and tapes, they had come to know the folks involved—John Bertrand, Alan Bond, Ben Lexcen, et al—but it was the thing now that had become more fascinating than even those colorful Australian characters of the Newport waterfront.

And so the line of people would file through the gate and stand around in silent, somewhat reverential regard of the thing. Some would whistle through their teeth and shake their heads. Some would pretend to be unimpressed. They took pictures and swapped theories about the thing quietly, so as not to disturb it somehow in its morning quietude. And then the guard would hustle one group out again and let in more.

The night before, Monday at around 8, the Aussies came sailing home victorious and amid the explosive madness of the dockside celebration, they did an amazing thing. The slings were drawn tight and up came their sleek white 12-meter hull. But no one hustled to draw the secret skirts about her bottom, no one tried to brush away crowds and photographers. Slowly as the hull rose, even the most champagne-soaked soul there had to be a little dazzled.

Here was a close encounter with the thing. The weapon fought over and agonized over all summer that had finally lived up to its billing as an American beater. Here at last was the keel. . . .

Narrowing a story down to an idea and then narrowing the discussion initially to one or several main people provide focus and style, as Edward Hill, Jr., did in the Winston-Salem (N.C.) *Chronicle*. The article was one in the entry in sportswriting that helped the *Chronicle* (one of the best designed papers in the Southeast) to win first place in sportswriting in the annual competition of the National Newspaper Publishers Association (which represents predominantly black readership newspapers) in 1984. Note how Hill works *all* the necessary information in gradually and painlessly (with essential "what-is-it" information near the top). And he didn't settle for one interview, but talked with about eight persons, including participants.

In an era where there's emphasis on winning in athletics on all levels, one local group, the Road Runners Track Club, has chosen a different path.

"There is no pressure on the kids to win in our program," says DeVal Dean Penn, one of the coaches of the Road Runners. "We want to make it fun for them. We let them know that, whether they finished in first place or last place, we still love them all the same."

"Unlike other youth athletic organizations that take only the best athletes, we give everyone a chance to come out and make the team," says Al Edwards, who has been with the Road Runners for six years. "We de-emphasize winning and concentrate more on participation and having fun."

The Road Runners Track Club was organized in 1972 by Virgil G. Simpson, track coach at Winston-Salem State University. Local youngsters, ages seven through 18, participate in the summer-long program and compete in city, district, regional and state meets.

Many of the club members perform for their respective schools during the track season. Budding stars such as hurdler Charles Goins of Hill High School, who set a record in this year's 9-10 meet in the 110-meter hurdles, and Tomika Whitten of Kennedy High School, who set a new mark in the 1,600 meters for 9-10 girls, are just two of the many who use the club to improve their skills and techniques while at the same time testing their abilities against quality competition outside of the area.

But the club serves other purposes as well. For instance, since there is no track program in the city/county elementary schools, the Road Runners gives the younger members a chance to learn such basics as proper techniques, proper breathing and proper conditioning.

"I was coming from class one day and I asked Coach Penn if I could come out for the Road Runners," says 9-year-old Derrick Hicks, who is competing in track for the first time. "I won five first-places and one second in my first two meets. Already I've learned how to stride and build up my pace."

"I really like running," says 7-year-old Candace Crawford, one of the club's youngest members. "I came out for the Road Runners to learn, to have fun and to win."

"My mother signed me up for the Road Runners," says 9-year-old Kenya Turner, who is participating for the second year. "Already I've improved my speed and learned some techniques that I will be able to use once I get to junior high school."

The participants are broken down into five categories, according to age: the bantams (7-, 8- and 9-year-olds), the midgets (10- and 11-year-olds), the juniors (12- and 13-year-olds), the intermediates (14- and 15-year-olds) and the seniors (16-, 17- and 18-year-olds). The events range from the 100-meter dash to the 1500 meters and include various relays.

The bantams, midgets and juniors generally compete in regional and state meets, while the the intermediates and seniors can qualify for national meets.

Edwards, whose daughter Denita Cunningham is an up-and-coming 12-year-old sprinter with the club, says the organization also fulfills other needs.

"First of all, the kids develop a certain amount of discipline," says Edwards, an admitted "track fanatic." "There is something about the training and the nature of track that requires discipline. We've had kids come here who people said were problems, but once they understood our philosophy and what we were trying to do, they usually fell in line."

"But beyond the discipline, there is also the social and maturing process. We try to stress meeting other people in the meets in which they participate. That will help them grow and mature as individuals. By traveling and meeting other people, they get a form of education.

"And then there is the factor of working on helping them improve. Many of them are good performers on their school teams, but they get a chance with the Road Runners to work on various weaknesses and techniques. We monitor them during the track season and try to work on those things where they need improvement."

One club member who benefitted from the Road Runners is multitalented Tina Wilds, a junior high school star who will be attending Paisley High School in the fall.

"This is my second year with the Road Runners and I really saw improvement in my times from last year," says Wilds, who is already long jumping over 18 feet. "There are some other things I need to work on so I can be ready for better competition next year."

Another member who will use the Road Runners as a learning experience this summer is Whitten, the 9-10 champion in both the 800 and 1600 meters this past season.

"By being a part of the Road Runners, I will get a chance to work on improving my times and building up my endurance and strength," says Whitten.

The Road Runners Track Club is a

nonprofit organization and its funding for trips and other expenses comes from bake sales and other fundraisers. Coach Penn, who has been with the club for nine of its 10 years, remembers when things were not so stable.

"In the first years, Coach Simpson and I had to often come out of our pockets or secure small-term loans to get the team around," recalls Penn, who teaches at Hall-Woodward Elementary School. "Things are more stable now. We've come a long way."

The club is now chartered and has 25 members on its board.

Another encouraging development has been the increase in the number of coaches, which jumped from four last year to an all-time high of seven this year.

Yolanda James, a first-year member of the Road Runners, is a prime example of what the club is trying to do. She sums her experience by saying, "I really enjoy being with the Road Runners. I get a chance to go out and run, meet people and have a lot of fun. I don't think about losing or winning, just having fun."

THE SPORTS COLUMN

Successful sports columns invite the use of gimmicks, humor, and style. Here is a column—certainly not a stylistic one—but one that works with a gimmick and with humor, plus that useful angle of working in the local people. It was Christmastime, and Dewaine Gahan of the Fremont (Neb.) *Tribune* made a play on the names of the local folk.

Says Gahan:

> I take pride in writing a column different from any other my readers will ever come across. I welcome the opportunity to entertain, and that's what this column does. I also try to stay as local as possible, as this column shows. This compilation of names and formation into a story didn't take nearly as long as you might think.

The column was titled "Gahan's Game Plan: Santa Story Time Again."

Are you all done Christmas **CARDEN** (Tom, Midland)? Got gifts bought for every **PERSSON** (Mike, Blair) on your shopping list?

I hope so. Because Christmas is coming **MUNDY** (Jim, Bergan), and, boy is Santa going to be busy!

Here, then is another Gahan version of the "Santa Story," using names of area athletes and coaches:

"Get your **BOOTS** (Daryl, West Point) on, Dear, it's time you got on your **WAY** (Steve, Mead). You've got a long, hard trip ahead of you. So **HOPP** (Bobbie, Fremont) to it," Mrs. Claus said.

So Santa put his suit on, topped off by that **SULLY** (Tim, Blair)-looking **HATT** (Lisa, Elkhorn); presented his wife with their traditional Christmas **HAMM** (Dave, Oakland-Craig); and started to **WADE** (Yvonne, Prague) through the snow toward the reindeer.

In the time it took Mrs. Santa to put the potatoes on the **BERNER** (Ragena, Logan View) to **BOYLE** (Bob, Scribner), Old St. Nick loaded his sleigh with his bag of toys, hitched up the reindeer and departed the North Pole. This old boy may be fat and he's been around for a coon's age, but he's still the **BEST** (Tana, Valley) around when it comes to delivering the goodies.

He 'Reither' doubts it

"Do we **LACK** (Janet, Fremont) anything?" Santa asked Rudolph.

"I **REITHER**(Eric, Elkhorn) doubt it, Santa," the red-nosed leader of the pack said.

Santa looked a bit puzzled as he glanced at the first item on his **LONG** (Alice, Midland) list.

"What's this!" he shouted. "Another new washer and dryer for the Smiths? That rat **FINK** (Keith, Arlington). I don't even know if we can make that brand anymore. Check in the **SEARS** (Pat and Jackie, Decatur) catalogue, Rudolph."

Asked why the Smiths wanted a washer and dryer for the third straight year, Rudolph replied, "It seems thieves either **ROBB** (Dion, Arlington) them or the old man **REX** (Goracke, Oakland-Craig) the machines somehow."

Next stop on the journey was at the home of a **RICH** (Lagge, Oakland-Craig, and Brabec, Clarkson) man who lived in a **PALLAS** (Tom, Pender). He had money galore. a real high-**BROWER** (Frank, Leigh), you know?

For Mr. Filthy Rich's wife, a new **MINK** (Jerry, Valley) stole. For the old man himself? What else? A blank **CECH** (Tim, Midland; Russ and Rancy, Howells; Jeff and Mike, North Bend)!

"That blank check should have gone to Mr. Jones down the block. He seems to be **OWEN** (John Paul, Tekamah-Herman) everybody money," Santa said.

"Stop brooding, Jelly Belly. **LITZ** (Ron, Snyder) get going," Rudolph said.

He soon will, Son

As Santa and his sleighful of toys were flying over one house, he heard a little boy ask his father, "Is Santa Claus here yet?"

"He soon **WIL,SON** (Lawrence, Midland)," Daddy replied. "Now crawl back under the **SHEETS** (Larry, Blair) and get some shut-eye."

Santa overheard one skeptical little boy say, "I don't know whether I believe in Santa Claus or not. How can he get all the toys for all the boys and girls in the whole world into one little sleigh. You'd think he'd need at least a **TRAILER** (Greg, Midland) or two."

Santa paused for a moment to check over the list of the next house.

"Let's see now," he said. "Janice wants a **CUDLEY** (Dean, Leigh) teddy bear. Rita wants a **HULA** (Kevin, Logan View) hoop. And how 'bout this next request? Chris thinks he's Superman and wants **LOIS** (Liibbe, West Point) Lane for Christmas. Glen wants a sleeping bag since he likes to **KAMP** (Greg, Lyons) out. And Mike wants an electric razor from **GILLETT** (Mike and Joe, Gillett) because his manual keeps giving him a case of the **GOTTSCH** (Mich, Elkhorn, and Gary, Valley) 'yuhs."

Santa had to chuckle at the next item on the list. Paul, who was sacked more times than any other quarterback in the league, wanted a **WALLA** (Chris, Wahoo Neumann) blockers.

There was the request from the vegetarian who wanted nothing more than a big head of **CABBAGE** (Kathy, Elkhorn).

'Sok' it to me

Muhammad Ali already has everything, it would seem, but he, too, sent a letter to Santa.

"I want an opponent who's as easy as pie. Give it to me, Santa, or I'll **SOK** (Mike, Oakland-Craig) you in the eye," Ali said in his best poetic prose.

There were the usual orders to fill, such as new **KOLLARS** (Phil, Arlington) for ministers; **BRAND** (Craig, Wisner-Pilger) new bikes for little boys and girls everywhere; **BERT** (TePoel, Prague) and Ernie puppets for Sesame Street fans; boxes of Reg-gie candy bars for New **YORK** (Davy, Midland, and Jeff, Decatur) Yankee fans; Luke Sky-**WALKER** (Karen, Blair) toys for Star Wars fans; new **HARLEY** (Morrissey,

Bergan) Davidsons for the hippies; a baby **HUSKEY** (Greg, Prague) for practically every little Alaskan boy; and **COPPI** (Troy, Elkhorn) machines for the executives.

Lawrence Welk—the man who says, "**ANNA** (Anderson, Oakland-Craig) one anna' two . . ."—wants a new suit, one that's a double-**BRESTER** (Laurie, Howells).

Santa got a laugh out of the note from one cute little **LASS** (Lewis, West Point). After telling him what she wanted for Christmas, she closed her letter by saying, ". . . and Mommy told me to tell you to eat every last **CROM** (Debbie, Decatur) of the cookies I've set out for you . . . and please **SCHUTT** (Ken, Midland) the door when you leave."

On a serious note

When Christmas **DEA** (Mark and Mike, West Point C.C.) rolls around, let us all give thanks to God for sending his only Son to us.

Let us keep in mind that lovely manger scene that took place 1,978 years ago: the baby, Jesus; borne by **MARY** (Wiese, Lyons), watched over by **JOSOFF** (Debbie, Cedar Bluffs) and visited by the **WISEMAN** (Al, Decatur).

Here's wishing you and yours a holiday season filled with **BLISS** (Doug, Tekamah-Herman) and a new year full of **JOY** (Rich and Bill, Cedar Bluffs).

Thank you—every **GUY** (Mytty, Tekamah-Herman and Mathers, Lyons) and gal—for reading me this year:

And thanks for the candy **KANE** (Jim, Elkhorn Mt. Michael), Santa!

Sports Words

Sports editors and writers contributed words and definitions to this list.

Box-and-one defense: A basketball strategy with four men working the corners and one guarding the opponent's key scorer.

Cager: Basketball player.

Camber: The bow in a pair of snow skis.

Caroms: Referring to ball rebounds.

Charges: Those being coached.

Charity line: Also known as gift line or stripe, referring to the free-throw line in basketball.

Chip shot: Short kick from placement; easily hit ball or lobbed golf shot.

Chuck: In professional football, the lineman hitting the opponent on the head.

Double eagle: In golf, three under par on a hole (par five).

Double whitewash: Shutouts in a baseball double header.

Draws: Faceoffs (like basketball jump-ball), in hockey.

Dunk shot* or *stuff: In basketball, a high or two-handed slam shot downward into the basket.

Faceoff: Dropping of the puck by the referee between hockey centers, similar to basketball jump-ball.

Four blind mice: Umpires.

Frozen rope: A hard line drive in baseball.

Grappler: Wrestler.

Kick: In track, the finishing spurt.

Line shot* or *line drive: Hard-hit ball.

Mentor: Teacher or coach.

Monster back: Roving linebacker in football.

Offensive goal tending: In professional basketball, going above the rim on a rebound. (To touch the ball is a violation.)

Outer gardens: Outfield in baseball.

Par: Number of strokes in golf set as a score for an expert for each hole on the golf course.

Passed ball: In baseball, almost a wild pitch, but one which the catcher should have stopped.

Quintet: Basketball team.

Radius: The part of an ice skate blade that touches the ice.

Roundtripper: A home run.

Seed: Ranking among contestants based on past performance.

Shutouts: Keeping the opponent from scoring.

Sin bin: Penalty box in hockey.

Skip: The team captain on a curling team.

Slice: A golf shot which veers to the right for right-handed golfers and to the left for left-handers.

Splits: Individual legs—or breaks—during a track race.

Suck it up: Coaching term to encourage athlete to fight off fatigue or pain.

Thinclads: Track team.

Three-point play: When a player makes a basket and then a free throw after he was fouled while making the initial goal.

Two bagger: Two-base hit in baseball.

Wheel dog: The dog(s) in a dog team closest to the sled to help a musher steer around corners.

Whistles: Fouls. ("The Bluejays picked up 22 whistles.")

Zebras: Description of football and basketball officials.

If you use the preceding trade words, you should explain them periodically and also make them clear in context. The laziest way to write is to assume that all your readers understand the jargon.

It is bad practice, says Le Anne Schreiber of the New York *Times*, to write only for ". . . a clubby audience. One should strike a middle ground between the fanatically interested fan and the reader who is not a fan and who dips into the sport once or twice a year." And she warns about failing to identify each player mentioned in the story. "There's a lot of resistance in trying to change people (some old-timers) on this one." She counters by asking such writers if they can name all the members of the President's cabinet. "The real trick in sports writing is to aim at a broad audience," she says. Identifications, however, do not have to be direct. For instance, Schreiber says, "If you want to get across that a certain player is a third baseman, then include some action that makes it clear, such as having him throw from third."

Notes

[1]John L. Dougherty, ed., *Learning in the Newsroom: A Manual for Supervisors* (Reston, Va.: American Newspaper Publishers Association Foundation, c. 1973, 1975), p. 191.

[2]Grantland Rice, "The Four Horsemen," New York *Herald Tribune*, Inc., c. 1924. Reprinted in Herbert Warren Wind, *The Realm of Sport* (New York: Simon and Schuster, c. 1966), pp. 312–315.

Assignments

1. In order to demonstrate how a sports article often depends on perspective, such as where a reporter's orientation is, cover a sports event. One-third of the class should report it as if for the home team school's newspaper, one-third for the visitors, and one-third as if for a round-up story in an out-of-town paper.
2. Read the sports page for a week; each student should bring three of the best sports stories of the week. Have the class vote to determine the overall best story. (The class could also vote on the worst story.)
3. Write a sports story with a dramatic lead, starting with an anecdote of game action. (The class could also be divided to take different approaches to the same story.)
4. Write an interview with a coach or sports figure. In the first draft, do not use any quotes. In the second draft, a rewrite, you can drop in your best, most poignant quotes.
5. Write a sports story about an object: the football, the trophy or cup, the coin tossed in the game, the referee's whistle, a kicker's shoe, the basketball hoop, or a baseball bat.
6. Look through a Sunday sports section. Make a list of sports jargon. How many of these words does the reporter explain directly or indirectly?

16

Science—Consumer Health

Science and health matters receive considerable attention in U.S. newspapers. Even smaller newspapers carry their share of science and health news from wire stories and national syndication and through efforts of their own staff on general assignment. Science and health news items are related to readers' well-being and therefore merit considerable attention.

SCIENCE

Science news in general has been popular since mid-century. The coming of the atomic age in World War II brought nuclear power—and the fear of it. Then in the early '50s, the Soviets put the first satellite, Sputnik, in orbit. The schools began to emphasize science more.

Silent Spring, a book by Rachel Carson in 1963, brought environmental concerns to the attention of American readers. Then space exploration and the first man on the moon in July, 1969, further boosted the interest in science. And the search for new sources of energy—from solar energy to hydrogen and electric power for cars—continues to occupy national and international attention.

Science became big news when the "nuclear accident" at Three Mile Island near Harrisburg, Pa., sent terror around the country in early 1979. Some papers carried banner headlines on the nuclear issue for several weeks. The situation was so demanding that the Philadelphia *Inquirer,* for instance, put 39 reporters and eight photographers on the story. One of these reporters, Rod Nordland, commented that he had put in so much time that winter and spring that the paper had to give him much of the summer off. Science was certainly *the* news.

Hillier Krieghbaum, journalism educator at New York University and science writer, did an analysis of the New York *Times* coverage of the Three Mile Island incident. In the eight peak days (March 29–April 5, 1979), Krieghbaum noted that the *Times* used approximately 2,600 column inches in "its wall-to-wall coverage."[1]

In the mid-1980s, Three Mile Island was still news, not only as background for discussion on safety or the new moratoriums declared at other sites, but Three Mile Island itself. Nearly five years after the accident, a federal grand jury indicted the company, Metropolitan Edison, that operated the nuclear plant, on charges of falsifying safety-test results prior to the accident at the site. In 1983 reporters chronicled problems in testing and making serviceable a giant "polar crane" which eventually would lift the top off the badly damaged nuclear reactor at the plant.

Breaking Out of the Pack

A study, *Science Writers at Work,* by Sharon Dunwoody of Ohio State, points out that the "average" journalist writing on science is "highly dependent on press conferences," a situation that also exists on other beats.[2]

One newspaper which was not sitting back and waiting for things to happen in the Three Mile Island vicinity was the York (Pa.) *Daily Record*. Two weeks before the accident the York paper had a series which began with the headline, "Nuclear Accident: The Devastating Consequences." The lead story was entitled, "Grave Safety Defects Cited at 3 Mile." The second day of the series dealt with the unpreparedness for a nuclear disaster. Still, it had not happened. The events that followed showed that the paper was on the right trail; there was disaster impending at the island near Harrisburg, and officials were either almost totally unprepared—or unwilling—to deal with the developing disaster.

With science news vying for top priority with other news, science reporters cannot afford to wait for official press conferences. Enterprising newspapers and reporters go after their own stories. In the Three Mile incident, the *Inquirer* waited for workers between shifts at the plant, copied down license numbers of workers, and then secured the names and addresses from the state's motor vehicle department. Each person was sent a mailgram which said the *Inquirer* wanted "any observations, complaints or compliments you have about the construction, operation or repair of Unit 2 [which was damaged]. Please call or write us, confidentially if you wish." The paper listed four phone numbers. Some 50 persons gave interviews. Turning to union lists kept by the U.S. Department of Labor, the paper also sought out former employees.[3]

Back in 1964, when the U.S. Public Health Service was preparing to release its report on smoking and cancer, Scripps-Howard science writer John Troan knew that with the big science story pending, he could not wait for the official announcement and spoon-feeding of reporters.

In *Science and the Mass Media*, Hillier Krieghbaum recounts how Troan got his story without violating any confidences or embargoes:

> Five days before the United States Public Health Service released its historic report on the relationship between cigarette smoking and cancer, John Troan, then Scripps-Howard science writer in Washington, D.C., sought to pick up the details so that he could beat his fellow writers.
>
> On a Monday, January 6, 1964, the Public Health Service announced that the report, long awaited by both physicians and the general public, would be released the following Saturday. Troan started by calling some of the co-workers of committee members since he knew none of the top officials well.
>
> What happened is told as follows by *Understanding*, quarterly publication of the American Association for the Advancement of Science and the Council for the Advancement of Science Writing, Inc., in the Spring, 1964, issue:
>
>> A few phone calls to these acquaintances turned up nothing. So John appealed to their egos. "But, Bill, you don't mean to say that (committee member) hasn't told even his *friends* about the report, do you?" This technique opened buttoned lips.
>>
>> Now Troan checked with three people who had seen the report, asking them, "Of course you won't tell me what's in the report, but at least tell me what's in my story which is way off base." This they did, and John had his two-day jump. . . .[4]

Principles for Science Writing

In his book, *Writing Science News for the Mass Media*, David Warren Burkett suggests a list of practical guidelines for the science writer.

One list has positive suggestions, the other negative. (The positive ones come from various interviews and such books as Joel Hildebrand's *Science in the Making*.) Burkett, former science and space writer for the Houston *Chronicle*, gives credit to Science Service for the second list.

Positive Suggestions

1. Science and medicine stories compete with all other stories for space; your story must be timely, interesting, and understandable.

2. Try to tell your story in 800 to 900 words or less. Editors contacted by the World Book Encyclopedia Science Service prefer this length, equal to about one column of type. Wire services prefer 300 to 500 words. Anything longer becomes difficult to place in most newspapers and many magazines.
3. Illustrate stories whenever possible to increase understanding, another reason for keeping a story as short as possible to allow space for drawings or photographs.
4. Round off figures, remembering that in lay language there is no translation for the tenth decimal precision of mathematics in science.
5. Employ analogy and word pictures to associate the often invisible, remote, and unknown experiences in scientific research with a common, human experience.
6. Keep writing simple, clear, communicative and avoid writing down to your reader. It may help to conjure up a mental picture of some specific person you wish to reach.
7. Define unusual or technical terms and keep sentences short.
8. Get to the point immediately.
9. Translate the stiff, technical jargon of formal scientific papers and speeches; they often are badly written, poorly organized and presented to a captive audience.
10. Present one to three basic points per news story; interpretation of more than three "angles" requires a feature length piece.
11. Recognize the existence of more than one kind of "scientist"; differentiate between biologists, geologists, and so on.
12. Remember that new ideas in science do not always command instant acceptance. The findings of one scientist presented at a meeting may not be confirmed by other experimenters.
13. Also remember that the Laws of Science are not like laws enacted for murder, rape, and overtime parking. Scientific "laws" describe, but they do not give a cause-and-effect explanation; when a phenomenon does not obey a supposed law of nature, the law must face revision.[5]

Negative Suggestions

1. Don't overestimate the reader's knowledge, and don't underestimate his intelligence.
2. Don't try to tell all you know in 500 words. Leave some for another time.
3. Don't think that because a thing is old to you it is known to the public. Anything new to your readers is news to them if hung on a timely peg.
4. Don't forget that your reader is interrupting you every 10 lines to ask "Why?", "What for?", or "Well, what of it?", and if you don't answer his tacit question, he will soon stop reading.

5. Don't think that you can make your topic more attractive by tricking it out with fairy lore or baby talk or irrelevant jokes or extravagant language.
6. Don't say "This discovery is interesting" unless you can prove it, and if you can prove it, you don't have to say it.
7. You don't have to give bibliographical references to all the literature on a subject, but don't fail to give the reader a clue he may use to begin more reading.
8. Don't expect an editor to explain why he objects to your manuscript. He is probably right in his verdict, but if you would make him give a reason for it, he will have to invent one and it would probably be wrong.
9. Don't define a hard word by a harder word.
10. Don't think you must leave out all the technical terms; use them when necessary, without apology and without a formal definition where possible. People aren't as easily scared by these words as you may think, and if you use the term in the correct way within the context of your story, it will be understood.[6]

Burkett has three additional suggestions for maximizing science news coverage. First, noting that news is not only information, but understandable information, he encourages giving the background information on a story that is making big news by having scientists and psychiatrists explain the event. Second, he suggests the science reporter have a team sense: after scanning the journals and checking sources, ". . . provide scientific information, as stories or notes, to other newspaper departments."[7]

His third principle: "Combine science writing with another specialty that will reinforce or feed back on science writing."[8]

For example:

> Politics, particularly the politics of science and technology, cannot be considered as separated from a writer's normal coverage. At one point 50 universities had set up interdisciplinary institutes of science and public policy. These institutes, in turn, organized the Science and Public Policy Studies Group at Massachusetts Institute of Technology as a clearing house for their efforts. And the pressures and divisions of urban life have increased the interest in research performed by the social scientists.
>
> Jerry Bishop of *The Wall Street Journal* has noted how stock-shaking drug developments announced during a scientific meeting can set almost all of the science writers working for the business editors. . . . *Fortune* magazine regularly reports on scientific developments for its business-oriented readers. As Walter Sullivan, science news editor of *The New York Times*, noted, the technical process of

> desalting sea water is so intertwined with economics that the two cannot be separated. . . . The success of the American Telephone and Telegraph Co., as seen by *Time* magazine, hinges on swift application of basic science to communication. . . .[9]

John Lear, science editor of the *Saturday Review,* also encourages reporters to be familiar with more than one specialty. He says: "The interdisciplinary approach to research and teaching . . . is now well established on many campuses. Journalists must embrace this approach to science writing, too."[10]

The "Hype" Stories

There is always the temptation to overplay a science story, giving more credence than necessary to what testing has actually proved. Reporters have to be on guard about science information—some should not be in newspapers at all.

The excitement of the 1960s—with demonstrations and rebellions—gave way to a continued desire to play up the unusual and offbeat. Some reporters even turned their attention to gurus: to the boy Maharaj Ji, the "Moonies," and to epiphenomenal, out-of-this-world alleged happenings. Unidentified flying object (UFO) watchers abounded. The moon exploration confirmed that humans have access to outer space and possible encounters and companionship some day. Some scientists told attendees at a symposium during an annual convention of the American Association for the Advancement of Science in San Francisco that there are about 250 billion stars in our galaxy, the Milky Way, and about a billion trillion stars in the universe. A *Newsday* writer said "by sheer mathematical probability" there may be life out there on the "perhaps millions" of planets circling those stars.[11] A German scientist, Heinrich Faust, told the German Society for Space Research that without hesitation one could assume that there is life on 1,000 trillion earthlike planets. In a more recent report, the New York *Times* carried a report that said possibly no other planet anywhere sustains life.

The science writer has to be on guard against the individual—often reputable—scientist as well as the person who has "all the answers." The reporter must accurately spot unsubstantiated and improbable information on the one hand, and overconfident sources on the other. Too often editors and reporters are conned into using stories that "fall" their way, often through the efforts of clever publicists.

Can you recognize "hype" and separate it from actual news when you see it?

Consider this story distributed by the UPI:

CHICAGO (UPI)—Mankind did not originate in earth's primordial slime, but may have come from a giant planet "Marduk" which orbits the sun far beyond the last known planet—so says Zecharia Sitchin.

Sitchin, author of a recent book called "The Twelfth Planet," doesn't believe conventional theories of evolution.

Marduk is a hidden planet located beyond Pluto and is many times the size of earth, he said. It orbits the sun, passing near earth only once in 3,600 years.

Sitchin has devoted the past 25 years trying to convince others—through research, decipherings of 3,000-year-old charts and world travel—that Marduk was known to ancient civilizations. He said the technologically advanced inhabitants of Marduk may have genetically created mankind.

By his own admission, Sitchin said the theory "sounds crazy." But the 58-year-old New York businessman, in Chicago Wednesday for the Fifth World Conference of the Ancient Astronaut Society, said he is pleased to find United States Naval Observatory astronomers are beginning to share his view about the existence of another planet.

"There is mounting astronomical evidence that there exists one more planet within our solar system," he said. "It is a planet many times the size of earth and the discovery of this planet will confirm ancient beliefs in its existence.

"The big news of the week, however, is that astronomers of the Naval Observatory in Washington, D.C., confirmed the discovery by one of their colleagues, Dr. James W. Christy, that Pluto has a moon. They also calculated that Pluto is much smaller than hitherto believed.

"The orbits of Haley's Comet were suspected a long time ago to have been caused by Planet X, but the irregularities in the orbit of Uranus and Neptune were attributed to Pluto. But now, because Pluto is not as big as originally thought, Pluto can no longer account for these irregularities. They say there must be one more planet farther out than Pluto to account for it, just as I have been saying all along."[12]

The report brought this response in the National Association of Science Writers *Newsletter* (a letter to UPI president Rod Beaton from NASW president George Alexander):

> As a science writer with 18 years in this business, as a science writer for the Los Angeles *Times*, and as the current president of the National Association of Science Writers, I feel compelled to call your attention to the attached story, written by a Marcia Stepanek, moved out of your Chicago bureau.
>
> In its naivete and imbalance, this story is precisely the sort of journalism which make professional scientists grimace in disgust and science writers despair. Ms. Stepanek having obviously accepted Zecharia Sitchin's bizarre—to say the least—theory as credible and consistent with reality, she can only encourage similar erroneous beliefs among the impressionable readers in our society.
>
> Unless things have changed since I was a journalism student, it is a cardinal rule to make sure that controversial stories include some counter-balancing statement from one or more informed adversaries. Nowhere, however, in Ms. Stepanek's account is there a quote or a statement from a responsible scientist which would throw a pail of

cold logic on Mr. Sitchin's highly speculative ideas, or at a bare minimum, suggest that the silly claims of this individual be taken with a large shaker of salt.

I don't quarrel with UPI's decision to cover the Ancient Astronaut Society's meeting. But I do quarrel with Ms. Stepanek's uncritical handling of such a patently preposterous claim and her apparent ignorance of the old "10th planet" theory so long favored by the nuttier fringes of the UFO crowd. If Ms. Stepanek is too young or too inexperienced to bring such a balance to a story, then it seems to me that someone on UPI's desk should have been responsible enough to do so.

In any event, this kind of story does no one any good—UPI, Ms. Stepanek, science, science writing or the average reader. I would appreciate knowing how you feel about this story.[13]

UPI's editor in chief, H. L. Stevenson, answered:

It would have been prudent certainly to include at least a line in the Chicago story on Zecharia Sitchin's claim about a twelfth planet, to the effect that recognized scientists discredit it. There were several references in the story which would give the reader fair warning that his theory should be taken with a grain of salt.

Specifically:

. . . "Sitchin . . . doesn't believe conventional theories of evolution."

. . . "Sitchin has devoted the past 25 years trying to convince others. . . ."

. . . "By his own admission, Sitchin said the theory 'sounds crazy.' "

Your point is well taken and I assure you and your colleagues in NASW that United Press International shares your zeal for accuracy and balance in all science copy, just as we strive to achieve it in other areas.

Al Rossiter Jr., our science editor, checks all of our regular Science Today columns, as well as other major stories. It is SOP to ask him to review any copy dealing with announcements of major advances in the field of medicine.

Patricia McCormack, our family health editor, does the same for stories in that area.

Senior editors in our various regions also are under instructions to check copy reporting sensitive or highly technical scientific or medical developments.[14]

Some stories are obvious "hypes," and yet you have to cover or at least take notice of them, just because everybody else does.

One such situation was the arrival a few years ago of a book, *In*

His Image: The Cloning of a Man, by David Rorvik, published by a major publisher, Lippincott. Although questionable, it could not be ignored.

You can always use the apparent "hype" story or look for a legitimate discussion, and in so doing, acknowledge that the news value exists, although the story might be a hype or total hoax. Tipping your hat to it, since the reports are out, you can proceed to discuss relevant ethical and philosophical considerations.

Reader's Digest illustrates one way of hitching onto the current fad, triggered by a questionable source (the Rorvik book), while at the same time separating itself from that source. Note the article by Emily and Per Ola D'Aulaire declines to mention the Rorvik book while obviously hitching onto the subject:

> Take a cell, practically any cell, from your body, the theory goes, and through appropriate biological tinkering you can cause it to grow into a duplicate of yourself—identical from eyelashes to toenails. No need for procreational sex anymore; with this system, you can neatly reproduce yourself without a partner. Human cloning, it's called.
>
> Science fact or science fiction? Last spring, a book was published telling the supposedly true story of an elderly millionaire who, at great expense, succeeded in producing a clone—an exact genetic copy of himself. According to the account, the clonal offspring, now two years old, is living with his "father" in California.
>
> The book caused a small uproar. Clone movies and clone jokes sprang up overnight. A group of scientists demanded that the federal government disclose all the studies it has funded on cloning and the related area of cell biology. . . .[15]

The article proceeds to discuss the pros and cons of the possibility of cloning.

With all the comment on "hypes" in hand, science writers should probably also entertain the idea that the unexplainable might just exist.

After an alleged "out of the body experience" in which he says he was able to aid his distraught wife, Henry W. Pierce, science writer for the Pittsburgh *Post-Gazette*, reports the experience in the NASW *Newsletter* and asks the delicate questions:

> Are we justified in dismissing every strange account out-of-hand merely because it is strange?
>
> Granted that there is no way scientists can repeat unique experiences in their laboratories, and granted that many such experiences may indeed be hallucinations and outright lies; does this, however,

justify scientists who heap scorn and ridicule on anyone who tries to tell them about anything that doesn't fit their preconceptions?

Wouldn't the most appropriate response for a scientist, in such a case, merely be to indicate that he has no way to test the person's claims and that therefore his story, while interesting, is beyond science? This, it seems to me, would be far better than the systematic attempts to discredit anyone who tries to report such an experience.

Another question: Is there such a thing as a "scientific establishment"? If so, is that establishment ideologically and dogmatically opposed to any consideration of truly strange phenomena?

A related question, of course: Would a really well-done experiment in parapsychology stand a chance of being reported in *Science* magazine if the results were positive?

I do not know the answers to these questions. I do know that if you've ever had a really far-out experience, and if you shared the experience with another person (ruling out the possibility that you had imagined the whole thing), you may find your orientation to science—and scientists—dramatically changed.[16]

When scientists are "onto" something, it can be news, even when the research has not run its course and is not conclusive. The mere uniqueness of a topic can make it news, especially when it involves the work of top researchers. How often have you heard "prime numbers" discussed on the front page? The Los Angeles *Times*, with an article by *Times* science writer Lee Dembart, did in September 1983. (See Chapter 20 for a discussion of media and computer technology.)

Computer scientists using one of the world's fastest computers believe they have found the largest prime number yet—one that contains nearly 40,000 digits.

A prime number is one that has no divisors other than itself and 1. Euclid proved that there are infinitely many primes, starting with 2, 3, 5, 7, 11, 13 and 17 and going on forever. But there is no formula for generating them.

Knowing a prime number larger than all others doesn't offer much benefit to society, nor anyone but a handful of mathematicians, but it is a feather in the cap of the supercomputer that finds it—in this case, a Cray XMP, which sells for about $9 million.

The new prime number, which has yet to be verified, is 2 raised to the 132,049th power minus 1, a number with 39,751 digits. If printed in this newspaper, the number would fill more than one entire page. Because of its special form, it is called a Mersenne prime, named for a 17th-Century monk who investigated them. This would be the 29th Mersenne prime known. The 28th Mersenne prime, which was found last year, is 2 raised to the 86,243rd power minus 1, a number with 25,692 digits.

The makers of supercomputers, which operate thousands of times faster than the run-of-the-mill variety, view the search for large primes as a way of marketing their machines.

"It's like racing computers," said David Slowinski of Cray Research, Inc. in Chippewa Falls, Wis., makers of the Cray XMP and its predecessor, the Cray-1.

Using these machines, Slowinski found the two previous largest primes as well as the latest one, which was found the other day on an experimental machine in the company's offices.

There are about 60 Crays in use in the United States, most of them in defense-related, top-secret applications. Some of them, at Slowinski's request, spend their idle seconds here and there running his prime number program. That's how the previous Mersenne prime was found.

Not everyone is happy that the marketing of supercomputers has overshadowed the mathematical research involved, and a gritty rivalry has developed among the participants.

'They Want Publicity'

"Some people are more interested in the world record than in the mathematics of it," said Curt Noll, who, with Laura Nickel, discovered the then-largest prime in 1978 while they were students at Hayward High School in the San Francisco Bay area.

"They want publicity, I guess, more than cooperation with the mathematical community, which, I think, is sad," Nickel said.

Slowinski responded: "This is an old problem for mathematicians, but for myself, I only pursue it as an interesting game, as a race."

The Cray XMP has two processors, each of which is capable of doing 200 million computations a second. One of the processors took 3,900 seconds (65 minutes) to find that 2 raised to the 132,049th power minus 1 is prime.

Slowinski said his new program for testing large primes is running about 12 times faster than the program he used last year to prove that a 25,692-digit number is prime. . . .

Mersenne primes have a unique structure that makes it possible to test their primality much more easily than any other number. For that reason, Mersenne primes are by far the largest primes known. Only simple arithmetic is needed to run the test for Mersenne primes—albeit a lot of it.

In the case of the largest Mersenne prime, the test for primality required multiplying the 39,751-digit number by itself over and over again. Modern supercomputers are uniquely suited to the task. They run about 200,000 times faster than an IBM personal computer, for example.

Mersenne primes are primes that are 1 less than a power of 2. They are generated by raising 2 to a prime power and subtracting 1. The first Mersenne prime is 3, which is equal to 2 raised to the second power (4) minus 1. The next Mersenne prime is 7, which is 2 to the third power (8) minus 1. The next Mersenne prime is 31, which is 2 to the fifth power minus 1. . . .

The advent of computers has greatly facilitated the search for Mersenne primes. The first four Mersenne primes (3, 7, 31 and 127) were mentioned in Euclid's Elements. The next one, 8,191 (which is 2 to the 13th power minus 1) was found in the 15th Century. The next two were found in the 16th Century, and one each was found in the 17th and 18th centuries. . . .

The Language of Science

If yesterday's science reporters needed to know a lot, today's journalists have to know much more. It was said of Thomas Aquinas in the Thirteenth Century that he knew all there was to know, and he wrote thick tomes embracing all the understanding of the time in science and philosophy. Now it is impossible to know everything, even in one area. Experts estimate that the total amount of scientific knowledge in recent times doubles in less than 10 years.

If you do much scientific reporting—and who can really avoid it—you will want to file clippings and other materials on topics and vocabulary.

Here are some terms from the New York *Times* that are useful in reporting nuclear plant operations:

Cladding: The material that surrounds the nuclear fuel material; in many reactors, the cladding is a metal shielding.

Condenser: Heat exchanger in which steam is transformed into (liquid) water by removing heat and transferring it to a cooling river or pond.

Coolant: The fluid that removes the nuclear-generated heat from the core. Most plants are termed liquid water reactors because the coolant is water.

Core: The region of a reactor containing the nuclear fuel. It is in this region that the nuclear reactions occur, with the exception of those caused outside the core by escaping radiation or radioactivity. This region may be distinguished from the "blanket," which is intended primarily to contain fertile material in which fission material can be generated by neutrons escaping from the core.

Decay heat: The heat produced by radioactive decay of materials that are primarily the remnants of the chain reaction.

Emergency core cooling system: Any engineered system for cooling the core in the event of failure of the basic cooling system; may include core sprays and/or injectors.

Fission: The splitting of a heavy atomic nucleus to form two lighter "fission fragments," as well as less massive particles, such as neutrons.

Fuel pellets: The basic form in which the uranium is contained.

Meltdown: Considered one of the more catastrophic events in a nuclear accident, second only to an explosion. This could involve either the melting of the metal rods in which pellets of enriched uranium fuel are contained, or of the pellets themselves. This could occur when the radioactive material in the core of a reactor loses the cooling water that keeps its temperature within controllable limits. In this event, the core would melt into a glowing radioactive mass, which could break through the containment walls of the reactor or sink deep into the ground. The sinking into the ground is what is known as the China Syndrome (presumably going through the Earth to China). In either case, the meltdown results in a massive release of radiation.

Primary coolant system (or loop): The entire circuit through which the fluid that actually cools the core passes, including all piping, vessels and components such as the reactor vessel, coolant pump and steam generator.

Rad: The standard unit of radiation absorbed dose, a term that supersedes the roentgen as the unit of dosage. A millirad is a thousandth of a rad. Doses of a few millirads are now considered safe, but there is still debate over the threshold between a safe and a hazardous dose.

Radioactivity: The spontaneous disintegration of the nucleus of an atom (uranium, for example) with the emission of radiation. The radiant energy is in the form of particles or rays known as alpha, beta, and gamma rays. Alpha rays are positively charged particles. Beta rays are negatively charged electrons. Gamma rays are elements of electromagnetic radiation resembling X-rays, and much more penetrating than other forms of radiation.

Reactor: The core and its protective container shell, sometimes called a vessel.

Rem: For "roentgen equivalent, man." A measure of the quantity of any ionizing radiation with the same biological effectiveness as one rad of X-rays.

Rods: Stainless steel tubes that hold the uranium fuel pellets.

Roentgen: A measure of the quantity of X-ray or gamma ray radiation in the air.

Zircaloy: An alloy of zirconium used as fuel rod cladding in water-cooled reactors because of its low thermal neutron cross-section and good heat-transfer properties.[17]

While scientific language needs simplifying for the layman, reporters make the mistake of oversimplifying ideas. "There are no simple answers [for the science writer]," says Ed Edelson, the New York *Daily News* science writer who has also been the president of the NASW. He operates out of a quiet corner in the modern feature room of the *Daily News*. "If someone offers simple answers, be suspicious," he says. "If you're young and eager, it is easy to accept magical cures. As you grow older, you increasingly take things with a grain of salt."

Lou Hudson, city editor for the Fort Worth (Tex.) *Star-Telegram*, has these three suggestions for the science writer: "(1) Don't write anything you don't understand; (2) explain everything (it is easier to cut stuff out than add it in); (3) read everything you can on every area of science you can."

The science writer—and any technical writer—is advised to check out the latest books from the library on any specific science matter that is coming up. Do some vocabulary building whenever you can: study definitions while you wait for a plane, for example. Or go back to school to bone up on the specialized beat. Says Blair Justice, winner of various awards in science and health reporting as a writer for the Fort Worth (Tex.) *Star-Telegram:*

> A young Associated Press staff man aspiring to become a science writer asked a number of scientists this question at a seminar not long ago:

"What do you expect of a reporter who comes to you for a story?"

The most frequent answer: "Some ability to speak our language. . . ."

The most obvious way for a reporter to gain a grasp of science, of scientific language and concepts is to go back to school. This is exactly what the AP man planned to do. He had a Ford Foundation fellowship and he was going to take a leave to return to college and enroll in science courses. Columbia University Graduate School of Journalism is now returning practicing reporters to school with its advanced science writing program.

I myself have been back at school for four years, taking one course a semester in an evening college and concentrating on just one field I think is applicable to my job in writing medical news—psychology.

But how many reporters doing science writing can, or want to, return to school?[18]

CONSUMER HEALTH

Closely related to the science beat is the consumer health beat. A growing public awareness of the effects of contemporary civilization on health and the insistence that manufacturers be held accountable for the safety of their products have increased consumer interest in health. And so newspapers are reporting on health issues more.

Using Agencies

Sources for stories in this area are many. The Food and Drug Administration, with regional offices throughout the U.S., offers a wealth of information and usually cooperates with the press. The FDA depends on the press to disseminate information to the public about possible harmful foods, drugs, or other products. The press must get the word out about asbestos in hair dryers, nitrites in hot dogs, sulfites as a food preservative, or harmful ingredients in drugs that can lead to miscarriage. "Basically," says Terry Rubenstein, consumer reporter for the Baltimore *Sun*, "I try to keep abreast of what's going on at the FDA and Federal Trade Commission."

Other governmental agencies which consumer health reporters will deal with are the Environmental Protection Agency (again, there are regional offices where you can obtain information), state environmental protection agencies, and some local agencies in larger cities.

Though perhaps less accessible to the press, the Center for

Disease Control in Atlanta, Ga., and government-funded private agencies dealing with specific subjects such as cancer can also be helpful.

Nonprofit health organizations can create frustration with their self-serving press releases and annual reports. Sometimes, however, reporters can develop information in those reports into good, in-depth consumer stories for the layman.

The American Cancer Society funds various researchers for both large and small projects on campuses, at hospitals, and in laboratories. The American Lung Association's concern with air pollution makes that group a good source in this area. Consumer watch groups, including Ralph Nader's well-publicized group, can provide information. Reporters should be aware, however, that advocates are often extremely subjective about a particular health subject. An antinuclear power group, for instance, will be blind to many arguments in favor of nuclear power plants. Reporters will find they are not only dealing with different philosophies and politics, but also with highly emotional causes.

Finding Stories

Consumer health stories can range from the very simple to the complex. A breakout of head lice in the local school may not call for much in-depth reporting but is a subject of much importance to the readers whose children attend that school. The reporter may find, in fact, that the head lice story may draw more reader interest than an in-depth examination of the carcinogenic (cancer-causing) effects of a chemical found in well water in the area. Parents can see head lice and the effect is readily apparent; a harmful chemical may be tasteless, odorless, and colorless, and its effects on the body are questionable and long term.

The "big" stories, however, require analysis, forethought, and extreme care with objectivity. Reporters must be sure that they do not create panic in readers—but reporters should give consumers adequate warning.

In two populous counties in southeastern Pennsylvania, near Philadelphia, a man-made chemical, trichloroethylene (TCE), was detected in well water—the only source of water for the area—in quantities that the EPA labeled as possibly unsafe. Because it was the first time such a widespread contamination of TCE had been found in the United States, government agencies had little information pertaining to it and to its possible carcinogenic effects on humans.

After several stories telling of wells being shut down because of contamination and the state's search for an industrial polluter (all the stories stated that the chemical had been found to cause internal damage to animals and was suspected of causing cancer in animals), the Doylestown (Pa.) *Intelligencer* did a four-part series in an attempt to answer some questions.

The first part provided a wrap-up of what had happened so far: the detection, the government's stepping in to find a cause, and the dilemma of some water companies which had to shut down some of their wells. The second related the new situation with better-known health hazards. The third part dealt with the chemical itself, listing the household products and the industrial products in which it could be found. The fourth told what the government was doing to control the use of the product in the future and described the government's efforts to find a way to clean up the water.

Follow-up stories are important in consumer health reporting. A school board may announce that contractors have used asbestos in the construction of a high school auditorium ceiling. What about the health hazard for students and parents who have been using that auditorium? If contractors used asbestos in one public building, perhaps they used it in other public buildings erected around the same time. Saccharin, the FDA proclaims, may cause cancer, but what about the diabetics who must either use it or go without "sweets"?

The reporter need not wait for a "crisis" to report on consumer health issues. Stories that you can do in any community at any time include: a look at the "contemporary" school lunch menu, its nutritional value and variety; an inquiry into the amount of contamination of toxic materials, such as dioxin or polychlorinated biphenyls (PCB's) in fish in local bodies of water; and house plants that are poisonous to animals and humans. You could look back at the bomb shelters of the early 1960s—do any still exist in your community, and what happened to the food and water stored in them, or, with new nuclear holocaust fears in the 1980s, are there new shelters? If fluoride is in the community's drinking water, what do dentists say about the effect on teeth, compared with the years before it was put in the water? And the old "should doctors be allowed to advertise" controversy usually has strong proponents and opponents in every community.

Reporters have the responsibility to tell both sides of such stories as those above. People's emotions run extremely high in the area of health and things in the environment which can affect it.

Conflicting Answers

One difficulty to watch for is the problem of receiving different answers to health questions. Peter Hackes of NBC News, in a speech before the American Association for the Advancement of Science, a few years ago emphasized the problem of conflicting answers given reporters in health and science. He cited different answers on the use of phosphates in detergents and the existing or nonexisting danger to the environment. Then:

> Remember "Get the lead out!?" It was a campaign begun by some scientists . . . a campaign soon picked up by environmentalists and politicians—with government encouragement even to the point of proposing a tax on leaded gasoline. The proposal was to phase out lead in gas because that's what was causing smog. Along came another science group whose experiments indicated that eliminating lead from gasoline might even create more smog in some areas—not less.
>
> Remember the outcry against mercury [as a health hazard]? It put the swordfisherman out of business. For a while it stopped the tuna boats. That too was a science-generated government ban. Based on more information, it wasn't long before the government soon relaxed its ban against tuna fish. Comes now a scientist who tells us the amount of mercury in our environment is not on the increase as we had thought, but is, in fact, decreasing. He goes so far as to theorize that the presence of traces of mercury may even be essential to life, although he admits ". . . the whole field is in ignorance."
>
> I think you can get a feel for the problem that faces us . . . the people who must go to science for the answers. What *are* the answers? Is there only one? If there are three answers—which is most correct?[19]

Medical Writing

Some newspapers have a medical beat. On most papers, however, this area is usually combined with others, such as consumer health and science writing.

While representing all sides fairly may be the most difficult task for the consumer health reporter, medical writers find their frustration and biggest challenge in adapting the highly sophisticated and technical medical information into readable language. Most journalism professors and editors tell new reporters that they should never submit the written story back to the source for reading prior to publication. Exceptions exist for nearly every rule, and at times the medical writer—particularly one who is new in the field—will want to check the wording of something with a source.

For example, the local clinic may have just acquired a highly sophisticated piece of machinery. For the sake of accuracy, the reporter may wish the physician or the medical technician interviewed to double-check the part of the story which describes just how the machine works.

With health-related organizations funding research projects throughout the country, reporters in most communities have access to either a college professor or a medical professional involved in important research. Most researchers are more than willing to explain their pet projects, but the reporter should not go into an interview without some basic knowledge of the field.

The psychological problem of personal involvement in health reporting, as with science and other areas, may prove difficult for some journalists: science writers have to watch that their personal biases do not infiltrate their writing. If they grew up on farms, they might have special interests in preserving the countryside and pursuing ecology; if they grew up in the city or are working there, perhaps some will be especially interested in looking at the result of exhaust pollution and the problems of additives in preserving food. But reporters also have to resist another kind of personal involvement when they cover health matters. John Troan of the Scripps-Howard News syndicate told a symposium at the University of West Virginia:

> Like most medical students, most reporters who cover health news experience, at first, every symptom they hear or write about. This business of collecting symptoms is a hazardous hobby of the medical writer; before he becomes a full-fledged health news reporter, he may suffer the agonies of every ailment from brain tumor to gangrene of the toenail. Eventually, however, the reporter manages to develop an immunity to such symptoms and this particular headache of health sciences reporting ceases.[20]

Fear, unfounded or real—such as concern with radiation when assigned to nuclear "accident" stories, undue anxiety if riding a first general flight of a new aircraft, or an expectation of contamination—can have a subconscious effect on a reporter's approach, and the health journalist should be aware of such fears in order to avoid them.

Among medical references useful to reporters:

Albercrombie, George, et al, eds. *Encyclopedia of General Practice*. 6 vols. London: Butterworth & Co., 1963.
Diseases and treatments.

Dorland, William Alexander, comp. *Dorland's Illustrated Medical Dictionary*. Philadelphia, Pa: Saunders, 1981.
Terminology and treatments defined and illustrated.

Dox, Ida, Bragio John Melloni, and Gilbert M. Eisner, eds. *Melloni's Illustrated Medical Dictionary*. Baltimore: Williams and Wilkins Co., 1979.
Definitions and information with pictures.

Grupenhoff, John T., ed. *National Health Directory*. Rockville, Md.: Aspen Systems Corp., 1982.
Names, titles, and addresses of information sources on health programs and legislation. Local, state, and regional health offices; congressional health committees.

Hughes, Harold K., ed. *Health Sciences*. Lexington, Mass.: Lexington Books, D.C. Heath & Co., 1977.
Names of drugs, technical terms, and meanings of abbreviations.

Kruzas, Anthony T., ed. *Medical and Health Information Directory*. 2nd ed. Detroit: Gale Research Co., 1980.
A guide to state, national, and world agencies, hospitals, research centers, data banks, and libraries.

Rothenberg, Robert E., ed. *New Illustrated Medical Encyclopedia for Home Use*. 4 vols. New York: Abradale Press, 1976.
Organized in form of questions and answers, with illustrations.

Sainer, Elliot A., ed. *Who's Who in Health Care*. 2nd ed. New York: Hanover Publications, Inc., 1982.
Biographies and addresses of doctors, health administrations, and educators.

American Medical Directory: Update to the 27th Edition. 4 vols., Chicago: American Medical Association, 1982.
Names and addresses of U.S. and world physicians.

Directory of Medical Specialists. 19th ed. 3 vols. Chicago: Marquis Who's Who, Inc., 1979.
Medical specialists in U.S. and overseas.

NIH Factbook. 1st ed. Chicago: Marquis Academic Media, Marquis Who's Who, Inc., 1976.
A guide to National Institute of Health programs and activities.

Physician's Desk Reference for Nonprescription. New York: Van Nostrand Reinhold, 1980.
All about drugs and how they work.

Standard Medical Almanac. 2nd ed. Chicago: Marquis Academic Media, Marquis Who's Who, Inc., 1980.
Statistics related to medicine—average doctor salaries, number enrolled in Medicare, and so on.

Covering Hospitals

The reporter often needs information from a hospital immediately following a car accident, a train wreck, a fire, or a tornado. Readers want to know how serious the injuries were, how the patients are doing, and sometimes even who the victims are. Since hospital information is usually available after other information, reporters with deadlines can't wait: they need the information immediately.

When an area athlete was killed and another injured in a construction accident, Leslie Champlin, health writer for the Topeka (Kans.) *Capital-Journal*, needed information from the hospital right away. The story, she said:

> . . . broke about 15 minutes before first edition deadline. The accident victims had been rushed to the hospital, but the emergency room personnel were too busy working on them to be of much help to me. They would confirm only that one man had been killed and would not elaborate on the circumstances or identify the dead man.
>
> At that point, we called the ambulance service that transported the men. Ambulance attendants confirmed the death. We then called the hospital public relations office to request help in identifying the men. About 10 minutes after we made our request, the PR people gave the men's names to us, identified which had been killed, then asked us to hold off on publication until the families had been notified. The first edition article did not carry the men's names; the second edition did:

A University of Kansas football player was killed and a former player was injured when a 10-foot trench at a construction site southeast of Topeka caved in on them shortly after 9:30 a.m. today.

Pronounced dead on arrival was Dennis Balagna, 21, starting offensive guard for KU, Stormont-Vail Regional Medical Center officials said. Balagna would have been a senior at KU this fall.

Treated at the hospital emergency room for a bruised chest was John Mascarello, 22. Hospital officials said he was released. Mascarello was an offensive guard on last year's KU team and he was graduated last spring.

Balagna and Mascarello, who were employed by M. S. Watson Inc. Constructors, 3333 E. 21st, apparently entered the trench and were waiting for wood to shore up the walls, according to Shawnee Sheriff's Det. Sgt. Farrell Fouts.

The trench connected two sewage lagoons under construction about a quarter of a mile south and a mile east of S.E. 21st and Croco Road. Fouts said pipe was to have been installed in the trench after its walls were reinforced.

Construction superintendent Bill Dinkel told sheriff's department officials that workers were about to install forms when the trench walls gave way, completely covering both victims.

The wall "completely blew out, like a tire would, according to the machine operator," Fouts said. "It started about two feet from the top. Within seconds they were covered, the operator said."

Phil Schell, 1713 Mission, a construction worker at the scene, said, "We heard them yell, and I saw everybody running over there. We ran and tried to dig them out."

A backhoe operator working at the east end of the trench saw that the trench was about to cave in, yelled to fellow workers, and turned the machine toward the trench, Fouts said. Witnesses rushed to the trench and began digging with their hands, shovels and the backhoe, he added.

By the time ambulances arrived, both men, who had been standing "fairly close together," were partially uncovered, Fouts said.

"They weren't there more than five minutes when the first (rescue) truck arrived," a second witness said.

Rescuers pulled Mascarello from the trench shortly before 10:20 a.m. Ambulance attendants administered oxygen to Mascarello as he was being transported from the scene.

Using shovels, workers frantically began digging dirt from around Balagna's knees while others administered cardiopulmonary resuscitation in an attempt to save him. At 10:40 a.m., the county coroner was called.

Workers pulled Balagna from the trench at 10:45 a.m. . . .

On some occasions, the reporter may want to seek information from a hospital in person, if time permits. When a wad of cash and a substantial stash of marijuana were found on a plane which crashed near Durham, N.C., Bob Kolin, a student at Duke University and a stringer before becoming a reporter for the Raleigh, N.C. *News and Observer,* went directly to the hospital. He figured that the switchboard operator had been advised not to give out any information on the patient. "I just went on over without calling," he said. "I stopped at the desk, asked for the room number of the injured person." He proceeded to walk across the lobby and asked for the person by room number. Kolin told the injured man that police had discovered the marijuana and had some questions. Kolin asked the man if he would like to comment. "When he knew the police version was out," Kolin said, "he wanted to give his own version. I told him I knew he wasn't feeling well, but I was concerned about getting his side of the story."

Hospital Guidelines

Reporters should be aware of guidelines on the release of information about patient conditions. Sometimes reporters will need to have the guidelines in hand to remind reluctant hospital staffs of what can and cannot be released.

In a booklet, *Guidelines for the Release of Information to the Communications Media,* the Hospital Association of Pennsylvania Board of Trustees has outlined ways of proceeding and general rules and considerations for the media in an action typical of efforts by other associations. Keep in mind, however, that the source of such guidelines is the public relations offices of the hospitals. The suggestions may not be absolute in terms of law, but rather state what the hospital officials consider to be the rules.[21]

Confidentiality of Patient Information

Medical information is private and confidential. Hospital medical records may be inspected by written authorization of the patient or his guardian or legal representative or as directed by law or court process. To be absolutely certain of utmost legal protection, consent should not be accepted from any person other than the patient.

Patient Information in the Public Domain

Cases of public record, or in the public domain, are those cases which by law are reportable to public authorities, such as police, coroner, public health officer, or governmental agency.

Events In the Public Domain Include:

a. Accidents (automobile, employment related) and police cases (shootings, stabbings, and so on.)

   Patients who are most often the subject of information released to the press are those treated for injuries sustained in accidents or police cases. On these patients, the hospital may release the name, address, age, nature of injury, condition if determined, and the disposition of the patient, whether hospitalized or released, following notification of next of kin. The hospital cannot pledge that all information is accurate, since accident victims frequently are admitted in haste and information immediately available may be incomplete.

   The hospital should never attempt to describe the event that caused the injury. This must come from the police officer investigating the incident. For example, the hospital should not make a statement on whether a person was intoxicated; whether injuries were the result of assault, attempted suicide, or accident; whether a patient was poisoned (deliberately or accidentally); whether a patient is suspected of being a drug addict; the circumstances through which the patient was shot or stabbed; or the circumstances relating to an automobile accident.

b. Fires.

c. Natural disasters (floods, tornadoes).

d. Man-made disasters.

e. Civil disorders.

f. Coroners' cases.

Requests for details on any patient must be referred to the coroner on any of the following:

—Any death wherein the body is unidentified or unclaimed.

—All sudden deaths not caused by readily recognized disease, or wherein the cause of death cannot be properly certified by a physician on the basis of prior (recent) medical attendance.

—All deaths occurring under suspicious circumstances, including those where alcohol, drugs, or other toxic substances may have a direct bearing on the outcome.

—All deaths occurring as a result of violence or trauma, whether apparently homicidal, suicidal, or accidental (including those due to mechanical, thermal, chemical, electrical, or radiational injury, drowning, cave-ins), and regardless of the time elapsing between the time of injury and time of death.

—All fetal deaths, stillbirths, or death of any baby within 24 hours after its birth, where the mother has not been under the care of a physician.

For "Events in the Public Domain" categories, the hospital may release the following information:

- Name.
- Address.
- Age.
- Sex.
- Occupation.
- Marital status.
- Condition of patient:

  —GOOD—Vital signs are stable and within normal limits. Patient is conscious and comfortable; indicators are excellent.
  —FAIR—Vital signs are stable and within normal limits. Patient is conscious but may be uncomfortable; indicators are favorable.
  —SERIOUS—Vital signs may be unstable and not within normal limits. Patient is acutely ill; indicators are questionable.
  —CRITICAL—Vital signs are unstable and not within normal limits. Patient may not be conscious; indicators are unfavorable.

- Disposition of patient:

  —Treated and released.
  —Admitted.
  —Admitted to critical care unit.

- Nature of accident or injury.

Special Considerations

a. Burns—A statement may be made that the patient is burned, but the degree must be determined after treatment by a physician.

b. Fractures—If there is a fracture, it is not to be described in any way except to state the member involved.

c. Head Injuries—A simple statement may be made that the injuries are of the head. It is not to be stated that the skull is fractured until definitely determined by a physician.
d. Internal Injuries—It may be stated that there are internal injuries, but no information may be given as to the location of the injuries unless definitely determined by a physician.
e. Intoxication, Drug, or Alcohol—No statement may be made as to whether the patient is intoxicated.
f. Poisoning—No statement may be made concerning either motivation or circumstances surrounding a patient's poisoning.
g. Sexual Assault—No statement may be made concerning the nature of the incident or injuries. Condition of the patient may be given.
h. Shooting or Stabbing—The number of wounds and their location may be stated if definitely determined by a physician. No statement may be made as to how the shooting or stabbing occurred.
i. Suicide or Attempted Suicide—No statement may be made that there was a suicide or attempted suicide.
j. Unconsciousness—If the patient is unconscious when brought to the hospital, a statement of this fact may be made.
k. Child Abuse—In suspected child abuse cases, no statement is to be made to that effect.
l. Psychiatric Admissions—Patients admitted to a neuro-psychiatric unit are to be regarded as any other patient. No statement should be made concerning treatment, nor should the name of the physician be released in this type of hospitalization.
m. Communicable or Rare Diseases—No statement is to be made. The media should be referred to the county health department. NOTE: No statement is to be made regarding prognosis.
n. Abortions—No statement may be made concerning abortions, whether therapeutic or criminal (self-induced or otherwise).
o. Operative Deaths—No statement may be made concerning operative and peri-operative deaths.

Death

Announcement of death is not routinely made by the hospital. However, such announcement may be made available to the communications media upon notification of next of kin and with their permission. Information of the cause of death must come from the patient's physician.

If a death becomes the object of a coroner's or medical examiner's investigation, inquiries as to the cause and circumstances of death should be directed to the appropriate office.

The name of the mortician receiving a body may be released to the press.

Patient Information: The Inpatient

The following information may be released upon request to the communications media or public in the case of inpatients:

—Name.
—Unit and room number.
—Condition.

It is recommended that consent be obtained from the patient. . . .

Consent Policies

The distinction between "consent" and "informed consent" should be recognized prior to the adoption and implementation of formalized consent policies.

The concept of informed consent is not necessarily satisfied by having the patient sign a document. Whether consent is informed or not is dependent upon the quality of the consent and not upon the format of any particular piece of paper. It is dependent upon the circumstances existing at the time that the consent should in fact be required, including the full disclosure of all information, including alternatives, which a reasonable person would require to decide whether or not a request for the release of information should be honored and the information released. Furthermore, to the extent that the hospital intends to formalize its policies concerning the patient and the release of information, appropriate hospital personnel should be instructed and understand the steps which must be taken in order to insure that the patient's consent is as legally meaningful as possible.

Consent forms should be signed prior to patient photography.

Since many hospitals traditionally make available to the public certain information on inpatients via telephone or information center (usually name, room and unit, and condition), an authorization procedure to disseminate this information publicly should be incorporated into the hospital consent policy. . . .

Access Restrictions

Hospitals are bound by certain regulations and policies that limit access to certain service areas or departments in the hospital building. This may apply particularly to the emergency and maternity departments and operating rooms. In some instances, requests by media that may seem to be in conflict with regulations or ordinances must be cleared with the administration.

The hospital emergency department is an example of a treatment area, access to which is usually limited to patients and persons engaged in their care. Emergency department personnel should not be permitted to release information on patients to the media. If reporters want to speak to persons being treated in the emergency area, permission must be granted by the patient and the hospital.

Medical Society Policies

Medical societies generally have a formal statement of media relations policies. These are policies established as guidance for member physicians in their dealings with media. The hospital and its agents are not obligated to abide by such a code, but as a rule, they honor it. A hospital may give newsmen the name of the attending physician only after obtaining his permission. Newsmen should be requested not to use the physician's name without his specific consent.

Local medical societies generally will make a copy of their codes available to concerned parties. . . .

AHA/ACHA Code of Ethics

Among the factors on which this guide is based is the nationally-endorsed American Hospital Association-America College of Hospital Administrators (AHA/ACHA) Code of Ethics. Pertinent paragraphs of this code state:

"Fully recognizing that the press, radio and other communications media are excellent vehicles of public education and have a responsibility to disseminate information to the community, the hospital must appreciate its moral obligation to the patient and to the professional groups represented in its organization. Consequently, information about patients, except as required by law or where privileged communication is involved, should not be given without consent. . . .

"Information about research and scientific projects should be made public only with the consent of the individuals concerned and in a manner consistent with the ethics of the professional group involved.

"Information on the activities or facilities of a hospital should not be designed to secure advantage over any other hospital by unfavorable comparison or for the personal aggrandizement of any individual.

"At all times, the hospital must adhere strictly to the truth, undistorted either by exaggeration or by incomplete and misleading statements. . . ."

Enterprising Hospital Stories

The best medical—and science—writers can think independently. Imaginative, creative reporters can turn a routine beat into an exciting one.

Says Arthur J. Snider, science writer for the Chicago *Sun-Times*:

> In addition to the routine news of emergencies, disasters, and illnesses of prominent persons, hospitals are great sources of stories dealing with the battles of children and adults against unusual diseases. I never go home at night without believing that the best story of the day lies unknown in some hospital.

Here's one of Snider's stories in the *Sun-Times* (copyright News Group Chicago, Inc., 1979) that arose from a tip and appeared on page one with the headline "At Last . . . A Mother Can Kiss Her Baby":

> Nine-month-old Olga Cisneros at last beheld her mother's face as Mrs. Josephine Cisneros Tuesday entered a germ-free hospital room, deliberately removed a sterile mask and protective hair covering, and showered the child with a mother's first kisses.
>
> Olga, born with an immune-deficiency disease that had prohibited contact with any contamination in the outside world, gazed transfixed by her pretty mother's red lips, gleaming teeth and flowing black hair, all hidden by strict septic regulations in the past.
>
> The child reached out, touched her mother's nose, smiled and posed patiently for photographers shooting through the hallway window.
>
> Doctors at Wyler Children's Hospital on the University of Chicago campus believe Olga's body now has developed enough germ-fighting equipment to withstand the wild outside world of ever-present infectious agents as a result of a bone marrow transplant from 12-year-old brother Jessie.
>
> The bone marrow, produced in a canal in the long bones of the body, is responsible for manufacturing white blood cells and other agents that fight off infections.
>
> In asking Mrs. Cisneros, 35, to remove her mask for the first time, doctors wanted the child's initial exposure to germs of the natural environment to be those of the mother's in the hope that any infection would be a benign one.
>
> "We believe the baby is immunologically normal," said Dr. Richard M. Rothberg, professor of pediatrics and pathology.
>
> It apparently was the first successful outcome in the 16 cases of the disease, called Severe Combined Immunodeficiency Disease, seen at Wyler thus far.
>
> Rothberg attributed much of the success to the ideal match of brother and sister marrow biochemistry and sterile conditions that were the equivalent of the "bubble" used to house such children elsewhere.
>
> The father, Jessie, an industrial worker, said he will be "overjoyed" to have his first daughter at home in suburban Lincoln Estates when she is released from the hospital sometime in April.

Julia Wallace, medical reporter for the Norfolk (Va.) *Ledger-Star*, came across the idea for this story "while walking around the hospital one day." The subject didn't want to be interviewed, so Wallace constructed her story from information from others.

> NORFOLK—A round-the-clock armed guard watches a hospitalized female prisoner paralyzed from the waist down by injuries suffered during an escape attempt.
>
> "People think it's kind of silly to

guard a woman who can't move her legs," said a sheriff's deputy guarding her. "They look at her and say, 'She ain't going anywhere.'

"But that's what they said when she was on the eighth floor of the jail, too," the deputy said.

The woman, Fayleta D. Patterson, is in Norfolk General Hospital. She received the injuries a month ago when she fell while attempting to escape after exiting an eighth floor window of Norfolk city jail. She has been in traction at the hospital ever since.

When she was hurt she had been in jail four days. She is wanted for an alleged probation violation in Ohio and is awaiting a hearing in Norfolk Circuit Court on two charges of forgery, one charge of uttering and one charge of failure to appear in court.

On Dec. 19, Ms. Patterson left a jail Christmas party, knotted several bedsheets together and attempted to scale down the side of the building after climbing out a window on the eighth floor.

The makeshift rope broke and she fell about seven stories, police said. She suffered multiple broken bones, shock and a collapsed lung. Her spine also was injured from the impact of the fall.

Orthopedic doctors are now working with her to determine if she will ever walk again. So far, she has no feeling in her legs.

Since she was admitted to the hospital, an armed deputy has been posted outside her door. An extra deputy from the jail is sent to the hospital or, if no one else is available, a deputy gets paid on his day off to watch Ms. Patterson, also known as June Marie Thornton.

"It's a pretty boring job," said the deputy. "There's nothing to do at all."

The guard is there to make sure she doesn't escape or is brought anything which could harm her or others, said chief deputy Claude Miller.

"It's just good common sense to have her guarded. She's been charged with a felony and she did try to escape before," Miller said.

State law says that the sheriff's department can be found liable of felonious conduct if a prisoner is wrongfully released from custody. If a prisoner were left unguarded in a hospital, that prisoner could be considered to be no longer in custody, according to assistant city attorney Daniel Hagermeister.

Ms. Patterson declined to be interviewed. Physicians said they are not sure how much longer she will need to be hospitalized.

Once she is able to be moved, Ms. Patterson will be transferred to a guarded section of the Medical College of Virginia Hospital in Richmond, which normally houses injured prisoners, or to a state prison for the handicapped, Miller said.

Until then, there'll be an armed guard outside her hospital room door.

While a snakebite incident captures the interest of the reader, a good reporter will research it further and recreate the drama moment by moment for greater interest. Dennis Hetzel of the *Journal Times* in Racine, Wis., talked to a number of people:

Death from rattlesnake bites was thwarted for a Racine man early Saturday when serum was rushed here from Milwaukee County Zoo.

The acting director of the Milwaukee County Zoo helped save the man about 4:30 a.m. Saturday by going to the zoo's reptile house to get serum needed by doctors at St. Luke's Hospital.

Jerry Albright, 26, of 513 8th St., was listed in very serious condition in the hospital's intensive care unit Saturday night.

Officials said Albright's pet snake bit him once on each hand about 4 a.m. Saturday.

Albright, whom neighbors described as a medium built motorcycle buff, told police he was petting the snake and was starting to place it back in its cage when it bit him.

Albright's ailment set off a chain of events early Saturday that started shortly after he walked into the emergency room. There followed phone calls across the country and a police escort from Milwaukee.

"We needed anti-venin serum," said Barry La Duke, director of pharmacy at St. Luke's, who was awakened by a phone call.

"They called me about 4:10 a.m. We don't normally keep that in our pharmacy. I've been there 10 years and we never had a case of snake bite. I called St. Luke's in Milwaukee and they didn't have any."

According to doctors who handled the case, others at the Racine hospital called a national center in Oklahoma City, and were given the name of Dr. Barry Ramacke of Denver, an authority on treatment of snake bites.

Meanwhile, La Duke called the Milwaukee County Zoo, and was quickly routed to Acting Director Robert Bullermann, who was sleeping in his Milwaukee home.

"We keep serum for every poisonous reptile we have," Bullermann said Saturday night. "I talked to our curator in charge of the reptile building, then I went to the zoo and got four doses."

Bullermann hopped in his own car and drove to the mass transit parking zone of I-94 and College Avenue, south of Mitchell Field.

Minutes later he was met by a Racine County Sheriff's Department squad car and La Duke, who signed for four doses of the serum and left. By 5:15 a.m., La Duke was at the hospital with the serum.

"We got hold of Dr. Ramacke right away," said an attending physician who asked that his name not be used. "It was a beautiful demonstration of man's humanity to man. People helping people."

The doctor said Dr. Ramacke instructed hospital officials to apply tourniquets to keep the venom localized in Albright's hands until the serum arrived.

Applying the serum as quickly as possible is thought to be crucial in treating snakebite victims, and rattlesnake bites can be fatal if they aren't treated, he said.

"He (Albright) was fine," the doctor recounted. "We had the snake venom localized. After we administered the anti-venin, we released the tourniquets."

The serum is made by having rattlesnakes bite horses and then drawing blood that contains antibodies the horses develop, he said.

Dr. William Stone, a Racine physician who was called into the case, said Albright now is "doing pretty well" but is experiencing considerable pain as his body and the anti-venin fight the poison.

He also faces a possible reaction of fever, pain or rashes later because half the persons who get the serum react allergically to it, Stone said.

Police said the snake still is caged in Albright's home, and a police spokesman said residents who have rattlesnakes could be violating a city ordinance that forbids keeping of wild or vicious animals.

Some of Albright's neighbors expressed surprise when they learned about the snake Saturday night.

"It's not loose, is it?" asked one woman.

As for Albright, Bullermann said, "He's a fortunate person. A hospital would not normally have it. We have plenty and we were able to get everyone moving at the same time."

Spending a night in an emergency room produces its own dramatic story. Nancy Wood of the Lake Charles (La.) *American Press* sat it out in Lake Charles:

About seven o'clock, they start to trickle in. By eleven, it becomes a steady stream.

The first to come in are patients who are merely ill and probably need to see their private physicians. A baby with a gradually worsening fever and a woman whose stomach pains haven't gone away as she anticipated waiting to see the doctor on duty. The RN, one of three nurses on duty, says that about 75 percent of the patients they see are nonemergency or nontrauma cases.

The RN says that an average of 40 patients will be treated during the night. And this one night will be repeated again and again. In 1978, more than 32,000 patients visited the emergency rooms of the three hospitals in Lake Charles, and were treated by doctors and nurses working three shifts a day, seven days a week.

One of those patients—the complaining baby—is undergoing treatment now, as her anxious parents sit in the waiting room. The mother, with red-rimmed eyes, sits clutching a baby blanket and bloodstained towel in the chair nearest the swinging doors of the treatment room. The father gets up, paces the floor, goes outside, returns, and walks toward the swinging doors.

"Don't go over there," the mother says to him. "You can hear her crying through the door."

"Why don't you wait outside instead of sitting here and listening?" he asks tersely.

The mother shakes her head and remains at her post. The father runs a hand through rumpled hair and resumes pacing, periodically stopping to peer through the small window in the door to the treatment room.

Across the room, a middle-aged woman—mother of the young woman with stomach pains—waits quietly. A few chairs down from her sits a man with a little girl on his lap.

He leans toward the middle-aged woman and says confidentially, "She's my little girl. That's my baby boy in there."

The woman recoils slightly and nods her head at him.

Encouraged at this slight show of interest, he goes on. "I'm Banjo Pete. You may have heard of me. You may have some of my records. I play a pretty good banjo. I played at a pizza place last night, but my baby got sick today. So, I stayed home to spend some time with my family."

The recipient of his confidence gives him a weak smile.

The swinging doors open and a nurse beckons to the young parents.

Minutes later, the father emerges, holding the door for the mother. In her arms, wrapped in the blanket, is a doll-like, two-year-old with long blonde hair and a large bandage across her forehead. Leaning her head against her mother, she gives a long, shuddering sigh. One hand clutches a balloon made from a rubber glove. One of the nurses has blown it up and inked a smiling face on the surface.

The mother sits, waiting for the father to pay the bill. The pain and tension leave her face. Exhaustion takes their place. Wrapping the blanket more closely around the child, they leave.

A man in his thirties leaves the treatment room and limps toward the payment desk. He is wearing jogging clothes and shoes. "Thirty-five dollars!" he exclaims. "Just for the doctor to walk in, look at you, and walk out?" He pays and limps out the door.

Banjo Pete's wife returns with the feverish baby. As they leave, he turns to the middle-aged woman and says, "Good-bye, Missus. Nice talking to you. Maybe I'll send you one of my records."

The waiting room is quiet now, as an elderly couple enter. They are from out of town, the husband tells the clerk. Their small hospital doesn't have an orthopedic surgeon, so they have come here for treatment.

The woman supports an elbow with her other hand, grimacing now and then with pain. The husband tells the clerk that she injured it in a fall on the golf course.

The woman is taken back for X-rays, and an orthopedist is called. The waiting room is deserted except for the woman's husband and the middle-aged woman.

In a small office located adjacent

to the treatment area, the staff takes advantage of the lull in activity. The young doctor sits at a desk reading a medical journal. Two nurses open boxes of pizza that have just been delivered. The doctor looks up, reaches over and takes a pinch of topping from one of the pizzas.

"Stop that," says one of the nurses, good-naturedly. "You know that's bad for your ulcer."

The doctor grins, leans back and resumes his reading.

Also seated in the small room are two tall, good-looking young men wearing hospital blues. In between bites of pizza, the RN tells them about the woman with the dislocated elbow.

The two men are Lake Charles city policemen who are taking an emergency medical course at Sowela. They have completed 81 hours of course work and are here to spend one of their two five-hour shifts observing emergency treatment. . . .

The quiet of the room is broken as a siren is heard. The doctor jumps to his feet, and he and the nurses converge at the door of the treatment room. Ambulance attendants quickly wheel in a stretcher. The doctor and nurses are instantly at the side of the stretcher, checking the middle-aged man lying there.

The ambulance attendants lead another middle-aged man out of the room. The man leans against the wall, sobbing.

"My brother. He's dead. Is he dead?" The man looks hopefully at the noncommittal faces of the two attendants. "He's dead," the man continues. "We walked in and he shot him. He wanted to shoot me. He shot my brother. He's dead. Is he dead?"

The young attendant says, "I don't know."

"There's gonna be one more," the man says. "He's gonna do the same to me. He killed my little brother I swear I'm going to kill him. I'm going to kill him tonight. It was me he wanted to shoot, but he shot my brother. Stepfather shot him."

The doctor emerges from the room. "Sorry," he says. ". . . not breathing when he came in, extensive damage, brain dead, so we didn't try to revive him." The doctor returns to his office as two detectives enter. . . .

It's now eleven o'clock—time for the shift to change. Along with the change in personnel comes a change in the type of patients. Soon they get the victims of fights, mostly barroom brawls and domestic disturbances. Then come the car wreck victims, as people with too much to drink pile into their cars and head for home.

And the drunks start coming in—some under their own power, some picked up by police, and others brought in by their families for detoxification.

The new RN comes in for duty. "How is it tonight?" she asks her predecessor.

"Same as usual," sighs the tired RN, putting on her jacket.

Outside, the middle-aged woman and daughter with stomach pains pause to watch the attendants load the stretcher of the dead man in the ambulance.

So it goes, until the rising sun displaces the full moon and ends Saturday night—the bloodiest night of the week in the emergency room.

Notes

[1]Hillier Krieghbaum, "Three Mile Island Coverage: A Crash Course for Readers," *Mass Comm Review,* Spring 1979, p. 2ff.

[2]Sharon Dunwoody, "Science Writers at Work" (Research Report No. 7, G. Cleveland Wilhoit, ed., School of Journalism-Center for New Communications, Indiana University, Bloomington, Ind., Dec. 1978), p. 2.

[3]Cf. Peter M. Sandman and Mary Paden, "The 'Inquirer' Goes for Broke," a sidebar to a study, "At Three Mile Island," *Columbia Journalism Review* (July–Aug. 1979): p. 48.

[4]Hillier Krieghbaum, *Science and the Mass Media* (New York: New York University Press, 1967), pp. 127, 128.

[5]David Warren Burkett, *Writing Science News for the Mass Media*, 2nd ed. (Houston, Texas: Gulf Pub. Co., c. 1956, 1973), pp. 72, 73.

[6]Burkett, pp. 73, 74.

[7]Burkett, p. 105.

[8]Burkett, p. 108.

[9]Burkett, pp. 109, 110.

[10]John Lear, "The Trouble With Science Writing," *Columbia Journalism Review* (Summer 1970): p. 34.

[11]David Zinman, "Search Just Beginning for Life in Outer Space," *Newsday* syndicated article in St. Paul (Minn.) *Pioneer Press*, May 26, 1974.

[12]"The UPI Story," National Association of Science Writers *Newsletter*, (Sept. 1978) 26: 2, p. 8.

[13]"The Protest," NASW *Newsletter*, pp. 7, 8.

[14]"UPI's Answer," NASW *Newsletter*, pp. 8, 9.

[15]Fmily and Per Ola D'Aulaire, "Clones: Will There Be 'Carbon Copy' People?," *Reader's Digest* (March 1979): p. 95.

[16]Henry W. Pierce, "Narrow-Mindedness and the 'Strange Experience,'" National Association of Science Writers *Newsletter* (Dec. 1978) 26:3, p. 16.

[17]"A Nuclear Plant Glossary," New York *Times*, Apr. 1, 1979, p. 32, col. 2.

[18]Blair Justice, "Advice for Science Reporters," *Quill* (Aug. 1960): p. 12.

[19]Peter Hackes, "The Uncommunicative Scientist: The Obligation of Scientists to Explain Environment to the Public" (Speech given at a symposium at the annual meeting of the American Association for the Advancement of Science, Dec. 27, 1971).

[20]John Troan, "Newsmen Find Health Sciences Headaches" (Speech given at a symposium held at the University of West Virginia).

[21]*Guidelines for the Release of Information to the Communications Media*, a booklet prepared by the Hospital Association of Pennsylvania, P.O. Box 608, Camp Hill, Pa. 17011.

Assignments

1. Look through a new book on science in the library, and prepare a news story about the book. If possible, localize your story by checking with an expert in the same scienific area for comment on the main point of your article on the book.
2. Some science writers, particularly at the New York *Times*, watch the new issues of scientific journals for human interest articles on all aspects of science. The *Times* often runs such items on the front page. These range from telling about an obscure insect in danger of extinction to the latest progress in the war on cancer. Go to the library, peruse health, medical, anthropology, scientific, and psychology magazines, and write an article telling about the information on a timely and/or high-interest topic in one of the magazines.
3. Check with a key researcher in such fields as science, technology, medicine, or psychology in your college or university, and write a news article on a recent discovery or conclusion of that researcher for the

student paper or other media. (Even wire services and national magazines are interested in such information.)

4. Analyze a newspaper science story by making an outline and listing its sources (and suggest some additional sources).
5. Have a "grab bag" of scientific words. Each student draws out a slip of paper with a scientific or high-technology word on it. After checking with books and authorities on its meaning, prepare a two-page article explaining the term; assume the article will be a boxed sidebar next to a main article using the term.
6. Prepare an article on the quality of water in your area by providing samples of water to respective city, county, and state agencies for testing. Secure interpretation from authorities, and report the results.
7. Follow through on information in the media about an accident, fire, or disaster by checking with the hospital(s) about the conditions of those injured, and write an update on the victims.
8. Plan and prepare over a period of time an "action" science story (such as accompanying an archaeologist on a "dig" or riding with a new ambulance or rescue unit), or plan and prepare an article on an issue or topic of science (such as prospects of death and survival in a nuclear attack or the newest developments in search for a cure for cancer or other diseases).

17

Entertainment: Drama, Music, and Film

Few papers are without entertainment or amusement sections. And most papers, even those with small staffs, appoint one or several reporters who do reviews of drama, music, or film.

If you are creative, intellectual, enjoy saturating yourself in one or several subjects, and like night work, an arts beat might be for you. Again, a rule follows: you must want to do it more than anything else.

"The main thing to understand is that it's 10 times, or 20 times, as hard as it looks," says William H. Honan, New York *Times* arts and leisure editor.

DRAMA REVIEWING

On the subject of preparation, listen to Clive Barnes, drama critic for the New York *Post*, describe what being a drama critic takes, and you will realize being a good one is more difficult than you might think:

Persistence: "You have to wear out lots of seats of pants in theaters. You go, go, go, and go to performances."

Dedication: "I kept a theater diary from age of 12. I knew at age of 14 what I wanted to be."

Professionalism: "Some people feel a critic should be a failed actor, but I believe a critic should be a critic."

Personal writing—a diary: "Maybe, even critique TV shows in the diary. Be a critic to yourself, and write as though it is going to be published."

Published material: "You can be a Phi Beta Kappa, which is all right, baby, but what did you do? It doesn't matter where you publish, but publish."

Other critics tell how a person can train to be a drama critic:

- Take classes in drama history, take part in drama productions, read scripts of plays to be reviewed, write features on plays and—for newspaper reviews—learn newspapering, especially spot news writing.

—William L. Hoffman, arts-entertainment editor, Albuquerque *Journal*

- Possibly take a college or university theater course and attend plays as often as possible. Knowing what's going on is only half the task, however; one must be able to write interestingly about what one has seen.
—Kenneth Shorey, movie and theater critic, Birmingham (Ala.) *News*

- Start as a sports reporter. I'm at least half serious when I say that. My point is that at the *Times* we consider our critics as men and women of the widest experience and, we hope, wisdom. And the way you acquire those qualities is by living intensely and long. How do you train to be President of the United States? Many routes are possible, and those which seem most direct are not always direct at all.
—William H. Honan, arts and leisure editor, New York *Times*

- READ, READ, READ—theater history; see every available play everywhere; train the mind to watch critically, engage the capacities needed; read the best criticism in the country; practice the art of writing in concise terms—in short, train the eyes and the mind.
—Sara Morrow, theater editor, Nashville *Banner*

Elements of a Review

Clive Barnes suggests that would-be critics ask themselves these questions that German poet Johann Wolfgang von Goethe expected literary critics to ask:

- What was the artist or author trying to do?
- How well did he or she do it?
- Was it worth doing?

Barnes adds a question for the critic to ask himself or herself: "'Did I have a good time, or didn't I?'—It's as simple as that."

Other critics discuss points a review should make and the direction the review should go:

- What happened? What's the quality of the experience? Increasingly, I've come to the view that a much neglected function of the critic is reporting. I want a critic to be a trusty scout out there looking and listening and recording the event itself as well as his or her own inner feelings. He should be part investigative reporter, too, seeking out the undiscovered. Then, too, of course, I want to know his or her expert opinion about whether it was any good, and if so, how so, and if not, how not.
—William H. Honan, arts and leisure editor, New York *Times*

- I agree with Lehman Engel (composer, author) when he says, "It seems to be possible that—without resorting to perjury or incriminating the reviewer himself or herself—reviews might be slanted toward the general group that would find satisfaction in a particular presentation."
—Kenneth Shorey, movie and theater critic, Birmingham (Ala.) *News*

- Is the show worth the price of admission? Does the production achieve what it sets out to do? Does the company meet its usual standards? What is exceptional or disappointing? Is the script dated? How have my reactions differed from the audience's?

—William L. Hoffman, arts-entertainment editor, Albuquerque (N.M.) *Journal*

- If a play is well known, concentrate on the performance only. If the presentation is of new material, concentrate on content, then the performance. Readers of a review are chiefly interested in whether to see the play.

—Sara Morrow, theater editor, Nashville *Banner*

Does Sara Morrow, in the review below, answer the basic question she proposes: Will the reader like the play?

Advent Theater's performance of *Period of Adjustment* is a keen disappointment.

First, this is not one of Tennessee Williams' better plays. Nor is it likely that Williams set this action in Nashville. Constant mention is made about the house being situated on a "subterranean cavern."

Where, in East Nashville, is a huge cavern? A simple deduction from program notes makes Williams two or three years old during the time he was in Nashville. How could this experience have made such a deep impression on his playwriting?

If Advent is to insist that the play is set here, why does Ralph say he invited his war-time buddy, George, who lives in Texas, to "come on down here?" Is Nashville "down" from Texas?

The set is designed functionally and artistically, but the Christmas motif seems odd at Eastertide. *Annie*, the New York hit show, gets away with this oddness, but the exquisite performance carries it off.

One serious fault (causing several to leave at the first intermission) is Miss Carole Lockwood's inaudibility. On the first few rows, she is probably understandable, but not so in the tenth. Miss Lockwood takes some awkward poses and does not handle her scenes of grief well. One is never sure whether she is laughing or crying about her wedding night fiasco. She spends the night, fully clothed, in a chair while shaking, unstable George gets in bed. Sobbing and weeping into a handkerchief does not cause the audience to cry instead—which should be the result of grief onstage.

The play is about two married couples who are having marital difficulties. Miss Lockwood, as Isabel, is married to George Haverstick, a role by Steve Simpson. The pair arrives in Nashville during a snowstorm to visit Ralph and Dottie Bates, who are portrayed by Tom Spillers and Laura Gardner. Dottie has left Ralph on Christmas Eve when the honeymooners arrive. Spillers' performance is loose and relaxed in a likeable way. Simpson's finger-stabbing, childish acting is both unpleasant and unconvincing.

The respective troubles of the pairs are illuminated in separate sequences. The action has no style and a serious lack of pace until Dottie's parents, by K. Lype O'Dell and Marian Baer, arrive to collect their daughter's belongings. The pace picks up and the audience wakes up to pay attention, especially when Ralph tells off his father-in-law, a loud-mouthed bigot.

If we hear "this is a period of adjustment" once, we hear it a dozen times. The playwright, in absentia, should hang his head in shame.

Director John Goings can make this a better performance if he will attend more to detail. One time, Miss Lockwood goes out to the car without a coat. Other times, she wraps up well for the snowy cold. Spillers says he will put on his shoes (he does) and go out to help with the bags. He stays in the house. The large bags are patently empty and lightweight when carried. Why not put some weight in them to make the scene valid?

Morrow also has some views on covering community theater:

> I do not believe that community theater and professional should be judged by the same standards. The first is an act of love; the second is performing for money. I get more tolerant about community theater, but when a company sets up as professional, I get pretty stern.

Some books useful to the drama critic include:

Freedley, George, and Reeves, John. *A History of the Theater.* New York: Crown, c. 1955, 1968.

Hartnoll, Phyllis. *The Oxford Companion to the Theater.* New York: Oxford University Press, 1951.
A dictionary.

Herbert, Ian, ed. *Who's Who in the Theater.* Detroit: Gale Research Co., 1981.

Hughes, Catharine, ed. *American Theatre Annual.* Detroit: Gale Research Co., 1980.
Play descriptions and excerpts from reviews.

Rigdon, Walter, ed. *The Biographical Encyclopedia and Who's Who of the American Theatre.* New York: James H. Heineman, Inc., 1966.

Willis, John. *Theater World.* Vol. 38. New York: Crown, c. 1983.
1981–82 season. Published annually.

New York Times Theater Reviews. New York: New York Times and Arno Press, 1920 to present.

MUSIC REVIEWING

Music reviewing is especially inviting as a journalism career. But again, unless you have an insatiable passion for music and are sure that music is the one thing you want to pursue, you should not enter the field. Robert C. Marsh, music critic of the Chicago *Sun-Times,* advises: "Lie down until the impulse goes away! The field is hopelessly overcrowded."

Music reviewing, in addition to requiring a wide appreciation of music, can be very demanding. How much work do you think went into this review of Verdi's opera, "La Traviata?"

Opera returned to Oklahoma City—colorfully, flamboyantly and lyrically—with the joint Tulsa Opera-Oklahoma Symphony Orchestra production of "La Traviata."

The production, the first ever collaboration between the Tulsa Opera and the Oklahoma Symphony and the first professional opera in five years in Oklahoma City, was witnessed by about 1,500 people Tuesday.

In spite of the major hardship of performing in the large and acoustically difficult Civic Center Music Hall, the cast was not miked and singers projected clearly and cleanly throughout the hall. And the minor orchestra chorus coordination problems in the first act had all but vanished by the conclusion of the opera.

For its production of Verdi's "La Traviata," the Tulsa Opera borrowed sets and costumes from a new Cincinnati Opera production. These were lush, 19th century gowns and suits and elegant, ornate furnishings.

Particularly spectacular was the third act masked ball with red and black Spanish costumes and a dark, cabana-like set seductively lit with many candelabras.

Conductor Judith Somogi, performing her second opera for Tulsa Opera (she debuted in 1976 with "The Ballad of Baby Doe"), capably coordinated orchestra and chorus. She led a dramatic and rhythmic "Traviata," emphasizing the opera's great romance and tragedy with sometimes off-guard and thrillingly rapid tempo and elsewhere, paces of sheer poignancy.

Especially Violetta's dying scene, in which the rhythms and vocal dynamics build to a wrenching crescendo, showed an understanding of Verdi's drama and showed off an exceptionally well-paced interpretation.

New York City Opera soprano Diana Soviero starred as the tragic heroine Violetta, a frail Parisian courtesan who falls in love with Alfredo, son of a nobleman, Germont. Germont orchestrates the dissolvement of the affair, discovering in the process his son's rash and bitter nature as well as Violetta's nobility.

Miss Soviero gave a touching, tragic performance, succeeding with both the saucy, freedom-loving nature of her character as well as her faithful, simple and doomed approach to love.

The soprano accomplished this largely by her successful transition from the high coloratura demands of the first act to the more emotional, dramatic singing the opera requires in the latter half. Also, her strong voice projected fully yet delicately throughout the hall.

English tenor John Brecknock was a rash and emotion-plagued Alfredo; his portrait worked nicely next to Miss Soviero's more rational, worldly Violetta.

Brecknock's singing was pure and smooth. His second act aria, "Wild My Dream," was a performance peak.

As Germont, Michael Devlin delivered his character's tenderness and humanity as well as the social snobbery. In the second act, where Germont persuades Violetta to leave his son for his family's honor, Devlin moved convincingly from an angered, righteous father to a man awed and humbled by the great honor of a frail woman.

"La Traviata" was an important performance for Oklahoma City, not only because the production was artistically excellent but for its implications for the future. . . .

Nancy Gilson, entertainment editor of the *Oklahoma* (Oklahoma City) *Journal,* explains just how much work went into this review.

I prepared for reviewing "La Traviata" by listening to several recordings (also I had seen several productions before). I also researched the

> opera in music and opera books. I was familiar with both the Oklahoma Symphony and Tulsa Opera, so I had some basis for criticizing the production in comparison with other works by the groups. Also, I did interviews with the conductor, soprano, opera director-manager and symphony conductor prior to the performance, and learned through this (approach) of special problems in the production.

Music—with its technical and intellectual side as well as ethnic and cultural—can lead the reviewer to write dully and over the heads of the general reader. Critics agree that the best writing is determined not by how erudite the writer might seem, but by how well the reader understands the article. Says Gene Grey, arts reporter for the *Evening Press* in Binghamton, N.Y.:

> I never try to write for the academic or musically knowledgeable person. First and foremost, I'm writing for a newspaper audience. That does not mean I write "down" to them; it merely means I try to avoid getting technical in a review.

Grey also offers advice on which concerts not to attend:

> Never go to a concert if you are patently disposed to dislike it. I never review hard rock, for example. A reviewer can be critical, and ought to be, but he or she also must have a basic liking of the art-form.

There's no doubt that Mary Ann Campbell, of the Medford (Ore.) *Mail Tribune*, likes music:

> The performance of Mozart's Requiem Mass in D Minor by the Rogue Valley Chorale in its spring concert this weekend marked a highlight in the Chorale's already distinguished record of fine concerts.
>
> With a quartet of impressive voices for the solo passages, the chorus showed its professional quality in such moving parts of the mass as the "Kyrie eleison, Christe eleison" double fugue at the beginning and in the majestic Sanctus, with its glorious fugue on the word "Hosanna."
>
> The soloists were Anne Turner Bunnell, soprano; Cathleen A. Long, contralto; Steve Simmons, tenor; and Nick Tennant, bass.
>
> In the moving Tuba mirum, accompanied throughout by the solo tenor trombone, the four voices blended and separated to provide beautiful music. Mrs. Bunnell's voice dominated and provided inspiration for the other singers, but Ms. Long and the men acquitted themselves expertly and with strong musical finesse.
>
> In the serenely beautiful Benedictus for solo quartet and chorus, Mrs. Bunnell led the triumphant joy expressed in the music.
>
> In the Agnus Dei at the end of the mass, Mrs. Bunnell again contributed a glorious musical passage in the Lux aeterna, and the final statement of promise of eternal rest, Requiem aeternam dona eis, showed a dramatic and moving contribution from the chorus.
>
> The rest of the program was devoted to two marvelously Romantic songs for men's chorus by Franz Schubert, a salute to spring for

women's voices by Claude Debussy, and another fine example of 19th century German Romanticism, Robert Schumann's "Zigeunerleben," a song of praise to the mysterious, fascinating life of the gypsies.

In the first of the two Schubert songs, "Widerspruch," or "Contradiction," the contrast between the overpowering sunset seen from a mountaintop and a tiny room is described.

The "Standchen," or Serenade, is a romantic conversation between the chorus and a solo soprano, in this case, Jo Ann Pilicler, who contributed a gentle lyricism to the love story. The "Salut Printemps" by Debussy gave the women's chorus an opportunity to show its abilities, but Karen Foster's soprano solo, though clear and light, showed a slight shrillness in the high notes and a small tremor occasionally.

Campbell adds:

This is an average review, just about the sort of concert usual in this area. I am not always so kind. If there are bobbles, I mention them. In this case, the soprano is very professional, and she appears with the Seattle Opera in the annual Ring Cycle and similar productions.

In music reviewing, there is room for the interpretative piece, for putting a certain work into perspective historically and culturally. Nelson George of the *Village Voice* in New York City put Lionel Richie in context:

To truly appreciate the rise of Lionel Richie and the bittersweet taste it has for some of his early fans, you have to go back to 1976, the year of the Commodores' first platinum album, when they were one of the best party bands in pop. Without the spiritual verbiage of Earth, Wind & Fire's Maurice White and the cosmic jive of P-Funk's George Clinton as media hooks, the Commodores were the black equivalent of Journey or REO Speedwagon—dedicated professionals whose group identity obscured their individuality, making them seem decidedly bland.

Throughout that era the Commodores maintained a delicate balance between thumping funk-rock tracks written collectively and Richie's growing sophistication as a ballad composer. Funk jams such as "Slippery When Wet," "Fancy Dancer," and the instrumental "Machine Gun" made Commodores' concerts big fun, with Richie and drummer Walter Orange exchanging lead vocals, and bassist Ronald LaPread, guitarist Thomas McClary, keyboardist Milan Williams, and trumpeter William King leaping about with the raunch & roll vigor you expect from six Southern boys on a Saturday night. Despite Richie's ballads, the group was very much a musical democracy. Richie never dominated the group the way White or Clinton did. When the Commodores were interviewed, Richie often had to squeeze comments between Orange and the loquacious King. The Commodores' real leader was the late Benny Ashburn, the Harlem-based manager who was father, brother, and boss man to them. Ashburn made the Commodores maintain their balance by preaching community, keeping egos in line, and fighting off the wolves who tear into the soul of every successful band. Equally significant was that Ashburn was one of the few truly independent black capitalists prospering in the music industry. For all the propaganda spewed forth about Earth, Wind & Fire and

P-Funk as exponents of black culture, both groups have been controlled by white managers, unlike the more superficially conservative Commodores.

But by 1977 Richie's slow-tempo love songs were superceding the funk, attracting older, more integrated audiences. With its slow modulation from quiet piano and vocal passages rising to crescendos of strings, horns, and choral harmonies, "This Is Your Life," from 1975's *Caught in the Act*, set the standard for subsequent Richie ballads like "Zoom," "Sweet Love," and "Just To Be Close To You," all still exciting fusions of country, soul, and MOR. Richie's voice, oozing with country melancholy, projected lyrics as sentimental and courtly as roses on the first date. The key to Richie's ballads isn't their undistinctive parts, but the gosh-darn wholesomeness of the whole. A Richie ballad is never sexy, occasionally romantic, and almost always incredibly nice. Richie has been the archetype for a new breed of black pop vocalists, singers who owe as much in vocal attack and material to MOR and adult contemporary as to soul. Listen to James Ingram, Stacy Lattisaw, Jeffrey Osborne, or the Peabo Bryson-Roberta Flack duet on "Tonight I Celebrate My Love" and you hear voices that aren't based on cliched reinterpretations of gospel music. This is a vision that encompasses Billy Eckstine, Sam Cooke, Jerry Butler, and Otis Redding's "Sitting on the Dock of the Bay"—not to mention Perry Como.

By the time of "Easy," a wonderfully realized Southern landscape in sound, and "Three Times a Lady," the ultimate testimony to the sweet and the sappy (and the start of a dull, dull period in Richie's writing), it was clear that Richie's early funk voice was just a facade. He wanted to be Kenny Rogers and didn't care how hokey that sounded. The Commodores' equilibrium was snapping. The break became irreparable on *Midnight Magic* with "Still" and "Sail On," two number-one ballads that made Richie's solo career inevitable. Soundwise they are completely different; "Still" has the ponderous strings and flowing French horns of MOR, while "Sail On" somehow fused corny chord changes, Latin percussion, and country into an inventive little "I'm hitting the road" song. Richie was hot now, but it wasn't until Orange injured his leg in an accident, postponing a national tour, that he had time to write "Lady" for Kenny Rogers. "Lady," an awesomely redundant song (see "Three Times a Lady"), got Richie the kind of establishment respect Motown acts have craved since the Supremes first played the Copacabana. In rapid succession Richie produced a lukewarm Kenny Rogers album; Rogers's high-powered manager Ken Kragen started seducing Richie; Ashburn's health began to deteriorate, and rumours of dissension within the Commodores family grew. Even after the terrible "Endless Love" Richie might have stayed closer to the Commodores if a heart attack hadn't felled Ashburn in 1982. The glue that had held the Commodores together was gone. So was a genuine black success story.

The Commodores hired another black manager, ex-television executive Chuck Smiley, and then spent a great deal of time in Europe, polishing a new stage show, writing new material, and seeking a voice. The logical choice is Orange, the lead singer on the single "Only You" and four other cuts on *13*, the Commodores' first full post-Richie album. He sounds good on the churning funk tune "Touchdown," but doesn't have the flexibility to front a band with the musical range of the Commodores. My choice is Harold Hudson, member of the Commodores' backing band, Mean Machine, cowriter with Richie of "Lady (You Bring Me Up)," and possessor of a cool, smart pop tenor. On "Painted Picture," a studio single released on a post-Richie greatest hits package, he impressed with control and tone. On *13*'s "I'm in Love," an excellent mid-tempo pop song with a sensitive, elaborate arrangement, "Turn Off the Lights," and "Welcome Home," Hudson gives the Commodores the freshness needed to mold a new personality.

Richie didn't need a new one. We

all knew his "gosh, golly gee" persona from *People*, *Jet*, and the Grammy Awards. What Richie did need after leaving the Commodores was some uptempo material with a pop sheen. "All Night Long (All Night)" from *Can't Slow Down* and "Serves You Right" and "You Are" from his self-titled debut greatly enlivened his performance at Radio City Music Hall two weeks ago. During Richie's last performance with the Commodores at Radio City, the ballads turned a once fiery funk band into Barry Manilow.

But Richie's bottom line is still ballads and *Can't Slow Down* showcases his best batch since *Midnight Magic*. While "Truly" was in the maudlin style of "Endless Love," here "Hello" takes that overblown approach in a more subtle direction. The arrangement is understated, highlighted by a tasty acoustic guitar bridge and a Carmichael string chart that supports one of Richie's best melodies. "Penny Lover," like "You Are" written with wife Brenda, is sung with Richie's customary commitment. The album's closer, and my personal favorite, "Stuck On You," sways with the Southern flavor of "Sweet Love" and "Easy." Richie, in an era when cynicism is fashionable, leads with his heart. I just wish it was still beating for the Commodores.

David Stabler, arts editor of the Anchorage (Alaska) *Daily News*, has a light touch and makes sure the reader knows what he is talking about:

You may have heard of the Fixx, but can you describe the band's music?

Those in the know, like David Oliver, say their music sounds like English rock 'n' roll with a funky beat.

"You don't have to rack your brains listening to heavy metal," he says. "It's very catchy. The guitar lines aren't screaming."

And, says the local record salesman, the group's two albums are popular with a cross section of people. "I sell them to people over 35, under 16, male, female."

The group's first album, "Shuttered Room," contained the songs "I Found You" and "Some People." On the second album, "Reach the Beach," released last year, the most popular songs were "One Thing Leads to Another" and "Saved by Zero."

The Fixx comes to the Sullivan Sports Arena with Mickey Thomas (lead singer with Jefferson Starship) and the Red Rockers for one concert at 7:30 p.m. Saturday. Tickets for Winter Jamm '83, produced by Ralph Streano and radio station KWHL-FM, are $17.50 and $18.50, on sale at the arena box office.

Earlier this year, Thomas put together a band called Little Gadget and the Soulful Twilites to sing rhythm and blues. "I thought it would give me a chance to get back to my roots, rekindle my original influences," he said in a recently published interview. Before joining Starship, Thomas sang with Elvin Bishop and a gospel singer named Gideon Daniels.

"I figure it will improve my performing with the Starship, because that's the kind of singing I do best," he said.

Joining Thomas and the Fixx are the Red Rockers, whose recent chart-hit "China" is from their album "Good as Gold." According to promoter Ralph Streano, the group appeared on "American Bandstand" last week.

Some useful books:

Apel, Willi, ed. *Harvard Dictionary of Music*. Cambridge, Mass.: Harvard University Press, 1969.

Cross, Milton, and Ewen, David. *Encyclopedia of the Great Composers and Their Music.* Garden City, N.Y.: Doubleday, 1962.

Ewen, David. *Ewen's Musical Masterworks.* New York: Arco Pub. Co., c. 1954, 1958.

Feather, Leonard. *The Encyclopedia of Jazz.* New York: Horizon Press, 1956.

See also *The Encyclopedia of Jazz in the Sixties* (1966) and *The Encyclopedia of Jazz in the Seventies* (1976).

Naha, Ed, comp. *Lillian Roxon's Rock Encyclopedia.* New York: Grosset & Dunlap, c., 1969, 1978.

Scholes, Percy. *The Oxford Companion to Music.* New York: Oxford University Press, 1950.

FILM REVIEWING

The Ideal Critic

Film critics were asked: "If you were the Creator and could create the best film critic in the world, what would he or she be like? Why?"

They responded that such a person would be:

- Honest. Period. That's all any critic has to offer—honesty in giving his or her opinion of a film.

  —Robert Butler, arts and entertainment editor, Kansas City *Star*

- A writer who has wit and taste—because quite a lot of film criticism written is a dreadful bore.

  —Carol Otten, film critic, San Diego *Union*

- A completely neutral intelligence without prejudice or preference or expectation. The critic would allow a film to explain what it sets out to do—make people laugh, cry, think, whatever. The critic to write an opinion as to whether it succeeds or not solely on that basis.

  —Susan Stark, Detroit *News*

- Above all, a person with an open mind, willing to examine different kinds of films on their own merits, without crossing off whole categories of work (experimental, documentary, and so on, which just don't interest many critics who should know better). Literate, committed, and more interested in understanding than just accumulating opinions.

  —David Sterritt, film critic, *Christian Science Monitor*

The Love of Film

The best film critics are those who love films, according to Roxanne Mueller of the Cleveland *Plain Dealer* and former film critic of the Ft. Wayne (Ind.) *Journal Gazette*. And Pauline Kael, critic of *The New*

Yorker magazine for years, once observed that her success as a film critic was due to her sympathy toward all films.

Mueller says:

> I like them all. Even the rotten ones. Some are so awful, they're almost good as camp or melodrama. A bad critic is one who does not love film.
>
> If all you read in a review is a summary of the movie, then you know that person (1) doesn't have much interest in the movie or (2) doesn't know how to write. Bad critics might spend all of the space downgrading the movie. They might play up themselves in the review. A bad critic might not pay attention to the movie and just comment on the stale popcorn.

There are, of course, times when the movie theater itself dominates the experience because of falling plaster, rowdy crowds, and children urinating in the aisle (as one Detroit critic once noted). Responsibility to the public sometimes may require more be said about the theater than the film.

Some find it helpful, if possible, to look at all the available reviews (in magazines or other papers) before writing. Others work independently, consulting nothing. A good compromise is to read nothing ahead of time, see the production without any prior opinion, and form an opinion on the basis of one's own experience, but afterwards, before writing, read reviews and other clippings (as time permits). You will have already formed an opinion, but the reading of other works might temper your view or open up some new vistas with which to interact before you actually write. This approach allows the best of both worlds: independent judgment and judgment in comparison to the judgments of others.

Mueller adds: "Before starting to write, think out the theme of the movie in your own mind." She begins her reviews with attention to the basic theme. Then she deals with "style" or techniques of the movie, then the acting, the script, and the "look" of the film (the visual impact).

"The purpose of any film is to entertain," she says. "Look at the movie, and decide if it achieves that. If style takes away from the plot and deadens the main point—if the director is more interested in the camera angle—then the director has definitely failed."

What a Film Says

Reviewers can go beyond the theme to ask what a film means. Few reviewers attempt what might be called a "message" review, but film, as art, often says something important.

Consider the attention to "message" in these three reviews:

Few films have ever been so unrelentingly preoccupied with death as "Last Tango in Paris," which is scheduled to open to a reserved seat only audience at the Studio 8 next week.

And hardly is there a movie more preoccupied with symbolism. Every gesture, every word in this Bernardo Bertolucci film hints of something, namely death and loss of identity. The viewer is led to speculate at what point identity and involvement in life itself invite death.

The story centers on Marlon Brando, as Paul, whose wife has just committed suicide, and newcomer Maria Schneider, as Jeanne. In the film, she plans to marry a young film producer who is more concerned with capturing her every emotion on film than understanding her.

Brando and Schneider meet as both are looking for an apartment, and join up in the spooky, zombie-like apartment for a week.

Brando, in shock and crying at times because of his wife's death, wants no names. In a very humorous scene, the two imitate the sounds of nameless jungle animals, and Brando asks: "What was your last name again?" and the answer is more jungle gibberish.

The two act out and unmask death wishes, all the while yearning for some hope and meaning in life.

With its interest in death and steady use of symbols, "Tango" may be, as some viewed Federico Fellini's "La Dolce Vita" of nearly 15 years ago, one of the most religious movies ever made.

In fact, Bertolucci seems to borrow scenes from "La Dolce Vita," as he does from many other movies going all the way back to the '20's.

In La Dolce Vita, a young man, despairing of meaning after his revelries, tried to call across a gap to a beautiful angelic girl, but could not cross the gap.

In "Tango," Schneider, as Jeanne, the young Parisian girl in childlike floppy hat, calls across subways to her fiance, the young movie producer who sees her as only a figure to frame on his film. And she talks across great rooms in the apartment to Brando.

Death stalks Schneider, even in her memories of childhood. She returns to her home, pauses by the grave of her dog, and later climbs under a table, as if it's a smaller tomb.

Death stalks Brando. Even the camera appears dead as he dialogs with his dead wife who's in a coffin. The camera for long periods does not move, as dead as the first cameras set on stages at the start of filmmaking. Yet Bertolucci, as in his "Prima della Rivoluzione," and other films, suddenly zooms in backward, from a closeup at times to capture a thought, and frame it, usually some expression of death.

Bertolucci borrows a classic comedy gag from Buster Keaton's 1927 film, "Steamboat Bill, Jr." In "Steamboat," a life-preserver is tossed off of a rickety steamboat and the life-preserver sinks—a comedy gesture about the state of the ship.

In "Tango," a life-preserver tossed into a park pond sinks, too, and gets a few half-hearted laughs, but not any guffaws as with Keaton, for here even this little gesture is a symbol of death.

"I've had enough of death," says Brando's mother-in-law in grief.

But Bertolucci never stops with his death images. Brando cleans up the blood in the bathtub from his wife's suicide, ghostlike sheets cover furniture in the apartment, he jokes with a dead rat and torments Schneider with it, the dance-hall figures at the end are all like corpses in a wax museum, and they move stiffly, more reminiscent of Fellini's grotesqueness with life.

The sets recall Ingmar Bergman's contrast and simplicity, with figures on the floor in a great plain room, or at the side by a small lamp next to a great expanse of darkness.

There is no meaning or happiness "until you look death in the face," intones Brando, "until you find a womb of fear."

"Your solitude weighs on me, you know," says Schneider. "You know, I feel like I am talking to a wall."

And walls there are in this film.

Always towering walls, so much higher than human figures. The walls in the rented apartment are higher than life. Brando hits walls in desperation with his fists, and his suicide wife had tried to tear wallpaper off of the walls before she died.

On the street, even the walls around construction sites are gigantic, much larger than in real life.

And never does the camera look down, until the tragic ending, from a balcony onto rooftops.

Schneider intones a litany . . . "I don't know who he is . . . I don't know his name . . ." and she repeats it, over and over again. . . .

—Detroit *Free Press*

DETROIT, Mich.—"The Godfather" is not just a glorified gangbuster movie about a post-World War II era of mobster rubouts.

In its highly stylized, meticulous concern with the life of one man and his family, it is the story of any human being seeking control, power and expression.

Specifically, it deals with ambition and quest for power in an underworld, mob setting and was based on the best-selling novel by Mario Puzo.

At the beginning, Marlon Brando as Don Corleone, head of the family, makes it clear that his thoughts are in the best of American rags-to-riches tradition. He even labels his actions very American.

Actor Brando himself has described the film as dealing with the broad concept of "The Corporate Mind." Author Puzo generalizes his intent with a quote from Balzac at the front of the novel: "Behind every great fortune there is a crime."

Puzo might have added that also behind absolute power and secrecy there is crime.

The killing by men like the Corleones, whom some will consider good men, God-fearing men and churchgoers, also raises the comparison to "good" modern nations and their vague undeclared wars.

In some respects, the Corleones are much more likeable than politicians who acquiesce in the deaths of war, not only indirectly through unknown soldiers but through faceless means such as bombing.

In the movie, the Corleones know why they are killing. Murder becomes deeply personal, and given their rules of the game, the Corleone decisions are deeply justified.

Thus through their eyes you can see how power in the hands of mobsters or in governments or in church dominions have justified killings. . . .

Wherever there is an institution . . . there is something to learn from "The Godfather."

The film comes out more symbolic than the book, particularly at the end where the reluctant Michael, heir to the godfather's kingdom, agrees to be the religious godfather for his sister's child. And shortly afterwards, he has the child's real father murdered.

During the church baptismal scene, as the priest asks if Satan has been properly renounced, and the mobster godfather, Michael, repeats the pledges of faith, the camera switches back and forth catching glimpses of neatly planned executions: the murder of the remaining individuals who pose a threat to Michael Corleone's power.

Ritual imposed or ritual life is a weave of rituals, and the varying shades of rituals converge. Baptism as the film points out is a preparation for death.

Those who are personally troubled with the relation of good or evil, how God can appear to be bad and allow death, while loving men and blessing him on the other hand—will find ground for reflection here.

How Michael, the talented, the good, the outsider in the family, with no taste for the family business, becomes involved in the killings and is eventually the king-pin, is a riddle to contemplate.

For he starts toward his evil end by good motives—a deep love for his dad and a desire to revenge his father's would-be killers.

—Detroit *Free Press* and *Miami Herald*

In *The Moon in the Gutter*, Jean-Jacques Beineix defies the laws of physics by placing an atmosphere inside a vacuum.

The feat is accomplished with all the verve and technical panache one would expect from a filmmaker who made a stunning international debut last year with *Diva*. But in the final analysis, *The Moon in the Gutter* is the victim of its own emptiness and Beineix's unwillingness to devote as much attention to the probing of his characters as he does to the milieu that they inhabit. It is not difficult to understand the reception accorded Beineix's movie at the Cannes Film Festival last spring. There were both cheers and jeers, and the movie was even disparaged by its star, Gerard Depardieu.

The Moon in the Gutter is the kind of film that resists any label. It attempts to fuse elements of late 19th-century romanticism with existentialism, which are not views of life one generally finds advanced in the same movie. The results are daring, gorgeous to look at and exasperating.

Beineix has spoken of liberating the language of film from the conventions of literature. In *The Moon in the Gutter*, he is groping toward a new form of expression, but he has nothing noteworthy to say. The movie is an adaptation of the 1953 novel by David Goodis, an American writer who enjoys a bigger following in France than in the United States.

Its dreamlike locale is described as "in a port nowhere in particular, in a dead end in the dockside area." The opening sequence proclaims the eerie power and the basic problem of the film. A young woman, her heels clicking on a deserted sidewalk, hurries down an alley. A man, his shoes tapping in menacing counterpoint, follows. She is next seen sprawled and lifeless on the sidewalk. Her blood seeps from razor-inflicted wounds and spills into the gutter where it mingles with the scummy water.

It is a tremendous beginning, both as an exercise in tension and an image of beauty and innocence defiled. What ensues is a disappointment. The woman is the sister of a stevedore, Gerard (played by Depardieu), who becomes obsessed with finding the murderer and avenging her death. The police, having scant interest in the human flotsam washed up at this port, close the case. Gerard comes nightly to the scene of the crime and stares at the fading bloodstain on the pavement as if it were a blot upon his honor.

He lives with an insufferable family and a very jealous girlfriend. At night he adjourns to a sleazy cafe where the main dish is despair, and the chief exercise of the clientele is to look on glumly as the clouds form in their glasses of Pernod. One of the customers is a slumming, rich alcoholic named Newton Channing, who comes to the docks to wallow in his failure and make cryptic remarks. Gerard's suspicions focus on him.

Two of the protagonists in *The Moon in the Gutter* are thus prisoners of the kind of depression that is so extreme that the victim is unaware of it. The movie itself becomes suffused with their ennui, and the only thing keeping the audience from succumbing is Beineix's active camera and sensuous imagery. These come into play when Channing's sister (Nastassia Kinski) makes an erotic entrance into the movie and quickens Gerard's interest.

I take the title of the movie to indicate the ray of hope that penetrates into the unrelieved gloom of Gerard's life as well as a metaphor for the two worlds that meet in the film. The other images Beineix lavishes upon this frail story really don't mean very much. They are both striking and ephemeral.

Beineix did much more with obsession and impossible love in *Diva*. In *The Moon in the Gutter* he reminds us that he has talent to burn but shows us that it could be put to better use.

—Desmond Ryan, *Philadelphia Inquirer*

The noted critic Pauline Kael searches for a meaning in film but does not divorce meaning from technique. Unless the art form and the theme(s) work together to form one effective tapestry, she is content to hold back in her judgments, as in her review of "Le Boucher," a moving tragic story of love and murder, a film that has deeply moved other critics. Note how she treats the movie as a whole, as she expresses her reservations:

Claude Chabrol's *Le Boucher* has everything but what ultimately counts. Back in 1948, Alexandre Astruc predicted that artists would be able to express themselves in films as they do in essays or novels; he called the coming age the age of *camera-stylo*, when directors would use the camera as writers use a pen. That is indeed how Chabrol uses his medium, and he has the grace and fluency of a master, but, unfortunately, *Le Boucher* is penmanship, not literature. In *Le Boucher*, as in *La Femme Infidele*, there's a remarkable consistency of tone; everything seems on the same level of interest to Chabrol—the vase of flowers that balances a composition, a wedding scene, a funeral (the bride's) in the rain, the look of schoolchildren in a Cro-Magnon cave, the cinematographer Jean Rabier's Perigord landscapes. Perhaps Chabrol gives a shade more than his usual decorous, unblinking gaze to the numerous eating scenes, and there's a leg of lamb that the butcher brings to his beloved like a bouquet, but nothing in the movie is very exciting, just as nothing is boring.

You know that Chabrol knows exactly what he's doing as he shows us the beautiful loner schoolteacher (Stephane Audran) who has been hurt in love and doesn't want to risk another hurt, and the butcher (Jean Yanne) who hated his butcher-father and went into the Army for fifteen years. And the serenely quiet village is a perfect storybook setting for murder. Everything in the movie is just about perfect. Chabrol was once the coauthor of a book on Alfred Hitchcock; now his films are like a learned but slightly dense aesthete's commentaries. He provides all the elements for a thriller except the kicker. He seems to cherish the atmospheric elements without quite getting the point of them; Hitchcock used them to prepare us for something. Chabrol makes tone poems on thriller themes. The ambiguities fabricated for the come-on have become the essence; for Chabrol, the atmosphere is everything. Even the one thriller centerpiece—a corpse on a cliff above a children's picnic drips blood on a little girl and she asks if it's raining, and then the blood falls on the bun she's eating—is such a recognizable piece of Hitchcockery that it seems a homage. One can see how Chabrol thinks—he is more interested in the personalities involved in murders, and in the ambience, than in the crude simplicities of whodunit and why. But as the inscrutable characters do not have any more depth or complexity than the characters in a typical thriller, what one gets has neither the zings of a thriller nor the richness of art.

The acting, too, is remarkably even. Stephane Audran and Jean Yanne seem unforced—incarnations rather than performers. Miss Audran (who is Chabrol's wife) has the elegance of a goddess but no range; her acting is a function of beauty, not of soul, and perhaps her husband's camera is too consciously adoring. Her beauty has become almost the subject of this film, and she isn't quite spiritual enough for that. Jean Yanne, a television talk-show host whom Godard induced to turn actor to play the aggressive, self-centered husband of *Weekend* (the man cannibalized by his luscious wife), is astutely cast here, because he suggests a man whose civilization is something put on, like a workman's Sunday clothes. But the melancholy of this unhappy pair and the perhapses that are the substance of the story—perhaps killing is the butcher's only release for his feelings, perhaps the schoolteacher might have saved him from committing murders if she had not been so fearful of a new love, and so on—are just faintly titillating hints, and the hints don't develop into recognitions. The film's point of view is so flexible that it doesn't seem to matter whether the movie is saying she could have saved him or saying nothing.

A director who uses the camera as fluently as if it were a pen may settle down (perhaps for a period) to being a minor master, turning out movies like the annual output of a detective-fiction writer. Chabrol's restrained surface blocks off the passions that cause murder, and in recent years nothing new seems to have come into his world. In film after film, one waits for Chabrol's revelations. At the end of *Le Boucher*, one doesn't feel cheated, exactly, but feels: Is that all?[1]

Creative Wrap-ups

Reviewers have some techniques for doing "wrap-ups" of the myriad films. Vincent Canby of the New York *Times* decided to use a travel motif and described all the places you could "visit" by seeing the current crop of films, including the latest wide-wheeling James Bond movie.

Ernest Leogrande of the New York News Service decided to discuss nonverbal language when a caveman flick came out:

You don't have to know the language to follow the conversation in *Quest for Fire*. As a matter of fact, before the movie was made, nobody knew its language.

This adventure tale about the dawn of man is one of a rare breed, a movie that sets out to tell its story in a way that will not need a translator. The fact that *Quest for Fire* has played in Paris, Rome and New York with the dialogue exactly the same is proof that it works.

By the end of the movie, though, if you don't know that *atra* means "fire," you have not been paying attention. This key word and others impress themselves on you the way strange words like *droog* ("friend") and viddy ("to see") did in the 1971 movie *A Clockwork Orange*. There is a link to this. The language for both was devised by writer Anthony Burgess.

Certain similarities have been pointed out between *Quest for Fire* and last year's *Caveman*, but the latter, starring Ringo Starr, was played for laughs all the way through and its made-up language was deliberately crude: only about a dozen words that included such obvious ha-ha's as *ca-ca* and *zug-zug*.

The famous *One Million B.C.*, made in 1940, and its remake, the 1966 *One Million Years B.C.*, used grunts and groans rather than vocabulary to get across their stories of prehistoric man and woman, but today they are remembered primarily for the fights with animated animals and the displays of cheesecake and beefcake: Carole Landis and Victor Mature in the former, Raquel Welch and—well, what was his name?—in the latter.

Quest for Fire has its flaws, like most of us. Nevertheless, it aims at being both enlightening and entertaining, trying to demonstrate some of the stages by which man learned to be human, which includes both making fire and making love. Desmond Morris, zoologist, behavioral theorist and author of *The Naked Ape*, was hired to create physical movements that would distinguish the evolution of the primates and be a form of communication for them. Burgess' assignment was to create a basic spoken vocabulary and grammar for the Ulam people, who are the central figures in the movie.

Burgess went back to a language called Indo-European, which existed more than 50,000 years ago, a language that acted as a tributary for the Romance and Germanic languages of today. Burgess' *A Clockwork Orange*, which appeared first as a novel, contained a language he called Nadsat, created from Russian, rhyming cockney slang and the sort of combination words that Lewis Carroll was fond of making up.

Another ambitious artificial language was created by Ruth Rose for the 1933 *King Kong*. She mapped out a language for the inhabitants of Skull Island, where Kong lived, patterned after the language on the island of Palau Nias in the Indian Ocean. (*Kow bisa para Kong! Dana, tebo malem na hi?* translates as "A gift for Kong! Strangers sell woman to us?" The Hays censorship office insisted on a translation of all this dialogue to make sure no indecencies slipped by.

It is rare, however, for anyone to get this involved in writing a new vocabulary for the screen. Most of the time it is only fragments, such as the unforgettable *Klaatu barada nikto*! from the 1951 *The Day the Earth Stood Still*.

Going without a recognizable language is not an appealing experiment in today's moviemaking psychology, where the choice is either subtitles or dubbing. Don't bring up Mel Brooks' 1976 *Silent Movie*, either; although the movie had exactly one spoken word, mime Marcel Marceau's "No," the narrative would not exist without the explicit title cards.

I would rather bestow my praise on a high-risker called *The Thief*, filmed in 1952, when studios were meeting the threat of television with super-stretch screens, stereophonic sound, three dimensions and even some basic smelloramas. This drama, starring Ray Milland, Rita Gam and Martin Gabel, was about a scientist who passed nuclear secrets to a "subversive power" and then had a change of heart. It dared to be experimental by being simple, telling its story only through facial expressions and background noises.

The Thief was not a critical success, but it went down in film history books with these words: Good try.

New ways of looking at God were presented in a round of science-fiction and fantasy films in 1983, an occasion for a topical discussion of film in *USA Today*:

"The grandfather and father images of God don't do anything for me," says Lenny Starck, 17, a high school student from Barryton, Mich. "God is more of a spirit, like The Force in *Star Wars* and *The Return of the Jedi*. In those movies, God is like all-powerful in the universe, and that is how God is on Earth. Nothing can stand up to that."

Seven-year-old Mark Ksiazek of St. Paul, Minn., sees God in much the same way. "When Ben (Obi-Wan Kenobi) goes 'Run! Run!' to Luke and you can't see him, it makes me think about God, cause you can't see God and you just hear him."

The old ways of looking at God—conjuring up images of a hoary-bearded old patriarch—are changing. And the direction of that change is being influenced in no small part by today's popular fantasy and science fiction films.

"In our church, kids see God as anything but the grandfather type," says the Rev. Walter Pulliam, minister of the Judson Baptist Church in Minneapolis. "They see God as a force, and if not as a force, then a kind of spirit from *E.T.* visiting the Earth. And we utilize these themes from these movies in our teaching."

The Force in *Star Wars* and the kindly E.T. are not the only new movie symbols that evoke the attributes of God. For instance, in *Krull*, Prince

Colwyn climbs to the top of a sacred mountain, where he receives a blessing and a weapon in a scene reminiscent of Moses on Mount Sinai. And generals in *War Games* stand in awe before an altarlike super-computer that, reacting to human error, is ready to destroy the world.

Far from causing a storm of protest by theologians anxious to preserve a "God-the-father" image, the new, movie-spawned conceptions of God seem to have won the clergy's approval.

"These new movies are good because they're symbolic of a transcendent being and the power of God in life today," says Pulliam, who also is president of the Ministers Council of the American Baptist Churches, USA. "And in these movies, the spirit of transcendence brings goodness and wholeness."

The mysterious forces in many of today's films emphasize that the ultimate power is a spirit, adds the Rev. Earl D. C. Brewer of the Candler School of Theology in Atlanta. And the computer—another of today's popular movie themes—can be symbolic of God. "We've already endowed the machine with divinity, no question about it," he says. "We've endowed the computer with intelligence and control ability, both characteristics of divinity."

Rabbi David Wortman, executive director of the Board of Rabbis of Greater Philadelphia, agrees that the new movie mythologies have some value. "Some of these things can be used in talks and seminars. People can relate to them."

"We are seeing a revival of theology under a different name: *E.T.*, *Star Wars*, *War Games*, *Superman*, whatever," observes Rabbi James Rudin, director of interreligious affairs for the American Jewish Committee in New York. "In each of these movies there is profound religious value at the heart, imparted in a positive way. They raise the issues of the universe: why we are here, what's our purpose, what's our role in the universe."

Among books on film:

Armour, Robert A. *Film: A Reference Guide*. Westport, Conn.: Greenwood Press, 1980.

Cowie, Peter, ed. *International Film Guide*. New York: A. S. Barnes, 1964.
Selected biographies and information on films of important directors, festivals, and awards.

Gertner, Richard, ed. *International Motion Picture Almanac*. New York and London: Quigley Publishing Co., 1983.
A compendium of facts and addresses.

Halliwell, Leslie. *The Filmgoer's Companion*. New York: Hill and Wang, 1967.
A dictionary of people, films, settings, and themes.

Halliwell, Leslie. *Halliwell's Film Guide*. New York: Scribner's, 1980.
Survey of 8,000 English language movies.

Knight, Arthur. *The Liveliest Art*. New York: Macmillan, c. 1957.
Reprinted in paperback by the New American Library, New York, n.d.

Kuhns, William. *Movies in America*. Dayton, Ohio: Pflaum, 1972.
A pictorial history.

Michael, Paul, ed. *The American Movies Reference Book*. Englewood Cliffs, N.J.: Prentice-Hall, 1967.

Sarris, Andrew. *The American Cinema: Directors and Directions, 1929–1968.* New York: E. P. Dutton, 1968.

New York Times Film Reviews. New York: New York Times and Arno Press, 1913 to present.

Useful magazines include *Film Journal* (1600 Broadway, New York, N.Y. 10019) and *Filmfacts* (P.O. Box 69610, West Station, Los Angeles). Both of these provide the full cast listing for each new movie—information that must be checked in a review. *Variety,* (154 W. 46th St., New York, N.Y. 10036), *Hollywood Reporter,* (6715 Sunset Blvd., Hollywood, Calif. 90028), *Billboard,* (1515 Broadway, New York, N.Y. 10036), and others help you to keep up with the developments in the industry, and they sometimes give the locations for the shootings of new movies (it always makes a fun story to drop in on a film in progress during your vacation or other travels).

Notes

[1]Pauline Kael, *Deeper Into Movies* (Boston: Little, Brown and Co., c. 1969, 1972), pp. 403–405.

Assignments

1. Go as a group to one production; write reviews immediately afterwards without discussion. Compare reviews in class with the professional review in the newspaper.
2. Hold a competition for the best review during the term or semester, with a local professional critic as judge.
3. Identify through the alumni or information office of your school one graduate who is now an entertainer, actor, or actress of some note. Contact that person (using a *Who's Who* address if the address is not forthcoming from the university offices). Present a list of questions prepared by the class. If and when the questions are answered, submit them as a Question and Answer article to the student newspaper or other publication.
4. Examine many reviews over a period of time—two or three weeks. Collect 20 reviews, each of them being of a different type. Create your own classification (for example, classified by kinds of humor, by use of topics treated, or by political or ideological tone or message). Present these in a booklet with table of contents.
5. Research and write up a review on the best movie you have ever seen; do the same for the worst.

6. Write advance biographical material—one page each—on the composers, film directors, and playwrights now represented in the entertainment field in your town or area. As a second assignment, do a review using this material.
7. Study the writings of one reviewer for several weeks. Write a critique column on that reviewer as if it were for a monthly magazine.
8. Go as a class to a production, with each student assigned to do an article on a different subject. Several could do interviews (with cast, projectionist, or conductor); others could deal with the audience, the setting (both stage and decor of building), the history of the production or the genre, the social or other implications of the production, the lighting, and current trends and how the production fits in.
9. Make a booklet of reviews that are all on the *same* film or production. See the production yourself. Write a three-page assessment of only the reviews you have collected.

San Diego (Calif.) *Tribune* Reporter Preston Turegano consults with Assistant City Editor Janette Mitchel. Photo by Joe Holly, San Diego (Calif.) *Union Tribune*

PART 5

Miscellaneous Writing

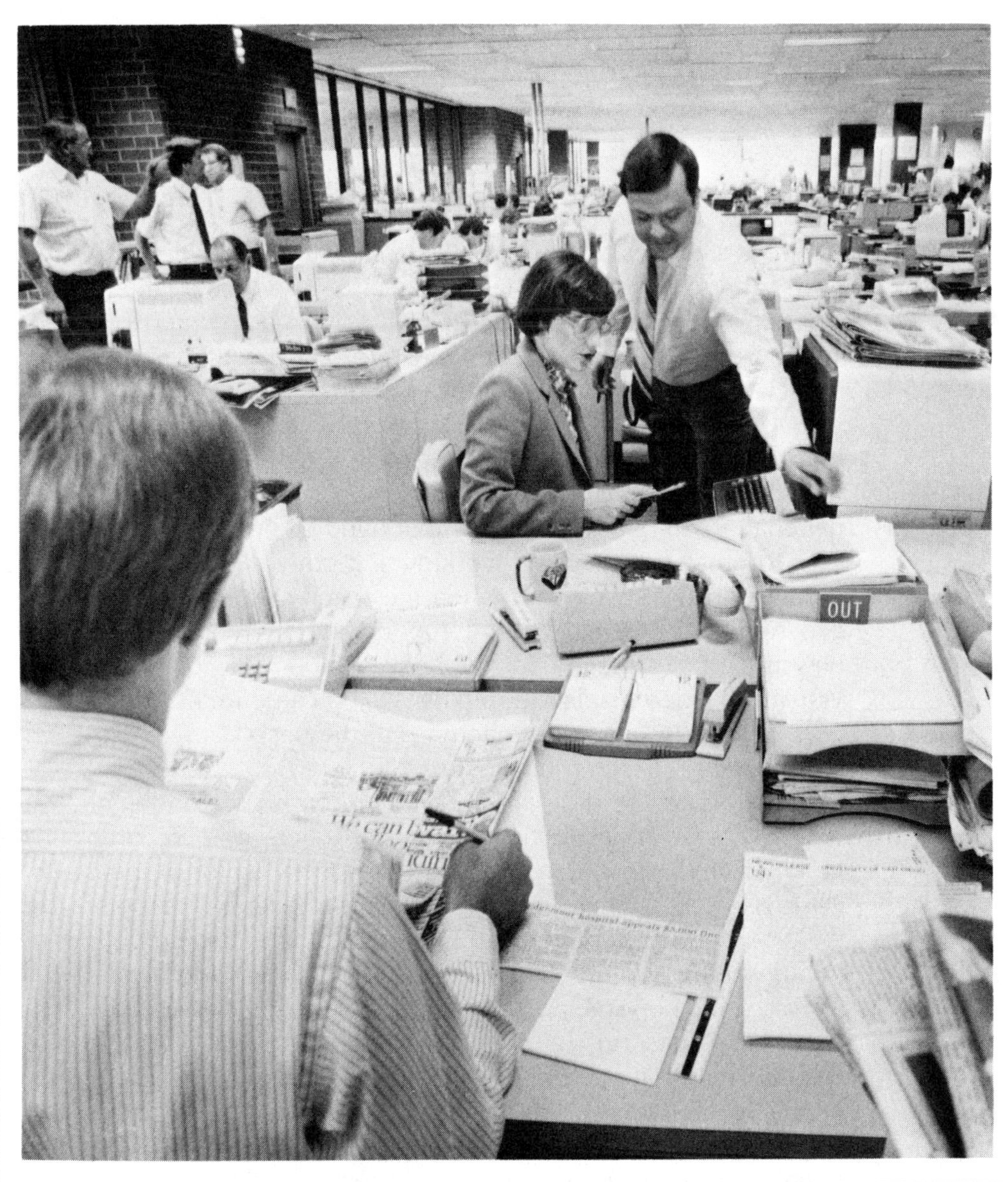

18

Writing at the Rim: The Copy Desk

An important location at a newspaper is the copy desk. On many newspapers, the "desk," shaped like a "U" and called the rim, has a slot person or a chief copv editor who sits at the center. This person supervises the writing of headlines and picture cutlines or captions, as well as supervising the editing of copy.

A senior desk person may lay out the front page after consultation with top editors. A "universal" desk is one through which all news copy flows. Larger papers have special desks—sports, features, national, foreign, and lifestyle—that handle copy for special areas.

You may find yourself working at a copy desk on your first job, perhaps on the swing shift when the regular staff is not there. Desk experience sharpens a future reporter's skills and, indeed, many newspapers put their reporters back on the desk for short periods. When the video display terminals (VDTs) came in, many staff members learned to use these machines at the desk as they jostled copy around with the electronic keyboard.

Writers on the rim can have a major influence on the quality of newswriting. "Good writing, no matter where it is prepared, is still good writing," says Alan Buncher, chief copy editor of the St. Louis *Post-Dispatch*. "Rim editors, like their comrades on the other side of the city room, are encouraged to take the stuffiness and dullness out of our writing. We think that is what readers want and need."

At some newspapers, in addition to editing, desk people handle typeblocks (descriptive paragraphs that go with photo features), weather information, promos (newspaper promotion items), blurbs, liftouts (paragraphs or sentences taken out of a story and repeated in larger type for layout and attention purposes), and a regular column of tidbits about famous people.

THE "CATCH-ALL" PEOPLE COLUMNS

There is a certain sameness in the "people" columns that have become popular in prime news space in major newspapers. The way one person writes for one of these sections would probably work for others. Depending largely on wire photos as well as wire copy, the columns in different papers look alike. In the Dallas *News*, one people column was topped by a photo of "Minnie Mouse" kissing band leader Count Basie. The cutline says: "Band leader Count Basie gets a kiss from Minnie Mouse" in celebration of Basie's 75th birthday. In Minneapolis, the *Tribune* topped its people column with the same picture: "Band leader Count Basie got a kiss. . . ."

The Minneapolis *Tribune*, the Dallas *News*, the Chicago *Tribune*, and many other papers call the corner column "People." The Washington *Post* calls its column "Personalities"; the Detroit *Free Press*, "Names and Faces"; the Philadelphia *Inquirer* and Los Angeles *Times*, "Newsmakers"; and the New York *Times*, "Notes on People." The tabloids (half-size papers) tend to give a whole page to the people briefs—the New York *Post* calls its full page "Page Six," which has its own staff. The tabloid Philadelphia *Daily News* has a "People" page with a corner, "Names in the News."

Typical of middle size papers, the *Courier-Post* in Camden, N.J., calls its column "People," places it on the second page along with other personality stories, includes six to eight one-paragraph items in a box, and moves the box around the page from day to day.

One person on the copy desk—Laurie Stuart—handles the *Courier-Post* column. When she begins work at night, she looks at the Associated Press wire material. A VDT, which makes looking through stacks of paper unnecessary, eases this task. She "scrolls" along the wire copy on the VDT with its TV-like screen and picks out suitable material. She also uses a syndicated service from *US* magazine.

From these, she selects what she might use for the morning paper. Later, she whittles down the material until she has six to eight items. Since she must limit each item to one paragraph, she rewrites each piece from copy that may be as long as 40 lines. "What I have when I'm finished is the essence of the story," she said. Because she rewrites the material, she receives a byline at the bottom of the box.

The Wilmington (Del.) *Morning News*, a member of the same Gannett newspaper chain as the Camden paper, uses another approach. Rather than having one person in charge of the column, it staggers the job among the people on the copy desk. One desk person handles the duties for three nights before the job switches to the next person.

The *Morning News* calls its column "People in the News" and includes six to eight two-inch stories. Relying on editing paragraphs, this paper does not rely on rewriting as much material as the *Courier-Post*. The Wilmington paper uses material from the New York *Times* Press Service and the AP.

The *Morning News* column appears at the beginning of the second section. Other articles on the page are personality-oriented and include some offbeat material. "It's known around here as the 'flake' page," said Evelyn Nilsson of the paper's copy desk. "The page has a certain personality. It's the kind of page people turn to while riding on the bus or train." Nilsson said that when she has charge of the column, she likes to balance it with stories on different kinds of personalities and not have white males predominate.

On the Wichita *Eagle*, the copy desk prepares a "catch-all" column about people based on wire copy each evening for the morning editions. The responsibility of this column rotates between three or four persons, with each one doing it on a different day. The idea is to break up the routine, give each person a chance to be creative, and add variety to the column from day to day.

With the miscellaneous people column, the principle of news as conversation works well—what will people talk about? Certainly such items as the President, the President's family, odd happenings to unfamiliar people, coincidences, where people formerly in the news are now, a movie star's unknown hobby—in short, the gossipy or gee-whiz side of the news. Says Alan Buncher, chief copy editor of the St. Louis *Post-Dispatch*: "These [items] are written in the language that people speak, not the way they write. It's breezy, easy to read, enjoyment-reading."

Some of the considerations a desk person would follow in writing people items:

1. ***Keep a singleness of idea.*** There isn't room in a short item to tell a person's whole life story.
2. ***Be brief.*** A few sentences or paragraphs at the most are sufficient.
3. ***Put names at top of the item,*** in the first line if possible. The reader should see clearly the shift from one person to the next. If the name appears too far down in the item, the reader may not make the transition from the previous paragraph. To facilitate reading, the names also often appear in boldface type, inviting a quick once-over so the reader can elect to read about whomever he or she wants.
4. ***Be picture wise.*** Select some items about people whose pictures might be in the newspaper "morgue," or files. Such "mug" shots enliven a column. Ideally each column should have at least one good action picture to provide visual relief.

5. ***Look for humorous items and material on human foibles:*** the youngster who outsmarts the scientist, the mother-in-law who gets her comeuppance, the miser who built a playground for children, or the sad clown who laughed by mistake.
6. ***Don't overwork the same celebrities.*** Everything that Princess Diana or Prince Andrew, perennial candidates, Presidents, and ex-Presidents do seems to get into the news, but at some point too much is too much.
7. ***Watch out for really old material.*** While no time limits exist for items that go into people column folders, journalists should be careful not to hold them too long. Dating each item as it goes into a folder helps to keep it in perspective. Using an item two weeks after it appears in other papers reduces a column's credibility. In one instance the person was already dead, but the unaware journalist used information buried in a folder.
8. ***Plan the column.*** Lay out the items in the order you want to use them. Apply whatever organizing principle you think will work; for example, grouping items on the same subject or items that elicit the same emotional response, such as those that bring fear—or laughter.
9. ***Hook items together with transitions.*** For example, you could follow an article on twins with an item on quadruplets: "Twin twins—or quadruplets—it was in Buenos Aires, . . ." or the 1984 item—reported by the Associated Press—about the woman in Rio de Janeiro who gave birth to her tenth set of twins.

   Says James Siepman, copy desk chief of the Milwaukee (Wis.) *Sentinel*:

   > Look for combinations, such as new jobs, retiring and resigning, day in court, the sick list, [but] avoid the trap of using an item just because it fits into a combination or offers one more "name" if that item would otherwise not be newsworthy.

10. ***Watch how subheads fall.*** You will likely be expected to put in the subheads—for example, three or four different one-line italic heads as you go along. Mark them on your layout as you do so. Avoid having subheads butt against each other in adjoining columns, resulting in "tombstone" heads. Also allow three or four lines of text after a subhead at the bottom of a page so you won't have a subhead by itself at the end of a column.

If you are working at a desk where the VDT system is not completely trustworthy, preparation of a people catch-all column on a tight deadline may sometimes aggravate you. You may lose the column if a mechanical defect erases it before you have a chance to store and print it. You may have to compose it all over again.

One backup technique to prepare for such an eventuality is to jot down on paper the first few words of each paragraph as you go along so you can recall what you have put on the screen. Another way is to send the copy on to the storage disk every few minutes; in case of mechanical defect, you will have your copy in storage. But sending small chunks "home," waiting for them to "take" (or register on a disc), and then calling them back out on the screen can be time-consuming. Another problem is that in some systems, at times you may have difficultv getting new copy to "take" or register, and you will lose the story in the transfer process. (Some reporters will hook the story onto another story already in storage in the VDT system and split the new story off later, once a storage record of it exists.)

WEATHER

'The daily weather report is simple enough to put together," says Joseph Hopkins of the Springfield (Mass.) *Morning Union*, "as long as the reporter remembers that he or she is writing for lay people and not meteorologists." He suggests: "Watch out for redundancies [such as rainy, wet weather]. Some weather forecasters are pretty sloppy in their phrasing. Translate terms—when in doubt, ask—and keep the report simple, factual, and accurate."

Bert O. Tucker of the *Daily Ardmoreite* in Ardmore, Okla., advises: "Keep a 'year-old' file—include in your story a fact or two for comparison." Secondly, he says, "It may be easier to use 'hedge' words: the weather 'calls for,' the weather 'outlook,' the weather 'should be,' the weather 'on tap for'—instead of 'the weather will be.'"

The weather information—a national roundup with regional and local temperatures—comes with maps and pictures over the wire services. The information originates in Washington in the National Weather Service of the National Oceanic and Atmosphere Administration, a section of the Department of Commerce. The agency is popularly known as the Weather Bureau. It has representatives in local areas across the country, and you can contact these people for information directly.

Editors are always on the lookout for angles on the weather. The variations on the theme of the change of seasons are endless. The desk person will likely be writing typeblocks for photographs concerning the weather.

The following typeblock that appeared with a picture in the Wichita *Eagle* demonstrates a nose for significant details—how the various plants around the civic auditorium hold up in the midst of cold snaps after nice weather.

These plants at Century II were tough enough to stand up to the cold temperatures that hit Wichita last Friday and Saturday, and they flourished in the 80 and 90 degree weather Sunday, Monday and Tuesday. Cynthia Chestnut of the city's park department watered them Tuesday in preparation for the predicted high of 70 today. Skies should remain mostly fair, with little chance of precipitation.

Reporters have to be on guard against overstatement in weather reporting. When the biggest snowstorm or the wettest summer on record comes, people tend to exaggerate such weather out of proportion.

This memo from a United Press International vice-president and editor, Roger Tatarian, points out the need for extra caution, particularly during weather-caused disasters—in this case a hurricane:

> Rumors are everywhere, and sometimes they are repeated by persons in official capacity—a sheriff, a coroner or a mayor.
>
> Here is where a reporter's sense of responsibility can be put to great test. Does the mere fact that it is an official who relays a particularly alarming report or rumor make it news? I think most newspapermen would agree that an unqualified yes can never be the answer. The report, if used, should be used only with proper caution flags; there should be a clear statement that this is unconfirmed and an indication made as to how it compares with the most reliable information otherwise available at that time.
>
> There were some urgent consultations between New York and New Orleans on questions such as these concerning hurricane Betsy. One telegraph editor telephoned the general news desk in New York and asked if we could match a published dispatch reporting 400 dead without qualification.
>
> He obliged us with a fill-in. The dispatch began: "Authoritative sources said today about 400 bodies had been counted by law enforcement officers in flooded regions in the New Orleans area."
>
> It quoted the New Orleans coroner as saying that a message from an amateur radio operator had reported 250 bodies en route to New Orleans by truck from Plaquemines parish. It quoted other sources that an additional 150 bodies "could be expected" in New Orleans itself. This was the basis for the 400 "body count" in the lead paragraph.
>
> New York quite properly did not ask New Orleans to "match" the story. Rather it simply advised the bureau what the opposition was saying. New Orleans replied that it did not feel justified to go beyond the story then standing on our wires. This dispatch began: "The coroner of New Orleans said today he had received reports that hurricane Betsy had killed 250 persons in devastated Plaquemines parish. The reports via amateur radio said the bodies would be sent to New Orleans.

"'We have no real confirmation of this,' said the coroner, Dr. Nicholas Chetta."

It then noted the "known" death toll as 45, and recalled that the coroner had previously expressed fear of a death toll of 200 in New Orleans alone.

Following these consultations it was decided to subordinate rather than play up the coroner's information in subsequent leads. . . .

When there is too much of one kind of weather, a "wrap-up" story can pull together reports and examples from the wire to make the point. *USA Today,* which gives its whole back page to colorful weather maps and reports, summed up a widespread drought and other weather ills in one report:

Farmers throughout much of the USA aren't likely to get much-needed rain this week.

While thunderstorms will be scattered around many parts of the nation, including the parched Great Plains today, they won't bring enough rain to make much difference to many farmers.

Some of the Gulf of Mexico moisture the Corn Belt so badly needs is making Southern California muggy instead.

In addition to temperatures in the 90s and 100s, the moist air is pushing humidities to steamy levels more like those normally found in the East.

• A line of thunderstorms with winds up to 77 mph swept across the Tucson, Ariz., area Sunday afternoon, knocking out power to hundreds of homes and businesses.

• More than 250,000 people jammed the beaches of Los Angeles County Sunday as temperatures climbed into the 90s with humidity around 50 percent.

• Fifteen small fires caused by lightning Saturday in Riverside County, Calif., were out by Sunday.

• Unhealthful air is expected today in most parts of Southern California except along the coast and in the mountains and deserts.

To the east, "We see no major changes in the conditions over the Plains," said Joel Myers, president of Accu-Weather, Inc.

The strong high pressure area over the West, which is blocking Gulf moisture from the Plains, is showing no signs of moving or weakening.

In addition, "drought breeds drought," Myers said. As the top layer of the soil dries out, less moisture is available to evaporate into the air to make clouds and rain.

Only a few thunderstorms were reported around the nation Sunday, mostly in the Southeast.

One of the thunderstorms hovered over Wilmington, N.C., dumping more than four inches of rain between noon and 2 p.m. and leaving up to three feet of water in a few streets.

—Jack Williams

Weather Terms

Some weather terms you should know are:

Alto-stratus clouds: Dense gray layer above fog.

Anemometer: Measures the speed of wind.

Baguio: Hurricane in the Philippines.

Barometer: Measures pressure of the atmosphere.

Blizzard: Technically, winds over 45 miles an hour, with temperature below 20° and visibility less than one-fourth of a mile.

Ceiling: Height above the earth of the lowest dense layer of clouds covering half the sky.

Cirrus clouds: Very high clouds, about 33,000 feet; thin, filmy, white.

Cold front: Line of cold air moving into a mass of warm air.

Conduction: Transfer of heat by molecular movement.

Contrail: Cloud which develops behind airplanes at high altitude.

Coriolis force: Deflecting force caused by the rotation of the earth.

Cumulus: Very thick clouds with horizontal base, but with extensions; look like cauliflowers.

Cyclone: Grouping of winds with a wide spread, ranging from 50 to 1,000 miles in diameter. The winds rotate between 90 and 130 miles an hour. A cyclone travels 20 to 30 miles an hour.

Dew: Moisture in the atmosphere that condenses at night after a warm day.

Dew point: The temperature at which air cools and condenses into liquid.

Fog: Clouds on the ground, with water drops suspended in air.

Frost: Ice particles caused when moisture condenses on cold nights.

Haze: Condition of atmosphere which makes air nontransparent.

Humidity: Amount of moisture in the air.

Hurricane: Raging tropical cyclone forming over water, with winds of 75 miles an hour or more.

Inversion: Increasing of temperature with height.

Jet stream: High speed core, up to 100 miles an hour, in high westerly wind.

Mist: A thin fog.

Monsoon: Seasonal winds over all or part of a continent.

Ozone: A blue gas, a form of oxygen, usually caused by exposure to sun or by an electrical discharge in air.

Precipitation: Water or ice particles falling to the ground.

Relative humidity: Ratio of water particles in air to the amount the air would hold if completely saturated; expressed in percentages.

Smog: Industrial haze; "smog" comes from "smoke" and "fog."

Squall: Sudden strong wind, especially at sea, accompanied by thick clouds and sometimes storms.

Tornado: Tiny, drastic storm developing locally in flat open lands. Whirling is counterclockwise in Northern Hemisphere and clockwise in Southern

Hemisphere. Concentrated wind creates a central vacuum. Speed of rotation is up to 500 miles an hour, moving forward at 25 to 60 miles an hour.

Troposphere: Layer of atmosphere nearest the earth, with temperature decreasing with altitude.

Waterspout: Tornado over a body of water.

PHOTOS AND WRITING

The desk person, as well as the photographer and the reporter, must know what makes a good photo and how to use it effectively.

Although normally a newswriter does not make photo assignments, the reporter needs to be able to relate to the picture side of the story. The reporter may write on one angle of the story and let the pictures present another angle. Or the reporter may coordinate the emphasis in the story with the photos in one dramatic package. How the journalist develops a story is often an individual decision.

At the copy desk, reporters also sometimes take part in selecting pictures or, on occasion, the editor will ask for their advice about which photos to use. On smaller newspapers the reporters may also take many of the pictures; even on larger papers with American Newspaper Guild contracts that limit overlapping functions, reporters may take pictures, especially when they are in a remote location—such as in the wilds doing a camping feature—without a photographer. In any event, the reporter profits from having some ideas on how to make pictures more interesting.

How to Avoid Dull Photos

Look through newspapers and make a list of the ten worst—the ten dullest—pictures. Chances are that the following will be among the worst:

1. Person pointing to a map.
2. Teacher or scholar holding a book.
3. Governor or executive signing a check or document.
4. Coach and team holding trophy.
5. Officials shaking hands.
6. Shots of new buildings.
7. Participants at groundbreaking ceremony or ribbon cutting.
8. Speaker standing at lectern.
9. People standing in line or sitting on a podium.
10. Scene from high school or college play.

While this group forms a deadly list, it nevertheless represents subjects that reporters and photographers must cover and photograph. When you are responsible for pictures—as a reporter with input into the assignment or as an editor or photographer—watch out for the "deadly ten." Look for ways to turn posing and deadly props into pictures of strength and interest.

Here are some ideas for putting new life into the dullest photos:

Person with a map. An executive or student is planning a long trip. A new missionary is assigned to a distant jungle. If you must use a map, don't have the person pointing to it. Take a closeup of the face off-center, possibly filling the lower right quarter of the picture with the map in the background.

Person with a book. If an author is in town with an important new book, photograph the book side by side with the face of the author. Or just photograph the face—in a series of candids—and the book by itself, and use them separately. Don't use a photo of the book if it has nothing to do with the story.

Check signing. Look for an interesting angle, such as shooting from the pen up into the face of the principal signer. Photos of other signers, if necessary, can appear separately as half-column pictures.

Coach, team, and trophy. Focus on the trophy—in front of the group. Or place it artistically at the top of the stadium where it catches a gleam of light against a broken sky. This can become the main picture, with photographs of the coach and a few team members appearing in one-column or thumbnail-sized head shots.

Handshaking and dead space. Pose the people with their heads close together—shoot only from shoulders up—or shoot over the shoulder of one into the face of another. If stuck with a picture of several people with a lot of dead space (such as speaker and moderator at a banquet lined up against a ballroom curtain), cut the picture apart and use only head shots, each one column or one-half column in size.

New building. Unless the new building is of unusual significance or is architecturally unique, use two pictures. For the main photograph, play up some interesting feature of the building. For example, a new library may have an interesting area such as a lounging area for young readers in the children's corner. Then in addition, you can use a second, small picture of the outside of the building. Imagination can go a long way: try a shot of automobile lights blurred in interesting streaks in front of a new building. One Detroit photographer achieved a three-dimensional effect by showing the curator of a historical building holding a model of the building while standing in the middle of the traffic-filled street in front of the building itself.

Groundbreaking. To achieve interesting perspectives, shoot low, from a spade of dirt, or high, from a garage or water tower. Perhaps you can arrange people in an interesting pattern. One picture in Detroit showed a youngster building a sand castle next to his grandfather while a dull groundbreaking ceremony went on in the background.

Speaker at lectern. Wait for an interesting gesture, preferably a gesture not too sweeping, so the picture of the person can be used as a close-up.

Groups of people. Decide who are the most important people, and put them in the center so that you can trim off the others later. Once, for a feature on a Russian festival in Detroit, the family which was the subject of the article insisted on having Grandpa and others in the picture. The reporter told the photographer to keep the added relatives at the edge of the picture. The family was eventually disappointed that several aunts and the ailing grandfather were not in the picture; they had to be cropped in order to keep the picture more limited and interesting. As a newsperson, you are preparing the article for your newspaper, not a scrapbook. (One story in this connection: When the editor of a small Minnesota weekly prepared a picture of three people, the editor crossed out the man on the right and wrote across him "leave him out." The production cameraman neglected to delete this, and the newspaper carried the picture with the deletion instruction printed across the man on the right!)

Scene from a play. Nothing can make a picture of a scene from a stage play interesting. Try instead to concentrate on the faces of actors; take candid shots using natural props—have an actor smoking a pipe or drinking coffee in a restaurant interview. Actually, anachronistic photography also has possibilities—you've seen the impact of record album photos showing the musical group performing on a beach or in a forest—try taking close-ups of the cast outdoors.

Writing Cutlines

According to Alan Buncher, chief copy editor of the St. Louis *Post-Dispatch*:

> The cutline should tell what the picture can't. It is pointless to write in a cutline, "The President waves to the welcoming crowd. . . ." Of course he's waving. That is what the picture shows. What did he say? That is the question that the cutline should answer.

Cutlines (sometimes called captions) vary in size. Basically, variations include: (1) name lines, usually the last name under a thumbnail half-column face picture; (2) full lines under a one-column picture, with a second line picking up two or three key words (first line—"John Smith," second line—"Died in battle . . ."); (3) full lines, two or more lines indentifying the person or event and giving some basic facts (these lines may start with one word capitalized or bold-faced—it is important that the first word be interesting); and (4) streamer lines, one-line cutlines that are usually set in slightly larger type under multicolumn pictures.

Whatever the style and length, using space wisely is important to convey information interestingly. David L. Russell, chief copy editor of the Niagara (Niagara Falls, N.Y.) *Gazette*, advises that cutlines "should not repeat what's in an accompanying story" and "should not contradict in any way what is in the story."

John P. Sulima, assistant city editor of the Westerly (R.I.) *Sun*, suggests that a deskman should know "who or what is in the picture, when it was taken, how the picture was taken (in case of special effects), where and why. In other words, treat a cutline as a story, only be BRIEF!!!"

Joseph Hopkins of the Springfield (Mass.) *Morning Union* suggests these tips:

- *Brevity is a must.* A cutline, if it stands alone, is a capsule story. Irrelevant details are best left out. Of course, the five Ws are necessary, as in any report. But a caption should never be so long that it pulls attention away from the photo.
- *Tense is important.* The photo cutline should be in the present: "The President boards his helicopter . . ." NOT "boarded his helicopter," even though the publication date may be different from the picture's action. The trick is to make the picture alive; it's happening, and the reader is seeing it happen.
- *A cutline's mood should match the picture's.* A photo of a girl riding a horse across a misty meadow should be poetic, whimsical: "A canter

through the morning mists—a perfect way to start the day. . . ." This instead of: "A girl rides her horse through the fields. . . ." Similarly, a tragic picture should be reported soberly and factually; a happy picture calls for lilting lines.

One of the problems of writing cutlines for pictures with breaking news stories is that often the picture has been sent on to mechanical photocomposition for reproduction and you have to write lines from the information that was with the wire photo. Usually this information is three or four lines of type torn off from the bottom of the picture. Sometimes the lines can go awry in this process. For example, when a Chicago politician died after being stricken outside a Chicago restaurant, the wire service cutline mentioned the sidewalk and restaurant. One deskman writing the cutline assumed that the picture showed the scene and so indicated that. When the picture and lines were matched up on the front page, the lines were pointing out the tragedy scene, but the picture showed only the face of the politician. Stay with the exact information; perhaps the lines mentioned the restaurant and sidewalk where the politician collapsed without saying explicitly that the restaurant and sidewalk were in the picture. In case of doubt, even under deadline pressure, a walk over to—or a shout to—the wire editor would likely confirm what was or was not in a picture you don't have in hand as you write your cutline.

Typeblocks

Among the miscellaneous copy that desk persons may write, a typeblock to describe a set of pictures can be the most demanding: it has to say either a little or a lot, it has to be brief, it has to be general, and it sometimes has to be inclusive without telling it all, leaving something to the pictures and picture cutlines.

In some cases, the story the reporter prepares may be killed in favor of running a descriptive block of type along with the set of pictures that turn out to be more powerful than the story. Desk persons may have to cut a lengthy story into a few paragraphs, or they may have to start from scratch, garnering information from handouts or bits of information the photographer has brought back from the scene. Or they may prepare the typeblock from information the wire service supplies.

For the typeblock, you may want to try to capture the mood or one theme that pulls the picture display together. Avoid a lot of detail, yet include enough to be precise and convincing.

The St. Paul (Minn.) *Pioneer-Press* could have expanded the following typeblock into a full feature, but the paper settled for a half-dozen pictures with a typeblock. This typeblock makes the dolls sound human:

> There's never a lonesome moment at True's Jewelry & Doll Shop in Isanti. At any hour of the day or night, 1,600 tiny faces peek from glass display cases, waiting to charm anyone who loves dolls. The proud owner of the collection is Mrs. Marion True, who can instantly recite the era, type and special attributes of each of her prized possessions. For pure delight, the elfish Whimsie . . . which dates to 1963, is hard to beat. This particular model has three faces, which change by turning the knob on the top of his head. Mrs. True has purchased many of her dolls from area women who tucked them away in attic trunks and forgot about them over the years.

PROMOS, BLURBS, AND LIFTOUTS

"Promos"—short promotional copy blocks to help sell the idea of reading the article—include just enough information to explain who an author is or provide other essential information before the reader begins to read the article. Usually a few lines above the byline or at the end of the story are enough to establish the authority of the writer or to give some reason for the article. Usually a title and a few facts about the person are enough: "John Smith, author of a novel on rodeos, grew up on a farm near Centertown. He's been riding since he was three." If this note accompanies the article, it is called an "editor's note"; if it stands separately—at the front of the section in which the article appears, for example—it is called a "promo."

"Blurbs" help to set the scene before one reads an article and make a page look good with their larger type. On a Memorial Day story, the Washington *Post* had the following blurb which set the mood, added some design interest to the page by being set apart, and helped to hold the story about various facets of the holiday together:

> Some people gathered at emotional wreath-laying ceremonies at Arlington and other area cemeteries yesterday, while some spent the day alone at gravesites with their private memories.
>
> But for other Washington-area residents, the three-day weekend that ended yesterday marked little more than a time to relax.
>
> Regardless of the way it was observed, there was little hustle or bustle on this average presummer weekend.

"Liftouts" come right from the article and can also serve as a second headline. In a Washington *Post* story about a plastic surgeon being sued for showing pictures of a patient on TV, the headline said, "New Look Leads to $33 Million Suit." The two liftouts, one from the plaintiff and one from the defendant, each appeared on opposite sides of the article and called attention to the conflict.

One liftout said:

> "Good God, no. I never gave him permission to use those photographs."
>
> —Mary Vassiliades

The other liftout, in contrast to the first, said:

> "She gave me and members of my staff gifts because she said she was so happy with the job . . . she told me to feel free to discuss her case or show photographs of the results to anyone who wanted to see what could be done with plastic surgery."
>
> —Dr. Csaba Magassy

While promos, blurbs, and liftouts require little original writing, nevertheless the deskman must be aware of good journalism techniques—what people will read, what will get their attention, or what is significant.

WRITING HEADLINES

Usually deskpersons write headlines at the rim—the copy desk—although on a big newspaper editors and writers of special sections such as real estate, food, travel, religion, and lifestyle may write their own heads.

Headline writing is a rigid task. For one thing, the words must fit into a very narrow range—two or three words to a line, half a dozen words for lines of multiple column length. Elaboration in this area is best left for the editing books.

The headline character count will vary from newspaper to newspaper, dependent largely on the kind of type and whether it has serifs. Short prepositions may not be capitalized in some styles. Some "up" styles may say prepositions are capitalized at the beginning of a line or with a verb (for example, "Grow Up"). "Down" or lower-case style would, of course, capitalize only the first word of a head and proper names.

The width of the column will determine how many letters you fit in a column. The number of letters of the alphabet you can get into a head also depends on how big the type size is. Type is described by how high it is. Type height is measured in "points" (each point equivalent to a pencil dot)—72 points equal one inch. Type height comes in these variations for headline: 12 point, 14, 18, 24, 30, 36, 42, 48, 60, 72, and some special larger sizes.

Headlines have a character count. Wide letters take more space than narrow letters, so you have to leave more space for them. This is done by ascribing so many counts to a letter (character). Thus:

Capital M, W	2
Capital I	1
All other capitals	1½
Lowercase m, w	1½
f, l, i, t, j	½
All other letters	1
Number 1	1
Other numbers	1½
Space, punctuation	½

"Smith Elected Council Head"—24 character count
"River Stocked with 1,000 Trout"—28½ character count
"BANG: The Race Is On"—21 character count

Your type specification card or chart will often give you the character count for a particular type size for a desired width.

Here are some rules for writing sharp headlines:

1. ***Match the head with the lead.*** Make sure they say the same thing.
2. ***Use emotive words*** . . . and positive words. The headline in a Pennsylvania paper that said "Students Review Sewers," with the top "Find Some Problems," could be more specific and more positive. It could mention "fish" since the article reports a student study showed that new sewers did not improve living conditions for fish: "Run-off Endangers Fish?" with the top "Students Study Sewers."
3. ***Use monosyllabic words.*** "Crash" or wreck" is shorter than "accident."
4. ***Don't be afraid of a "soft" headline on features and discussion pieces.*** An article in *Today's Spirit* in Hatboro, Pa., dealt with those who helped pioneer in space and quoted Isaac Newton, who explained his success by saying, "I stood on the shoulders of giants." The headline: "Standing on the Shoulders of Giants" with the top "Our View of the Universe." When Walter Mondale chose Geraldine Ferraro to be his running mate

on the Democratic ticket in 1984, the Detroit *Free Press* put a quote from Ferraro in the headline: "Vice-President 'Has Nice Ring to It.'" The lower-deck headline read: "Mondale announces choice of Ferraro as 'American dream.'" Reporting Mondale's acceptance speech, the Doylestown (Pa.) *Intelligencer* had as a headline: "Mondale's warning: 'I mean business.'"

5. ***Avoid male chauvinism.*** The story under "Ex-Democrat Leader Squawks" was about a woman politician. The headline writer would probably not have used "squawk" in reference to a male.
6. ***Avoid cuteness.*** Here is an example of too much alliteration: "Area Inventors Push Incentive to Invent."
7. ***Be consistent.*** Select one spelling and keep it. One paper had "2" and "two," "Boro" and "borough" in the same issue.
8. ***Check for page unity.*** One word may be used too much: "Crash" appeared in three headlines in a row in a summary of the day's news. "200 Killed in Peking Plane Crash," "Qatar Crash Leaves 45 Dead," and "Runaway Barges Crash Ships, Docks"—one "crash" too many.
9. ***Be accurate.*** "Mideast Peace Ok'd" is not the same as the approving of two provisions that pave the way for discussions.
10. ***Start the head with an action word.*** "Board May Increase False Alarm Penalties" would be better if "False Alarm" came first: "False Alarm Penalties May Increase," or "Fire Alarm Devices May Bring Fine if Faulty."
11. ***Avoid double meanings.*** "Nursery Blocks/INA's Proposal."
12. ***Don't split adjectives and nouns.*** "SAGA Schedules Two/Flower Show Trips." "Two" and "Show" should be on the same line.
13. ***Look for personal words***—nouns and pronouns. "Meet the New Mayor:/He's a New Breed."
14. ***Stay with a single idea in the head in most cases.*** "Travel Easy:/Pack Light" could have played up the specific idea and made the other words secondary: "PACK LIGHT: Travel Can Be Easy."
15. ***Go easy on question heads.*** An occasional one is permissible, but if six appear on the same page, readers will think they are taking a quiz.
16. ***Avoid mixed metaphors.*** "City Makes Plans/For Fuel Squeeze"—do you squeeze gas?
17. ***Be specific.*** "Thousands/In Egypt/Cheer Plan." Neither "thousands" nor "plan" are very specific. The lead said they cheered the U.S. President. Better, tell how many thousands cheer or hail President (use his last name, if it is short; otherwise initials).
18. ***Solve layout problems.*** Heads stacked next to the logo or nameplate, without a screen overlay or shading over the nameplate, can be confusing. Single column heads should not be next to each other; multicol-

umn heads, if they butt up to each other, should be set in different size type so they do not look as if they read into each other. Use of white space should be on the outside and not "trapped" or surrounded on all sides.

19. ***Avoid Latin derivative words ending in -tion, -ness, -ty.*** "Condition, humaneness, sexuality" are too long.
20. ***Avoid prepositions at the end of the first line.*** Some newspapers accept a preposition at the end of the second line, but others argue against the use of the preposition at the end of any line.
21. ***Avoid initials.*** The initials of a noted politician, such as FDR (Franklin Delano Roosevelt), JFK (John Fitzgerald Kennedy), and HHH (Hubert Horatio Humphrey) were acceptable when they were alive. Some will know that Upper Moreland is meant in "U.M. to Go Back to Court" and Willow Grove in "W.G. Man Guilty in Stabbing," but there are always some who won't know. Besides, initials, especially in a lot of heads, give the paper a cluttered look.
22. ***Avoid auxiliary verbs.*** "Is" is a good example. Eastern newspapers seem to allow "is" more than editors in the rest of the country. Sometimes "is" helps with readability: "Security Is Target of Boro Unit" vs. "Security Target of Boro Unit." Another possibility here would be "Boro Unit Targets Security."
23. ***Avoid labels.*** "Citizens Patrol" as a head with a typeblock acts like a label, with "patrol" as noun or verb. It is clearer and more exciting to round it out: "Citizens/Patrol/at Night."
24. ***Avoid meaningless words.*** Special, area, recent, and words such as these don't mean much: "Area PTA Sets Special Session." This is better: "PTA to Review Parking Plans."
25. ***Develop a list of taboo words.*** Refusing to use certain words in headlines makes the writer think and sharpens his or her style. Taboo words could include honor, meet, met, set, held, increase, board, and man. Also included here could be trite, slangy words such as rap, cop, solons, and hit.

Assignments

1. Select a group of people stories—look for high human interest, timeliness, and variety. Boil the stories down to a paragraph each, and string them together as a people column.
2. Put subheads in a copy of a newspaper that has a lot of uninterrupted gray columns.
3. After getting information from the weather bureau, write a weekend or long-range weather forecast, or write a story on the "reasons" for the current kind of weather the area is experiencing.

4. After browsing through a newspaper, suggest how you would improve some of the pictures; identify the best—and the worst—picture in a paper, and explain why.
5. Write cutlines for several pictures that go with stories, using only the story information that is available; or secure a group of wire service photos with lengthy blurbs and adapt them to specified newspaper formats—decide what should be a caption or a typeblock.
6. Identify what you think would be the best liftouts in a lengthy story of your choice.
7. Write a half dozen headlines for your next story, each using specified different measures.
8. Photographers do not always agree with editors and reporters, and vice versa. Have an editor and photographer debate these topics in class: When is an article more important than the picture? How does an editor deal with the problems of space limitations and conforming pictures to preconceived layouts?

Cable News Network Senior Correspondent Daniel Schorr consults with Moscow Bureau Chief Stuart Loory and Washington Anchor Bernard Shaw prior to broadcast. Photo by Adam's Studio/HBJ Collection

PART 6

The Electronic Age

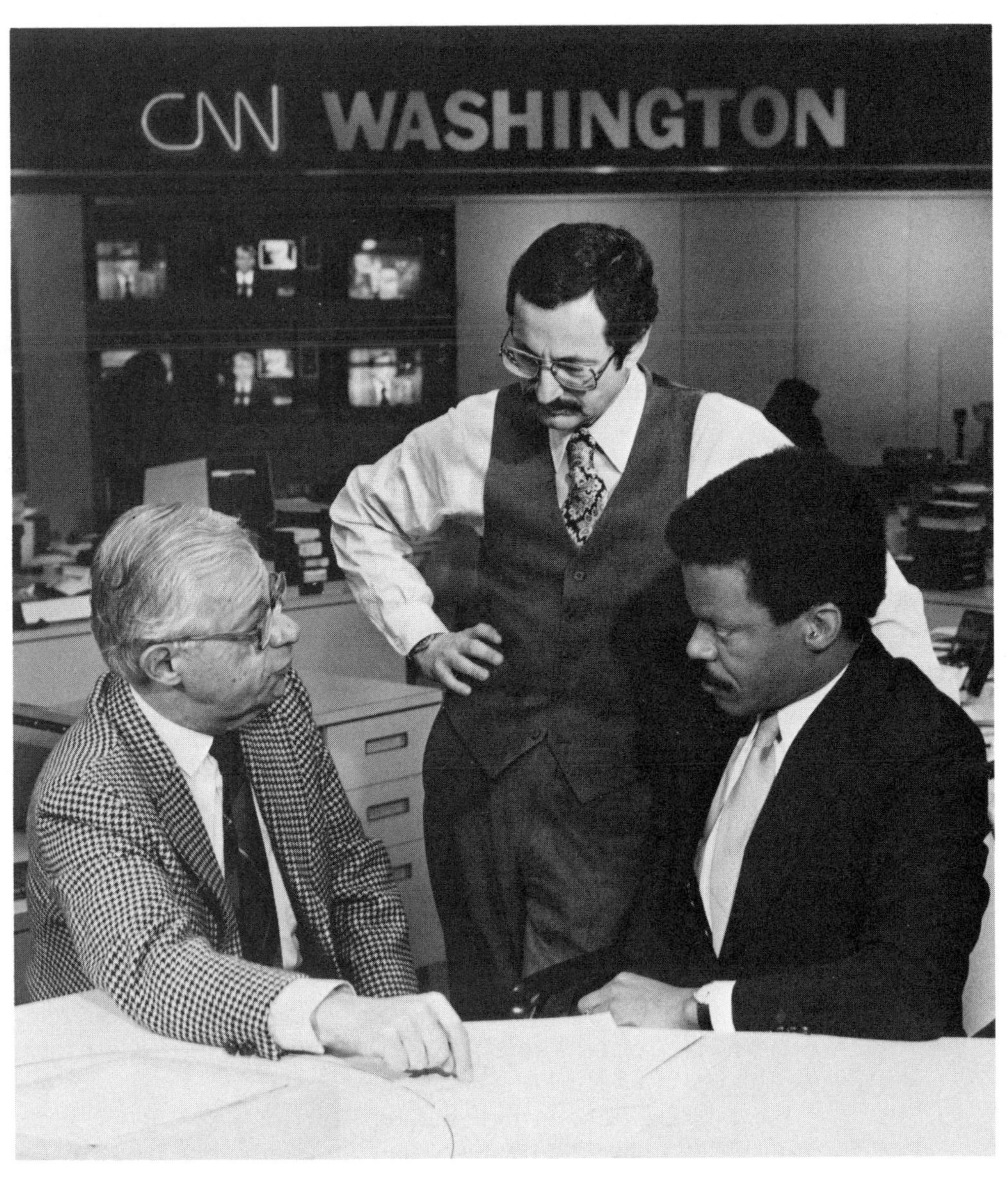

19

Writing Broadcast News

Barry Nemcoff, former senior producer of ABC News and now a public relations executive, is the author of this chapter.

Many present journalism students will be working in radio and television at some time in their careers. Certainly, print media reporters must work side by side with radio and television reporters, so understanding of the electronic media is useful for all journalism students.

The United States alone has over 8,600 radio stations and nearly 1,000 television stations. These broadcast facilities are licensed to operate by the Federal Communications Commission. Since the stations use the airwaves, which belong to the public, to transmit their signals, the F.C.C. requires them to devote a portion of their programming to serve the public interest. In order to keep their licenses, broadcast stations must devote a percent of their total programming to news, documentaries, and other public affairs programs.

One of the principal differences between *print* news media and *broadcast* news media is the emphasis on current information. Newspapers and news magazines are solely concerned with gathering and reporting news and news features. Radio and television stations devote only a part of their time to news. In recent years, however, a growing number of radio and television stations program what is called "all news," that is, broadcasting news and news features around the clock. There have been attempts to develop "videotext," all-day news-feature programming serving up printed words and pictures. But some of the pioneers, such as Time, Inc., have decided that the market is not ready for this approach that allows the television set to be treated like a newspaper, with controls allowing the viewer to select which stories appear on the screen.

Even if most stations and channels still don't give up all or most of their time to news and public affairs programming, newscasts are becoming more frequent and of longer duration. This is a reflection of growing popular interest in the events around us that affect and shape our lives: popular interest translates into larger audiences which bear directly on sponsor interest. Prospective sponsors who want to reach large audiences with their commercials are finding that news programs are attractive vehicles for their messages. Stations and channels are more than happy to oblige—by making more and longer news programs available to those who provide the profits.

Despite more broadcast time being devoted to news, news staffs, even on the largest radio and television stations, are generally much smaller than on newspapers covering the same territory. On the other hand, the networks have large staffs to gather and report radio and television news. The ABC, CBS, and NBC networks employ hundreds of reporters (called correspondents), writers, editors, producers, cameramen, and other technical personnel to man news bureaus at home and abroad. The three principal networks, in effect, serve as the national news and public affairs medium in the United States.

Although the principal goal of both print and broadcast journalists is the same—to report the news—they use different means. The differences are the news gathering tools, the media used for communicating, and how these media affect the senses. Print is for the eye, radio is for the ear, and television for both the eye and the ear.

Print journalists need little more than paper and pencils to record the raw information that they will work into their stories. Broadcast journalists—radio and television reporters—must rely on an assortment of electronic gadgetry to "get" their stories. Of course, working with a pad and pencil when interviewing a news source is much easier than using audio or video tape recorders, cameras, sound amplifiers, and lights.

News sources reluctant to submit to interviews will be even more reluctant when confronted with broadcast media equipment. However, news sources generally believe that broadcast media will present their key statements in the broadcast story just as recorded in the interview. But like print reporters who organize their notes and select the most interesting or timely facts, broadcast reporters use the same criteria to edit material recorded on tape or film. And much the same as print reporters, those working in broadcast news experience disgruntled interviewees. Just as sources accuse print reporters of "misquoting," they also accuse broadcast reporters of using recorded statements out of context.

One difference between print and broadcast journalism concerns the impact on each of the senses of the readers/listeners/viewers. Newspaper readers review—reread—an article for clarification. Radio listeners and television viewers cannot "re-hear" or "re-see" information. When words and pictures emerge from electronic boxes, they have only one chance to get the message, unless they use video tape recorders.

Understanding the limitations as well as the advantages of their medium, good broadcast journalists constantly try to present material in its most cogent form. Broadcast news reporters and writers, as do many good newspaper writers, strive to use "people talk": everyday words and expressions as much like conversational English as possible. They try to keep sentences short and clear. Simple declarative statements are usually best. Some comparisons follow.

1. Sentences tend to be shorter in broadcast news writing, although many print journalists argue they should be this way in print also. Nevertheless, in comparing the two, you find differences.
2. Broadcast news writers avoid the inverted structure found in much of newspaper writing.
3. Broadcast news writers often drop subordinate clauses to keep subjects and verbs close together.
4. In radio and television news writing, identification of the subject by title, age, and any other pertinent information precedes the name, while the practice will vary in print journalism.
5. In broadcast news writing, whenever possible, journalists use the present tense to give the story a sense of immediacy. Of course, print journalists also use the technique when writing captions and some features.

Because radio and television stations always employ fewer reporters than newspapers do, broadcast news journalists have to carefully select the stories they cover first hand. And in preparing television news, the number of camera crews and visual appeal govern the selection of stories staff reporters cover. In television, events that provide "moving pictures" get priority coverage.

Radio and television stations have to report all the news if they are to compete with newspapers. With limited electronic equipment and short staffs, they have to rely on more than just their own reporters; sometimes they rely on the local newspapers for information, and they often rewrite newspaper stories. Also, newspapers have comparatively extensive beat systems which can supply many leads which radio and television reporters then run down.

The radio reporter who gets a lead from a newspaper looks for opportunities to record interviews with the principals in the story. Later, regularly scheduled newscasts will air portions of the interview. Television reporters look for newspaper stories they can make into visually interesting news reports. Of course, good journalists in any medium look for a fresh angle or a new development in a story which other media have already reported. Good radio and television reporters endeavor to do the same when using newspaper stories as their leads.

The newspaper probably will remain broadcast journalism's unwitting and unwilling best ally. How else can radio and television cover all the beats that newspapers do?

Space and time differences in the various media also determine coverage. A newspaper devotes considerable space to an important story. A radio or television newscast will give considerable time to the same story. A very important story may get as much as two minutes of coverage in the newscast, the equivalent of about a page of double-spaced copy. The same story in a newspaper may run a half-dozen typewritten pages or more. So the broadcast journalist rewriting newspaper stories can tell only the bare essentials.

Skillful rewriting of a complicated newspaper story requires a high degree of editorial judgment and language ability. The essence of good broadcast news writing is the careful selection of essential information and the critical use of words to boil down a long story into a short one that *tells it all*. For the novice broadcast newswriter who must boil down a handful of notes, a long newspaper story, or wire copy to a 30-second report (about eight lines of copy), here are five useful rules to follow:

1. Read the original material thoroughly until you fully understand the information.
2. Take short notes on the essential information, and devote one sentence to each important element in the story.
3. Put the original source material face down to avoid the temptation of plagiarizing.
4. Organize the notes made in step two into the order in which you will present the facts of the story.
5. Write the story, and check it for accuracy against the original source material.

Too often what passes for rewriting in broadcast news is a mere transposition of a few words or sentences in the lead paragraphs of a newspaper story.

The wire services, the Associated Press and United Press International, provide much of the raw as well as "finished" material for radio and television newscasts. In addition to their regular services, both AP and UPI offer broadcast clients their respective "radio wires." They also provide broadcasters with "actualities," recorded interviews with newsmakers around the world. They transmit these to client stations over telephone line feeds from central wire service facilities at specified times every day.

The AP and UPI radio wires carry most of the news found on their regular wires, except it has been rewritten and packaged for broadcast. An example is the five-minute news summary that covers world events which news sources make available for newscasts on the hour and on the half-hour. And the one-minute news summaries may include as many as five stories given headline treatment. Of course, the services also provide independent pieces devoted to the top breaking stories of the day and to special daily and weekly features.

A good broadcast news organization, however, prides itself on not using wire service copy "as is." Broadcasters refer to the use of unrewritten wire copy as "rip and read." Most regard this practice as something only the smallest radio stations with no news staffs do. On such stations, the lone disc jockey, who may also be the station manager and engineer, stops his banter long enough to read an hourly five-minute AP or UPI news summary—just enough to satisfy F.C.C. requirements for keeping the station's license. Most radio stations have a sense of pride and do not want to sound the same as their competitors. They rewrite all wire service material including the packaged news programs.

The three major networks also provide sources of news for broadcasters. Since most commercial stations are affiliates of either ABC, CBS, or NBC, they get worldwide news coverage from network news operations. The network news product may come to the stations in two ways: 1) the complete world news program with the station as the window for it and 2) packages of daily syndicated news and sports stories for inclusion in the news programs produced by the affiliate stations themselves. Of course, local stations and channels can also tape and use any of the radio or television news reports found in the network news programs in subsequent locally produced newscasts.

This relationship between station and network news operations in effect gives the affiliates a worldwide staff of reporters, whose voices and faces become popular and become identified with the station on which they appear rather than with the network that employs them.

Personalities play a big part in the success of broadcast news. Most listeners and viewers of broadcast news can quickly identify their favorite reporters and anchor people. The fight for top ratings peculiar to the broadcasting industry goes beyond the entertainment programs. The battle for news followers is evident in every American city and hamlet where radio and television stations compete for supremacy. Has anyone been spared from commercials which promote a station's own news programs by emphasizing how "friendly" the anchor people and reporters are rather than how good the news operation is?

If a picture, indeed, is worth a thousand words, what is a moving picture worth? We have no way to estimate the worth of the "moving pictures" of the tragedy of an attempted Presidential assassination, of the drama of man's first landing on the moon, or of the excitement of Olympic sports competitions broadcast live from the scene of the events. No news medium can compete with the credibility of television news when pictures tell the story. But the visual aspects of television news are at once the strength of the medium as well as its weakness.

Because television news needs exciting visuals, television cannot easily report many important news stories adequately because of lack of visual appeal. Physical action makes a story perfect for television. But if a story focuses on an important conference, the results of which may critically affect all of us, and reporters can come up with nothing more than "talking heads," television may slight this conference. Such a consideration creates important imbalances in television news reporting.

A visually interesting story that is of less consequence to viewers usually gets more time in a newscast than one that is visually uninteresting. The latter, no matter how important, often is relegated to the status of a "reader"—a story read by the newscaster with little or no visual support. In the perception of most viewers, the story reported on film or videotape becomes a more memorable event than the story an anchorperson covers in a few spoken lines.

Covering news for television is much more of a team effort than it is for newspapers or even radio. The newspaper reporter can work alone with his pad and pencil. The radio news reporter doesn't need help to carry his compact tape recorder. But the television news reporter, in his quest for visual material, needs the support of a cameraman, a sound technician who may also handle lighting, and sometimes a lighting technician if the station's labor contract demands it. Network television news crews even include a "field producer" who shares responsibility with the correspondent in getting the story. The field producer arranges the interviews, selects locations for shooting film or tape, makes sure the required physical and technical facilities are there when needed, and is responsible for feeding the story to New York in time for inclusion on the network newscast. In addition, a correspondent usually appreciates a good field producer's input about editorial content.

Since the picture is the dominant factor in television news, the words or narration play a supporting role. Television news viewers respond first and more strongly to what they see and second to what they hear. Thus, in writing a script for a television news story, the good reporter will list the visuals (on tape or film) he has available to tell the story. He will then arrange the shots so that the opening scene will have the kind of impact that serves the story best, much as a newspaper story lead does. That opening shot should make the viewer want to see more. Subsequent shots should elaborate on the story and appropriately close it. The good television reporter who understands his medium will never use narration that repeats the obvious information the picture makes clear. Television newswriting is much the same as photo caption writing in print journalism. The caption elaborates on the picture by supplying information the picture lacks.

A simple story about a fire, covered for television news, can serve as an example. Against a shot of firemen climbing ladders to enter an upper story of the burning building, the narrator should *not* say: "Firemen used ladders to gain access to the upper stories of the burning building." The viewer *can see* that! The narration should be used to tell *why* firemen used ladders to enter the building, information that the camera was not able to capture. Thus, the narration might read: "Firemen fought to reach *the sixth floor of the burning building where they believed the fire had trapped a number of people*. Their efforts paid off with *the rescue of three women employees. . . .*" The italics indicate information provided *only* by the copy. And as the narrator begins to give details of the rescue, the picture changes to show the women being led out of the building.

Let's use our imaginary fire story to lay out a simulated television news script:

NEWSCASTER: The courage and quick action of Philadelphia firemen today averted tragedy in an office building fire. Reporter Bill Smith has the story:

VIDEO:	AUDIO:
FIREMEN CLIMBING LADDERS	Firefighters fought to reach the sixth floor of the burning office building, at Sixth and Tioga streets, where a number of people were believed to be trapped.
WOMEN BEING LED FROM BURNING BUILDING	Their efforts paid off when they rescued three women and led them down an inside fire escape to the ground floor.

FIREMEN PLAYING HOSES ON BURNING BUILDING	It took firemen from three companies nearly an hour to bring the blaze under control.
ASST. FIRE COMMISSIONER TALKING TO SMITH	Assistant Fire Commissioner Joe Burke says there are suspicions about the origin of the fire:
BURKE SOUND ON FILM	IN CUE: "We found some . . . OUT CUE: . . . by the investigation." TIME: 18 seconds.
POLICE CONTROLLING PILED-UP TRAFFIC	The fire played havoc with rush-hour traffic as home-bound drivers had to use narrow side streets to avoid the area.
BILL SMITH SOUND ON FILM IN FRONT OF GUTTED BUILDING	When it was all over . . . what had been the six-month-old, 10-story Ajax office building was a gutted ruin.

No other news medium could have captured the drama of the fire as well as television. Since people often equate "seeing" with "believing," television news continues to capture top honors for credibility. If a prominent person says something important in a television news report, more often than not the viewer not only *hears* it said, but *sees* it said by the newsmaker—and that makes the story believable.

Of course, getting pictures can present some unexpected problems. Since so much depends on equipment in getting the broadcast news story, sometimes cameras and recorders suddenly stop working at a crucial moment in the coverage. Then again, sometimes the extraordinary resourcefulness of reporters and other news crew members can save the day.

ABC News, among many others, covered Jimmy Carter's first trip abroad as president of the United States. The scene was London, the event, an economic conference where Europe's leading heads of state were meeting President Carter for the first time. President Valéry Giscard d'Estaing of France emerged as Carter's antagonist on several important issues. ABC News was on its way to scoring a beat by getting the French president to agree to an exclusive interview. The interview was to be fed live via satellite to ABC's "Good Morning America" program originating out of New York.

Giscard agreed to the interview on the condition that it would not take more than 15 minutes at a place of his choice. The place was to be the French ambassador's residence in London where the French president was scheduled to host an important dinner for the West German prime minister immediately after the interview. Therefore, getting everything off on time was critical.

ABC News correspondent Steve Bell, assorted producers, cameramen, and technicians, standing in a forest of equipment and cables, were ready to go at the designated hour. The network had ordered the satellite, which was to transmit the interview, a half-hour ahead of time to assure that everything would be ready to go as soon as Giscard arrived. Suddenly word came that the French president would be late—no telling how late since the conference was deadlocked about the language in the final communique.

Satellites, those modern marvels of broadcast communications, spinning in space after being booked by a client, are costly by the minute. The senior producer, after consulting by phone with program producers in New York, cancelled the satellite with the understanding that ABC News could have it again on five minutes' notice. It would take at least that long to put makeup on the French president once he arrived.

But no sooner was the satellite unavailable than in swept Valéry Giscard d'Estaing. "Are you ready for me?" he demanded to know. "I have very little time," he declared.

The senior producer fought hard to hide panic as he contacted the British Post and Telegraph authorities who are responsible for satellite operations. They told him in typical British understatement that they were "experiencing minor technical difficulties" and that it might take some time to correct the situation.

Correspondent Bell, veteran television newsman that he is, read the signs of trouble in his producer's eyes. He moved in and began charming the French president. Bell realized that none of the European heads of state really knew much about Jimmy Carter, the new American president. All of them were eager to know more about Carter so they could deal better with him. Bell spent several years at the ABC news bureau in Atlanta covering Jimmy Carter when he was governor of Georgia. Bell knew a lot about Carter and began to tell Giscard all about the new American president.

Giscard became so engrossed in what Bell had to say, he completely forgot he was short on time. Getting the satellite working took about 20 minutes, and another five to get the go-ahead from New York. Finally, the producer told the president of France the interview could begin.

An alert correspondent saved the day.

As new communications technology makes it possible for television news to move more and more toward "live" reporting directly from the news scene, alert reporters will be in greater demand. Live reporting often calls for more than a good reporter who can write a good script to go with good film or videotape carefully edited into a "packaged" news story. Live feeds directly from the scene of a breaking story will challenge reporters' ability to ad lib their information as cameras move from shot to shot without advance notice. Advanced technology will challenge the reporter to be so good that his audience will believe he is presenting his report from a carefully prepared script.

Broadcast Journalism Glossary

ABC: American Broadcasting Company.

Actuality: The actual voices and sounds of people and events in the news incorporated into radio news stories.

Assignment Desk: The source of news coverage assignments in broadcast news operations.

Assignment Editor: The staff person responsible for making news coverage assignments in broadcast news operations.

Audio: Synonym for sound in radio and television.

Audio Tape: Magnetic tape used to record sound.

Beeper: Telephone interview in which a periodic "beep" is audible to conform to FCC regulations that require an indication that the material is being recorded.

CBS: Columbia Broadcasting System.

Communications Act: The body of regulations governing the conduct of broadcasting activities and operations as enforced by the Federal Communications Commission.

Crew: Cameramen and sound technicians involved in covering a television news story.

Director: The staff person responsible for getting the television program on the air from the control room.

Editor: The staff person responsible for editing audio tape, film, or videotape into a news report under the direction of the producer or reporter.

ENG: Electronic news gathering as it applies to the use of electronic equipment such as videotape cameras and recorders in television news gathering.

Fairness Doctrine: FCC regulation designed to ensure fair and unbiased reporting of important social and political issues.

FCC: Federal Communications Commission, the government agency charged with regulating the broadcast industry.

In Cue: The first few words in a recorded or filmed statement made by a subject in a radio or television news story.

Lead-in: The in-studio lead read by the newscaster in introducing a radio or television news story reported from the scene.

Mini-documentary: A short documentary report usually incorporated within a radio or television news program.

NBC: National Broadcasting Company.

Network: A broadcasting organization that supplies programming to a network of affiliated stations.

News Bulletin: A short summary report of an important breaking news event inserted due to its urgency into radio and television programming in progress.

Newscast: Any radio or television news program.

News Director: The principal executive in charge of a radio or television station's news department.

Pad Copy: Additional copy provided for a radio or television newscast to ensure against the news program running short of required time.

Producer: The staff person responsible for producing a radio or television news program.

Out Cue: The last few words in a recorded or filmed statement made by a subject in a radio or television news report.

Ratings: The popularity of broadcast programming as measured by rating services such as Nielsen and Arbitron.

Rewriting: Rewriting wire service or newspaper stories for radio or television news presentation.

Rip and Read: Ripping and reading wire service radio newscast copy without the benefit of rewriting or editing.

Section 315A: The FCC regulation governing "equal time" provisions for political candidates appearing on nonnews radio and television programs.

Standup: The on-camera lead and/or close to a television story by a reporter on the scene.

Video: The visual portion in a television news story or program.

Videotape: Magnetic tape used for recording the visual aspects of a television news event at the scene.

Voicer: Voice reports from radio newsmen on the scene describing the event or incident.

20

Editing and Reporting Machines

Contributing to this chapter were Joan Bastel, managing editor, Montgomery County (Pa.) Record, *Bill Gloede of* Editor & Publisher, *and Paul Sullivan of Temple University, with material provided by the systems editor of the New York* Times, *Howard Angione, in an interview. Bill Gloede also supplied the glossary of newsroom computer terms.*

The majority of the newspapers in this country have installed "electronic" newsrooms. There are two basic systems of electronic newsrooms: those which input from OCRs and those which input from VDTs.

OCR is the term used to describe an "optical character recognition" scanner. In this system a reporter types his or her copy on a typewriter equipped with a typing element containing characters which an optical scanner can recognize. The paper story the reporter originates feeds through an OCR device which either sends the words to a typesetter or places them in storage for electronic editing. But this system is giving way to the VDT on which reporters create and edit copy.

VDT means "video display terminal." This device, resembling a television screen with an expanded typewriter keyboard attached, uses no paper. No paper is used with this system. The reporter sees his or her keystrokes displayed in lines on the video screen. The reporter can pass the story directly to a typesetter or move it through the system to another VDT an editor operates.

Before electronic editing, one of the most time-consuming and expensive parts of news operations involved typesetters' rekeyboarding stories as they passed through different stages. An OCR or a VDT captures the reporter's original keystrokes and the story does not have to be rekeyed. Editors like these systems because they move deadline times forward. Publishers like these systems because they save labor on typesetting and proofreading.

THE OCR

Working on an OCR scanner system, a reporter prepares copy on an ordinary typewriter, typically an IBM Selectric, which has a typing element compatible to the system and a slightly modified line spacing gear. Scanner copy is typically prepared on special paper with margins and line counts printed in red. Most scanners are blind to red so that all instructions that are not to be read by the machine are printed or written in that color. (All scanners are blind to one color for this purpose.)

Scanners are programmed so that reporters can use symbols to delete a letter, delete a word, or delete a line. They can even add copy in limited amounts once they have typed a page by using special symbols to allow the reading of copy they have added between the lines. This need for extra space between the lines is the reason for the modified line spacing gear. The scanner system requires accurate typing, but most reporters learn this quickly.

The scanner copy the reporter prepares will probably pass to an editor for corrections and the addition of a headline. The editor can block out copy with a black pen and can make additions between the lines on another typewriter. Copy is then fed to the OCR device.

Most OCR scanners have an automatic feeding device so that 8½ x 11 sheets of copy paper run continuously into the system. An electric eye which recognizes all the letters and symbols reads the lines of copy at high speed. The scanner turns this information into electronic impulses and sends them either directly to an electronic phototypesetter or to the memory disk of a computer for use at a later time.

Although some papers still use OCRs, their use is not expanding rapidly for two reasons. First, they are expensive devices and must be used in pairs since a newspaper cannot risk being shut down by a single device going out of order. Second, they require extensive maintenance to avoid mistakes such as the misreading of letters and the repetition of lines. In addition, the VDTs permit instant recall of copy on a screen without involving a lot of paper. Editing is also much easier.

THE VDT

Although working on VDT systems is a new experience, most people find them easy to operate. The keyboard which operates a VDT has all the keys of a regular typewriter plus specific command keys and keys to move the cursor. The cursor is a highlighted area the size of one character which shows the point at which the reporter is working on the screen. When the reporter strikes a letter key on the keyboard, the letter will appear under the cursor and the cursor will then move to the next space. With a set of special keys, the reporter can move the cursor in all directions all over the screen.

One of the advantages of a VDT is that the reporter can move the cursor to correct mistakes easily: one key will delete a character at a cursor position, one will delete a line, and another will delete a paragraph. Another key will allow the reporter to insert material at the cursor position without disturbing the rest of the typed copy. These functions make preparation of "clean" newspaper copy simple. Making extensive changes without time-consuming rekeyboarding of the information is also possible.

The heart of every individual VDT is a microprocessor, a wonder of the computer revolution which stores thousands of pieces of data on tiny silicon chips. Single terminals usually handle units of from 5,000 to 12,000 bits of information. Wire stories and individual assignments for reporters tend to average three "takes," which is approximately 4,500 characters (or bits of information). This means that editors usually ask reporters to write material in units—generally about three "takes."

Most VDT systems are set up so that when reporters have completed a story on their individual terminals they can pass that story out of their machine and farther on into the system. Individual VDTs are usually "hard wired," that is they have only a certain number of memory chips, and when the chips are filled with electronic information they will no longer accept material. The reporter might want to send the information to a line printer so that he will have his own hard copy of the story, but if this is the only place that the story is sent then the original keystrokes will be lost. The story should also be sent to a storage system so that an editor can retrieve it at a later time.

When a reporter's story moves from the individual VDT, it passes through another microprocessor and is placed in a larger memory unit. Many newspapers attach a floppy disk storage unit to the microprocessors to file stories. A floppy disk is a soft piece of plastic that looks much like a 45-rpm record and costs only a few dollars. A floppy disk will file and store 250,000 pieces of information on a single side. Several disks being used at once will store all of the data needed to publish a medium-sized newspaper, including the wire service.

At a large newspaper a story may pass into the memory system of a larger minicomputer which will handle millions of pieces of information. What is ultimately important, though, no matter what the size of the system, is that the reporter can store the original story for later use exactly as he or she has typed it into the system. The reporter can retrieve and rework the story if necessary before sending it to the typesetter. Retrieving the story takes only seconds on most systems since all that the system requires is a file name and a single command.

There are both advantages and disadvantages for the reporter working with an OCR or a VDT. Making corrections, especially on a VDT, is quite simple, but both systems work best when the reporter types accurately. One disadvantage is that these systems place more responsibility on the individual. The reporter's original keystrokes provide the basic information that enters into the memory system. No one will rekey the material to take out careless mistakes. In effect, the reporter becomes the typesetter.

On small newspapers, which may have a limited number of editors, the reporter is really responsible for the story as it appears in type. Traditionally the reporter, the editor, the typesetter, and the proofreader handled each story. Many mistakes on the original copy were caught in the last two steps. Most operations today omit the last two steps. If the reporter is inaccurate, the final printed story will be inaccurate. Editors today demand greater accuracy on copy preparation than ever before.

More on the OCR

The problems that are inherent in an OCR system stem from the limitations of the typewriter. Paper must be aligned in the typewriter exactly since the scanner reads copy only along predetermined lines. If the writer is not an accurate typist who catches keystroke mistakes as they are made, the correction procedure can be cumbersome. Eliminating a character or a word immediately is simple, but if the reporter doesn't catch the error until later, then the reporter must cross it out in black and type the correction between the lines. Corrections or additions can be no longer than a single typed line at any time. On OCR all corrections must be typed in a predetermined fashion since the scanner only reads typed characters.

Also the reporter cannot feed copy into the scanner until it has been properly prepared. If the reporter does, the result will be a mess that will take longer to unscramble than the original correction would have taken. There is also the additional problem that copy with too many corrections will confuse the scanner. What this ultimately means is that editors often send copy back to reporters to retype accurately, which slows down the process.

More on the VDT

VDTs are much easier for reporters to use than OCRs. The biggest initial problem is getting accustomed to paperless typing and the lack of the familiar typewriter noise.

In operating any electronic equipment, there is one principle to keep in mind that often gets the uninitiated into trouble when they don't follow it: for every action there is a reaction. This simple rule of physics means that whenever you touch a key something happens, even if nothing appears on the screen. It is not uncommon for newcomers to VDTs to strike too many keys at once and lock up the electronics as a result. If you are a neophyte, you must learn procedures and then follow them to operate the equipment effectively.

While it is relatively simple for an editor to work with copy on a VDT and to make corrections, it is not always easy for reporters to see simple mechanical errors when scrolling through their stories. Since reporters have a responsibility to make sure that the originally entered copy is clean, they have to discipline themselves to reread copy carefully.

The two greatest enemies of the novice operator are fear and frustration. You can overcome both of these through careful orientation and some practice.

"The system" takes a lot of verbal abuse in newsrooms, and that abuse increases as deadlines draw near. Both reporters and editors are frustrated when they are ready to produce—only to have the system prevent them from producing because of a software or a hardware problem.

Newsroom staffers—who have always found stress to be part of the job description—deal with a new kind of stress today. They deal with it sometimes with humor: "If this response time gets any slower, I'll be eligible for retirement before I get this police brief done"; sometimes with sarcasm: "It's okay. If they want to pay me for staring at a blank screen, that's fine with me"; and sometimes with anger: system snafus have caused more than one near-rebellion in newsrooms across the country.

Imagine you are writing a three-part series on the county's financial situation over the last 10 years. Your stories include considerable statistics, some touchy quotations, and a lot of darn good writing. Poof! Your VDT screen goes blank!

Or you are doing an interview over the telephone and taking notes on your VDT. Poof! It's gone.

In the first case, you still have your notes and you can recreate your story or stories. In the second, you have no notes. They've gone to that great computer graveyard in the sky.

Reporters working VDTs soon learn to safeguard their work to prevent such catastrophies. Reporters should know to periodically "save" the work they have done on stories in progress so that at least portions of their stories are safe in the computer memory and thus can't be eliminated by electrical failure or hardware problems.

Yet "down time" is frustrating, and a lot of it costs manhours or morale.

"Most of us would never go back to the days of upright typewriters and 'takes' of copy with smeared pencil scratches," says Joan Bastel, managing editor, Montgomery County (Pa.) *Record*. "We'd never accept the days of the OCR when the scanner would read just a crinkle in the paper and make it gibberish in the middle of a story."

Back in the early 1970s, when the newspaper industry began phasing in a new technology known as "cold type composition," it met with a great deal of resistance. ("Cold type" referred to pages prepared photographically for offset printing rather than by using type formed by melting metal.) The resistance came not only from newspaper unions, which were concerned with safeguarding the jobs of their members, but also from journalists. It was a new procedure in a business never known for its ability to adapt to rapid change.

For publishers, the new technology offered a way to cut production costs in a very labor-intensive industry. With readership declining, costs increasing, and advertising dollars leaving the print media for television, publishers sorely needed a way to cut costs. As a result, in less than 10 years, the new technology had not only been accepted, but embraced.

The computer made the new technology work, and the computer eventually drove that new technology into obsolescence. "Cold type" has become "electronic imaging." The computers that drove the early cold-type composition systems have long since been replaced by machines a fraction of their size with an exponential increase in processing power. In fact, computers are advancing so rapidly that an analyst considers a three-year technological forecast a long-term outlook.

Computers have revolutionized the way newspapers and magazines are put together once, and they will probably do it again.

For this reason, the aspiring print journalist should learn as much as possible about computers. Computers, equipped with word-processing/text-editing software, have effectively replaced typewriters as the primary tool of the journalist. But, more importantly, computers have made access to vast information resources possible.

Besides knowing how to use the computer as a tool, a journalist who understands computers can become the most valuable person in the newsroom when the system "goes down" an hour before deadline in the middle of the night. Knowing what happened and how to correct it can make the difference between a minor hassle and a missed edition. A journalist need not learn to program or design computer systems. But understanding how a computer works and knowing a few basic principles can make the job easier and the work better.

The computer is similar to the human nervous system. To function, both depend on electricity. In trying to understand the way a computer works, think of the entire writing process as a series of events spurred by electrical impulses.

Thoughts move from the reporter's mind to the reporter's hand to the reporter's pen or keyboard via electrical impulses sent from the brain through the nervous system to the fingers. The computer takes electrical impulses from a keyboard, processes them according to a set of human instructions (the program), and eventually translates these electronic impulses into type. In that sense, the link between the keyboard and the computer is almost a natural extension of the nervous system. Moreover, computers can turn almost anything into an electronic impulse, including the human voice (voice recognition and synthesis), the elements contained within a picture, the elements that make a type font, and even the nervous system's electrical impulses. Someday scientists may achieve a direct link between the human brain and the computer through the nervous system, allowing a reporter to literally "think" a story into print!

Certainly the computer will to some extent change almost every job in the newspaper and magazine businesses as in most other businesses. The computer is and will continue to be a primary tool for journalists from news clerks to executive editors, and it will in some ways define the parameters within which journalism functions.

Computer technology has already allowed reporters to spend more time in news gathering. In the future it will likely allow even more time. The Associated Press Stylebook, the style and usage manual that provides the guidelines for writing and editing at most American newspapers, has been successfully programmed into the AP's main computer system. The stylebook program actually alters a reporter's copy, automatically, to fit AP style.

Many newspapers and magazines have installed their own spelling-corrector and grammar-corrector programs that largely make misspellings and poor grammar impossible. A major benefit of these programs, aside from achieving uniform style, is that they allow the reporter to spend more time researching the story and polishing the writing; the computer does some of the copyediting.

Some publishing systems allow reporters to access the publication's morgue—on line—as they are writing a story and, using a split screen on a video display terminal, transfer information into the story on the other side of the screen. Multiple-source databases also permit this, allowing a reporter to search any of hundreds of newspapers and magazines for a particular subject.

For the news editor, the computer has put the entire newsroom staff less than an arm's length away. The news editor can access, edit, file, and cue a story in less time than it used to take the copy paper to get from the reporter to the desk. The editor can communicate with newsroom staff members through the computer system with electronic memos. The editor can also analyze a reporter's performance by checking a reporter's file in the system and noting what that reporter has written in the past week, month, or even year.

Computers have made it possible for the photo editor to eliminate film entirely, though it will probably take some time for this technology to filter into the publishing industry. A digital image camera, like a film camera, captures reflected light to form an image. But in a digital picture, each element of the picture—called a picture element (Pel)—is represented by a byte of information, that is, a series of negative and positive electrical charges strung together to represent a unique code. That code can then be altered electronically. Hence, photographers can enter the picture directly into a high resolution graphics computer system, where it can be manipulated electronically. Cropping, sizing, rotating, airbrushing, enhancing, outlining, reversing, and so on can be handled electronically at far greater speeds with much greater quality than was ever possible manually.

For the production editor, the computer has made the "pagination" system possible. A true graphics-handling pagination system eliminates all interference with the final product from the layout editor to the platemaking department. This eliminates the opportunity for a line to get lost, for a photo caption to run with the wrong photo, or for lines not to be justified across the page. With a pagination system, an editor simply pulls text files from the text system and digitalized photos and artwork from the graphics system and then creates the page, with text justified and graphics in place, on a computer screen. The photos appear, in scale, just as they will in the finished product. The computer wraps text around graphics, justifies, and even jumps text to another page.

In some systems, the type faces actually appear on the monitor in their true font, point size, and measure. Once the page is together, it progresses to an output device (a typesetter or computerized printing/platemaking machine), and out it comes, with all elements in place.

So what does this mean to journalism students? They cannot become too familiar with computers! Computer manufacturers are constantly striving to develop systems that are "user friendly" so the people who run them can do so without extensive knowledge or training. A goal of the aspiring journalist should be the *inverse* of that: to become "computer friendly."

Getting to know how a computer works and how to make it perform specific tasks is only one goal. Consider also career goals.

Many newspapers and magazines, among them the largest and most prestigious in the country, have created a new class of newsroom executive, the so-called "systems editor," in response to the need for someone who understands how to tailor the editorial process to computer systems, and vice versa. While computer people may understand computers, few understand what goes into the production of a newspaper or magazine.

The systems editor's function is to act as a buffer between the news department and the equipment it uses. When the executive editor says "we need to do things this way," the systems editor determines how to perform the task without causing unnecessary problems for the news staff. It is an up-and-coming job category—and at many publications, a highly paid job category.

For the journalism student, computer-programming courses may not be necessary. But courses dealing in computer concepts may be very valuable. For the journalism student who aspires to become a systems editor, programming and even some electrical-engineering courses are a necessity. "Above all, get to know computers," says Bill Gloede, associate editor at *Editor & Publisher* magazine in New York. "With personal computer prices declining steadily and expected to fall even further, buying a computer equipped with a good word-processing software package is a good idea."

Not only will it familiarize the journalism student with computer logic, says Gloede, it will also serve as a potential profit center. With a good personal computer and the necessary equipment to send stories over telephone lines, a freelance writer can increase productivity while selling more stories to more publications. It's much easier to sell an editor on a story you can send now as opposed to a story that will take several days to reach its destination.

One of the most prominent "systems editors" in the nation is Howard Angione of the New York *Times*. He rides herd over 439 terminals directly logged onto newsroom computers. The editing network, or system, is really nine separate computers that are interlinked, each of the computers able to store 4.5 million words of copy (or three weeks' worth of the *Times*). Each of these computers can store an additional four million words of copy coming in by wire, namely from Associated Press, where Angione previously worked (he edited the widely circulated Associated Press Stylebook).

However, as sophisticated as the *Times* system or network is, the paper still has its equivalent of "erasures" or "lost" copy. Angione was sitting back talking about the system in his office when an urgent call came in from a reporter covering the President's visit to Japan. It seems his story sent on line had been lost somewhere.

Angione wondered if ". . . the damn purge [the elimination of old stories from the system] got it. I could fish it out," he said, referring to its possible presence in another computer. "But your circuit is sound. I want you to rely on that circuit. . . ."

After reflection, he wondered if AP was the culprit. It was a day after the national elections in November 1983.

"I'll tell the foreign desk not to use system four but system six, which is not being pounded by AP, which washes out everything," he decided. "I don't know what AP did last night—they must have transmitted the whole election all over again." He told the reporter to get some sleep, he would find his story somewhere.

Angione left his office to check other news hubs in the buzzing third-floor operation and returned; he rang up the reporter in Tokyo again, and comforted the reporter: "I found it letter-perfect in news service." Angione thought the problem was a misplaced letter in the "header," or lead-in code information, told the reporter how it should be coded in the future, ". . . and I told foreign service to check news service next time [that a story can't be found]."

Angione believes that every newsperson will fall in love with the computer technology if they compare it to the typewriter of olden days. But he has some fond memories of the sports staff learning to make the adjustments—among them, the distinguished Red Smith not too long before he died. Angione would go to the games and assist the writers with the new equipment. He remembers Red Smith saying, "I think I've done something very stupid. . . . I cleared the screen before I saved it."

"Red, you never pressed the save key?" was Angione's reply. "Well, Red, you're right. There is no way to retrieve it." In newer equipment, only the most awkward combination would lose a story; it would still be somewhere even though a button wiped it from the screen.

Angione tells of another sports writer who lost his story. Angione advised him that he would just have to write it over. "It was a lousy feature," said the sports reporter of his own work. "I don't know what I wrote!" Angione recalls that the reporter, when he wrote it over the next day, said the second attempt was a better story.

New York *Times* reporters out on assignment carry the 15-pound box unit, the Teleram Portabubble/81. These use "bubble" memories as compared to the larger awkward disks of earlier units. Bubble memories consist of "thin wafers" of synthetic material, which, once they are magnetized, form minute magnetic fields, or bubbles, on the surface. By altering the direction of the magnetism, the bubbles can be routed to different locations (resulting in the "off" and "on" or 0 and 1 in computer coding).

New York *Times* reporters—such as Charles Austin, sitting in the newsroom at the convention arena in Pittsburgh—can compose stories on the screen and store them in the bubble memory. Then, when they are ready to send them, they use a phone connection, and, with special coding, lay the receiver on top of the Portabubble/81 (fastening the phone receiver into two rubber receptacles on top of the unit), press the right buttons, and relay the story electronically by phone lines to the "systems" at the New York *Times*.

Angione, like Gloede, advises students to learn as much general technology as possible, but he says that learning specific computer languages is not necessary, since they vary considerably. However, he does see value perhaps in learning BASIC, because it is a basic computer language, and even advanced equipment can run BASIC.

He encourages students to get used to working on a word processor—writing on a TV screen—instead of a typewriter. "The word processor encourages you to rewrite yourself and edit yourself more," he said. "You don't have to tear up a whole sheet of paper: just change what needs to be changed."

He believes students should not necessarily spend a lot of time on courses that teach VDT use, a skill he believes is a mere transfer of good typing. "I would spend time on searching data banks and learning electronic research tools which are available now and learning how to use computers in research," he said. "Increasing skills in science to interpret data can be meaningful."

He also urges a study of logic, rhetoric, and the works of such men as Edmund Burke and Cardinal John Henry Newman "in order to organize systematic thought processes and to refine ideas," and thus better relate to the very orderly and consistent computer.

Glossary of Newsroom Computer Technology

Access: To locate and process an area of main or auxiliary storage. See also Random access and Serial access.

Access time: The time interval between the instant at which data is called for and the instant at which delivery is completed. Access time is the sum of the waiting time and the transfer time.

Address: An identification as represented by a name, label, or number for a register, location in storage, or any other data source or destination.

Alphanumeric: Pertaining to a set that contains both letters and numerals, and usually other characters.

ASCII: American Standard Code for Information Interchange. A standard electronic code that represents common characters adopted to facilitate the interchange of data among various types of data processing and data communications equipment.

Auxiliary storage: Any peripheral devices (magnetic tape drives, floppy disks, hard disks, or optical disks) on which data may be stored. Augments the computer's internal storage.

Baud: A unit of signalling speed equal to the number of discrete conditions or signal events per second. One baud equals one half-dot cycle in Morse code, one bit per second in a train of binary signals, and one three-bit value per second in a train of signals each of which can assume one of eight different states.

Binary: A base-two numbering system using the digits 0 and 1. Widely used in computer systems because it can be represented by a single on/off switch.

Bit: The smallest unit of information in a computer. It represents one binary digit, 0 or 1.

Byte: A group of adjacent bits operated on as a unit. It can represent one complete character.

Central processing unit: The unit of a computing system that includes the circuits controlling the interpretations and execution of instructions.

Character: Any single unit of type that is type high, that is, not spaces; a written or printed alphabetic, numeric, or other symbol.

Computer program: A set of instructions which, when converted to machine-readable format, causes a computer to perform specified operations to solve a problem or complete a task.

Core storage: The memory of a computer, as opposed to storage on peripheral devices. Also called main memory.

Digital: Data in the form of digits, rather than in analog form.

Digitize: To express any kind of data in digital form.

Disk drive: The system or device that physically reads information from or writes information to a storage disk.

Downtime: The time during which a computer is not functioning properly.

Dump: To copy the contents of a set of storage locations, usually from an internal storage device to an external storage medium or output device. For example, a computer dumps processed text to a typesetter.

Duplex: Pertaining to a twin, a double, or a two-in-one situation. A channel or computer that allows simultaneous transmission in both directions.

EBCDIC: Extended Binary Coded Decimal Interchange Code. An electronic code, similar to ASCII, with which computers and peripherals communicate with one another. Used in IBM computers.

Execute: To perform the operations indicated by a machine instruction.

Field: An area within a record (tape, disk, or core storage) allocated to hold a specific amount and/or type of information.

File: A collection of related records, usually (but not always) arranged in sequence according to a key contained in each record.

Fixed storage: A storage device that stores data not alterable by computer instructions. A computer's operating system usually is contained in fixed storage.

Gigabyte: One billion bytes of data.

Hardware: The physical equipment that makes up a computer system.

Head: A device that reads, records, or erases data on a storage medium (disks or tape).

Header label: A line at the beginning of a file containing data identifying the file and data used in file control.

Initialize: To set counters, switches, and addresses to zero or other starting values at the beginning of or at prescribed points within a computer routine. Often denotes the erasure of a complete set of files.

Interface: A common boundary between systems or parts of systems; in computer nomenclature it usually refers to some type of electronic device that allows one piece of equipment to interact with another.

Kilobyte: One thousand bytes of information.

Laser optical disk: A storage medium, similar in appearance to a magnetic disk, on which information is written, erased, or retrieved by a laser instead of a head. Has much greater storage capacity than magnetic disks.

Line printer: A printer that, when linked with a computer, is capable of accepting one line of data at a time from a computer, then printing it.

Load: In programming, to place data into internal storage.

Loop: A sequence of instructions that is executed perpetually until terminated.

Mainframe: A class of computers, usually those with the greatest processing power, that contains both a central processing unit and large amounts of internal storage.

Megabyte: One million bytes of data.

Menu: A listing of elements, items, stories, or references of any nature that can be called up or accessed.

Microchip: A silicon chip containing integrating circuits that executes programmed instructions, sorts, and stores data within a computer.

Microcomputer: A computer that processes information using only one silicon microchip. Also contains relatively little internal storage.

Microprocessor: A system of electronic circuitry that executes computer instructions. Constitutes the central processing function of micro and mini computers.

Minicomputer: A computer designed with integrated circuitry that generally has less memory capacity and processing power than a mainframe yet performs many of the same functions.

Microsecond: One-millionth of a second.

Millisecond: One-thousandth of a second.

Modem: A device that provides the appropriate interface between a communications link (telephone line or coaxial cable) and a data processing machine or system by serving as a modulator and/or demodulator.

Nanosecond: One-billionth of a second.

Off-line: Pertaining to equipment or devices that are not in direct communication with the central processor of a computer system.

On-line: Pertaining to equipment or devices that are in direct communication with the central processor of a computer system.

Operating system: A set of programs for the overall monitoring, control, and maintenance of a computer system.

Output: Data that has been processed.

Pagination: A complete computer system, often consisting of several computers and related peripherals, that allows a publication to assemble, view, and edit complete pages electronically before outputting the full page with graphics in place.

Peripheral equipment: The input/output units and secondary storage units of a computer system. The central processor and its associated storage and control units are the only part of a computer system that are not considered peripheral equipment.

Picosecond: One-trillionth of a second.

Processor: A device or system capable of performing operations on data.

Program: A plan for solving a problem; to devise a plan for solving a problem; a computer routine, a set of instructions arranged in proper sequence to cause a computer to perform a particular process; to write a computer routine.

Random Access Memory (RAM): A system of file management in which a record or file is accessible independent of its file location or the location of the previous record accessed.

Run: To process, as a program or system.

Serial Access: The process necessary to obtain data from or to place data into storage when there is a time sequence relationship that governs access to the successive storage location.

Software: A collection of programs and routines that cause the computer to perform specific tasks.

System: An integrated assembly of hardware and software designed to implement a given application or set of applications.

Terminal: A point in a system or communication network at which data can be either entered or retrieved.

Word: One storage location in memory or on a peripheral. Usually eight, twelve, sixteen, thirty-two, or sixty-four bits make up a word.

Word length: The number of bits or characters in a word.

Write: To transfer data from a terminal, main computer memory, or peripheral to a data recording device.

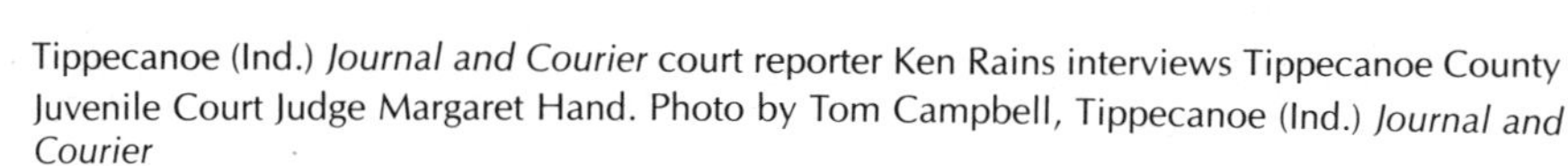

Tippecanoe (Ind.) *Journal and Courier* court reporter Ken Rains interviews Tippecanoe County Juvenile Court Judge Margaret Hand. Photo by Tom Campbell, Tippecanoe (Ind.) *Journal and Courier*

PART 7

What's Right

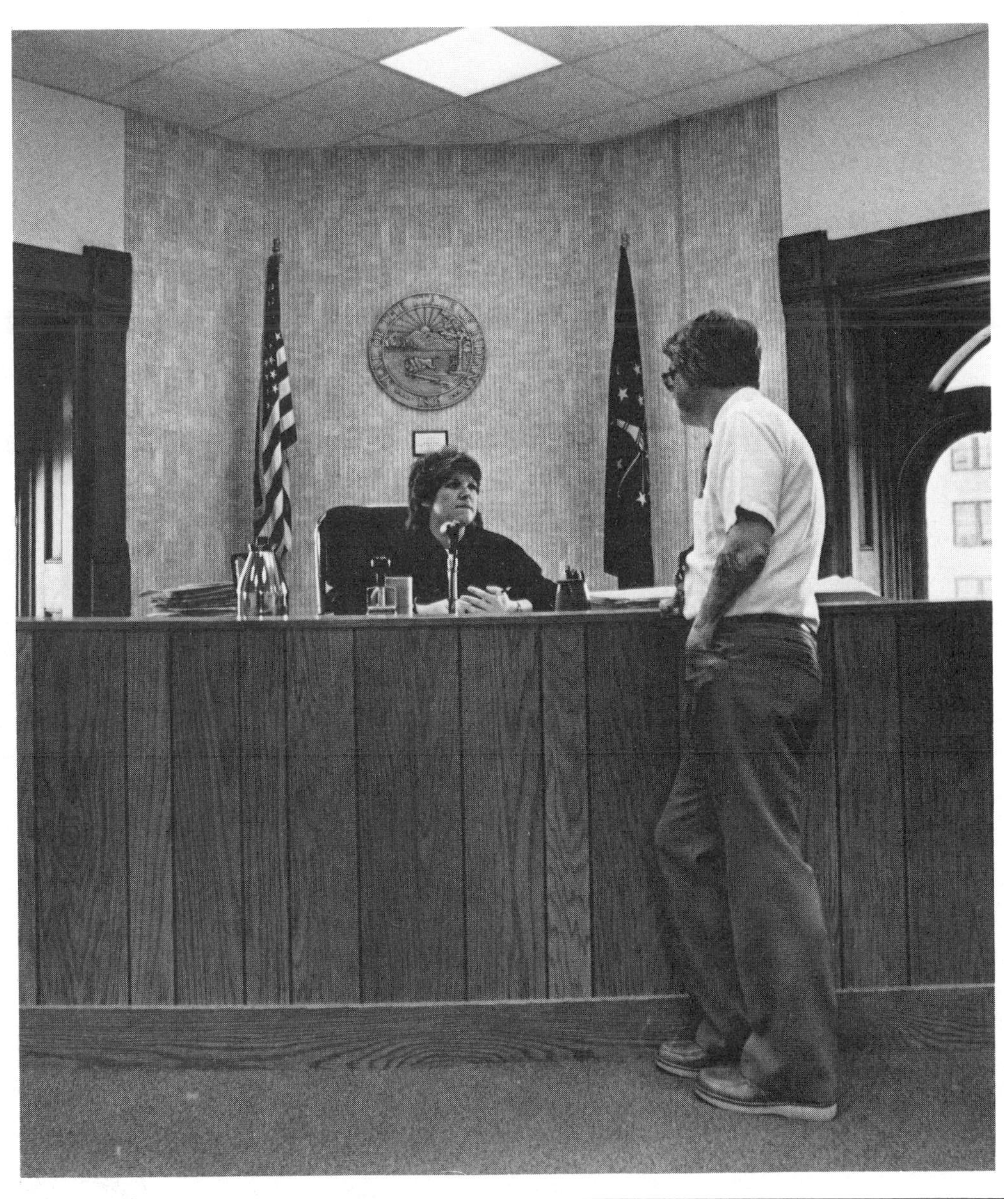

21

Law and Ethics

Fred Behringer, vice president of the Montgomery Publishing Co. in Fort Washington, Pa., and a teacher of a media law course at Temple University, wrote part of this section on reporting and the law.

Reporting would be much simpler if people were more alike, if they believed the same things, spoke the same language, understood words the same way, and experienced events the same.

But no two people are physically alike (not even identical twins—one is often left-handed, the other right-handed), and no common deposit of belief unites people. (There are some 1,700 religious groups and cults in the U.S.) Various people around the world speak 4,000 languages. Words in the same language have many connotations: even words such as town and city have disparate meanings in different places.

No two people hear the same words or sounds the same—if you think they do, take any group of reporters and compare their reports. Even their quotes have variations.

People don't see things the same way. People viewing an event, such as an accident from different perspectives at an intersection, will not always agree.

People even perceive concepts differently. Although people yearn for universal ethical and moral guidelines, answers to the most basic questions are blurred at worst and complex at best.

Humans are still trying to find consensus on fundamental issues. And so we still ask: What is the law? What is ethical?

KNOWING THE LAW

In the United States, law, in deciding disputes, means guidelines and regulations adopted according to the basic positions the U.S. Constitution established.

The U.S. Constitution originated at the Constitutional Convention which convened in Philadelphia in the summer of 1787 to work out a new binding document to succeed the earlier Articles of Confederation. James Madison, of Virginia, drafted most of the Constitution, drawing from Greek philosophy as well as from diverse contemporary thinking. To many the Constitution emerged as a patchwork document, but 39 of the 55 delegates signed it on Sept. 17, 1787. After the necessary number of nine states had ratified it, the Constitution took effect in March 1789.

When the new Congress met on Sept. 25, 1789, members presented 12 amendments to the Constitution in the interest of clarifying rights of individuals and states. Ten of the amendments (numbers 3 to 12) eventually were ratified by the states.

The following amendments directly affect how journalists practice their profession.

The First Amendment

The First Amendment originally did not mention the press. Reference to the press was added only after a committee headed by Madison presented the amendment to the convention, which returned it to that committee for corrections and additions.

The First Amendment explicitly says that Congress shall make no laws abridging freedom of the press. While protections here are great, the amendment does not mention protection from state legislatures or the courts. Nor does it define the terms, rank, or balance of the guarantees with other guarantees of the other amendments which speak of special rights of individuals.

The First Amendment says:

> Congress shall make no law respecting an establishment of religion, or prohibiting the free exercise thereof; or abridging the freedom of speech, or of the press; or the right of the people peaceably to assemble, and to petition the Government for a redress of grievances.

The Fourth Amendment

The person's right to privacy, with which aggressive news reporting may at times contend, is explicit in the Fourth Amendment:

> The right of the people to be secure in their persons, houses, papers, and effects, against unreasonable searches and seizures, shall not be violated, and no warrants shall issue, but upon probable cause, supported by oath or affirmation, and particularly describing the place to be searched, and the persons or things to be seized.

The Sixth Amendment

Much of the conflict between press and authorities occurs because of the inherent conflict between the First Amendment, with its guarantees for the press, and the Sixth, with its guarantees to a fair and impartial trial. Several legal questions here are hard to answer. For example, in the interest of due process and to create a climate without prejudicing the case against the defendant, can a judge bar the press from some of the proceedings, especially in sensational cases? Can a judge determine how much the press can or cannot report? Should judges allow cameras in the courtroom? Are the right to know and the right to access available to the press? Says Clark Mollenhoff:

> Whether you like it or not, you will have to live with the reality of the bench's concern for the Sixth Amendment and stop dreaming of any special status as a journalist. A nation unwilling to give an unqualified executive privilege to the President is not very likely to approve an absolute privilege to someone who calls himself a journalist.[1]

The Sixth Amendment says:

> In all criminal prosecutions, the accused shall enjoy the right to a speedy and public trial, by an impartial jury of the State and district wherein the crime shall have been committed, which district shall have been previously ascertained by law, and to be informed of the nature and cause of the accusation; to be confronted with the witnesses against him; to have compulsory process for obtaining witnesses in his favor, and to have the assistance of counsel for his defense.

The Fourteenth Amendment

The Fourteenth Amendment, adopted in 1868, says that rights guaranteed in the national Constitution apply to the states, including guarantees of freedom of speech and press, thus making applicable the guarantees of the First Amendment:

> All persons born or naturalized in the United States, and subject to the jurisdiction thereof, are citizens of the United States and of the State wherein they reside. No State shall make or enforce any law which shall abridge the privileges or immunities of citizens of the United States; nor shall any State deprive any person of life, liberty, or property, without due process of law; nor deny to any person within its jurisdiction the equal protection of the laws. . . .

> The Congress shall have power to enforce, by appropriate legislation, the provisions of this article.

Understanding the First Amendment

The First Amendment remains vague and, of course, it does not guarantee absolute freedom (or license) to the press. There are limitations to the First Amendment when it is balanced with other amendments.

For example, the Thirteenth Amendment (adopted in 1865), prohibiting slavery and seemingly unrelated to freedom of press guarantees, was cited in the defense in a celebrated case before the U.S. Supreme Court in 1919. The case grew out of an incident of a socialist editor circulating an anti-draft booklet in 1917 during World War I. The argument in the booklet was that conscription was a form of slavery, and the government could not compel conscription.

Justice Oliver Wendell Holmes, who handed down the opinion of the court against Socialist Charles Schenck, enunciated a doctrine which would be used in future attempts to justify censorship of the press:

> We admit that in many places and in ordinary times the defendants in saying all that was said in the circular would have been within their constitutional rights. But the character of every act depends upon the circumstances in which it is done. The most stringent protection of free speech would not protect a man in falsely shouting fire in a theatre and causing a panic. It does not even protect a man from an injunction against uttering words that may have all the effect of force. The question in every case is whether the words used are used in such circumstances and are of such a nature as to create a clear and present danger that they will bring about the substantive evils that Congress has a right to prevent. It is a question of proximity and degree. When a nation is at war many things that might be said in time of peace are such a hindrance to its effort that their utterance will not be endured so long as men fight and that no Court could regard them as protected by any constitutional right.[2]

The question of national security and the later definition of the existence of "clear and present danger" (in the form of threat of sedition or subversion) has served as a reason to suppress editors and reporters beginning with the Alien and Sedition Acts of 1798 (used against enemies of the Federalists). Then came the Espionage Act of 1917 and the Sedition Act of 1918 (one editor, Congressman Victor Berger, was sentenced to 20 years). The government was concerned about alleged threats to security by the publication of the Pentagon Papers (concerning Vietnam War policy) and the publication of H-bomb "secrets" in the small Wisconsin magazine, the *Progressive*. The government's case against the *Progressive* collapsed when another paper, the Madison *Press Connection*, carried the same basic information gleaned from a library in a letter to the editor. However, the secrecy provisions of the Atomic Energy Act of 1954 are still on the books. Military censorship has existed in various forms, even to the point of initially blacking out a war, as was the case in the 1983 invasion of Grenada in which reporters were banned.

The Thirteenth Amendment, used in the Schenck defense to challenge government coercion, says:

> Neither slavery nor involuntary servitude, except as a punishment for crime whereof the party shall have been duly convicted, shall exist within the United States or any place subject to their jurisdiction. . . .

Constitutional historian Leonard Levy maintains that the First Amendment is extremely limited and the only thing it upholds for the press is freedom from prior restraint—a government's attempt to prohibit publishing a report it considers harmful or undesirable. Says Levy:

> We do not know what the First Amendment's freedom of speech-and-press clause meant to the men who drafted and ratified it at the time that they did so. Moreover, they themselves were at that time sharply divided and possessed no clear understanding either.[3]

If a choice had to be made, Levy said, these same men would probably have been supportive of the repressive Alien and Sedition Acts of 1798–1800.

Justice William Douglas, who was one of the most liberal justices, admitted that "secrecy in government is not fully eliminated by the First Amendment."[4]

Tension between press and government over the meaning of the First Amendment continues into the 1980s. A First Amendment Congress of educators and journalists which met in Philadelphia in January 1980 and in Williamsburg, Va., in March of the same year kept the focus on the problems ahead in interpreting the First Amendment. CBS television correspondent Dan Rather warned the delegates in the Philadelphia meeting that the whole public—not just the media—has a stake in the First Amendment. If press rights are eroded, he said, so are the public's.

However, at that meeting New York *Times* columnist Anthony

Lewis, winner of two Pulitzer prizes, noted that many of the cases the press has lost in the courts were not really protection of rights cases but rather "tests to gain new legal advantages" for the press.[5]

Beginning journalists should think carefully about what the First Amendment means. As a starter, they may want to consider the views of noted journalism educator John C. Merrill of the Louisiana State University in Baton Rouge. Merrill rankles absolutists by suggesting three myths dealing with freedom of the press and the First Amendment:

> Three of the most popular and sacred of these myths are: (1) that the "people have a right to know"; (2) that the people have a right "of access to the press"; and (3) that the press is a "fourth branch of government." All of these slogans are used by those who call them into service in "defense" of freedom of the press. But, actually, they are *destructive of press freedom*; in fact, they are subtle myths which contradict journalistic autonomy by placing obligations on the free press.
>
> All three of these myths, as "American as apple pie," are extremely popular today and one opens himself to charges of seditious activity, disloyalty to journalism, acute myopia—of even insanity—when he dares to question one or all of them. But even at the risk of spoiling the "pie" by looking at the apples in it, let us consider briefly these three myths and their relationship to libertarianism.[6]

Concerning what he calls the myth of the "right to know," Merrill says:

> In the United States, . . . large numbers of citizens and journalists (and occasionally, even a government official) assume the "right" and believe they have a basis for it (even a legal one). But if such a "right" does exist, what is its source? Is it implicit in the First Amendment to the Constitution as we are often told? Where is there the slightest insinuation in the Bill of Rights that the people have a *right* to know? The right of the press to freedom is there; the right of the people to know is not there. But the myth persists. And related to it is another assumption: that the press has the obligation (responsibility) to see to it that people know. Where did the press acquire this obligation? The First Amendment only forbids laws abridging press freedom; it places *no* obligation on the press—not a single one! If there is some theoretical right of the people to know, the obligation to grant it would fall on Government, not on the press.[7]

Concerning the second alleged myth, the "right of access to the media," Merrill says:

> The whole attempt to "redefine" the First Amendment press freedom . . . has stemmed from the belief that the "people" have some kind of inalienable *right* to have someone else publish their opinions. This "myth" of people's rights in this area is increasingly potent in America, but it is not accepted by everyone. One of the foremost writers in recent years to take issue with it is the late Ayn Rand.[8]

Merrill then quotes Ayn Rand's *Virtue of Selfishness*:

> The right of free speech means that a man has a right to express his ideas without danger of suppression, interference or punitive action by the government. It does not mean that others must provide him with a lecture hall, a radio station or a printing press through which to express his ideas.[9]

Adds Merrill:

> This whole subject of the people's right to access was, to Ayn Rand, contrary to the concept of individual freedom. Carried very far this "right of access," as Miss Rand sees it, would mean that a publisher has to publish articles (or books) he considers worthless, false or evil, and that the owner of a newspaper must turn his editorial pages over "to any young hooligan who clamors for the enslavement of the press."
>
> Perhaps we try to make the term "freedom of the press" cover too much. If we were to understand it narrowly, in the sense clearly indicated by its syntax, we would emphasize the *press* and its *freedom* from restraint or control. This would mean that the "freedom" belongs to "the press." The press alone, in this definition, would be in the position of determining what it would or would not print. The press would have no prior restrictions or directions on its editorial prerogatives; this would be press freedom. . . .
>
> The person, however, who is concerned about what does not get into the press is not primarily a supporter of the concept of press freedom stated above; he is not overly concerned that the press should make editorial determinations. However laudable his reasons for such a stance might be, he must recognize that his position is potentially *authoritarian*—or even basically authoritarian. . . . Naturally this "anti-press's-freedom" person justifies his position on the basis that it is what is "best for society" and contends that the press must be willing to give up its freedom in order to be socially responsible.[10]

Concerning the third alleged myth, that the press is a kind of a "fourth estate" or "fourth branch of government," Merrill notes:

> . . . the press likes to think of itself as a part of government—or a check on government, or a "watchdog" of some kind. In effect, the press (or

> portions of it) is a self-appointed governmental branch, check or watchdog. The U.S. Constitution certainly does not give the press such a status, although many persons claim they can "read into" the Constitution such responsibilities for the press. . . .
>
> But, on even superficial analysis, we can see that this is not the case.
>
> The "people" do not own the press; it cannot, therefore, be their watchdog. It has no specific duties—except those which the press people themselves want to accept. Why should the press "watch" the government any more than it should watch the people? The metaphoric myth of a "watchdog" is as meaningless as is its companion, the concept of the "fourth branch of government." Certainly *the press* does not recognize any such function. We see all around us newspapers and other media which like to consider themselves part of the "press" not serving as "watchdogs" on government, checks on government or critics of government. Some, in fact, tend to be apologists for government. They do not consider themselves "watchdogs" on anybody; or, if they do, they see themselves as dogs belonging to no master and having no leashes.
>
> Related very closely to this concept, of course, is the idea that the press has an "adversary" relationship to government—that press and government are natural enemies. Many writers and speakers have stressed this adversary role of the press. What is rather interesting is that it is usually journalism people who allude to this relationship and what they mean usually is that the press is to be an adversary to government—but not the other way around. The prospect of government being an adversary to the press is, of course, a natural part of a press-government adversary relationship, but it does not seem to occur to most journalists. They want it all one way. We fight you; but you don't fight us. We try to get information from you, but you don't have the right to try to withhold information from us. This is really not much of an "adversary" relationship. If the press values so highly this role of government adversary (a myth!), it should recognize that the government, then, has an equal right to be a press adversary. Otherwise there really is not any meaning to the concept, and journalists would do well to forget it.[11]

Merrill, author of books on the foreign press, is perhaps influenced by his work with international press systems which regard the responsibility of the press in many ways, from a press that follows a doctrine of "social responsibility" for educating the masses, as in communist and socialist and new emerging nations, to the sensational Japanese press, with fewer restrictions, that allows reporters to even climb into windows of private dwellings.

Merrill, along with coauthor Everette Dennis, former dean of the School of Journalism at the University of Oregon in Eugene and now head of a new Gannet-funded research center at Columbia University, reiterates much of this classic discussion in *Basic Issues in Mass Communications*, published by Macmillan in 1984.

Libel

"Libel," which comes from the Latin *libellus*, "a little book, writing, or lampoon," is "any written or printed statement, or any sign, picture, or effigy, not made in the public interest, tending to expose a person to public ridicule or contempt or to injure his reputation in any way."[12]

"Defamation" is a general term which means to harm the good name or reputation of a person. Spoken orally, it is "slander"; in writing, print, picture, or film, it is "libel," as determined by law.

Libel is one of the most significant and potentially most confusing areas of press law. Libel is a tort—a civil wrong not involving a contract, in the same category as trespass, assault or negligence. As such it varies from state to state. In Indiana, for instance, it is difficult to get a libel judgment against the press, but next door in Illinois it is easy. For example, a local businessman in Alton, Ill., hit the Alton *Telegraph* with a $9.2 million libel suit for a memo, never published, by two reporters to a U.S. Justice Department investigator. The reporters set forth their suspicions that money was going from the Mafia to a local builder in the form of loans. The tip was never confirmed, but the memo was passed along to federal bank regulators in Chicago, who forced the local savings and loan association to cut off the builder's credit. The builder charged that his business failed because of the memo. The suit was settled out of court in 1982 for $1.4 million, one of the largest libel settlements in history.[13]

Telling the truth is a near absolute defense in a libel case, but the burden of proving the truth is theoretically on the defendant. The other traditional common law defenses—privilege and fair comment—are not as clear-cut and present more hazards for journalists.

An additional protection against libel, the "New York *Times* Rule" defense, has developed since 1964, when the U.S. Supreme Court ruled that public officials suing for libel must prove actual malice (*New York Times v. Sullivan*). A group of civil rights leaders in an ad in the New York *Times* had said unkind things about certain Alabama officials, including Montgomery Police Commissioner L. B. Sullivan. Some information was not correct, and Sullivan sued. He won in the lower courts, but lost before the U.S. Supreme Court. The majority opinion said:

> The constitutional guarantees (the First and Fourteenth Amendments) require, we think, a federal rule that prohibits a public official from recovering damages for a defamatory falsehood relating to his official conduct unless he proves that the statement was made with "actual malice"—that is, with knowledge that it was false or with reckless disregard of whether it was false or not.

Public figures also have the added burden of showing actual malice, the court said in 1967 (*Associated Press v. Walker*), but the definition of a public figure is difficult to pin down. The court extended the actual malice test to anyone involved in a public issue (*Rosenbloom v. Metromedia 1971*) but reversed itself three years later (*Gertz v. Welch 1974*). In the Gertz case, the court again limited the rule to public officials and "public figures" and not to private persons unwillingly involved in public issues. It reinforced this decision in 1976 (*Time v. Firestone*) by deciding that a socially prominent woman was not a public figure even though she held press conferences during a divorce dispute and maintained a clipping service to keep track of her publicity.

In 1979 the U.S. Supreme Court ruled that an employee of a state—specifically a scientist working at a state hospital where he had received substantial federal funds for research—could not be regarded as a public figure in a libel suit filed against U.S. Senator William Proxmire (D-Wis.). Proxmire awarded his "Golden Fleece of the Month Award" to federal agencies that helped to fund research on stress in monkeys and other animals by Dr. Ronald R. Hutchinson of the Kalamazoo (Mich.) State Mental Hospital. Hutchinson filed a libel suit saying that he was not a public figure and Proxmire's announcement and remarks had hurt his professional reputation and were inaccurate. The U.S. Supreme Court eventually ruled in Hutchinson's favor, that he was not a public figure, and that Proxmire's protection from libel as a point of privilege as a senator applied only inside the walls of Congress. The court said Hutchinson ". . . did not have the regular and continuing access to the media that is one of the accouterments of having become a public figure . . . [his] access was limited to responding to the announcement of the . . . Award."

Commented Carol E. Rinzler, an author and a lawyer, in *Publishers Weekly* in 1983:

> The first step in identifying a limited purpose public figure, the cases suggest, is to identify a public controversy. It's not clear how substantial a controversy must be in order to qualify. Tempests in teapots—the firing of a tennis pro by a country club, for instance—won't do; the

> firing of a town librarian will. That's not to say, however, that the controversy must be either political or earthshaking. In one recent case, a manufacturer of loudspeakers sued *Consumer Reports* for stating falsely that instruments heard through the plaintiff's speakers "tended to wander about the room." The court found a public controversy concerning "the relative merits" of various loudspeaker systems. In another recent case, in which the plaintiff was president of a large food cooperative, "unit pricing, open-dating [and] the cooperative form of business" was sufficient. In theory, at least, the controversy must be pointed, not merely a matter of general public interest. In a leading Supreme Court case, a scientist using government funds to study, among other things, why monkeys clenched their jaws, received Senator William Proxmire's Golden Fleece Award and sued. Among the reasons the Court gave for finding the plaintiff not a public figure was that the controversy—the public's concern about government spending—was too general. To hold otherwise would subject all recipients of government grants to public figure status. True, Proxmire's award had created a specific controversy around the scientist, but "those charged with defamation cannot . . . create their own defense by making the claimant a public figure."[14]

Although the constitutional defense which started in 1964 has somewhat broadened journalists' protection against the charge of libel, there is a narrowing in the rulings, and the court's changing interpretation makes the risk of libel greater.

Making the possibility of more libel cases going against the publishers were two unanimous decisions by the U.S. Supreme Court in March 1984. The court ruled that a person seeking redress for libel against a national publication can file suit in any state where the publication is generally sold, thus allowing the plaintiff to shop around for states where the laws might seem more favorable to their suits.

One of the rulings that has troubled journalists was the decision of the U.S. Supreme Court in *Herbert v. Lando* in 1979. It said that in libel suits editors may be questioned about their thoughts and reasons for decisions in the process of printing a story. Retired Army Lt. Col. Anthony Herbert, in a suit against CBS "60 Minutes" producer Barry Lando, CBS correspondent Mike Wallace, and *Atlantic Monthly* magazine, sought the right to look into the editorial process to establish whether there had been knowing or reckless printing of falsehood. Herbert won his case. The right of "discovery" achieved in the Herbert case has received support in a case involving Gen. William C. Westmoreland against CBS.

CBS sought to show in its documentary, "The Uncounted

Enemy: A Vietnam Deception," that the commander in Vietnam, Gen. William Westmoreland, had deliberately distorted a document, the "Order of Battle," in order to understate the number of enemy soldiers in Vietnam for fear of showing the war was not being won. A brief filed by CBS in May 1984, presented interviews and depositions from CIA aides and military intelligence officers who served with Westmoreland and that said the charges were true. Westmoreland's lawyers followed in July 1984 with a 365-page memorandum that calls the alleged deception a legitimate intelligence "debate." Westmoreland, using an affidavit of former Defense Secretary Robert McNamara, argues "the debate" was fully aired and had the full knowledge of President Lyndon Johnson. Seeking to show malice, Westmoreland is asking $120 million. He cites 27 different examples of malice as determined by previous rulings and maintains that the CBS documentary manifested them all. CBS was also arguing that Gen. Westmoreland should not be suing because, as a commander for the military, he represented the government. "Any attack upon plaintiff's conduct in his official capacity is indistinguishable from an attack on the Government's military conduct of the war," an important area of free speech protected from libel suits, according to the CBS brief. The CBS brief argues that such freedom is necessary to review the real and potential involvement of U.S. troops in the Middle East, Central America, and elsewhere.

If you give opinions, you must be sure to label them opinions. Says *Editor & Publisher*:

> There is one defense that will defeat a libel suit regardless whether the plaintiff is considered a public or private figure. The key is to characterize the alleged defamation as "opinion," as opposed to statements of fact. Following the Supreme Court rubric that "there is no such thing as a false idea," a newspaper cannot generally be held liable even for the harshest of opinions.[15]

In the appellate courts, the Palm Beach (Fla.) *Post* survived a $1 million libel challenge when the article said a school superintendent was characterized by "incompetence." The courts held that the reference was mere opinion or "rhetorical hyperbole." The Supreme Court declined to rule otherwise.

Certain words and subjects suggest special caution. Watch stories about arrests and investigations; quoting the unofficial comments of a police officer, even if the quote is accurate, is not always legally safe. Watch stories that may affect a person's professional or business reputation. Be careful about words that relate to a person's honesty, personal habits, religious beliefs, political affiliations, and the like. Remember that the word "alleged" does not remove the danger from publishing a libelous statement.

Journalists should be just as watchful of the short, routine story as they are of the major investigative report. Many, probably most, libel actions result from seemingly minor, uncontroversial reports. Unconfirmed engagement announcements, letters to the editor, and items from the police blotter are examples of items requiring special attention to accuracy.

One small mistake in a story in the *Kentucky Post* in Covington, Ky., led to a $32,500 libel judgment against the paper. The story told of a fist fight between a 12-year-old and an 11-year-old who was killed in the fight. The article said the younger boy was repeatedly struck by the older boy, but, in fact, only one blow occurred. Since the 12-year-old was a private figure, the prosecutor did not need to show actual malice.

Headlines must be as accurate as stories; libel plaintiffs have received damages for an erroneous headline on a story that was completely accurate. An article in the New Orleans *States-Item* about an architectural firm preparing designs for a new state school for the deaf was accurate, but a headline suggesting that bids were rigged—which is not what the story said—cost the paper $10,000 in damages to an official whose reputation the court felt was maligned.

You should handle complaints about stories with care. Respond to complaints courteously, of course, but do not admit error or explain how you developed the information. If the complaint comes from a lawyer, immediately refer it to your own attorney.

Still one of the best rules in handling material which may damage a person's reputation is to make sure it is provably true.

Reporters might try pretending they are the publisher for a moment when deciding whether to write a story that might be considered libelous. Alexander Greenfield, former attorney for the New York *Times*, suggested 16 rules for protection for publishers against libel. Greenfeld, a University of California law professor, made his remarks at a workshop of the California Newspaper Publishers in Berkeley, Calif. As a publisher (which you may be someday), you will:

1. Always use a libel lawyer, not a general practitioner. It is far less expensive in the long run to use a libel lawyer because it takes the libel lawyer less time to handle your case than it does a general practitioner.
2. When beginning a highly sensitive investigative story, go over the

parameters of it with your attorney so that he can spot potential problems.

3. Do not allow your reporters to break the law.
4. Use the following test for determining potential libel problems: (a) Is the story accurate? and (b) Is the story fair? What would you do if the story were written about you?
5. Forget the retraction statute. It is useless and we would be better off without it.
6. Double check pictures of criminals and indicted persons.
7. Have photographers and reporters get written releases from institutions and minors.
8. Have your copy editors check to make sure that the story reflects the headline.
9. Always get a comment from the subject of the story who is being pictured in a bad light.
10. Do not allow editors and reporters to make private disparaging remarks about the story subjects. Make sure their discussions are fit to be tape recorded. This advice is given as a result of the recent Supreme Court decision in *Herbert v. Lando* in which the court said that the plaintiff in the libel action has the right to examine the thought processes of the reporter and editors.
11. Be careful when reporting about private companies that are on the verge of bankruptcy.
12. Beware of making remarks about the competency of professionals, such as lawyers and doctors.
13. Know the names of your sources, and be prepared to defend on the basis of truth.
14. Make sure that your confidential sources make an accusation but not in your paper (for example, "Law enforcement officials revealed that an indictment is expected soon against Johnny Jones.")
15. Avoid guilt by association. If you have an accurate story that Smith is a crook, do not mention his prominent friends when there is no evidence that they are aware of his illegal activities.
16. Play lawyer when you are involved in a sensitive story. Ask for the sources. If the reporter will not give you the names, tell him to print the story in his own newspaper. Confidentiality is not damaged by giving the names to editors and lawyers.[16]

Privacy

While provable truth is always a defense in libel, in the case of privacy law even the truth can get journalists into legal trouble.

Privacy law, like libel law, has been developing on a case-by-case basis, and the trend has not been an encouraging one for journalists. Recently many individuals have sued over their rights to be let alone and to keep their names and activities out of the public domain. Something as apparently innocent as a paragraph in a "years ago" column drawn from back files of a newspaper can result in damages for invasion of privacy.

Even publicizing the facts of a conviction can lead to a ruling charging invasion of privacy. In Alexandra, La., a laundromat owner put up a poster which told of a conviction of a burglar of his laundromat—an attempt to discourage other would-be burglars. The owner had captured Michael Norris on film through a hidden camera in the act of theft. Norris, who pleaded guilty, received a one-year-suspended sentence. The laundromat continued to be burglarized and so came the poster entitled, "Caught in the Act," with the hidden security camera picture of Norris burglarizing the laundromat. Norris was identified and his address included. The owner pleaded that under the First Amendment he had the right to publicize information about a crime of public record. A Louisiana court of appeals in 1978 upheld a lower court injunction against the owner and levied a fine of $500 against the owner. The court said the owner's action was "harassment" and "unreasonable and seriously interfered with . . . privacy." The Supreme Court declined to review the case.

Journalists must beware of four separate wrongs which they may commit under privacy law:

1. ***False light:*** Making individuals appear different than they really are, often through fictionalizing a story or embellishing facts.
2. ***Appropriation:*** Using someone's name or photograph without a model release or proper permission, as in a testimonial ad. This category is sometimes referred to as "misappropriation" or "commercialization."
3. ***Intrusion:*** Trespassing, such as eavesdropping on a conversation in the course of pursuing a story.
4. ***Using private information:*** Public disclosure of information which is not newsworthy and which may be considered sensational prying into someone's life.

Journalists and the Courts

Court decisions in the 1970s drastically affected the relationship of reporters to the criminal justice system. In these decisions, which began in 1972 with *Branzburg v. Hayes*, the Supreme Court rejected reporters' claims of First Amendment protection against testifying about confidential sources (see Chapter 4). The court continued to try to balance First Amendment rights against what it saw as the rights of defendants and prosecutors, and it most often decided against the news media.

Both the Branzburg case and the 1978 *Zurcher v. Stanford Daily* case, in which the court upheld a surprise police search of the Stanford University newspaper for information from its files, resulted in considerable sentiment for legislation to overturn the court decisions. In regard to shield laws which protect sources, journalists, as we have seen in Chapter 4, have trouble agreeing among themselves whether such legislation is desirable, and if so, what form it should take. But in regard to the Stanford *Daily* decision, the Congress began action in early 1980 aimed at overturning the U.S. Supreme Court ruling of May 1978, which gave police the right of surprise searches. The Senate Judiciary Subcommittee on the Constitution approved a bill which would overturn the Supreme Court decision. The bill was passed, and then-President Jimmy Carter signed it into law.

News media attorneys generally advise reporters not to appear voluntarily as witnesses in any court proceeding and not to give information informally to attorneys who ask about stories. Reporters are advised to report subpoenas immediately to their editors.

While many journalists have found themselves in court against their will, there are also times when they want access to the courtroom and cannot get it. Their claim that the "public trial" provision of the Sixth Amendment applies to the general public, not just the defendant, conflicts with judges' and lawyers' concern for the defendants' rights. This continuing "free press-fair trial" controversy frequently has gone to the Supreme Court for balancing.

The court in 1976 (*Nebraska Press Assn. v. Stuart*) struck down restrictive orders against reporting open court proceedings and indicated that the court will find such orders unconstitutional unless clearly justified and narrowly written.

The lower courts were more successful in restricting comments by court personnel and in closing the courtroom to the press and the public, especially in pretrial proceedings.

On July 2, 1979, the Supreme Court widened judges' power to bar reporters and the public from pretrial hearings upon request of the defendant when the judge thought the publicity might adversely affect the chance of a fair trial.

In the *Gannett v. DePasquale* case, the Court, in a 5 to 4 decision, said: "To safeguard the due process of the accused, a trial judge has an affirmative constitutional duty to minimize the effects of prejudicial pretrial publicity." Although dealing with pretrial proceedings, the ruling also said that neither public nor press has a constitutional right to be on hand at a regular criminal trial.

The case came from pretrial hearings in the murder of a policeman in the Rochester, N.Y., area in which a 16-year-old Texan was charged. At the hearing Judge Daniel DePasquale barred the press and public. The Gannett Newspaper chain took the matter to court.

In the several months that followed this decision, some 40 attempts to bar the press elsewhere were reported. A reporter stood up in a courtroom in Minneapolis and persuaded a judge to reconsider when the judge, on the advice of the defendant's attorney, sought to bar the press. Sam Newlund, the reporter from the Minneapolis *Tribune*, asked that his paper's attorney be allowed to argue that the pretrial hearing not be closed. The judge agreed, and the paper's attorney was there in a half hour. After hearing the attorney, the judge ordered the court to proceed to bar the public and the press. The paper appealed to the state supreme court which met that afternoon. Since the prosecutor himself favored the hearing to be open, the state supreme court ruled in favor of the paper and the hearings stayed open. The prosecutor argued that, as in *Gannett v. DePasquale*, the prosecutor and judge had to agree on the closing of the hearing. The *Tribune* developed pocket-size cards with a statement to read in court in event a judge seeks to close a proceeding of the court. The statement asks that the newspaper be permitted to present arguments through its attorney for an open proceeding.

Gannett v. DePasquale has been partially superseded by *Richmond Newspapers v. Virginia* and *Globe Newspapers v. Superior Court*, media law observers point out. Basically, trials must universally be open. Pretrial hearing rules vary from state to state although there is presumed to be a heavy burden of proof to close a session.

The Associated Press, concerned about the increased attempts to close court proceedings, put out the following guidelines to its bureaus to be used when a pretrial hearing closure is filed:

> May it please the Court. I am ______________ of The Associated Press. I respectfully request the opportunity to register on the record an objection to the motion to close this proceeding to the public and to representatives of the news media. The Associated Press requests a hearing at which its counsel may present to the Court legal authority and arguments that closure in this case is improper.
>
> The plurality opinion of the United States Supreme Court in *Gannett Company v. DePasquale* sets out the proper standards for deciding this motion. As Justice Powell stated in his concurring opinion, closure of the pretrial hearing infringes upon the First Amendment guarantee that the public and the press have *access* to courtroom

> proceedings. In some cases, this consideration may be outweighed because publicity resulting from an open hearing may prejudice a party's right to a fair trial.
>
> The party seeking to close the hearing, however, has the burden of establishing that the right to a fair trial will be prejudiced by an open proceeding.
>
> The Associated Press takes the position that defendants should be required to make the following showing in order to prevail on a motion to close this proceeding:
>
> First, they must demonstrate that conducting this proceeding in public will damage the right to a fair trial, when that trial eventually takes place. They must demonstrate therefore that disclosures made in this hearing will prejudice the case and that these disclosures would not otherwise be brought to the attention of potential jurors.
>
> Second, they must demonstrate that none of the alternatives to an order closing this proceeding would effectively protect their right to a fair trial. Among the alternatives available to protect the defendant's rights are: continuance, severance, change of venue, preemptory challenges, sequestration, and admonition of the jury.
>
> Third, they must demonstrate that closure will be effective in protecting the right to a fair trial. In the present case there has already been substantial publicity concerning the facts. The defendant must demonstrate that any prejudice to the right to a fair trial would result from publicity given to disclosures made in this proceeding, and not to previously published facts or allegations.
>
> The Associated Press believes that there has been substantial public interest generated by this case. The public has a right to be informed of future developments, and the Court should avoid conveying any impression that justice is being carried on in secrecy. The public has a right to know how the court system is handling criminal matters, what kind of deals may be struck by prosecutors and defense lawyers, what kind of evidence may be kept from the jury, and what sort of police or prosecutorial acts or omissions have occurred. For these reasons, The Associated Press objects to the motion for closure and respectfully requests a hearing in which it can present full legal arguments and authority.[17]

The constantly changing legal atmosphere for journalists obviously requires a systematic effort to stay current with press law developments. Publications such as *The Associated Press Stylebook and Libel Manual* and Scripps-Howard's *Synopsis of the Law of Libel and the Right of Privacy* provide sound basics, while trade journals such as *Editor & Publisher* and *Publishers' Auxiliary* report on new cases. The *News Media and the Law,* published six times a year by the Reporters' Committee for Freedom of the Press, is particularly useful.

UNDERSTANDING ETHICS

Although people are taught early "what is right and what is wrong," life is not always a simple yes or no. Can an evil—such as telling a lie—serve a good end? Consider the saving of a life: a very old person might be near death and could not stand the shock of learning that his or her mate has just succumbed. Should the person be told the truth or be buoyed with a lie? What is right?

Decisions as to what is right or wrong have been compounded by the complexities new technology has introduced. How does one make a decision concerning the availability of transplant organs? Who gets the available organ? Who is left to die?

Perhaps no profession has more ethical decisions to make than journalism. And the pressure of deadlines compounds the making of decisions. Journalists face the temptation of shortcuts—and shortcuts can mean half-truths, the little lie, misrepresentations, and stolen information.

Other issues—apart from deadlines—strain personal ethics: what can a journalist accept in good conscience—free meals, tickets, plane tickets, or the use of a car?

"Freebies"

Times have changed since leading editors and newspaper organization executives coerced, if not threatened, railroad magnates into giving them free travel tickets. And times are different from those when papers, among them college papers, regularly gave free news space to public relation stories from advertisers.

Yet gray areas persist. Some theater critics accept free tickets. Does it really matter whether a journalist goes to a free press preview of a play (a situation comparable to a press conference) or accepts a free ticket for another night? Are intangibles, such as airline and theater tickets, different than tangibles, such as a free television set? One Detroit newspaper had the policy that its journalists could accept what they could eat in one sitting or could carry alone, or which had a value of $15 or under. This, of course, allowed for free tickets, free ballpoint pens, but not TV sets.

Some quibbling over what may be proper and what may not is amusing. The Wichita *Eagle* and *Beacon* sweated this one out—first an innocuous memo from the employee relations director announcing a whole day of freebies (somewhat substantial) for newspaper personnel, their families, and others at an area amusement park:

> TO: EMPLOYEES OF THE WICHITA EAGLE-BEACON
>
> Once again, the management and staff of Joyland Park have invited Eagle/Beacon employees and their families to the 4th annual Media Appreciation Day at Joyland Park. The date is *Saturday, April 30, from 7:30 P.M. 'til closing.*
>
> DO NOT GO WITHOUT THIS LETTER. It's your identification and provides free admission to the park. Each person will receive a hand stamp and a ticket good for one ride on the Whacky Shack. Go-Karts are not included but all other rides are without limit.
>
> The only stipulation—ALL CHILDREN MUST BE ACCOMPANIED BY A PARENT.

Six days later (and three days before the event), a memo from a top news executive sought to ease consciences that might be troubled by such entertaining of news people and their families.

> Folks:
>
> Some questions have arisen again this year about the "media day" at Joyland, and how that fits into the newsroom's guidelines for acceptance of gifts.
>
> Joyland has many sorts of special promotional days—for Boeing, for instance, and for Cessna. This promotion is for the entire Eagle-Beacon as a business in the community, like those other businesses.
>
> I am not personally comfortable with the idea, but since it involves more than the newsroom people and since Joyland does these promotions for a number of major businesses and institutions, companywide—as opposed to newsroom—policy prevails.
>
> Use your own judgment in use of the notes in your paycheck.

This memo shows how easy it is to justify any action, right or wrong, and the ease—and techniques—by which editors scoot out of making decisions as to what is right or wrong.

Can there be any guide to ethical conduct for newspersons? Are there any firm principles, any system or group of rules, or any inviolate codes?

Do you agree with—or disagree with—this statement of Robert W. Greene, a Pulitzer prize editor at *Newsday* and former president of the national Investigative Reporters and Editors organization?

> I believe that there is no absolute answer to most of the ethical questions raised by my colleagues in the craft. But I would firmly disagree with the New York *Times* reporter who recently told *More*

magazine that he would "lie, cheat and steal" to get a good story. The inference here is that this reporter would lie, cheat or steal to get *any* good story. Although it is against my personal ethic, I can conceive only a few rare occasions on which I might do any of the three to get a story. There would be two prerequisites: 1) I would have to exhaust every honorable way of getting the story; 2) the story itself would have to answer the test of compelling public urgency.

For example: I know where a mob loan shark keeps his books and records. If I illegally enter his office by night through the window I can steal the books and records and publish the details of his crimes. Should I? Personally I would say no, because 1) I could tell law enforcement about the location of the books and records and law enforcement could get them legally; 2) my means (burglary) is as heinous a crime as criminal usury. I am no better than the loan shark and the future of our society will hardly be affected whether he is arrested or not.

But, suppose I am waiting in the Pentagon office of a high-ranking general. He has left the office for a moment and I am alone. On his desk is a file. I read the file and it contains details of a coup d'etat to be pulled against the United States government by this and other generals 16 hours from now.

If I leave the file there, I am highly ethical.

If I steal the file and run, I am a good newsperson.

I would steal the file and publish its contents. I would do this because—given the time limit—there is no other way in which to prove my case convincingly. And, more importantly, I would do this because in helping to save our democracy I am meeting the test of compelling public urgency.

Not every case, however, has such clear demarcations. Where is the exact line on our ability to get a story through legal means? What are the exact components of a compelling public urgency? These are largely personal decisions and their correctness is always subject to historical revision. . . .[18]

The Journalism Codes

Codes of professional news organizations offer some help to new journalists seeking to outline patterns of behavior in the profession. These organizations include the Society of Professional Journalists, Sigma Delta Chi; the Associated Press Managing Editors Association; the American Society of Newspaper Editors; the American Newspaper Guild; and a Canadian news organization.

These codes have their supporters and their critics. Supporters believe that journalism is a profession and, like the legal and medical professions, should have at least standards for behavior if not an actual disciplinary code. Critics feel such codes are always incomplete, invite exceptions, if not violations, are self-righteous, and fail to allow for the diversity of human nature and the complexity of human situations in which reporters, as others, must act on the basis of certain principles or values apart from or in spite of a code.

What do you think of these codes? Which is the best code? Even accepting these codes in part or in full, what else can you do to make yourself more ethical than the confines these codes require?

The Society of Professional Journalists, Sigma Delta Chi, code:

> THE SOCIETY of Professional Journalists, Sigma Delta Chi, believes the duty of journalists is to serve the truth.
>
> WE BELIEVE the agencies of mass communication are carriers of public discussion and information, acting on their Constitutional mandate and freedom to learn and report the facts.
>
> WE BELIEVE in public enlightenment as the forerunner of justice, and in our Constitutional role to seek the truth as part of the public's right to know the truth.
>
> WE BELIEVE these responsibilities carry obligations that require journalists to perform with intelligence, objectivity, accuracy and fairness.
>
> To these ends, we declare acceptance of the standards of practice here set forth:
>
> RESPONSIBILITY:
>
> The public's right to know of events of public importance and interest is the overriding mission of the mass media. The purpose of distributing news and enlightened opinion is to serve the general welfare. Journalists who use their professional status as representatives of the public for selfish or other unworthy motives violate a high trust.
>
> FREEDOM OF THE PRESS:
>
> Freedom of the press is to be guarded as an inalienable right of people in a free society. It carries with it the freedom and the responsibility to discuss, question and challenge actions and utterances of our government and of our public and private institutions. Journalists uphold the right to speak unpopular opinions and the privilege to agree with the majority.
>
> ETHICS:
>
> Journalists must be free of obligation to any interest other than the public's right to know the truth.
>
> 1. Gifts, favors, free travel, special treatment or privileges can compromise the integrity of journalists and their employers. Nothing of value should be accepted.
> 2. Secondary employment, political involvement, holding public office and service in community organizations should be avoided if it compromises the integrity of journalists and their employers. Journalists and their employers should conduct their personal lives

in a manner which protects them from conflict of interest, real or apparent. The responsibilities to the public are paramount. That is the nature of their profession.

3. So-called news communications from private sources should not be published or broadcast without substantiation of their claims to news value.
4. Journalists will seek news that serves the public interest, despite the obstacles. They will make constant efforts to assure that the public's business is conducted in public and that public records are open to public inspection.
5. Journalists acknowledge the newsman's ethic of protecting confidential sources of information.

ACCURACY AND OBJECTIVITY:
Good faith with the public is the foundation of all worthy journalism.

1. Truth is our ultimate goal.
2. Objectivity in reporting the news is another goal, which serves as the mark of an experienced professional. It is a standard of performance toward which we strive. We honor those who achieve it.
3. There is no excuse for inaccuracies or lack of thoroughness.
4. Newspaper headlines should be fully warranted by the contents of the articles they accompany. Photographs and telecasts should give an accurate picture of an event and not highlight a minor incident out of context.
5. Sound practice makes clear distinctions between news reports and expressions of opinion. News reports should be free of opinion or bias and represent all sides of an issue.
6. Partisanship in editorial comment which knowingly departs from the truth violates the spirit of American journalism.
7. Journalists recognize their responsibility for offering informed analysis, comment and editorial opinion on public events and issues. They accept the obligation to present such material by individuals whose competence, experience and judgment qualify them for it.
8. Special articles or presentations devoted to advocacy or the writer's own conclusions and interpretations should be labeled as such.

FAIR PLAY:
Journalists at all times will show respect for the dignity, privacy, rights and well-being of people encountered in the course of gathering and presenting the news.

1. The news media should not communicate unofficial charges affecting reputation or moral character without giving the accused a chance to reply.

2. The news media must guard against invading a person's right to privacy.
3. The media should not pander to morbid curiosity about details of vice and crime.
4. It is the duty of news media to make prompt and complete correction of their errors.
5. Journalists should be accountable to the public for their reports and the public should be encouraged to voice its grievances against the media. Open dialogue with our readers, viewers and listeners should be fostered.

PLEDGE:
Journalists should actively censure and try to prevent violations of these standards, and they should encourage their observance by all newspeople. Adherence to this code of ethics is intended to preserve the bond of mutual trust and respect between American journalists and the American people.

The Associated Press Managing Editors Association code:

This code is a model against which newspaper men and women can measure their performance. It is meant to apply to news and editorial staff members, and others who are involved in, or who influence, news coverage and editorial policy. It has been formulated in the belief that newspapers and the people who produce them should adhere to the highest standards of ethical and professional conduct.

RESPONSIBILITY

A good newspaper is fair, accurate, honest, responsible, independent and decent. Truth is its guiding principle.

It avoids practices that would conflict with the ability to report and present news in a fair and unbiased manner.

The newspaper should serve as a constructive critic of all segments of society. Editorially, it should advocate needed reform or innovations in the public interest. It should vigorously expose wrongdoing or misuse of power, public or private.

News sources should be disclosed unless there is clear reason not to do so. When it is necessary to protect the confidentiality of a source, the reason should be explained.

The newspaper should background, with the facts, public statements that it knows to be inaccurate or misleading. It should uphold the right of free speech and freedom of the press and should respect the individual's right of privacy.

The public's right to know about matters of importance is paramount, and the newspaper should fight vigorously for public access to news of government through open meetings and open records.

ACCURACY

The newspaper should guard against inaccuracies, carelessness, bias or distortion through either emphasis or omission.

It should admit all substantive errors and correct them promptly and prominently.

INTEGRITY

The newspaper should strive for impartial treatment of issues and dispassionate handling of controversial subjects. It should provide a forum for the exchange of comment and criticism, especially when such comment is opposed to its editorial positions. Editorials and other expressions of opinion by reporters and editors should be clearly labeled.

The newspaper should report the news without regard for its own interests. It should not give favored news treatment to advertisers or special interest groups. It should report matters regarding itself or its personnel with the same vigor and candor as it would other institutions or individuals.

Concern for community, business or personal interests should not cause a newspaper to distort or misrepresent the facts.

CONFLICTS OF INTEREST

The newspaper and its staff should be free of obligations to news sources and special interests. Even the appearance of obligation or conflict of interest should be avoided.

Newspapers should accept nothing of value from news sources or others outside the profession. Gifts and free or reduced-rate travel, entertainment, products and lodging should not be accepted. Expenses in connection with news reporting should be paid by the newspaper. Special favors and special treatment for members of the press should be avoided.

Involvement in such things as politics, community affairs, demonstrations and social causes that could cause a conflict of interest, or the appearance of such conflict, should be avoided.

Financial investments by staff members or other outside business interests that could conflict with the newspaper's ability to report the news or that would create the impression of such conflict should be avoided.

Stories should not be written or edited primarily for the purpose of winning awards and prizes. Blatantly commercial journalism contests, or others that reflect unfavorably on the newspaper or the profession, should be avoided.

No code of ethics can prejudge every situation. Common sense and good judgment are required in applying ethical principles to newspaper realities. Individual newspapers are encouraged to augment these guidelines with locally produced codes that apply more specifically to their own situations. . . .

The American Society of Newspaper Editors code: A Statement of Principles.

PREAMBLE

The First Amendment, protecting freedom of expression from abridgement by any law, guarantees to the people through their press a constitutional right, and thereby places on newspaper people a particular responsibility.

Thus journalism demands of its practitioners not only industry and knowledge but also the pursuit of a standard of integrity proportionate to the journalist's singular obligation.

To this end the American Society of Newspaper Editors sets forth this Statement of Principles as a standard encouraging the highest ethical and professional performance.

ARTICLE I—Responsibility

The primary purpose of gathering and distributing news and opinion is to serve the general welfare by informing the people and enabling them to make judgments on the issues of the time. Newspapermen and women who abuse the power of their professional role for selfish motives or unworthy purposes are faithless to that public trust.

The American press was made free not just to inform or just to serve as a forum for debate but also to bring an independent scrutiny to bear on the forces of power in the society, including the conduct of official power at all levels of government.

ARTICLE II—Freedom of the Press

Freedom of the press belongs to the people. It must be defended against encroachment or assault from any quarter, public or private.

Journalists must be constantly alert to see that the public's business is conducted in public. They must be vigilant against all who would exploit the press for selfish purposes.

ARTICLE III—Independence

Journalists must avoid impropriety and the appearance of impropriety as well as any conflict of interest or the appearance of conflict. They should neither accept anything nor pursue any activity that might compromise or seem to compromise their integrity.

ARTICLE IV—Truth and Accuracy

Good faith with the reader is the foundation of good journalism. Every effort must be made to assure that the news content is accurate, free from bias and in context, and that all sides are presented fairly. Editorials, analytical articles and commentary should be held to the same standards of accuracy with respect to facts as news reports.

Significant errors of fact, as well as errors of omission, should be corrected promptly and prominently.

ARTICLE V—Impartiality

To be impartial does not require the press to be unquestioning or to refrain from editorial expression. Sound practice, however, demands a clear distinction for the reader between news reports and opinion. Articles that contain opinion or personal interpretation should be clearly identified.

ARTICLE VI—Fair Play

Journalists should respect the rights of people involved in the news, observe the common standards of decency and stand accountable to the public for the fairness and accuracy of their news reports.

Persons publicly accused should be given the earliest opportunity to respond.

Pledges of confidentiality to news sources must be honored at all costs, and therefore should not be given lightly. Unless there is clear and pressing need to maintain confidences, sources of information should be identified.

These principles are intended to preserve, protect and strengthen the bond of trust and respect between American journalists and the American people, a bond that is essential to sustain the grant of freedom entrusted to both by the nation's founders.

The American Newspaper Guild code of ethics:

RESOLVED:

1. That the newspaperman's first duty is to give the public accurate and unbiased news reports, and that he be guided in his contacts with the public by a decent respect for the rights of individuals and groups.
2. That the equality of all men before the law should be observed by the men ot tne press; that they should not be swayed in news reporting by political, economic, social, racial or religious prejudices; that they should be guided only by fact and fairness.
3. That newspapermen should presume persons accused of crime to be innocent until they are convicted, as is the case under the law, and that news accounts dealing with accused persons should be in such form as not to mislead or prejudice the reading public.
4. That the Guild should work, through efforts of its members or by agreement with editors and publishers, to curb the suppression of legitimate news concerning "privileged" persons or groups, including advertisers, commercial powers and friends of newspapermen.
5. That newspapermen shall refuse to reveal confidences or disclose sources of confidential information in court or before other judicial or investigating bodies, and that the newspaperman's duty to keep confidences shall include those he shared with one employer even after he has changed his employment.

6. That the news be edited exclusively in the editorial rooms instead of in the business office of the daily newspaper.
7. That newspapermen shall behave in a manner indicating independence and decent self-respect, in the city room as well as outside, and shall avoid any demeanor that might be interpreted as a desire to curry favor with any person.

WE CONDEMN:

1. The carrying of publicity in the news columns in the guise of news matter.
2. The current practice of requiring the procuring or writing of stories which newspapermen know are false or misleading and which work oppression or wrong to persons and to groups.

Code of ethics for Canadian Newsmen:

Montreal: L'Union Canadienne des Journalistes de Langue Francaise (The Canadian Association of French Language Journalists) adopted this "Charter of Professional Integrity."

The charter is to be the basis of a more detailed code of ethics. The charter says that any newspaperman worthy of the name must:

1. Work actively to obtain exact information and to ensure the distribution of facts; multiplying methods of investigation in order to reach a maximum of certainty and truth;
2. Take the moral responsibility of his work and neither demand nor accept tasks not worthy of his professional dignity;
3. Maintain that defamation, blackmail and accusations without proof are the gravest professional faults; make no accusations, even if well-founded, nor reveal facts of a personal nature, except in the public interest;
4. Refuse to use disloyal means, such as fraud, blackmail and intimidation, to obtain facts or to learn the truth; unless circumstances justify it, must not conceal or falsify his identity to obtain information which would otherwise be refused him;
5. Never accept bribes; refuse gratuities, gifts or personal advantages susceptible of affecting his independence and alienating his freedom of thought or action;
6. Not take part in any commercial activity prejudicial to the free exercise of his profession or contrary to its interests;
7. Not guarantee with his signature a text the insertion of which is paid and, in practicing his profession, must not accept publicity undertakings;
8. Not commit any plagiarism;

9. Never request to take over a colleague's position nor provoke his dismissal by offering to work for lesser conditions;
10. Strive for objectivity, that is to say strive to reveal all the facts of a given situation, all the opinions in a conflict, all the particulars of a problem; but, in reporting a fact (reality), must not omit under any pretext to cite the explanations and to relate the circumstances without which this fact would be unintelligible;
11. Strive constantly, by use of all the techniques and methods available to the press, by personal effort or sustained work, by research and innovation, to make information available to the public;
12. Undertake, if he abandons his profession, no longer to take advantage of the rights or the titles to which he has no further title;
13. Maintain professional accuracy.

There are some common themes in the codes. J. Edward Gerald of Minnesota University's School of Journalism once reviewed the codes of professional conduct or ethics adopted by newsmen and other journalists around the world. In most of these codes, he found, were these seven principles:

1. Accuracy in reporting: a journalist must neither distort nor suppress news.
2. A journalist must separate news and comment.
3. A journalist must write comment or criticism in a constructive spirit to serve the public interest; the critic must avoid calumny.
4. A journalist must respect confidences.
5. A journalist must keep faith with the public; when published information is found harmful or inaccurate, the journalist should rectify it immediately.
6. If charges are made against reputation or moral character, the journalist should give the accused the opportunity to reply.
7. A journalist rejects both plagiarism and the acceptance of payment calculated to influence his or her writing.

For a review of some hard editorial decisions in journalism ethics, you might want to consider Frank McCulloch's *Drawing the Line: How 31 Editors Solved Their Toughest Ethical Dilemmas,* published in 1984 by the American Society of Newspaper Editors Foundation, P.O. Box 17004, Washington, D.C. 20041.

Starting With Values

The ultimate formula for conduct in any endeavor, including the profession of journalism, comes down to what the individual or the newspaper considers important values and how these values rank in importance.

For example, an artist may pay more homage to artistic or aesthetic values; a businessman may prize economic values; an athlete, values of physical condition and attainment; or a philosopher, the value of the joy of knowing or searching.

Some values are in conflict at times, and so sorting out ahead of time what you consider the most important is useful. Then, in a conflict of values, you can opt for the one(s) ranked highest in your value system.

To precede formulating or adopting a code of ethics—such as the five codes of press organizations quoted in this chapter—you might prepare a "preamble" which (1) summarizes the views of a philosopher or writer in the history of ethics which most appeals to you, and (2) you might cite several of the most important values (and/or goals and standards of judgment) as you see them, with a ranking as to importance, in the event you are faced with a complex decision in which ethical values might cancel one another out unless they are ranked.

The Appeal of Conscience

In case of doubt, you should follow the dictates of your conscience—what you know deep inside is right.

Since the Watergate scandals, when consciences proved to be of little help to men bent on serving authority, moralists have been rethinking the value of conscience in preserving ideals and eliciting the right value judgments in making tough decisions. It turns out that conscience is more than the "still small voice" of last appeal.

A discussion in a class on "Conscience, a Contemporary Appraisal," at the University of Detroit, reported in the Detroit *Free Press*, suggests some of the rethinking going on concerning conscience. Instead of conscience being defined as "a judgment of the intellect," as one dictionary has it, conscience is being seen as the "direction" that grows out of a prior human commitment. If one is committed to a relationship, to living for another, a sense of conscience is instructive, dependable, and beyond moral reprehension.

Among the graduate students in the University of Detroit class, some students struggled with a new definition of conscience. Colette Purdy, 21, said:

> Conscience is the moral awareness of self. It's me. I used to think of conscience as I was taught as being something inside of me that was called forth when a decision had to be made concerning right or wrong. At that time my conscience, I was told, spoke to me.

> Now I realize conscience to mean listening to the "real" me to the point that I'm always aware of myself. And it's not something that I "call forth on occasion." If I can listen to myself and understand that, then I can listen to others and see my relationship to them.
>
> It is in terms of this that I can make decisions concerning what's right or wrong not only in terms of myself but also in terms of my relationships with others.

Mark Springer, 26, said:

> Conscience for me is an ongoing, living and growing process.
>
> It is not apart or just a part of me, but it is me both at the core of my being and my present experiencing.
>
> I don't believe conscience is formed or is static, but rather, ever-changing as I am more aware of myself and others and my many experiences.

The Rev. Kevin McBrien, a Carmelite priest from Englewood, N.J., studying at U-D, put it this way:

> Conscience is a movement of the whole person, emotions as well as intellect without coercion or facade. It is a movement toward a decision or an option considered vital to a person's life situation but in relationship to others.

Said Sister Mary Ellen McClanaghan, a Dominican nun: "Ten years ago I thought conscience was a more narrow reality for me, a little voice that registered actions right or wrong." Now she views conscience as ". . . the person at his core. Conscience might be explained as the composite of all experiences, both real and vicarious, that have been internalized."

Another class member, 21-year-old Jim Rossie, said:

> When I was younger, I was under the impression that you only had a conscience when you did something wrong.
>
> And then, its main purpose was to make you feel guilty. Its only purpose was to decide your innocence or guilt in a particular situation. "Examine your conscience before you go to confession" used to be heard frequently in grade school. The implication being that wrong-doing and evil were intimately associated with conscience, not good and happiness.
>
> [Now] I believe that conscience is more than just the traditional "voice" in the back of your mind that lets you know when you've done something wrong.
>
> Moreover, it's a way of life that dictates your daily decisions, 24

> hours a day. It is not on duty only when a major "moral" question is raised, but it's there in all of your actions.
>
> It's your reaction to life—how you will deal with the people and events in it.

The professor in the class, the Rev. John W. Glaser, a Jesuit, summed up his new thinking of conscience:

> Twenty years ago I would have given a "traditional Roman Catholic" definition. Ten years ago I was on my way to understanding that conscience is not primarily a function, but one way of understanding the whole me from a specific point of view.
>
> Conscience is "me-listening" to (1) the complex unity of my neighbor, his situation, needs here and now; (2) myself related to this here-and-now other person; (3) the mystery at the heart of this encounter which we call God, but which we need not name in any way.

Help From the Great Thinkers

Questions journalists wrestle with often are not different from those great minds have dealt with over the centuries. Each philosopher and ethical thinker offers something for consideration. A reporter who identifies with a great philosopher or religious leader will have a lot of help in knowing what to do in difficult situations.

Without going into the complexities of their thinking, here is a key idea from each of a few great thinkers.

> *Socrates* (470–399 B.C.) is probably best known for this advice: Know thyself.
> Journalists: Ask yourself how you feel about everything from traditions to the status quo.
>
> *Aristotle* (384–322 B.C.) held that there is a happy middle ground between the far ends of everything.
> Journalists: Avoid going to extremes.
>
> *Marcus Aurelius* (121–180), who believed that everyone has a conscience, argued against making judgments about others and for the spirit of forgiveness.
> Journalists: Do not condemn people for their ideas, and forget personal grudges.
>
> *Anselm* (1033–1109) emphasized that motives are important.
> Journalists: Examine the reasons you want to do something.
>
> *Francis of Assisi* (1182–1226) wrote: ". . . where there is hatred, let me sow love; where there is injury, pardon; where there is doubt, faith;

where there is despair, hope; where there is darkness, light; and where there is sadness, joy. . . ."
Journalists: Be sensitive, and try to do what is good for others as well as for yourself.

Niccolo Machiavelli (1487–1527) said that if you want something badly enough, and you believe in it, then you should do whatever is necessary to get it.
Journalists: The ends can justify the means. But beware, for this is not generally the case, and it is especially risky when the ends are for personal gain.

Thomas Hobbes (1588–1679) insisted that life is a jungle.
Journalists: Do not trust anyone.

Rene Descartes (1596–1650) could well be the saint of investigative reporters. He believed everything must be questioned, and that what is understood clearly must be true.
Journalists: Doubt, doubt, doubt. . . . And when something seems absolutely true, do not hesitate to act on it.

Immanuel Kant (1724–1804) developed this maxim: Do something only if you would have no objections to everyone else doing it, too. For example, he said it is wrong to borrow money, because if everyone did so there would be no money left for anyone to borrow.
Journalists: Act only according to maxims which you would wish to see become widespread practice.

John Stuart Mill (1806–1873), as the father of Utilitarianism, contended that if something is useful, it is worthwhile.
Journalists: Pursue ideas that promise practical results.

Jean-Paul Sartre (1905–1980) was a leader of the Existentialist movement, which put forth the idea of existence before essence. That is, you are cast into the world with complete freedom and totally responsible for what you do with that freedom. A journalist, for instance, cannot pass the blame for inaccuracies to his sources or editors.
Journalists: Remember that actions speak for themselves, and loudly.

Albert Camus (1913–1960) said there are limits to everything, even if one does not choose to talk about absolutes.
Journalists: Know your limits—professionally, personally, and legally.[19]

For further reading, consult the following: Kurt Baier and Nicholas Rescher, *Values and the Future;* Edgar Sheffield Brightman, *A Philosophy of Religion;* Norman Feather, *Values in Education and Society;* C. W. Morris, *Varieties of Human Value;* Milton Rokeach, *The Nature of Human Values;* and Morris Rosenberg, *Occupations and Values*.

A Simple Creed

Ethics need not be as complicated as both the philosopher and news executive often make them. Knowing what is right and how to act in situations of conflicting principles can come from implied or explicit ranking of values in conjunction with the world view and/or commitments in life.

Actually, there is a common theme in most ethical systems, from the Greek idealists to the radical freedom existentialists: do that which is most human in every situation.

It is surprising how many decisions can be pigeonholed into categories of questions such as: what is the custom, what is legal, what is institutional policy, what's in it for me, and what is human?

A "human" categorical imperative—to borrow a phrase from Immanuel Kant—might suggest you go to bat for an unpopular person or cause; it might suggest that a law, such as in the underpinning of an unnecessary war, needs to be challenged; or it might suggest that you treat minority groups with more respect. Journalists strive to stay out of stories, but the mere selection of topics can betray or suggest their commitments.

In preparation for a sensitizing to the human condition and a human ethic, young journalists might develop a sense of giving of self, ranging from signing on in a service corps for a term (a New York *Times* editor has suggested this) to regularly entertaining the poor and aged and outcasts in their homes. One New York *Times* editor—when she was a reporter in another city—spent many of her evenings visiting an elderly neighbor who was dying. Such involvement can influence one's outlook and ethics. It is hard to imagine that people who get involved in such endeavors will have any major problems in ethical decisions.

In John Irving's remarkable novel, *The World According to Garp*, the hero, T. S. Garp, finds his way out of a floundering ethic and lifestyle by taking in an unfortunate child, the beginning of a wider commitment for Garp:

> In the car north, on the dark road to Steering, Ellen James slept like a kitten curled in the back seat. In the rear-view mirror Garp noted that her knee was skinned, and that the girl sucked her thumb while she slept.
>
> It had been a proper funeral for Jenny Fields (Garp's mother, a nurse and women's rights crusader), after all; some essential message had passed from mother to son. Here he was, playing nurse to someone. More essentially, Garp finally understood what his mother's talent had been; she had right instincts—*Jenny Fields always did what was*

> *right*. One day, Garp hoped, he would see the connection between this lesson and his own writing, but that was a personal goal—like others, it would take a little time. Importantly, it was in the car north to Steering, with the real Ellen James asleep and in his care, that T. S. Garp decided he would try to *be* more like his mother, Jenny Fields.[20]

In summary, a Ten Commandments for the reporter and editor, combining both functional work-a-day considerations and ethics, could simply be stated:

1. Be accurate.
2. Be first.
3. Have a sense of humor.
4. Respect the law.
5. Be humble.
6. Respect all confidences—from principals at press conferences, personal sources, and requests for embargoes.
7. Consider the effect of a story—will somebody be hurt? (Will a political exile be in trouble, will hostages be harmed, or will a community be unnecessarily inflamed to violence?)
8. Don't be obligated—avoid freebies.
9. Accept all people—as sources and in friendship; avoid classism; and be fair.
10. Do that which is human, whether to protect or to expose, never forgetting acts of charity.

Notes

[1]Clark R. Mollenhoff, "You'd Better Know What You're Getting Into," *Quill* (Mar. 1979): p. 27.

[2]Donald M. Gillmor and Jerome A. Barron, *Mass Communication Law* (St. Paul, Minn.: West, c. 1969, 1979), pp. 11, 12.

[3]Leonard Levy, *Freedom of Speech and Press in Early American History: Legacy of Suppression* (New York: Harper & Row, c. 1960, 1963), p. 248.

[4]William O. Douglas, *The Right of the People* (Garden City, N.Y.: Doubleday, 1958), p. 78.

[5]Cf. Andrew Radolf, "Press Urged to Explain First Amendment Rights," *Editor & Publisher* (Jan. 26, 1980): p. 14.

[6]John C. Merrill, *The Imperative of Freedom* (New York: Hastings, 1974), p. 99. See also John C. Merrill and Everette E. Dennis, *Basic Issues in Mass Communications* (New York: Macmillan, 1984).

[7]Merrill, p. 101.

[8]Merrill, p. 111.

[9]Merrill, p. 111. See also Ayn Rand, *Virtue of Selfishness* (New York: New American Library Signet Books, 1964), p. 97.

[10]Merrill, pp. 111, 112.
[11]Merrill, pp. 117, 118.
[12]*Webster's New World Dictionary: College Edition* (New York: World, c. 1951, 1966), p. 843.
[13]John Curley, "How Libel Sapped the Crusading Spirit of a Small Newspaper," *Wall Street Journal* (Sept. 9, 1983): p. 1.
[14]Carol E. Rinzler, "Who Is That Public Figure—And Why Can You Say All Those Terrible Things About Him?," *Publishers Weekly* (June 24, 1983): p. 19.
[15]*Editor & Publisher* (Jan. 6, 1979): p. 32.
[16]"Sixteen Ways to Protect Against Libel," *Editor & Publisher* (Dec. 29, 1979): p. 66.
[17]"Burger Says Courtroom Closure Rule Applies Only in Pretrial Hearings," *Editor & Publisher* (Aug. 18, 1979): p. 8.
[18]Robert W. Greene, "Exploring the Impossible—A Search for Journalism Ethics," in Louis W. Hodges, *Social Responsibility: Journalism, Law, Medicine* (Lexington, Va.: Washington and Lee University, 1978), vol. 4, p. 27.
[19]Hiley H. Ward, "Precepts for Journalists," *Quill* (Jan. 1981): p. 15.
[20]John Irving, *The World According to Garp* (New York: Pocket Books, c. 1976, 1978), p. 510.

Assignments

1. Libel law is constantly changing and developing. Clip the latest report on a libel case from your daily newspaper, *Editor & Publisher*, or a newsmagazine, and as a class suggest how it might finally be decided on appeal on the basis of information in this chapter and media law books.
2. Have a debate on the pros and cons of a media ethics code, such as the SPJ/SDX code, or others in this chapter.
3. Invite a publisher to class to discuss what protection his or her paper takes against libel and what precautions he or she expects the paper's writers and editors to take.
4. Can you suggest any other "myths" in regard to journalism practice and ethics beyond the concerns of John Merrill? Explain your views in three or four pages, with the use of several sources. (These can be used for short discussion and debate in class.)
5. Using excerpts of transcripts, reenact a libel or privacy trial involving a reporter in your area.
6. Think of a basic principle or two which guide your life. (All follow some principles—even anarchists follow a principle of having no principles.) Apply your principle(s) to a concrete reporting situation.
7. In the movie *Under Fire*, a photographer—not used to being forced to make an ethical decision and who assumes all pictures are neutral—finds that if he takes pictures as they are he will be aiding the oppressors, but if he takes a picture of a dead rebel leader as if he were alive, he can help the good guys. What should he do? Can a journalist—

reporter or photographer—ever be neutral? Nick Nolte, as the photographer Russell Price, later found the repressive Central American nation was using his pictures to identify peasant rebels whom the government proceeded to mark for death. Did photographer Price have any responsibility, or is a picture a picture?

8. How far can you go in creating the news? Just to ask about something may create a story. For instance: a Wichita State journalism student asked local officials about pornography in a bookstore and it resulted in a raid and banner headlines. She was later criticized for creating a story, but she never filed a complaint; rather, she merely asked a question. Was she right or wrong?
9. Write a memo governing "freebies," as if you were an editor.
10. Write a 10-part code of journalism ethics for yourself. Compare the different codes in class, and work together as a class on a consensus version.

Applicant Jeffrey Remez talks with Asa Cole, executive editor, Middlesex (Mass.) *News* during a job interview. Photo by John McDonnell, Middlesex County (Mass.) *News*

PART 8

Working

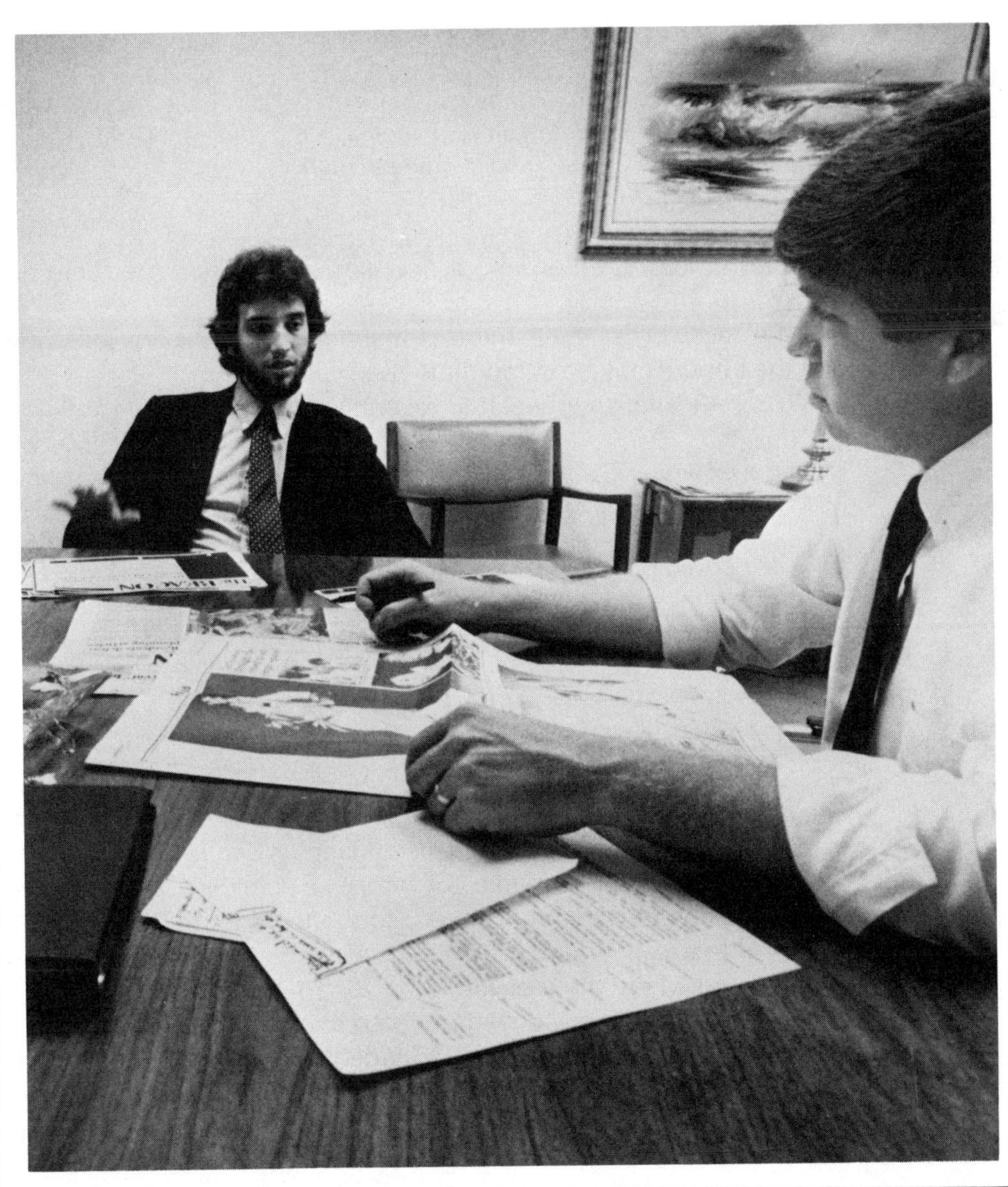

22

Getting and Keeping a Job

Jean Brodey, who teaches public relations courses at Temple University and is the author of a book on career planning, wrote the part of this chapter dealing with resumes and interview preparation.

The most-asked question about newspaper work is: "Are there any jobs?"

The answer is: "Yes, there is a sufficient number of jobs now, and the trend should continue into the 1990s."

Editor & Publisher declared recently:

> The experience of most of the last class of graduates from the nation's schools and departments of journalism indicates newspaper editors and publishers are gearing up for bigger and better news departments and coverage. . . . It is predicted there will be 25% more families in this country by 1990 which favors solid newspaper growth. It looks like newspapers are gearing up to handle it.[1]

JOBS ARE WAITING

There are jobs—for qualified young journalists. They must be able to read well, write grammatically, type efficiently, and use word processors effectively. And, of course, they must be able to report accurately and interestingly. They must have a good measure of common sense and be able to take initiative. Jobs are available for students who are willing to go where the jobs are.

One journalism professor has noted that journalism students as a group are—like Caesar's Gaul—divided into three parts. Students making up one third sign up in journalism programs because they don't know what profession they want to follow. Some of them feel that a journalism program might be easier than another major. These are the dropouts. If they don't drop out or flunk out of the program, they certainly will drop out of the job market before they find a newspaper that will hire them.

Students in another third are capable and talented, but for some reason will not exert any real effort to find a job and certainly will not go to any place in the country to take their first jobs. These also are lost to the journalism job market.

Students in the last third—talented, skilled, with some experience, willing to work anywhere in the country, and aggressively seeking a job—will find jobs.

A joint report of educators and newspaper publishers underscores this fact: there are jobs for the motivated and the skilled student. The group's report declared in its opening statement: "Reports from all over the nation indicate that there is no shortage of jobs for journalism graduates who can say, 'Have newspaper skills, will travel.'"[2]

The report was based on a nationwide survey of journalism schools sponsored by the AEJ (Association for Education in Journalism)-ANPA (American Newspaper Publishers Association) Foundation Cooperative Committee on Journalism Education.

Prepared on the threshold of the 1980s, the Syracuse University School of Public Communications survey reports on views from 46 accredited journalism schools. All said that placement of graduates in newspaper jobs was "good to excellent." More than one fourth said there were more jobs than students.

One of the educators replying, Joe W. Milner, chairman of the Department of Mass Communication at Arizona State University, said: "I have left several editors speechless lately when I told them that I have no one to recommend for entry-level jobs as all our graduates who wanted employment in the media are employed."

Said Neale Copple, director of the University of Nebraska School of Journalism, "We still fail to produce enough students to fill all the jobs listed directly with us."

Other reactions which should cheer the serious journalism student:

> All of our . . . news editorial graduates are placed. We could have placed twice the number easily.
>
> —William H. Melson, dean, School of Communication, University of Alabama

> Everyone who was motivated enough and smart enough to get a degree and go look for a job, got one.
>
> —Harry D. Marsh, chairman, Department of Journalism, University of Arkansas

> Quickly put, we had 435 job opportunities for 138 graduates. . . .
>
> —Robert S. Kahan, chairman, Department of Journalism and Mass Communications, Iowa State University

> Since January 1, more than 230 jobs have been listed with the school's placement director. We haven't been able to fill a large percentage because candidates weren't available.
>
> —Del Brinkman, dean, William Allen White School of Journalism, University of Kansas

> . . . we had about 20 jobs at the end of the spring semester which went begging. . . .
>
> —Ronald G. Hicks, director, School of Journalism, Louisiana State University

> Jobs in the Montana-Idaho-Wyoming region seem plentiful. Graduates are finding satisfactory positions. I continue to have trouble filling the openings.
>
> —Warren J. Brier, dean, School of Journalism, University of Montana

> Our overall job picture is good. There are unemployed education majors and there are, cyclically, unemployed engineering graduates. We simply do not have the experience of large numbers of unemployed communications students, which would be the case if all the scare stories were true.
>
> —Ralph L. Lowenstein, dean, College of Journalism and Communications, University of Florida

> We're doing very well. We have more jobs in journalism than we can fill.
>
> —Kelly Leitter, associate dean, College of Communications, University of Tennessee[3]

WHOM EDITORS HIRE

Two other questions prospective journalists often ask are: "Must I go to college in order to get a journalism job? And if a college education is important, should I major in journalism?"

Maria K. Thompson, who takes ads and writes for the Warsaw (Mo.) *Benton County Enterprise*, did not major in journalism, but does have a degree in marketing from Penn State. "Too many people lock themselves in with a journalism major," she said. "I suppose it is OK, but it may not make them any good for anything else. Sufficient is a background in English and writing." She continued, "Practical experience means as much [as a journalism major]. You start at the bottom anyway [with or without a journalism degree]."

Larry D. Names, sports editor of the Broken Arrow (Okla.) *Daily Ledger*, describes himself as a high-school dropout and is doing well:

> I am a high school dropout, but I do have a GED [general education diploma, a high school equivalency degree earned later by special work] and 17 hours of college. I have risen from a high school stringer to sports editor of a daily newspaper, albeit our circulation is still less than 10,000. I am only 32, and I have already had four books pub-

> lished—all novels. I lecture high school classes on sports writing and fiction writing. I encourage young people to get as much experience as possible in writing as they go through high school and college. The student who does is one hundred miles ahead of the student who only works on his school newspapers. How I got where I am thus far is possibly a very different story than most in an equal position.

Experience, as Names indicates, is still the name of the game. You can get a journalism job in some cases without a standard college degree. The Philadelphia *Inquirer* hired a feature writer and the Philadelphia *Bulletin*, before it folded, hired a general assignment writer (later an editorial page writer), both in their late 20s who had not completed degrees, but who had experience. However, these two are also working on journalism degrees on the side.

Some papers will hire a person with "comparable" experience. The Detroit *Free Press* once hired a writer with some magazine background and several books published, but with no formal journalism education and only a few weeks of work on a newspaper (a weekly). The consideration was that the magazine and book experience equaled about five years of reporting experience.

Experience still counts, although times have changed. Gone are the days when persons without college background, such as printer apprentice Horace Greeley, mule-driver-turned-German-language-reporter Joseph Pulitzer, college dropout William Randolph Hearst, and writers such as sailor-janitor Jack London dominated the scene. Yet even in those days, Richard Harding Davis was college trained, and Lincoln Steffens did graduate study overseas.

Jobs are there for the young person, but because competition is great, a journalism education can give an aspiring reporter an extra edge. A meaningful journalism education includes a liberal arts background, plus some training in skills and in understanding the issues of the media.

Says a journalism career booklet of the Newspaper Fund:

> The day is passing when an aspiring journalist without a journalism education background can easily find media work. It can be done, though. A newsperson may advise you to avoid journalism subjects in college because he or she did. But chances are that person is not aware of what is happening in modern journalism education. Most young people who find media jobs today have studied journalism in college, had a professional media internship during college, or both. . . .
>
> Routes taken to various journalism careers are remarkably diverse. Some professionals have virtually stumbled into the field, while others have succeeded as a result of careful planning and preparation.

> Professionals who have been in the business many years took different routes to success in journalism. But young journalists today are finding that careful educational preparation improves their chances of finding media work soon after graduation.
>
> Competition for the better jobs is fierce. Editors closely scrutinize the educational and job backgrounds of applicants to find sure signs of applicants' training for and interest in a media job. A journalism education gives editors one of those "signs," and a graduate with a journalism degree usually gets the job over grads without academic and practical preparation. . . .[4]

Many factors help in getting a job. Knowing the editor may pay off; if you are seriously job hunting, get out and meet editors. Drop in on them, go to the front of an auditorium to meet them at a convention, sit next to them at various social functions, even invest a few dollars to invite them out to lunch (all people have to eat, one Chicago editor, willing to accept lunch invitations, once said on a panel). Or take a staffer at a paper where you want to work out to lunch and find out the best way to meet the editor; that staffer might also later write a recommendation for you.

According to Jo Johnston, managing editor of the *Daily Forum* in Maryville, Mo., editors do hire those whom they know:

> The last person we hired in the newsroom is a general assistant reporter who is also backup to the managing editor. She has a degree in English/journalism from a university here in town and was editor of a weekly paper a few miles from here for a year and a half before we hired her. She came to our attention because we knew her and knew she was interested in moving up. We asked her to apply.

Knowing the area where you plan to work can be useful, and for some papers it is essential. Craig Ammerman, when he was managing editor of the New York *Post*, said, "The reporter has to be from New York, or we are not interested. We want people who already know a hell of a lot [about the city] and how to get a story."

Journalism in some respects is an old-fashioned craft with an apprenticeship system. You start low, then begin to move up after your "dues," or apprenticeship, are paid. Many students start paying their "dues," so to speak, through internships and writing for small papers (or clerking—doing tasks such as writing obituaries—or doing sports listings) for large papers during their school years. Beginning low is the way up.

Big papers and wire services often like the newcomer to have a broad background in "little," or grassroots, America. Robert H. Johnson, assistant general manager of the Associated Press in New York, says:

> It is rare for AP to hire right out of college. We prefer two years in a daily newspaper or a large broadcasting newsroom. The reason is that working for AP and [large] newspapers is a difficult thing. The best AP staffers are those who understand what happens at the other end [in the newspapers which use the service]. My advice: get a job on a small newspaper, which often is preferable to working on a large metropolitan paper. On the small paper, the nature of the operation forces you to do a lot of things [and thus understand the whole news operation].

EDITORS TELL HOW TO GO ABOUT IT

Editors were asked, first, how can a journalism student or graduate proceed to get a job on your paper; second, what is a profile of the last person you hired in the newsroom, what is his or her background concerning experience and training; and third, how did that person come to the attention of your newspaper?

Frank E. Johnson, managing editor of the *Arizona Daily Star* in Tucson, said:

> We generally do not hire people without two years daily newspaper experience. If they have that type experience, we are not too concerned whether they have a journalism education. On rare occasions we do hire beginning reporters, but they usually are among the top graduating seniors in journalism.

Mike Middlesworth, managing editor of the *Advertiser* in Honolulu, Hawaii, replied:

> The best way for a journalism graduate to get a job on the *Advertiser* is to go somewhere else and get about five years experience on a daily paper. Because of the small difference in pay for beginners and five-year minimum, we hire few rookies. Those we do take on are generally local graduates of the University of Hawaii who have interned with us.

Said John Robertson, managing editor of the *Gazette* in Cedar Rapids, Iowa:

> We maintain a list of resumes, all unsolicited, from which we draw when we need a staff member. An applicant should send us, with a cover letter, a complete resume plus samples of his/her work. Sloppy resumes—complete with misspellings—surprisingly come along quite

often. They go to the bottom of the pile. We look at a resume the same way we look at a story: for clearness, accuracy, and completeness.

Our most recent employee had a resume on file when an opening occurred. She was employed on a weekly paper in the area. We called her in for an interview and looked over her tear sheets. She made a good impression in the interview and her work looked good.

Ray Call, managing editor of the *Gazette* in Emporia, Kans., said:

> . . . We hired two reporters this week. One was a summer intern last year, the other a Kansas University graduate who had sent in an application, complete with resume and samples.

Don Pieper, assistant managing editor of the *Journal* in Lincoln, Neb., replied:

> We appreciate a complete resume and clips showing a variety of skills. Applicants in whom we become more than casually interested will be invited to personal interviews with the editors. At that time, we conduct some testing. References are important to us. We are interested in professional skills and breadth of knowledge, so persons who can react to those aspects of an applicant's background are more valuable than character references.
>
> An additional tip: persistence is a valuable trait for a reporter. We tell applicants here to keep checking with us about the progress of their applications. We tell them it won't be scored against them unless they are unreasonable, and, in fact, will be evidence that they might pursue a story even when the going is tough.

Said Tom Kelsch, editor of the *Foster's Daily Democrat* in Dover, N.H.:

> I am looking for the applicant who, even though a recent J-grad, stands out. I look for these things: (a) honors or grade-point average above 3.5, (b) an editorial position with the student paper or magazine, (c) an advanced degree, not necessarily in journalism, (d) a second major in an advantageous field (poly sci, history, English lit, economics, psychology), (e) an internship with a daily, (f) clips of free-lance material published, (g) *strong* recommendations from more than one professor, (h) persistence in the application process, and (i) anything that lifts the applicant above the mass of good journalists.

Jim Schottelkotte, managing editor of the *Enquirer* in Cincinnati, Ohio:

> It would be most rare for us to hire a journalism student or graduate directly out of college, unless that student or graduate has been an intern at our paper. . . . Our last hiring was for the copy desk—a 57-year-old former public relations executive who has been out of newspapers for nearly 20 years but who was a reporter and copyeditor for a metropolitan daily early in his career. His knowledge of the city, its people, its history, and his general background were extremely attractive.

Ray McDonald, publisher of the *News-Free Press* in Chattanooga, Tenn.:

> I would have to presume my procedure will not follow big paper practice elsewhere. We still operate a good deal like a country weekly. We have very little turnover and hence no opportunity to hire new people. We like young people with majors in English and history as much as we do those with journalism degrees. They come to see us, and the editor or I will talk with them. If we like what we see and hear, we try them out for four to six weeks. We rarely employ writers with experience elsewhere.

Don Pickels, managing editor of the *Chronicle* in Houston, Tex.:

> The Houston *Chronicle* looks for two attributes in an applicant: intelligence and writing talent. We don't pay much attention to degrees, journalism or otherwise, unless we are filling a vacancy for coverage of the fine arts, religion, medicine, or science. We also rely upon references, both those listed by the applicant and others. . . .
>
> The last person hired in our newsroom was a reporter: a woman, a journalism graduate of the University of North Carolina with six years experience on medium-size dailies. She moved to Houston when her husband was transferred. She applied for a job but there were no vacancies. She worked for a suburban newspaper and began working part-time as an area correspondent for us. She was hired as a full-time reporter after about a year.

Getting a job at either *Time* or *Newsweek* is not impossible. It's just difficult because of the competition.

The first step is to gain experience somewhere else. *Newsweek*'s general editor, Stuart A. Seidel, says:

> This may be old and mundane, but it's true. The best way to get a job at *Newsweek* is to work your way up.
>
> I was reading the cover of David Halberstam's book [*The Powers*

> *That Be*] and it said that he started on the smallest daily in Mississippi. People have to be willing to do that.
>
> Also, you have a chance to learn and make your mistakes there. You make a mistake at a smaller paper, and it won't be as crucial as making a mistake at a larger organization.

People just out of college may be hired as researchers and then possibly work their way up to a reporter or writer position, Seidel says.

Using a mailroom job as a foot-in-the-door approach to get a reporting or writing job is a "myth," says *Time*'s Rudolph S. Rauch III, deputy chief of correspondents.

> We do not hire someone just out of college unless the individual is extraordinary. Better yet, we would like someone to get at least two years experience, especially with the wire services. This helps people learn to write well under pressure, which we have at the magazine.
>
> . . . someone's writing must be interesting. The writer must show the certain unexplainable ability to get people to say something interesting.

Rauch, who started with the *Time-Life* organization in Europe in 1969, advises students to learn through practical experience.

Learning a specialty helps. John Lee, New York *Times* financial editor, began his journalism career as editor of his sixth grade newspaper. He continued writing throughout school and worked on the Duke University newspaper.

Starting on general assignment at a Richmond (Va.) newspaper, he did have a chance on Saturday to open the mail of the business editor, who had the day off. When the business editor left, Lee was the natural choice to take his place. From there, business and finance became his specialty.

At the New York Financial Writers' seminar, he outlined three maxims for students to follow: learn something, do something, and write a lot. "By learning something, I mean learn something other than journalism. Journalism is like a craft but you must bear down on the substantive material." Everyone should have some special area of knowledge such as law, labor, physics, science, medical health, anything, Lee said, noting that someone on the *Times*' financial staff had a literature major in Dickens and Milton. "You should start now . . . to learn something as an undergraduate."

The student should also "do something," something else besides studying. "I look for a sense of adventure," such as Peace Corps experience, work on a political campaign, or a cross-country trip.

This shows "versatility, a sense of being able to cope with life and a variety of experiences."

The third maxim is to write a lot. "There is no substitute for constant writing. Write for every publication that you can." Even writing letters and essays helps. At the *Times*, Lee said, people who can write well are considered able to think well. Writing well shows that a person can think in an orderly fashion.

The emphasis on experience prevails. This means primarily that the student must be able to show some clippings with his or her bylines.

"Ninety percent of my decisions in hiring are based on reading the clips," says New York *Times* sports editor Le Anne Schreiber. "I don't care where they appeared." She likes a mixture of kinds of stories—some games, features, and personalities. She looks for "good prose, logic, thoroughness [several sources], sensibility—the tone of writing, the personality coming through naturally."

Says Robert Maynard, managing editor of the Oakland (Calif.) *Tribune*:

> You must build a clip file—from clippings from college papers, from community papers. The key thing the editor always asks is whether the applicant has potential, and the only way to decide is with clips. I see so many bright young people, but there is no way to tell [what they can do] without clips.

Maynard made his comments at an annual meeting of the National Association of Black Journalists in Washington. Other editors in a panel there suggested: "Clips must be professional-looking, with substance and quality," and "Don't just gather the clippings, but know where you are going. Study the ads, ask around, know something about a paper before you show up with the clips."

RESUMES AND LETTERS

A resume is a concise description of the life experiences of an individual, particularly those experiences that have career relevance. Among the many different styles of resumes, there is no one correct form. However, an individual should bear several things in mind when writing a resume:

1. The purpose of the resume is to obtain an interview.
2. Most prospective employers spend less than a minute reading each resume received.

What this means is:

1. The material selected should make the prospective employer want to call the candidate in for an interview (for example, information about job experiences and skills, as well as abilities that relate to the job).
2. The prospect should present the material in a way that the prospective employer can easily read and understand it.

After an individual has been working for a while, he or she should have a complete chronology of jobs held. (All the years must be accounted for.) The college student can select those experiences that seem relevant.

Some rules for resumes:

1. ***Choose material carefully.*** Select and emphasize those parts of your experience that will be of greatest interest to the prospective employer.
2. ***Be brief.*** Use as few words as possible. Keep the resume to one page.
3. ***Choose words with care.*** Use mainly verbs. Use phrases rather than complete sentences. Be sure to use parallel construction in your listings—all verbs in the same tense, all gerunds, and so on. Organize your material in such a way that the reader can get an overall picture very quickly.

Here are two sample resumes, written especially for graduating college seniors. The first perhaps is the best suited to recent graduates because of the graduate's limited experience. The second resume is standard and allows for more experience. Comments follow each resume.

Val J. Brecclehaus
1754 Mirk Lane
Yeston, Pennsylvania 19011
(215) 734-7376 (after 6 p.m.)

PROFESSIONAL EXPERIENCE

1979–present
temporary and part-time

UNITED PRESS INTERNATIONAL – Philadelphia Bureau
Trainee
Responsibilities: wrote copy, supervised

interns, edited copy, served as office manager

YESTON LEDGER — (weekly newspaper)
Assistant to Editor
Responsibilities: assigned beats and stories to trainees, covered county courthouse and other political stories, wrote regular column, assisted in layout of paper, supervised delivery boys and girls

STATE COLLEGIAN — (college newspaper)
Editor
Responsibilities: planned paper, supervised staff, handled layout, assigned stories, wrote copy, served as liaison with college administration

SPECIAL ACCOMPLISHMENTS:
First editor ever to serve two successive years; expanded paper to four days a week from twice a week

OTHER EXPERIENCE
1979–present
temporary and part-time

CHARLIE'S CONSTRUCTION — carpenter's assistant

EDUCATION

State University
B.S. in Journalism, 1984
Dean's List 6 out of 8 semesters

FREE-LANCE PUBLICATIONS
1976–present

ON THE SLOPES — A Student's Guide to Skiing
Carrying A Camera
Emergency on The Slope
THE BUSINESS PAPER — selected articles

OTHER INTERESTS
[use one or the other of the following but not both]

```
[A] Skiing – spend almost every holiday on the
    slopes; teach beginners
    Cooking – am considered by some as a gourmet
    chef
    Reading – devour historical novels
[B] My interests are varied. I enjoy all kinds of
    outdoor activities but especially winter
    sports. However, if I have a good book in my
    hands I'm happy to be curled up by the
    fireplace. Most of all I like to write about
    all my experiences.

OTHER SKILLS AND ABILITIES

     Can handle all standard cameras and can
     develop film
     Speak fluent Spanish

REFERENCES AND PORTFOLIO AVAILABLE ON REQUEST
```

(All of these categories can be used, but each student may not use all: some may delete the sections on free-lancing, other skills, and so on.)

Note these things about the Val J. Brecclehaus resume:

1. ***The name and address should be at the top of the page.*** If a prospective employer is not likely to get an answer to a phone call during the day, the best calling time should be indicated.
2. ***Unless only one specific job is acceptable, the objective should be kept for the cover letter.*** General objectives are meaningless and specific ones may keep a candidate from being considered for alternative jobs of interest.
3. ***Professional experience.*** Many college students have a variety of work experiences, some lasting for only several months. Therefore, indicating exact months can lead to unnecessary confusion. It also downplays the value of a job experience that may only have lasted for a couple of months. At this stage of a career, it is a good idea to list the total time frame and indicate all the jobs held. This also allows a student to order jobs with the most impressive at the top of the list.

   List placement of employment, *job title*, and responsibilities with different lettering. This makes it easier to scan. Single out special accomplishments from routine responsibilities.
4. ***Other experience.*** For the college student who has limited paid-professional experience, a brief listing of paid jobs, even if they are not

career-related, can show that he/she is familiar with the responsibilities of the world of work. No details are needed for nonprofessional jobs.

5. ***Education.*** List college and date of graduation. If marks are very good, or if the student has attained academic honors or participated in campus activities, this is the place to say so.
6. ***Free-lance publications.*** List articles that have appeared in publications not listed in the professional experience section.
7. ***Other interests.*** These need not be listed, but they can add dimension to a resume. However, if a list of activities is included, it should say something about them. A list such as reading, sports, music, and painting means nothing.

   A brief paragraph as indicated on the sample is an acceptable way of presenting this material if one feels comfortable with it.
8. ***Other skills and abilities.*** Included in this section should be skills and abilities you have acquired, perhaps in class, but that you have not used in a job situation. List as many skills as possible under the specific job where you have actually done them.

Here is the second resume, a standard form with dates:

```
Leslie K. Fernley
4438 Woodmere Pike
Merton Point, Pennsylvania 19022
(215) 754-7163

PROFESSIONAL EXPERIENCE
temporary and part-time

1979-1981

     WYATTSVILLE WEEKLY
     Reporter
     Responsibilities: covered all beats, assisted
     with layout, did rewrites

1981-present
part-time

     WYATTSVILLE HOTEL
     Assistant to Manager
     Responsibilities: supervised staff, hired and
     trained staff, wrote monthly reports, handled
     budgets, worked with customers, handled
     complaints, wrote and placed ads
```

```
     THE WYATTSVILLE COLLEGIAN-(college paper)
     Entertainment Page Editor
     Responsibilities: covered college and
     township productions, edited press releases,
     took pictures of local productions

     SPECIAL ACCOMPLISHMENTS

     Expanded coverage to include record coverage,
     obtained guest articles by well-known critics

OTHER EXPERIENCE

1979-1981  CAMP WISSAHICKON - swimming counselor
1981-1982  KEN'S PLACE - waiter
1982-present  LIZ'S LOUNGE - bartender

EDUCATION

     WYATTSVILLE STATE COLLEGE
     B.S. in Communications

     Member of varsity fencing team
     Society of Professional Journalists (student
     chapter)
```

Page two of this resume (the standard form) parallels that of the first (the recent college graduate resume).

Concerning the Leslie K. Fernley resume, note that most of the sections are the same as in the previous resume. However, the professional experience is listed in chronological order. This is useful if the student has only had one or two positions and has held them for a year or more. It is usually more appropriate for someone who is already working.

Cover Letters

You should be aware of two general kinds of cover letters:

1. A cover letter that accompanies a resume sent by an applicant who is applying for a specific, advertised job.
2. An exploratory cover letter that accompanies a resume where there is no specific advertised job, but the sender is sending out a copy of his credentials in the hope that some employer may be interested in talking to him/her.

In either case, there are certain basic rules:

1. Learn as much as possible about the organization in which you are interested. Write to a specific person, and make sure that you have the name spelled correctly. The only exception would be if you are applying for a job where you have only the box number.
2. Write each letter specifically for the person to whom it is addressed. Form letters rarely bring about the desired result.
3. Indicate in the letter why you are writing the letter: you would like an interview. Don't repeat what you have written in the resume. It may be a good idea, however, to call attention to certain items that are particularly applicable.
4. Be specific in what you say. Stay away from generalities. Mention accomplishments, not personality traits.
5. Write an interesting letter. How you say something can be as important as what you say. It will help you to get a hearing for what you are saying, and it will also show that you do, indeed, write well.

Following are four cover letters: a good and a bad example of a job application letter, and a good and a bad example of an exploratory cover letter. First, a good example of a job application letter:

Andrea Burgess
Editor
Swamp City Journal
Swamp City, New York 87605

Dear Ms. Burgess:

Your ad in the April 4 issue of the Daily Courier seemed especially written for me. The enclosed resume will give you a complete picture of my related experience. I do, however, want to call your attention to the fact that most of my writing and editing experience has involved sports coverage, which, of course, is the type of experience you are seeking.

I have read the Swamp City Journal regularly, and the quality of reporting and the interesting appearance of the paper have always impressed me. To be associated with such a paper would be especially pleasing to me, and I feel that I could make a positive contribution to your publication.

Clips are enclosed; if you would like to see any more, I will be more than happy to forward them. I will contact you soon to see if you are interested in speaking to me about a job.

Sincerely,

Kenneth R. West

This letter is succinct, the opening is original and shows some thought, it indicates an awareness of the paper and the specific job, and it doesn't repeat what is in the resume but calls attention to specifically relevant sections. It makes no assumptions regarding the granting of an interview.

Here is a poor exploratory letter:

October 27, 1984

Editor
Bay City Journal
Bay City, New York 87605

Dear Sir:

I am a recent college graduate who is anxious to pursue a career as a newspaper reporter. My experience as editor of my college paper will, I am sure, make me a valuable addition to your staff.

I am hard working, diligent, and thrive on challenges. I got good marks in all my courses and have gotten some nice compliments from many professors about my writing.

I am anxious to work in Bay City because I have many friends there so a job with your paper would be just perfect for me.

My degree in journalism involved taking three courses in newswriting, the history of journalism, editing the news, principles of media, introduction to advertising and other journalism courses. I also had a lot of political science courses.

So if you have been looking for a bright, young, eager addition to your staff, look no more. Just contact me. I will be awaiting your response.

Sincerely,

Kevin C. Rose

This letter emphasizes what Kevin wants and shows no concern for the person to whom he is writing. "I am a recent college graduate" is a standard phrase and may cause the editor to stop reading right there. Generalities about personality sound like one is bragging. Details of course work are not of interest, he assumes the person will contact him, he hasn't taken the trouble to find out the editor's name, and "Sir" may be a woman.

Here is a good exploratory letter:

Mr. Harold Lederly
Ocean City Journal
Ocean City, New York 87605

Dear Mr. Lederly:

My credentials are good — (resume enclosed). You can judge my writing ability from the enclosed clips. I am ready to start my newspaper career and am writing this letter to you to see if you might, perhaps, have an opening.

I want to share my opinion of the Ocean City Journal with you. Several of my professors showed us copies in class and indicated that it had the best business coverage of any paper in the state.

Since business reporting is my special interest and my strength, I would like the opportunity to help you in any modest way I can.

I am planning a trip to the northern part of the state in several weeks and, if it is convenient, I would like to stop in to see you and to discuss possible employment either now or in the near future. I will call you beforehand to arrange such a meeting if your schedule permits.

Sincerely,

Elizabeth U. Winters

This letter shows that the writer knows the paper to which she is writing and is not just sending out a form; it starts off in an interesting manner and not with the same tired old phrase as most letters. Elizabeth doesn't assume the editor will see her.

And now, a poor example of a job application letter:

Mr. Lester Z. Questenheimer
Sand City Journal
Sand City, New York 87605

Dear Mr. Questenheimer:

I saw your ad in the paper on Sunday and so I decided to write to you and see if you would hire me. I graduated from the state university and although I don't have any real experience on a paper I have written for the college paper.

I am hard working and eager to learn and think that your paper would be a good place for me to get started. Here is a list of my courses and I think that what I learned from them will be helpful to me on the job should you decide to hire me which I hope you will: history, political science, economics, English, biology, chemistry, a lot of gym courses, a course on women writers, and, of course, all of my journalism courses.

It is my desire to stay close to home so that is why I would like to work for your paper.

I know you want a year's experience and I don't have that but what I lack in experience I can make up for in enthusiasm. And I did write for the college paper.

Please call me and let me know when I can come in for an interview. I am anxiously waiting your reply.

Sincerely,

Eva J. Smith

This letter is wordy and rambles on; it has poor organization; it emphasizes what's in it for Eva and shows no concern of what the editor needs; it emphasizes lack of qualifications rather than builds up experience; it deals in generalities; it assumes that Mr. Questenheimer will grant an interview; and it doesn't list Questenheimer's title.

Places to Look for Jobs

To find out where to send your resumes and cover letters, here are some publications worth checking for job listings: *Advertising Age, Editor & Publisher, Matrix* (Women in Communications, Inc.), *Public Relations Journal, Publishers' Auxiliary* (weekly newspapers), *Publishers Weekly* (books), *Quill, Writer,* and *Writers' Digest.* Also state press associations put out regular newsletters which have listings of positions open in the state. Some of these, along with *Publishers' Auxiliary,* carry free ads every spring from journalism students who are graduating seniors.

STRINGERS

Part-time correspondents who write articles for newspapers on a per story basis are called stringers. These people allow a newspaper to "string" out into areas—often suburban or rural—where there is no regular staff to cover all of the stories. National newspapers, such as the New York *Times* and the Washington *Post,* and the news magazines, *Time* and *Newsweek*, use stringers across the country. Even in cities where they have a news bureau, these publications depend on "moonlighting" reporters, homemakers, and students to augment coverage.

Nearly all papers use stringers to some degree—especially in sports departments which must compile scores of many games overnight. By stringing for a newspaper, a beginning newswriter can help pay his or her way through school as well as provide the much-needed clippings necessary to get a job.

Some editors and educators encourage students to keep a "stringbook," a scrapbook or some kind of booklet or portfolio for organizing clippings. Students can show the stringbook to prospective employers. Better advice perhaps is to keep a file of clippings. Students can paste these items on letter-size paper and accumulate them in one or a number of folders. Students can easily photocopy the unbound, mounted clippings for submission to editors. Such loose sheets are easier for an editor to handle and file than cumbersome books.

A good filing system and a file drawer or file cabinet serve better in the long run than an accumulation of scrapbooks: a file system encourages students to extend space to developing topical and other files useful in reporting topics in the future.

Some papers do not have a definitive policy for assigning stringers to cover stories. For example, says Dennis A. Britton, national editor of the Los Angeles *Times*:

> As a general rule, the Los Angeles *Times* does not use stringers on news assignments. We do, on occasion, use free-lance work in our View sections and Opinion sections. We have no written guide sheets; we try to remain flexible.

Wire services are generally poor sources for stringing opportunities. They depend on their own networks of bureaus and, as cooperatives, on client newspapers which share duplicates of their stories and from which the wire editors and reporters draw stories for their own use.

United Press International New York-New Jersey editor Richard A. Hughes say UPI seldom uses stringers, in the accepted meaning of the word. Being a wire service, each state has at least one bureau, unlike the news magazines. Also, UPI can use its subscribers—both radio stations and newspapers—to provide information from places its bureau staffers cannot reach.

Associated Press works on a story-by-story basis with various individuals, many of them in broadcasting. They call in facts as they happen. AP pays $5 to $15 a story, and desk editors write the story from the facts called in, according to Jim Donna, who heads the New York bureau for AP. Some police "buffs," he said, also call in information. One of them has 25 different police scanner radios in his home.

Becoming a stringer for *Time* or *Newsweek* is not impossible for a college student, but both magazines like to use stringers who have more experience.

If you want to work as a stringer, write the specific bureau chief for the area in which you live. Include clips and a resume. What is most likely to happen is that your name will be placed on a list of possible stringers. Being given an assignment is another matter. Both magazines, when they are unable to use someone from their staff, will first use their more experienced stringers.

College students have an edge if they attend a college away from major cities. This increases the chance that bureau staffers cannot cover the area, thus needing a stringer. When *Time* does a national round-up story, for example, on the economy, the editor may want to include "color" from small towns and will then call a stringer in an obscure place.

Time magazine's Rudolph S. Rauch III, deputy chief of correspondents and former Atlanta bureau chief, says the magazine generally hires stringers who are working journalists and who have access to a newspaper's files, but being a working journalist is not a prerequisite. Whoever the stringers are, they have to be available on short notice, he says.

The policies at *Newsweek* are not much different, says Stuart A. Seidel, general editor. The magazine has at least one stringer in each state, although some large states, such as Texas, have more.

Newsweek uses its stringers not only for stories, but as listening posts to provide tips and background information. Seidel recalls a time when he used a stringer for a story that eventually did not run.

> We were doing a story on sex and prostitution, and I went to New Hampshire to check with our stringer in Concord. He was very valuable in telling me which people to talk to . . . and saved me a lot of time. We never did the story, though.

Newsweek keeps some special stringers on small monthly retainers, like the stringer who covers NASA headquarters in Houston.

"It's worth it for us because these people can be called any time for a quick check on information. How do you pay someone for a five-minute phone call that may have gotten him out of sleep?" He says *Newsweek* pays stringers by assignment, and the pay depends on the amount of money the bureau chief has in a budget as well as on the amount of information provided by the stringer. *Time* magazine pays varying hourly rates, Rauch says.

Newspaper Stringer Guidelines

Papers which encourage and use stringers have definite guidelines. Some of the suggestions of editors concerning whom they hire, whom to contact for a job, how the system works, and how to go about writing on a stringer (free-lance, correspondent) basis follow.

James E. Jones, Jr., assistant metro editor of the Birmingham (Ala.) *Post-Herald*:

> Our stringers either cover stories for us on their own initiative or are assigned to do so by the paper. They usually call us every day on a special WATS line. Most of our correspondence is done this way in dealing with spot news. Stringers either mail or send by bus features or stories that we do not need to use immediately.
>
> A stringer who is a student is usually recommended to us by someone we have dealt with, such as the director or employee of the school's news bureau, a journalism faculty member, and so on. At the present time, we have only one correspondent who is a student. Frankly, we have found students to be unreliable for the most part; either they don't have enough time or are not interested enough to do a very good job. They seem to want to do the stories they want to do and forget about what you have asked them to do.
>
> We now have approximately 12 correspondents who work for us on a regular basis. They are stationed in the larger areas of North Alabama such as Huntsville, Florence, Gadsden, Anniston and Tuscaloosa. We have one correspondent who covers the Huntsville-Athens-Decatur area who does as much as a full-time employee and is paid accordingly. The others work only a few minutes or a few hours a day.
>
> Most of our stringers are male, with an average age of about 35 years. Most have had some college education and have worked for either newspapers or radio.
>
> We require our correspondents to report in about 2 p.m. daily to let us know what they have coming, if anything. They have two deadlines to meet for state editions, about 5:30 p.m. for the first, and about 9:45 p.m. for the sunrise. We have no limit on length of copy, but encourage them not to be too longwinded.

Robert P. Hey, assistant managing editor of the *Christian Science Monitor* in Boston, Mass.:

Almost without exception stringers for *Monitor* news departments are experienced and practicing journalists. The *Monitor* uses very few national news stories from stringers, due to the *Monitor*'s network of staff correspondents stationed in the U.S.; on the other hand, the *Monitor* uses a substantial number of stories from overseas stringers. Stringers are well known to the news editors. Thus there is virtually no opportunity for students to become stringers for news stories.

Feature stories are another question. Although most feature pieces also are staff written, the *Monitor* does accept a number of stories from nonstaff members for various feature pages—Travel and Home Forum particularly.

Anyone who desires to submit feature stories on speculation should send the story or idea to the editor of the particular feature page for which the story is aimed—such as Arts, Sports, Travel, and so on.

Monroe Dodd, state editor of the Kansas City (Mo.) *Times*:

On rare occasions, I or someone else will travel around Kansas and Missouri, visiting towns and especially the local newspapers, to dig up a correspondent. I haven't had tremendous luck doing that; many of the newspapermen and women will agree to notify us in case of news and do an occasional feature, but few ever call. More often, we get calls from people who want to be stringers. They are housewives, students, and sometimes young reporters for small dailies who want a little extra money. So our stringer network is established in large part by luck.

If a potential stringer is from outside the metropolitan area—Kansas, Missouri and a slice of Nebraska—he or she should call me. If in the metro area, the metropolitan editor. If in another part of the country, or overseas (and we have a couple of those), the telegraph editor.

Our 20 correspondents are spotted around the two states, most in western Missouri or Eastern Kansas. Our stringer network does not blanket the area, because sometimes it's just impossible to find someone competent and willing to do the job. Stringers include housewives, students, reporters for small dailies and weeklies.

Generally, we want stringers to tell us what's going on, as many details as he or she can, and we'll follow up. Stringers generally do not write publishable news stories—their stories are too localized or poorly organized—so we have staff members rewrite them and call the local officials to pump up the stories. Deadlines: the earlier the better, but we have to have stories for the state edition by 10:30 p.m.

and the main by 11:30 p.m. Twenty to 25 inches is about as much as we'll want to run from a stringer, and usually even a feature will wind up being rewritten.

Carl Keith, night managing editor of the Omaha (Neb.) *World-Herald*:

> Contact the regional editor.
>
> We require no experience. We use juniors in journalism school.
>
> We use about 50. They come from across Nebraska and the southwestern corner of Iowa.
>
> They include reporters at radio stations and on smaller newspapers; also students and housewives.
>
> There are no requirements. Nearly all the stories are in a timely category, of a spot nature—deaths, bad weather, election results, accidents; these are usually brief. Stringers phone most stories to our regional desk. We also use features of a timeless nature in state editions.

David J. Oestreicher, national editor of the New York *Daily News*:

> Most of the stringers who file for the *News* come to our attention when a big story breaks, and we seek special coverage beyond that provided by the wire services. I am referring to such events as airplane crashes, natural disasters, major crimes. We often call a paper, get in touch with the person who covered the story and request whatever additional material is needed.
>
> We generally look for experienced journalists who can provide exclusive information and write a story accurately and concisely.
>
> The *News* has a half a dozen or so stringers who offer stories as the need arises. We have a full-time staff correspondent in Los Angeles who uses stringers from time to time.
>
> On most big stories, of course, we rely on our own people to get to the scene as quickly as possible. An example was the crisis at Three Mile Island. We had a three-man team there for more than a week.
>
> As for deadlines, we have four major editions. The deadline for the first edition is 4 p.m. and that for the last is 2 a.m.

Irvin M. Horowitz, assistant national editor of the New York *Times*:

> Someone gets to be a stringer by asking or by being recommended by someone who is giving up that job.
>
> At the *Times*, a prospective stringer should contact the editor of the department for which he or she wants to work—foreign, national,

metropolitan, and so on. In just about every case an assistant to that editor deals with stringers.

If a student still in school is going somewhere where we have no stringer, as likely as not we will take him/her on, particularly someone who has been a campus stringer for us.

The national desk has more than 200 stringers, in all parts of the country, including a number on college campuses.

A typical stringer is a reporter or editor for a local paper or a freelancer.

The *Times* has no stringers on retainer. It is entirely piecework, payment for each piece that is ordered. We discourage over-the-transom material; we like to talk over a story and give a yes or no answer on the spot.

Here is a basic document once distributed to stringers by a major metropolitan newspaper, but which has recently been withdrawn. However, a spokesman for that newspaper suggested that it might be instructive to include it here as an example of how a large operation works with its stringers (references to the particular newspaper have been omitted). The national desk said it wanted:

1. Stories of more than local interest in such fields as interfaith cooperation, public welfare, scientific advances, conservation, public power, education, and so on. These stories may concern progress in these fields, retrogression or disputes.
2. Local stories that may contain a lesson for others, such as traffic advances, municipal taxation, major civic improvements, elections for city and statewide offices, building or major bridges and tunnels, and public housing. These stories, too, may concern progress or lack of it or disputes.
3. Anything not covered by the above instructions that you think readers . . . would be interested in. If you have any doubts about what we want, query us.

Sunday stories:

1. We have a special interest in regional stories that cannot be fully explained in a brief daily story. These pieces may run as long as 500 to 700 words.
2. No story—daily or Sunday—should be sent in unless ordered. On proposed Sunday pieces, you may query by airmail or telephone as soon as you can—on Monday, if possible.
3. Stories so ordered must reach us not later than Thursday, unless other arrangements are approved.

This is how we want stories:

1. Query us by telephone . . . on all spot stories as early as possible in the day, starting at 10:30 a.m. Eastern time. We will try to give you an immediate answer on what we want.

2. On stories without a definitive time element, we would like to be queried by mail. We will answer as soon as we can.
3. On spot stories, after receiving an order, file by phone to our Recording Room, after 11 a.m. and before 6 p.m. On a really important story, of course, file to the Recording Room when you can.
4. If you are a "trend" stringer—or have matters dealing with our trend operation—call us. The trend operation relies on memos from many sources, to be incorporated into a story by a . . . staff reporter.
5. All queries and files should be addressed to "National News Editor," . . . not to any individual by name.
6. Never file a story without getting an order to do so. Unsolicited pieces cause extraordinary grief [because] time is wasted checking on who ordered it.

Payment.

1. We pay for all stories ordered, whether or not used. If we ask for a picture, we will pay for that. . . .
2. The rate is flexible. . . .
3. We ask correspondents to file a bill if, after about three weeks, a story has not been paid. This will be checked against our clippings. We want only a listing of the stories ordered with the wordage.
4. If you have unusual expenses or if you do not think the wordage ordered covers your work on the story, a statement should be sent in together with your bill.

A three-by-five file card is kept on each stringer. It contains information such as name, address, newspaper with which connected, position on that paper, office and home telephone, social security number, working hours, days off, and date.

With the guidelines, the newspaper sends memos such as these:

Memo to regular contributors

The copyright law requires that we spell out the basis for transactions with you. This memorandum governs all assignments, whether we make them over the telephone or in writing. This is necessarily an all-inclusive statement and covers those who write for the daily paper, the Sunday magazine, . . . and so on.

Our standard agreement with contributors is that all their material accepted . . . is considered "work made for hire." This gives us all rights in the material throughout the world for which they are paid the regular fee, per diem page rate or whatever is agreed at the time of the assignment.

This does not change the fact that when you write for [this paper] you do so as an independent free-lance contributor, not as an employee. . . . Acceptance of your next check constitutes acceptance of this policy.

Please refer any questions to the editor with whom you regularly deal.

Memo to editors

As you know, stringers are not employees of [this paper]. To help maintain this distinction, it is important that stringers do not take on the aspect of temporary employees.

It will help if you try to build up a pool of stringers in each area so that you are not forced to go back to the same person on too regular a basis, although I realize that this is sometimes difficult.

Except in emergencies, stringers should not use the . . . office facilities. They are expected to use their own telephone and type their articles at their homes or anywhere else of their choosing outside of the . . . offices.

At no time should stringers be used to fill in for (temporarily replace) regular reporters or others who are sick or on vacation without prior approval. . . .

Attached is a memo I would like each department head to send or give to old and new stringers. It is important that they understand their relationship and that we all abide by our understanding.

Memo to all stringers

This is to notify you of the terms under which [this paper] accepts material for publication from stringers.

You and we do not have an employment relationship. [This paper] has no obligation to give you assignments. And you, on your side, have no obligation to be available for or accept assignments. . . . You are free to work for anyone else, including other newspapers.

Even though [this paper] may pay you for articles you submit, we have no obligation to publish your articles.

You may work at home or at any other location of your choice, but you may not use the . . . offices or facilities. You are expected to pay for your telephone calls and other incidental expenses incurred in writing. . . . If you anticipate unusual expenses, you should obtain prior approval from an editor on the desk which gave you the assignment. No expenses will be reimbursed without such prior approval.

> If you accept an assignment, we expect you to meet our publication deadline. Otherwise, you are free to work on any schedule you set for yourself.
>
> You are not an employee of [this paper] and therefore have no right to receive employee benefits from us. Since you are not an employee, we will not withhold taxes from any payments we may make to you for your articles. You are responsible for all taxes owed on such payments.

The Washington *Post* puts out an extensive 31-page booklet for stringers. Edited by Joel R. Garreau, assistant national editor, it outlines organization of the paper, the needs of special sections, and "what is expected of a stringer." The paper has a "live" list of 200 names and a secondary list of another 200. A third file contains resumes and letters from people who want to write for the paper but have not done so.

Here is an excerpt from the *Post*'s booklet:

> Since it is rare for anybody to be equally adept at political, spot and feature reporting, it is not unusual for us to have more than one stringer in a given city or geographical area. This is not necessarily a reflection of our esteem for you. . . .
>
> In normal times, a stringer should carry on as if the *Post* had no bureaus and no roving staff reporters. That means that stringers should never assume that the *Post* knows about any event, and never assume that a bureau plans to cover it. Stringers should call in story ideas. . . .

INTERNSHIPS

Most journalism schools have, and often require, journalism internships. These are supervised work assignments in area media arranged by a member of the journalism department staff. Students should contact the intern supervisor to find out what requirements to fulfill before the school can arrange work and to determine how much academic credit they will receive and under what conditions (the kind of evaluating procedures, and so on).

The intern supervisor has to be sure the right person—usually one with the necessary prerequisites and some demonstrated ability and interest—gets to the right place. Students should not sit back and wait for internship assignments but should seek out a place themselves. Some schools make the students find the internship on their own.

Summer internships are usually very competitive, and newspapers will line up their summer interns very early, usually in November.

Schools vary as to how much pay, if any, interns should receive. Some schools insist on full minimum salary rate in exchange for the experience.

The Kansas City *Times* and *Star* expect prospective interns to do the following:

> Send a typewritten letter in 500 words or less telling why you want to be an intern, your ambitions and interests, and any experience you have had in journalism. Include a statement about your typing ability, and specify whether you are a freshman, sophomore, junior, or senior.
>
> Include no more than four published clippings. If you do not have published material, please send no more than four unpublished pieces. Clippings cannot be returned.
>
> Include a photograph of yourself. Any size will do.
>
> Prepare a typewritten resume, including professional and personal references.

Entry-level positions for journalists are available—part-time, intern, and full-time—but you have to go after them. Such jobs belong to the talented, the trained, the eager, the dedicated. The jobs, of course, bring their frustrations, as most jobs do—difficult deadlines, tensions, and confusion—but few professions offer more challenge, excitement, and sense of personal satisfaction. Remember, though, to get a journalism job and to be successful at it,—you've got to want the job more than anything else in the world. If you do, you will succeed.

Notes

[1]"Graduates and Jobs," *Editor & Publisher* (Feb. 24, 1979): p. 6.

[2]Henry F. Schulte, *Newspaper Jobs for Journalism Grads* (Washington, D.C.: American Newspaper Publishers Association Foundation, n.d.), p. 1.

[3]Schulte, p. 2.

[4]*A Newspaper Career and You* (Princeton, N.J.: Newspaper Fund, Inc., n.d.), p. 3. See also the Newspaper Fund's *1984 Journalism Career and Scholarship Guide* (P.O. Box 300, Princeton, NJ 08540).

Appendix

Spelling, Grammar, and Copy Preparation

Professional newswriting begins with being able to use the language. A baseball player is not much good without a bat, a football player without a helmet, a trapeze artist without a trapeze. You must have the tools of the trade and they must be trustworthy. Communication is a language game you cannot play without words.

Learning to use the language correctly is probably not the most popular activity for would-be newswriters. After all, you signed up for a course in reporting and not in third-grade grammar. But for whatever reasons, many people do not use the language effectively, and certainly not even professional writers use it perfectly. If you are proficient in spelling and grammar, use this appendix as a review; if you are less than proficient, then this appendix is for you.

Among more specific books on using the language are *Grammar for Journalists* (Chilton) by E. L. Callihan, *Language Skills for Journalists* (Houghton Mifflin) by R. Thomas Berner, and *The Elements of Style* (Macmillan) by William Strunk, Jr., and E. B. White.

Although this appendix cannot present a complete English course, it can treat some common problems. It makes sense to learn how to handle the language right away.

SPELLING—COPY EDITORS' LIST

Before they hire you, many editors will ask you to write something. An editor of a weekly may ask only that you write a page or two about yourself, as the editor of the Berrien County (Mich.) *Record* does. Or you may be asked to write some short news items, such as a write-up of an accident story or a "brite" about drunken robins (who ate fermented apples), as Associated Press does with new applicants in New York. The news magazines make you produce a story or two of your own and evaluate you on how you handle the stories. If you do not write good English, you can expect to have difficulty—especially if other applicants use the language better.

Some prospective employers even give spelling tests. Marshall L. Stone, managing editor of the Bangor (Me.) *Daily News*, outlines how important spelling can be to an editor in this column:

> . . . with me, spelling's a passion. It's one passion, I might add, that doesn't fade with advancing age—except that I can no longer be in spelling bees.
>
> For another thing, some people out there still read. Not everybody listens all the time to their own and others' yakkety-yak. People who write owe it to their readers to use the tools of the trade correctly. Misspelling words or otherwise misusing them is the surest way of casting doubt on the reliability of the message we're trying to convey.
>
> If a reporter, for example, doesn't know how to spell Furbish lousewort, can I trust the accuracy of the rest of his story on an environmental controversy? If he writes principle when he means principal, can he hold my interest?
>
> If an editor allows Pittsburgh to get into print without the h, he sends my thoughts flying out west to Oklahoma, Kansas and Texas—but not to the Pennsylvania city that's the home of steel and the Steelers.
>
> A pronounced part of me has always thrilled to the challenge of sorting out averse from adverse, affect from effect, its from it's, who's from whose; and of tripping rhythmically through Nebuchadnezzar and antidisestablishmentarianism.
>
> I tend to think it's sheer beauty when by just learning the combination "ough" you can thereby master the correct spelling of such diverse pronunciations as bough, dough, sought, tough, through and cough. Not to mention hiccough. . . .
>
> Some years ago I interviewed several people for a reporter job. I had narrowed it down to one young man when I received a fatal follow-up thank-you letter from him.
>
> "Dear Mr. Stone," he wrote, "I want to thank you for the opportunity of meeting with you, and hope I can find a birth on your estimable newspaper."
>
> More recently, the last couple of months, we've been searching for a copy editor at the BDN. A copy editor edits stories for accuracy, sense, readability, libel, taste, punctuation, grammar, and so on, and then puts headlines on them. He obviously should know how to spell at least as well as the writer he's editing.
>
> It so happened that of the eight people interviewed and tested, we had to reach all the way to Cape Girardeau, Mo., for someone who missed only four of the following 50-word spelling quiz, which is part of an editing and writing test I gave.

On the honor system, without benefit of dictionary or help from schoolmarm, would you like to see how you do?

In this list, some words are spelled correctly; others are not. Can you leave the correct ones alone, and correct the wrong ones?

assessment	sizible	municiple
sherriff	seize	indictment
synonomous	subsidiary	separately
phenomenon	conscience	comparable
hemorrhage	liaison	weild
guage	rhumba	infallable
observent	naptha	resurrection
abreviate	accomodate	deductable
permanent	occurrence	possession
rarified	comparatively	restaurateur
occassion	exhorbitant	weird
questionaire	subpoena	sargeant
embarass	preponderence	barrel
coroner	proceedure	perennial
misspell	diptheria	incredable
committment	arraignment	parallel
recommend	disastrous	

If you get all 50 correct, please knock on my door. I'd like to visit a spell with you.

Some 250 copy editors and their deskmen around the "rim"—a table, often U-shaped, where the copy editors sit—were asked for this book to identify "five words newcomers misspell most often."

On nearly everyone's list in the questionnaires returned was "accommodate," two c's, two m's.

Here are the 12 most misspelled words by beginning reporters, according to the editors who responded. The words occur in order of frequency.

1. Accommodate
2. Occurred
3. Judgment
4. Harass
5. Commitment
6. Embarrass
7. Separate
8. Liaison
9. Cemetery
10. Its, it's
11. Affect, effect
12. Consensus

Other words the copy editors cited as among the words most misspelled by newcomers were:

achieve
admissible
adviser
aid, aide
allege
all right
amendment
amount
appropriate
argument
bettor
buoy
canceled
canister
canvas (cloth)
canvass
committal
competitive
complement, compliment
consistent
council, counsel, consul
defendant
definitely
desperate
detente
dilemma
diphtheria
disburse
dispel
disperse
drunkenness
environment
existence
extension
forego
forward, foreword
gardener
gauge
gray
halves
homemaker
homicide
impressario
inaugurate
infeasible
innocuous
inoculate
Israel
kindergartner
license
lightning
maintenance
mantel
marshal
necessary
occasion
offered
paraphernalia
pari-mutuel
paycheck
predominantly
privilege
Philippine, Filipino
pleurisy
pompon
proceed
protector
pursue
questionnaire
quite, quiet
referee
relevant
restaurant
resuscitation
sacrifice
seize
sheriff
siege
similar
sizable
spacy
supersede
teen-age
under way
warrant
weird
withhold

The same copy editors were also asked in a more general question, apart from the failings of beginners, "what are 10 misspelled words you have seen in copy in recent weeks?" In addition to the preceding words, they include:

abscess
absence
access
accidentally
accusation
accused
acquit
adamant
admissible
aggravate
aggressive
anonymous
appalling
apparent
arctic
ascension
ax
believable
believe
benefiting
berm
brilliant
Britain
calendar
caliber
capital, capitol
chauffeur
chastise
commemorate
commissary
concede
confident
consolidate
dearth
deliberate
desperate

disastrous
dispel
enforceable
ensure
entrepreneur
exception
exuberant
expenditure
extinguish
eyeing
fiance
fiercy
forcible
fluctuating
frivolous
galley
genuine
gigolo
guerrilla
haled (into court)
hangar
hierarchy
idiosyncrasies
incumbent
independent
innovator
input
interference
interim
interrupt
jealousy
laid
lambaste
led
lens
levee, levy
litigation
lose
lovable
mandatory
maneuver
Manhattan
mechanic
minuscule
missile, missal
moot, mute
municipal
offered
omission
opposed
ordinance, ordnance
pageantry
pamphlet
pastime
Peking
politician
possessor
precede
prerogative
principle, principal
procedure
publicity
quarantine
quarrel
receive
recommend
refrigerator
renaissance
renege
renovate
repentance
respiratory
saxophone
sclerosis
sensitive
sepulcher
severely
shaky
significant
silhouette
speech
strictly
subpoena
success
symptom
tablespoonfuls
their
totaled
trailer
traveled
Tucson
tread
udder
vacuum
venereal
waste, waist
wondrous
yield

Doubling Letters

The endings of words present special spelling problems. Consider these rules:

When the ending of a word is changed by adding another syllable, often the original final consonant is doubled. (Consonants are all the letters that are not vowels. Vowels are a, e, i, o, and u.)

Double the final consonant before an ending . . .

. . . if the ending starts with a vowel: *shop* PLUS *ing* = *shopping*.

. . . if the word originally ended in one consonant preceded by a vowel: pre*fer*, pre*ferred*.

. . . if there is a need to keep the previous vowel short (as in *hop* vs. *hope*):

hop PLUS *ing* = *hopping;*
hope PLUS *ing* = *hoping.*

Do not double the final consonant . . .

. . . if the ending begins with a vowel and the accent is shifted when the ending is added: con*fer*, *con*ference, but con*ferr*ing.

. . . if the accent does not fall on the last syllable: bene*fit*, bene*fited*.
(Some words can go either way; worshipping, worshiping; kidnapping, kidnaping, and so on; some newspapers that lean toward using the simplest form prefer not to double the final consonant.)

. . . if the ending begins with a consonant: fi*t*, fi*tness*.

More About Spelling and Word Endings

When words end in *c*, add *k* before an ending beginning with *e*, *i*, or *y*: panic, panicky; picnic, picnicked; traffic, trafficking.

When verbs end in *ie* change the *ie* to *y*; die, dying; lie, lying.

When words end in *y* after a consonant, the *y* usually becomes an *i* when an ending is added: beauty, beautiful; bounty, bountiful; happy, happiness.

When a word ends in *e*, drop the *e* when adding an ending starting with a vowel: blue, bluish; guide, guidance; love, lovable; size, sizable; stone, stony. Exceptions: dye, dyeing; hoe, hoeing; eye, eyeing; and so on. But words ending in *ce* or *ge* do not give up the *e* when *ous* or *able* is added: courage, courageous; notice, noticeable.

A spritely little booklet on spelling put out by General Motors for company personnel warns about the tricky endings of *-ify* and *-efy*. "Every common English verb which allows of such a choice," says the author, Norman Lewis, "ends in *-ify* except four archdemons that even the most educated writers are likely to come a cropper on." The four archdemons are: liquefy, putrefy, rarefy, and stupefy. "Rarely, if ever," says Lewis, "will you find a person who spells these words correctly, or even doubts that he is spelling them correctly when he misspells them." Keep these four in mind, and end other such words with *ify*: clarify, classify, edify, mortify, quantify, and testify.

Plurals

Most nouns form a plural by adding *s*, but there are also variations:

- Nouns ending in *y* (preceded by a consonant) drop the *y* and add *ies*: country, countries; library, libraries.

- Some nouns ending in *f* take a *-ves* ending: leaf, leaves; thief, thieves—some, however, keep the *f*: beliefs, chiefs, roofs.
- Nouns ending in *o* vary, some adding *s*, some *es*: echoes, embargoes, heroes, mosquitoes, potatoes, tomatoes; with *s* only: banjos, dynamos, pianos, zeros; some can be either way: buffaloes, buffalos; tornadoes, tornados.
- Foreign words keep the plural in the original languages: datum, data; medium, media; phenomenon, phenomena; kibbutz, kibbutzim; alumnus, alumni (masculine); alumna, alumnae (feminine); thesis, theses. Some can be either: syllabus—syllabi or syllabuses.
- Some nouns have their own special plural form: man, men; woman, women; child, children.
- Letters of the alphabet, numbers, and conjunctions referred to as nouns use apostrophes: the ABC's, DC 10's, no but's accepted. Dates, however, do not use the apostrophe: the 1970s.

POSSESSIVES

The apostrophe confuses many students, and nothing looks so out of place as a misplaced apostrophe.

The apostrophe is used basically for contraction, such as *don't* for *do not* (be sure to put it in the right place), and for forming possessives, that is, to show that something belongs to somebody or something. In many foreign languages, possession is shown by a "genitive" ending on a word. In English, it is the use of *of* or the apostrophe, usually with *s*.

- Singular nouns not ending in *s* usually add *'s*: the banquet's flowers, the president's speech.
- Singular nouns ending with *s* take *'s* unless the next word starts with an *s*: witness's testimony, a witness' story.
- Singular proper names ending in *s*. The practice of newspapers in recent years (with an emphasis on simplicity and uncluttered style) has been simply to add an apostrophe: Jones' house, Dickens' novels. The new Associated Press stylebook follows this approach. However, the style on many major papers is returning to an older style of adding *'s*. Learn these distinctions to begin with, and you can simplify them if the style of the paper you work for so dictates. Thus: Jones's, Dickens's, Charles's, and so on.
- For plural nouns ending in *s*, just add the apostrophe: the Davises' house, the Joneses' driveway.
- Several famous, historical names ending in *s* may take only an apostrophe: Moses', Jesus'.

- Nouns plural in appearance but singular in meaning add an apostrophe: mathematics' tables, the physics' lab.
- When two people own the same thing, only the last noun takes on the possessive form: John and Henry's boat. But if each owns a distinctive part, use apostrophes for both: John's, Henry's, and Mike's claims were staked out.
- In compound words, make the last word possessive: his mother-in-law's house.
- Don't overlook the use of the possessive for inanimate objects and in expressions of time: an hour's wait; a day's pay; two weeks' vacation; a hair's breadth; his money's worth. You can avoid the use of the possessive if you wish by making the phrase into an adjective; for example: "He has a two-week vacation coming."
- A double possessive exists and *of* is used, if the word after *of* is animate, such as a name, and if the word before the *of* represents only a part of that which is possessed. Thus, "a friend of Mary's"—obviously she has some other friends. In "he is a friend of the city," city is not treated as a possessive because it is inanimate.
- Remember, a word that looks as if it might be a possessive might really be an adjective merely describing a noun: an old folks home, a farmers seminar. Beware of trade names. Use the name as the organization or product uses it: Veterans Administration, Diners Club, *Reader's Digest*.

COMMAS

Just as many people misunderstand and abuse apostrophes in usage, they also misuse commas. Don't overuse commas, but make sure that you use enough. If something is set off from something else, then there is a comma on each side of the material. Some students develop the unbelievable habit of putting commas between subject and verb. Knowing parts of sentences and their relationships can also help in determining where commas go.

Use commas:

1. ***To separate words in a series.*** The flag is red, white and blue. (Some stylebooks, particularly in book publishing, permit another comma before "and," but most newspaper stylebooks do not.)
2. ***To separate phrases in a series.*** Flying like an eagle, digging like a mole, swimming like a shark—he's done all of these.
3. ***To separate proper names and address information.*** John J. Jones, 1111 Main St., Centerville, Ill.
4. ***To separate a proper name from a descriptive phrase.*** Ima Nutt, a young woman with problems, stood up to speak.

5. ***To separate a name when the name is added information.*** It's time you meet my partner, Ida Wrathernot.
6. ***To separate an opening phrase or comment.*** As I understand it, he should have been put away years ago.
7. ***To separate a nonrestrictive clause, the kind of clause which does not really restrict or affect the meaning and could be dropped.*** The newspaper, which has 30 pages, will now be sold in all towns in the county.
   (A restrictive clause has information which cannot be dropped: The rail-splitter who became president will long be revered in history.)
8. ***To separate parenthetical or interruptive words.*** She did, indeed, speak up when she had a chance.
9. ***To separate words that add a thought at the end of a sentence.*** Miserable Mike decided he wanted to come along, too.
10. ***To separate standard transitional words at the start of a sentence.*** However, the other side had its opinion.
    Nevertheless, she knew what she was doing.

When a quote is followed by words outside the quotes, use the American style of putting commas and periods inside the closing quotation marks.

British: "You won't", he said.
American: "You won't," he said.
British: "I know", she added, "but I can't give it to you".
American: "I know," she added, "but I can't give it to you."

QUOTATION MARKS

Quotation marks can cause confusion especially since they must relate to other punctuation.

- Capitalize the first letter of a full sentence in a quote: The governor said, "Get off my back, will you?"
- If it is a partial sentence, do not capitalize the first letter: The governor said the problem is "too complex for anyone to understand."
- Punctuation (namely, period and comma) go within the quotation marks. An exception is when the punctuation is a part of the quotation and the quotation ends a sentence: John said, "Shouldn't you challenge Mary's view that 'the world is going to hell'?"
- Always start a new paragraph when speakers change.

- If a quotation goes on for more than one paragraph, do not put quote marks at the end of the first paragraph. Put marks at the beginning of the quote, at the beginning of each paragraph that is part of the quote, and then at the end of the total quote.

The AP stylebook also takes up three very practical matters:

> UNFAMILIAR TERMS: A word or words being introduced to readers may be placed in quotation marks on first reference:
>
> *Broadcast frequencies are measured in "kilohertz."*
>
> Do not put subsequent references to *kilohertz* in quotation marks.
>
> AVOID UNNECESSARY FRAGMENTS: Do not use quotation marks to report a few ordinary words that a speaker or writer has used:
>
> Wrong: *The senator said he would "go home to Michigan" if he lost the election.*
>
> Right: *The senator said he would go home to Michigan if he lost the election.*
>
> PARTIAL QUOTES: When a partial quote is used, do not put quotation marks around words that the speaker could not have used.
>
> Suppose the individual said, *"I am horrified at your slovenly manners."*
>
> Wrong: *She said she "was horrified at their slovenly manners."*
>
> Right: *She said she was horrified at their "slovenly manners."*
>
> Better when practical: Use the full quote.[1]

HYPHENS AND DASHES

People tend to confuse the hyphen and the dash. As R. Thomas Berner puts it in his *Language Skills for Journalists*, "The difference between the hyphen and the dash is a difference in function: a hyphen connects, a dash separates." The hyphen on the typewriter is - and the dash is two hyphens --.

The hyphen connects in two ways: (1) to join words and (2) to connect syllables when a word is split at the end of a line and continued onto another line.

In the first instance, a compound modifier or two adjectives preceding a noun take a hyphen: two-part series, well-known entertainer, the gray-haired candidate, yellow-red tinge. Some magazine editors put a hyphen in general names of institutions that become adjectives: the high-school cheerleaders, the Sunday-school class.

Do not use hyphens with an adverb (ending in *-ly*) or an adjective: the happily married man, the dismally lit room.

The hyphen is used to help clarify meaning. The Associated Press Stylebook has this interesting notation:

Use a hyphen whenever ambiguity would result if it were omitted: *The president will speak to small-business men.* (Businessmen normally is one word. But *The president will speak to small businessmen* is unclear.) Others: *He recovered his health. He re-covered the leaky roof.*[2]

The use of a hyphen at the end of a typed line to break a word which is continued to the next is not as important to reporters in the computer age—VDTs do the work for you. Concerning electronic scanners which read lines on paper, the reporter simply types right up to a guiding mark, then uses a symbol, such as a bracket sign, to instruct the scanner-computer to join the letters that continue on the next line. The computer searches its memory for the right syllabication and "justifies"—spaces out or tightens up—the line accordingly. Nevertheless, reporters must still know how to use syllabication in their writing. They may have to type magazine pieces to a specification and divide words, or they may have to divide words in memos and letters.

Among the rules regarding word division are (1) divide only between syllables: *ex-er-cise* (not *ex-erc-ise*); (2) do not divide a syllable of one letter: *a-bout* is wrong; (3) do not divide a monosyllable: *th-ough* is wrong; (4) when there are two consonants, divide between them: *Cincin-nati*; (5) divide after a vowel when the pronunciation permits it: *ca-pitulate, sepa-rate*; and (6) do not divide a pair of letters which form a single speech sound: *anot-her* and *splas-hing* are both wrong.

The dash can be used to set off something repetitious or parenthetical for which normal punctuation seems difficult to come by: I thought—by God, I thought!—why did Mark do this to me?

If there is a change in the sentence direction, a dash helps to signify it: When the siren began, Karen was asleep—at least everybody thought she was.

As Berner indicates, you should not use the dash indiscriminately; frequent use too easily becomes a substitute for more appropriate punctuation.

VERBS

These few pointers on verbs and their use should help:

- Some terms: *Tense* refers to the time of action—thus, *present* means it happened in the present, *past* in the past, and so on. Some languages—

namely the classical languages—divide these categories more precisely. For instance, a continuing past action ("was doing") vs. a completed past action ("he did"), as in the Greek aorist tense.

Voice tells something about the subject—in the active voice, the doer of the action is the subject: *I ran the race*. In the passive voice the subject is acted upon: *The race was run by me*.

Mood (or mode) tells the manner of the action. There are three main moods: indicative (states a fact or asks a question), imperative (gives a command), and subjunctive (expresses such things as a wish, a doubt, improbability, or condition contrary to fact). Examples:

I went downtown. (indicative)
Go downtown, right away! (imperative)
If he were downtown, he would understand. (subjunctive)

Note the switch of *were* for *was* in the last example. Sometimes *be* is used for *is* in the subjunctive:

If he be as mean as you say, then we must do something. (expresses improbability—indicative also could be used here)

- Historical present. You can give a sustained account that retells a historical event—such as the conquering of Iwo Jima, the invasion of the coast of France, or the attack on Pearl Harbor—by reliving an anniversary of the event in the present tense for effect. Early chroniclers, notably Julius Caesar, are noted for telling history in the present—with Caesar, it was his account of the Gallic wars told as if they were just happening.
- Will, shall. Purists insist that *will* in the future tense be used with *you, he, she,* and *it*. The first person, *I* and *we*, uses shall.

  You will be there. I shall be there. The words are reversed for an imperative emphasis:

  You shall be there. I will be there.
- Split infinitives. An infinitive uses *to* with the root form of the verb: *To be or not to be*. To split an infinitive is to put another word between *to* and the verb: *He wants to with as much haste as possible fix the plumbing*. Rather, *He wants to fix the plumbing with as much haste as possible*.

COMMON ERRORS—A SUMMARY

A writing and editing committee of the Associated Press has put together a list of common errors in newswriting. The list includes problem-spelling words, word usage, and violations of grammar rules.

Dick Reid, an assistant managing editor of the Minneapolis *Tribune*, compiled most of the items. The 50 items summarize—and add some new dimensions—to the discussion above on spelling, punctuation, and grammar.

1. *Affect, effect.* Generally, *affect* is the verb; effect is the noun. "The letter did not *affect* the outcome." "The letter had a significant *effect*." BUT *effect* is also a verb meaning *to bring about*. Thus: "It is almost impossible to *effect* change."
2. *Afterward, afterwards.* Use *afterward.* The dictionary allows use of afterwards only as a second form. The same thinking applies to *toward* and *towards*. Use *toward*.
3. *All right.* That's the way to spell it. The dictionary may list *alright* as a legitimate word, but it is not acceptable in standard usage, says Random House.
4. *Allude, elude.* You *allude* to (or mention) a book. You *elude* (or escape) a pursuer.
5. *Annual.* Don't use *first* with it. If it's the first time, it can't be annual.
6. *Averse, adverse.* If you don't like something, you are *averse* (or opposed) to it. *Adverse* is an adjective: *adverse* (bad) weather, *adverse* conditions.
7. *Block, bloc.* A *bloc* is a coalition of persons or a group with the same purpose or goal. Don't call it a *block*, which has some 40 dictionary definitions.
8. *Compose, comprise.* Remember that the parts *compose* the whole and the whole is *comprised* of the parts. You *compose* things by putting them together. Once the parts are put together, the object *comprises* or is *comprised* of the parts.
9. *Couple of.* You need the *of.* It's never *"a couple tomatoes."*
10. *Demolish, destroy.* They mean to do away with *completely.* You can't partially demolish or destroy something, nor is there any need to say *totally* destroyed.
11. *Different from.* Things and people are different *from* each other. Don't write that they are different *than* each other.
12. *Drown.* Don't say someone was *drowned* unless an assailant held the victim's head under water. Just say the victim *drowned.*
13. *Due to, owing to, because of.* We prefer the last.
    Wrong: The game was canceled *due to* rain.
    Stilted: *Owing to* rain, the game was canceled.
    Right: The game was canceled *because of* rain.
14. *Ecology, environment.* They are not synonymous. *Ecology* is the study of the relationship between organisms and their *environment.*
    Right: The laboratory is studying the *ecology* of man and the desert.
    Right: There is much interest in animal *ecology* these days.
    Wrong: Even so simple an undertaking as maintaining a lawn affects *ecology.*
    Right: Even so simple an undertaking as maintaining a lawn affects our *environment.*

15. *Either*. It means one or the other, not both.
    Wrong: There were lions on *either* side of the door.
    Right: There were lions on *each* side of the door.
16. *Fliers, flyers*. Airmen are *fliers*. Handbills are *flyers*.
17. *Flout, flaunt*. They aren't the same words; they mean completely different things and they're very commonly confused. *Flout* means to mock, to scoff, or to show disdain for. *Flaunt* means to display ostentatiously.
18. *Funeral service*. A redundant expression. A funeral *is* a service.
19. *Head up*. People don't *head up* committees. They *head* them.
20. *Hopefully*. One of the most commonly misused words, in spite of what the dictionary may say. *Hopefully* should describe the way the subject *feels*. For instance: *Hopefully*, I shall present the plan to the president. (This means I will be hopeful when I do it.) But it is something else again when you attribute hope to a nonperson. You may write: *Hopefully*, the war will end soon. This means you hope the war will end soon, but it is not what you are writing. What you mean is: I *hope* the war will end soon.
21. *Imply and infer*. The speaker implies. The hearer infers.
22. *In advance of, prior to*. Use *before;* it sounds more natural.
23. *It's, its*. *Its* is the possessive, *it's* is the contraction of *it is*.
    Wrong: What is *it's* name?
    Right: What is *its* name? *Its* name is Fido.
    Right: *It's* the first time he's scored tonight.
    Right: *It's* my coat.
24. *Lay, lie*. Lay is the action word; lie is the state of being.
    Wrong: The body will *lay* in state until Wednesday.
    Right: The body will *lie* in state until Wednesday.
    Right: The prosecutor tried to *lay* the blame on him.
    However, the past tense of *lie* is *lay*.
    Right: The body *lay* in state from Tuesday until Wednesday.
    Wrong: The body *laid* in state from Tuesday until Wednesday.
    The past participle and the plain past tense of *lay* is *laid*.
    Right: He *laid* the pencil on the pad.
    Right: He *had laid* the pencil on the pad.
    Right: The hen *laid* an egg.
25. *Leave, let*. *Leave alone* means to depart from or cause to be in solitude. *Let alone* means to be undisturbed.
    Wrong: The man had pulled a gun on her, but Mr. Jones intervened and talked him into *leaving her alone*.
    Right: The man had pulled a gun on her, but Mr. Jones intervened and talked him into *letting her alone*.
    Right: When I entered the room I saw that Jim and Mary were sleeping, so I decided to *leave them alone*.

26. *Less, fewer.* If you can separate items in the quantities being compared, use *fewer.* If not, use *less.*
    Wrong: The Rams are inferior to the Vikings because they have *less* good linemen.
    Right: The Rams are inferior to the Vikings because they have *fewer* good linemen.
    Right: The Rams are inferior to the Vikings because they have *less* experience.
27. *Like, as.* Don't use *like* for *as* or *as if.* In general, use *like* to compare with nouns and pronouns; use *as* when comparing with phrases and clauses that contain a verb.
    Wrong: Jim blocks the linebacker *like* he should.
    Right: Jim blocks the linebacker *as* he should.
    Right: Jim blocks *like* a pro.
28. *Marshall, marshal.* Generally, the first form is correct only when the word is a proper noun: John *Marshall.* The second form is the verb form: Marilyn will *marshal* her forces. The second form is also the one to use for a title: *Fire Marshal* Stan Anderson, *Field Marshal* Erwin Rommel.
29. *Mean, average, median*: Use *mean* as synonymous with *average.* Each word refers to the sum of all components. *Median* is the number that has as many components above it as below it.
30. *Nouns.* There's a growing trend toward using them as verbs. Resist it. *Host, headquarters,* and *author,* for instance, are nouns, even though the dictionary may acknowledge they can be used as verbs. If you do, you'll come up with a monstrosity like: "Headquartered at his country home, John Doe hosted a party to celebrate the book he had authored."
31. *Oral, verbal.* Use *oral* when use of the mouth is central to the thought; the word emphasizes the idea of human utterance. *Verbal* may apply to spoken or written words; it connotes the process of reducing ideas to writing. Usually, it's a *verbal* contract, nor an *oral* one, if it's in writing.
32. *Over* and *more than.* They aren't interchangeable. *Over* refers to spatial relationships: The plane flew *over* the city. *More than* is used with figures: In the crowd were *more than* 1,000 fans.
33. *Parallel construction.* Thoughts in series in the same sentence require parallel construction.
    Wrong: The union delivered demands for an increase of 10 percent in wages and to cut the work week to 30 hours.
    Right: The union delivered demands for an increase of 10 percent in wages and for a *reduction* in the work week to 30 hours.
34. *Peddle, pedal.* When selling something, you *peddle* it. When riding a bicycle or similar form of locomotion, you *pedal* it.
35. *Pretense, pretext.* They're different, but it's a tough distinction. A *pretext* is that which is put forward to conceal a truth: He was discharged for tardiness, but this was only a *pretext* for general incompetence. A

pretense is a "false show"; a more overt act intended to conceal personal feelings: My profuse compliments were all *pretense*.

36. *Principle, principal*. A guiding rule of basic truth is a *principle*. The first, dominant, or leading thing is *principal*. *Principle* is a noun; *principal* may be a noun or an adjective.
Right: It's the *principle* of the thing.
Right: Liberty and Justice are two *principles* on which our nation is founded.
Right: Hitting and fielding are the *principal* activities in baseball.
Right: Robert Jamieson is the school *principal*.

37. Redundancies to avoid:
Easter Sunday. Make it *Easter*.
Incumbent Congressman. *Congressman*.
Owns his own home. *Owns his home*.
The company will close down. *The company will close*.
Jones, Smith, Johnson, and Reid were all convicted. *Jones, Smith, Johnson, and Reid were convicted*.
Jewish rabbi. Just *rabbi*.
8 p.m. tonight. All you need is *8 tonight* or *8 p.m. today*.
During the winter months. *During the winter*.
Both Reid and Jones were denied pardons. *Reid and Jones were denied pardons*.
I am currently tired. *I am tired*.
Autopsy to determine the cause of death. *Autopsy*.

38. *Refute*. The word connotes success in argument and almost always implies an editorial judgment.
Wrong: Father Bury *refuted* the arguments of the pro-abortion faction.
Right: Father Bury responded to the arguments of the pro-abortion faction.

39. *Reluctant, reticent*. If he doesn't want to act, he is *reluctant*. If he doesn't want to speak, he is *reticent*.

40. *Say, said*. The most serviceable words in the journalist's language are the forms of the verb *to say*. Let a person *say* something, rather than declare or admit or point out. And never let him grin, smile, frown, or giggle something.

41. *Slang*. Don't try to use "with-it" slang. Usually a term is on the way out by the time we get it in print.
Wrong: The police cleared the demonstrators with a sunrise *bust*.

42. *Spelling*. It's basic. If reporters can't spell and copy editors can't spell, we're in trouble. Some ripe ones for the top of your list:
It's *consensus*, not concensus.
It's *restaurateur*, not restauranteur.
It's *dietitian*, not dietician.

43. *Temperatures*. They may get higher or lower, but they don't get warmer or cooler.

44. *That, which. That* tends to restrict the reader's thought and direct it the way you want it to go; *which* is nonrestrictive, introducing a bit of subsidiary information. For instance:
    The lawnmower *that* is in the garage needs sharpening. (Meaning: We have more than one lawnmower. The one in the garage needs sharpening.)
    The lawnmower, *which* is in the garage, needs sharpening. (Meaning: Our lawnmower needs sharpening. It's in the garage.)
    Note that *which* clauses take commas, signaling they are not essential to the meaning of the sentence.
45. *Under way*, not underway. But don't say something got under way. Say it *started* or *began*.
46. *Unique*. Something that is unique is the only one of its kind. It can't be very unique or quite unique or somewhat unique or rather unique. Don't use it unless you really mean unique.
47. *Up*. Don't use it as a verb.
    Wrong: The manager said he would *up* the price next week.
    Right: The manager said he would *raise* the price next week.
48. *Who, whom*. A tough one, but generally you're safe to use *whom* to refer to someone who has been the object of an action. *Who* is the word when the somebody has been the actor:
    A 19-year-old woman, to *whom* the room was rented, left the window open.
    A 19-year-old woman, *who* rented the room, left the window open.
49. *Who's, whose*. Though it incorporates an apostrophe, *who's* is not a possessive. It's a contraction for *who is*. *Whose* is the possessive.
    Wrong: I don't know *who's* coat it is.
    Right: I don't know *whose* coat it is.
    Right: Find out *who's* there.
50. *Would*: Be careful about using *would* when constructing a conditional past tense.
    Wrong: If Soderholm *would not have had* an injured foot, Thompson wouldn't have been in the lineup.
    Right: If Soderholm *had not had* an injured foot, Thompson wouldn't have been in the lineup.[3]

The copy editors responding to the spelling questionnaire mentioned earlier were also asked to identify common grammatical errors that they see in the copy they edit. A number of the problems they see are on the AP list, but the copy editors also call attention to the following as well.

1. Disagreement of noun and pronoun. *The team won their game* is wrong. *The team won its game*. Team is singular, and so are such words as committee, council, and association.

2. Incomplete sentences. *He is going to town. Which is good.* Although people do talk this way, in writing, a subordinate clause must be in a sentence with a main clause. *He is going to town, which is good.*
3. Misplacement of *only.* A seemingly innocuous little word, *only,* depending on where a writer places it, can change the meaning of a sentence. It can be an adverb, an adjective, or a conjunction. Adverb: *Mike had only 30 cents to spend.* (It goes with the verb, as "merely.") Adjective: *Only Mike had 30 cents to spend* (as Mike "alone"). Conjunction: *Mike would have gone, only he had 30 cents* (as "except"). The conjunction appears more in spoken speech.
4. Splitting verb forms. It's acceptable to put an adverb between the auxiliary verb and the principal part of the verb; in fact, it is preferred: *she will not go; he will always be there.* What is objectionable is the insertion of a prepositional phrase or clause between the auxiliary and rest of the verb: *Astronaut Will B. Thayer will with a steady hand place a flag on the planet's surface.* Better: *With a steady hand, Astronaut Will B. Thayer will place a flag on the planet's surface.*
5. Dangling participles, gerunds. A participle is a verb form ending with *-ing.* Participles serve as adjectives and must stand close to the nouns they modify. Thus: *Foaming and whining, the wild animal was snared by the zoo attendant.* Not: *Foaming and whining, the zoo attendant snared the wild animal.* A gerund is much like a noun—a verbal form that can have modifiers, can be the object of a verb, and can be part of a prepositional phrase: *Instead of watching a movie, John ate in a restaurant.* Not: *Instead of watching a movie, a meal was eaten in a restaurant.*
6. Confusing *around, about.* About refers to an estimate; around is used to demonstrate motion: *they will be here about 6 p.m.; they walked around the park.*
7. *No sooner . . . when.* Bad: *No sooner had we arrived when the music started.* Better: *No sooner had we arrived than the music started.*
8. Overuse of *that.* Bad: *John said that in coming to the party, that Jane would find some friends.* Better: *John said that Jane, in coming to the party, would find some friends.* With verbs of attribution with indirect quotes, the *that* may be left out but should be included when needed to make the meaning clear. Thus, if left out in the first example, it would sound as if *John, in coming to the party. . . .*

STYLEBOOKS

There are differences among newspapers and differences between newspapers and wire services. Language is never absolute, and even if it were to freeze, people would still use language differently. One paper will say "per cent" and another "percent." One will use a second comma in a series of three items—"red, blue, and green"—others will not. Other differences, such as the use of the apostrophe, have already been noted. A point of comparison over the years was the "downstyle" vs. the "upstyle." Downstyle newspapers capitalize only necessary words. Advocates of such style prefer dropping the final capital: William Jewell college, Northwestern university, 1258 Main st. Upstyle seems to be more prevalent now. Words such as street, college, and university are more likely to appear in capitals.

The wire service stylebooks help to keep newspaper policy in spelling, punctuation, and grammar reasonably consistent. The Associated Press and United Press International stylebooks are basically the same, but they have some differences. The AP book contains a "libel manual"; the UPI book is better edited and uses crisp, shorter sentences. Few newspapers follow the stylebooks precisely.

Some newspapers have their own stylebooks. While these individual newspaper stylebooks tip their hats to the AP stylebook, they like to make the differences known. The Omaha *World-Herald* included a list of "Errata AP Stylebook 1977." It notes some misspelled words; for example, canister was misspelled in an entry on chemical mace; Maccabees in a story about Hanukkah; and naphtha and trampoline were also misspelled.

The extensive Bangor (Me.) *Daily News* stylebook warns:

> Beware of the Bangor *Daily News's* exceptions to wire service style and of reversals in style from the old wire service stylebooks: percent instead of per cent, employee instead of employe, kidnapped instead of kidnaped, goodbye instead of goodby, firefighter instead of fire fighter, whiskey instead of whisky.
>
> For spellings, capitalizations, abbreviations and word usages not in this book, use the first-listed reference in *Webster's New World Dictionary of the American Language, Second College Edition*.

Some areas of style are still being debated. One is how to identify women. For a while, "Ms." seemed destined to replace the traditional identification of women as "Miss" or "Mrs." The New York *Times* now does not use "Ms." at all, unless in a quote. The *Times* argues that many women object to "Ms." Geraldine Ferraro, married to John Zaccaro, is referred to as "Mrs. Ferraro" by the *Times*. William Giles, in one of his columns as editor of the Detroit *News*, says, "Ms. merely provides editors more chance to make more people mad." Newspapers do use "Ms.," however, when women indicate a preference. "When confounded by the choice," says Giles, "we usually ask the source which title she prefers.

The Duluth (Minn.) papers, the *Herald* and *Tribune*, take another approach. In first references to a woman, a woman's first and last name are used, as in the case of men. In second references, only the last name is used. When a couple is mentioned, both first names are used: "Mary and John Smith." In obituaries, the first name is used with the spouse in parentheses: "Mary (John) Smith." In second reference in obituaries, Mr., Mrs., or Miss is used. The marital titles are omitted for survivors.

The Associated Press style retains *Miss, Mrs.*, and *Ms.* for identifying women on second reference. The titles are not used on first reference unless a woman requests it. Thus a married woman on first reference would be *Susan Smith*. "On second reference," says the Stylebook, "use *Mrs.* unless a woman initially identified by her own first name prefers *Ms.*: *Carla Hills, Mrs. Hills*. If a married woman uses her maiden name, precede it by *Miss* on second reference unless she prefers *Ms.*: *Jane Jones, Miss Jones*." Unlike the New York *Times* stylebook, which calls for the retention of *Mr.*, the AP says: "Do not use *Mr.* in any reference unless it is combined with *Mrs.*: *Mr. and Mrs. John Smith, Mr. and Mrs. Smith*."[4] This modified old-fashioned approach has little sympathy in Missoula, Mont. "We do not use courtesy titles such as Mr., Mrs., and Ms.," says Gayle Shirley, copy editor of the *Missoulian*. "They are archaic, and I think it would insult sources to ask which title is accurate." The style is generally evolving to this simpler format.

In fact, the AP style itself is constantly evolving. It might be useful for you to send for the annual revisions to the Associated Press Stylebook and Libel Manual that AP issues. You can obtain the revisions, eventually incorporated in future printings, from AP Newsfeatures (Louis D. Boccardi, executive editor and vice president), The Associated Press, 50 Rockefeller Plaza, New York, N.Y. 10020. Changes range from making entries more precise—as with the definition of "epicenter" in connection with earthquakes (it is now "the point on the earth's surface above the underground center" instead of merely being the center of an earthquake, as was previously logged)—to updating, as in the case of the latest vote on the Equal Rights Amendment, and to adding new entries, such as Legionnaires' disease. There's the new style for Chinese names, a name change (U.S. Information Agency giving way to U.S. International Communication Agency), and a return to tradition, such as deleting the "Gulf of Iran" and replacing it with the "Persian Gulf": "Use this long-established name for the body of water off the southern coast of Iran. . . ."

At the Los Angeles *Times*, copy editor Frederick S. Holley says:

> We are in the process of completing a new stylebook. I have devoted most of the last year to looking into style problems. How will it differ from the AP?
>
> In many ways, it is attacking some grammatical questions such as sequence of tenses, which the AP ignores.
>
> It is blazing new trails in such matters as ethnic designations, courtesy titles, and obscenity-profanity-vulgarity.
>
> It is making a serious effort to achieve some degree of uniformity in the transliteration, spelling and use of Arabic and Asian names. [The Los Angeles *Times* uses Khomaini for the Iranian leader; others use Khomeini. Both are acceptable.]

The AP stylebook has persisted in keeping Western—if not colonial—spellings, and reporters following a newspaper style using AP and UPI can be expected to be taken to task by unhappy members of ethnic groups. "Cracow" instead of "Krakow" prevailed as the town where the Pope once served. The newer U.S. atlases vary on this, but Poles prefer "Krakow." Muslims react to *Moslem*. AP and UPI continue the bias to blacks here by insisting that *Muslims* be used only for black Muslims, even though Arab-nation Muslims prefer the Muslim spelling and are not worried about distinguishing between black and white. Muslims also prefer *Qur'an* instead of the AP and UPI's *Koran*, and *Muhammad* instead of *Mohammed*.

To determine style in local areas, find out what ethnic groups themselves prefer in their own publications, and try to persuade the management of your paper to use the same terminology (and this might vary from region to region). For example, if the local Jewish paper is using Hanuka, as some Jewish papers do, then you might want to suggest that that spelling replace an older form, such as Chanukah or the AP and UPI's Hanukkah.

As a newswriter, the style for you to follow is that which your newspaper uses—either the AP-UPI style, the paper's own, or a mixture. The AP stylebook is 276 pages, the UPI is 200 pages; you should have one or the other. Both are reasonably comprehensive, and other stylebooks are based on them. Sections you should check and become familiar with in the AP and UPI stylebook include abbreviations, state names, titles (check also "academic titles"), "doctor," religious titles, capitalization, ages, and numerals.

For example, here are a few items from the AP stylebook, in summary:

- *Numbers:* One to nine are spelled out; 10 and over use numerals. There are exceptions: Do not start a sentence with a number—spell it out or get around it with "More than 1,000."

- *Ages:* Use figures, but note the variations—A 7-year-old girl, but the girl is 7 years old. A girl, 7, has a sister, 11.
- *Dates:* If you have just the month and year, then there is no comma—September 1985—but if there is a date, then it is Sept. 15, 1985. No apostrophe in 1890s, 1960s, 1990s, and so on.
- *Time:* Never "o'clock" or 8:00. Say 8 a.m. or 8 p.m.
- *Titles:* Capitalize a precise title just before a name: Attorney General John Jones, but John Jones, attorney general.
- *Commas:* In a series, do not put a comma before the "and"; thus, "They listened to the singing of the three sisters—Mary, Myrtle and Misty." (In book publishing, however, the extra comma may prevail, as it does in this book.)
- *Addresses:* Spell out the street if there is no number. "He lives on Sunset Boulevard." If there is a number: "He lives at 1900 Sunset Blvd."

MARKING COPY

There are standard ways to mark changes in your news copy. The markings serve a purpose: telling other editors and typesetters (manual or computers) how the copy should be set. There is nothing mysterious about the marks, and marks should be as readable as possible. It takes only one mistaken letter to change a meaning. So mark your copy clearly, using these symbols:

Set bold face

By Mary Smith

Set italics

Staff writer

Center

] By Mary Smith [

Move to the right

By Mary Smith]

Move to the left

[By Mary Smith

Align left

|| John H. Smith
|| Accountant

Align right

John H. Smith ||
Accountant ||

Align left, center unit

John H. Smith
Accountant
Springfield, Ill.

Capitalize

John smith will be here.

Small capital letters

by lance davidson

Insert letter

The instructor was on tme.

Delete letter

The instructor was not on tiime.

Add word new

The instructor was on time.

Delete word

The ugly substitute teacher was on time.

Separate words

It snowedall day.

Transpose

The surfer from Ventura in California southern wsa wiped out.

Close up

Her mother was a go od cook.

Close, leave one letter space

The election was   much too close.

Run in together

Shortly after the sun came up, Marty and Mary were on the beach and began surfing.

Abbreviate

The United Nations committee began its work.

Do not abbreviate

The U.S. and the Soviet Union continued strategic arms limitations talks.

Spell out number

9

Use figure

one thousand

Insert period

F. T. Davis teaches advertising.
J. P. Fishbein teaches magazine writing.

Insert comma

American colors are red, white and blue.

Insert apostrophe

Smith's hours are too long.

Insert hyphen

She has an apple-red nose.

Insert dash

When all is said and done—if it is ever done—all will know she was right.

New paragraph

Once upon a time, the little people of the tree lands gathered around a Christmas tree. It was a night of snow and sparkle. Then it happened. A great wind of the north came in like an avalanche and. . . .

Here are the copyediting symbols applied:

```
"congress shall make no new law respecting an establish-
ment of re ligion, or prohibiting
the freedom of sppeech, or of the press; or the right
of the people peaceably to assemble, and to peti-
tion the government for a of redress grievances.
   This is the First Amendment of the U.S.
Constitution and appears in a book, Your
Constitution. More than one hundred thousand
copies have been printed in 6 editions. Doctor
Henry Smith is editor. A year's supply is available.
You may order—if you're early—from:

        Everyman Printing Service
        1111 Main Ave.
        Somewhere, Pa. 18976
      $1; only 50¢ for order of 10 or more
```

Proofreading Marks

Students sometimes confuse proofreading marks with copyediting marks. In typed copy there is room between lines to make changes with the word itself. When copy is set in type, the lines are too close together and you must indicate changes with symbols in the margin. So proofreader symbols are more elaborate:

bf	Put in bold face
lf	Put in light face
ital	Reset in italic
rom.	Reset in Roman (non-italic)
caps	Reset in capitals
s.c.	Reset in small capitals
lc.	Reset in lower case
9	Turn inverted letter
×	Defective letter
ℊ	Delete
◡	Use less space
◯	Close up entirely
∧	Insert at this place
⊙	Insert period
∧,	Insert comma
⊙:	Insert colon
]	Move to right
///	Straighten lines
[	Move to left
□	Indent 1 em (letter "m" width)
1/em	One-em dash
2/M	Two-em dash
∧=	Insert hyphen
∨'	Insert apostrophe
∨"	Enclose in quotation marks
stet	Let it stand
⌒	Run in
¶	Paragraph
no ¶	No paragraph
w.f.	Wrong type font
tr.	Transpose
?	Verify
sp	Spell out

Here are the proofreading symbols applied.

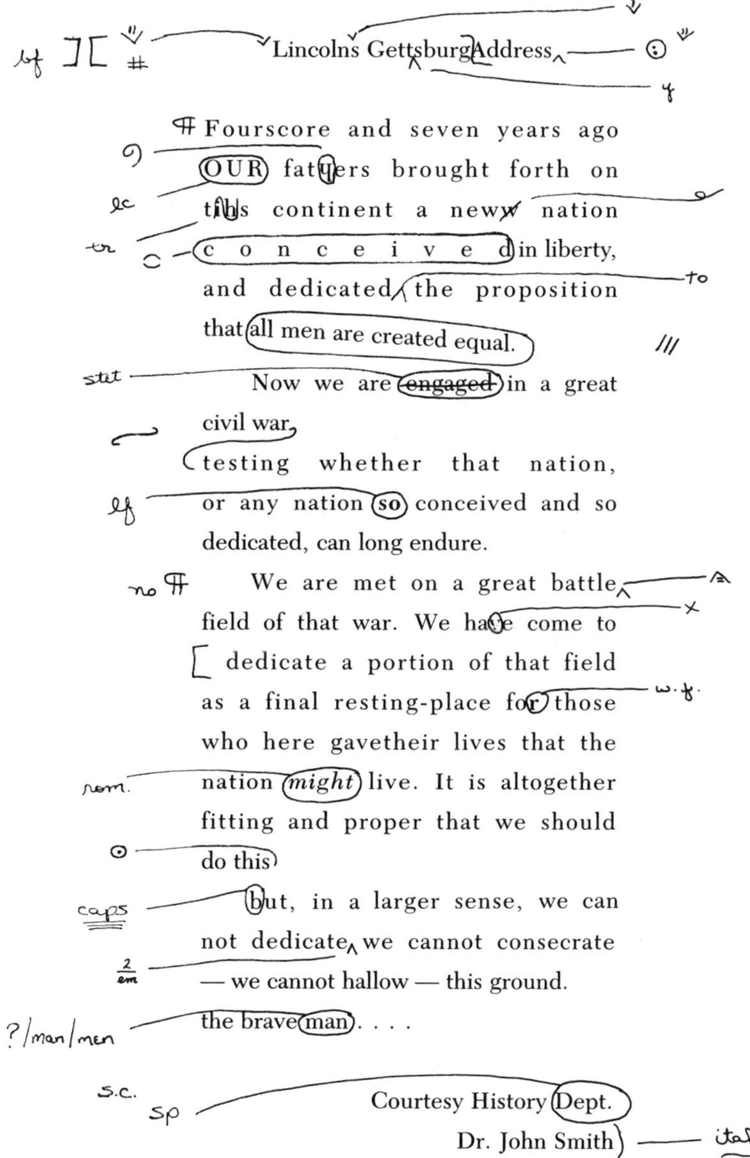

Lincolns Gettsburg Address

Fourscore and seven years ago OUR fatuers brought forth on tihs continent a neww nation c o n c e i v e d in liberty, and dedicated the proposition that all men are created equal.

Now we are engaged in a great civil war, testing whether that nation, or any nation so conceived and so dedicated, can long endure.

We are met on a great battle field of that war. We have come to dedicate a portion of that field as a final resting-place for those who here gavetheir lives that the nation *might* live. It is altogether fitting and proper that we should do this but, in a larger sense, we can not dedicate we cannot consecrate — we cannot hallow — this ground. the brave man. . . .

Courtesy History Dept.
Dr. John Smith

SCANNER COPY

Although you should know this basic manner of pencil pushing, a scanner reading copy will require its own special marks. The optical character reader (OCR) looks at letters and symbols electronically and translates them into type of specified size and arrangement. The scanner machine requires special kinds of marks.

Reporters now more likely compose copy on the video display terminal (VDT) and make corrections on the TV-like screen by manipulating letters and instruction buttons on a keyboard. Chapter 20 discusses this technology.

The following box shows symbols which were used on typed copy prepared for the scanner at the Mankato (Minn.) *Free Press*.

ΔCM — regular body type, over regular column width (10.6 ems)
ΔCI — regular body type, over wide column width (14 ems)

ΔBC — bold face caps
ΔBF — bold face, must end this coding with a ΔLF (lightface)
ΔCO — 10 pt. body type
ΔC2 — column width (this would be two regular column widths) — 21 ems
ΔWC2 — column width (two wide column widths) — 29.6 ems

Δ14 — 14 pt. type, one regular column
Δ18 — 18 pt. type, one regular column
ΔW14 — 14 pt. type, one wide column (14 ems)
ΔW18 — 18 pt. type, one wide column, and so on for 24 pt. and 36 pt. (14 ems)
ΔCT23 — italic body face (9 pt.) or whatever the body type is
ΔCT27 — light headline face (used on Accent pages) up to 36 pt.
ΔC — centers line
ΔL — puts line flush left
ΔR — puts line flush right
ΔPD — "paragraph defined" — this means that as long as the typist starts each new paragraph at the same place on the paper, then the paragraph indentations will be put in
ΔPF — "paragraph forced" — if the beginning of the paragraph should happen to start somewhere else, this code must precede it (then next pph put PD again)
ΔCW23 — if copy, or head is to be set a width different than the normal column widths, this coding is used — this copy, for instance, would be 23 ems wide — (CW18, CW28, etc. also)
ΔS — puts in one slugline of space before next line
ΔS2 — puts in two sluglines of space before next line, and so on
ΔΔ — tells scanner there is nothing more to read on the page
ΔCV — coding used for bylines on narrow measures

A page of scanner copy marked with these symbols looks like this:

ΔCM police log cath thursday T18 ΔS4

Δ14 Thefts ΔL

ΔCM ΔCW21 ΔPD Hardean Bonkrude, 115

Parkway Apt. 306, told Mankato police someone

broke into his ~~apatment~~ apartment and stole

$274.95 worth of merchandise. Items reported

stolen ~~inl~~ include a model ship, two bows, a

typewriter, vacuum cleaner and ~~taperecorder~~

/tape recorder./

Jeff Clay, 520 James Ave.,

Apt. 104, told police ~~sone~~ someone stole $132

worth of record ~~alm~~ albums and a set ~~a~~

/ / /of/

headphones from his ~~apr~~ apartment

sometime between Saturday and Wednesday. ΔS4

Δ14 Breakin ΔL

ΔCM ΔCW21 ΔPD Police said someone broke

into Mankato Cold Storage, 216 W. Elm St.,

sometime ~~Tued~~ Tuesday night and stole $120

worth of butter and french ~~fir~~ fries. Police

said a padlock and hasp were pried off one of

the doors. ΔS4

ΔΔ

Here is a sample of scanner copy at the Wichita *Eagle* during one stage of its system development. The *1a means the photo credit line will be set one column in agate (6 points high), and the *19d means the copy will be set in 10 points on a column and a half. The (□) symbols instruct the scanner to wipe out the preceding error, and the bracket ({) tells the machine that the word continues on the next line.

```
*1a
Staff Photo by Anthony Reed/¦
*19d/Em1803/


These plan-s □□ plants at Century II were

tough eng □  ough to stand up to the cold

temperatures that hit  Wichita  last Friday

and Saturday, and they flourished in the 80

and 90 degree weather Sunday, Monday and

Tuesday. Cun □□Cynthia a□Chestnut

of the city's park work department watered

them Tuesday in preparation for the

predicted high of 70 today. Skies should

ramina □□ remain mostly fair, with

little chance of precipitati{

on./¦$t
```

TYPING FORMAT

If you are using typewriters for your class stories (you may be using VDTs), use newsprint or—if your instructor prefers—mimeograph paper, which is very white and allows duplication for additional instructional purposes. Never use erasable bond—it smears and is hard to write on with a ballpoint or grading pencil.

Follow this format: Put a "slug," or identifying word, in the upper left-hand corner of the first page. Number the second page FIRST ADD SMITH (or whatever one-word slug you choose to identify your story), the third, SECOND ADD SMITH, and so on. Other ways of numbering the second page include TAKE 2 and 2-2-2-2-2-2. Your instructor will probably suggest a system for you to use. Start typing in the middle of the first page and at the top on subsequent pages.

Here are some additional guidelines:

- Indent widely (a fourth of the page indentation to start a paragraph is not too much).
- Do not continue a paragraph at the bottom of the page to the next page. (Historically, the custom developed because when a story was being rushed through, each page might be set on a different machine to speed things up. Split paragraphs set by separate units are difficult to assemble.)
- Put "more" at the bottom of the page when there is more to come.
- At the end of your story, put "end," #, or "30." (Why "30" has been used has many explanations—among them, writers used to sign off with "XXX," the end of an old-fashioned typesetting line was the 30th character, or the early telegraph messages were 30 words.)

Notes

[1]Howard Angione, ed., *The Associated Press Stylebook and Libel Manual* (New York: The Associated Press, c. 1977), pp. 183, 184.

[2]Angione, p. 110.

[3]"Fifty Common Errors in Newspaper Writing," *Editor & Publisher* (Dec. 7, 1974): pp. 16, 20.

[4]Angione, p. 59.

Assignments

1. Make note of words you misspell in class assignments, and keep a list of words to learn.
2. Copyedit a double-spaced page of unedited copy. (You could also take a page or a story by a newspaper person—perhaps a duplicate file copy—edit it, then compare the editing—both the markings and the adjustments, and the rewrite—with that of the edited copy that appeared in the paper.)
3. Using an AP or UPI stylebook, compare three or four paragraphs of a

news story in the local paper with the style suggested in the AP or UPI stylebooks. To what extent is the local paper following AP and UPI style?

4. Take a copy of a news release, perhaps from the college or university; then, consulting an AP or UPI stylebook, edit the release to conform with AP-UPI style.
5. Some more assignments: (1) discuss colloquialisms, phrases common to your area which other reporters across the country might not know; (2) make a list of "trite" phrases or cliches to avoid. These include such phrases as "from time immemorial" and "ever since the dawn of time"; (3) look at the AP or other stylebooks and decide if you would add or change anything based on your experience and background; and (4) how should the confusion over the use of women's names on first and second references be resolved?

Copyrights and Acknowledgments

For permission to use the following selections reprinted in this book, the author is grateful to these publishers and copyright holders:

CHAPTER 1 Bernard C. Cohen, *The Press and Foreign Policy*. Copyright © 1963 by Princeton University Press. Excerpt, p. 13. Edwin Emery, Michael Emery, excerpt from *The Press and America: An Interpretative History of the Mass Media*, 4th Ed., © 1978, p. 4. Adapted by permission of Prentice-Hall, Inc., Englewood Cliffs, N.J. Robert Gless, "Ex-Rhodes Scholars Mark Anniversary," Associated Press in the Burlington (Vt.) *Free Press*. Michael Schudson, excerpt from *Discovering the News*, copyright © 1978 Basic Books, Inc. Don C. Seitz, excerpt from *Joseph Pulitzer: His Life and Letters*. Reprinted by permission of Simon & Schuster, Inc. Dorothy Storck, excerpt from the "James Guttmann and the Nazis" clipping from *The Philadelphia Inquirer,* 2/23/79. Reprinted by permission.

CHAPTER 2 Thomas Boswell, excerpt from " 'Roofers' Have Chicago Hopping." Reprinted by permission of the *Washington Post*. Kitty Caparella, excerpt from the "Anti-Nuclear Groups" clipping. Reprinted by permission of the *Philadelphia Daily News*. Peter G. Chronis, excerpt from the "Dear Judge" clipping reprinted by permission of the *Denver Post*. Colin Covert, excerpt from the "Dull Men's Club" clipping. Reprinted by permission of the Knight-Ridder News Service in the *Miami Herald*. Al Cross, excerpt from the "Ryder Cemetery" clipping from the Louisville *Courier-Journal*, © 1984. Reprinted with permission. Paul Feldman and Jan Klunder, excerpt from "Trees: Lovely, Untrimmed—Funds Lacking," published Sept. 15, 1983 by the *Los Angeles Times*, and Patt Morrison, "Dinosaur Bones Among Bargains at Epochal Sale," published Sept. 23, 1983 by the *Los Angeles Times*. Copyright 1983, *Los Angeles Times*. Reprinted by permission. Ann LoLordo, excerpt from "City bus passenger finds baby girl." Reprinted by permission of the *Baltimore Sun*. Mike McNamee, "Wall Street Wednesday" clipping. Reprinted by permission of *USA Today*. Timothy McQuay, excerpt from "A diplomatic end" clipping. Reprinted by permission of *USA Today*. Edward Moran, excerpt from "City Honors a 'Name.'" Reprinted by permission of the

Philadelphia Daily News. Helen Pauly, excerpt from the "Sentry welcomes Kohl's customers" clipping. Reprinted by permission of the *Milwaukee Journal*. Carlin Romano, excerpt from the "Umberto Eco" clipping. Reprinted by permission of *The Philadelphia Inquirer*. Marylyn Schwartz, excerpt from the "Dallas" clipping. Reprinted by permission of the *Dallas Morning News*, in the *Denver Post*. Diane Sechrest, excerpt from "The ducks at the Furman University lake" clipping. Reprinted by permission of the Greenville (S.C.) *Piedmont*. Edward J. Smith, excerpt from "Screw Model has advantages over inverted pyramid." Reprinted by permission of the *Journalism Educator*. Judy McConnell Steele, excerpt from the "Romance!" clipping from the Gannett News Service in the Boise (Idaho) *Statesman*. The *St. Louis Globe-Democrat*, excerpt from the "Female hockey buffs take note" clipping, reprinted by permission of the *St. Louis Globe-Democrat*. Bill Thomas, excerpt from the "Dan Greenburg and Suzanne O'Malley" clipping, reprinted by permission of the *Baltimore Sun*. Gene Wojciechowski, excerpt from the "Denver Broncos" clipping, reprinted by permission of the *Denver Post*.

CHAPTER 3 Carl Bernstein and Bob Woodward, excerpt from *All the President's Men*. Copyright © 1974 by Carl Bernstein and Bob Woodward. Reprinted by permission of Simon & Schuster, Inc. Evan Hill, excerpt from "Accuracy Is a Winner's Policy," *Reader's Digest*, Oct. 1973. Reprinted with permission of *Reader's Digest* and *Christian Herald Magazine*, where the article originally appeared, June 1973. Alleyne Ireland, excerpt from *An Adventure with a Genius: Joseph Pulitzer*, pp. 110-111 Copyright © 1914 by E. P. Dutton, Inc. Reprinted by permission. James L. Kilgallen, excerpt from *It's a Great Life: My 50 Years as a Newspaperman* (New York: International News Service, 1956), pp. 6, 7. Reprinted by permission.

CHAPTER 4 David Anderson and Peter Benjaminson, excerpt from *Investigative Reporting* (Bloomington, Indiana: Indiana University Press, 1976), p. 63. Reprinted by permission. Carl Bernstein and Bob Woodward, excerpt from *All the President's Men*, p. 214. Copyright © 1974 by Carl Bernstein and Bob Woodward. Reprinted by permission of Simon & Schuster, Inc. Excerpts from items by Charlotte Burrows, Margaret Martin and Lynn Stewart and by Martin and Stewart, *The Shreveport Times*, April 25 and 27, 1976. Excerpts reprinted by permission of *The Times*, Shreveport, Louisiana. *Media Survival Kit*, Pennsylvania First Amendment Coalition, prepared by Samuel E. Klein (Philadelphia: Kohn, Sarett, Marion & Graf), cf. pp. 5-10. William Metz, excerpt from *Newswriting: From Lead to "30,"* pp. 91-93, Prentice-Hall, Inc. Copyright © 1977. Reprinted by permission of Prentice-Hall, Inc. *New York Times Stylebook* excerpts. Copyright © 1976 by the New York Times Company. Reprinted by permission. Hiley Ward, "The Brief Career of Rev. McGovern," from *Newsday*. Reprinted by permission.

CHAPTER 6 Jane Evinger, excerpts from "Dirty tricks teach interview pitfalls," from the *Journalism Educator*, Winter, 1984, p. 28. Reprinted by permission. Georgie Anne Geyer, excerpt from "Securing the Elusive Interview—Geyer Tells How She Does It," *Editor & Publisher* (Feb. 10, 1979), 112:6, p. 28. Reprinted by permission. Ida M. Tarbell, excerpt from *All in the Day's Work* (New York: Macmillan, 1939), p. 235. Reprinted by permission of Ella Tarbell Price.

CHAPTER 7 Tom Ahern, "Governor Ella T. Grasso" clippings from the Danbury *News-Times*, 1/3/79 and 1/4/79. Reprinted by permission of the *News-Times*, Danbury, Conn. Susanne Burks, excerpt from the "Mayor David Rusk" clipping from the *Albuquerque Journal*. Reprinted by permission. Will Fehr, "Utah's attorney" clipping from the Salt Lake (Utah) *Tribune*. Reprinted by permission. Ron Herron, excerpts from clippings from the Frankfort (Ky.) *State Journal*, 6/17/77 and 1/14/79. Reprinted by permission. Emery Hutchison, "Church Board Spat Begat by its Cat," reprinted from the Chicago *Daily News* by permission. William K. Marimow, Bob Frump and Dick Cooper, excerpt from the "State Rep. Milton Street" clipping from *The Philadelphia Inquirer*, 2/9/79. Reprinted by permission. Pat Ordovensky, "Industry to Schools: You Fail," reprinted from *USA Today*, 7/21/83, by permission. Hiley Ward, excerpt from the "convention" clipping from *The Philadelphia Inquirer*, 7/1/78. Reprinted by permission.

CHAPTER 8 Kent W. Cockson, "Guidelines for Writing Obituaries," from the Pensacola (Fla.) *News-Journal*, a Gannett newspaper in Florida's Panhandle. Reprinted by permission of Mr. Cockson, executive editor of the *News-Journal*. The Hawaii *Tribune-Herald*, various obituaries, reprinted by permission. Inquirer Wire Services, Reynolds and Durante obituaries, *The Philadelphia Inquirer*, 7/21/83 and 2/20/80. Reprinted by permission. Ida Leiby, Karen Korman, personals, from the Centre (County) *Democrat*, Bellefonte, Pa. Reprinted by permission. The *Los Angeles Times*, Dozar Obituary, copyright 1983, *Los Angeles Times*. Reprinted by permission. Anita Manning, "Viral hepatitis" clipping reprinted by permission of *USA Today*, 7/21/83. *The New York Times*, Wedding and Engagement Announcements. Copyright © 1979 by The New York Times Company. Reprinted by permission.

CHAPTER 9 Mark Arax, excerpt from "Her pink fur-lined coffin . . . ," clipping reprinted by permission of *Insight*, California State University, Fresno. Louise Boggess, excerpt from *Fiction Techniques That Sell*. Reprinted by permission of Curtis Brown Associates, Ltd. Copyright © 1964 by Louise Boggess. Lucille DeView, excerpt from "Old Men with Time to Kill," reprinted by permission of the *Detroit News*. Richard Eastman, excerpt from *Style*. Reprinted by permission of Oxford University Press. Tom French, excerpt from "Harold McDermit keeps a pig." Reprinted by permission of the *Daily Student*, Indiana University. Joe Heaney and Bill Dooley, "The Parakeet Murder Case," from the *Boston Herald American*. Reprinted by permission. Bob Krauss, "body building" clipping from the *Honolulu Advertiser*. Reprinted by permission. Alan M. Kriegsman, "Roots in Dance, Rites of Fall" from *Writing in Style*. Published by the *Washington Post*. Reprinted by permission. Stewart Dill McBride, excerpt from "Highbrows in Hard Hats" from *The Christian Science Monitor.* Reprinted by permission from *The Christian Science Monitor.* © 1980 The Christian Science Publishing Society. All rights reserved. Henry Mitchell, excerpt from "Samurai Surrender" from *Writing in Style*. Published by the *Washington Post*. Reprinted by permission. Billy Reed, excerpt from "A Grand Lady Sees Her Grand Colt Win" from the Louisville *Courier-Journal*. ©1984. Reprinted with permission. Robert Schwabach, "massage parlor" clipping from *The Philadelphia Inquirer*, 4/23/78. Reprinted by permission. Items by Jon Roe and by Craig Stock from the *Wichita Eagle*. Reprinted by permission. Jerome Thale, "Style and Anti-Style: History and Anti-History," *College English*, 19 (January 1968), pp. 286-302. Reprinted with the permission of the National Council of Teachers of English. Hiley Ward, excerpt from "Last Hours of a Tiny Goldfish," from the *Detroit Free Press*. Reprinted by permission.

CHAPTER 10 Ken Blum, of the *Courier-Crescent*, Orrville, Ohio, "Police Scanner" clipping from *The Byliner*, a bulletin of the National Newspaper Association. Reprinted by permission. John Covaleski, "List of abused drugs and their street names," clipping reprinted by permission of the Doylestown (Pa.) *Daily Intelligencer.* Doris Flora, "The body of a 28-year-old . . . ," clipping reprinted by permission of the *Tuscaloosa News*. Gary Hines, "'Good Samaritan' Is Critically Injured," reprinted by permission of the Shreveport (La.) *Journal*. Tom Jackson, "Durant man" clipping reprinted by permission of the Lawton (Okla.) *Constitution*. Art Latham, excerpt from the "Death of a 2-year-old boy" clipping reprinted by permission from the *New Mexican*, Santa Fe, N.M. Steve Patton, excerpt from the "South Coatesville fire" clipping from the Coatesville (Pa.) *Record*. Reprinted by permission. Gresham M. Sykes, excerpt from *Crime and Society*, Second Edition, reprinted by permission of the publisher, Random House, Inc. Copyright © 1956 by Gresham Sykes and the publisher.

CHAPTER 11 Carolyn Bower, "Deliberations Expected to Begin in Damage Suit," from the Riverton (Wyo.) *Ranger.* Reprinted by permission. Jim Deal, "Three-year sentence . . ." clipping from *The Argus*, Rock Island, Ill. Reprinted by permission. Jim Dowd, "Drunk Driving Conviction Cover-Up Admitted," from the Janesville (Wis.) *Gazette*. Reprinted by permission. Robert K. Entriken, Jr., five short clippings from the Salina (Kan.) *Journal*. Reprinted by permission. Vicki Ferstel, "Suit Challenges Racial Separation of Funeral Homes," from the *Daily Iberian*, New Iberia, La. Reprinted by permission. Mary R. Heffron, excerpt from "Investigators Muffed Case Jurors Say," from the Orlando *Sentinel Star*, Orlando, Fla. Reprinted by permission. Doug Higgs, "Dismissal South in Theft Charges," from the Klamath Falls (Ore.) *Herald and News.* Reprinted by permission. Aline L. Jacobs, "District Court," from the Laconia (N.H.) *Evening Citizen*. Reprinted by permission. Steven C. Lachowicz, "Judge Takes Obscene Shirt with Probation Ruling," from the Wenatchee (Wash.) *World*. Reprinted by permission. Emilie Lounsberry, "Man Pleads Guilty to Raping 10-year-old Girl," from the Doylestown (Pa.) *Daily Intelligencer.* Reprinted by permission.

CHAPTER 12 Warren J. Brier and Howard C. Heyn, excerpt from *Writing for Newspapers and News Services* (New York: Funk and Wagnalls, 1969), p. 23. Maria Crape, editor-in-chief, Helen Redfern, editor, *Key to the Keystone State: Pennsylvania*, League of Women Voters (Philadelphia: League of Women Voters of Pennsylvania, © 1972, 1978), pp. 31-32. Excerpt reprinted by permission. Clancy DuBos, excerpt from the "Elections and Cockfights" clipping from the New Orleans *Times-Picayune*, New Orleans, La. Reprinted by permission. Margaret Edds, excerpt from the "Private Profit" clipping from the *Virginian-Pilot*, Norfolk, Va. Reprinted by permission. Bob Kolin, excerpts from four news clippings from the Raleigh (N.C.) *News and Observer*. Reprinted by permission. Janice Law, excerpt from "Overflow Turnout Forces Wallace to Speak Twice," and "Tamarac" clipping from the Fort Lauderdale (Fla.) *News*. Reprinted by permission. Leonard Levy, excerpt from *Freedom of Speech and Press in Early American History: Legacy of Suppression* (Cambridge, Mass.: Harvard University Press; New York: Harper & Row, © 1960, 1963), p. 248. Reprinted by permission. Mildred Parten, excerpt from *Surveys, Polls, and Samples: Practical Procedures* (New York: Harper, 1950), p. 219. Reprinted by permission. Jewell Case Phillips, excerpt from *State and Local Government in America*. Copyright © 1954 by American Book Company. All rights reserved. Peggy Rector, excerpt from "Braddock Chosen Board Attorney," from the Vicksburg (Miss.) *Evening Post*. Reprinted by permission. Frank Van Riper, "McGovern: Freeze!," from the New York *Daily News*. Copyright 1983 New York News, Inc. Reprinted by permission. Earle Stern, excerpt from "Kennedy packs 'em inside . . . ," from the Lynn (Mass.) *Item*. Reprinted by permission. Harry Stoffer, "Harrisburg" clipping from the Doylestown (Pa.) *Intelligencer*. Reprinted by permission of the *Intelligencer* and Calkins Newspapers. Mason Taylor, "A New Ball Game," in Dougherty, *Learning in the Newsroom: A Manual for Supervisors*. Reprinted by permission of the American Newspaper Publishers Association Foundation. Paul Williams, from *Investigative Reporting and Editing* (Englewood Cliffs, N.J.: Prentice-Hall, 1978), pp. 228, 229. Reprinted by permission.

CHAPTER 13 Donna Moore Whitaker, excerpt from the "Springdale School District Policies" clipping, reprinted by permission from the Springdale (Ark.) *News*. Dru Wilson, excerpt from "Involvement Part of Education," from the Colorado Springs (Colo.) *Gazette Telegraph*. Reprinted by permission. Joe Wilson, excerpts from education clippings, reprinted by permission of the Gainesville (Ga.) *Times*.

CHAPTER 14 Charley Blaine, "Real Estate" clipping from *USA Today*. Reprinted by permission. Philip Heckman, excerpt from "Come to Terms with Credit," from *Everybody's Money*, © 1983, n.d., pp. 16-18. Published by The Credit Union National Association. Reprinted by permission. Marge Higgins, excerpt from "Beetlemania: Pesky critters here in force," from the Kent-Ravenna (Ohio) *Record-Courier*. Reprinted by permission. Kathie Jarmon, excerpts from miscellaneous clippings, from the *Northeast Mississippi Daily Journal*. Reprinted by permission of The Journal Publishing Company, Tupelo,

MS. David J. Mahoney, "On Ending an Adversary Relationship," from *The New York Times*. Copyright © 1977 by The New York Times Company. Reprinted by permission. Jack Miller, excerpt from "Contractors' State License Board" clipping from the *San Francisco Examiner*. Reprinted by permission. Patty Moore, excerpt from the "farming" clipping from the Atchison (Kan.) *Daily Globe*. Reprinted by permission. Joseph Poindexter, excerpt from "The Great Industry-Media Debate," from *The Saturday Review*. © 1976 Saturday Review Magazine Co. Reprinted by permission. Sue Robinson, excerpts from clippings from the Greensboro (N.C.) *News and Record*. Charles H. Turner, "Iron worker 'trick' cited by employer," from the *Honolulu Advertiser*. Reprinted by permission. Gary Washburn, excerpt from a real estate clipping from the *Chicago Tribune*. Reprinted by permission. Gayle Zubler, excerpt from an Action Line column, from the *South Bend (Ind.) Tribune*. Reprinted by permission.

CHAPTER 15 Ralph D. Berenger, "Upset bid fails in last second," from the Shelley (Idaho) *Pioneer*. Reprinted by permission of Ralph D. Berenger, publisher, the *Pioneer*. Bob Buckel, "Jaycees Fall to Wharton Here," from the El Campo (Tex.) *Leader-News*. Reprinted by permission. Tony Chamberlain, excerpt from "They're head over keels in Newport," from the Boston *Globe*, 9/28/83. Reprinted courtesy of the Boston *Globe*. Randy Cummings, "Colts Catch Rebs Off Guard," from the Arlington (Tex.) *Citizen-Journal*. Reprinted by permission of the *Citizen-Journal* and Randy Cummings, sports editor. Dewaine Gahan, "Gahan's Game Plan . . ." clipping from the Fremont (Neb.) *Tribune*. Reprinted by permission. Ron Green, excerpt from the "face of Danny Ford" clipping from the Greenville (S.C.) *Piedmont*. Reprinted by permission of the *Piedmont* and Ron Green, assistant sports editor. Edward Hill, Jr., "Road Runners" clipping reprinted by permission of the *Winston-Salem Chronicle*. Harry McFarland, "One Cheeseburger and a Championship, Please!," from the *Westside Record-Journal*. Reprinted by permission of Harry McFarland, news editor, *Westside Record-Journal*, Ferndale, Wash. Mike Newell, excerpt from "Local Soccer Games Heat-up," from the Hobbs (N.M.) *Flare*. Reprinted by permission. Grantland Rice, "The Four Horsemen," © 1924, from the *New York Herald Tribune*. Reprinted by permission. Jim Satterly, excerpt from "Down, But Not Out," from the DeKalb (Ga.) *News-Sun*. Reprinted by permission of Jim Satterly, sports editor, and the *News-Sun*. Herbert Warren Wind, excerpt from *The Realm of Sport* (New York: Simon & Schuster, © 1966), pp. 312-315. Wind's comments are on "The Four Horsemen," by Grantland Rice, © 1924, *New York Herald Tribune*.

CHAPTER 16 Warren Burkett, excerpt from *Writing Science News for the Mass Media*, Second Edition. Copyright © 1973 by Gulf Publishing Company, Houston, Texas. All rights reserved. Used with permission. Leslie Champlin, excerpt from "KU football player killed," from the *Topeka Capital-Journal*. Reprinted by permission. Emily and Per Ola D'Aulaire, excerpt from "Will There Be 'Carbon Copy' People?," *Reader's Digest*, March 1979. Reprinted by permission. Lee Dembart, excerpt from "Scientists Find New High in

Prime Numbers Game," from the *Los Angeles Times*. Copyright 1983, The *Los Angeles Times*. Reprinted by permission. Dennis Hetzel, "Death from rattlesnake" clipping from the *Journal Times*, Racine, Wis. Reprinted by permission. Blair Justice, excerpt from the "Advice for Science Reporters" clipping from *The Quill*, August 1960, p. 12. Reprinted by permission. Hillier Krieghbaum, excerpt from *Science and the Mass Media*. Copyright © 1967 by New York University. Reprinted by permission. David J. Mahoney, from "A Nuclear Plant Glossary," from *The New York Times*. Copyright 1979 by The New York Times Company. Reprinted by permission. Henry W. Pierce, excerpt from "Narrow-Mindedness and the 'Strange Experience'" *Newsletter*, NASW, Vol. 26, No. 3, December 1978, p. 16. Reprinted by permission. Arthur J. Snider, "At Last . . . A Mother Can Kiss Her Baby," from the Chicago *Sun-Times*. © News Group Chicago, Inc., 1979. Reprinted with permission of the Chicago *Sun-Times*. Marcia Stepanek with comments by H. L. Stevenson, "The UPI Story," *Newsletter*, National Association of Science Writers, vol. 26, no. 2, September 1978, p. 8. Reprinted by permission. Julia Wallace, "Hospitalized female prisoner" clipping from the Norfolk (Va.) *Ledger-Star*. Reprinted by permission. Nancy Wood, "Saturday bloodiest night in emergency room" clipping from the Lake Charles (La.) *American Press*. Reprinted by permission.

CHAPTER 17 Mary Ann Campbell, "RV Chorale impressive in spring concert," from the Medford (Ore.) *Mail Tribune*. Reprinted by permission. Nelson George, "Lionel Richie" clipping from the *Village Voice*. Reprinted by permission. Pauline Kael, excerpt from "Killer and Thieves," pp. 403-405, from *Deeper into Movies* by Pauline Kael. Copyright © 1972 by Pauline Kael. Reprinted by permission of Little, Brown and Company in association with the Atlantic Monthly Press. Ernest Leogrande, "Quest: Still another language," from the New York *Daily News*. Copyright 1982 New York News Inc. Reprinted by permission. Sara Morrow, review from the Nashville *Banner*. Reprinted by permission. Desmond Ryan, "The Moon in the Gutter" review, from *The Philadelphia Inquirer*, 10/31/83. Reprinted by permission. David Stabler, "English band Fixxin' to play," from the Anchorage (Alaska) *Daily News*. Reprinted by permission of David Stabler, arts editor, Anchorage *Daily News*. Hiley Ward, "Films foster view of God as 'force,'" from *USA Today*. Reprinted by permission. Hiley Ward, "'Godfather' Power a Pitfall for Church," from the *Miami Herald* and *Detroit Free Press*. Reprinted by permission. Hiley Ward, excerpt from "Last Tango: It's About Death," from the *Detroit Free Press*. Reprinted by permission.

CHAPTER 18 *USA Today*, "Farmers and the Weather" clipping. Reprinted by permission.

CHAPTER 21 Associated Press, guidelines for journalists. Used by permission of The Associated Press. Donald M. Gillmor and Jerome A. Barron, excerpt from *Mass Communication Law* (St. Paul, Minn.: West, © 1969, 1979), pp. 11, 12. Reprinted by permission. Robert W. Greene, excerpt from

"Exploring the Impossible—A Search for Journalism Ethics," in Louis W. Hodges' *Social Responsibility: journalism, Law, Medicine* Vol. IV (Lexington, Va.: Washington and Lee University, 1978), p. 27. Reprinted by permission. John Irving, excerpt from *The World According to Garp* (New York: E. P. Dutton, Inc., © 1976, 1978). John C. Merrill, from *The Imperative of Freedom*, copyright 1974 by John C. Merrill, permission by Hastings House, Publishers. Carol E. Rinzler, from "Who Is That Public Figure—And Why Can You Say All Those Terrible Things About Him?," *Publishers Weekly*. Reprinted by permission. Hiley Ward, excerpt from "'Conscience' Is Changing in the Church," from the *Detroit Free Press*. Reprinted by permission. Hiley H. Ward, excerpt from "Precepts for Journalists," in *The Quill*, January 1981, p. 15. Reprinted by permission.

CHAPTER 22 Dow Jones Newspaper Fund Inc., "A Newspaper Career and You" booklet, Princeton, N.J. Reprinted by permission. Henry F. Schulte, "Newspaper Jobs for Journalism Grads," ANPA Foundation. Reprinted by permission of the ANPA Foundation.

APPENDIX Howard Angione, excerpts from "Ex-Rhodes Scholars Mark Anniversary," from *The Associated Press Stylebook and Libel Manual*. Reprinted by permission of AP Newsfeatures. *Editor & Publisher*, "Fifty Common Errors in Newspaper Writing," (Dec. 7, 1974). Reprinted by permission.

Index

A 4
B 5
C 6
D 7
E 8
F 9
G 0
H 1
I 2
J 3